CRIMINAL EVIDENCE
PRINCIPLES AND CASES

Ninth Edition

Thomas J. Gardner
Attorney at Law and Former Assistant District Attorney

Terry M. Anderson
Creighton University School of Law

CENGAGE
Learning·

Australia • Brazil • Japan • Korea • Mexico • Singapore • Spain • United Kingdom • United States

Criminal Evidence: Principles and Cases,
Ninth Edition

Thomas J. Gardner and Terry M. Anderson

Product Director: Marta Lee-Perriard

Senior Product Manager: Carolyn Henderson Meier

Content Developer: Michael B. Kopf,
S4Carlisle Publishing Services

Product Assistant: Julia Catalano

Media Developer: Ting Jian Yap

Senior Marketing Manager: Kara Kindstrom

Senior Content Project Manager: Christy Frame

Managing Art Director: Andrei Pasternak

Senior Manufacturing Planner: Judy Inouye

Production Service: Lynn Lustberg, MPS Limited

Photo Researcher: Kalaivani Periassamy,
Lumina Datamatics

Text Researcher: Pinky Subi, Lumina Datamatics

Copy Editor: Laurene Sorensen

Text and Cover Designer: Brenda Carmichael,
Lumina Datamatics

Cover Image: A. T. Willett/Alamy

Composition: MPS Limited

For product information and technology assistance, contact us at
Cengage Learning Customer & Sales Support, 1-800-354-9706.

For permission to use material from this text or product,
submit all requests online at **www.cengage.com/permissions**.

Further permissions questions can be e-mailed to
permissionrequest@cengage.com.

Library of Congress Control Number: 2014946140

ISBN: 978-1-285-45900-4

Cengage Learning
20 Channel Center Street
Boston, MA 02210
USA

Cengage Learning is a leading provider of customized learning solutions with office locations around the globe, including Singapore, the United Kingdom, Australia, Mexico, Brazil, and Japan. Locate your local office at **www.cengage.com/global**.

Cengage Learning products are represented in Canada by Nelson Education, Ltd.

To learn more about Cengage Learning Solutions, visit **www.cengage.com**.

Purchase any of our products at your local college store or at our preferred online store **www.cengagebrain.com**.

Printed in the United States of America
Print Number: 04   Print Year: 2019

CONTENTS

PREFACE

In 1791, just four years after the writing of the U.S. Constitution, representatives from the original thirteen states ratified the first ten amendments to the Constitution. These amendments, collectively called the Bill of Rights, reflect concerns of the Founding Fathers that the strong, central federal government would usurp rights then enjoyed in the American states. Although the first American Congress considered more than 145 proposed amendments to the Constitution, the ten that were adopted established the core of basic individual rights in the United States. Relevant selections from the Constitution and the Bill of Rights appear in Appendix A.

The Bill of Rights, as interpreted by the U.S. Supreme Court and state courts, has historically been the basis for the rules of evidence used in criminal trials in the United States. The federal government has promulgated the Federal Rules of Evidence, which many states have adopted outright or used as a pattern for their rules of evidence. These rules incorporate more than 200 years of judicial and legislative debate on the proper evidentiary rules to be used in court trials in the United States. We have added, as Appendix C, the most recent version of the Federal Rules of Evidence, which were amended effective December 1, 2011, to be more readable and understandable. Today, as in 1791, the Bill of Rights continues to be the beginning point for an understanding of the rules of evidence in criminal trials.

In criminal trials, rules of evidence have as a primary goal securing a defendant's constitutional right to a fair trial. What is meant by a "fair trial" has varied over the years. What was considered a fair trial in the witchcraft trials in Salem, Massachusetts, in 1692 would not be regarded as such in any democratic nation in the world today. Most of the evidence introduced in those trials, as a result of which nineteen people were executed, would not be admissible today under the Bill of Rights and the Federal Rules of Evidence.

Rules of evidence are not only important for the protection of the fundamental rights of persons accused of crimes, but also are necessary in seeking to secure the interests of the American public in an efficient and effective criminal justice system. To accomplish those goals, a necessary trade-off must be made between the protection of individual rights and judicial efficiency. Understanding this trade-off adds greatly to the student's appreciation of the dynamics of the criminal justice system. As in previous editions, we continue in this edition to try to identify this trade-off between the legitimate requirements of an efficient criminal justice system and individual rights.

ORGANIZATION OF THE BOOK

This book is divided into eighteen chapters and organized into four parts. Part 1, which includes Chapters 1–4, focuses on the historical basis for the American criminal justice system and evidentiary rules. Part 2 (Chapters 5–8) examines in detail the role of witnesses in that system. In Part 3 (Chapters 9–15) we discuss some of the many facets of the exclusionary rule and related issues, such as the use of confessions, the legal requirements for searches and seizures, and the "special needs" rules. In Part 4 (Chapters 16–18) we concentrate on the techniques used in gathering evidence for use in criminal trials and the legal rules to which those techniques must conform.

NEW TO THIS EDITION

In the ninth edition we strive to present the key rules of evidence, the rationale behind these rules, and the applicability of these rules in criminal prosecutions in a manner that is not encyclopedic or overwhelming to the student. We hope the text's clear explanations, accessible writing style, coverage of current issues, and numerous pedagogical aids combine to help students understand and be engaged by complex legal topics. Toward this same end, we use interesting, news-based examples wherever possible to help students understand and retain concepts. Boxes and charts are extensively incorporated to illustrate new and important developments in the rules of criminal evidence. Case discussions help add detail to the judicial decision-making process. Learning how laws evolve helps students to understand the laws themselves.

We have retained changes we made to the eighth edition of *Criminal Evidence*. These include revised Learning Objectives, which will help professors and students target specific subjects, and a "bullet" approach to chapter-ending summaries that attempts to align the summaries with the learning objectives. We also highlight the "Key Terms" feature by including them at the end of each chapter, together with a related feature, "Key Cases," which lists some of the important cases discussed in each chapter. We have retained the chapter-ending problems in all the chapters. We have retained the "Case Analysis" feature in this edition, and in all chapters we have added more recent cases to the feature.

The text addresses up-to-the-minute topics such as obtaining evidence from computers and smartphones, attaching GPS tracking devices to automobiles, and using social media like Facebook as evidence in criminal trials. The topic of search and seizure has been expanded, and historical coverage has been streamlined throughout the text. Subjects that have traditionally been confusing, such as the discussion of husband-wife privilege, have been retooled to be as clear to students as possible. We continue to try to improve the materials in certain key chapters, such as Chapters 8–10, and 14, which have in the past proved difficult for students to master. In this edition we discuss important recent changes to the subjects discussed in those chapters, and we continue to try to make that material more understandable to our readers. Where possible, we have incorporated recent developments that will be of interest to students who are associated with law enforcement.

We have added a new feature to many of the chapters in the ninth edition. Titled "You Be the Judge," this feature invites students to don the trial judge's robe and decide motions to admit or exclude evidence. Trial judges are routinely asked to decide difficult questions on admissibility of evidence, and we hope students will profit from doing the same.

In addition to the enhancements listed above, and the substantial changes to the eighth edition retained in this edition, the ninth edition also features the following chapter-by-chapter changes:

- In Chapter 1 we expanded the discussion of how federal courts handle habeas petitions, based on requests from some of those who use our book. This includes a 2011 Supreme Court case on the subject. We updated boxes, such as the enemy combatant and 48-hour boxes, as well as the sections on the presumption of innocence and speedy trial doctrine. We included a 2013 case that is very helpful on how courts determine if the speedy trial right has been infringed. We also included two 2012 Supreme Court cases on when and how claims of ineffective assistance of counsel should be considered in criminal appeals.

- In Chapter 2 we updated several cases, like the *Bond* case mentioned in the box on the Tenth Amendment and Individual Rights. The Supreme Court considered the underlying criminal case in *Bond* in 2013. We also updated the SORNA material with a 2013 Supreme Court case that gave a partial answer to the power of Congress to pass legislation like SORNA. Our first "You Be the Judge" box appears in this chapter.

- In Chapter 3 we expanded, in various parts of the chapter, our discussion of guilty pleas. For example, we updated the fast-track plea box to reflect the Justice Department's plan, announced in 2012, to make such pleas available in all districts for re-entry prosecutions. We added a new box that discusses the ability of a defendant to withdraw a guilty plea. We deleted old and added new cases on nolo contendere pleas, and added a new case on the consequences of making an *Alford* plea. One of the case analysis assignments invites students to study two recent Supreme Court cases and see how the Court is split on some important issues.

- As the new vignette in Chapter 4 illustrates, we are using this feature as more of a discussion tool, and less of a current example exposition. We rewrote many sections in this chapter to improve understanding, including the "bad acts" rules. Recent legislative acts and court decisions have made changes in the admissibility of that type of evidence in sexual assaults. We also expanded the section on silence/self-incrimination to include a 2013 Supreme Court case on the subject, as well as 2013 federal cases that show how the rules about use of a defendant's silence have developed. We added a "You Be the Judge" box to include "Be the Jury" in a 2012 murder case.

- In Chapter 5, in response to helpful suggestions from our readers, we expanded the voir dire section to make it clearer. We also added a new subsection, "Vouching", as a limit on permissible testimony of a witness. We discuss at some length the practice of using police officers as both expert and lay witnesses, and include a "You Be a Judge" box on that issue.

- In Chapter 6 we clarified the attorney-client privilege where a third party was present during a communication. We also added a new box on the survival of the attorney-client privilege following the death of the client. We expanded the discussion of the crime/fraud exception to the attorney-client privilege, with a new case showing how judges respond to claims the privilege should be lost. We added a "You Be the Judge" box on the psychotherapist-patient privilege.

- The Confrontation Clause jurisprudence continues to evolve, as the Supreme Court and lower courts provide guidance on the "testimonial" vs. "non-testimonial" distinction. In Chapter 8 we added a new box that provides guides to students seeking Confrontation Clause solutions. We address specific examples of the testimonial-non-testimonial hearsay problem, including the 2012 Supreme Court decision on forensics reports as hearsay; a new box on autopsy reports; the child-sexual abuse exception; and examples of hearsay testimony that is non-testimonial, and thus not subject to the Confrontation Clause.

- In Chapter 9 we rewrote the text's historical exposition of the exclusionary rule, in response to helpful suggestions from some of our readers. If, as many believe, the role of the exclusionary rule is changing, it is important that students see its origins. We have a "You Be the Judge" box in this chapter that focuses on live witness testimony as derivative evidence for purposes of the exclusionary rule.

- In Chapter 10 we highlight the 2014 Supreme Court case that places limits on the ability of a co-resident, under *Georgia v. Randolph*, to prohibit another co-resident to give consent to search their shared residence. We added a new box on abandoned real estate for search purposes, and added new cases on what constitutes a private search. We added a new section on good faith and changes in the law. A number of courts have considered whether the good faith exception to the exclusionary rule first identified in *United States v. Leon* should apply to good faith reliance by police officers on existing practices that subsequently are held invalid by a reviewing court. We discuss those cases.

- In Chapter 11 we updated many sections with recent cases. These include the sections on random searches of luggage at airports, school searches of students' backpacks and cell phones, and sham roadblocks. We also discuss the 2013 decision of the Supreme Court on collection of DNA samples in *Maryland v. King*.

- In response to requests from some readers, we have added materials to the corpus delicti rule section in Chapter 12. Specifically, we have a new box, "Making Sense of the Corpus Delicti Rule," that examines problems for courts in those states that retain the requirement of corroborating evidence in cases of confessions of child sexual abuse. We focus on two recent Illinois Supreme Court cases, and ask students to compare the results in those cases. Our "You Be the Judge" box in this chapter invites students to make the voluntary-involuntary decision for the admissibility of confessions in several situations taken from recent cases. We retitled the section on invoking the Fifth Amendment right to remain silent, and discuss several recent cases that highlight the need for those in custody to clearly invoke the right to remain silent. We deleted older cases and added four new cases that illustrate how the public safety exception is applied to pre-*Miranda* questioning. Finally, we extensively rewrote the Silence, *Miranda*, and Impeachment section, and added a chart that explains how and when silence of a defendant may be used in a criminal trial.

- In Chapter 13 we deleted the chapter-opening photograph of a police lineup. As one reader suggested, it created the wrong impression of how a lineup is done. We hope the photograph in this edition is better. We added, at various places, new cases on how courts are treating eyewitness identification evidence, and expert testimony about the limits of such testimony.

- The vignette that opens Chapter 14 updates the status of the New York Police Department's controversial stop-and-frisk policy. We extensively rewrote the section on *Terry* stops based on reasonable suspicion. We hope we better show the difference between reasonable suspicion and probable cause, and to that end include recent cases that analyze the requirement in the context of common police operations. We also discuss the 2014 Supreme Court decision in *Navarette v. California* on anonymous 911 callers and reasonable suspicion. The "You Be the Judge" box in this chapter asks students to evaluate the quantum of suspicion police had in several settings, and decide if evidence discovered should be excluded. Under a new section title, "Searches without

Warrants: Detentions and Arrests", we reorganized materials that previously appeared under several different titles. We hope the reorganization makes this area more understandable. We added important recent Supreme Court decisions on police actions without warrants: the 2014 decision in *Riley v. California* for searches of cell phones incident to an arrest; the 2013 decision in *Missouri v. McNeeley* on nonconsensual blood samples in DUI arrests; and the 2013 decision in *United States v. Bailey* on detentions, without probable cause or reasonable suspicion, of persons leaving premises subject to a search warrant.

- We reorganized the material in Chapter 15 so that search warrants come before, rather than after, computer searches. That seems more logical. We added recent cases to the section on extended detention of articles lawfully seized to focus on the permissible length of such detentions. The "You Be the Judge" box for this chapter examines the technical requirements for getting a search warrant, and asks students to respond to challenges by a defendant that the search warrant was not properly obtained or issued. We added new cases on computer search protocols, a subject courts continue to find vexing. We also added cases decided after *California v. Riley* that distinguish between a search of a cell phone and other ways a suspect's cell phone may be used by police. We greatly expanded the section on state and federal wiretapping laws, with cases illustrating when evidence will be excluded for violation of those laws. Finally, we continue to add cases that discuss the introduction and authentication of evidence obtained from social media locations.

- As suggested by a reader, we added cases on "staging" crime scenes to Chapter 16's discussion of the crime scene and chain of custody. For similar reasons, we included a summary of what most experts regard as the mistakes in the crime scene and chain of custody requirements made by the prosecution in the Casey Anthony trial.

- In Chapter 17 the new vignette looks at the ubiquitous use of cell phones as video recorders, and how a video can be used in the prosecution of crimes captured in the video. We also added a new box on the crime of "video voyeurism," with a 2014 case showing how that crime is committed and proved.

- In Chapter 18 we updated the section on DNA testing in light of the Supreme Court's decision in *Maryland v. King*. We also added new information on familial DNA searches. We updated CODIS statistics, and highlighted some of the recent scandals at private and state-run crime labs.

ANCILLARIES FOR THE INSTRUCTOR
Instructor's Resource Manual With Test Bank

An improved and completely updated *Instructor's Resource Manual with Test Bank* is available. The manual includes learning objectives, detailed chapter outlines and summaries, key terms, and Internet resources. Each chapter's test bank contains questions in multiple-choice, true/false, fill-in-the-blank, and essay formats, with a full answer key. The test bank is coded to the learning objectives that appear in the main text and includes the section titles in the main text where the answers can be found. Finally, each question in the test bank has been carefully reviewed by experienced criminal justice instructors for quality, accuracy, and content coverage.

The manual is available for download on the password-protected website and can also be obtained by e-mailing your local Cengage Learning representative.

Cengage Learning Testing

Powered by Cognero, the accompanying assessment tool is a flexible, online system that allows you to

- Import, edit, and manipulate test bank content from the Gardner/Anderson test bank or elsewhere, including your own favorite test questions.
- Create ideal assessments with your choice of fifteen question types (including true/false, multiple choice, opinion scale/likert, and essay).
- Create multiple test versions in an instant using drop-down menus and familiar, intuitive tools that take you through content creation and management with ease.
- Deliver tests from your LMS, your classroom, or wherever you want— and import and export content into other systems as needed.

PowerPoint® Lecture Slides

These handy Microsoft® PowerPoint® slides, which outline the chapters of the main text in a classroom-ready presentation, will help you in making your lectures engaging and in reaching your visually oriented students. Newly revised, the presentations are available for download on the password-protected website and can also be obtained by e-mailing your local Cengage Learning representative.

ANCILLARIES FOR THE STUDENT
CourseMate

Cengage Learning's Criminal Justice CourseMate brings course concepts to life with interactive learning, study, and exam preparation tools that support the printed textbook. CourseMate includes an integrated eBook, quizzes mapped to chapter learning objectives, flashcards, videos, and more, and EngagementTracker, a first-of-its-kind tool that monitors student engagement in the course. The accompanying instructor website offers access to password-protected resources such as an electronic version of the instructor's manual and PowerPoint® slides.

ACKNOWLEDGMENTS

We would like to thank the many reviewers of the eighth and previous editions for their thoughtful suggestions and gracious comments on the organization and subject matter of our book. They are Ken Aud, Oakland Community College; Don Bernardi, Illinois State University; Tim Bragg, Mississippi County Community College; Mark S. Brown, University of South Carolina; Marjie Britz, The Citadel; Valerie Brown, DeKalb Technical College; Harry Bruno, Thomas College; Tod W. Burke, Radford University; Eric Burnham, Denmark Technical College; John Clark, University of Texas at Tyler; Elaine F. Cohen, Broward College; Milo Colton, St. Mary's University; Jean Comley, Ball State University; Chris De Lay, University of Louisiana at Lafayette; Jim Doyle, Chaffey College; Janine Ferraro, Nassau Community College; Michael Goodwin, Solano Community College; John Grimes, University of Alabama at Birmingham; Don V. Haley, Tidewater Community College; Craig Hemmens, Boise State University; Taiping Ho, Ball State University; Maria F. Howell, Stevenson University; Marianne Hudson, College of Western Idaho; Pearl Jacobs, Sacred Heart University; Carolyn Johnson, Stevenson University; David Jones, University of Wisconsin, Oshkosh; Mark A. Jones, Palm Beach State College; Njoroge Kamau, Quinsigamond Community College; Raymond Kessler, Sul Ross State University; David Kotajarvi, Lakeshore Technical College; Walter Lewis, St. Louis Community College at Meramec; Jerry Maynard, Cuyahoga Community College; Michael Meyer, University of North Dakota; Robert E. Mongue, University of Mississippi; Tom O'Connor, North Carolina Wesleyan College; Sam Newton, Weber State University; Karren S. Price, Stephen F. Austin State University; Jennifer Riggs, Eastern New Mexico University-Ruidoso; David P. Schwartz, University of Las Vegas, Nevada; Anita Sedillo, Virginia Commonwealth University; Sandy Self, Hardin-Simmons University; Diane Sjuts, Metro Community College; Steven Sondergaard, Defiance College; Dave Stout, Cedarville University; David Stumpf, Minnesota School of Business; Kelli Styron, Tarleton State University; Sharon Tracy, Georgia Southern University; Robert Vaughn, Cedarville University; Arnold R. Waggoner, Rose State College; Carroll T. Wagner, Harrisburg Area Community College; Ruth Walsh, Washtenaw Community College; Tamra Watts, Kean University; Thomas White, University of Texas-Pan American; Jack Williams, Western New England College; and Rickey Williams, Sr., Danville Area Community College.

We also would like to thank the staff at Cengage Learning, in particular Carolyn Henderson Meier and Christy Frame, as well as the production service editor for this edition, Lynn Lustberg of MPS Limited. As always, the publishing part of this endeavor has played a vital role in the book's progress.

Tom Gardner and Terry Anderson would like to thank their families for their patience and understanding while they worked on this edition of *Criminal Evidence*.

Terry Anderson would also like to thank Creighton Law School for the logistical support given him while he worked on this edition.

Thomas J. Gardner

Terry M. Anderson

CHAPTER 1

History and Development of the Law of Criminal Evidence

KING JOHN SIGNS THE
MAGNA CARTA

duncan1890/iStockphoto.com

CHAPTER CONTENTS

LEARNING OBJECTIVES

In this chapter we provide a summary of the history of the use of evidence in criminal trials, with a special focus on criminal defendants' rights contained in the U.S. Constitution. The learning objectives for this chapter are

Explain the importance of the Magna Carta.

Explain the function of the writ of habeas corpus.

Identify how the U.S. Supreme Court made the Bill of Rights applicable in state court criminal cases.

List the rights identified and made available to a criminal defendant under the U.S. Constitution.

In 2012 David Rivera pled guilty in U.S. District Court in California to the federal crime of transportation of 214.4 grams of methamphetamine. Under the plea agreement reached with the prosecution, the parties stipulated that Rivera would be sentenced at base level 31 under Federal Sentencing Guidelines, but that each side could argue to the District Court judge for a reduction or increase of that base level. The base level plays a significant role in the length of the sentence imposed under Federal Sentencing Guidelines.

At the first sentencing hearing Rivera brought his 7-year-old son with him to the hearing. There, his lawyers argued Rivera should be given a "minimal role" reduction in his sentence because of his limited role in the crime. The district judge expressed displeasure about the presence of Rivera's son in the courtroom, stating that he (the judge) would not be manipulated by such actions. The judge continued the sentencing hearing, and told Rivera he could not bring family members to the continued hearing.

At the continued hearing, where only Rivera and his attorney were present, the Judge declined to give Rivera the "minimal role" reduction, and sentenced him to 97 months in prison. Rivera appealed to the Ninth Circuit Court of Appeals, contending his Sixth Amendment right to a "public trial" was violated when the District Judge excluded his family members from the hearing.

What do you think are the reasons for the "public trial" requirement? Does the First Amendment play a role? Should "public trial" include the sentencing part of the trial? Why did it matter if Rivera's family, including his young son, were excluded from the sentencing hearing? Can you think of good reasons for a judge to order a closed hearing? Were the judge's reasons in Rivera's case good enough? *See United States v. Rivera*, 682 F.3d 1223 (9th Cir. 2012).

In this chapter we examine the history of rules of evidence, and show their relationship to many of our most important Constitutional guarantees and privileges. One of those guarantees, the Sixth Amendment right to a "speedy and public trial," was invoked by Rivera in the case cited above.

HISTORY OF THE RULES OF EVIDENCE

One cannot understand the rules of evidence applicable in criminal trials today without some appreciation of the historical development of those rules. Evidentiary rules are the gates through which information flows into our judicial courtrooms; the size and shape of the gates have varied over the life of the United States and other English-speaking nations.

The United States and England share a common judicial heritage. Most of the early rules of evidence were made by English courts, although some were made by English parliaments. These early rules of evidence were brought to the American colonies and used by the first English settlers. The same rules were used by other English-speaking colonies, such as Canada and Australia, and were known as common-law rules of evidence.[1] Because of this common heritage, many similarities exist even today in the laws of evidence used in English-speaking countries. The following account of the first murder trial in the American colonies would also describe the court proceedings used in other English colonies:

> The first reported murder in the American colonies occurred in 1630. John Billington, one of the original band of 102 Pilgrims to sail on the Mayflower, waylaid a neighbor and killed the man by shooting him with his blunderbuss. As the colonies had no written criminal laws, Billington was charged with the English common-law crime of murder and tried using the English common-law rules of evidence and criminal procedure. After a prompt trial and conviction, Billington was sentenced to death and hanged.[2]

Rules of evidence are an important part of all criminal justice systems, just as rules are important in baseball, football, and basketball games. In a democracy, rules of evidence are important not only to safeguard the rights of accused persons in a fair trial but also to ensure the interests of the public in the proper functioning of the criminal justice system. Some rules of evidence are highly controversial and cause arguments over what would best serve the overall needs of society.

Early Methods of Determining Guilt or Innocence

Today, persons charged with criminal offenses are presumed innocent until proven guilty. Defendants may admit or deny a criminal charge, and if the charge is denied, place the burden of proof on the government to come forward with sufficient, credible, and admissible evidence proving guilt beyond a reasonable doubt.

But the rights we enjoy today did not always exist. They developed slowly over the centuries and were incorporated into the common law. Many were made part of the U.S. Constitution by our Founding Fathers.

ordeal A medieval method of proof that was an appeal to God to determine guilt or innocence.

At the time the Normans conquered England in 1066, the use of **ordeals** to determine guilt or innocence was a common practice. A titled person or one of noble birth could demand trial by battle to determine his guilt or innocence. Winning a sword fight would prove innocence, whereas losing would show guilt. Because the loser was often killed or seriously injured, the case would ordinarily be disposed of by the outcome of the battle.

The guilt or innocence of a common person was determined by other types of ordeals. The nineteenth-century English judge Sir James Stephens described these ordeals in his treatise *History of the Criminal Law of England:*

> It is unnecessary to give a minute account of the ceremonial of the ordeals. They were of various kinds. The general nature of all was the same. They were appeals to God to work a miracle in attestation of the innocence of the accused person. The handling of hot iron, and plunging the hand or arm into boiling water unhurt, were the commonest. The ordeal of water was a very singular institution. Sinking was the sign of innocence, floating the sign of guilt. As any one would sink unless he understood how to float, and intentionally did so, it is difficult to see how anyone could ever be convicted by this means. Is it possible that this ordeal may have been an honourable form of suicide, like the Japanese happy despatch? In nearly every case the accused would sink. This would prove his innocence, indeed, but there would be no need to take him out. He would thus die honourably. If by accident he floated, he would be put to death disgracefully.[3]

The ordeals adjudicated guilt by appeals to God (or the supernatural). People living in the Middle Ages believed in frequent divine intervention in human affairs and thus were content to leave questions of guilt or innocence to such interventions.

All this changed in England, however, at the Lateran Council of 1215, when clergy were prohibited from taking part in ordeals. Without the clergy, one could not be sure God had ordained the result of the ordeal. Indeed, in the reign of King John (1199–1216), the ordeal went from being the standard of proof to completely nonexistent.

In its place came the oath and oath-helpers. Although still an appeal to divine guidance, the oath, in which the accused swore before God his innocence, began the journey toward trial by jury. To support his oath, the accused gathered oath-helpers to swear to his innocence. Over time, these oath-helpers began to swear not to the ultimate guilt or innocence of the accused but to facts relevant to his guilt or innocence. In essence, they became witnesses.

presentment juries
English forerunners to grand juries; gave information that crimes had been committed.

At the same time, itinerant justices holding court around England began to impanel groups of local residents into **presentment juries**, whose purpose was to inform the justices of crimes committed by other residents. The accused then put himself "on the oath" of his fellow residents (often referred to as the "petit" jury), rather than producing his own oath-helpers. Over time, it came to be realized that those serving on the presentment jury should not serve on the smaller petit jury. By the fourteenth century, the origins of our grand jury and trial jury system were firmly established in English law.

As the use of presentment and petit juries became widespread in England, rules developed to control and direct the tasks of those juries. Then, as now, the presentment jury had few evidentiary limitations. The petit jury, however, became charged not only with determining the guilt or innocence of the accused but also with finding the facts upon which its determination depended. Once the jury was established as a fact-finding body, rules of evidence controlling how facts could be presented to the jury began to develop.

In the long period between the fourteenth century and today, rules governing the introduction of facts into criminal trials developed slowly and inconsistently. For example, even though hearsay evidence was regarded as unreliable even in the early thirteenth century,[4] such evidence was still widely permitted in the American colonies. Other nonjudicial forces helped move the nature of criminal trials and rules of evidence forward.

WHEN EVIDENCE OF WITCHCRAFT WAS PERMITTED IN THE COURTS OF THE AMERICAN COLONIES

Not too many years prior to the signing of the American Declaration of Independence, evidence of the crime of witchcraft was permitted in the criminal courts of some of the American colonies. Massachusetts, Connecticut, and Virginia permitted prosecutions for the crime of witchcraft based on superstition and ignorance.

Witchcraft was first prosecuted as a crime in the Roman Empire. Over the years, thousands of people in Europe were tried, convicted, and put to death for being witches or practicing witchcraft. For example, in 1431 Joan of Arc was convicted in France of being a witch and burned at the stake by a tribunal under the direction of English invaders. The English used the accusation of witchcraft as a convenient way of eliminating a very effective French military opponent.

A crop failure, a sickness, or an epidemic within a community could lead to accusations that a local person was a witch and the cause of the problems. The Salem, Massachusetts, witchcraft trials of 1692 resulted in the execution of 19 people and the imprisonment of over 150 others. Arthur Miller's famous play *The Crucible* is a modern dramatization of the Salem witchcraft trials. In Miller's play, the accusations were not of crop failure or an epidemic but of sexual improprieties, and were made by teenage girls. The book form of Miller's play contains commentary by the author. Miller observes in the introduction to his play that after the accusations by the teenage girls were made, "long-held hatreds of neighbors could now be openly expressed ... one could cry witch against one's neighbors ... old scores could be settled ... and any envy of the miserable toward the happy could and did burst out in the general revenge."[a]

The crime of witchcraft no longer exists, and under the American criminal justice system could never be resurrected.

[a]Arthur Miller, *The Crucible* (New York: Viking Press, 1953).

MAGNA CARTA AND HABEAS CORPUS

In twelfth-century England, people could be jailed based on anonymous accusations of wrongdoing, or they could be seized on mere suspicion or on the whim of a government official. English kings suppressed political opposition by jailing anyone who dared criticize the Crown or the government. Absolute loyalty was compelled by the arrest of those suspected of antigovernment sentiments or statements.

Because of these abuses by English kings, the great barons of England revolted against the Crown. After many years of fighting, King John met with the barons in 1215 at a field in Runnymede, England. An agreement between the parties to stop the fighting resulted in the king and the barons signing a document called **Magna Carta**, or the Great Charter. Among other clauses, Magna Carta stated that there would be no criminal "trial upon ... simple accusation without producing credible witnesses to the truth therein" and that "no freeman shall be taken, imprisoned ... except by lawful judgment of his peers or the law of the land." Magna Carta was a historic first step toward democracy and the establishment of minimum standards for arresting and imprisoning people accused of crimes. Under this new concept of law, no one could be taken into **custody** on mere suspicion, on a whim, or without substantial good cause. Magna Carta began the development of the concept in law that there had to be **probable cause**, or "reasonable grounds to believe," to justify arresting or holding a person in custody.

Magna Carta deeply affected the drafters of the American Declaration of Independence:

> The event became the rallying cry of individual liberty in England during the 17th century, and so influenced the Founding Fathers of our country that the Seal of the Magna Carta was emblazoned on the cover of the *Journal of the Proceedings of the First Continental Congress*, held in Philadelphia on September 5, 1774, where our forefathers laid the foundation stone of individual liberty in the United States.[5]

Another important milestone in the protection of personal liberties was the development of the Writ of Habeas Corpus. This famous writ is believed to date to the fourteenth and fifteenth centuries. The Writ of Habeas Corpus was and is a safeguard against the illegal or improper holding of a person against his or her will. The word *writ* means a "writing," and **habeas corpus** is a Latin term meaning "have the body." This writ, when signed by a judge, is served upon the government official who has custody of a person and orders that official to appear before the court and show cause for holding the person. If such cause is not shown the person may be released.

Magna Carta and habeas corpus not only are very important legal concepts in the English-speaking world but also have had an important impact worldwide. Magna Carta first expressed the idea that a person should not be jailed or held without just cause. The Writ of Habeas Corpus was the earliest legal procedure by which illegal or improper jailing or detention could be challenged in a court of law. If a person is held without just cause and legal authority, the judge presiding at the habeas corpus hearing must order his or her release.

The American Founding Fathers guaranteed the right of habeas corpus in the U.S. Constitution. ARTICLE I, SECTION 9 of the U.S. Constitution provides that "The privilege of the Writ of Habeas Corpus shall not be suspended, unless when in Cases of Rebellion or Invasion the public Safety may require it." The original 13 states, and all those that subsequently joined the union, did the same. Some states

Magna Carta The Great Charter signed by King John of England and his barons in 1215; created the first standards for arresting and imprisoning those accused of crimes.

custody Under police control, whether or not physically constrained.

probable cause The quantum (amount) of evidence required by the Fourth Amendment to make an arrest or to issue a search warrant; greater than reasonable suspicion but can be less than proof or reasonable doubt.

habeas corpus Latin name of the writ used to compel a government official, such as a prison warden, to show cause why the official is holding a person in custody.

strengthened the constitutional guarantee by statutes, such as Wisconsin statute 782.09, which provides that "any judge who refuses to grant a writ of habeas corpus, when legally applied for, is liable to the prisoner in the sum of $1,000." Other statutes impose penalties for "refusing papers" ($200), "concealing" or "transferring" the prisoner ($1,000 or six months' imprisonment), and "reimprisoning party discharged" ($1,250 and misdemeanor violation).

The famous English writer Sir William Blackstone wrote that habeas corpus is "the most celebrated writ in the English law." Chief Justice Marshall of the U.S. Supreme Court called the writ a "great constitutional privilege," and the U.S. Supreme Court has stated a number of times that "there is no higher duty than to maintain it unimpaired."

Habeas corpus writs provide a form of review of criminal convictions and sentences in addition to the normal appeal process. Every state has some form of appellate review for those convicted of crimes. In addition, so-called "direct review" of a state conviction is possible in the U.S. Supreme Court, though petitions for such review are not commonly granted by the Supreme Court. Federal convictions may be appealed to the appropriate U.S. Court of Appeals, and again direct review by the U.S. Supreme Court is possible, but infrequent.

U.S. courts, mainly federal district courts in whose jurisdictions prisons are located, are authorized under 28 U.S.C. § 2254 to hear petitions for habeas corpus by persons convicted in state courts. 28 U.S.C. § 2255, called post-conviction relief, provides similar procedures for federal prisoners. Generally speaking, habeas corpus petitions and petitions under 2255 are filed after the normal appeals process through the state (or federal for 2255) appellate system has been exhausted. Section 2254 specifically requires that the petition show that state remedies have been exhausted. Petitions must allege that the prisoner is being held in violation of federal law or the U.S. Constitution.

Prior to 1996 federal courts hearing habeas petitions by state prisoners reviewed questions of law under "de novo" review, which gave little deference to the decision of the state court. Purely fact questions, however, were reviewed with great deference to the findings of the state court. The Antiterrorism and Effective Death Penalty Act of 1996 made important changes in how habeas corpus petitions by state prisoners were reviewed in federal courts, if the petitioners' claim had been "adjudicated on the merits" in the state courts. That Act, now codified as 28 U.S.C. § 2254(d) (1) (2), limits application of the writ to cases where the conviction or sentence was contrary to, or an unreasonable application of, a "clearly established Federal law, as determined by the Supreme Court of the United States," or based on an "unreasonable determination of the facts" in light of evidence admitted at the state court trial. If the claim of a violation of federal law or the U.S. Constitution had not been "adjudicated on the merits" in the state courts, the pre-1996 form of review is used.

Cullen v. Pinholster, 131 S. Ct. 1388 (2011) is an important case on how federal courts are to review the claims in the habeas petition. (Citations in criminal cases typically include the name of a state or the federal government: e.g. *State* (or *People,* or *Commonwealth*) *v. Smith*, or *United States v. Smith*. In habeas cases the person seeking relief is incarcerated. As a result, the name of the other party in the habeas petition is typically the warden of the penitentiary where the prisoner is held. "Cullen" is the name of the warden of the penitentiary where Pinholster was incarcerated.)

In *Cullen*, a petitioner claimed a murder conviction and resulting death sentence were flawed because his attorney failed to adequately raise the petitioner's mental condition at the penalty-phase of the trial. The petitioner introduced new medical evidence at the habeas hearing that supported his claim that he had mental problems that should have been a factor in his sentence. The full Ninth Circuit Court of Appeals sitting *en banc* agreed and granted the petition.

The U.S. Supreme Court reversed. It held that when reviewing a decision of a state court, the "record" for review was the evidence before the state court at the time it made its decision. Evidence introduced at the habeas hearing on an issue already reviewed in the state court could not be considered.

Thaler v. Haynes, 130 S. Ct. 1171 (2010) illustrates how the "clearly established Federal law, as determined by the Supreme Court" also serves as a limit on habeas petitions. In that case a federal circuit court of appeals ordered a retrial in a Texas murder case, based on the defendant's claim that the trial judge should not have accepted the state's "race-neutral" reason for using a peremptory challenge to exclude a Black juror. (See the discussion of peremptory challenges in Chapter 2.) The prosecution gave its reason for excluding the juror as based on the juror's demeanor. The trial judge who accepted that as an adequate reason did not personally conduct the *voir dire* (jury selection), and thus did not see the juror's demeanor. The circuit court held that "demeanor" cannot be an adequate "race neutral" reason unless the trial court personally observed the juror in *voir dire*. The Supreme Court reversed, stating that such a legal principle is not a "clearly established" rule because no Supreme Court opinion actually reached such a result.

 LEGAL CASES

Habeas Corpus and Enemy Combatants

Since 2001, the U.S. military has detained alien enemy combatants at Guantanamo Naval Base in Cuba. Some of these detainees have sought to obtain review of their detentions by use of the habeas corpus writ. The U.S. government initially contended that federal courts had no jurisdiction over the naval base, but in *Rasul v. Bush* [542 U.S. 466 (2004)], the U.S. Supreme Court held that under existing jurisdictional statutes, federal courts did have jurisdiction over the naval base.

In response to that decision, Congress passed the Military Commissions Act of 2006 [28 U.S.C. § 2241 (e)], which contained a clause stating that federal courts had no jurisdiction to hear habeas corpus claims made by alien enemy combatants detained at military installations. Several detainees appealed dismissal of their habeas corpus petitions. On review the Supreme Court held that enemy combatants detained at military installations had the constitutional right to bring habeas corpus petitions, and as a result section 2241(e) was an unconstitutional violation of the Suspension Clause [Art. I, § 9, cl. 2], which prohibits the suspension of the writ except in cases of "Rebellion or Invasion." See *Boumediene v. Bush* [128 S. Ct. 2229 (2008)].

Suspected enemy combatants detained at Guantanamo were tried in military tribunals during the Bush administration. President Obama initially ordered the military tribunals to cease such trials, but in 2011 revoked that order to permit the military trial of Khalid Sheik Mohammed, the suspected mastermind of the 9/11 attacks. Although the Justice Department stated it wished to try Mohammed in federal district court in New York City, the anticipated cost for such a trial—in the hundreds of millions of dollars—led the Justice Department to reopen the military tribunals. Mohammed remains detained at Guantanamo. Some suspected terrorists have been tried in federal court. Abu Gaith, the son-in-law of Osama bin Laden, was tried in federal court in New York in March 2014, and was convicted on terrorism charges on March 26, 2014.

THE AMERICAN DECLARATION OF INDEPENDENCE

When students are asked where their personal freedoms come from, they will often answer that personal freedoms come from government. This answer was correct hundreds of years ago, when it was believed that kings received their authority to rule from God. What few personal rights the ordinary person had in those days came from the ruler. This was known as the divine right of kings. Generally accepted and promoted throughout the world in the Middle Ages, this doctrine stated that monarchs received absolute authority to govern from God and that their subjects had only such personal freedoms as fit their status under their sovereign.

SOME ABUSES LEADING TO THE SIGNING OF THE DECLARATION OF INDEPENDENCE

The American Declaration of Independence, celebrated each year on the Fourth of July, lists more than 25 abuses by the "King of Great Britain" against the American colonies. It was these abuses that caused the colonies to declare their independence from Great Britain. About two-thirds of the abuses concerned the English mercantile system, which Great Britain forced upon the American colonies. Under this system, Americans had to buy only English products and goods at prices set by the English. The system was enforced against the colonies by military force and heavy taxation, which led to the famous cry "No taxation without representation" and incidents like the Boston Tea Party. The famous Scottish economist Adam Smith, who wrote the *Wealth of Nations* in 1776 and opposed the English policy of mercantilism, became known as the father of the American economic system. The following is a brief summary of the remaining one-third of the abuses listed in the Declaration of Independence:

Abuses Concerning Liberty, Freedom, and the Judiciary	Correction of the Abuse in the U.S. Constitution
"He has made Judges dependent on his will alone ..."	Article III, creating an independent judiciary
"He has kept among us in times of peace Standing Armies ... [and] has quartered large bodies of armed troops among us."	Third Amendment to the Bill of Rights (Soldiers may not be quartered without consent)
He "... protect[s] [the armed troops], by a mock trial, from punishment for any Murders which they should commit on the Inhabitants."	The establishment of an independent judiciary, an elected president and Congress, and grand juries
"... depriving us in many cases, of the benefits of Trial by Jury."	"... the accused shall enjoy the right of a ... trial ... by an impartial jury" (Sixth Amendment)
He "... transport[s] us beyond the Seas to be tried for pretended offenses."	The right to an "indictment by a Grand Jury" and the right to be tried in "the State and district where the crime shall have been committed ..." (Fifth and Sixth Amendments)
"He has plundered our seas, ravaged our Coasts, burnt our towns, and destroyed the lives of our people."	The establishment of an independent judiciary, an elected Congress and president, and grand juries
"He is at this time transporting large Armies of foreign Mercenaries to compleat the work of death, desolation and tyranny ..."	Limiting the powers of the president and the Congress to those specifically set forth in Article I and II, and the protection of the Third Amendment

This theory, actively promoted by those in power, helped monarchs rule and maintain control over their subjects.

Early American documents show that the American colonies did not accept the European concept of the divine right of kings. The 1641 Massachusetts Body of Liberties commenced by discussing the "free fruition of such liberties, Immunities and privileges ... as due every man."[6] The 1765 Declaration of Rights spoke of "inherent rights and liberties," "freedom of a people," and "the undoubted rights of Englishmen."[7]

The American Declaration of Independence of 1776 specifically repudiated the doctrine of the divine right of kings, pointing out that personal freedoms do not come from government or kings. Every Fourth of July, we celebrate the signing of the document that established the following propositions:

- That the United States is independent from Great Britain (the document details the "history of repeated injuries and usurpations" of the king of Great Britain, who sought to establish "an absolute Tyranny over these States")
- That "Governments are instituted among Men, deriving their just powers from the consent of the governed"
- That "all men are created equal, that they are endowed by their Creator with certain unalienable Rights, that among these are Life, Liberty, and the pursuit of Happiness"

THE U.S. CONSTITUTION AND THE AMERICAN BILL OF RIGHTS

When the American Founding Fathers met in Philadelphia in 1787, many of the wrongs of the past had been eliminated. For example, trial for witchcraft had been abolished, and people accused of crimes no longer had to prove their innocence by ordeal or battle. The delegates set about writing a constitution for the new American democracy that would embody the spirit of the Declaration of Independence and create a workable, practical government to serve the people. They stated their goals in the preamble to the new U.S. Constitution:

> We the People of the United States, in order to form a more perfect Union, establish justice, insure domestic Tranquility, provide for the common defense, promote the general Welfare, and secure the Blessings of Liberty to ourselves and our Posterity, do ordain and establish this Constitution for the United States of America.

The U.S. Constitution sought to protect the privilege of habeas corpus and prohibited such abuses as the passing of bills of attainder and ex post facto laws. The right of trial by jury was protected, and *corruption of blood* (punishing a family for the criminal acts of another family member) was forbidden. The drafters of the Constitution knew that such abuses had occurred in England and were determined that they would not occur in the new American nation.

As a further protection, the Constitution provided that all federal officials, including the president of the United States, could be removed upon "Impeachment for, and Conviction of, Treason, Bribery, or other high Crimes and Misdemeanors" (ART. II, SEC. 4).

When the Constitution was presented to the states for ratification, it was criticized as not going far enough to protect the people from possible abuses by the new federal government. The people understood their state governments and believed

The delegates to the Constitutional Convention set about writing a constitution that would embody the spirit of the Declaration of Independence, create a working, practical government to serve the people, and protect the people from abuses by government.

Bettmann/Corbis

ANCIENT WRONGS THAT INFLUENCED THE AMERICAN CRIMINAL JUSTICE SYSTEM

Wrong	Resulted In	Led to the Following Development	U.S. Constitution
The practice of English kings jailing persons for no good reason, on mere suspicion or on simple accusation by another.	The English civil war of the late 1100s and early 1200s, which was settled by King John signing Magna Carta in 1215, abolished this practice.	Magna Carta provides that there will be no criminal "trial upon … simple accusation without producing credible witnesses to the truth therein." Magna Carta led to the development of the great English Writ of Habeas Corpus, which requires law officers to show probable cause to a court in order to hold a person in custody.	The Fourth Amendment requires probable cause to arrest and to issue a search warrant. Habeas corpus is guaranteed by Article I, Section 9 of the Constitution.
The use of torture and coercion to obtain confessions.	The English Parliament abolished the inquisitorial court, the Star Chamber, in 1640s. [See *Miranda v. Arizona*, 384 U.S. 436 (1966).]	The development was the privilege against self-incrimination and the right to remain silent while in police custody.	The Fifth Amendment contains privilege against self-incrimination, and the Sixth Amendment the right to an attorney.
The use of general warrants, which gave British officials power to search anywhere and anything they wished.	The practice was discontinued in England but continued to "bedevil" the American colonies.	The continued practice of the British to search "where they pleased" was the "most prominent event" that led to the Declaration of Independence and the American Revolutionary War. [*Stanford v. State of Texas*, 85 S. Ct. 506, 510 (1965).]	The Fourth Amendment forbids "unreasonable searches and seizures" and requires probable cause and search warrants.

Wrong	Resulted In	Led to the Following Development	U.S. Constitution
The practice of English courts of convicting persons on hearsay and written statements or testimony by persons who did not appear in court and who were not identified to the accused.	This practice was used to "frame" Sir Walter Raleigh in 1603 and send him to prison for treason.	The hearsay rules were developed, along with the requirement that the government prove criminal charges with witnesses who testified in court in the presence of the accused.	The Sixth Amendment makes it a requirement that "… the accused shall enjoy the right to be confronted with the witnesses against him…" Article II, Section 3 of the Constitution prohibits conviction for treason except on "the testimony of two witnesses."
Charging a person with a trumped-up criminal charge and then putting pressure on the jury to convict the person.	William Penn was charged in this manner in 1670. When an English jury would not convict him, the jury was held for two days without food, water, or toilet facilities.	When the jury would not give in to the pressures of the judge and the king, they were fined for their conduct. This case was important in the development of a system of independent juries. William Penn left England and founded the state of Pennsylvania.	Persons charged with crimes have a right to "an impartial jury" (Sixth Amendment) and "due process of law" (fundamental fairness requirement of the Fourteenth Amendment).

Bill of Rights The first 10 amendments to the U.S. Constitution.

they could control them, but they were suspicious of the new central government. As a result, prior to ratification of the new Constitution, it was agreed that additional protections would immediately be added to the Constitution. The U.S. Constitution was ratified in 1788, and 10 amendments, now known as the **Bill of Rights**, were added in 1791.

In a 1991 U.S. Supreme Court opinion, Justice Scalia pointed out that "most of the procedural protections of the federal Bill of Rights simply codified traditional common-law privileges (that) had been widely adopted by the states." Justice Scalia used the following quote from 1878: "the law is perfectly well settled that the first ten amendments to the Constitution … were not intended to lay down any novel principles of government, but simply to embody certain guarantees and immunities which we had inherited from our English ancestors."[8]

The Bill of Rights (see Appendix A) originally applied only to the federal government. Beginning in 1961, however, the U.S. Supreme Court began to make the Bill of Rights applicable to the states through the Fourteenth Amendment. (See the case of *Mapp v. Ohio* and the material in Chapter 9 on the use of the American exclusionary rule.)

BASIC RIGHTS UNDER THE U.S. CONSTITUTION TODAY

The United States celebrated the 200th anniversary of the U.S. Constitution in 1988. This remarkable document, which includes the Bill of Rights, has received worldwide attention and has been a model for many countries. It sets forth the foundation and requirements for the law of criminal evidence used throughout the United States.

The people of the United States may change, abolish, or modify any part of the Constitution; polls show, however, that the great majority of Americans want to keep the Constitution and the Bill of Rights intact. Although individual rights in criminal prosecutions are articulated in various parts of the Constitution and Bill of Rights, the Fifth and Sixth Amendments contain an extensive list of those rights. The Fifth Amendment states:

> No person shall be held to answer for a capital, or otherwise infamous crime, unless on a presentment or indictment of a Grand Jury, except in cases arising in the land or naval forces, or in the Militia, when in actual service in time of War or public danger; nor shall any person be subject for the same offence to be twice put in jeopardy of life or limb; nor shall be compelled in any criminal case to be a witness against himself, nor be deprived

PROCEDURES & PROCESSES

The 48-Hour Requirement of a Probable Cause Hearing (The "Promptness Rule")

When an arrest warrant is issued, there has already been a determination that probable cause exists for the arrest. However, when an arrest occurs without a warrant, no such determination is made before the arrest. In *County of Riverside v. McLaughlin* [500 U.S. 44 (1991)], the U.S. Supreme Court held that a suspect arrested without an arrest warrant must have a probable cause hearing before a judge or magistrate "promptly," within 48 hours of the arrest, including weekends and holidays. If such a hearing is held within 48 hours, the probable cause hearing will "as a general matter, comply with the promptness requirement." However, even a hearing held within a 48-hour period can be unreasonable if the delay was "for the purpose of gathering additional evidence to justify the arrest [or] motivated by ill will against the arrested individual, or delay for delay's sake."

If the probable cause hearing is delayed beyond the 48-hour period, the burden is on the government "to demonstrate the existence of a bona fide emergency or otherwise extraordinary circumstance." For example, in the 2012 case of *Waganfeald v. Gusman*, 674 F.3d 475 (5th Cir. 2012) the court held that Hurricane Katrina, which hit New Orleans on the day an arrested person's 48-hour limit was reached, was a sufficient emergency justifying a longer wait before a probable cause hearing was held.

If that burden is not met, many states now provide that the arrested person must be released on his own recognizance. Also, evidence obtained during the delay may be excluded from any resulting trial, if the delay in some way contributed to obtaining the evidence. However, most courts hold that evidence obtained during the 48-hour period is admissible, even if a subsequent delay occurred. *See e.g. State v. Lawrence*, 154 S.W.3d 71 (Tenn. 2005). Courts will not normally order dismissal of the criminal charge as the remedy for a violation of the promptness rule, although the court in *State v. Larson*, 776 N.W.2d 254 (S.D. 2009) remanded to the trial court a conviction of a defendant who was held 18 days before getting a probable cause hearing to determine if that remedy should be invoked.

Because of the "promptness" rule, writs of habeas corpus are generally not needed to secure the release of persons arrested without a warrant.

of life, liberty, or property, without due process of law; nor shall private property be taken for public use, without just compensation.

The Sixth Amendment states,

In all criminal prosecutions, the accused shall enjoy the right to a speedy and public trial, by an impartial jury of the State and district wherein the crime shall have been committed, which district shall have been previously ascertained by law, and to be informed of the nature and cause of the accusation; to be confronted with the witnesses against him; to have compulsory process for obtaining witnesses in his favour, and have Assistance of Counsel for his defence.

The following sections summarize some of the most basic rights protected or created by the Bill of Rights. Many of these rights will be discussed more fully in later chapters of this book.

The Presumption of Innocence Until Proven Guilty

beyond a reasonable doubt The burden that the prosecution must meet in proving guilt in criminal cases; applies to every element of the crime charged.

presumption of innocence The legal presumption required in all criminal courts that the defendant is innocent until sufficient credible evidence is produced to carry the burden of proving guilt beyond a reasonable doubt.

One of the most deeply rooted traditions of modern Anglo-Saxon law is that an accused is innocent until proven guilty **beyond a reasonable doubt**.[9] In *Estelle v. Williams*,[10] the U.S. Supreme Court stated, "The **presumption of innocence**, though not articulated in the Constitution, is a basic component of a fair trial under our system of criminal justice." A violation of this right can occur when the jury is not properly instructed on the presumption of innocence and the burden of the prosecution to overcome the presumption by competent evidence. In *Taylor v. Kentucky*,[11] the Supreme Court held that the failure of the trial court to give a requested instruction on the presumption of innocence was, under the facts of that case, a violation of the right to a fair trial. The Court stated that every criminal defendant has the right to have guilt or innocence determined solely by evidence adduced during trial, and the presumption of innocence serves to impress upon the jury the importance of that right.

A violation can also occur through statements made by the prosecution. For example, in *Pagano v. Allard*,[12] the court held that, after a prosecutor referred to the presumption of innocence as a "cloak" that protected a defendant, the prosecutor's statement in the closing argument to the jury that "... now that cloak comes off" violated the right to a fair trial.

The Right to a Speedy and Public Trial

The Sixth Amendment provides that "the accused shall enjoy the right to a speedy and public trial." The right to a public trial means all court sessions must be open to the public, unless sufficient, specific reasons for closing the courtroom are given by the trial court. In the 2010 case of *Presley v. Georgia*, 130 S. Ct. 721, the U.S. Supreme Court held that the "public trial" right includes *voir dire*. It reversed a defendant's conviction for cocaine trafficking because the trial court ordered the courtroom cleared during *voir dire* without giving a sufficient reason for doing so, or considering alternatives.

In *Barker v. Wingo*[13] the U.S. Supreme Court held that "speedy trial" right could not be defined in any specific time period, but depended on the circumstances of each case. Factors to be considered when the right is invoked include (1) the length of the delay between accusation and trial, (2) reasons for the delay, (3) whether the defendant asserted the right during the delay, and (4) whether the defendant was prejudiced by the delay. In the 2013 case of *United States v. Ghailani*[14] the court held the speedy trial right was not violated by a five-year delay. The defendant, a member of the terrorist group al Qaeda, was captured by the CIA in 2004, and interrogated concerning the terrorist attacks on U.S. embassies in Nairobi, Kenya, and Tanzania in 1998, in which 244 people were killed. He was held by the CIA outside the United States for two years, where he was subjected to "enhanced" interrogation. In 2006 Ghailani was brought to the detention facility at Guantanamo Bay, Cuba. In October, 2012, Ghailani was tried in federal court in New York, and convicted of terrorist acts against U.S. property that took human lives. He was sentenced to life in prison. The appeals court rejected Ghailani's claim that the speedy trial clause was violated, mainly because the delays were not caused by the bad faith of the government, and did not prejudice his ability to prepare for his trial.

There is some question whether a delay in sentencing a convicted defendant should be included under the "speedy trial" rule of the Sixth Amendment or under the Due Process Clause of the Fifth and Fourteenth Amendments. At least one federal court of appeals has held the speedy trial rule inapplicable to sentencing delays. In *United States v. Ray*, 578 F.3d 184 (2d Cir. 2009), *cert denied* 130 S. Ct. 2401 (2010) the Court held that "trial" in the Sixth Amendment does not include sentencing, but that an unreasonable delay in imposing sentence would violate the due process clause.

A defendant may waive the right to a speedy trial with the permission of the court. The federal government and many states have enacted statutes that state the time within which a trial must be held. The federal government's Speedy Trial Act requires a trial within 70 days for a felony and within 60 days for a misdemeanor, unless the requirement of a speedy trial is waived.[15]

The Right to an Indictment

About half of the states follow the system imposed upon the federal government by the Fifth Amendment, requiring a grand jury indictment for a "capital, or otherwise infamous crime." In the other states, elected prosecutors (district attorneys or state attorneys) make the decisions about whether to charge and what crimes to charge. Defendants charged by a district or state attorney have the right to a preliminary hearing if they are charged with a felony.

In the case of separate trials of multiple defendants, many courts have held that the prosecution cannot charge each defendant with the same criminal act. For example, in the trial of *A,* the prosecutor cannot allege that *A* pulled the trigger on the murder weapon, and then in the trial of *B* allege that *B* did so. In 2004, a federal circuit court of appeals held that doing so violated the Due Process Clause.[16] In 2005, the U.S. Supreme Court reversed,[17] holding that the use of inconsistent charges did not prejudice the defendant because he could have been convicted under the state aiding and abetting statute. (This aspect of this decision is discussed in the guilty plea section in Chapter 3.) The Supreme Court remanded the case to determine whether the use of inconsistent charges prejudiced the defendant in the sentencing process, where he was given the death sentence.

The Right to a Fair (Not Perfect) Trial

In any trial, mistakes can be made. The U.S. Supreme Court and state courts have repeatedly held that under the Due Process clauses of the Fifth and Fourteenth Amendments "the law does not require that a defendant receive a perfect trial, only a fair one."[18] As a result, a defendant convicted in a trial where harmless error has occurred has received a fair trial, though not a perfect trial. However, if the error was harmful, reversible, or plain, the defendant has not received a fair trial and is entitled to a new trial or to have the criminal charges dropped.

A defendant is not entitled to a new trial if it is shown that the error was harmless beyond a reasonable doubt. An error is harmless if it did not in any meaningful way contribute to the defendant's conviction. Where the error is the improper admission of evidence, the U.S. Supreme Court has held that "the test for harmfulness is whether there is a reasonable possibility that the improperly admitted evidence contributed to the conviction."[19] For example, the use of a confession obtained by force would be reversible (harmful or plain) error when the conviction rests only on this evidence. But if the crime charged is bank robbery, and ten eyewitnesses testified and the bank's video also showed the defendant robbing the bank, an appellate court could hold that the use of the coerced confession was harmless error.

The Right to Assistance of Counsel

Persons charged with a state or federal crime (or juveniles where a delinquency petition has been filed against them) have the Sixth Amendment right to counsel. If the defendant (or juvenile) cannot afford an attorney, one will be provided by the state or federal government.[20]

The right to assistance of counsel means the right to effective assistance. If the attorney is ineffective, the right has been denied. A convicted defendant who claims he was represented by an inadequate or ineffective lawyer must prove that (1) the lawyer's defense fell below an objective standard of reasonableness and (2) a reasonable probability exists that, but for the lawyer's unprofessional errors, the results would have been different. *Strickland v. Washington,* 466 U.S. 668, 104 S. Ct. 2052 (1984).

The U.S. Supreme Court has held that the right to effective assistance of counsel applies at all stages of a criminal prosecution,[21] including during plea negotiations.[22] Those Supreme Court decisions all involved claims of ineffective assistance of counsel made after a plea bargain was accepted by the defendant. In two 2012 cases the Supreme Court considered the role of the right to effective assistance of counsel where the plea offer from the prosecution was not accepted because it was not communicated to the defendant by his counsel (*Missouri v. Frye*[23]) and where the defendant's attorney recommended refusal of a plea bargain (*Lafler v. Cooper*[24]). In *Frye* the defendant pled guilty to the charges, and received a sentence substantially greater than that contained in the uncommunicated plea offer. In *Lafler* the defendant went to trial, was convicted, and received a prison sentence three times greater than the sentence made part of the plea offer.

The Supreme Court held that the right to effective assistance of counsel applied to both situations. This was true, the court said, even though the defendant received a full and fair trial in *Lafler*, and that the defendant in *Frye* made a fully informed decision to plead guilty. The Court noted that plea bargaining was an integral part of the criminal process: 97 percent of federal prosecutions and 94 percent of state prosecutions are resolved by guilty pleas.[25] In both cases, the Court remanded the cases to the state courts to determine if the second prong of *Strickland* was satisfied. That would depend on whether the defendant could show the plea bargain offer would have been accepted by the trial judge, a question of state law.

The Right to Be Informed of Charges

A defendant charged with a crime has a right to be informed of what he or she is alleged to have done and what specific crime or crimes are being charged. The Sixth Amendment provides that "the accused shall enjoy the right ... to be informed of the nature and cause of the accusation." This right may become an issue when a defendant has made a guilty plea that he or she later seeks to retract because it was not "voluntary and intelligent." In *Bousley v. United States*,[26] the Supreme Court stated that a guilty plea is constitutionally valid only if it is made voluntarily and intelligently. That requires that the defendant be realistically informed of the charges against him. The Court stated that while giving the defendant a copy of the indictment creates a presumption that the defendant has been informed of the charges against him, if the circumstances indicate the defendant was misinformed by the court or the prosecutor, the plea is invalid.

The Right of the Defendant to Compel Witnesses

The Sixth Amendment provides that "the accused shall enjoy the right ... to have compulsory process for obtaining witnesses in his favor." If there are witnesses who can help a defendant's case, the accused may compel their appearance by use of subpoenas. Such witnesses, however, can be very uncooperative. They may make efforts to avoid service by a subpoena, fail to appear in court, or state that they do not remember or did not see or hear the incident. They may also use the Fifth Amendment privilege against self-incrimination.

The Right of the Defendant to Testify or Not Testify

In criminal cases the burden is on the government to come forward with sufficient credible evidence to prove guilt beyond a reasonable doubt. It is the choice of the defendant to take the witness stand and testify in his or her own defense. Most defendants, however, do not testify for various tactical reasons. The most important of these reasons is that a defendant who testifies is then subject to cross-examination, which could be disastrous to the defendant's case. Therefore, many defense lawyers do not want their clients to take this risk.[27]

The Right of the Defendant to Confront and Cross-Examine Witnesses

The Sixth Amendment's Confrontation Clause provides that "the accused shall enjoy the right ... to be confronted with the witnesses against him." The U.S. Supreme Court pointed out that the famous London trial of Sir Walter Raleigh in 1603 was one of the reasons the Confrontation Clause was included in the Sixth Amendment of the Bill of Rights.[28] (See the discussion in Chapter 7.)

The Right to Be Free of Unreasonable Searches and Seizures

The Fourth Amendment forbids unreasonable searches and seizures by officers of the federal and state governments. Therefore, law officers must have a search warrant or must show that a search or seizure is justified by an exception to the search warrant requirements.

The historic roots of the Fourth Amendment go back to Magna Carta and the development over the centuries of the probable cause requirement. In 1965, the U.S. Supreme Court traced the events that led to the American Revolution against British rule:

> Vivid in the memory of the newly formed independent Americans were those general warrants known as writs of assistance under which officers of the Crown had so bedeviled the Colonists. The hated writs of assistance had given customs officials blanket authority to search where they pleased for goods imported in violation of British tax laws. They were denounced by James Otis as "the worst instrument of arbitrary power, the most destructive of English liberty, and the fundamental principles of law, that ever was found in an English law book" because they placed "the liberty of every man in the hands of every petty officer." The historic occasion of that denunciation in 1761 at Boston has been characterized as "perhaps the most prominent event which inaugurated the resistance of the colonies to the oppressions of the mother country." "Then and there," said John Adams, "was the first scene of the first act of opposition to the arbitrary claims of Great Britain. Then and there the child Independence was born."[29]

The Right to an Impartial Jury

The Sixth Amendment of the U.S. Constitution guarantees defendants the right to "an impartial jury of the State and district wherein the crime shall have been committed." Juror challenges, either for cause or peremptory, are a procedural device designed to help ensure that the jury is impartial. However, the challenges themselves are not of constitutional dimension. Thus, in *United States v. Martinez-Salazar*,[30] the Supreme Court held that a wrongful refusal by a trial judge to excuse a juror for cause, forcing the defendant to use a peremptory challenge, was not by itself a constitutional violation, so long as the jury actually chosen was impartial.

Excusing jurors for cause has long been an issue in death penalty cases. A defendant can argue persuasively that excusing any juror who expresses doubt about capital punishment denies him an "impartial jury" because the resulting jury will consist only of those who favor capital punishment. The prosecution's response is that a jury made up of those opposed to capital punishment would be unwilling to apply the law correctly because of the possible death sentence for a guilty verdict.

In the 2007 case of *Uttecht v. Brown*,[31] the U.S. Supreme Court reversed the Ninth Circuit Court of Appeals, which had overturned the conviction of a defendant charged with murder because a prospective jury member had been excused for cause based on his statements about the death penalty. In holding that the juror had been properly excused by the trial court judge, the Supreme Court stated that four principles must be used to determine whether a juror has been properly excused for cause in capital cases:

1. The defendant has a right to have a jury that is not tilted in favor of capital punishment, which means the prosecution may not challenge for cause any juror who expresses doubt about capital punishment.

LEGAL CASES

Peremptory Challenges and Discrimination

In jury trials, the parties are generally entitled to strike any prospective juror for cause, such having some relationship to the defendant, or having already formed opinions about guilt. They may also strike a limited number of potential jury members without giving a reason for the decision to strike. The prosecutor often uses this "peremptory challenge" to exclude a potential juror who might be reluctant, for one reason or another, to find the defendant guilty of the crime charged. Defendants can use the challenge to exclude a juror who is otherwise qualified but who, the defendant believes, might not be sympathetic to his case.

Peremptory challenges are determined by state law, and are not required by the U.S. Constitution. *See United States v. Martinez-Salazar*, 528 U.S. 304 (2000). Moreover, even if a trial judge erroneously refuses to exclude a juror based on a defendant's peremptory challenge, the refusal is not a violation of due process. In *Rivera v. Illinois*, 129 S. Ct. 1446 (2009) the Supreme Court held that so long as the jury seated was impartial and properly instructed, a criminal defendant has received "precisely what due process required," even though the trial court erred in refusing to allow the defendant to use a peremptory challenge to exclude a juror.

In most instances, the prosecution does not have to explain the reasons for exercising a peremptory challenge. In one area at least, the U.S. Supreme Court has said the prosecution cannot use peremptory strikes to exclude potential jurors. In *Batson v. Kentucky,* 476 U.S. 79 (1986), the Court held that if a defendant in a criminal case makes a prima facie case showing that jurors were excluded because of their race, the prosecution must provide "race-neutral" reasons justifying the challenges. In a 2005 decision (*Johnson v. California,* 545 U.S. 162), the Court reversed the murder conviction of a black male because the prosecution used its peremptory challenges to exclude the only three black prospective jurors. The Court said that all that the defendant needed to produce to force the state to show a race-neutral reason for the challenges was evidence that supports the inference of a discriminatory purpose. The California Supreme Court, like many other state courts, had interpreted *Batson* to require the defendant to show discriminatory purpose by a preponderance of the evidence. The Supreme Court rejected that interpretation.

The "race-neutral" reasons advanced by the state as the justification for the peremptory challenges are themselves reviewable by federal courts. *See Miller-El v. Dretke*, 125 S. Ct. 2317 (2005). Such justifications must not be mere pretext. In *Snyder v. Louisiana*, 552 U.S. 472 (2008) the Supreme Court reversed a murder conviction of a black defendant because all five black jurors who survived challenges for cause were excluded by the prosecution using peremptory challenges. The Court said that the reasons given by the prosecution for the challenges (one juror "looked nervous" and was "worried about his student teaching duties") were insufficient. The Court noted that at least 50 prospective jurors expressed concerns about the trial interfering with school or work. The Court also said that excluding even one juror for a discriminatory purpose was a constitutional violation. 552 U.S. at 478.

The U.S. Supreme Court has not extended *Batson* to include peremptory strikes based on other factors, such as the religious affiliation of a prospective juror. Some lower federal courts have approved the use of such strikes where the religious views of the juror would hamper the ability of the juror to sit in judgment of others. [See *United States v. Brown*, 352 F.3d 654 (2d Cir. 2003).] Some state courts have held that peremptory challenges based on religious affiliation are prohibited. [See *Thorson v. State*, 721 So.2d 590 (Miss. 1998).]

2. The state has a legitimate interest in having jurors who are willing to apply capital punishment where the law so permits.
3. Unless a juror is "substantially impaired" in his ability to impose the death sentence, his excusal for cause is improper.
4. The trial judge is entitled to deference in the determination of when a prospective juror is "substantially impaired."

The Common Law Right of a Defendant to Be Present at the Defendant's Criminal Trial

It has long been a guiding principle of the common law that a defendant had the right to be present at his criminal trial, and that trials *in absentia* were prohibited. *See* W. Mikell, *Clark Criminal Procedure* 492 (2nd ed. 1918). In *Crosby v. United States*, 506 U.S. 255 (1993) the U.S. Supreme Court stated the reason for the common law rule: "The canon was premised on the notion that a fair trial could take place only if the jurors met the defendant face-to-face and only if those testifying against the defendant did so in his presence." 506 U.S. at 259.

In the *Crosby* case the Court held that Rule 43 of the Federal Rules of Criminal Procedure requires in a felony trial that a defendant be present at the beginning of the criminal trial, and forbids a trial *in absentia* of a defendant who was not "initially present." The Court also held that under Rule 43 a defendant's intentional flight before trial did not constitute a waiver of the right. The *Crosby* court expressly stated it made no determination on the defendant's claim that the "trial *in absentia* was also prohibited by the Constitution." Also, whether waiver of the right could constitutionally occur in other circumstances was not decided in *Crosby*: the Court specifically stated "we express no opinion on that subject" 506 U.S. at 261.

Many state courts have interpreted *Crosby* to permit defendants to make a "knowing waiver" of the right to be present at their criminal trial. *See, e.g., Reeves v. State*, 994 A2d 469 (Md. App. 2010). That is so even if the state has adopted a rule similar to Rule 43, interpreted in *Crosby*. In *State v. Padilla*, 46 P.3d 1247 (N.M. 2002) the court held an express, knowing waiver by a defendant who was not initially present at his trial was sufficient to waive the right to be present.

Defendants charged with a felony in the United States and are present at the beginning of their trials can lose their right to be present at their trials in either of the following situations:

1. If the defendant is present at the commencement of a criminal trial but flees during the trial, Rule 43 (c) of the Federal Rules of Criminal Procedure treats the mid-trial flight as "a knowing and voluntary waiver of the right to be present." *Crosby,* 506 U.S. at 261. The trial may then proceed without the presence of the defendant in such a case.
2. If a defendant continuously disrupts the criminal trial, a trial judge may rule (after warning the defendant) that the defendant has waived the right to be present in the courtroom. The defendant would then be placed in another room and observe the trial from there. In the bank robbery case of *United States v. Prince*, 938 F.2d 1092 (10th Cir. 1991) the defendant "exposed himself and began to urinate in the courtroom ... and the ... began moaning and screaming ..." Five marshals were needed to take the struggling defendant from the courtroom.

Some states have laws that permit attorneys to appear for a defendant in minor criminal matters, with the permission of the trial judge. Some European countries permit felony trials *in absentia* of defendants who are not in custody. European countries do not have the same "common law" as England and the United States, and thus have different procedures in some areas.

SUMMARY

1. **Explain the importance of the Magna Carta.**
   - The Magna Carta was an important limitation on the rights of English kings, including how criminal trials were to be held. It profoundly influenced the drafters of the Declaration of Independence, and served as the beginning point for many of the individual rights in the Bill of Rights. Original copies of the Magna Carta are displayed in the National Archives in Washington, D.C., and in London, England.

2. **Explain the function of the writ of habeas corpus.**
   - The writ of habeas corpus is issued by a court and directed to a government official, such as a warden of a prison, to appear before the court and show cause why the person seeking the petition is being held. In federal courts the writ can be used to review criminal convictions from state courts, but only to determine if the convictions violated the U.S. Constitution or federal laws.

3. **Identify how the U.S. Supreme court made the bill of rights applicable in state court criminal cases.**

   - The U.S. Supreme Court made the Bill of Rights, the first 10 amendments to the Constitution, applicable to the states through the doctrine of "selective incorporation." Using the Due Process Clause of the Fourteenth Amendment, which is binding on the states, the Supreme Court over time incorporated the rights in the first 10 amendments into the Fourteenth Amendment, and thus made them binding on the states.

4. **List the rights identified and made available to a criminal defendant under the U.S. Constitution.**
   - While some individual rights in criminal prosecutions are identified in the U.S. Constitution, such as the two-witness testimony requirement for conviction of treason in Article III, Section 3, most individual rights are found in the first 10 amendments. These rights have been incorporated into the Fourteenth Amendment at various times, most recently in *McDonald v. City of Chicago*, 130 S. Ct. 3020 (2010), where the Supreme Court held that the Second Amendment's right to bear arms was made binding on the states under the Fourteenth Amendment.

KEY TERMS

beyond a reasonable doubt, 13	custody, 5	ordeals, 3	presumption of innocence, 13
Bill of Rights, 11	habeas corpus, 5	presentment juries, 4	probable cause, 5
	Magna Carta, 5		

KEY CASES

Batson v. Kentucky, 476 U.S. 79 (1986): Prohibited use of peremptory challenges to exclude jurors based on race of juror.

Bousley v. United States, 523 U.S. 614 (1998): Guilty pleas must be knowingly and intelligently made to be valid.

Carey v. Musladin, 594 U.S. 70 (2006): Stated when the prejudicial effect of courtroom conditions denies a defendant a fair trial.

County of Riverside v. McLaughlin, 500 U.S. 44 (1991): Stated 48-hour rule for "prompt" probable cause hearing in criminal cases.

Crosby v. United States, 506 U.S. 255 (1993): Identified common law right to be present at criminal trial, and applied Rule 43 of Federal Rules of Criminal Procedure to prohibit *in absentia* trials for felony cases in federal courts if the defendant was not present at commencement of the trial.

Lafler v. Cooper, 132 S. Ct. 1376 (2012): Held Sixth Amendment right to effective assistance of counsel applies to plea offers rejected by defendant based on advice of counsel.

Presley v. Georgia, 130 S. Ct. 721 (2010): Held "public trial" right applies to all aspects of a criminal trial, including *voir dire*.

Thaler v. Haymes, 130 S. Ct. 1171 (2010): Defines "clearly established rule" for purposes of habeas corpus review of state court criminal convictions.

Uttecht v. Brown, 127 S. Ct. 2218 (2007): States the four principles used to determine if a juror was properly excused for cause in a capital case.

PROBLEMS

Refer to Appendix A, which contains the Bill of Rights and applicable sections of the U.S. Constitution, and answer the questions about rights and privileges in the United States by choosing one of the following available answers. You may also have to use the index for further information on a few of the questions.

Available Answers

a. This is a right or privilege protected by the U.S. Constitution.
b. This is not a right or privilege protected by the U.S. Constitution.

A Person Charged with a Crime Has a Right To

1. A perfect trial.
2. A speedy trial.
3. A private (not public) trial.
4. The assistance of a lawyer for his or her defense.
5. Compel witnesses to appear in his or her defense.
6. Not be tried more than once for the same offense and the same conduct.
7. Due process of law (fundamental fairness).
8. An impartial jury.
9. Not take the witness stand in his or her criminal trial (right to remain silent).
10. Make false statements in court under oath.
11. See and hear witnesses as they testify in court.
12. Cross-examine witnesses.
13. Be informed of the charge or charges.
14. Be tried in the county in which the crime was committed.
15. An unbiased judge.
16. A defense lawyer who believes the defendant to be innocent.
17. Reasonable bail if bail is set.

All Persons Have the Following Rights or Freedoms (Answer True or False):

1. Freedom to say, print, or write anything and everything they wish (absolute freedom of speech).
2. Freedom from any and all government searches.
3. The right to have *Miranda* warnings given when in police custody.
4. The right to a habeas corpus hearing if held illegally or improperly.
5. Freedom of movement without interference by a government official unless there is lawful authority.
6. The right to remain silent when a person is an important material witness to a serious felony and is not incriminating him- or herself.
7. Freedom to move from one state to another or from one city to another.
8. The right to block sidewalks.

CASE ANALYSIS

Read Appendix B, Finding and Analyzing Cases (p. 499). With these guidelines in mind, please continue with the Case Analysis selections for Chapter 1.

1. In this chapter, we stated that criminal defendants are entitled to a "Fair (Not Perfect) Trial." This means that sometimes mistakes can be made in a criminal trial, but the trial is nonetheless "fair." Mistakes during a trial have historically been classified as either "structural" or "non-structural" errors. Structural errors require reversal of a verdict of guilty, and the doctrine of harmless error is not applicable. Denials of the right to counsel, or racial discrimination in jury selection, are examples of structural errors requiring reversal. Admission of inadmissible evidence is normally not a structural error, and harmless error applies. A guilty verdict will be reversed if the error contributed to the verdict, but not otherwise. In *Pierce v. Com.,* 652 S.E.2d 785 (Va. App. 2007) a trial judge admitted evidence the defendant, charged with possession of marijuana, had committed perjury in a prior case. In *State v. Rodriguez,* 254 S.W.3d 361 (Tenn. 2008) a trial judge admitted evidence a defendant, charged with sexual battery, possessed child pornography. Both courts found the evidence inadmissible; in *Pierce* the harmless error doctrine upheld the conviction; in *Rodriguez* it did not. Why did the courts reach different results?

2. At the end of a criminal trial, after all the evidence has been admitted, the case goes to the jury for its verdict. Before the jury goes to the jury room to deliberate, the trial judge gives the jury instructions. Jury instructions address many aspects of the trial, such as the elements of the crime charged, and what the prosecution's burden is to prove those elements. Trial judges also give the jury an instruction on the presumption of innocence. The content of jury instructions are frequently the subject of an appeal of a guilty verdict.

   In *Tillman v. Massey*, 637 S.E.2d 720, 722 (Ga. 2006) the trial judge gave this instruction to the jury in defendant's murder trial: "Our law provides that every person charged with the commission of a crime is presumed innocent under our law until proved guilty beyond a reasonable doubt. *That presumption in our law is for the protection of the innocent. It is not intended to be a cloak behind which guilty persons may hide.* Whether that presumption has been overcome by the State is for you, the jury to decide."

   Assume you represent the defendant on appeal. Can you make an argument that this instruction deprived the defendant of a fair trial? How does the presumption of innocence help to make sure a trial is fair? Did this instruction help or hinder securing a fair trial?

3. Defendant was convicted of "increasing speed to escape" a police officer after he failed to stop when a police cruiser pulled up behind him with flashing lights. At defendant's trial, the prosecutor said in the state's summation argument to the jury that "If I'm going to convict someone, I better well have a good case. And I think we do." In a summary of the evidence, the prosecutor also said to the jury "What would you do? What is your normal reaction when you see flashing red lights in the rearview mirror?" Are these statements proper? If not, why are they improper? Has the defendant been deprived of a fair trial? *State v. Daniel G.*, 84 A.3d 9 (Conn. App. 2014), *cert. denied* 311 Conn. 931 (Conn. 2014).

4. All courts agree that requiring a defendant to appear at trial in identifiable prison clothing violates the fair trial right. Why does the defendant's compelled appearance in prison clothes have that effect? Should the same result be reached if the witnesses for the defendant, who at the time of trial were incarcerated in prison, were compelled to testify in prison clothes and shackles? Does this have anything to do with the presumption of innocence? If not, what right of the defendant is involved? *Stacey v. Com.*, 396 S.W.3d 787 (Ky. 2013).

Notes

1. Common law is sometimes referred to as "unwritten law." In early England and during American colonial times, legislatures did not meet often to enact statutory law. Courts made most of the laws, usually based on the custom and usage of the community. This judge-made law became known as "common law." Because printing presses were rare and few people could read and write, law for the most part in those days was unwritten and carried in the minds of judges, lawyers, and government officials. Today, written law is recorded in statutes enacted by legislative bodies, and common law is found in court reports, court transcripts, and other written material.

2. See *Bloodletters and Sudmen: A Narrative Encyclopedia of American Criminals from the Pilgrims to the Present* by Jay Robert Nash (New York: M. Evans & Co., 1974).

3. *A History of the Criminal Law of England*, vol. 1, p. 73 (London: MacMillan & Co., 1883).

4. F. Pollack and F. W. Maitland, *History of English Law*, 2nd ed., vol. 2, p. 622 (Cambridge, U.K.: Cambridge University Press, 1968).

5. J. Few, *In Defense of Trial by Jury*, vol. 1, p. 1 (Greenville, SC: American Jury Trial Foundation, 1993).

6. See *The Harvard Classics*, vol. 43, p. 70 (Boston: Collier & Son, 1910).

7. See *The Harvard Classics*, vol. 43, p. 70 (Boston: Collier & Son, 1910).

8. Pacific Mutual Life Ins. Co. v. Haslip, 499 U.S. 1, 111 S. Ct. 1032 (1991).

9. T. Cooley, *Constitutional Limitations*, chap. 10 (4th ed., 1878). Abraham's widely used text makes the statement that all democracies use the presumption of innocence until proven guilty. See Abraham, *The Judicial Process*, 2nd ed., p. 101 (New York: Oxford University Press, 1968).

10. 425 U.S. 501, 503 (1976).

11. 436 U.S. 478 (1978).

12. 218 F. Supp. 2d 26 (D. Mass. 2002).

13. 407 U.S. 514 (1972).

14. 733 F.3d 29 (2nd Cir. 2013).

15. 18 U.S.C. § 3161.

16. *Stumpf v. Mitchell*, 367 F.3d 594 (6th Cir. 2004).

17. *Bradshaw v. Stumpf*, 125 S. Ct. 2398 (2005).

18. *Lutwak v. United States*, 344 U.S. 604, at 619, 73 S. Ct. 481, at 490 (1953).

19. *Chapman v. California*, 386 U.S. 18, 87 S. Ct. 824 (1967), *rehearing denied*, 386 U.S. 987, 87 S. Ct. 1283; *State v. Jones*, 575 A.2d 216 (Conn. 1990); and *Schneble v. Florida*, 405 U.S. 427, 92 S. Ct. 1056 (1972).

20. In the 1975 case of *Faretta v. California* 422 U.S. 806, 95 S. Ct. 2525, the U.S. Supreme Court recognized the right of a criminal defendant under the Sixth Amendment to act as his or her own attorney. Denial of this constitutional right of self-representation is reversible error unless it is shown that (1) the request was untimely, (2) the defendant abused the right of self-representation, (3) the request was made solely for the purposes of delay, (4) the case is so complex that it requires the assistance of a lawyer, or (5) the defendant is unable to voluntarily and intelligently waive her right to a lawyer. See also *McKaskle v. Wiggins*, 465 U.S. 168, 177 n. 8, 104 S. Ct. 944, 950 n. 8 (1984).

21. *Rothgery v. Gillespie County*, 128 S. Ct. 2578 (2008).

22. *Padilla v. Kentucky*, 130 S. Ct. 1473 (2010).

23. 132 S. Ct. 1399 (2012).

24. 132 S. Ct. 1376 (2012).

25. *Frye*, 132 S. Ct. at 1407.

26. 523 U.S. 614, 619 (1998).

27. Witnesses and prosecutors cannot comment on the fact that a defendant in a criminal case has exercised the constitutional right to remain silent. Such comments or statements would in most instances be reversible error should the defendant be convicted. Such comments could also be grounds for charging the lawyer before a bar association.

   In 1993 the U.S. Supreme Court held that "defendant's right to testify does not include a right to commit perjury." However, a defendant who only enters a not guilty plea does not commit perjury if the defendant is found guilty after a trial (see Chapter 6). [See *United States v. Dunnigan*, 507 U.S. 87, 113 S. Ct. 1111 (1993). Also see *United States v. Havens*, 446 U.S. 620 at 626, 100 S. Ct. 1912 at 1918 (1980).

28. *California v. Green*, 399 U.S. 149 (1970).

29. *Stanford v. Texas*, 379 U.S. 476, 85 S. Ct. 506 (1965).

30. 528 U.S. 304 (2000).

31. 127 S. Ct. 2218, 2224.

CHAPTER 2

Important Aspects of the American Criminal Justice System

Library of Congress Prints and Photographs Division Washington, D.C.[LC-D416-444]

ALEXANDER HAMILTON (UPPER) AND JAMES MADISON (LOWER), THE PRIMARY AUTHORS OF THE FEDERALIST PAPERS, WHICH WERE INFLUENTIAL IN THE ADOPTION OF THE CONSTITUTION.

Library of Congress Prints and Photographs Division Washington, D.C.[LC-USZ62-80104]

LEARNING OBJECTIVES

In this chapter we discuss some aspects of the American criminal justice system, specifically the notion of federalism and the adversary system. The learning objectives for this chapter are

> Know the meaning of *federalism* as it applies to criminal justice.
>
> Identify the constitutional basis for the exercise of federal criminal jurisdiction.
>
> Identify the limits of federal criminal jurisdiction under the Interstate Commerce Clause.
>
> Know the meaning of reliable, relevant, and competent evidence.
>
> List some differences between accusatorial and inquisitional systems.
>
> State the requirements of the *Brady* rule.
>
> State the requirements of the U.S. Supreme Court's rule for lost or destroyed evidence.

Devin Parsons and other members of the "Courtlandt Avenue Crew," a racketeering enterprise in the Bronx, were arrested and charged with drug trafficking and murdering rival gang members. Parsons agreed to be a cooperating witness for the government against other members of the crew in exchange for a plea agreement.

While in prison prior to the trial of the other defendants, Parson convinced a friend to establish a Facebook account for him under an alias, with the friend controlling the account. Using a contraband cellphone, Parsons made posts to the account, some of which mentioned the benefits he planned to obtain from his agreement with the prosecution. The other defendants discovered the existence of these posts and the secret Facebook account, and filed a motion demanding that the prosecution (1) compel Parsons' friend, who controlled access to the account, to grant such access to the prosecution to see all posts by Parsons, and (2) turn over all Facebook posts and information discovered to the defense. The defense relied on the *Brady* rule (discussed in this chapter), which requires the prosecution to disclose to the defense any exculpatory information possessed by the prosecution or its agents. If you were the trial judge, would you grant the motion? Is there a difference between exculpatory information held by a police officer who investigated a crime and a witness for the prosecution of that crime? *See United States v. Meregildo*, 920 F. Supp. 2d 434 (S.D.N.Y. 2013).

FEDERALISM IN THE UNITED STATES

federalism Division of power between state governments and the federal government, in which the federal government has specified powers delegated to it, with the remaining powers vested in the states.

The United States uses a form of government based on a division of powers called **federalism**, which was first presented to the original states at the 1787 Constitutional Convention in Philadelphia. The people of the original thirteen states thought of themselves as being primarily citizens of their states. They were familiar with the political and civic leaders of their local communities but knew little of the leaders of the proposed central government. They thus were reluctant to grant complete authority to a national government. However, the people recognized they needed a strong central government to provide for national defense, to create a national currency and central banking system, to establish a postal system, to regulate trade with foreign nations, and to establish a taxation system to pay the expenses of the new national government. The resulting system, federalism, is generally regarded as a compromise between the competing ideas of a strong central government and independently run state governments.

The United States was the first country in the world to use a federal form of government.[1] Under a federal system, the central government has the power and authority to handle national problems, while the states have the power to regulate local needs and problems. Federalism provides diversity and flexibility at both the state and local levels of government. The needs and problems of states such as Maine or Colorado, for example, differ from those of, say, New York, California, or Illinois. Under American federalism, states are primarily responsible for public safety and can enact laws that they believe are most effective in providing for public order and an efficient, effective criminal justice system.

Federalism and the Law of Evidence

The keystone of American federalism is the U.S. Constitution. ARTICLE VI of the Constitution provides that "This Constitution ... shall be the supreme Law of the Land; and the Judges in every State shall be bound thereby." The powers of the U.S. Congress, the president, and the U.S. Supreme Court are limited to those powers granted in the Constitution. The Tenth Amendment provides that "The powers not delegated to the United States by the Constitution are reserved to the States … or to the people."

Each state is sovereign, and the officials of each state have the powers granted to them by the constitution of that state. Each state has its own criminal codes, and each has enacted a code of criminal procedure and evidence. These codes and the rulings of state courts must conform to the requirements of the U.S. Constitution. However, state laws and state court rulings may provide additional rights to the people of the state and to criminal defendants within that state, beyond those extended by the Constitution.

In 1975 Congress enacted the **Federal Rules of Evidence** (see Appendix C). Since that time, most states have adopted rules of evidence almost identical to the Federal Rules, with local modifications. However, each state retains the power to interpret and modify those rules of evidence. Thus, the meaning and application of the

Federal Rules of Evidence Codification in 1975 of common-law rules of evidence; applicable only in federal courts but provide the model for most state evidence codes.

THE TENTH AMENDMENT AND INDIVIDUAL RIGHTS

The Tenth Amendment to the U.S. Constitution states that powers not delegated to the United States are reserved to the states or the people. It thus reinforces the basic concept of federalism: two sovereigns exist, and their powers are separated. The federal government is sovereign in those areas where the Constitution has delegated specific powers to that government, and the states are sovereign in the other areas, subject to constitutional prohibitions on their power.

States have often attacked federal statutes alleging violations of the Tenth Amendment. (*See* e.g., *New York v. United States*, 505 U.S. 144 (1992).) In such cases the state is both enforcing the Constitution's limits on federal power, and protecting its own sovereignty guaranteed by the Tenth Amendment. To what extent, if at all, may an individual attack a federal statute based on her claim that the statute violates the Tenth Amendment?

In *Bond v. United States*, 131 S. Ct. 2355 (2011), the U.S. Supreme Court held that in the proper circumstances, where an individual alleges direct injury from governmental action, that individual may claim the federal statute violates the Tenth Amendment. In that case, a woman was charged with violation of 18 U.S.C. § 229, a federal statute prohibiting use of a chemical that could cause death or serious injury. Section 229 was passed as part of an act implementing a chemical weapons treaty. The woman alleged her actions were totally local in nature, and were thus reserved to the states or the people under the Tenth Amendment. She entered a conditional guilty plea, reserving the Tenth Amendment issue for appeal. The court of appeals held she could not raise the Tenth Amendment as a defense. The Supreme Court granted certiorari, and reversed the court of appeals. In doing so, the Court said this about the role of the Tenth Amendment:

> Federalism also protects the liberty of all persons within a State by ensuring that laws enacted in excess of delegated governmental power cannot direct or control their actions…. By denying any one government complete jurisdiction over all the concerns of public life, federalism protects the liberty of the individual from arbitrary power. When government acts in excess of its lawful powers, that liberty is a stake. The limitations that federalism entails are not therefore a matter of rights belonging only to the States. States are not the sole intended beneficiaries of federalism…. An individual has a direct interest in objecting to laws that upset the constitutional balance between the National Government and the States when the enforcement of those laws causes injury that is concrete, particular, and redressable. Fidelity to principles of federalism is not for the States alone to vindicate.[2]

Federal Rules of Evidence can vary between federal courts and state courts and among the states.

The Federal Rules of Evidence and most state rules of evidence apply in both civil and criminal trials. However, some rules or parts of rules may apply differently in criminal cases.[3]

State and Federal Jurisdiction over Crimes in the United States

The great majority of crimes committed in the United States are violations of state criminal codes. Some crimes are federal offenses in violation of the federal criminal code. A small percentage of criminal offenses are violations of both the federal criminal code and a state criminal code.

Because each state is sovereign and has the power and authority granted to it by its residents, it may enforce its criminal laws against anyone who violates them.[4] The federal government is also sovereign, having the power and authority to enforce violations of federal law.

The U.S. Constitution does not grant to the federal government a general police power, nor has there ever been federal criminal common law. All federal crimes therefore have to be statutory crimes enacted by Congress.[5] States have general police power in providing for domestic tranquility. Common law, both civil and criminal, has always been part of the legal systems of the states. **Common law**, or unwritten law, consists of the rules developed over many years by courts and judges. Common-law crimes and common-law rules of evidence were used for years during the early history of the United States. Today, criminal codes and rules of evidence are enacted by state legislatures and are found in the codified laws of each state.

common law Legal rules that evolved over many years in English and American court opinions.

To enact federal criminal law, the U.S. Congress must act within the powers granted to it by the U.S. Constitution. Criminal laws may be enacted by the federal government in the following areas:

- To protect itself, its officials and employees, its property, and the administration of its authorized functions
- To regulate interstate and foreign commerce
- To protect civil rights
- To enact criminal laws for places beyond the jurisdiction of any state, such as the District of Columbia, federal territories, and federal enclaves such as military bases and national parks

Defendants in prosecutions for violations of federal criminal law sometimes attack the jurisdiction of the federal government to make their conduct criminal—in particular, when the basis of that jurisdiction is the Commerce Clause. Congress may pass criminal laws under the Commerce Clause only if (1) the prohibited actions use the "channels" of interstate commerce, such as actions taking place in more than one state; (2) the activity uses the "instrumentalities" of interstate commerce, such as telephone lines or the postal service; or (3) the activity has a "substantial effect" on interstate commerce. The Constitution gives Congress the power to pass all "necessary and proper" laws in regulation of interstate commerce. The 2005 U.S. Supreme Court case of *Gonzales v. Raich*, discussed below, raised the issue of the constitutionality of a federal criminal statute passed under the Interstate Commerce Clause.

Gonzales v. Raich

United States Supreme
Court, 125 S. Ct. 2195 (2005)

Raich and other users and growers of marijuana for medical purposes brought an action to declare the federal Controlled Substances Act (CSA) unconstitutional. The CSA regulates the production, sale, and use of various controlled substances, including marijuana. Violation of the CSA's provisions is a federal crime. Raich and other California residents produced and used marijuana pursuant to a California statute, the California Compassionate Use Act. This act permitted the production and use of marijuana where the user had a medical condition that might be made less burdensome by the use of marijuana and a physician had prescribed the use of the drug. Federal agents seized and destroyed marijuana plants grown by persons claiming coverage under the California Compassionate Use Act, and they sought an injunction against further federal actions, including criminal prosecutions under the CSA. The Ninth Circuit Court of Appeals granted the injunction, but the U.S. Supreme Court reversed the Ninth Circuit, holding that the Commerce Clause permitted Congress to regulate even purely intrastate production of marijuana.

Marijuana is a Schedule I substance, and under the CSA all use or production of the substance is prohibited. Raich did not contend that Congress could not regulate or prohibit the interstate commerce in a Schedule I controlled substance such as marijuana. However, she did contend that Congress had no jurisdiction under the Commerce Clause to make purely intrastate production or use of the substance illegal. She argued that since the marijuana was only for her personal use under a physician's care, she could not affect interstate commerce.

The Supreme Court disagreed. It held that Congress could reasonably conclude that the presence of a permitted local market for a Schedule I substance would adversely affect efforts to totally eradicate the interstate market for marijuana, and that under established case law the Commerce Clause permits Congress to regulate activity that "substantially affects" interstate commerce. Among other things, the Court said that producers of marijuana for medical purposes might be induced by higher prices to re-route their product to the interstate market, thus frustrating the congressional goal of total eradication of the substance.

The Supreme Court held that the reasonable possibility of such an effect gives Congress the authority to make the CSA applicable to those who use or produce marijuana under the California Compassionate Use Act.

The scope of federal criminal jurisdiction under the Commerce Clause has continued to be contentious since the decision in *Gonzales v. Reich*. For example, several federal courts have decided cases where it was contended Congress lacked the power to enact certain provisions of the Sex Offender Registration and Notification Act (SORNA), 18 U.S.C. § 2250(a), and registration requirements set out in 42 U.S.C. § 16913.

Under section 16913, all persons convicted under state sex offender laws are required to register in the state where they were convicted and any state to which they travel.[6] Section 2250(a) then makes it a federal crime for a sex offender to travel to another state and fail to register as a sex offender in the arrival state. In the resulting cases that came before federal district courts, convicted sex offenders who were required to register in one state traveled to another state and failed to register on that state's sex offender list. They were then charged with violation of section 2250(a), and often contended that Congress lacked the power to pass the SORNA laws.

CAN CONGRESS MAKE ACTIONS IN FOREIGN COUNTRIES A CRIME?

Assume that a U.S. citizen travels to a foreign country on a personal vacation trip. While there, with knowledge of her age, he has sex with a female under the age of 18. When he returns to the U.S. he is charged with violation of 18 U.S.C. § 2423 (c), which makes it a crime for U.S. citizen to have "illicit sex" abroad. "Illicit sex" is defined as any act that would be a crime if committed within U.S. jurisdiction, which includes having sex with a minor under the age of 18.

Should Congress make actions taken in other countries violations of U.S. law? If so, does Congress have the power to do so? Look back at the list of powers granted to Congress in Article 8 of the Constitution that are discussed in this chapter. Where would the power to pass 18 U.S.C. § 2423 (c) fit in that list? Does the "foreign commerce clause", Article 8, cl. 3, give Congress that power? One court thinks so: *United States v. Pendleton*, 658 F.3d 299 (3rd Cir. 2011), *cert denied* 132 S. Ct. 2771 (2012). Can you see a problem with that conclusion? Does it help that in 2000 President Clinton signed a treaty with several countries, ratified by the U.S. Senate, designed to eliminate the international illicit sex trade? How does the "necessary and proper" clause, Article 8, cl. 18, apply? *See United States v. Bollinger*, 966 F. Supp. 2d 568 (W.D. N.C. 2013).

Most federal courts have upheld the power of Congress to pass SORNA, either under the Commerce Clause or the Necessary and Proper Clause of the Constitution.[7] A few federal courts have reached the contrary conclusion, illustrated by the decision in *United States v. Waybright*.[8] In that case the federal district court held that, although the Interstate Commerce Clause supports federal jurisdiction to make an activity a crime where the person charged actually travels in interstate commerce, the clause does not give the federal government the power to require every convicted sex offender to register on a state's sex offender list. The *Waybright* court then reasoned that a person could be convicted under section 2250(a) only because section 16913 mandated sex offender registration in the first place, and because sex offenses are purely local crimes with no interstate economic impact, Congress lacked the power to require sex offenders to register. That being so, Congress could not make it a crime to travel from state to state and fail to do some act that Congress lacked the initial power to mandate.

In 2013 the U.S. Supreme Court upheld a challenge to SORNA brought by a former military serviceman who was convicted of failing to register under SORNA based on a conviction of a sex offense while he was in the U.S. Air Force.[9] In *United States v. Kebodeaux* the court held that Congress had the power to enact SORNA under the Necessary and Proper Clause, which authorizes Congress to pass laws necessary to obtain the object of permissible legislation.[10]

Law Enforcement in the American Federal System

The United States has more than 17,000 law enforcement agencies. Most of these are at the local levels of government (cities, counties, towns, and so on). All 50 states have law enforcement agencies working at the state level of government. At the federal level are the federal law enforcement agencies created by Congress to enforce specific federal laws.

Local law enforcement agencies such as police and sheriff's departments enforce city and county ordinances in addition to the criminal laws of their state. They bring

PROCEDURES & PROCESSES

Courts and Trials in the United States

The U.S. Department of Justice, Bureau of Justice Statistics, each year conducts the National Crime Victimization Survey (NCVS). The 2010 survey report released in September 2011 gave the following national crime statistics: From 2000 to 2010 violent crimes dropped by 34 percent, and property crimes decreased by 29 percent. In 2010 the survey showed that 18,700,000 violent and felonious property crimes were experienced by U.S. residents age 12 or older. However, the NCVS report issued in October 2013 for 2012 showed an increase in both violent crimes and property crimes over the previous year (see Figure 2.1). This number does not include misdemeanors and offenses charged as ordinance violations throughout the United States, such as shoplifting and traffic violations. Reported crimes that lead to criminal prosecutions are tried in the following manner:

Federal and State Courts	Military Courts	Military Commissions
(handling about 95 percent of all criminal trials in the United States)	(for members of the U.S. Armed Forces)	(established in 2004 for "enemy combatants" held by the U.S. military)[a]
Trial: Can be held by jurors selected at random	Before a panel of military personnel appointed by the military authority	Before an appointed military officer
Presiding Official: Independent judges either elected or appointed	Appointed military officer	Appointed military officer
Appeals: Independent legal courts	Military appellant courts	Panel appointed by U.S. Secretary of Defense
Hearsay: Federal or state rules apply	Federal Rules of Evidence apply	Hearsay evidence allowed
Exclusionary Rule: Federal and state rules apply	Only federal rules apply	Most federal rules do not apply
Exculpatory Evidence Proving Innocence: In both federal and state courts, must be provided to defense	Same	May be withheld if deemed classified
Right to Confront Witnesses: Defendants in all criminal trials have right to confront witnesses against them	Same	Not guaranteed to enemy combatants
Right to Speedy Trial: Sixth Amendment guarantees this right, and state and federal courts have speedy trial rules	Same	Enemy combatants may be held until end of war without trial
Right to Habeas Corpus Hearings: U.S. Constitution and most state constitutions protect the right to habeas corpus	Same	In 2008 the U.S. Supreme Court held that alien enemy combatants had the right to habeas corpus and that federal courts had jurisdiction to hear their claims[b]

[a]Prisoners of war are protected under the Geneva Convention Treaties, which were signed by the United States and over 100 other nations. Prisoners of war are entitled to a basic level of humane treatment and may refuse to answer questions other than name, rank, and serial number. If POWs violate the laws of war, they can be tried for criminal violations.

[b]In one of the first hearings brought by 6 of the 270 detainees held for six years at the Guantanamo Naval Base, a federal court of appeals held that a military tribunal had improperly classified a detainee as an enemy combatant. In *Bensayah v. Obama*, 610 F.3d 718 (C.A.D.C. 2010) the court found the government failed to show a detainee held at Guantanamo was an "enemy combatant" based on the government's claim the detainee was "part" of al-Qaeda.

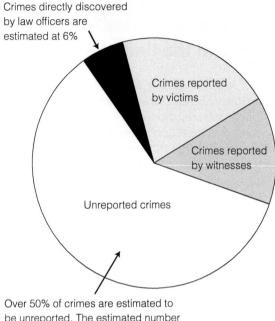

Crimes directly discovered
by law officers are
estimated at 6%

Crimes reported
by victims

Crimes reported
by witnesses

Unreported crimes

Over 50% of crimes are estimated to
be unreported. The estimated number
of violent crimes committed in 2012
was 7,679,050, and the estimated
number of serious property crimes was
19,792,450. (See NCJ 243389
(October 2013).

Figure 2.1 | Estimates of Reported Crimes in the United States

their cases to city attorneys and state attorneys (district attorneys) for charging and prosecution. Municipal police officers often spend more time in municipal courts on ordinance violations than they spend in state courts appearing in criminal cases. Both municipal and state courts use state rules of evidence.

Law enforcement agencies working at the state level of government are generally created by state law to enforce state criminal laws or to enforce hunting, fishing, health, sanitation, fire, and other state codes. Typical state law enforcement officers are state troopers; state traffic patrol; game wardens; and health, sanitation, and fire inspectors.

Federal law enforcement officers work in the many federal law agencies created by Congress. They enforce specific federal laws assigned to their agencies and take most of their cases to federal prosecutors for trial in the federal court system. Some of the many federal law enforcement agencies are the Federal Bureau of Investigation (FBI), the Drug Enforcement Agency (DEA), Immigration and Customs Enforcement (ICE), the Secret Service, the U.S. Marshals Service, and the U.S. Postal Inspection Service. ICE is the newest of the large federal law enforcement agencies and runs the Criminal Alien Program. In 2007 that program identified 164,000 criminals who were in this country illegally and were serving time in jails and prisons in the United States.

THE AMERICAN ADVERSARY SYSTEM

adversary system The judicial system in which opposing parties present evidence, and an impartial judge or jury weighs the evidence; contrasts with the inquisitorial system, where the judge actively questions the accused and witnesses.

In the American court system, the function of a criminal trial is to provide a venue for determining the facts upon which the guilt or innocence of the accused is based.

The main actors at the trial are the judge, the jury, the prosecutor, and the defense attorney. Each has a well-defined role to play in the trial. In the American **adversary system**, the prosecutor and the defense attorney assume adversarial roles; that is, they do not seek to establish the facts in cooperation with each other, but in opposition. Each side has two goals: to present the facts most advantageous to their position, and to seek to prevent and make it difficult for their opponent to do the same. (See Figure 2.2.)

Figure 2.2 | The American Adversary System

Note: In most civil and criminal jury trials, the names and addresses of jurors are available from public records for people with the interest and knowledge of how to go about obtaining them. It does not occur to most people sitting on juror panels that this could be a problem. However, jurors sitting on criminal cases where defendants are potentially dangerous or retaliatory should have some concerns for their families and themselves.

Trial courts can restrict the disclosure of juror information if the court determines that jurors need protection. Courts have held that factors that could justify restricting jury information include "… but are not limited to: (1) the defendant's involvement in organized crime; (2) the defendant's participation in a group with the capacity to harm jurors; (3) the defendant's past attempts to interfere with the judicial process; and (4) extensive publicity that could enhance the possibility that jurors' names would become public and expose them to intimidation or harassment." See *United States v. Darden* [70 F.3d 1507, 1532 (8th Cir. 1995)] and *United States v. Ross* [33 F.3d 1507 at 1520 (11th Cir. 1994)].

This system—which "sets the parties fighting," in the words of former U.S. Supreme Court Justice Jackson—gives the adversaries clearly defined roles. The prosecutor, though obligated to "seek justice, not merely to convict," attempts to have the defendant "found guilty beyond a reasonable doubt by a unanimous jury."[11] The defense counsel's duty is "to represent his client (the defendant) zealously within the bounds of the law."[12]

The two adversaries (the prosecutor and the defense lawyer) approach the facts in the case from entirely different perspectives. Each advocate comes to the trial prepared to present evidence and arguments. The trial judge and the jury come to the trial uncommitted. Within the framework of the rules of evidence and the rules of court procedure, witnesses and evidence are presented. Witnesses are cross-examined and evidence is challenged.

The trial judge presides neutrally at the criminal trial and has the responsibility for safeguarding both the rights of the accused and the interests of the public in the administration of criminal justice. The adversary nature of the proceedings does not relieve the trial judge of the obligation of raising, on his own initiative, at all appropriate times and in an appropriate manner, matters which may significantly promote a just determination of the trial. The only purpose of a criminal trial is to determine whether the prosecution has established the guilt of the accused as required by law, and the trial judge should not allow the proceedings to be used for any other purpose.[13]

Because a criminal trial "is in the end basically a fact-finding process,"[14] questions of fact must be determined in all contested criminal cases.[15] The Supreme Court stated in the case of *Tehan v. U.S. ex rel. Shott*[16] that "(t)he basic purpose of a trial is the determination of truth." Therefore, after the adversaries have presented all their evidence and made all their motions and arguments, the trier of fact must make the determination as to whether the government has carried the burden of proving the defendant guilty beyond reasonable doubt.

The determination of truth is the function of the jury. The jury must make that determination based only on the (often) conflicting versions of the truth presented by the adversaries. As a result, the adversary system has elaborate rules to control how those versions of the truth are presented. The purpose of the rules of evidence is to ensure that each adversary's version of the truth is put before the jury by relevant, reliable, and competent evidence.

THE ADVERSARY SYSTEM AND BATTLES OVER WHAT IS RELEVANT, RELIABLE, AND COMPETENT EVIDENCE

Each adversary (prosecution and defense) seeks to present the facts that are most advantageous to its position. Each adversary also seeks to prevent and make it difficult for the opponent to do the same.

The parties often battle over what is relevant, reliable, and competent evidence. To be admissible in a trial, evidence must be relevant, reliable, and competent. If evidence is not relevant, not reliable, or not competent, it is not admissible and cannot be used in a trial.

Relevant Evidence

relevant evidence
Evidence that has a tendency to make a material issue before the court more or less probable; see Chapter 5.

Relevant evidence is direct or circumstantial evidence[17] that has "any tendency to make the existence of any fact that is of consequence to the determination of the action more probative or less probative than it would be without the evidence."[18] Non-relevant evidence is inadmissible (see Federal Rule of Evidence 402 in Appendix C).

Examples

- To show that the defendant was benefiting from illegal drug operations, evidence that he purchased expensive cars and jewelry and that his assets (net worth) far exceeded his wages from legitimate employment was relevant.[19]
- To show that the defendant knew illegal drugs were in his rental truck, evidence that the defendant traveled with his wife in prior drug transportations was relevant and admissible. But evidence that the defendant's children had been involved in illegal drug operations was held not relevant and not admissible evidence.[20]
- In a charge of sexual assault, evidence that the defendant operates an X-rated movie theater is not relevant because, even if true, the evidence has no logical basis as tending to increase the probability that the defendant did any acts constituting the sexual assault.
- In a charge of transporting stolen property, evidence that the defendant has a gambling addiction is not relevant to that charge. Addiction does not logically support the inference that the defendant lacked the ability to refrain from non-gambling crimes.[21]

Under Rule 403 (see Appendix C) even relevant evidence may be excluded and held not admissible if the evidence may (1) unfairly prejudice a party, (2) confuse

In the American adversary system, the prosecutor and the defense attorney assume adversarial roles; that is, they seek to establish the facts not in cooperation with each other, but in opposition. Each side has two goals: first, to present the facts most advantageous to their position, and second, to seek to prevent and make it difficult for their opponent to do the same.

AP Images/Mark Duncan

the jury, or (3) waste the court's time. Trial judges are generally given great discretion in striking the balance between the evidence's probative value and its likely prejudicial or confusing potential.

Examples

- In child pornography prosecutions, photographs of child pornography are highly probative and outweigh prejudicial effects on the jury that views such photographs.[22]
- If the admissible child pornography pictures that were the basis of the criminal charge did not show violent and gruesome sexual practices, then sexually explicit narratives in the defendant's possession that described the violent and gruesome practices were not admissible because of the prejudicial effect of such narratives.[23]
- In a prosecution for making false statements on a passport application, evidence of the defendant's marriage to a Japanese citizen were held inadmissible because such evidence was likely to confuse the jury and create sympathy for the defendant, who sought a passport to return to his wife in Japan.[24]

You be the JUDGE

Trial judges are often asked, through pretrial motions by the prosecution or the defendant, to decide if certain evidence a party plans to introduce at the trial is relevant and admissible. Some kinds of evidence, such as prior convictions for similar crimes, or that the defendant was subjected to abuse as a child, are generally not relevant. This kind of evidence invites the jury to convict the defendant based on prior bad acts, or acquit the defendant out of sympathy for the troubled past. Sometimes, inadmissible evidence gets admitted; when that happens and a defendant is convicted by a jury, the trial judge is often asked to order a new trial.

In the first two examples below, consider (1) why the moving party might want to introduce the challenged evidence, and what argument could be made for relevance, and (2) would you as the trial judge admit the evidence. In the third example, consider what should happen if inadmissible evidence is admitted. Following each example is the citation to the trial judge's decision.

Example: Defendants were charged with distribution of methamphetamine. They seek to introduce evidence they were drug addicts. Admissible? *United States v. Norita,* 2010 WL 1752673 (D. Mar. I. 2010).

Example: Defendant, a physician, was charged with illegal drug sales through his Pain Management Clinic. The prosecution seeks to introduce evidence that (a) the defendant had a baseball bat at the clinic; (b) he had large sums of cash at the clinic; (c) many patients at the clinic were drug addicts. Admissible? *United States v. Gerlay,* 2010 WL 2867940 (D. Alaska 2010).

Example: Defendant was charged with and convicted of two bank robberies. In one case, several witnesses identified the defendant as the robber. In the other, only one bank teller was able to identify the defendant as the robber. The prosecution caused an exhibit to be entered into evidence that disclosed to the jury the defendant had committed a prior robbery. This evidence was inadmissible. What would you do as the trial judge when the defendant moved for a new trial? *United States v. Martinez Santiago,* 2006 WL 1167865 (E.D. Pa.)

Rule 404 (Appendix C) limits the use of "character" evidence, including evidence of other crimes or acts, if the purpose of admitting the evidence is to prove the criminal actions charged are in conformity with such character or other actions.

- The prosecution may not introduce evidence by a witness that a defendant charged with drug possession had on other occasions been seen by the witness with drugs in his possession.
- The prosecution may introduce testimony of a witness that a defendant had illegal guns and drugs in his apartment the day before the defendant discharged a gun and hit a police officer who was attempting to enter the apartment. Because the defendant offered a self-defense justification for discharging the gun, the fact that he had illegal drugs and guns in his apartment was relevant to prove motive and the reasonableness of the decision to discharge the gun. *State v. Payano*, 768 N.W.2d 832 (Wis. 2009).

Reliable Evidence

reliable evidence

Evidence that possesses a sufficient degree of likelihood that it is true and accurate.

Reliable evidence is evidence that possesses a sufficient degree of believability—that is, it is likely that the evidence is true and accurate. An adult witness's testimony about what he actually saw or heard is generally reliable. A statement by a witness about what another person said she saw or heard is generally unreliable. (This is the hearsay rule, discussed in detail in Chapter 7 and Chapter 8.) Unreliable evidence is inadmissible.

Example

A witness to a robbery who testified at a defendant's trial for robbery identified her as the driver of the getaway car. Earlier, the witness had identified the defendant in a photograph array (see Chapter 13) that was subsequently found to be improperly suggestive. Because the prosecution failed to independently prove the reliability of the witness' in-court identification by establishing the conditions prevailing when the witness saw the robbery and the accuracy of her descriptions of the perpetrator, her identification was determined to be unreliable, and the defendant's conviction was overturned.[25]

Reliable and admissible evidence is needed to justify charging a person with a crime. The U.S. Supreme Court pointed out in the 1986 case of *Holbrook v. Flynn*[26] that central to the right to a fair trial, guaranteed by the Sixth and Fourteenth Amendments, is the principle that "one accused of a crime is entitled to have his guilt or innocence determined solely on the basis of the evidence introduced at trial, and not on grounds of official suspicion, indictment, continued custody, or other circumstances not adduced as proof at trial."[27]

Each state has authority to commence a criminal prosecution if sufficient evidence is available to justify the criminal charge. The U.S. Supreme Court pointed out that the authorities of the states "derive from separate and independent sources of power and authority originally belonging to them before the admission to the Union and preserved to them by the Tenth Amendment."[28]

Each state also "has the power, inherent in any sovereign, independently to determine what shall be an offense against its authority and to punish such offenses, and in doing so each 'is exercising its own sovereignty, not that of the other.'"[29]

Under the American federal system, each state has its own constitution, court system, and other governmental units. States have the principal responsibility of maintaining public order within their boundaries.

Fry v. Piller

United States Supreme
Court,
127 S. Ct. 2321 (2007)

It is not uncommon for a defendant in a criminal case to attempt to present evidence that a third person committed the crime of which he is charged. The prosecution often seeks to exclude such evidence because, to the extent the jury believes the evidence is credible, it is less likely to convict the defendant even if strong evidence of his guilt exists. Ultimately, a trial court must determine whether such evidence is admissible based on its relevance and reliability. In *Fry v. Pliler*, the Supreme Court considered two important questions raised when a trial court excludes such evidence: How are decisions excluding such evidence reviewed in appellate courts? Should that review be the same for direct review and review under habeas corpus?

After two mistrials ended in hung juries, the defendant Fry was convicted of two counts of murder by a third jury. At his trial he introduced the testimony of several witnesses that a third person had committed the murders. However, the trial court excluded the testimony of one witness, holding that the defendant had not provided sufficient evidence linking the excluded testimony to the murders. The California Supreme Court affirmed the conviction, and the defendant filed a petition for habeas corpus in the federal courts. The district court denied the petition, and the Ninth Circuit Court of Appeals affirmed.

The U.S. Supreme Court granted certiorari to consider the scope of review of constitutional error in habeas corpus cases, taking into account its decision in *Holmes v. South Carolina*, 547 U.S. 319 (2006).

In *Holmes v. South Carolina* a defendant was charged with murder. He attempted to introduce evidence that a third party had committed the murder, and offered witnesses who were prepared to testify that the third party told them he had killed the victim. The trial court excluded the testimony, based on a court-made rule that evidence that another person committed the crime should be excluded if it creates a "bare suspicion" and the case against the defendant is strong. Holmes was convicted of murder and sentenced to death; his conviction was affirmed by the South Carolina Supreme Court.

On review, the U.S. Supreme Court held that Holmes was deprived of his constitutional right to "a meaningful opportunity to present a complete defense," and the Court reversed his conviction. The Court reasoned that although evidence of a third party's involvement may be excluded if it bears little logical connection to the crime, the South Carolina rule went much further than this. It operated to exclude evidence that might have a logical connection to the crime if the jury doubted the credibility of the prosecution's evidence, which in effect made the decision to exclude the evidence depend on the strength of the prosecution's case. The Court held that this was a violation of Holmes's constitutional right to present a complete defense.

The *Fry* court concluded that even if the testimony of the witness was wrongly excluded by the trial court in habeas corpus cases, unlike cases of direct review as in *Holmes*, where the "harmless beyond a reasonable doubt" rule of *Chapman v. California* applies (see Chapter 1), a trial judge's decision to exclude evidence would be overturned, even if wrongful, only if it had a "substantial and injurious effect" on the jury verdict. The court of appeals had concluded that even if the witness should have been permitted to testify, her evidence was merely "cumulative" because other witnesses had been permitted to testify about the same facts, and thus the exclusion of her testimony could not have had an adverse effect on the jury's decision. The Supreme Court affirmed the lower courts' holdings denying habeas relief.

Competent Evidence

competent evidence
Any evidence that
is relevant and reliable
and not otherwise
excludable;
see Chapter 5.

Competent evidence is a catch-all term that includes relevant, reliable evidence that is not otherwise rendered inadmissible. Relevant, reliable evidence may also be incompetent.

Examples
- Evidence that a defendant in an armed robbery told a treating physician that the injury occurred during the robbery is inadmissible. Though clearly relevant and reliable, the communication between patient and treating physician is privileged.[30]
- Evidence seized in violation of the Fourth Amendment's probable cause requirement, though relevant and reliable, is usually inadmissible under the exclusionary rule adopted by the U.S. Supreme Court to promote the purposes of the Fourth Amendment.[31]

THE AMERICAN ACCUSATORIAL SYSTEM

The United States and most of the English-speaking democracies in the world use the accusatorial system in criminal investigations and in criminal trials. The U.S. Supreme Court stated in the case of *Rogers v. Richmond*[32] that

> ours is an accusatorial and not an inquisitorial system—a system in which the State must establish guilt by evidence independently and freely secured and may not by coercion prove its charge against an accused out of his own mouth.

Under the accusatorial system, suspects and defendants have an absolute right to remain silent about matters that could incriminate them. If a defendant chooses to remain silent, the state must carry the burden of proving guilt beyond a reasonable doubt—using evidence obtained elsewhere in a manner that did not violate the rights of the suspect.

Most European countries and other democracies of the world do not use the accusatorial system but use instead an inquisitorial system. Under the inquisitorial system, defendants do not have an absolute right to remain silent. In some European countries, special judges become responsible for investigating serious crimes and questioning witnesses and suspects.

Although countries that use the inquisitorial system rely more heavily on obtaining confessions to solve crimes, the U.S. Supreme Court expressed a different philosophy in the 1964 case of *Escobedo v. Illinois*[33] and the 1966 case of *Miranda v. Arizona*.[34]

DISCLOSING INFORMATION IN THE ADVERSARY SYSTEM

When a criminal charge has been made, the prosecution and the defense begin separate investigations of the facts supporting or opposing the charge. (See Chapter 3 for a discussion of the charging process.) As adversaries, neither the prosecution nor the defense is inclined to share information with the other side. However, the U.S. Supreme Court has placed limits on this unwillingness to share:

> The adversary system of trial is hardly an end in itself, it is not yet a poker game in which players enjoy an absolute right always to conceal their cards until played.[35]

Many of the rules that compel disclosure apply to the prosecution, but some compel a defendant to disclose information to the prosecution.

Notice of Alibi Statutes

In using the alibi defense, a defendant is alleging that he or she physically could not have committed the crime that is charged because the defendant was at another place at the time the crime was committed.

Example

X is charged with robbing a liquor store and has been identified by two witnesses and an employee of the store as the man who robbed the store. *X* uses the defense of alibi and states that at the time of robbery, he was at his mother's home 100 miles away. *X*'s wife and mother corroborate *X*'s story, stating that they were with *X* at the time of the robbery.

Because an alibi can easily be fabricated, it must be carefully investigated. Most states have notice of alibi statutes that require defendants who plan to use an alibi defense to serve notice on the prosecutor before trial. These statutes are meant to safeguard against the wrongful use of alibis and to give law enforcement agencies and prosecutors necessary notice and time to investigate the merits of the proposed alibi.

Notice of alibi statutes require a defendant to disclose the place where the defendant claims to have been at the time the crime was committed and the names and addresses of witnesses to the alibi, if known. In the 1973 case of *Wardius v. Oregon*,[36] the U.S. Supreme Court held that if a defendant is compelled to disclose information, then the state must also make similar disclosures so that discovery is a "two-way street." The Court held in the *Wardius* case that

> [In] the absence of a strong showing of state interests to the contrary, discovery must be a two-way street. The State may not insist that trials be run as a "search for truth" so far as defense witnesses are concerned, while maintaining "poker game" secrecy for its own witnesses. It is fundamentally unfair to require a defendant to divulge the details of his own case while at the same time subjecting him to the hazard of surprise concerning refutation of the very pieces of evidence which he disclosed to the State.

The Duty to Disclose Evidence Tending to Show the Innocence of an Accused (the *Brady* Rule)

Brady rule The rule that requires the prosecution to disclose, upon request, evidence favorable to the accused.

Exculpatory evidence is evidence that tends to show innocence. The following cases establish the well-recognized rule that a prosecutor has a duty to disclose evidence favorable to an accused upon request, where the evidence is material to guilt or innocence (the **Brady rule**). Where such evidence is in the exclusive possession of the prosecution, it must be disclosed even when there is no request for disclosure by the defense if such evidence is "clearly supportive of a claim of innocence."[37] For discovery purposes, it has been held that law enforcement officers are part of the prosecution and also have a duty of disclosure. (See *Kyles v. Whitley*, 514 U.S. 419 (1995).)

In *Steckler v. Greene*,[38] the U.S. Supreme Court reviewed its decisions after *Brady* and stated that (1) the duty to disclose exists even if the defense makes no request for disclosure, (2) the duty includes evidence useful in impeachment as well as exculpatory evidence, and (3) evidence is material if there is a reasonable probability that, if the evidence were known to the defendant, the result in the trial might have been different.

In the 2004 case of *Banks v. Dretke*,[39] a capital murder case, the U.S. Supreme Court held that the failure of the prosecutor to inform the defense that a key witness was a paid informant violated the *Brady* rule. The prosecution told the defense that it would not have to ask for exculpatory information, as the prosecution would give them everything they had. Nonetheless, a paid informant testified against the defendant, and, when asked whether he had any agreements with the prosecution, he stated he did not. The prosecution permitted that false testimony to stand. The Court said those actions violated the *Brady* rule and ordered a new hearing to determine whether the defendant should have a new trial.

Brady v. Maryland

United States Supreme Court, 373 U.S. 83, 83 S. Ct. 1194 (1963)

The defendant testified that he had participated in the robbery charged but stated that his accomplice had killed the victim. Despite a request for exculpatory evidence from the defense lawyer, the prosecutor withheld a statement by the accomplice admitting the killing but claiming that the defendant had wanted to strangle the victim, whereas the accomplice had wanted to shoot him. After a jury sentenced the defendant to death, the case was remanded for retrial on the question of punishment, but not on the question of guilt. The Supreme Court quoted the Maryland Court of Appeals as saying that there was "considerable doubt" about how much good the undisclosed statement would have done the defendant, but that it was "too dogmatic" to say that the jury would not have attached "any significance" to the evidence. The Court held that

> the suppression by the prosecution of evidence favorable to an accused upon request violates due process where the evidence is material either to guilt or to punishment, irrespective of the good faith or bad faith of the prosecution.

In *Smith v. Cain*, 132 S. Ct. 627 (2012) the U.S. Supreme Court held that failure to disclose to the defense the fact that the sole witness identifying the defendant in a murder case had made prior contradictory statements violated the *Brady* rule. All states have passed statutes adopting the *Brady* requirements.

The U.S. Supreme Court has held that the *Brady* rule does not require the prosecution to disclose evidence a defendant could use to impeach a government witness before making a plea agreement with that defendant; *United States v. Ruiz*.[40] The Court did note in that case that the government had agreed that even if a plea agreement was reached, it would disclose any information bearing on the factual innocence of the defendant.

Lost, Misplaced, and Destroyed Evidence

Hundreds of thousands of criminal cases are handled every year by thousands of law officers. Sometimes evidence is lost, misplaced, or accidentally destroyed. In the investigation of a violent crime, an item of clothing or other potential evidence can be overlooked in the rush to render medical assistance to the victim or to apprehend the offender. These problems have occurred over the years and raise the question of the government's duty to collect and preserve evidence that might assist a defense lawyer in defending a client.

A SUMMARY OF THE BRADY RULE BY THE NATIONAL INSTITUTE OF JUSTICE

The following is the summary of the *Brady* rule presented by the National Institute of Justice in a May 2002 publication (NCJ 191717):

- Under the *Brady* rule, the state is required to turn over any and all exculpatory evidence to the defense.
- In most states, "missing" evidence or failure to turn over evidence violates the *Brady* rule only if it is found to have been done in bad faith, which requires a showing that it was known that (a) the evidence was exculpatory and (b) the evidence was intentionally withheld.
- Potentially useful but not conclusively exculpatory information does not necessarily need to be turned over.
- To prevail on a *Brady* claim, the defendant must prove a conscious effort to suppress exculpatory evidence.

Law enforcement officers are part of the prosecution and have a duty of disclosure, as does the prosecutor.

In the 1984 case of *California v. Trombetta*[41] and the 1988 case of *Arizona v. Youngblood,*[42] the U.S. Supreme Court established rules concerning the government's duty to preserve evidence. In the *Trombetta* case, California law officers followed routine procedure in not saving the breath samples of persons charged with driving while intoxicated where the chances were very low that the samples would have helped defense lawyers. In the *Youngblood* case, Arizona law officers did not properly refrigerate evidence of a sexual assault. The Supreme Court held that a violation of **due process** has not occurred unless the following is shown:

due process The minimum procedural protections courts must afford those charged with crimes; guaranteed by the Fifth and Fourteenth Amendments to the U.S. Constitution.

- *Bad faith on the part of the police or other law enforcement official:* The Court held that "unless a criminal defendant can show bad faith on the part of the police, failure to preserve potentially useful evidence does not constitute a denial of due process of law."[43]
- *The evidence also would be of likely significance to the defendant's defense:* The Court held that "[the] evidence must both possess an exculpatory value that was apparent before the evidence was destroyed, and be of such a nature that the defendant would be unable to obtain comparable evidence by other reasonably available means."[44]

In both the *Trombetta* and the *Youngblood* cases, the Supreme Court held that there was no bad faith on the part of the law officers and that both convictions were based on other strong, credible evidence.

If a *Brady* violation occurs, the penalty often will be more severe, and could be a new trial or, in a severe case even a complete dismissal of the criminal charges. In *United States v. Chapman*, 524 F.3d 1073 (9th Cir. 2008), the court noted that dismissal of the charges, while not the usual remedy, is appropriate if the prosecution was guilty of "flagrant or willful" suppression of exculpatory evidence. A *Brady* violation occurred in *Ouimette v. Moran,*[45] where a state prosecutor's chief witness had an extensive criminal record and the state failed to disclose that record, which the defense lawyer needed for cross-examination. A new trial was ordered. A new trial was also ordered where, because of the improper handling of a murder weapon, blood and fingerprint evidence was lost.[46]

Other lesser penalties could include forbidding the state to use some of its evidence, warning the state in court, or filing a complaint with the employer of the person causing the problem.

Use of False or Perjured Evidence

The deliberate use of false or perjured evidence in an attempt to obtain a criminal conviction is a crime. Such conduct could also be the basis for a civil lawsuit in which large compensatory and punitive damages could be awarded. If the prosecution knowingly permits a witness to give false evidence, any resulting conviction must be reversed if there is a "reasonable likelihood" the evidence may have affected the judgment of the jury. *United States v. Agurs*, 427 U.S. 97 (1976). However, if the prosecution does not know a government witness has given false testimony, due process is denied only if the evidence is material and the reviewing court concludes it is "most likely" the defendant would not have been convicted without the false testimony. (See e.g., *Ortega v. Duncan*, 333 F.3d 102 (2d Cir. 2003).)

In a 2007 case, the Ninth Circuit Court of Appeals held that a prosecutor's obligation to reveal known perjury by a state witness to the defense applied to allegations that a state witness committed perjury. In *Morris v. Ylst*,[47] a defendant appealed his murder conviction based on a report made available to the prosecution in which a legal assistant in the prosecution office stated that a co-defendant perjured herself at the defendant's trial. The circuit court held that the state had a duty to investigate an allegation of perjury, and the failure to do so could be a violation of a defendant's rights. Here, however, the court concluded that the defendant did not show that correcting any falsehood would have changed the result at his trial. The defendant's murder conviction was affirmed. In the following U.S. Supreme Court cases knowing use of false testimony by the prosecution constituted a denial of due process.

Mooney v. Holohan

United States Supreme Court, 294 U.S. 103, 55 S. Ct. 340 (1935)

The Supreme Court made it very clear that a conviction obtained by the knowing use of false testimony or false evidence is a denial of due process of law and will be reversed. The Court held that

> if a state has contrived a conviction through the pretense of a trial which in truth is but used as a means of depriving a defendant of liberty through a deliberate deception of court and jury by the presentation of testimony known to be perjured. Such a contrivance by a state to procure the conviction and imprisonment of a defendant is as inconsistent with the rudimentary demands of justice as is the obtaining of a like result by intimidation.

Miller v. Pate

United States Supreme Court, 386 U.S. 1, 87 S. Ct. 785 (1967)

The Supreme Court reversed and remanded the defendant's murder and rape conviction. The prosecutor referred to and exhibited to the jury a pair of "blood-stained shorts" that were an important link in the chain of the circumstantial evidence case against the defendant. The prosecutor knew but did not tell the jury or the defense lawyer that the reddish-brown stains on the shorts were not blood, but paint. The Court held that the prosecution "deliberately misrepresented the truth" and that

> More than 30 years ago this Court held that the Fourteenth Amendment cannot tolerate a state criminal conviction obtained by the knowing use of false evidence.... There has been no deviation from that established principle. There can be no retreat from that principle here.

CIVIL COMMITMENT: EVIDENCE NEEDED TO COMMIT A PERSON WHO MIGHT BE VIOLENT

Involuntary confinement of a person usually involves the criminal justice system discussed previously. However, under some circumstances civil commitment is authorized under state or federal statutes. Where that is the case, those seeking an involuntary commitment order must present evidence supporting the statutory requirements for such commitment. Persons who present danger to themselves or others because of mental health problems or sexual predator histories are among those for whom statutory, civil commitment is authorized.

Millions of Americans have mental health problems. Although experts point out that most people with mental health problems will never be violent, those same experts agree there is an increased risk of violence presented by persons with serious mental illnesses. Moreover, substance abuse or failure to take prescribed medications can increase the risk of violence. (See the July 2, 2011 *New York Times* article "Mixing Guns and Mental Illness.")

All states have mental health laws that authorize involuntary, short-term mental observation (often called "MOing") of persons with mental illness. These emergency procedures permit a law enforcement officer or a physician to place in a mental health facility a person who exhibits signs of a mental illness and who poses a danger to self or others. Most state statutes require only that the person seeking commitment have a reasonable belief the person to be committed is potentially dangerous. The initial commitment based on such a belief is usually for only 24 or 48 hours. If during that time the person is found to be mentally ill and dangerous, longer detentions for observation and treatment can be made. Longer commitments require a court order, and under most state statutes the person seeking commitment must prove mental illness and potential for violence beyond a reasonable doubt.

Sometimes the person being committed must be forcibly taken to a mental health facility. If it is determined the person does not require commitment, a civil action against those instituting the emergency commitment procedures might be brought by that person. An example of the issues in such a case is *Chathas v. Smith*.[48] There, a former Illinois police officer was undergoing psychiatric treatment for mental problems. He had misused firearms, and his wife reported that he was in a "highly nervous state." When a dispute occurred over his pension rights, he stated to his psychiatrist that he would "blow away" the persons threatening his pension. Based on this information, police officers used force to take the former officer to a mental hospital, as provided in the Illinois Mental Health Code. However, the mental hospital concluded there was insufficient evidence of mental illness and dangerousness to admit the former officer, and he was released. He then sued the officers who forcibly took him to the mental facility, alleging they violated his civil rights. The trial court and the court of appeals held against the former officer because the police officers who forcibly took him to the mental facility had probable cause to believe he was mentally ill and dangerous, and could not be liable absent severe injury or malice.

Persons convicted of sexual offenses who continue to pose a danger of sexual crimes after release from prison can be detained indefinitely for treatment. In *McKune v. Lile*, 536 U.S. 24 (2002) the U.S. Supreme Court wrote:

> Sex offenders are a serious threat in this nation.... When convicted sex offenders reenter society, they are much more likely than any other type of offender to be rearrested for a new rape or sexual assault.... The rate of recidivism (repeat offenders) of treated sex offenders is fairly consistently estimated to be around 15%, whereas the rate of recidivism of untreated (sex) offenders has been estimated to be as high as 80%.... 536 U.S. at 31.

In *United States v. Comstock,* 130 S. Ct. 1949 (2010), the U.S. Supreme Court again affirmed that the detention of mentally ill, sexually dangerous prisoners beyond the date the prisoner would ordinarily be released was constitutional. To detain such a prisoner, the Supreme Court stated it must be shown that the prisoner

1. Had previously committed sexually violent acts or child molestation;
2. Currently was suffering from a serious mental illness, abnormality or disorder; and
3. As a result of the mental illness or disorder, is dangerous to others and if released would have serious difficulty in restraining from sexually violent conduct or child molestation.

SUMMARY

1. **Know the meaning of *federalism* as it applies to criminal justice.**
   - Federalism as applied to criminal justice means the federal government may pass criminal laws only in the specific areas delegated to the federal government by the U.S. Constitution. States have the power to pass criminal laws in all other areas, unless such laws conflict with rights protected by the Constitution.

2. **Identify the constitutional basis for the exercise of federal criminal jurisdiction.**
   - The Constitution gives the federal government power to pass criminal laws to protect itself, its property, and its employees and agents. It is authorized to pass laws, including criminal laws, in areas or activities that affect interstate commerce, including all "necessary and proper" laws that are related to interstate commerce. It also may pass criminal laws governing places outside the jurisdiction of a state, such as a federal territory, military base, and so forth.

3. **Identify the limits of federal jurisdiction under the Interstate Commerce Clause.**
   - The Commerce Clause power extends only to activities that affect interstate commerce, as opposed to activities that affect only a single state. It includes activities that occur in only one state, but have a substantial effect on interstate commerce.

4. **Know the meaning of reliable, relevant, competent evidence.**
   - Reliable evidence is evidence that possesses a sufficient degree of likelihood that it is true and accurate; relevant evidence is evidence that has a tendency to make a contested fact more or less probable than if the evidence is not admitted; competent evidence is any relevant and reliable evidence that is not excludable for some other reason.

5. **List some differences between the accusatorial and inquisitional systems.**
   - In the accusatorial system suspects cannot be required to testify, and the prosecution has the

duty to develop evidence of guilt from other sources. In an inquisitorial system a suspect may be required to answer questions and provide information that may lead to his conviction.

6. **State the requirements of the *Brady* rule.**
   - The *Brady* rule requires the prosecution to disclose exculpatory information or evidence to the defendant, even if a request for such information or evidence is not made. It includes evidence that goes to the credibility of a government witness, such as evidence the witness has made inconsistent statements to

investigators. A violation of the *Brady* rule does not occur unless the evidence withheld is material and a reasonable probability exists that the result in the trial might have been different if the evidence had been disclosed to the defendant.

7. **State the requirements of the U.S. Supreme Court's rule for lost or destroyed evidence.**
   - A failure by the government to preserve evidence violates due process only if done so in bad faith, the evidence possesses some exculpatory value apparent to the government when it was lost or destroyed, and the defendant cannot independently obtain comparable evidence.

KEY TERMS

adversary system, 33
Brady rule, 40
common law, 28

competent evidence, 39
due process, 42

Federal Rules of Evidence, 27
federalism, 26

relevant evidence, 35
reliable evidence, 37

KEY CASES

Bond v. U.S., 131 S. Ct. 2355 (2011): Tenth Amendment permits individual citizens to claim federal statute violated principles of federalism.

Brady v. Maryland, 373 U.S. 83 (1963): Prosecution must disclose potentially exculpatory evidence to defendant.

Fry v. Pliler, 127 S. Ct. 2321 (2007): Established when evidence that third parties may have committed the crime charged can be excluded at a trial, and also the scope of review by an appeals court of such exclusions.

Gonzales v. Raich, 125 S. Ct. 2195 (2005): Commerce Clause gave Congress power to apply federal drug laws to wholly intrastate use of controlled substances.

Holbrook v. Flynn, 475 U.S. 560 (1986): Trials and judgments must be based solely on admitted competent, relevant, reliable evidence.

Miller v. Pate, 386 U.S. 451 (1967): Explains when use of false evidence by prosecution requires reversal of conviction.

United States v. Kebodeaux, 133 S. Ct. 2496 (2013): Necessary and Proper Clause gives Congress power to pass SORNA registration requirements for former military members convicted of sexual crimes while in the military.

PROBLEMS

Finish each sentence using one of the available answers provided.

Available Answers (Problems 1–6)

a. An accusatorial system
b. An inquisitorial system
c. A totalitarian system
d. All of the above are correct.
e. None of the above is correct.

1. The United States uses
2. Most European countries use
3. Defendants charged with a crime have an absolute right to remain silent under
4. Defendants charged with crimes do not have an absolute right to remain silent under
5. More confessions are obtained and used as evidence under
6. Confessions and incriminating statements cannot be used as evidence under

Available Answers (Problems 7–13)

a. Relevant evidence
b. Reliable evidence
c. Competent evidence
d. All of the above are correct.
e. None of the above is correct.

7. To be admissible, evidence must be
8. Most hearsay is not admissible because it is not
9. Testimony that the defendant's son has a long criminal record is not admissible because it is not
10. Evidence obtained by a police burglary of the defendant's home is not admissible because it is not
11. A voluntary confession is not ordinarily admissible because it is not
12. An eyewitness who saw *X* commit the armed robbery he or she is charged with cannot testify as to what the witness saw because it is not
13. Testimony of a defendant's wife about a confession to the crime charged is not admissible because it is not

Discussion Problem: The Casey Anthony Verdict

The first-degree murder trial of Casey Anthony ended in a not-guilty verdict on July 5, 2011. No case since the O. J. Simpson trial has attracted as much public attention, particularly focused on the limitations of the prosecution's case. Using a source such as Google or Bing, make a synopsis of the prosecution's evidence and the defense offered to rebut that evidence. What evidence did the prosecution offer to prove the elements of first-degree murder? Why was it insufficient? What theory or theories did the defense propose as an alternative explanation of Caylee Anthony's death? Would evidence supporting such theories be admissible?

CASE ANALYSIS

Read Appendix B, Finding and Analyzing Cases (p. 499). With these guidelines in mind, please continue with the Case Analysis selections for Chapter 2.

1. In *United States v. Tavera*, 719 F.3d 705 (6th Cir. 2013), a defendant convicted of drug distribution charges discovered after the trial that a chief prosecution witness had initially told prosecutors prior to trial that the defendant was not involved in the drug distribution ring. At the trial, the witness testified the defendant was part of the distribution ring. On appeal, the defendant argued the prosecution violated *Brady* by not informing him the witness had made the prior statements. The appeals court reversed the conviction, stated it was abandoning the "due diligence" rule in *Brady* cases. The due diligence rule holds that if the defendant could have unearthed the exculpatory material possessed by the prosecution by his own efforts, any *Brady* violation is excused. The majority stated it was compelled to abandon the due diligence rule because of the decision of the U.S. Supreme Court in *Banks v. Dretke*, discussed in this chapter. Do you agree? Or do you agree with the opinion of the judge who wrote a dissenting opinion?

2. The U.S. Supreme Court said in the *Ruiz* case, discussed in this chapter, that the prosecution has no duty to give impeachment information to a defendant during the plea bargaining process. Thus, if the prosecution knows a key government witness has made contradictory statements relative to a defendant's guilt, that information need not be disclosed. Should the same result be reached if during the plea-bargaining process the prosecution possesses exculpatory information that tends to show the innocence of the defendant? Why or why not? *State v. Huebler*, 275 P.3d 91 (Nev. 2012).

3. Notice of alibi statutes require a defendant who intends to present such a defense to give notice to the prosecution. The notice typically must list the witnesses who will support the defendant's claim he was not present when the crime occurred. Assume a defendant in a murder case files an alibi notice with the names of several witnesses who will testify they saw the defendant at a party when the murder took place at a different location. The prosecution discovers that some of the named witnesses were out of town on the date they were supposed to have seen the defendant at the party. At trial,

defendant does not pursue the alibi defense, and thus does not list any of the alibi witnesses as witnesses for the defense. The prosecution seeks to introduce the alibi notice, which includes the names of witnesses who clearly could not provide an alibi for the defendant. Is that notice admissible? Is it relevant? Does it have probative value, i.e. did it render more probable the fact of the defendant's guilt? *See State v. Simms*, 25 A.3d 144 (Md. 2011).

4. The "knowing use" by the prosecution of false evidence is a denial of due process requiring a new trial, if the false evidence may have affected the jury verdict. In *Ramirez v. State*, 96 S.W.3d 386 (Tex. App. 2002) a police officer was charged with sexual assault. The alleged victim, a woman with a long criminal record, had contacted a lawyer on the day she reported the alleged assault. Shortly before trial, her attorney filed a civil suit against the officer's employer, the City of Austin. The prosecution knew of the civil action, but on direct examination did not ask the alleged victim about it. Was that a violation of the "knowing use" of false evidence? What was "false"? Why did it matter?

Notes

1. Since the beginning of federalism more than 200 years ago, other democratic countries have also adopted forms of federalism, including Canada, Mexico, Australia, and the Federal German Republic. Democratic nations also use two other forms of government: (a) The *unitary form*—used by England, France, Ireland, Norway, and other countries—has one center of power (the central government), which creates smaller units, such as cities and provinces, to provide services. Countries that use unitary forms of government are generally small in both size and population. (b) The *confederate form* of government, which Switzerland has used for more than 700 years, bands together provinces and states in a loose organization called a confederacy. The United States used this form of government from after the American Revolution until 1791. Because it was not working, the Constitutional Convention was convened in Philadelphia in 1787 to draft a new constitution and to invent a workable system of government acceptable to all 13 states.

2. After remand, the federal court upheld Bond's conviction under the chemical weapons statute. The U.S. Supreme Court granted review of that decision, 133 S. Ct. 978 (2013).

3. See, e.g., Federal Rules of Evidence 201(g) and 404(b).

4. In the 1985 case of *Heath v. Alabama*, 474 U.S. 82, 106 S. Ct. 433, the U.S. Supreme Court ruled that under the dual sovereignty doctrine, a defendant who "in a single act violates the 'peace and dignity' of two sovereigns by breaking the laws of each ... has committed two distinct 'offenses.'"

   In the *Heath* case, the defendant confessed that he hired two men in Georgia to kidnap his pregnant wife from their Alabama home and kill her. After his wife was murdered in Alabama, the defendant (and the men) was convicted of crimes in both Alabama and Georgia. The Supreme Court affirmed the criminal convictions under the dual sovereignty doctrine, holding that "(t)o deny a State its power to enforce its criminal laws because another state has won the race to the courthouse 'would be a shocking... deprivation of the historic right and obligation of the States to maintain peace and order within their confines.'"

   Dual sovereignty also applies when criminal acts violate both state and federal laws. The 1993 trial of four Los Angeles police officers for beating Rodney King is an example. When federal prosecutors were not satisfied with the outcome of the California trial (the officers' acquittals resulted in a large-scale riot in Los Angeles), criminal indictments were sought under federal law, and the officers were tried again in a federal court for the same conduct. The second trial resulted in conviction of two of the officers and acquittal of the other two.

   Some states, however, have enacted statutes that forbid criminal prosecution for a criminal act (or acts) already prosecuted in another state or in the federal courts. Wisconsin Statute 939.71 is such an example.

5. See the 1812 U.S. Supreme Court case *United States v. Hudson and Goodwin,* 11 U.S. (7 Cranch) 32, and the 1949 Supreme Court case *Krulewitch v. United States,* 336 U.S. 440, 69 S. Ct. 16, where Justice Jackson stated, "It is well and wisely settled that there can be no judge-made offense against the United States and that every federal prosecution must be sustained by statutory authority."

6. In *Carr v. United States*, 560 U.S. 438 (2010) the Supreme Court held that SORNA did not apply to convicted sex offenders whose interstate travel occurred before SORNA's effective date.

7. *See United States v. Romeo*, 647 F.3d 184, 189 (S.D. N.Y. 2009).

8. 561 F. Supp. 2d 1154 (D. Mont. 2008).

9. 133 S. Ct. 2496 (2013).

10. The holding in *Kebodeaux* may be limited to cases involving former military persons convicted of sexual offenses while in the military. The Court's decision upholding Congress's power to pass SORNA was closely tied to the Court's conclusion Kebodeaux was subject to sexual registration requirements under prevailing military law, and thus the Necessary and Proper Clause would permit Congress to make Kebodeaux responsible under SORNA. Whether the same result would be reached for others convicted of federal crimes is not clear.

11. American Bar Association (ABA) Standards Relating to the Prosecution Function and the Defense Function, 1.1(c).

12. ABA Code EC 7-1.

13. *General Responsibility of the Trial Judge,* p. 167, ABA Standards Relating to the Administration of Criminal Justice.

14. *Herring v. New York,* 422 U.S. 853, 95 S. Ct. 2550 (1975).

15. Questions of fact are determined by the fact finder. The fact finder is a jury in a jury trial or the trial judge when a case is tried without a jury. Questions of law are always determined by the trial judge.

16. 382 U.S. 406, 416, 86 S. Ct. 459, 465 (1966).

17. See Chapter 4 for definitions of *direct* and *circumstantial.*

18. Federal Rules of Evidence, sec. 401. Evidence, even though relevant, may be excluded under evidentiary rules like Rule 403 of the Federal Rules if it is unduly prejudicial or may tend to mislead the jury. This is sometimes referred to as the "legally relevant" test.

19. *United States v. Burgos,* 254 F.3d 8 (1st Cir. 2001).

20. *United States v. Espinoza,* 244 F.3d 1234 (10th Cir. 2001).

21. *United States v. Garcia,* 94 F.3d 57 (2d Cir. 1996).

22. *United States v. Becht,* 267 F.3d 767 (8th Cir. 2001).

23. *United States v. Grimes,* 244 F.3d 375 (5th Cir. 2001).

24. *United States v. George,* 266 F.3d 52 (2d Cir. 2001).

25. *Hull v. State,* 607 So.2d 369 (Ct. Crim. App. Ala. 1992).

26. 475 U.S. 560, 106 S. Ct. 1340.

27. *Taylor v. Kentucky,* 436 U.S. 478, 485 (1978).

28. *Heath v. Alabama,* 474 U.S. 82 (1985).

29. *Id.*

30. See Chapter 6 for a discussion of privileged communications.

31. See Chapter 9 for a discussion of the Fourth Amendment exclusionary rule.

32. 365 U.S. 534, 540–41, 81 S. Ct. 735, 739–40 (1961).

33. 378 U.S. 478, 84 S. Ct. 1758.

34. 384 U.S. 436, 86 S. Ct. 1602.

35. *Williams v. Florida,* 399 U.S. 78, 90 S. Ct. 1893, 1896 (1970).

36. 93 S. T. 2208 (1973). See also *Williams v. Florida* [399 U.S. 78 (1970)] and *Taylor v. Illinois,* 484 U.S. 400 (1988).

37. *Brady v. Maryland,* 83 S. Ct. 1194.

38. 527 U.S. 263 (1999).

39. 540 U.S. 668 (2004).

40. 536 U.S. 622 (2002).

41. 467 U.S. 479, 104 S. Ct. 2528.

42. 37.488 U.S. 51, 109 S. Ct. 333.

43. 488 U.S. 58, 109 S. Ct. 337.

44. 467 U.S. 489, 104 S. Ct. 2534.

45. 942 F.2d 1 (1st Cir. 1991).

46. *Sanburn v. State,* 812 P.2d 1279 (Nev. 1991).

47. 447 F.3d 735 (9th Cir. 2007), *cert. denied,* 127 S. Ct. 957 (2007).

48. 884 F.2d 980 (7th Cir. 1989), *cert. denied,* 493 U.S. 1095 (1990).

CHAPTER 3

Using Evidence to Determine Guilt or Innocence

ENTERING A PLEA

Frances Twitty/iStockphoto.com

LEARNING OBJECTIVES

In this chapter we discuss pleas and plea bargaining in criminal prosecutions. The learning objectives for this chapter are

  Outline the criminal court process.

  List the pleas a defendant may enter to a criminal charge.

  Evaluate the pros and cons of plea bargaining.

  Compare the use of evidence at various stages of a criminal trial.

As we discuss in this chapter, the great majority of criminal cases, both in the federal courts and in state courts, are resolved by guilty pleas entered after plea agreements between the defendant and the prosecution have been reached. In the federal courts, and virtually all state courts, the trial judge does not participate in the plea bargaining, and is not bound to accept the plea agreement agreed to by the prosecution. However, if the trial judge elects to reject the plea agreement, the defendant is given the right to withdraw the guilty plea and enter a plea of not guilty.

What if the trial judge, contrary to the rules, enters into plea negotiations with a defendant in open court, accepts the defendant's guilty plea, and imposes a sentence as agreed with the defendant, all over the objections of the prosecution? Can the state appeal the sentence as an illegal sentence? In *State v. McMahon*, 94 So. 3d 468 (Fla. 2012), the prosecution objected to the plea agreement the trial judge reached with the defendant because the prosecution planned to seek a longer prison sentence under the Florida habitual offender statute. The state appealed the shorter sentence imposed by the trial judge. Should the state be permitted to appeal the trial judge's sentence? Should the ability of a state to appeal decisions made by trial judges in criminal cases be limited? If so, why, and in which situations?

EVALUATION AND REVIEW OF EVIDENCE

The rules of evidence ultimately decide what evidence will be presented to the judge and jury for evaluation and what evidence will not. However, at various stages of the investigatory and criminal court process, evidence may be evaluated in a variety of settings. In many of these settings, the rules of evidence do not apply. Consider the stages in a shoplifting case:

1. Store employees or security personnel are usually the first to evaluate and judge the information and evidence available to them before detaining a person for shoplifting. Probable cause based on firsthand information by a reliable adult employee is the standard required. Store employees are told, "If you did not see it, it did not happen" and "When in doubt, let him go."
2. After a suspect is detained for shoplifting and the police are called, the officer evaluates the available evidence before proceeding. If the evidence is insufficient, the suspect is immediately released.
3. Evaluations made in stages one and two are often reviewed immediately by superiors (store managers and police sergeants).
4. If the case is presented to a prosecutor (a city attorney or a district attorney), the prosecutor reviews the available evidence to determine whether further proceedings are warranted.
5. If a charge or citation is issued, a defense lawyer often reviews the evidence, looking for weaknesses in the case. Insufficient or questionable evidence, use of improper procedure, or lack of probable cause based on firsthand information are some of the weaknesses for which a defense lawyer would look.

motion to suppress evidence A written or oral request to a judge to keep out evidence at a trial or hearing; often made when a party believes the evidence was unlawfully obtained.

6. A **motion to suppress evidence** and dismiss could bring the matter before a judge. To rule on the motion, the judge must review the evidence.
7. If the defense motion is denied, the case may be tried before a jury, which evaluates the evidence and determines guilt or innocence.
8. A convicted defendant can appeal the case and argue to an appellate court that the evidence was not sufficient to support a finding or a judgment of guilt. The appellate court then reviews the evidence.

The defendant in the 1984 case of *Lee v. State*[1] did not argue insufficient evidence, but in his appeal argued instead that a shoplifter had to leave a store in order to be convicted of larceny (theft). The Maryland Court of Special Appeals, however, affirmed the defendant's conviction, holding that it was not necessary for a state to show that a defendant left a store to be convicted of shoplifting. Stating that they found no court decision holding otherwise, the court held that once "a customer goes beyond the mere removal of goods from the shelf and crosses the threshold into the realm of behavior inconsistent with the owner's expectations, the circumstances may be such that a larcenous intent can be inferred."

Obtaining evidence to infer "larcenous intent" when a customer remains on the premises of a store can be difficult. In response to this, in some states the shoplifting crime is divided into "theft" and "willful concealment." (See e.g., N.H. Stat. 644:17 (I) and (II).) Proof of willful concealment is sufficient if the customer has concealed goods while in the retail store. Theft requires proof of the completed shoplifting, such as taking goods through a cashier line without payment or changing the sticker price of goods. Concealment is a misdemeanor, whereas shoplifting/theft can be a felony depending on the value of the goods stolen. (See *State v. Thiel*, 999 A.2d 367 (N.H. 2010).)

In the process of review and evaluation of evidence, weaker cases are filtered out of the system or lesser charges are used. Not all cases go to court and trial. A merchant might recover the stolen merchandise from a shoplifter and, after warning the person, take no further action. A police officer might take a teenaged shoplifter home to his or her parents. After the parents have been informed of the incident, the matter may be dropped.

Team Evidence Reviews and Clearance Rates

In the investigation of both major and minor crimes, a determination must be made about whether sufficient evidence exists to obtain a conviction or more investigation is needed. A February 2008 *FBI Law Enforcement Bulletin* article, "Homicide Investigations: Identifying Best Practices," points out that almost 40 percent of criminal homicides committed in the United States are not cleared. Police departments that use the practice of team review of evidence within a short time after the discovery of major crimes have a higher clearance rate than the national average, the article concludes.

Team reviews allow for better communication and exchange of information between officers involved in an investigation, who might work different shifts. Whether done informally or pursuant to established department policy, evidence reviews can increase the efficiency of investigations and lead to higher clearance rates. The following list suggests some of the methods and questions that are raised in a team review. (Most of these topics are developed more fully in this book.)

1. What physical evidence is available?

DNA	Documents
Latent prints	Videos or photos
Weapons	Sexual assault evidence
Ballistics	Illegal drug evidence
Stolen property	Test results

GOALS OF THE CRIMINAL JUSTICE SYSTEM

The most basic function of any government is to provide for the security of the individual and her or his property [U.S. Supreme Court in *Lanzetta v. New Jersey*, 306 U.S. 451, 455, 59 S.Ct. 618 (1939)]. The generally recognized overall goals of the criminal justice system are

- To discourage and to deter people from committing crimes
- To protect society from dangerous and harmful people
- To punish people who have committed crimes
- To rehabilitate and reform people who have committed crimes

2. Was the physical evidence obtained in a manner that may be seriously attacked or suppressed under the exclusionary or derivative evidence rule? Are there problems with the chain of custody of the evidence?

3. What witnesses are available, and how reliable and dependable are the witnesses? Have the witnesses categorized below been evaluated (on a scale from excellent to poor, or unknown) on their reliability, dependability, credibility, willingness to testify, and importance of their testimony, as well as their age and appearance?
    Eyewitnesses
    Victim(s)
    Other civilian witnesses
    Police/sheriff/law enforcement personnel
    Expert witnesses (qualifications?)

4. What are some likely ways the witnesses may be attacked on cross-examination? What evidence is available to corroborate statements made by witnesses, especially eyewitnesses?

5. Is there a suspect or suspects? What are the reasons for targeting the suspect? Are any persons related to the case in police custody? If so, on what charges? Are charges for an offense other than the crime under investigation? If so, are the offenses related? Is there an opportunity for multiple clearances?

6. Are confessions or incriminating statements available as evidence? If so, where and when were the statements made?
    Were they recorded on audio or video? If so, by whom?
    Can they be seriously attacked as made involuntarily?
    Are there omissions, false statements, or inaccuracies in the statements?
    Are there any violations of the *Miranda, Massiah,* or *Bruton* rules?
    Were departmental or state standards for taking confessions followed?

THE CRIMINAL COURT PROCESS

In this text, we study the rules of evidence as they apply in formal judicial proceedings, principally jury trials. Included here is a short discussion of the criminal court process. In misdemeanor cases, the process typically begins with the filing of

criminal complaint
The formal charge made by the prosecution against a defendant, which begins criminal proceedings.

initial appearance The first appearance by an accused before a judge or magistrate; a plea is entered and bail is set at this hearing.

preliminary hearing
Full adversarial hearing with a lawyer present.

criminal indictment
The formal charge issued by a grand jury, listing crimes believed to have been committed by the named defendant.

grand jury A jury that hears evidence presented by the prosecution and determines whether to charge persons with crimes; used in federal and many state criminal proceedings.

arraignment The formal proceeding following the indictment or information, where a plea is entered and the case is bound over for trial.

a **criminal complaint** with a magistrate or other judicial official. The complaint can come before or after the defendant is placed under arrest. The magistrate determines only whether probable cause exists to believe that a crime has been committed and that the named defendant committed the crime.

Following the issuance of the complaint, a warrant may be issued for the defendant's arrest if he or she is not already in custody. The **initial appearance** before the magistrate is then promptly held. At this appearance, the charges are read to the defendant, a plea is entered, and bail is set.

If a felony is charged, in states that do not use the indictment system the next step is the **preliminary hearing**. This is a full adversarial hearing where lawyers are present, evidence is heard, and a judge makes the determination whether probable cause exists to believe the defendant committed the crime charged. Although this hearing is more detailed than the initial appearance, it is not a full trial. At this juncture, however, a judge may dismiss the charges if the prosecution's case is weak. If sufficient evidence is introduced to show probable cause, the defendant is bound over for trial.

Federal and many state courts use the indictment system for felonies instead of public prosecutors issuing criminal complaints. In some states, such as Texas, the prosecutor issues a criminal complaint and then proceeds through the indictment process. A **criminal indictment** is a list of criminal charges issued by a **grand jury**, which has heard evidence presented by a U.S. Attorney or state prosecuting attorney. The grand jury proceedings are held in secret, are not adversarial, and include only evidence presented by the prosecution.

In states that do not use the grand jury system, a criminal case can begin with the filing of an *information*, which is a statement by the prosecution detailing the basis on which it is believed the defendant committed a crime.

After an indictment or information has been issued, the defendant is *arraigned*. At the **arraignment**, the defendant enters a plea and the case is bound over to the appropriate criminal court for trial.

During the period between arraignment or preliminary hearing and full trial, the defendant may reevaluate the evidence and either change a simple not guilty plea or begin plea bargaining. Because of the prevalence of such practices, the following section discusses the plea and plea-bargaining process in greater detail.

PLEAS A DEFENDANT MAY ENTER TO A CRIMINAL CHARGE

After a defendant has been charged with a criminal offense, the defendant and the attorney must evaluate the evidence available to the state to support its criminal charge. Their evaluation of the evidence could determine what defenses they will or will not use and what plea they will enter. The following pleas are available to defendants:

- *Not guilty plea.*
- *Guilty plea:* This may be a regular guilty plea or an Alford guilty plea in states that permit the Alford plea.
- *An insanity plea (or defense):* The usual insanity plea is not guilty by reason of mental disease or defect. This plea may be joined with a plea of not guilty. If it is not joined with a not guilty plea, the defendant then admits committing the offense but pleads a lack of mental capacity.

A jury or a judge may, if the evidence permits, find a defendant guilty but mentally ill under the statutes of thirteen states.[2] Such a person is not legally insane but at the time of the offense had serious mental or emotional problems. Under this verdict, prison authorities must provide necessary psychiatric or psychological treatment to restore the offender's mental and emotional health in an appropriate treatment setting.

- *No contest (nolo contendere) plea:* This plea is permitted if the statutes of a state allow it, subject to the approval of the court. A defendant who uses this plea seeks to avoid admitting guilt in the hope of successfully denying the truth of the charges in a subsequent civil lawsuit.
- *Standing mute or refusing to enter a plea:* This plea ordinarily causes the court to direct that a plea of not guilty be entered on behalf of the defendant.

PROCEDURES & PROCESSES

Purposes of Rules of Evidence

- ***Rules of evidence that are designed to be of assistance to the judge or jury in the search for the truth***
  Examples are rules that exclude and keep evidence out of court:
  i. Rules requiring that evidence be relevant, reliable, and competent
  ii. The opinion evidence rule
  iii. The hearsay rules

  These rules of evidence guard against unreliable evidence that could be prejudicial, misleading, inaccurate, or distracting.

- ***Rules of evidence that expedite trials and move them along without unnecessary delays***
  i. Rules concerning *judicial notice* that relieve parties to a trial of the burden of proving uncontested facts that are of common knowledge to the community or are available in a reliable text or other publication
  ii. Rules concerning presumptions and inferences that give directions to judges and juries and also determine in criminal and civil trials which of the parties has the burden of proof and the burden of coming forward with evidence

- ***Rules of evidence that are not designed to be of assistance in the search for the truth but have other purposes; they often actually hinder the search for the truth***
  i. Testimonial privilege rules that have been created to protect relationships and interests, such as husband-wife, attorney-client, and physician-patient. These relationships have been determined to be of sufficient importance to justify sacrificing what might be reliable evidence from being used in criminal and civil trials.
  ii. The rule of the exclusion of evidence (the *exclusionary rule*) that is used to discourage and deter law enforcement officers from improper or illegal conduct or procedure. This form of "policing the police" sometimes prevents reliable evidence from being used in criminal trials.

The Not Guilty Plea

All defendants in criminal cases are presumed innocent until proven guilty through the use of evidence and witnesses presented during a trial. The burden of proof is always on the state or government to prove the elements of the crime charged.

The level of proof required in criminal cases is proof beyond a reasonable doubt. This is the highest level of proof the law requires in any kind of case. It means that the evidence presented during the trial must convince the fact finder (jury or judge) of the defendant's guilt to a moral certitude. It does not mean that the evidence must show that the defendant is guilty beyond *any* doubt, nor does it require evidence of absolute certainty of the defendant's guilt. The burden on the state is to prove the defendant guilty beyond any *reasonable* doubt.

Because of the constitutional presumption of innocence, the U.S. system of justice is an accusatorial system. The accuser must bear the entire burden of proving the charge by the use of competent evidence. The defendant does not have to do anything. The burden is on the state to come forward with sufficient evidence to carry the burden of proof beyond reasonable doubt.

The defendant can remain silent and inactive. Or the defendant can appear as a witness on his or her own behalf and may present evidence showing or tending to show his or her innocence. The defense may also actively attack or seek to hinder and minimize the state's evidence and case by the use of motions before, during, or after the trial.

The defendant can deny performing the acts charged or assert an affirmative defense. In an affirmative defense, a defendant in effect admits to performing the acts charged but claims that he or she had a lawful excuse for doing so and thus is not guilty of the crime charged. To assert an affirmative defense, the defendant must come forward with evidence showing a basis for it, and in some states must prove the affirmative defense by a preponderance of evidence.

An example of an affirmative defense is the claim of entrapment. Many states require that a defendant using an entrapment defense admit that he or she committed the criminal act or acts. The defense is that law enforcement officers used excessive or improper inducements that caused the defendant to violate the law. Other affirmative defenses are outrageous government conduct, frame-up, and coercion or duress ("I was forced to do it"). [For an explanation of affirmative defenses, see Chapter 7 of T. Gardner and T. Anderson, *Criminal Law: Principles and Cases*, 12th ed. (Cengage Learning, 2015).]

The Guilty Plea

In the United States, the great majority of the people charged with felonies plead guilty. The 2012 United States Attorney Annual Statistics Report (U.S. DOJ) states that in the federal courts in 2012, criminal cases against 87,709 defendants were completed. 80,963, or 93 percent, resulted in convictions. 78,647 of those convictions were by guilty plea. Only 3 percent of federal criminal cases in 2012 went to trial. Prosecutions in state criminal cases reach similar results.

The U.S. Supreme Court stated in *Boykin v. Alabama*[3] that "[a] plea of guilty is more than a confession which admits that the accused did various acts; it is itself a conviction; nothing remains but to give judgment and determine punishment."

Most guilty pleas are entered because defendants realize that the evidence that the state or government has against them will result in a conviction. Defendants therefore enter the guilty plea because of the standard practice of rewarding a defendant who acknowledges guilt in open court with a lighter sentence.[4]

The U.S. Supreme Court has held that the foundations of a valid guilty plea are the defendant's voluntary admission in open court that he committed the acts charged and the defendant's knowing consent to the judgment of guilt without a trial. Because the defendant stands before the court as a witness against himself in entering a guilty plea, the admission of guilt cannot be compelled but must be a voluntary expression of his own choice. And because a defendant's consent to judgment without trial constitutes a waiver of the constitutional rights attending a trial, his consent must be made with knowledge of the waiver of those rights.[5]

The defendant who offers a guilty plea must admit that he committed the crime charged. In the 2005 case of *Bradshaw v. Stumpf*,[6] the U.S. Supreme Court held that a guilty plea in an aggravated murder case was valid even with the defendant's "steadfast assertion" that he had not shot the victim. The Court stated that because under Ohio statutes one who aids and abets a murder can be charged the same as the person who actually does the killing, the defendant's admission that he did aid and abet satisfied the requirement that he admit a specific intent to cause death.

It must be shown that a defendant entered a guilty plea voluntarily and intelligently.[7] The trial judge must be convinced by the evidence presented that the defendant did in fact commit the criminal act of which she is charged. There is no constitutional right to plead guilty, but a state may create a statutory right to do so.[8] In *Boykin v. Alabama*,[9] the Court held that the following rights are waived by a guilty plea:

> Several federal constitutional rights are involved in a waiver that takes place when a plea of guilty is entered in a state criminal trial. First, is the privilege against compulsory self-incrimination guaranteed by the Fifth Amendment and applicable to the States by reason of the Fourteenth ....
> Second, is the right to trial by jury ....
> Third, is the right to confront one's accusers ....
> We cannot presume a waiver of these three important federal rights from a silent record.

The Federal Rules of Criminal Procedure, and the criminal procedure rules of every state, require the trial judge to inform the defendant entering a plea of guilty of various rights the defendant has and consequences of such a plea. Rule 11 of the Federal Rules of Criminal Procedure (F.R.Crim.P.) includes a list of fourteen specific topics the trial judge must address, including the right to plead not guilty, to have an attorney appointed, to a jury trial, and information about the possible sentence, such as a mandatory minimum that will be imposed.

Rule 11 specifically states that the trial judge "must address the defendant personally in open court" to provide the information mandated by Rule 11. This procedure presents problems when a large group of defendants enter pleas at the same time. For example, the federal court in Tucson, Arizona uses a procedure called "Operation Streamline" to deal with the large numbers of defendants brought before the court on illegal entry charges. In the 2011 case of *United States v. Escamilla-Rojas*,[10] the court held that taking pleas *en masse* in illegal entry cases can violate Rule 11. In that case, about 67 persons charged with illegal entry were brought before a federal magistrate. The magistrate informed the group *en masse* of each defendant's individual rights, and later questioned each defendant personally before accepting a guilty plea. The appeals court held that a two-hour gap between the time when the defendant was informed of her rights and the personal questioning by the judge violated Rule 11.[11]

The *Alford* Guilty Plea In the case of *North Carolina v. Alford*,[12] the U.S. Supreme Court held that a defendant "may voluntarily, knowingly, and understandingly consent to the imposition of a prison sentence even if he is unwilling or unable to admit his participation in the acts constituting the crime." The **Alford guilty plea** permits a defendant to enter a guilty plea while at the same time asserting his innocence. The Alford plea is not mandatory for states, but most states have adopted it. State judges, however, are generally not obligated to accept an Alford plea. Most judges do accept it because the sentence given is the same as the sentence given for a regular guilty plea under the state sentencing guidelines.

Most state courts hold that an Alford plea is the "functional equivalent" of a regular plea of guilty.[13] A defendant who enters a guilty plea, whether it is an Alford plea or a regular guilty plea, has lost almost all rights to appeal. Most courts hold that the only issues applicable are the voluntary and intelligent nature of the plea and the jurisdiction of the court.

There may be different consequences of a regular guilty plea and an Alford plea. In the 2014 case of *United States v. Williams*[14] the defendant was convicted of a federal crime and sentenced to 3 years of supervised release; one condition of the release was that he did not commit another state or federal crime during the release period. If he did, the release would be revoked and he would serve a prison sentence. Williams entered an Alford plea to a state assault charge during his release period. A federal judge held that was a violation of the release condition and sentenced Williams to 18 months in prison. On appeal, the court reversed that decision, holding that an Alford plea under Washington state law was not treated as final evidence of guilt for other purposes. As a result, the Alford plea by itself did not prove Williams "committed" a crime during the release period. The court noted that in other states, such as California, where Alford pleas are regarded as final proof of guilt of a felony for all purposes, the result would be different.

The No Contest or Nolo Contendere Plea Most (if not all) states also have statutes permitting the **no contest** or **nolo contendere plea**. In most states and in the federal court system, the plea may be made only with the consent of the trial judge.[15] Some states limit the plea to misdemeanors and ordinance violations. For purposes of punishment the plea has the same effect as a regular guilty plea. In some states, a nolo plea cannot be used as an admission of facts in subsequent civil or criminal proceedings.

The no contest plea has been called a troublesome legal creature. The advisory committee notes to the federal criminal procedure rules noted that the "defendant who asserts his innocence while pleading guilty or nolo contendere is often difficult to deal with in a correctional setting."[16] An example of this problem is *Betts v. State*,[17] where a defendant, after making a no contest plea to sexual assault, refused to discuss his actions in a court-ordered counselling program made a part of his probation. The defendant was held to have violated his probation, and sentenced to prison. The court said the nature of the plea did not limit the duty of the defendant to abide by the terms of his probation.

The Conditional Guilty Plea Defendants do not have a constitutional right to plead guilty and may be forced to go to trial. But because forcing a defendant to stand trial

---

Alford guilty plea
A guilty plea that permits the accused to maintain innocence.

no contest or **nolo contendere plea**
A plea in which the accused neither contests nor admits the charges against him; treated as a guilty plea.

PROCEDURES & PROCESSES

Withdrawal of Guilty Pleas

A guilty plea can be withdrawn "for any reason or no reason" before it has been accepted by the trial judge. *See United States v. Mendez-Santana*,[18] construing Fed. R. Crim. P. § 11 (d) (1). After acceptance of a plea by the trial judge, withdrawal of a guilty plea is not automatic. There is often a substantial time gap between when a guilty plea is accepted by the trial judge and when the sentence is imposed. To what extent, if at all, may a defendant who has entered a guilty plea that was accepted by the judge withdraw that plea, and substitute a plea of not guilty?

- **Before sentencing**: In federal prosecutions, Fed. R. Crim. P. § 11 (d) (2) (B) permits a defendant to withdraw a guilty plea for "fair and just" reasons. While federal courts generally are inclined to permit a withdrawal for reasons such as new evidence becoming available after the plea, or changes in the law, there is no absolute right to have a guilty plea withdrawn. *United States v. Andolini*, 705 F.3d 335 (8th Cir. 2013). Most states have similar procedures, and trial judges are counseled to grant a motion to withdraw if it appears the plea was entered by mistake, or any reasonable grounds exist for going to a jury trial. *Hubbard v. Com.*, 725 S.E.2d 163 (Va. App. 2012). A very few states make it an "absolute right" to withdraw a guilty plea before sentencing; *Franks v. State*, 748 S.E.2d 291 (Ga. App. 2013), applying Ga. Code Ann. § 17-7-93 (b).

- **After sentencing**: In federal prosecutions, there is no jurisdiction in the trial court to grant a motion to withdraw a guilty plea after sentence has been imposed. A guilty plea after sentencing can only be set aside in an appeal to a Court of Appeals. Fed. R. Crim. P. § 11 (e). Most states permit withdrawal of a guilty plea after sentencing only if there is compelling evidence of "manifest injustice" in making or accepting the plea. An example of "manifest injustice" is *State v. Dimmit*, 665 N.W.2d 692 (N.D. 2003), where the prosecution agreed during plea bargaining to recommend a 5-year sentence to the trial judge, but instead recommended a 10-year sentence, which the trial judge imposed.

rarely serves a useful purpose, all states have statutes and case law setting the procedure for accepting guilty pleas. Nor does a criminal defendant "have an absolute right under the Constitution to have his guilty plea accepted by the court."[19] Trial judges have the discretion under the laws of all states to refuse to accept a plea of guilty.

Defendants who enter a guilty plea in any form to a criminal charge lose most of their right to appeal. The U.S. Supreme Court ruled in 1973 that "[w]hen a criminal defendant has solemnly admitted in open court that he is in fact guilty of the offense with which he is charged, he may not thereafter raise independent claims relating to the deprivation of constitutional rights that occurred prior to the entry of the guilty plea."[20]

To preserve the right to appeal on any issue before a trial court, defense lawyers sometimes use the conditional guilty plea. They might do this, for example, after the defense has failed in a motion to suppress evidence, after an attack on the validity of a search warrant, or following a defense attack on the validity of an arrest. The defendant can enter a guilty plea conditioned upon the defendant's right to appeal the trial judge's ruling.

The Insanity Plea

insanity plea A plea to a criminal charge of not guilty because of mental disease or defect.

The plea of not guilty because of mental disease or defect (the **insanity plea**) is found in the criminal codes of most states. At least four states (Idaho, Kansas, Utah, and Montana) have abolished the insanity defense. If a defendant enters an insanity plea in a minor criminal matter, the state may agree and join the defendant in requesting the court to find the defendant legally insane. The defendant probably will then be held for mental observation and treatment for a much longer period than would have been the case had he or she been convicted of the crime charged.

Therefore, the insanity plea is used by defendants primarily in murder cases, for which sentences are severe. In using the insanity defense, most defendants also enter a not guilty plea. The trial is then bifurcated, with the first part of the trial determining guilt or innocence of the charge and the second part determining whether the defendant was legally insane when the criminal act was committed.

Because there is a legal inference that all people are sane and normal, most states place the burden on a defendant using the insanity plea to come forward with evidence showing that he or she was so mentally diseased or defective that he or she was unable to formulate the mental intent to commit the crime charged.

In 1981 John Hinckley, Jr., was charged with attempting to kill President Ronald Reagan. In a wild shooting spree in Washington, D.C., Hinckley seriously wounded the president and three others. At the time of the Hinckley trial, federal courts required the government to carry the burden of proving that the defendant was sane and normal. The government could not produce evidence showing that Hinckley was sane and normal and therefore, under the rule used then, Hinckley was found not guilty because of insanity.

In 1984 Congress passed legislation providing that the federal courts rejoin most of the state courts in requiring defendants using the insanity plea to prove by clear and convincing evidence that the defendant was insane at the time of the crime.

THE GUILTY PLEA SYSTEM, PLEA BARGAINING, AND VICTIM'S RIGHTS LAWS

plea bargaining Agreement to enter a guilty plea in return for a reduction in the charge or sentence. For example, first-offense shoplifters are often given the opportunity to plea to disorderly conduct in a municipal court instead of going to trial for a theft charge. First-offense drunk drivers are often permitted to enter a guilty plea in return for the dropping of one of the three or four criminal charges that they face.

U.S. criminal courts and prosecutors in metropolitan areas are extremely busy, particularly in the hot summer months. Police officers, sheriffs, and other law enforcement personnel work long hours bringing in new cases and spend a lot of time waiting in offices and courtrooms for those cases to advance. Prosecutors and defense lawyers struggle to manage their case loads and grasp the facts of their cases, with prosecutors depending heavily on briefings from the police and defense lawyers reading criminal complaints and seeking information from their clients.

The criminal court system is simply not set up to deal with this high volume of cases. There are not enough courts and staff personnel to provide either jury or bench (judge) trials for all criminal defendants. While using minimum sentences for non-violent offenders helps, there still remain far too many cases awaiting trial. Overcrowded jails and prisons in the United States exacerbate the problem, as do tight fiscal budgets. These fiscal problems have meant that as prosecutors and public defenders retire or leave for other employment, they cannot be replaced. These conditions make the criminal court system a "guilty plea" system, with **plea bargaining** at the center of the system. That bargaining occurs through either sentencing bargains or plea bargains.

Plea bargaining involves substituting a guilty plea to one offense for a trial on multiple offenses. Prosecutors often charge defendants with multiple offenses, such as charging a person accused of drunk driving with several related offenses, or a burglar with criminal trespass or criminal damage to property. As part of the plea bargain, the lesser or "add-on" offenses are dropped in exchange for a guilty plea to the principal criminal charge.

In all guilty plea hearings entered before a court, the defendant is entitled to an attorney unless that right has been waived. The trial judge questions the defendant to establish for the record that the defendant knowingly and voluntarily is pleading guilty to the criminal charge. The state must then introduce sufficient evidence for the record to show beyond a reasonable doubt the defendant committed the crime charged for which the guilty plea is entered.

The cooperation of witnesses and victims has always been very important in this process, and law officers, prosecutors, and courts have historically used best efforts to be helpful and courteous to victims. In addition, since the 1990s, every state has enacted crime victim rights laws, which give victims rights during the court process and must be respected by courts and prosecutors. These laws vary from state to state, but generally include the requirement that crime victims be informed of times, dates, and details for all court proceedings in their case, and also of the right to make a "victim impact statement" during sentencing. In many states crime victims may voice disagreement with a plea bargain agreement, which can cause a trial court judge to reject the plea agreement. This has long been the practice for experienced prosecutors in the criminal court system.

As can be seen from the high number of guilty pleas entered in criminal cases in the United States, plea bargains and sentence bargains have been a staple of criminal court cases for a very long time. It was stated in the 1967 President's Commission on Law Enforcement and Administration of Justice that "[w]hen a decision is made to prosecute, it is estimated that in many courts as many as 90 percent of all convictions are obtained by guilty pleas."[21] In appraising the amount and quality of the evidence against a client, the American defense lawyer often turns to plea bargaining if the government has a strong case. The defense lawyer usually informs the client that there is a strong likelihood of conviction and advises "copping a plea." Not all guilty pleas are plea bargained, however. Many guilty pleas are entered every day in U.S. courts without any assurance from a prosecutor concerning the penalty. Plea bargaining, or sentence bargaining, implies a situation in which a defendant receives (or is assured of) a consideration in return for a guilty plea. The following circumstances could cause a defendant to plead guilty:

- The defendant receives an agreed-upon sentence or penalty instead of running the risk of a more severe sentence.
- An agreement is reached in a case having multiple charges to drop one or more of the charges, which in most situations are then "read into the record" in court for sentencing consideration.[22]
- The defendant is permitted to plead guilty to a lesser charge.
- The court receives a recommendation that the defendant receive probation or a suspended sentence.
- The prosecutor agrees to drop charges against another person.
- Charges are reduced or dropped when the defendant agrees to testify as a state's witness (such as a burglar turning state's evidence against a "fence").
- The defendant receives reduced charges, probation, or a suspended sentence when he agrees to compensate the victim for damages or injuries that occurred.

- The defendant receives probation or a suspended sentence when she agrees to undergo psychiatric, drug, or alcohol treatment when the criminal conduct was caused by any of these conditions. (In some of these situations, the defendant agrees to commit herself to an institution for such treatment.)

Prosecutors list the following reasons why plea bargaining, negotiated pleas, and sentence pleading have become standard practice in most American communities:

- It clears the court calendar of cases by providing a rapid trial and punishment.
- Defendants participate and admit their guilt to the charges to which they plead guilty.
- The practice eliminates many appeals.
- It provides a certainty of adjudication.
- A guilty plea could be the first step toward genuine rehabilitation.

 ## IS THE INSANITY DEFENSE AN EFFECTIVE DEFENSE?

There has long been controversy about the insanity defense. Some of that controversy may be the result of the public's perception that significant numbers of criminal defendants who use the defense are found not guilty by reason of insanity (NGRI) and are released to prey on the public. However, virtually all the empirical studies done on this subject show that is not the case. Here are some results of these studies:

- The defense is used in only about 1 percent of the felony cases prosecuted and has a success rate of just over 20 percent. That means that for every 1,000 felony defendants, only 2 or 3 are found NGRI.[a]
- The defense is risky. Unsuccessful defendants who assert the defense but are found guilty go to prison for a period 22 percent longer than similar defendants charged with the same crime.[b]
- Among those defendants who are successful in raising the defense, only 1 percent are released after being found NGRI; 4 percent are placed on conditional release and 90 percent are hospitalized for a substantial period.[c]
- For defendants found NGRI in violent crimes other than murder, the period of confinement in a mental hospital or similar institution is twice as long as the confinement of a defendant convicted of a similar crime. For nonviolent crimes, the confinement period is ten times the sentence given defendants convicted of similar crimes.[d]

These studies suggest that the defense of insanity is really the last resort for most defendants; even if the defense is successful, it does not often result in the release of the defendant. Nonetheless, dissatisfaction with the defense continues, and some states—including Idaho, Montana, Kansas, and Utah—have abolished the defense.[e]

[a]Lisa A. Callahan et al., The Volume and Characteristics of Insanity Defense: An Eight-State Study, 19 *Bull. Am. Acad. Psychiatry & L.* 331 (1991).
[b]Joseph H. Rodriguez et al., *The Insanity Defense Under Siege: Legislative Assaults and Legal Rejoinders*, 14 Rutgers L. J. 397 (1983). The authors of this article suggest that the reason for longer sentences for the unsuccessful defendant asserting the insanity defense is the defense's obstacle to plea bargains.
[c]H. Steadman et al., *Before and After Hinckley; Evaluating Insanity Defense Reform* (Guilford Press, 1993), p. 58.
[d]Id.
[e]See T. Gardner and T. Anderson, *Criminal Law: Principles and Cases*, 12th ed. (Cengage Learning 2015), chap. 5, p. 121.

The President's Commission commented as follows in the 1967 report entitled "The Challenge of Crime in a Free Society":

> Many overburdened courts have come to rely upon these informal procedures to deal with overpowering caseloads, and some cases that are dropped might have been prosecuted had sufficient resources been available. But it would be an oversimplification to tie the use of early disposition solely to the problem of volume, for some courts appear to be able to deal with their workloads without recourse to such procedures....

> The main danger in the present system of nontrial dispositions is that it is so informal and invisible that it gives rise to fears that it does not operate fairly or that it does not accurately identify those who should be prosecuted and what disposition should be made in their cases. Often important decisions are made without adequate information, without sound policy guidance or rules, and without basic procedural protections for the defendant, such as counsel or judicial consideration of the issues. Because these dispositions are reached at an early stage, often little factual material is available about the offense, the offender, and the treatment alternatives.

> No record reveals the participants, their positions, or the reason for or facts underlying the disposition. When the disposition involves the dismissal of filed charges or the entry of a guilty plea, the case is likely to reach court, but only the end product is visible and that view often is misleading. There are disturbing opportunities for coercion and overreaching, as well as for undue leniency. The informality and flexibility of the procedures are sources of both potential usefulness and abuse.

PROCEDURES & PROCESSES

Fast-Track Trials and Fast-Track Plea Bargains

For years, many states and the federal government have had policies of putting criminal trials that have high public concern on a "fast track." Defendants in these cases must then prepare for a speedy trial or have the choice of "fast-tracking" plea bargaining. In federal prosecutions, fast-track programs were begun in the mid-1990s in judicial districts in states along the U.S.-Mexico border. These districts had a high number of illegal entry prosecutions; the fast-track program was designed to speed cases along by offering reduced sentences below the federal sentencing guidelines. As of December, 2009, there were twenty-five approved fast-track programs in seventeen judicial districts. (See *United States v. Lopez*, 650 F.3d 952 (3rd Cir. 2011).)

The ability of defendants to receive reduced sentences in federal districts that have fast-track programs has caused problems for judges sentencing defendants in other districts, where fast track plea bargains are not available. For example, in *United States v. Lopez-Macias*, 661 F.3d 485 (10th Cir. 2011), the court held that a trial judge sentencing a defendant in an illegal entry case should consider the disparity of sentences given in fast-track districts when determining the proper sentence. Other federal courts have held otherwise, *e.g.*, *United States v. Gonzalez-Zotelo*, 556 F.3d 736 (9th Cir. 2009). Because of this uncertainty, in March 2012 the United States Justice Department announced that in the future the fast-track program will be available in all federal districts in felony re-entry prosecutions.

Debates about plea bargaining have been going on for years. The practice was denounced as early as 1875.[23] Over the years, plea negotiation has continued, however. Some states have enacted statutes regulating the practice.

AN OFFER TO PLEAD GUILTY CANNOT BE USED AS EVIDENCE IF THE OFFER IS LATER WITHDRAWN

Both public policy and the judicial system encourage voluntary, intelligent guilty pleas. By admitting guilt in open court, the defendant acknowledges the wrongful conduct, which is the first step in rehabilitation. Guilty pleas also help to keep court calendars current.

To encourage guilty pleas, the federal government and many states have statutes such as Rule 410 of the Federal Rules of Evidence and Rule 11(6) of the Federal Rules of Criminal Procedure, which forbid the use of any of the following as evidence:

> evidence of a plea of guilty, later withdrawn, or a plea of nolo contendere, or of an offer to plead guilty or nolo contendere to the crime charged or any other crime, or of statements made in connection with any of the foregoing pleas or offers.

States with similar statutes also prohibit evidence of pleas offered in plea negotiations, including incriminating statements made in the offer, as the following cases illustrate:

- After a sex crime had occurred, Muniz (the defendant) offered to pay some of the victim's medical expenses. The State of California then charged Muniz

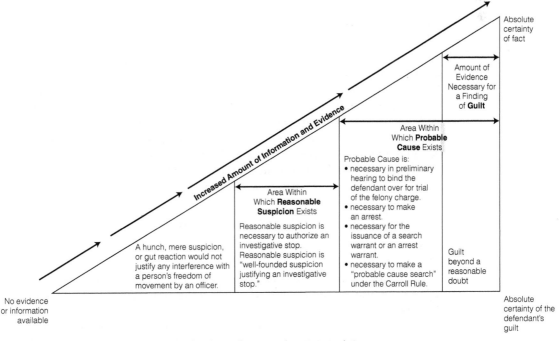

Quantums (Amounts) of Proof and Standards of Proof Required in Criminal Cases

PROCEDURES & PROCESSES

Use of Evidence at a Bail Hearing

The purpose of bail is to assure the defendant's appearance at trial. Bail hearings can become hotly contested—angry confrontations with defense lawyers arguing that high bail punishes a defendant and that defendants can be punished only after trial and conviction.

Another argument of defense lawyers is that high bail can be used as preventive detention, to unlawfully detain a defendant based on only the possibility that the defendant may be a threat to others. In most states, preventive detention in this sense is not regarded as a legitimate basis for setting bail.

In asking for high bail, prosecutors generally stress the seriousness of the crime, the viciousness of the criminal act, and the strength of the evidence against the defendant. Because the likelihood of flight by a defendant goes up with the probability of a long prison term, very high bail is often set in murder and other violent crime cases.

Although the past criminal record of the defendant is not admissible evidence during a trial, it is admissible evidence during both bail hearings and sentencing hearings. The prosecution must provide defense lawyers with the defendant's known criminal record (or lack of criminal record) prior to the bail hearing.

In bail hearings, both sides may present evidence of a defendant's roots in the community, such as whether the defendant has a family, close relatives, a good job, and a home, as well as his or her age and marital status.

The Eighth Amendment of the U.S. Constitution states that "Excessive bail shall not be required ...." However, as the U.S. Supreme Court noted in *United States v. Salerno*, 481 U.S. 739, 752 (1987), the Eighth Amendment "says nothing about whether bail shall be available at all." In *Salerno* the Court upheld the constitutionality of the Bail Reform Act, 18 U.S.C. § 3141, which permits a judge to order pretrial detention of persons charged with serious crimes who may be dangerous if released on bail. Detention orders are subject to "expedited appellate review" under the Act. In other situations either the defendant or the prosecutor could immediately appeal a bail ruling by a lower court and present arguments to a higher court seeking a different bail ruling.

Historically, about 60 percent of persons charged with felony crimes are released on bail. Of those released, about half are released on signature bonds, frequently with the requirement that the person report to authorities on a daily or weekly basis. The other half are released on bail bonds, either bonds from commercial bail bondsmen or full cash or property bonds. Bench warrants end up being issued in about one-fourth of the cases of persons released on bail because of their failure to appear in court for their trials.

Source: Bureau of Justice Statistics Report NCJ 14994, November 2007.

with the sex crime. Because Muniz's statements were not part of an offer to plead guilty, his statements were held to be admissible as an admission against interest.[24]

- When a plea-bargain agreement was not carried out due to a failure on both sides, the state sought to use incriminating statements the defendant had made during the negotiations. The Supreme Court of Louisiana held that the statements could not be used as evidence against the defendant on the basis of "equitable immunity."[25]

- During the sentencing hearing where the state was seeking the death penalty, the state sought to use as evidence the fact that the defendant offered to plea bargain to avoid the death penalty. It was held that such evidence was inadmissible. The defendant was nevertheless sentenced to death for murder and robbery by force.[26]

- Before going to trial, a drug-trafficking defendant wrote a letter to the prosecutor offering to plead guilty in return for sentencing concessions. The letter was held to be inadmissible against the defendant at trial.[27]

THE TRIAL

discovery Formal procedures used by prosecution and defense attorneys to gather documents, witnesses, and other evidence.

The vast majority of criminal charges result in guilty pleas after plea bargaining. Only about 8 percent of criminal cases in the United States actually go to trial. Of those, about 20 percent are tried before a judge, and 80 percent are tried before a jury.

Prior to the trial, the parties undertake **discovery**. In the discovery process in most states, both the prosecution and the defense gather evidence through formal questions put to the other side, depositions of witnesses, and examination of documents and records.

As a result of discovery, the parties can file various *motions*, such as to compel discovery, to dismiss for lack of jurisdiction or evidence, or to exclude evidence obtained in violation of a defendant's rights, such as violations of the defendant's Fourth Amendment rights. At this time or at any other time during the trial, the defendant may agree to enter a guilty plea ending the trial. The guilty plea may be based on a sentence or plea agreement, which would be subject to the approval of the trial judge.

If the trial goes forward, jurors are summoned and selected, and subpoenas are issued to compel witnesses to attend and testify at the trial. Jurors are selected from the community in which the court sits (the *venue*) from lists maintained by the court, such as registered voters. The jury may consist of six to twelve people, depending on the seriousness of the crime charged and state rules.[28]

prima facie case A civil or criminal case that is so strong that the opponent must respond with rebutting evidence to avoid losing the case.

The prosecution presents evidence first and must establish a **prima facie case**; that is, the evidence must be sufficient to permit a reasonable jury to believe the defendant was guilty beyond a reasonable doubt. A defendant may move for a judgment of acquittal after the close of the prosecution's case. If the judge concludes that the evidence is insufficient to support a reasonable jury verdict of guilty beyond a reasonable doubt, the case will be dismissed without going to the jury.

affirmative defense A defense that admits the defendant committed the crime charged but asserts that the defendant should not be convicted.

If the case is not dismissed, the defendant may present evidence either to cast doubt on the prosecution's case or to prove an **affirmative defense**. Affirmative defenses include insanity, immunity, entrapment, and double jeopardy. The defendant carries the burden of proving any affirmative defense raised, and the prosecution may offer *rebuttal* evidence to such defense and other new matters brought out in the defendant's case.

After all evidence is in and both sides have delivered closing arguments to the jury, the trial judge issues *jury instructions*. These instructions are the judge's explanation of the relevant law that governs the case. Following the trial judge's instructions, the jury begins its deliberations. Jury members weigh the evidence presented to them during the trial and vote on the issue of guilt or innocence of the defendant.

PROCEDURES & PROCESSES

Use of Evidence in the Stages of the Criminal Process

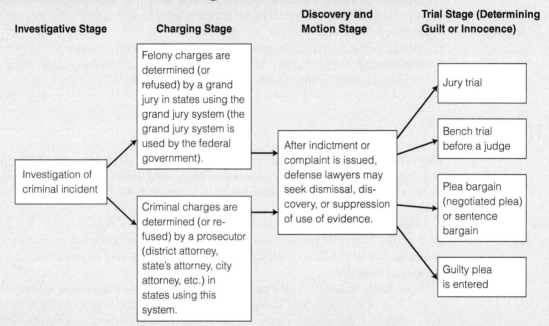

Investigative Stage	Charging Stage	Discovery and Motion Stage	Trial Stage (Determining Guilt or Innocence)
Investigation of criminal incident	Felony charges are determined (or refused) by a grand jury in states using the grand jury system (the grand jury system is used by the federal government).	After indictment or complaint is issued, defense lawyers may seek dismissal, discovery, or suppression of use of evidence.	Jury trial
			Bench trial before a judge
	Criminal charges are determined (or refused) by a prosecutor (district attorney, state's attorney, city attorney, etc.) in states using this system.		Plea bargain (negotiated plea) or sentence bargain
			Guilty plea is entered

If it is known (or suspected) that a crime or offense has been committed, law enforcement officers or private persons and investigators seek evidence of the offense. If competent evidence exists amounting to probable cause to believe that

- a crime (or offense) has been committed, and
- a specific person (or persons) committed the offense

then the matter can be taken to a prosecutor.

If it is determined that probable cause exists to prove

- corpus delicti (a crime has been committed), and
- the suspect was a party to the crime[a]

then a criminal charge or indictment can be issued.

The defense lawyer seeks to discover and obtain evidence helpful to his client. He may also make some or all of the following motions[b] before the court:

- Motion to dismiss because of insufficient evidence, etc.
- Motion to dismiss because of improper procedure, constitutionality of statute, etc.
- Motion to suppress evidence (statements, physical evidence, identification evidence, or procedure, etc.)
- Motion for discovery of evidence

The defense's decision on whether to try the case before a jury or a judge is generally based on the evaluation of the case and the evidence. Because weaker cases are filtered out of the system or charged as lesser offenses, most cases that reach the trial stage are strong governmental cases. In these cases, the defense may attempt to plea bargain or may enter a guilty plea. If the state has a weakness in its case at this stage, the state may attempt to plea bargain.

[a]A party to a crime may be (1) the person (or persons) who actually committed the crime; (2) a conspirator who hired, procured, planned, or counseled the crime; or (3) a person (or persons) who aided and abetted in the commission of the crime. Different evidence is required to carry the burden of proving each of the different categories of parties to a crime.
[b]A *motion* means an application for an order from that judge or other court.

If the jury reaches a verdict of not guilty, the case is over and the defendant is discharged from custody. If the verdict is guilty, the defendant may file post-trial motions in the trial court. These motions include motions for *judgment notwithstanding the verdict* (sometimes called **judgment NOV**) and motions for a new trial. Motions for judgment NOV are rarely granted because the trial judge has usually already heard motions for a *directed verdict* after the close of the prosecution and defense cases. Motions for a new trial meet with better success because the trial judge may have a better opportunity following the trial to consider errors that occurred during the trial.

If the defendant's motions are overruled, the defendant may appeal the criminal conviction and/or the sentence imposed upon the defendant. In state cases, the defendant's initial appeals go through the state appellate process, which frequently includes an intermediate court called a *court of appeals* and a final court called a *state supreme court.*

The state appellate court does not conduct a new trial. Rather, it looks at the evidence to see whether it supports the conviction and determines whether the judge made any **reversible errors**—such as permitting the use of damaging, inadmissible evidence.

The state appellate court also rules on other claims the defendant may make, such as a constitutional violation. Appellate courts give deference to decisions made by the trial court on most questions, such as a decision to admit evidence over an objection by a defendant. Such decisions are reversible only if they constitute an "abuse of discretion." Facts found by the jury will rarely be the basis for reversal

judgment NOV A post-trial judgment made by a judge changing or reversing the jury decision; literally, *non obstante verdicto* ("notwithstanding the verdict").

reversible error Errors that occur at a trial that might have had a bearing on the outcome. If the outcome clearly would have been the same without the error, it is not reversible error.

Following deliberations, the jury members vote on the guilt or innocence of the defendant. A head or presiding juror, sometimes called the foreman, then presents the verdict to the court.

2012 Bill Fritsch/Getty Images

on appeal. Decisions by the trial court on questions of law, such as whether a criminal statute applied to a defendant, are reviewed "*de novo*," which means the appellate court makes its own independent determination of the issue and is not bound by the trial court's ruling.

Generally, the appellate court will review only those issues raised by the defendant at the trial, such as by making a formal objection in the record of the trial to some ruling by the trial court or action by the prosecution. Thus, in most cases if an error occurred at the trial but was not brought to the trial court's attention in some manner, it will not be reviewed on appeal. The "plain error" rule is an exception to this general rule. All states, and Rule 52(b) of the F.R.Crim.P, permit appellate courts to consider issues not raised by a party in the trial court if they constitute "plain error." In *United States v. Marcus*, 130 S. Ct. 2159 (2010), the U.S. Supreme Court held that in federal prosecutions "plain error" requires a showing that the error was clear and obvious, and that there is a "reasonable probability" the error affected the outcome of the trial.

After the defendant has exhausted his or her state court appeals, the defendant may seek review in the federal courts but only for violation of federal constitutional rights. The defendant may file for a writ of certiorari in the U.S. Supreme Court or a writ of habeas corpus in U.S. district courts.

 ## REVIEW OF SENTENCING

Sentencing authority is granted to the trial judge (or jury) by the law defining the crime and by other statutes in the state or federal criminal code. The sentencing judge may be further guided by sentencing guidelines enacted by that state's legislature. Imposed sentences may be reviewed by the following authorities:

- *Trial judge:* On a motion by the defense attorney, the trial judge reviews his or her sentence of a particular defendant and may modify the sentence after hearing arguments presented by both the defense lawyer and the prosecutor.
- *Appellate courts (including the U.S. Supreme Court and state supreme courts):* On appeal, an appellate court may find that a particular sentence was not within the statutory authority of the trial judge to impose, or that the sentence violated the Eighth Amendment's Cruel and Unusual Punishment Clause.
- *Federal courts:* A state prisoner ordinarily uses a writ of habeas corpus in attempting to get his or her case into the federal courts. To do this, a violation of a right under the U.S. Constitution must be shown. Because there are very few violations (or errors) of this type, few habeas corpus hearings are granted.
- *State parole board or parole authorities:* Parole authority is granted by a statute of that state. State statutes might provide that parole eligibility for murder does not commence until after 16 years—or after 20 or 25 years. Whether the convicted person is released on parole (and the conditions of parole) is then determined by the parole board.
- *The president of the United States and state governors:* The president and state governors have broad power to pardon, grant amnesty, or commute a sentence. Such authority is constitutional, with additional statutory power often provided. Article II of the U.S. Constitution provides that the president "shall have Power to grant Reprieves and Pardons for Offenses against the United States, except in Cases of Impeachment."[a]

[a]See the case of *Murphy v. Ford* [390 F.Supp. 1372 (W.D. Mich. 1975)], in which a federal district court found that President Gerald R. Ford had the constitutional authority to grant a pardon to former President Richard M. Nixon before Nixon had been charged with a crime.

LEGAL CASES

Notable Cases Where Insufficient Evidence Has Resulted in Uncleared Crimes

Criminal Incident	Disposition
Deadly anthrax spores sent through the mail in 2001 killed five people and injured 17 others. One suspect scientist was cleared and later won a $4.6 million award from the federal government. Another suspect scientist, Dr. Bruce Ivins, committed suicide.	No other suspects have been identified by the FBI. It has been reported that some members of Congress are not convinced Ivins acted alone. See the September 18, 2008, New York Times article, "Senator, Target of Anthrax Letter, Challenges F.B.I. Finding."
The most followed murder trial of the 1990s was the charge against O. J. Simpson of murdering his wife and Ron Goldman.	Simpson was acquitted despite DNA evidence showing his blood was found at the crime scene. The Goldman family brought a civil lawsuit against Simpson, and the same evidence was used to acquire a judgment of $34 million; little of that judgment has been paid. The police have not identified any other person as a suspect in the murders. Simpson was convicted of being a party to armed robbery and sentenced to prison in 2006.
The 1996 homicide of 6-year-old JonBenet Ramsey in Boulder, Colorado, remains a mystery, reminding us that 40 percent of murder cases go unsolved.	In July 2008 DNA evidence was found to exclude JonBenet's parents as suspects. Despite extensive efforts by law enforcement agencies, no charges or indictments have been made.
No eyewitnesses to the 1963 assassination of President John F. Kennedy have ever been identified, and for some time after the incident there was confusion about where the gunfire originated. Strong circumstantial evidence established that Lee Harvey Oswald was the lone shooter; he was subsequently shot and killed in the basement of the Dallas Police Department.	No criminal trial was ever held; however, a factfinding commission headed by then–U.S. Supreme Court Chief Justice Earl Warren reviewed all the evidence available and concluded Oswald was the sole assassin. The conclusion remains controversial, however, and a book written by former prosecutor Vincent Bugliosi in 2007 was made into a 10-hour HBO miniseries starring Tom Hanks in 2009.
2-year-old Caylee Anthony disappeared in 2008 in Florida. Seven months later her remains were found in the woods near her home. Her mother, Casey Anthony, did not report Caylee missing for 31 days. No cause of death could be determined from the badly decomposed body. Casey Anthony was acquitted of murder and manslaughter charges by an Orlando, Florida, jury in 2011. Anthony was convicted of four counts of lying to police officers, but served only a few weeks in prison based on the time served while waiting for trial.	Not only was this a "dry bones" case with no "smoking gun," but also the State's theory of the cause of death was not supported by the evidence. The defense alleged that Caylee's grandfather found her body drowned in the family pool, and hid the child's body, although no evidence supported this theory. The investigation and trial was filled with a tangle of lies and allegations by the defendant.

writ of certiorari

Formal notice from the U.S. Supreme Court to a lower federal court or state court that a decision of that court has been accepted for review by the Supreme Court.

Writs of certiorari are limited to a review of state court rulings that violate the defendant's rights under the Constitution, such as the right to counsel, fair trial, confrontation of witnesses, and so on. Writs of certiorari are very rarely granted.

Habeas corpus writs, filed with a federal district court, ask the court to determine whether the defendant is being held in violation of his constitutional rights. Frequently, constitutional issues not reviewed by the Supreme Court under the certiorari power are raised in habeas corpus writs. The denial of a writ is itself appealable by the defendant through the federal appellate system.

In theory, the habeas corpus writ is the final stop in the criminal process. Filing successive habeas corpus writs is possible, however, so it is not accurate to say the process is ever truly complete.

SUMMARY

1. **Outline the criminal court process.**
   - Criminal cases begin with a criminal complaint filed in misdemeanor crimes, or indictments in felony cases where grand juries are used. After arrest, the defendant is arraigned before a judge or magistrate, a plea is taken, and the case is bound over for trial. A preliminary hearing is usually held, where a judge decides only if sufficient evidence exists to justify a trial.

2. **List the pleas a defendant may enter to a criminal charge.**
   - A defendant may always plead not guilty. He may also plead not guilty by reason of insanity, in all but four states that have the insanity defense.
   - A defendant can plead guilty, by a simple guilty plea, an "Alford" guilty plea (which does not admit wrong), or a "conditional" guilty plea (which allows for appeal of contested issues, like a refusal by the trial court to suppress evidence).
   - A "no contest" plea is treated as a guilty plea.

3. **Evaluate the pros and cons of plea bargaining.**
   - The principal gain of plea bargaining is avoidance of congestion in the courts. If every criminal case, or even a substantial percentage, went to trial the court system could not handle the volume.

   - The main objection to plea bargains is they often are reached without protections for the defendant, based on inadequate disclosure of evidence, and don't result in the proper disposition of those charged with crimes.

4. **Compare the use of evidence at various stages of the criminal trial.**
   - At arraignments and bail hearings almost no evidence is offered by either party. At preliminary hearings the prosecution introduces some evidence, but only to show there is some likelihood a crime was committed and the defendant committed the crime. At the trial, evidence is formally introduced and either admitted or excluded, based on the rules of evidence and objections by the parties.

   - The prosecution bears the burden of introducing evidence that proves guilt "beyond a reasonable doubt." Although this is normally a jury question, the trial judge has the power to direct a verdict of not guilty after the prosecution rests its case, if the evidence cannot support conviction as a matter of law. If a conviction results, evidence is admitted at the sentencing, sometimes of a type that would be inadmissible at trial, such as the defendant's criminal history.

   - On appeal, no new evidence is admitted, and only a limited review of the evidence admitted at the trial is made by the appellate court.

KEY TERMS

affirmative defense, 67

Alford guilty plea, 59

arraignment, 55

criminal complaint, 55

criminal indictment, 55

discovery, 67

grand jury, 55

initial appearance, 55

insanity plea, 61

judgment NOV, 69

motion to suppress
  evidence, 52

no contest or nolo
  contendere plea, 59

plea bargaining, 61

preliminary hearing, 55

prima facie case, 67

reversible error, 69

writ of certiorari, 72

KEY CASES

Boykin v. Alabama, 395 U.S. 238 (1969): Stated nature and consequences of a guilty plea in criminal prosecutions.

North Carolina v. Alford, 400 U.S. 25 (1970): Held a defendant may plead guilty while protesting his innocence.

United States v. Marcus, 130 S.Ct. 1259 (2010): States the meaning of the "plain error" rule in federal appeals of criminal convictions.

United States v. Mendez-Santana, 645 F.3d 822 (6th Cir. 2011): Under federal rules a defendant has an absolute right to withdraw a guilty plea before the trial judge accepts the plea.

United States v. Salerno, 481 U.S. 739 (1987): Pretrial detention is permissible in some circumstances under the Federal Bail Reform Act, and does not violate the Eighth Amendment.

PROBLEMS

Finish each sentence using one of the available answers provided.

Available Answers

a. Not guilty plea

b. Guilty plea

c. Alford plea

d. Insanity plea

e. Only a and d

1. Most felony cases in the United States conclude when the defendant enters a(n) ___.
2. When a defendant refuses to enter a plea or stands mute, the court enters a(n) ___.
3. A defendant who has evidence supporting a strong defense is likely to enter a(n) ___.

4. In most states defendants have the burden of producing evidence to prove a(n) ___.
5. The plea that is a not guilty plea is a(n) ___.
6. A defendant who acknowledges that sufficient evidence exists to convict but denies guilt might seek to enter a(n) ___.
7. All but three states are reported to have statutorized a(n) ___.
8. In drunk-driving cases, there is a very high percentage of ___.
9. The defense is likely to seek an expert witness to support a(n) ___.
10. Defendants entering a(n) ___ have the right to a jury trial in most states.

CASE ANALYSIS

Read Appendix B, Finding and Analyzing Cases (p. 499). With these guidelines in mind, please continue with the Case Analysis selections for Chapter 3.

1. When a plea agreement is made, the parties are expected to honor the agreement. In *Santobello v. New York*, 404 U.S. 257 (1971) the U.S. Supreme Court held that breach of a plea agreement by the prosecution makes the resulting sentence invalid, and the defendant must be resentenced in accord with the agreement or given the option to withdraw the guilty plea. Materiality of the breach is not relevant, and the harmless error rule does not apply. How did the prosecution get around *Santobello* in *United States v. Purser*, 2014 WL 747 F.3d 284 (5th Cir. 2014), where the government agreed to ask for a four-offense-level enhancement,

but then asked the judge for a six-offense-level enhancement?

2. What happens when a defendant breaches a plea agreement before sentencing? In *United States v. Hallahan*, 2014 WL 744 F.3d 497 (7th Cir. 2014) a defendant reached a plea agreement with the prosecution, but fled before sentencing. Twelve years later she was captured, and resentenced pursuant to the plea agreement. Although the plea agreement required the prosecution to recommend a lenient sentence, it refused to do so. Should the defendant be held to the terms of the plea agreement?

3. The Bail Reform Act, discussed in this chapter, sets the rules for federal judges and magistrates to follow when a defendant requests bail. When a federal magistrate sets bail, the magistrate's decision can be reviewed by the federal judge for that judicial district. What factors do the magistrate and judge look at when making the bail, no-bail decision? Who has the burden of proof on these factors? What is the standard of review the federal judge uses when reviewing the magistrates fact-findings on the relevant factors? *See United States v. Perez-Lugo*, 2013 WL 979 F. Supp. 2d 197 (D. Puerto Rico 2013).

4. Review of a state conviction in a federal habeas corpus hearing can create tension between the federal courts and the state. For example, a claim first asserted in a habeas hearing that could have been asserted in a state review of a conviction but was not properly raised by the defendant causes such tension. The U.S. Supreme Court has often held that a legitimate state procedural rule that prevented a defendant's claim from being reviewed by a state appellate court was an "independent" ground for refusing to grant the habeas petition. What if the procedural default in the state appeals process was caused by ineffective assistance of counsel? Since a criminal defendant has a constitutional right to effective assistance of counsel, including on direct appeal to the state appeals court, should a federal court when considering a claim of ineffective assistance of counsel ignore the state procedural default rule and hear the claim? What did the U.S. Supreme Court hold in *Trevino v. Thaler*, 133 S. Ct. 1911 (2013)? Why did Chief Justice Roberts in his dissent say the result was not required by the Court's earlier decision in *Martinez v. Ryan*, 132 S. Ct. 1309 (2012)?

Notes

1. 59 Md. App., 28, 474 A.2d 537, 35 CrL 2147 (1984).
2. The states that use the verdict of guilty but mentally ill are Michigan, Indiana, Illinois, Georgia, Kentucky, New Mexico, Delaware, Maryland, Oregon, Pennsylvania, South Carolina, South Dakota, and Alaska.
3. U.S. 238, 242, 89 S. Ct. 1709, 1711–12 (1969).
4. For many years, courts have encouraged guilty pleas by rewarding a guilty plea with a shorter sentence. Court time is saved, court calendars are not so overloaded, witnesses are not required to come to court more than once, and the interests of justice are served.

   In the 1992 case of *United States v. Jones* [973 F.2d 928 (D.C. Cir.)], the defendant received an additional six-month sentence when he took his case to trial instead of entering a guilty plea. The Federal Court of Appeals held that the procedure did not unconstitutionally burden the defendant's right to stand trial. The present federal sentencing guidelines (U.S.S.G. sec. 3 E 1.1) provide that a sentence may be reduced by two levels "if the defendant clearly demonstrates a recognition and affirmative acceptance of personal responsibility for his criminal conduct."

   Guilty pleas are particularly common in misdemeanor offenses such as drunk driving. The evidence in most drunk-driving cases is strong, and conviction rates in these cases are high. Many drunk drivers feel genuine remorse for what they have done and admit their guilt to get the matter settled quickly. Some drunk-driving defendants have said, "Why waste money on a lawyer? I'll save money by going into court and pleading guilty."

   Many prosecutors have established standard pleading and sentencing practices, which are explained to people charged with misdemeanor or ordinance violations. For example, people charged for the first time with shoplifting or soliciting for prostitution might be told that it is standard office procedure to permit first-time offenders to plead to a lesser charge, such as disorderly conduct, if they enter a guilty plea. Those who wish to go to trial are charged with the more serious offense.

   People charged with ordinance or misdemeanor offenses are also told the standard sentences if they enter a guilty plea. Another standard procedure is the practice of issuing multiple charges to an offense such as drunk driving. In return for pleading guilty to the drunk-driving charge and receiving the standard court sentence, the additional charge or charges are dropped.

5. Federal Rule 11c (3) of the Federal Rules of Criminal Procedure requires the judge accepting a guilty plea to inform the defendant of her constitutional rights at the time such plea is taken. Most states have a similar rule. In *United States v. Vonn*, 535 U.S. 55 (2002), the Supreme Court held that failure to give a defendant such advice permits withdrawal of a guilty plea only if the record as a whole shows the defendant was not informed of those rights. Thus, even though such advice was not given at the plea proceeding, the fact that the defendant was informed of her rights at the first arraignment showed that the defendant was aware of her rights when she entered her plea.

   The rule that guilty pleas be voluntary does not require the trial judge to inform the defendant of all the consequences of the plea. For example, in *Irala v. Connecticut,* 792 A.2d 109 (Conn. App. Ct. 2002), a defendant entered a nolo contendere plea to a charge that, under federal law, would result in deportation upon conviction. The trial judge informed the defendant only that conviction of the state crime might have deportation consequences. The defendant subsequently sought to withdraw the plea, but her request was denied. On appeal, the court held that the "voluntary" requirement does not require a judge to inform the defendant of all the "collateral" consequences of a plea.

6. 125 S. Ct. 2398.

7. *Irala v. Connecticut*, supra.

8. *United States v. Jackson*, 390 U.S. 570, 584, 88 S. Ct. 1209, 1217 (1968); *North Carolina v. Alford*, 400 U.S. 25, 38 n. 11, 91 S. Ct. 160, 168 n. 11 (1970).

9. 395 U.S. 238, 89 S. Ct. 1709 (1969).

10. 640 F.3d 1055 (9th Cir. 2011), *cert denied* 133 S. Ct. 101 (2012).

11. The Court of Appeals affirmed the defendant's conviction, finding that the magistrate's mistake was harmless error, because ample evidence showed the defendant was well aware of her rights when she pled guilty.

12. 400 U.S. 25, 37, 91 S.Ct. 160, 167 (1970).

13. *Ward v. State*, 575 A.2d 771 (Md. App. 1990).

14. 741 F.3d 1057 (9th Cir. 2014).

15. In *United States v. A.E.M., Inc.,* 718 F. Supp.2d 1334 (M.D. Fla. 2010) the court discusses the various factors a trial judge should consider when deciding whether to permit a nolo plea under Fed. R. Crim. P. 11 (a) (3).

16. Fed. R. Crim. P 11(b), Advisory Committee's Note to 1974 Amendment.

17. 983 A.2d 75 (Del. Super. 2009).

18. 645 F.3d 822 (6th Cir. 2011).

19. *North Carolina v. Alford*, 400 U.S. 25, 38 n.11, 91 S. Ct. 160, 168, n.11 (1970).

20. *Tollett v. Henderson*, 411 U.S. 258, 93 S. Ct. 1602 (1973).

21. "Task Force Report: The Courts," p. 4, President's Commission on Law Enforcement and Administration of Justice (Government Printing Office, 1967).

22. *Read-in* plea bargains are used most often in property offenses such as burglary and forgery when there is repetitious conduct on the part of the defendant. An example of a read-in plea bargain occurred in Milwaukee. A woman was charged with forging 10 checks. She pleaded guilty to two of the charges. The other eight charges were dismissed, and information that she had forged 628 checks was read into the record. The judge sentenced her to the maximum 20 years. Because the woman had young children, she stayed in prison long enough to cause the parole board to believe that she would not go back to forging checks again before they placed her on parole with the warning that any further violation would send her back to prison.

23. *Golden v. State*, 49 Ind. 424, 427 (1875), in which the Supreme Court of Indiana labeled a plea arrangement a "corrupt agreement" and compared the procedure to "corrupt purchasing of an indulgence."

24. *People v. Muniz*, 262 Cal. Rptr. 473 (Calif. App. 1989).

25. *State v. Lewis*, 539 So.2d 1199 (La. 1989).

26. *Thomas v. State*, 811 P.2d 1337 (Okla. Crim. App. 1991).

27. *Russell v. State*, 614 So.2d 605 (Fla. App. 1993).

28. Either the defense attorney or the prosecutor may challenge a member of the jury panel for cause and disqualify the person. Challenge for cause could be because the panel member is a friend or relative of one of the attorneys or because an answer to a question in voir dire disclosed prejudice in favor of or against a party. The parties are also allowed a limited number of *peremptory challenges*, in which a prospective juror is excused without cause. In *Batson v. Kentucky*, 476 U.S. 79 (1986), the Supreme Court held that the prosecution could not use these peremptory challenges in a discriminatory manner. An example of a prima facie case showing such discrimination is *Roe v. Fernandez*, 286 F.3d 1190 (2001), where the prosecution used most of its peremptory challenges to strike Hispanic and African American members of the jury.

Direct and Circumstantial Evidence and the Use of Inferences

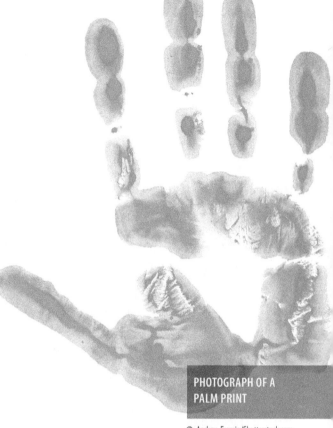

PHOTOGRAPH OF A PALM PRINT

© Andrey Eremin/Shutterstock.com

LEARNING OBJECTIVES

In this chapter we discuss the framework in which evidence, both direct and circumstantial, is used in criminal prosecutions. The learning objectives for this chapter are

Distinguish between the burden of production and the burden of persuasion.

Give a constitutionally acceptable definition of *reasonable doubt*.

Distinguish between direct evidence and circumstantial evidence.

List some examples of inferences that may be drawn from facts proved.

List some inferences that may not be drawn.

Define *presumption,* and state how a presumption may be used in a criminal prosecution.

A man assaulted another man in a New York City freight elevator, demanding the victim surrender his money. The victim complied and the other man fled. Police caught the assailant, and discovered he carried a toy gun and novelty handcuffs in his pocket, though these items had not been brandished during the assault. The assailant was charged with robbery. Prior to trial the defendant moved to exclude the toy gun and handcuffs from evidence at his trial. Why might the prosecution want to introduce that evidence? Are some of those reasons inappropriate in a criminal trial? What argument would you make for the prosecution in favor of admissibility of this evidence? Would it help that the New York robbery statute defines the crime as the intent to "use or threaten to use" physical force during the commission of a robbery? Is the toy gun direct or circumstantial evidence? *See People v. Alfaro*, 979 N.E.2d 1152 (N.Y. 2012).

EVIDENCE AND PROOF

What Is Evidence?

evidence The means of establishing the truth or untruth of any fact that is alleged.

Evidence is ordinarily defined as the means of establishing and proving the truth or untruth of any fact that is alleged. Evidence can be the testimony of witnesses, physical objects, documents, records, fingerprints, photographs, and so on. The famous English lawyer and writer Sir William Blackstone defined evidence in the 1760s as "that which demonstrates, makes clear or ascertains the truth of the very fact or point in issue, either on the one side or other." When the quality and quantity of the evidence presented are so convincing and are sufficient to prove the existence of the fact sought to be proved or disproved, the result is *proof* of the fact. **Proof** is therefore the result of evidence, and evidence is the means of attaining proof. Whether a fact has been proved is determined by the trier of the facts (jury or judge).

proof The result of evidence; evidence is the means of attaining proof.

In trials, the parties introduce evidence to satisfy the *burdens of proof* assigned to them. The burden-of-proof requirement is actually two burdens: the burden of production and the burden of persuasion. The **burden of production** requires the party with the burden on a factual issue to introduce sufficient relevant evidence to prove the fact at issue. Failure to do so means the fact has not been proved, which usually means the person with the burden loses. The **burden of persuasion** requires the party with the burden to produce sufficient evidence to persuade the fact finder that a fact exists.

burden of production That part of the burden of proof that requires a party to produce sufficient evidence to establish the fact at issue.

In criminal trials, both the burden of production and the burden of persuasion rest on the prosecution:

burden of persuasion That part of the burden of proof that requires a party to persuade the jury that a fact exists.

> The Due Process Clause protects the accused against conviction except upon proof beyond a reasonable doubt of every fact necessary to constitute the crime with which he is charged.[1]

Thus, for every element of an offense, the prosecution must produce evidence sufficient to establish the element and also to persuade the jury that no reasonable doubt exists about the fact's existence, based on the evidence produced. In most states, the defendant bears the burden of proof for an affirmative defense.

THE REASONABLE DOUBT STANDARD

reasonable doubt The standard for evidence that fact finders (juries or judges) must use in criminal cases to find a defendant guilty of the crime charged.

Every essential element of the crime charged must be proved by the government beyond a **reasonable doubt** in order to convict and punish a defendant for the crime charged. The requirement of "proof beyond a reasonable doubt" is one of the most familiar legal standards in our society. However, courts and legal scholars have not reached a consensus on the exact definition of that important term. As a result, the instructions trial judges give juries on the standard of proof they must apply to the evidence in order to convict a defendant in a criminal case varies from state to state, and even from court to court within a state. These differences in instructions have caused the U.S. Supreme Court in several cases to consider whether the Due Process Clause has been satisfied by a "reasonable doubt" instruction. Those cases, and the history of the reasonable doubt standard, help to explain the standard's meaning today.

As far back as the seventeenth century, English courts recognized that, in many cases, a criminal defendant's guilt could never be known with absolute certainty. That is, a jury could not be sure of a defendant's guilt beyond any doubt because a chance always existed, no matter how unlikely, that the defendant was innocent. English courts thus instructed juries to find guilt if they were morally certain of that guilt.

In the United States, influenced by decisions like that of Chief Justice Shaw of the Supreme Judicial Court of Massachusetts in 1850, judges began instructing juries to find guilt by use of a reasonable doubt standard. Shaw said the following about what constitutes reasonable doubt:

> What is reasonable doubt? ... It is not mere possible doubt; because everything relating to human affairs, and depending on moral evidence, is open to some possible or imaginary doubt.[2]

In 1970, the U.S. Supreme Court held in *In re Winship*[3] that the Due Process Clause requires that the prosecution prove each element of a crime beyond a reasonable doubt. However, the Court did not in *Winship* mandate any particular jury instruction on the exact meaning of *reasonable doubt*. In the 1994 case of *Victor v. Nebraska*,[4] the Supreme Court held that while jury instructions may attempt to define reasonable doubt, they need not do so; all the Constitution requires is that "taken as a whole, the instructions properly convey the concept of reasonable doubt."

The jury must be instructed to judge the guilt of the defendant according to a high degree of certainty. The Supreme Court has identified certain language in jury instructions that does not properly convey the concept of reasonable doubt. In *Cage v. Louisiana*,[5] the trial court instructed the jury that reasonable doubt meant "such doubt as would give rise to a grave uncertainty" and "an actual substantial doubt." The Supreme Court held that the instruction suggested to the jury that it must find a greater degree of doubt than the reasonable doubt standard requires.

The U.S. Supreme Court has also upheld definitions of reasonable doubt that spoke to the degree of doubt. In *Sandoval v. California*,[6] the Court upheld a jury instruction that defined reasonable doubt as "not a mere possible doubt." Thus, from these cases it can be said that reasonable doubt is less than "actual substantial doubt" but more than "a mere possible doubt." Jurors should not find a defendant guilty because they did not have "substantial doubt" about the defendant's guilt. However, they should not refuse to find that same defendant guilty simply because a "mere possible doubt" exists about the defendant's guilt.

The reasonable doubt jury instruction proposed by the Federal Judicial Center, and that Justice Ginsburg cited with approval in *Victor v. Nebraska*,[7] has been praised by several commentators.[8] That instruction has the advantage of clearly identifying the quantity of doubt the jury must possess, as well as informing the jury that the standard of reasonable doubt is stricter than the standard of proof used in civil cases. That instruction reads:

> The government has the burden of proving the defendant guilty beyond a reasonable doubt. Some of you may have served as jurors in civil cases, where you were told

that it is only necessary to prove that a fact is more likely than not true. In criminal cases, the government's proof must be more powerful than that. It must be beyond a reasonable doubt.

Proof beyond a reasonable doubt is proof that leaves you firmly convinced of the defendant's guilt. There are very few things in this world that we know with absolute certainty, and in criminal cases the law does not require proof that overcomes every possible doubt. If, based on your consideration of the evidence, you are firmly convinced that the defendant is guilty of the crime charged, you must find him guilty. If on the other hand, you think there is a real possibility that he is not guilty, you must give him the benefit of the doubt and find him not guilty.[9]

DIRECT EVIDENCE AND CIRCUMSTANTIAL EVIDENCE

direct evidence
Evidence that proves or disproves a fact in question with no need for inferences.

circumstantial evidence Evidence from which proof of the fact in question may be inferred.

The U.S. Constitution requires that in all criminal cases the state or the federal government prove each and every essential element of a crime beyond reasonable doubt. This can be done by the use of either **direct evidence** or **circumstantial** (indirect) **evidence** or, as occurs in most criminal cases, by a combination of both direct and circumstantial evidence (see Figure 4.1).

Example of Direct Evidence
A witness testifies that he or she saw the defendant commit the crime. Further questioning shows that the witness has good eyesight, the witness was close enough to observe the incident, the lighting was good, and the witness both accurately described the defendant to the police and in the courtroom identified the defendant without any doubt. This is an example of strong, direct, credible evidence that would be sufficient to convict unless the defense could produce evidence sufficient to impeach the credibility of the witness.

Circumstantial evidence is evidence that indirectly proves a fact in issue. Testimony that the defendant was at the scene of the crime and ran from the scene with a pistol in his or her hand is *circumstantial*, or indirect, evidence. Inferences have to be drawn for indirect evidence. If it were shown that no one other than the defendant had an opportunity to commit the crime and that the defendant and the victim were heard arguing angrily, the circumstantial evidence against the defendant would be stronger.

Although direct evidence can be used to directly prove facts, circumstantial evidence requires the fact finder to draw inferences. An inference is a conclusion that can be drawn from a fact.

Direct and circumstantial evidence are used not only to prove criminal conduct but also to prove mental elements that are required essential factors in many

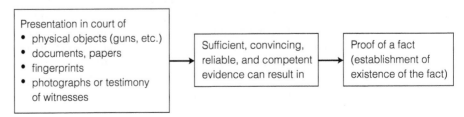

Figure 4.1 | Use of Evidence to Prove a Fact

crimes.[10] Mental elements that must be proved in many crimes of violence include intent, recklessness, and criminal negligence.

In the case of *Commonwealth v. Lee*,[11] the defendant testified that he did not intend to take the victim's life when he pointed a gun directly at the victim and pulled the trigger. In affirming the defendant's conviction, the Pennsylvania Superior Court held:

> [I]t is well settled that the intentional use of a deadly weapon on a vital part of the body raises a permissible inference of malice....

The finder of fact is not required to ignore this inference merely because the defendant testifies that he did not intend to take a person's life ....

... The law infers ... from the use of a deadly weapon, in the absence of circumstances of explanation or mitigation, the existence of the mental element—intent, malice, design, premeditation, or whatever term may be used to express it—which is essential as culpable homicide. [See generally 40 Am. Jur. 2d *Homicide* § 265 (1968).]

The Inference That People Intend the Natural and Probable Consequences of Their Deliberate Acts

In the proof of intent, recklessness, malice, or negligence, the law infers that people intend the reasonable, foreseeable consequences of their intentional and deliberate acts.[12] Such inferences must flow rationally from the evidence presented in court. The U.S. Court of Appeals, in the case of *United States v. Ortiz*,[13] pointed out that "jurors are neither required to divorce themselves from their common sense nor to abandon the dictate of mature experience.... [A] criminal jury [does not have] to ignore that which is perfectly obvious."

Attempted murder and assault with intent to cause serious bodily harm or death are examples of crimes that require proof of the defendant's intent. This intent can be inferred from the defendant's conduct and from the "deadly weapon" doctrine if the defendant uses an object likely to cause death or great bodily harm. A fist could be a deadly weapon if it were used in a way that could cause death or great bodily harm to the victim.

The "probable consequences" inference is often used for finding criminal liability of persons who "aid or abet" the commission of an attempt crime, as was the result in the 2011 case of *Nguyen v. Knowles*.[14] There, one defendant (the shooter) entered a house intending to kill A. The shooter's plan was to "spray" the room with bullets from a semiautomatic handgun. Other defendants aided and abetted the shooter by accompanying him to the front door of the house and handing him the handgun. A was killed by the "spray" of bullets, and B was wounded. The defendants were convicted of the murder of A and the attempted murder of B. The aiders and abettors claimed they could not be guilty of attempted murder, because that crime requires a specific intent to kill, and, they argued, they didn't intend to kill B. The court rejected their arguments, stating that since the shooter could be guilty of attempted murder of every person in the "kill zone" created by his intentional act of shooting into a crowded room, the aiders and abettors were charged with knowledge and thus intent of the natural and probable consequences of the shooter's criminal act.

DIRECT AND CIRCUMSTANTIAL EVIDENCE

Direct evidence is evidence that proves or disproves a fact in issue without the fact finder having to draw upon any reasoning or inferences. *Circumstantial evidence* is evidence that indirectly proves or disproves a fact in issue. The fact finder must reason or draw an inference from circumstantial evidence.

Types of Evidence	Direct Evidence	Circumstantial Evidence
Statements by a suspect or defendant	A full or partial confession by a suspect	A statement that the suspect was with the victim a short time before the murder (an incriminating statement, but neither a full nor a partial confession)
Testimony of witnesses or the victim	Identification of the suspect as the person who committed the crime	Evidence that links the suspect to the crime or that shows motive, means, or opportunity for the suspect to commit the crime (e.g., suspect seen fleeing from the crime scene)
Physical evidence	Contraband (drugs, stolen property, concealed weapons, etc.) when a suspect is charged with possession	Other physical evidence (fingerprints, blood stains, weapons used to commit the crime, bite marks, etc.)
Evidence obtained as a result of wiretapping or electronic surveillance	Statements directly showing who committed the crime	Statements that incriminate but do not directly show who committed the crime

Scientific evidence such as DNA and fingerprints are generally circumstantial evidence (see Chapter 18).

What are the natural and probable consequences of the conduct in the following examples? What common-sense conclusions could a fact finder draw about intent or malice?

- A man drops a 20-pound cement block from a highway overpass, hitting the windshield of a car traveling 60 miles per hour.
- An angry 70-year-old woman hits a 200-pound man with a folded newspaper.
- A strong young man in a rage hits a baby hard in the face with his fist.
- Two men of about equal strength are involved in a fistfight. One of the men hits the other as hard as he can in the face.

When Circumstantial Evidence Alone Is Used to Obtain a Criminal Conviction

In many criminal investigations, direct evidence is unavailable. One common reason for that unavailability is that the suspect controls the direct evidence. This has long been a problem for prosecutions for income tax evasion because often only the defendant has access to records that show total income. As a result, prosecutors use circumstantial evidence called the "net worth method." In that method, a defendant's net worth is calculated at a beginning point, and then for each succeeding year under investigation the defendant's net worth is recalculated to determine whether it increased in an amount greater than declared income. The increase in net worth is then used by the prosecution to prove the income tax evaded.

In 1954 the U.S. Supreme Court decided the case of *Holland v. United States.*[15] In that case, the federal government prosecuted a taxpayer for tax evasion and used the net worth method of proof as evidence of tax evasion. The defendant contended that evidence introduced to show growth of his net worth was inadmissible because other sources of funds besides income could explain the increase. The defendant argued that the prosecution was required to introduce evidence negating all the other possible ways the defendant could have increased his net worth. The Supreme Court disagreed and affirmed the defendant's conviction under the net worth method, stating

> Circumstantial evidence in this respect is intrinsically no different from testimonial evidence. Admittedly, circumstantial evidence may in some cases point to a wholly incorrect result. Yet this is equally true of testimonial evidence. In both instances, a jury is asked to weigh the chances that the evidence correctly points to guilt against the possibility of inaccuracy or ambiguous inference. In both, the jury must use its experience with people and events in weighing the probabilities. If the jury is convinced beyond a reasonable doubt, we can require no more.

In most criminal cases, the government uses a combination of direct evidence and circumstantial evidence to obtain convictions. However, in some cases, circumstantial evidence alone is used. As an example, in the case of *Anderson v. Hubert*[16] the defendants were convicted of murder based almost solely on forensics evidence. The bodies of two victims of gunshot wounds were found in boxes painted black, taped shut, and dumped in a bayou. Fingerprints taken from the defendants matched fingerprints on the paint covering the boxes, and on the adhesive side of the duct tape used to tape the boxes shut. The court upheld the jury verdict, stating the jury "need not find the evidence excluded every reasonable hypothesis of innocence, or was wholly inconsistent with every conclusion except that of guilt," so long as a reasonable jury could conclude the evidence established guilt beyond a reasonable doubt.

When only circumstantial evidence is used, many states do not follow a general rule like the rule stated in the *Holland* decision, but instead add requirements for criminal convictions that rely substantially or exclusively on circumstantial evidence. The following is the jury instruction used in California when the prosecution's case is based primarily on circumstantial evidence:

> Before you may rely on circumstantial evidence to conclude that a fact necessary to find the allegations in the Petition has been proved, you must be convinced that the People have proved each fact essential to that conclusion beyond a reasonable doubt. Also, before you may rely on circumstantial evidence to find the allegations contained in the petition are true, you must be convinced that the only reasonable conclusion supported by the circumstantial evidence is that the defendant is guilty. If you can draw two or more reasonable conclusions from the circumstantial evidence, and one of those reasonable conclusions points to the allegation being true and another to the allegation's being not true, you must accept the one that points to the allegation being not true. However, when considering circumstantial evidence, you must accept only reasonable conclusions and reject any that are unreasonable. (CALCRIM No. 224 (2011); *see People v. Contreras*, 108 Cal. Rptr. 3d 880 (Cal. App. 2011).)

In a few crimes, prosecutors are limited to direct evidence in proving the offenses. For example, ARTICLE III, SECTION 3, CLAUSE 1 of the U.S. Constitution states that "No person shall be convicted of Treason unless on the Testimony of Two Witnesses to the same overt Act, or on Confession in open Court."

Means—Opportunity—Motive as Circumstantial Evidence

When eyewitness evidence is not available, it has often been stated that investigators and officers should ask, as guidelines in investigating crimes, these questions:

- Who had the *means* of committing the crime?
- Who had the *opportunity* to commit the crime?
- Who had the *motive* to commit the crime?

When only circumstantial evidence is introduced in a criminal trial, most courts hold that proof only of motive, or only of opportunity, is insufficient to permit submission of the case to the jury.[17] If circumstantial evidence shows both motive and opportunity, a case can go to the jury for its determination of guilt. The jury must still be instructed that the circumstantial evidence must convince the jury the defendant was guilty beyond a reasonable doubt.

Motive evidence is generally not required to be introduced by the prosecution. Motive is seldom an element of a crime, and courts usually reject claims by defendants that failure to introduce proof of motive makes other circumstantial evidence insufficient.[18]

Conviction of a crime can require proof of motive. An example is 18 U.S.C.A. § 248. This federal statute makes it a crime to intentionally injure or intimidate a person working at or using a reproductive health clinic "because that person is … obtaining or providing reproductive health services." Thus, unlike most crimes that require proof of (1) a criminal act, and (2) a criminal intent, this statute also requires proof of (3) the reason or motive for that intentional act.

Evidence tending to establish a defendant's motive can take a variety of forms. Some are common, such as financial benefit a defendant receives as a result of the crime or personal animosity against a victim. In other cases, motive may be established in more unusual ways. For example, in a 2002 Wisconsin case,[19] the prosecution was permitted to introduce testimony establishing a cultural heritage that members of a Korean family would place family loyalty above other interests. The prosecution argued that the defendant, a Korean American, burned down his father's financially troubled business at his father's request out of loyalty to his father. The cultural tradition was thus used by the prosecution as evidence to show the son's motive.

If the prosecution does not introduce evidence of motive, defendants can argue to the jury that the failure to do so creates reasonable doubt. In *State v. Caruolo,*[20] the Rhode Island Supreme Court said a defendant is not entitled to a jury instruction that absence of motive evidence is a circumstance that shows innocence.

Defendants may also use circumstantial evidence. A defendant might show that she was 200 hundred miles away at the time the crime was committed, a fact from which a strong inference of innocence could be drawn. Some crimes require a great deal of skill, strength, or physical agility; therefore, a defendant lacking such traits has presented circumstantial evidence tending to prove innocence.

"Modus Operandi" ("MO") as Evidence and Investigative Tool

"Modus operandi" (literally, method of working or operating) is commonly used as an investigative tool to link crimes to suspects. As evidence in criminal prosecutions, modus operandi evidence, such as evidence of other crimes with similar elements, permits the jury to draw inferences of guilt where the other crimes can be tied to

You be the **JUDGE (AND JURY)**

In a murder case, the absence of direct evidence (e.g., witnesses, murder weapon, or physical evidence at the crime scene) makes proof of motive, means, and opportunity by circumstantial evidence necessary, and often difficult. Based on the circumstantial evidence listed below, would you as judge permit the case to go to the jury? If so, and you were on the jury, would you convict the defendant of murder?

Motive:

1. Victim owed defendant money.
2. Defendant made several attempts to obtain payment of money owed him by victim.
3. Defendant expressed rage at victim for nonpayment of money.
4. Defendant told friends he would kill victim if the debt was not paid.

Opportunity:

1. Defendant was in victim's neighborhood on night of murder.
2. Cell phone tower records show defendant was proceeding in direction of victim's home around time of death, based on calls made by defendant on his cell phone.
3. Victim's daughter observed large "square or box-shaped" vehicle near victim's home around time of death. Defendant owned an RV vehicle.

Means:

1. Victim was killed by .40-caliber gunshot to back of head from about 1 inch away.
2. Government witness testified he had "previously seen a .45 or 9 millimeter" handgun in defendant's possession.
3. The murder weapon was not found, and no registered weapon can be traced to defendant.

Should the case go to the jury? Should the jury convict the defendant of murder? This problem is based on the case of *State v. Miles*, 730 S.E.2d 816 (N.C. App. 2012). Read closely the dissent in that case, particularly the dissenting judge's discussion of the cellular phone evidence and the daughter's testimony concerning the presence of defendant's RV at the victim's home. Do you think the majority correctly characterized the circumstantial evidence? Do you think it is likely the defendant killed the victim? Do you think there is no reasonable possibility he didn't kill the victim? Which is the proper test in criminal cases?

the defendant. So-called "serial crimes" and "signature" crimes are so similar that they bear the mark of a common pattern, and that modus operandi can be used to connect a defendant to each crime.

Under Rule 404(b) of the Federal Rules of Evidence (see Appendix C), and in most state evidence rules, the prosecution may use evidence of past crimes to prove modus operandi only if the other crimes share peculiar or distinctive features with the crime or crimes charged. The features must be unusual and not often seen in other crimes. If the modus operandi evidence is admitted, the fact finder may draw inferences and conclude the crimes are the handiwork of the same person.

The "Green River" murders during the 1980s and 1990s in the Seattle-Tacoma area illustrate the use of modus operandi as an investigative tool. The bodies of dozens of women, many of them prostitutes, were found by the Green River in Washington. They had all been raped and then murdered by strangulation, either by hand or use of a ligature, and then abandoned near the Green River. Based on this modus operandi several suspects were identified, including Gary Ridgway. He was questioned in 1987, and DNA samples were taken, but he was not arrested. By 2001, however, with advances in DNA testing and increased efforts to solve the crimes, investigators were able to link Ridgway to sperm collected from the pubic hair of an early victim. Ridgway confessed to 48 murders, and claimed he had killed as many as 71 women. In 2003 he was sentenced to 48 life terms with no possibility of parole.

Modus operandi evidence must be distinguished from so-called "profile" evidence, where certain kinds of characteristics are believed to be indicative of criminal conduct. In drug courier crimes, for example, profile evidence includes clothes or jewelry worn by a person, the car driven, use of cash for transactions, and nervous actions by a person. While this profile evidence may sometimes permit police to stop and question a suspected drug courier, it is not admissible as proof of guilt. On the other hand, police experts are permitted to give testimony establishing the common methods used by criminals in drug transactions as modus operandi evidence, which the jury may then consider if similar conduct has been proved in the case before the jury. Thus, in the 2014 case of *State v. Garcia-Quintana*[21] the prosecution was allowed to introduce evidence (through expert police testimony) about how illegal drugs are moved through the Arizona desert by use of certain kinds of backpacks, similar to the backpacks carried by the defendant in that case.

Fingerprints and Shoe Prints as Circumstantial Evidence

Fingerprints and shoe prints are circumstantial evidence, and inferences can be drawn from their presence at a crime scene.

Example

Your home or apartment is burglarized. Fingerprints of a stranger are found at the site of the forced entry. The prints match those of a person with a long history of committing burglaries. A search warrant for his home results in the police seizure of many items taken from your home. The presence of the stolen articles supports the inference that the fingerprints were made during the crime.

In the case of *Commonwealth v. Hall*,[22] the Massachusetts Court of Appeals affirmed the conviction of the defendant for burglary, holding:

The presence of a fingerprint at a crime scene is insufficient by itself to support a guilty finding. "The prosecution must couple the [fingerprint] with evidence which reasonably excludes the hypothesis that the [fingerprint] [was] impressed at a time other than when the crime was being committed." *Commonwealth v. Fazzino,* 27 Mass. App. Ct. 485, 487, 539 N.E.2d 1060 (1989). We conclude that the evidence submitted in this case supports a reasonable inference that the defendant placed his fingerprint on the doorknob at the time of the crime.

Circumstantial evidence may produce inferences, and these inferences "need only be reasonable and possible, ... not necessary or inescapable."

This close-up of a numerical mapping technique links similarities between fingerprints on a computer monitor in a forensic crime lab. The software enables the identification of the owner of the fingerprints. The circumstantial evidence of fingerprints at a crime scene can lead to the inference that the fingerprint owner was involved in the crime.

Mauro Fermariello/Science Source

permissible inference
Inferences made from proof of facts that a fact finder may, but need not, draw.

Although inferences "need only be reasonable and possible," as the court in the above case observed, this means only that the jury may use such a **permissible inference** to reach a conclusion. The prosecution retains the duty to persuade the jury to make the inference.

Shoe prints differ from fingerprints because, unlike fingers, shoes are not part of the human body, and thus are not unique to each individual. As a result, even if evidence establishes (1) the make and model of shoe that made the shoe print, and (2) that the defendant owned such a shoe, the evidence is not conclusive of guilt. In the 2012 murder case of *Com. v. Foley*[23] the court admitted evidence that a shoe print at a crime scene was made by a size 10-12.5 Asics "Gel Creed" shoe, and that the defendant had purchased such a shoe. The defendant argued the evidence was inadmissible, because 25,000 pairs of such shoes were sold during the period he purchased his shoes, and thus 24,999 other shoes could have made the crime scene shoe print. The court said that went only to the weight of the evidence for the jury to determine, not its admissibility.

Courts routinely permit experts to testify about the similarities between a crime scene shoe print and shoes worn by a defendant; *e.g. Com. v. Mitchell*, 962 N.E.2d 246 (Mass. App. 2012).[24] Some courts permit lay testimony to show such similarities.[25]

In the case of *State v. Thompson*, 788 N.W. 2d 485 (Minn. 2010) the court upheld the murder conviction of a defendant based on circumstantial evidence. Part of the evidence was computer-generated images, reproduced based on crime-scene photographs, of bloody shoe prints and sock prints on the victim's floor. The court said the images were admissible to make it easier to understand how the shoe and sock prints matched the bloody tennis shoes worn by one defendant and the bloody socks worn by the other, all of which were admitted into evidence.

Rape Kits as a Source of Circumstantial Evidence

It is generally accepted among law enforcement officers that up to 80 percent of rapes go unreported. Where reports are made by a victim, it is important to collect and preserve physical evidence as quickly as possible. Since initial reports often occur at clinics or hospitals where a victim seeks treatment, hospitals and physicians, as well as police officers called by a victim, prepare rape kits to hold physical evidence such as body hairs, blood, semen, skin samples, or other evidence.

In rape cases that go to trial, rape kits can be a valuable source of circumstantial evidence. Rape kits could show that a sex act occurred, and DNA evidence from semen, blood, hair, or skin scrapings could be sued to identify the man involved. Photographs of the victim could show bruises, tears, cuts, and other injuries showing the use of force. Clothing of the victim could contain trace evidence of the attacker, or the location of the area where the attack occurred.

To encourage victims of rape or sexual assault to report their attacks, the Federal Violence Against Women Act, 42 U.S.C. § 13925, mandates that all states make forensic medical examinations available to victims free of charge. The purpose of the Act is both the health and safety of the victim, and to provide evidence to convict the attacker. The exams also test for sexually transmitted diseases, pregnancy, or other physical injuries. Victims have no obligation to report the sexual assault to police, but may do so anonymously to the police or to a hospital.

The Centers for Disease Control and Prevention provides information and publications about this Act, and can be reached at 1-800-956-7273, or at www.fcasv.org.

Inferences Drawn from Other Bad Acts or Other Convictions of Defendants

A defendant charged with a crime must answer for only that crime at his trial. Evidence of prior crimes or other bad acts is generally held to be inadmissible because of the prejudice it could cause in the minds of the jury or fact finder. In the case of *Thompson v. United States*,[26] the court pointed out that "the jury may condemn the defendant because of his prior criminal behavior and not because he is guilty of the offense charged."

Example

Admission made by defendant to police investigators that defendant had participated in prior robberies was inadmissible as invalid "other bad acts" evidence in murder trial arising out of convenience store robbery. Defendant's conviction of first-degree murder reversed. *Zuniga v. State*, 121 So.3d 640 (Fla. App. 2013).

However, there are exceptions to the rule forbidding evidence of prior crimes or bad acts. Most states have statutes similar to the federal "Other crimes, wrongs, or acts" statute (Federal Rule of Evidence 404[b]), which provides:

Other crimes, wrongs, or acts. Evidence of other crimes, wrongs, or acts is not admissible to prove the character of a person in order to show that he acted in conformity therewith. It may, however, be admissible for other purposes, such as proof of motive, opportunity, intent, preparation, plan, knowledge, identity, or absence of mistake or accident....

An example of evidence admissible under Rule 404(b) appears in the 2012 case of *State v. Torres.*[27] There, the prosecution was permitted to introduce evidence that the defendant in a kidnapping/murder trial had previously kidnapped another victim. The evidence was held admissible under rule 404 (b) because in the prior kidnapping a witness testified the defendant agreed to let the victim go only if the witness would drive the defendant to Texas. The state's theory was that the kidnapping and murder that subsequently occurred were committed by the defendant to acquire money to return to Texas, and thus the prior kidnapping was admissible as proof of motive.

In some circumstances, the defendant may introduce evidence of past violent acts by the victim. In *People v. Harris,*[28] the Michigan Supreme Court reversed a conviction for manslaughter because the trial court excluded evidence of the victim's reputation for violence. The court held that such evidence is relevant to create the inference that the victim initiated violence, a fact that would have some bearing on the culpability of the actions taken by the defendant. Moreover, the court held that the defendant need not have knowledge of that violent reputation because such evidence tends only to prove the likelihood of the victim's violent acts. The court also stated, however, that if the defendant offers evidence of the victim's past violence as part of a self-defense claim, the defendant must show he was aware of the victim's reputation.

PROCEDURES & PROCESSES

Everyday Use of Inferences and Deductions

We all draw inferences from observations in our everyday life. From observations you may conclude that a friend is angry or upset, that it is going to rain, that a motorist is driving recklessly, or that a pet is getting old or is sick. Consider the following example of an inference: You awake one morning to see snow falling in your backyard. In the newly fallen snow are animal tracks across your yard. From your observations and past experiences, you could conclude:

- A large dog crossed your yard a few minutes earlier.
- The dog was moving slowly from east to west.
- The dog probably belongs to your neighbor to the east, who lets his dog out every morning.

If you had seen the dog cross your yard, you would have direct information regarding the dog. But because you did not see or hear the dog, you made your deductions or conclusions based on the circumstantial facts available to you. Further investigation could either affirm or rebut the conclusions you have made.

Other Bad Acts Evidence in Sexual Assault Cases   In 1994, Congress passed the Violent Crime Control and Law Enforcement Act.[29] As part of its provisions, this law amended the Federal Rules of Evidence by adding Rules 413, 414, and 415. These rules make admissible in criminal cases evidence of prior sexual assaults (Rule 413) and child molestations (Rule 414) by a defendant charged with those crimes. Unlike the limited use of evidence of "bad acts" under Rule 404(b), evidence introduced under Rule 413 or 414 "may be considered for its bearing on any matter to which it is relevant."[30] This includes introducing such evidence to prove "a defendant's propensity to act in conformity therewith." *United States v. Lohse*, 993 F.Supp. 2d 947 (N.D. Iowa 2014).

Most states have similar rules for admissibility of past sexual offenses. In *People v. Villatoro*, 281 P.3d 390, 406 (Cal. 2012) the California Supreme Court gave the following justification for the California rule on propensity evidence in sexual assault cases, section 1108 of the California Rules of Evidence:

> By their very nature, sex crimes are usually committed in seclusion without third party witnesses or substantial corroborating evidence. The ensuing trial often presents conflicting versions of the event and requires the trier of fact to make difficult credibility determinations. Section 1108 provides the trier of fact in a sex offense case the opportunity to learn of the defendant's possible disposition to commit sex crimes.

The California rule, like the federal rules and most other similar rules, requires (1) that the prosecution give pretrial notice to a defendant of its intent to offer evidence of prior sexual offenses, and (2) the prosecution must prove those other offenses occurred by "clear and convincing" evidence.

In those states that have not adopted rules similar to Rule 413 or 414, there is often a "pedophile exception" to Rule 404 (b). An example is the exception to the Arkansas version of Rule 404 (b) discussed in the 2012 case of *State v. Craig*.[31] There, in a prosecution for performing oral sex on a 14-year-old boy, the prosecution was permitted to introduce evidence of the defendant's conviction 16 years earlier for performing oral sex on a 4-year-old boy. The Arkansas Supreme Court said that the "pedophile exception" to Rule 404 (b) required only that the two offenses involved similar sexual conduct, and that in both cases the defendant had a family or intimate friend relationship with the victim.

Some Inferences Should Not Be Drawn

Circumstantial evidence invites the fact finder to make inferences, often about the defendant's guilt. As we saw above, sometimes the inferences likely to be drawn from circumstantial evidence are inappropriate and prejudicial, and the evidence is not admissible. That is the reason for the "bad acts" limitation of Rule 404 (b) of the Federal Rules of Evidence. In some situations, the circumstantial evidence offered by the prosecution offends a Constitutional right. In others, the defense might seek to introduce circumstantial evidence that suggests an inference about a prosecution witness that is inappropriate. In the following situations, courts have ruled that certain circumstantial evidence is inadmissible, that inferences are **impermissible**, and that no inference of guilt or the victim's role in the crime may be drawn from them.

impermissible inference   An inference a fact finder may not draw; an example is inferring guilt because the defendant does not testify.

When a Defendant Exercises the Privilege Against Self-Incrimination   In a criminal trial, the prosecution might seek to introduce evidence that the defendant remained silent in the face of questions about the crime. The silence of the defendant, either during a trial or before the trial, might encourage the jury to make the inference that the defendant had something to hide. Evidence of a defendant's silence, or comments about that silence by the prosecution, even if relevant, is a potential problem because the U.S. Constitution in the Fifth Amendment gives criminal defendants the right to refuse to answer questions which might incriminate them.

The U.S. Supreme Court has held that an inference of guilt may not be drawn in criminal trials where defendants do not take the witness stand to defend themselves against criminal charges made against them. The U.S. Supreme Court held in *Griffin v. California*[32] that the Fifth Amendment prohibits a trial judge, a prosecutor, or a witness from commenting upon a defendant's failure to testify in a criminal trial.

The fact that a defendant remained silent during questioning prior to trial is also inadmissible under some, but not all, circumstances. To understand the different rules, one must distinguish between criminal trials where the defendant takes the witness stand to testify and criminal trials where the defendant does not take the witness stand to testify. In the former case, evidence that the defendant remained silent during pre-trial questioning might be used by the prosecution to **impeach** the testimony given at the trial. In the latter case, the prosecution seeks to introduce in its case-in-chief the fact of a defendant's silence to prove the guilt of the defendant.

The use by the prosecution of a defendant's pretrial silence has one clear dividing line: If the *Miranda* warnings, which must be given to a person who is in police custody (see Chapter 12), have been given, the defendant's silence or invocation of his Fifth Amendment rights may not be used for either impeachment if the defendant testifies, or proof of guilt if the defendant does not testify.[33]

If the *Miranda* warnings have not been given, the rules are less clear. The U.S. Supreme Court has held that silence by a person in custody in response to questions asked before the *Miranda* warnings were given may be used to impeach that person if he takes the stand to testify at a subsequent trial.[34] The same is true if the silence is in response to questions by police before the defendant is in custody.[35] The Supreme Court has not decided the question of the use of such silence by the prosecution in its case-in-chief to prove guilt. Lower courts have split on this question.[36]

In the 2013 case of *Salinas v. Texas*, 133 S. Ct. 2174, a divided Supreme Court held that the prosecution could use the pre-arrest, pre-*Miranda* silence of the defendant in the prosecution's case-in-chief as proof of guilt. In *Salinas* the defendant did not invoke his Fifth Amendment right, but simply remained silent in response to potentially incriminating questions by the police. The Court said the Fifth Amendment cannot provide protection for any purpose until it has been invoked. It specifically did not decide a question that had split lower courts[37] about the use of silence in the prosecution's case-in-chief where the defendant *did* invoke his Fifth Amendment rights. The various opinions written by the justices in *Salinas* may be a sign that if faced with such a case, the Court would hold that a defendant's silence after invoking the Fifth Amendment may not be used in the prosecution's case-in-chief.

When the Information Is Protected by the Rape Shield Law Before the enactment of rape shield laws, defense lawyers in rape cases were permitted to question victims about their past sex life in hopes that the jury and judge would draw the inference that a victim who was sexually active was more likely to have consented to sex.

In the case of *Commonwealth v. Nieves*,[38] the Pennsylvania Superior Court pointed out that "[r]ape shield laws were intended to end the abuses ... by limiting the harassing and embarrassing inquiries of defense counsel into irrelevant prior sexual conduct of sexual assault complainants."

---

impeach Use of evidence to challenge the credibility of a witness.

Rape shield laws enacted by the federal government and the several states contain exceptions where evidence of past sexual behavior may be admitted. Federal Rule of Evidence 412 b (1) (found in Appendix C of this book) contains the federal exceptions to the relevance of evidence as to the "alleged victim's past sexual behavior or alleged sexual predisposition." One common exception, found in Rule 412 b (1) (B) of the Federal Rules and in state rape shield laws, is evidence of past sexual conduct between the victim and the defendant, where consent is an issue. For example, in *State v. Yenser*, 889 N.E.2d 581 (Ohio App. 2008), *rev. denied* 891 N.E.2d 771 (Ohio 2008), the court reversed a conviction of anal rape because the trial court refused to permit the defendant to introduce evidence of prior consensual instances of anal intercourse with the victim. The court stated that the prosecution used the fact of bruising of the victim as proof of lack of consent, and that the defendant should have been permitted to offer evidence that bruising occurred in prior consensual acts as rebuttal to the prosecution's claims.

Cessation of Signature Crimes After a Suspect's Arrest   *Signature crimes* are crimes that are so similar that they bear the mark of a common pattern. Many cities and communities have faced the terrible problem of serial crimes. If a suspect is arrested and the serial or signature crimes stop, can this be used as evidence of the guilt of the person arrested?

Courts disagree on the relevance and admissibility of cessation evidence. In one case, *State v. Miller,*[39] an Arizona appeals court held that evidence of cessation, though not compelling, had some probative value, and that is all that is needed for admissibility. The Pennsylvania Supreme Court reached the opposite conclusion, and held that such evidence is inherently unreliable. In the case of *Commonwealth v. Foy,*[40] the court pointed out that there are many reasons why reports of signature crimes could stop:

> Further signature crimes may have been committed but never reported to the police. The true culprit may have died, or left the community, or been incarcerated on unrelated charges about the time of the defendant's arrest. Or perhaps the true culprit has decided to refrain from further acts of violence in order to shift suspicion onto the defendant and thereby escape detection.

USING DIRECT AND CIRCUMSTANTIAL EVIDENCE

In most criminal cases, both direct and circumstantial evidence is used. Following are some examples.

Finding Illegal Drugs in a Motor Vehicle

Illegal drugs are found in motor vehicles in a variety of situations. In a lawful stop of a vehicle, a law officer may see or smell illegal drugs. An informant or other source might provide probable cause to believe drugs are in the vehicle.

If the illegal drugs are in an open position in the vehicle and only the driver is in the car, the inference of knowledge and possession of drugs is easy. When more than one person is in the car, the inference of illegal possession is strongest against the owner and driver of the vehicle. It would be more difficult to convict a passenger in the vehicle because the inferences of knowledge and possession are weaker.

However, the location of the drugs in the vehicle, the amount of illegal drugs found, the criminal record of the passenger, and the passenger's relationship to the driver and owner would all be circumstantial factors in determining whether or not to charge the passenger.

The U.S. Court of Appeals, in the case of *United States v. Gibson*,[41] made the following observations in affirming the conviction of the defendant:

> It is well established in this circuit that in cases involving hidden compartments, reliance may not be placed solely on the defendant's control of the vehicle. In such an instance, possession can be inferred only if knowledge is indicated by additional factors, such as circumstances evidencing a consciousness of guilt on the part of the defendant. Inconsistent stories may constitute substantive evidence of a defendant's guilty knowledge. Circumstantial factors also include lack of knowledge of the name of the true owner and implausible explanations for one's travels.

Proving the Crime of Possession of Illegal Drugs with Intent to Deliver

A defendant apprehended in the act of selling illegal drugs usually can easily be convicted of the offense because strong direct evidence exists to prove selling, transferring, or delivering of the drugs.

When the crime of possession with intent to deliver is charged, the defendant usually has a large quantity of illegal drugs in his or her possession. State and federal governments argue that sufficient circumstantial evidence exists to prove that the defendant had the intent to sell, transfer, or deliver the illegal drugs to others and did not intend all of the drugs for personal use. The crime of possession with intent to deliver has higher penalties than mere possession.[42]

In the case of *State v. Morgan*,[43] the Supreme Court of North Carolina reviewed cases from North Carolina courts showing the many, various circumstances where intent to deliver was inferred from circumstantial evidence:

> A jury can reasonably infer from the amount of the controlled substance found within a defendant's constructive or actual possession and from the manner of its packaging an intent to transfer, sell, or deliver that substance. See, e.g., *State v. Williams*, 307 N.C. 452, 298 S.E.2d 372 (1983) (presence of material normally used for packaging); *State v. Baxter*, 285 N.C. 735, 208 S.E.2d 696 (1974) (amount of marijuana found, its packaging, and presence of packaging materials); *State v. Rich*, 87 N.C. App. 380, 361 S.E.2d 321 (1987) (20 grams cocaine plus packaging paraphernalia); *State v. Casey*, 59 N.C. App. 99, 296 S.E.2d 473 (1982) (possession of over 25,000 individually wrapped dosage units of LSD); *State v. Mitchell*, 27 N.C. App. 313, 219 S.E.2d 295 (1975), *cert. denied*, 289 N.C. 301, 222 S.E.2d 701 (1976) (possession of considerable inventory of marijuana plus other seized, "suspicious" items). *See also State v. James*, 81 N.C. App. 91, 344 S.E.2d 77 (1986) (cocaine of small quantity packaged in multiple envelopes); *State v. Williams*, 71 N.C. App. 136, 321 S.E.2d 561 (1984) (less than one ounce marijuana packaged in seventeen small bags); *State v. Francum*, 39 N.C. App. 429, 250 S.E.2d 705 (1979) (quantity of LSD unspecified, but found in plastic bags inside larger plastic bags).

probable cause The belief of guilt based on reasonable grounds made with particularized evidence of the guilt of the person to be searched or seized.

Other circumstantial evidence used to prove intent to deliver is mentioned in the case of *United States v. Solis*,[44] where drugs were found in Solis's luggage:

> As counsel for Ms. Solis conceded on appeal, her intent to distribute the cocaine found in her luggage was at issue. The government had to establish that intent through circumstantial evidence. Evidence of Ms. Solis' actions and of the other articles in her possession was therefore relevant on the issue of whether she intended to distribute

LEGAL CASES

Circumstantial Evidence and Probable Cause

In many situations, such as use of force, police officers must make decisions based on circumstantial evidence. Also, before a law enforcement officer may arrest a person, search a car, or take similar actions, the officer must have "**probable cause**" to believe a crime has been committed or evidence of a crime might be discovered. Probable cause (defined in Chapter One of this text) requires that the officer have "reasonable ground for belief of guilt, and that the belief of guilt must be particularized with respect to the person to be searched or seized," *Maryland v. Pringle*, 540 U.S. 366, 370 (2003). The officer usually must decide if probable cause exists based on circumstantial evidence, and reasonable inferences drawn from those circumstances. The U.S. Supreme Court and other courts have had many occasions to consider whether an inference drawn by a law enforcement officer was "reasonable" and satisfied the probable cause requirement. Here are some typical cases:

Case	Reasonable Inference Drawn
A car occupied by three men was stopped early one morning for speeding. After a computer check showed no outstanding warrants an officer asked for and was given consent to search the vehicle. The officer found $763 in rolled-up cash in the glove compartment, and five plastic bags of cocaine behind a backseat armrest. Can all three men in the vehicle be arrested and charged with possession of illegal drugs?	The U.S. Supreme Court held: "We think it an entirely reasonable inference from these facts that any or all three of the occupants had knowledge of, and exercised dominion and control over the cocaine .... We think it was reasonable for the officer to infer a common enterprise among the three men. The quantity of drugs and cash in the car indicated the likelihood of drug dealing." *Maryland v. Pringle, supra*. The Court distinguished the case of *Ybarra v. Illinois*, 444 U.S. 85 (1979), where a search of a patron in a bar by officers holding a search warrant for the bar was held unreasonable. The Court noted that the mere presence in the bar was not enough to give probable cause. The *Pringle* court said the small confines of the car and the proximity of the illegal drugs made the inferences of common enterprise reasonable there.
Police lawfully stopped a car for faulty taillights. The officer approached the car and saw a syringe in the shirt pocket of the driver. The officer determined the syringe was used for injecting illegal drugs, and searched the car, including the purse of a passenger in the car. The purse contained illegal drugs, and the passenger was convicted of illegal possession.	In concluding the officer had probable cause to search the passenger belongings that are capable of concealing the object of a search the U.S. Supreme Court said: "... it is reasonable to infer that ... a car passenger ... will often be engaged in a common enterprise with the driver and have the same interests in concealing the fruits of the evidence of their wrongdoing. *Wyoming v. Houghton*, 526 U.S. 296, 304–305 (1999).
Police officers stopped Brown at a drivers' license checkpoint, where it was discovered Brown did not have a valid driver's license. When Brown opened the glove compartment and fumbled the contents officer Maples saw suspicious evidence of illegal drugs, including a tied-off balloon, which the officer opened, revealing illegal drugs.	In holding Officer Maples had probable cause to open the balloon, the U.S. Supreme Court said: "Officer Maples testified that he previously made an arrest in a case where narcotics were carried in tied-off balloons similar to the issue here. Other officers had also told him of such cases.... We have recognized that a law enforcement officer may rely on is training and experience to draw inferences and make deductions that might well elude an untrained person." *Texas v. Brown*, 460 U.S. 730, 746 (1983), Justices Powell and Blackmun, concurring.

the contraband. For instance, evidence of repeated trips to Anchorage, paid for in cash by or on behalf of a woman living on Social Security, certainly provides important pieces to the government's evidentiary puzzle. The simultaneous presence of beeper numbers helps complete the picture—*if* the trier of fact is aware of the role that beepers often play in the conduct of illegal drug trade. The government was entitled to demonstrate through the use of expert testimony that someone traveling with two kilograms of cocaine under the conditions we have described would find access to beepers a useful means of effectuating the transportation and eventual distribution of her deadly cargo.

In addition to beepers, guns are tools of drug traffickers and can be used as circumstantial evidence from which fact finders can infer intent to deliver. The federal court in the case of *United States v. Carstens*[45] held that "courts have recognized that any gun is a 'tool of the trade' for drug traffickers. The presence of weapons is evidence of ... intent to distribute controlled substances."

Other circumstances common to the illegal drug trade have been found to support guilty verdicts of individuals charged with drug-related offenses. In the 2014 case of *Acosta v. State*, 429 S.W.3d 621 (Tex. Crim. App. 2014) the court held that the presence of over $500,000 in bundled-up cash hidden in a truck traveling from Illinois to Mexico was sufficient circumstantial evidence to support the jury verdict of money laundering, which includes transporting "the proceeds of criminal activity." The court noted that the money, though bundled in a manner meant to prevent its detection by drug dogs, nonetheless caused the dogs to alert when they sniffed the truck where the money was hidden. Legitimate businesses do not, the court said, carry cash of that amount hidden in secret panels of trucks travelling to Mexico.

Proving Use of the Internet in Child Pornography

Although possession of child pornography is both a federal and a state crime, federal prosecutors have more resources for prosecutions.[46] If a defendant is found to possess child pornography, the government must prove he received the images over the Internet to obtain a federal conviction (an interstate violation).

Internet use must often be proved by circumstantial evidence. An example of how circumstantial evidence can be used for such a conviction is *United States v. Dodds*.[47] The defendant was charged under 18 U.S.C. section 1462 after being found with more than 3,400 images of child pornography in his possession. The prosecution proved that the images were taken from the Internet by the following circumstantial evidence:

- The photographs were shown to be available on the Internet and traded there.
- Some of the children pictured were shown to live in states other than the defendant's.
- There was no evidence the defendant traveled to those other states.
- The defendant was shown to be familiar with using the Internet.

The court of appeals held that this evidence was sufficient and affirmed the defendant's conviction.

Congress has passed several acts designed to protect children from sexual exploitation on the Internet, but the U.S. Supreme Court has held many of these acts to be unconstitutional. [For a discussion of these cases, see T. Gardner and T. Anderson, *Criminal Law: Principles and Cases,* 12th ed. (Thomson Wadsworth, 2015), p. 350.] In the 2008 case of *United States v. Williams*,[48] the Supreme Court reversed the Eleventh Circuit Court of Appeals and held the PROTECT Act[49] constitutional. The PROTECT Act makes it a crime for a person to distribute information on the Internet in a manner that "reflects a belief" or is "intended to make another believe" the person was distributing child pornography.

Charges of distributing child pornography over the Internet can be difficult to prove because the U.S. Supreme Court had held that persons distributing pictures alleged to contain images of actual children in sexual poses, but who are in reality young-looking actors or computer-created animations, cannot be prosecuted as child pornographers. As a result, it is difficult for a prosecution to prove that images depicted in an Internet posting are actual children. The PROTECT Act alleviates this problem by making it a violation to post images in such a manner that suggests the person posting the image either believes it to be of an actual child or posts it in a manner designed to make others believe the images are real children. The Supreme Court upheld the statute, stating it narrowly prohibited conduct that relates to the depiction of sexual poses involving actual children, and did not operate to prohibit conduct that does not involve actual children.

Proving Physical and Sexual Abuse of Children

Thousands of babies and very young children are seriously injured every year, but are unable to tell investigators what happened. Adults caring for an injured child may not truthfully recount how the injuries occurred. As a result, testimony of medical professionals and the use of inferences become very important in determining if abuse occurred, and proving who committed child abuse, neglect, or sexual abuse.

Brutal injuries to babies and children range from cigarettes, hot stove and hot liquid burns, to ruptured internal organs such as the liver, spleen, kidney, or bowels caused by blows to the abdomen. They include missing teeth, multiple scars, and knife or gunshot wounds. When an adult has sole custody of a child and it is shown that the injury was not accidental or self-inflicted, a jury may infer that the adult inflicted the injury. In the case of *Commonwealth v. Earnest*,[50] the Superior Court of Pennsylvania relied on this rule, allowing

> [A]n inference of guilt where a child suffers a fatal injury while an adult has sole custody of the child. *Commonwealth v. Nissly,* 379 Pa. Super. 86, 549 A.2d 918 (1988). In *Nissly,* the defendant was not the only adult in the house when the fatal injury was inflicted, but the inference of guilt was still applicable, as the defendant was the only adult with the child when the injury had to have occurred. As in the instant case, the fact finder found the injury was not accidental or self-inflicted, therefore, the evidence was sufficient for the conviction, as we find it is here.

In the case of *Campbell v. Commonwealth*,[51] the victim was a 3-year-old child. The court of appeals held:

> [T]he trial judge could have inferred from all the facts and circumstances that the defendant intended to do exactly what he did—beat the child with such force that it left his back and side extensively marked and bruised. Further, the trial judge could have found that the probable and natural consequence of this act, given the force with which the blows were applied and the location of the marks near Cecil's spinal column and right kidney, was disfigurement or disablement of the child ....

A three-year-old child with no way to defend himself, except by screaming and crying, received a brutal beating from the much stronger defendant. We conclude that the trial judge could have inferred from all the evidence that this beating was delivered with the intent to disfigure or disable the child.

Medical studies in the past 10 years show that there can be many causes of injury to a baby in addition to injury caused by shaking the baby. Bleeding in or around the brain of a baby can be caused by a fall, an infection or other illness, problems during birth, or by shaking a baby. However, as this billboard in Florida urges, babies are fragile and should be handled with care.

© Mary Demett

For the foregoing reasons, therefore, we affirm the defendant's conviction of malicious wounding.

One area where inferences of guilt have been used is in "shaken baby syndrome" cases. Babies are very fragile, and should not be shaken because it could cause serious injuries to an infant's neck, spinal cord, or brain. In the past, where a baby was diagnosed as having such injuries, police investigators and prosecutors assumed that the presence of the injuries alone created the inference the baby was forcibly shaken (the "syndrome"), and thus charged the last person who cared for the child. Based on this inference hundreds of parents, baby-sitters and daycare providers were convicted of causing the serious injury or death of babies in their care.

In the past few years, medical studies have cast doubt on the reliability of the "shaken baby syndrome." These medical studies, which include the use of recent advances in technology such as medical resonance imaging (MRI), have shown that

- Bleeding in or around a baby's brain that had previously been assumed to be caused only by forcible shaking can also be caused by a number of other circumstances, such as a fall, an infection, an illness like sickle-cell anemia, or trauma experienced by the baby during birth.
- There can be a lag of hours, even days, between the time of an injury and the time when a baby shows signs of the injury, such as a loss of consciousness. As a result, the common inference that the last person caring for the baby was the cause of the injury is harder to draw. In *State v. Edmonds*, 746 N.W.2d 590 (Wis. App. 2008), *rev denied* 749 N.W.2d 663 (Wis. 2008) the court ordered a new trial of a babysitter convicted of causing the death of a seven-month-old child based on medical testimony on the "shaken baby syndrome." Experts had testified that the baby must have been shaken by the babysitter, because the baby was lucid when dropped off at the babysitter's house, and thus could not have been injured prior to that time. New medical evidence was introduced showing that assumption is now subject to doubt.

As a result of these new medical studies, in the May 2009 issue of *Pediatrics*, the American Academy of Pediatrics issued a policy statement that recommended the phrase "shaken baby syndrome" be replaced by the phrase "abusive head trauma" to avoid the implication that only forcible shaking could be the cause of a head injury to a baby or young child.

Some sexual abuse statutes require proof of *forcible compulsion.* When the victim is a child, the child often submits to the advances of adults who have parental or similar authority over the child.

The highest courts in Pennsylvania, North Carolina, and Alabama permit an inference of forcible compulsion where sexual intercourse or abuse is shown even if no physical force was used and no threats were uttered by the adult. In adopting this inference in the case of *Powe v. State,*[52] the Supreme Court of Alabama held:

> We note that our holding is limited to cases involving the sexual assault of children by adults with whom the children are in a relationship of trust. The reason for the distinction between cases involving children as victims and those involving adults as victims is the great influence and control that an adult who plays a dominant role in a child's life may exert over the child. When a defendant who plays an authoritative role in a child's world instructs the child to submit to certain acts, an implied threat of some sort of disciplinary action accompanies the instruction. If the victim is young, inexperienced, and perhaps ignorant of the "wrongness" of the conduct, the child may submit to the acts because the child assumes the conduct is acceptable or because the child does not have the capacity to refuse. Moreover, fear of the parent resulting from love or respect may play a role as great or greater than that played by fear of threats of serious bodily harm in coercing a child to submit to a sexual act.

Proving the Defendant Was the Driver of a Motor Vehicle

Thousands of drivers on American highways have had their driver's license suspended or revoked. Many others do not have a valid driver's license or are driving under the influence of drugs or alcohol. In 2012 in the United States, according to the November, 2013 report issued by the National Highway Traffic Safety Administration, 33,561 persons died in automobile crashes. Of those killed, 10,322 or about 32 percent, involved alcohol-impaired drivers. This means that once every 50 minutes someone in the United States dies in a drunk-driving crash or is hit by a drunk driver. When drugged drivers are added to the statistics, more than 50 percent of all traffic deaths are alcohol or drug related. Moreover, as of 2013, 18 states have passed laws making the medical or recreational use of marijuana legal. It is possible drug-related automobile deaths will increase. California, which has the longest-running medical marijuana use laws, saw the number of "high" traffic deaths where alcohol is not involved jump 55 percent over the 10 years ending in 2009.

Proof beyond reasonable doubt that the defendant was driving the vehicle is required and is central to the conviction of the defendant in many moving vehicle trials. The following cases illustrate only a few of those that come before American courts every year, where inferences drawn from circumstantial evidence are used to determine who was driving the vehicle in question.

Humphreys v. State 696 S.E.2d 400 (Ga. App. 2010)	Police officers making a random check of license plates determined that a vehicle's owner, a male, had a suspended driver's license. The person operating the vehicle was a male, and the police made the inference that the owner was driving the vehicle illegally. The Court held that the police had reasonable suspicion to make a stop of the vehicle, in the absence of evidence showing that someone else was driving the car.

State v. Fitzgerald
63 So.3d 75 (Fla. App. 2011)

Circumstantial evidence was sufficient to prove the defendant was driving a car while intoxicated, where the state trooper found the defendant in the driver's seat of a vehicle parked at an intersection. The motor was off, but the keys were in the defendant's right hand. This constituted physical control of the vehicle under Florida law, the court held.

PROVING CORPUS DELICTI BY DIRECT OR CIRCUMSTANTIAL EVIDENCE

corpus delicti The body of the crime; the requirement that the government must prove that the crime charged has been committed.

In all criminal cases, the state or government must prove that (1) a crime has been committed by someone (**corpus delicti**) and (2) the defendant(s) committed the offense. Most states have adopted a definition of *corpus delicti* similar to that used by the Supreme Court of California in the case of *People v. Jennings:*[53] "The corpus delicti of a crime consists of two elements, the fact of the injury or loss or harm, and the existence of a criminal agency as its cause."

The corpus delicti of most crimes is ordinarily proved by direct evidence, as when the victim or a witness tells the police of the crime. The corpus delicti of other crimes is proved by physical evidence; for example, the corpus delicti of a burglary is shown by a broken window and missing valuables. The corpus delicti of a murder could be proved by a dead body with a knife in the chest. The following examples illustrate common corpus delicti problems.

Examples

- A suspicious fire destroys a building housing a business that was in serious financial trouble. Investigators suspect arson but cannot prove corpus delicti (that the fire was deliberately started). The insurance company is unhappy because of the large amount of insurance. It can be shown that the owner of the building and business had the means, opportunity, and motive for "torching" the building, but if the state cannot prove corpus delicti, it cannot charge the owner with a criminal offense.

- In sexual assault or rape cases a common defense is consent of the victim. This is a "corpus delicti" defense because lack of consent is an element of the crime that must be proved by the prosecution.

- The "corpus delicti" defense is also a problem in determining if a death occurred, and if so was the result of criminal homicide, rather than natural causes. These cases include

  a) "Missing persons" cases which are present in all major cities. Is the person simply missing, or is the person dead? In the famous case of the disappearance of the labor leader Jimmy Hoffa, who many suspected was murdered and buried in a construction site somewhere, the FBI has spent hundreds of hours looking for his body, with no success.

  b) "Bodies without proof of death" cases, where a body is found but because of decomposition the cause of death cannot be determined. In the 2011 Florida trial of Casey Anthony for the alleged murder of her 2-year-old daughter the state was unable to prove Anthony killed her daughter because, due to the badly decomposed body of the child, it did not have evidence showing the cause of death. The defense offered a theory that the child drowned in a swimming pool and was secretly buried by her grandfather, though it had no real evidence to support this theory. Anthony, who led the police on a "wild-goose chase" for months, was convicted only of lying to the police, and served only a short time in jail. (In Chapter 16 we discuss the crime scene, chain of custody, and "junk science" aspects of the Casey Anthony investigation and trial.)

As a general rule, corpus delicti must be established beyond a reasonable doubt.[54] Corpus delicti may be proved by a combination of direct and circumstantial evidence or by either alone. When an attempt is made to prove corpus delicti by circumstantial evidence, the general rule is that the evidence must be so conclusive as to eliminate all reasonable doubt in concluding that a crime was committed. The following cases illustrate:

State v. Barker

945 N.E.2d 1107 (Ohio App. 2010)

Defendant was convicted of murder based in part on the testimony of two witnesses, who stated the defendant confessed to them that he killed the victim, his girlfriend. The defendant appealed, claiming insufficient independent evidence existed to prove the corpus delicti. The appeals court agreed that the corpus delicti rule required independent proof in addition to the confession, but held such proof existed. The court noted the victim had been missing for 3 years without contact with her mother or two young sons, had left her house on the day she went missing with the defendant, had not touched any of her bank accounts since she disappeared, and on the day she disappeared bought two pumpkins to make into jack-o'-lanterns for her sons. This evidence could have been found by the jury to be proof that the victim had not simply disappeared, but was dead.

Tetso v. State

45 A.3d 788 (Md. App. 2012), *cert denied* 52 A.3d 979 (Md. 2012)

On March 6, 2005, Tracey Tetso was to attend a Motley Crue concert with a man with whom she was having an affair. She did not attend the concert and was never seen again. In 2010 her husband, Dennis, was convicted of second-degree murder of Tracey, based only on circumstantial evidence. On appeal, the conviction was affirmed. The appeals court said that one corpus delicti requirement, proof that Tracey was dead, was satisfied by the evidence that Tracey was very excited to go to the concert, her dogs were left alone at her house, that she normally was in constant contact with her family, and that her credit cards had not been used since her disappearance. The court said the second corpus delicti requirement, that Dennis killed Tracey, was satisfied by the evidence that he knew of the affair and that Tracey wanted a divorce, that he was seen driving Tracey's car after her disappearance, and that shortly after her disappearance he told others he planned to buy a new boat with the money from a life insurance policy on Tracey.

In 1990 the Supreme Court of North Carolina affirmed the first-degree murder conviction of the defendant in the case of *State v. Franklin,*[55] holding that

> [When a] body is found with marks of violence upon it, as was the case here, such evidence establishes *corpus delicti.*
>
> Evidence of *corpus delicti* coupled with the testimony of a cell mate [Woolard] relating inculpatory statements made by the defendant is sufficient to support a conviction.

In this case, according to Woolard, defendant said that he had killed a girl, had been questioned about it, and had gotten away with it. He further told Woolard that the reason he had killed the girl was because she owed him money. The evidence shows that defendant had previously been questioned about Jean Sherman's disappearance but had not been charged with her murder. The evidence further conclusively shows that Jean Sherman owed defendant money for the cocaine she had stolen on the night before her disappearance. All of this evidence, taken as a whole, is sufficient to take the case to the jury, which was then entitled to evaluate its weight. We conclude that the State's evidence, when viewed in the light most favorable to the State, is sufficient to withstand defendant's motion to dismiss. This assignment of error is overruled.

THE SUFFICIENCY-OF-EVIDENCE REQUIREMENT TO JUSTIFY A VERDICT OR FINDING OF GUILT

sufficiency-of-evidence requirement
The demand for a reasonably substantial foundation of evidence to support a verdict or finding.

One of the most common grounds for appeal of a jury verdict or a judge's finding of guilty is insufficiency of evidence (**sufficiency-of-evidence requirement**). In this appeal, the defense argues that there was not sufficient evidence to support the verdict or finding of guilt beyond a reasonable doubt. In the 2012 case of *State v. Pavlicik*[56] the North Dakota Supreme Court said this about the role of an appellate court faced with a claim of insufficient evidence:

> [T]his Court merely reviews the record to determine if there is competent evidence allowing the jury to draw an inference reasonably tending to prove guilt and fairly warranting a conviction. The defendant bears the burden of showing the evidence reveals no reasonable inference of guilt when viewed in the light most favorable to the verdict. When considering insufficiency of the evidence, we will not reweigh conflicting evidence or judge the credibility of witnesses A jury may find a defendant guilty even though evidence exists which, if believed, could lead to a verdict of not guilty.
>
> Although an appeals court does not make an independent determination of the facts but rather defers to the jury findings, the jury's verdict or a judge's finding must be supported and based on legal and substantial evidence. Mere possibilities, suspicion, or conjecture will not support a verdict or finding of guilt. If the evidence is inherently incredible or is contrary to common knowledge and experience or established physical facts, it will not support a finding of guilt.

A defendant may move for a dismissal based on insufficient evidence after the prosecution rests its case, and the trial judge may enter such an order based on its own motion. However, after the jury returns a guilty verdict, generally only the defendant may move for a judgment of dismissal. The trial may not on its own behalf make such an order. Thus, in *State v. Deutscher*,[57] the appellate court reversed a dismissal by the trial judge on its own behalf based on insufficient evidence after a jury verdict.

Either direct or circumstantial evidence will support a finding of guilt if the evidence is legally sufficient to prove all of the essential elements of the crime charged. The Court of Special Appeals of Maryland held in the case of *Metz v. State*[58] that "we feel that the test for sufficiency is the same whether the evidence be direct, circumstantial, or provided by rational inferences therefrom."

THE USE OF PRESUMPTIONS AND INFERENCES
Presumptions

McCormick on Evidence, sec. 342 (Thomson, 6th ed. 2006) states that "presumption is the slipperiest member of the family of legal terms." This is because *presumption* is used in so many ways by different courts.

The following is an example of a jury instruction that must be given to juries in criminal cases. The presumption stated in the jury instruction is ordinarily referred to as the "presumption of innocence." However, some writers and McCormick prefer the term "assumption of innocence."

> The law presumes every person charged with the commission of an offense to be innocent. This presumption attends the defendant throughout the trial and prevails at its close unless overcome by evidence which satisfy the jury of his (or her) guilt beyond a reasonable doubt. The defendant is not required to prove his (or her) innocence.

Is the above presumption "rebuttable" (meaning that it can be "overcome" by evidence showing otherwise)? Yes, it can, but the state must carry this burden "throughout the trial."

Is the above presumption "mandatory" (meaning that the jury must "presume" or "assume" the innocence of the defendant "unless overcome by evidence which satisfy the jury of ... guilt beyond a reasonable doubt")? Yes, it is mandatory.

The terms *conclusive* and *irrebuttable presumptions* are used and defined in different ways by different writers and different courts. The old common-law presumption that a child under age 7 is incapable of committing a crime can be called an irrebuttable or conclusive presumption because it cannot be overcome by evidence showing otherwise. A state could statutorize this presumption as a law, but most states leave the concept in its common-law form.

Most states have a rule that limits the use of presumptions applicable in civil cases in criminal prosecutions. An example is Section 903.03 (2) of the Wisconsin Statutes, which states, "The judge is not authorized to direct the jury to find a presumed fact against the accused." Thus, though in a civil case exceeding the speed limit is presumed to be negligent, a trial judge, who instructed the jury in a homicide by negligent use of a vehicle that it must find negligence if it found the defendant was speeding, was in error, and required reversal of the conviction.[59]

The Supreme Court of Pennsylvania[60] and the Supreme Court of Indiana[61] defined the legal significance and nature of a presumption as follows:

> [A] presumption of law is not evidence nor should it be weighed by the fact finder as though it had evidentiary value. Rather, a presumption is a rule of law enabling the party in whose favor it operates to take his case to the jury without presenting evidence of the fact presumed. It serves as a challenge for proof and indicates the party from whom such proof must be forthcoming. When the opponent of the presumption has met the burden of production thus imposed, however, the office of the presumption has been performed; the presumption is of no further effect and drops from the case.

Inferences Conclusions that may be drawn from facts.

Inferences are reasonable conclusions or deductions that fact finders (juries or judges) *may* draw from the evidence presented to them. Fact finders should use common sense and their knowledge of everyday life in their reasoning process.

Inferences

Whereas a *presumption* is an assumption that the law expressly directs that the trier of fact *must* make, an *inference* is a conclusion that a jury or judge *may* make based on the evidence presented. Many crimes require proof of facts that are not susceptible to direct evidence, but must be inferred by the jury. For example, first-degree murder requires proof of a specific intent to kill. It is not common for witnesses to testify directly about the defendant's stated intent. Thus, in many cases circumstantial evidence must be used to prove the requisite intent. In *State v. White*, 17 A.3d 72 (Conn. App. 2011, the court affirmed a murder conviction based on

CLASSIFICATIONS OF EVIDENCE

Corroborative evidence	Corroborative evidence is evidence that adds weight or **credibility** to a case. In many instances, corroborative evidence is important in carrying the burden of persuasion in the mind of the fact finder. For example, in rape cases, corroborative evidence is important to reinforce the testimony of the victim.
Prima facie evidence	The term *prima facie* is Latin for "at first sight" or "on the face of it." Prima facie evidence is that amount of evidence or that quality of evidence that is sufficient in itself to prove a case. When the state presents a prima facie case, the defense must respond or accept a serious risk of conviction. A prima facie case is a very strong case with sufficient evidence to obtain a conviction.
Conclusive evidence and conflicting evidence	Conclusive evidence is evidence from which only one reasonable conclusion may be drawn. The term *conclusive evidence* is sometimes used in statutes where the legislature requires evidence so strong as to conclusively prove the fact or issue. The term *conflicting evidence* is usually used to indicate a situation where evidence both proving and disproving a fact or issue has been presented, and, depending on the weight and credibility accorded the evidence, the fact finder could find either way.
Cumulative evidence	Cumulative evidence is additional evidence of the same kind that proves the same point as evidence already presented. However, evidence from a different source or evidence of a different kind is not cumulative even though it tends to prove or disprove the same fact or issue. See the U.S. Supreme Court case of *Hamling v. United States* 418 U.S. 87 (2009), discussing cumulative evidence.
Positive and negative evidence	Most evidence is positive evidence in that it is presented in positive terms. Some evidence, however, is presented in negative terms and is referred to as negative evidence. For example, a motorist testifying that he saw a "Construction Ahead" sign on the road is positive evidence. However, another motorist testifying that he did not see any signs is negative evidence. The sign may have been there, but the motorist did not see it. (See 32 C.J.S. Evidence 1079 for discussion and case citations.)
Parole and testimonial evidence	Oral or verbal evidence is parole evidence. If a confession is only verbal, it is a parole confession. Testimonial evidence is the statement of a witness in court, under oath.
Real, tangible, or mere evidence	Tangible, or physical, evidence is evidence such as weapons, illegal drugs, or shoplifted items. Real evidence can be physically brought into court, as in the case of small items, or, in the case of large items like stolen vehicles, can be stored with authorities and photographs or videos of the large items can be brought into court. Clothing worn by the defendant, such as ski masks, sunglasses, hats, or jackets, can be used to link the defendant to the crime. In rape cases, the victim's clothing is often used as evidence.
Other evidence	See Chapters 7 and 8 for *secondhand evidence and hearsay*; see Chapter 16 for *trace evidence and demonstrative evidence*; see Chapter 17 for the best *evidence or original document rule*; and see Chapter 18 for *scientific evidence*.

credibility Believability.

circumstantial evidence. Based on testimony that the defendant and the victim were arguing most of the day of the killing, and that at one point the defendant said, "I'm going to get my gun," the jury could reasonably infer that the resulting gunshot was not an accident (as contended by the defendant) but instead was intentional.

Persons charged with a crime have a constitutional right to a jury trial. Juries in criminal trials, therefore, must decide all issues of fact presented by evidence in

PROCEDURES & PROCESSES

Res Ipsa Loquitur as an Inference

The phrase, doctrine, or rule *res ipsa loquitur* ("the thing speaks for itself") is used in both civil and criminal law. *McCormick on Evidence* (Thomson, 6th ed. 2006) points out that this doctrine is an inference that is permissible but does not require a jury to draw a conclusion.

Example

In a sexual or physical assault case where the victim has been terribly injured, photographs of the battered victim are introduced into evidence and a medical person who attended the victim verifies the accuracy of the photographs.

Whether or not the photographs are contested by the defense, the prosecutor can argue that the photographs speak for themselves in presenting strong evidence proving that the criminal harm and wrong charged in the criminal action did occur (proof of corpus delicti).

The only issue then remaining before the court and jury is the identity of the perpetrator. The defense lawyer could agree that corpus delicti has been proved and take the position "Yes, a terrible crime has occurred, but my client did not commit the crime and is innocent."

the trial. If a jury instruction interferes with or infringes upon the jury's obligation to determine and decide issues of fact, a violation of the defendant's right to jury has occurred.

The defendant's right to a jury was violated in the case of *Sandstrom v. Montana.*[62] The U.S. Supreme Court held that an instruction to a jury that "the law presumes that a person intends the ordinary consequences of his voluntary acts" shifted the burden of proof in Sandstrom's criminal case to the defendant. Because the state must prove all essential elements of the crime charged, the burden-shifting presumption as to the intent of the defendant violated his due process rights.

Juries may infer that a defendant intended "the ordinary consequences of his or her voluntary act," but they cannot be told by a judge in a jury instruction that they have to presume this.

SUMMARY

1. **Distinguish between the burden of production and the burden of persuasion.**
   - The burden of production requires the party with the burden to introduce some evidence of the fact to be proved. The burden of persuasion requires the party with the burden to convince the jury that the evidence is enough to prove the fact exists.

2. **Give a constitutionally acceptable definition of reasonable doubt.**
   - Reasonable doubt does not have to overcome every possible, though unlikely, doubt. Rather, it must be proof that is powerful enough to leave the jury firmly convinced of the defendant's guilt. If there is a real possibility that the defendant is not guilty,

that doubt must be resolved in the favor of the defendant.

3. **Distinguish between direct evidence and circumstantial evidence.**
   - Direct evidence is testimony or physical evidence that by itself proves a fact to be true. Circumstantial evidence is testimony or physical evidence that, if believed, creates a reasonable inference a fact is true.

4. **List some examples of inferences that may be drawn from facts proved.**
   - The fact that the defendant was asleep in the driver's seat of a vehicle parked on the side of a highway may create the inference the defendant drove the vehicle to that spot. The fact that the defendant hid a weapon near the spot he intended to confront the victim may infer intent to harm the victim. The fact that the defendant was seen with a child in one location, and later the child was recovered in another location may infer the defendant was responsible for moving the child between locations. The fact that defendant had a

bloody hand, had stolen goods in his possession, and that a window had been broken by a fist to enter a building may infer the defendant committed burglary.

5. **List some inferences that may not be drawn.**
   - Inferences from past bad acts of the defendant that the defendant has the propensity to commit the crime charged may not be drawn by the jury. Silence of the defendant cannot be used as an inference of guilt. Mandatory inferences are prohibited; the jury must make its own decision to conclude that a fact is proved by inference from other facts.

6. **Define presumption, and state how a presumption may be used in a criminal prosecution.**
   - A presumption is a rule that permits a party to satisfy a burden without introducing other evidence of the fact presumed. In criminal prosecutions, all presumptions relating to any element of the offence charged must be rebuttable, meaning the jury is not required to find the fact based only on the presumption.

KEY TERMS

burden of persuasion, 78

burden of production, 78

circumstantial evidence, 80

corpus delicti, 99

credibility, 103

direct evidence, 80

evidence, 78

impeach, 91

impermissible inference, 90

inferences, 102

permissible inference, 87

probable cause, 93

proof, 78

reasonable doubt, 78

sufficiency-of-evidence requirement, 101

KEY CASES

In re Winship, 397 U.S. 358 (1970): Requires beyond-a-reasonable-doubt standard in criminal prosecutions.

Sandstrom v. Montana, 442 U.S. 510 (1979): States that mandatory or irrebuttable presumptions are unconstitutional in criminal prosecutions.

State v. Barker, 945 N.E.2d 1107 (Ohio App. 2010): States corpus delicti rule and requirement of independent circumstantial evidence in addition to confessions in murder prosecutions.

Thompson v. United States, 546 A.2d 419 (D.C. App.1988): States why evidence of prior bad acts is

inadmissible if only offered to prove character or propensity of the defendant.

United States v. Roche, 916 F.2d 219 (5th Cir. 1990): States that Fifth Amendment prohibits trial court or prosecutor from commenting on silence of the defendant or the defendant's failure to testify.

United States v. Williams, 128 S. Ct. 1830 (2008): Held PROTECT Act constitutional.

Victor v. Nebraska, 511 U.S. 1 (1994): Gives the wording of a satisfactory jury instruction on the meaning of reasonable doubt.

PROBLEMS

1. A New York state trooper saw a car traveling at an excessive rate of speed on the New York Thruway. The officer overtook the speeding vehicle and stopped it. Four men were in the vehicle, two in the front seat and two in the back seat. While the officer was asking the driver for his license and vehicle registration, the officer smelled burning marijuana. The officer then saw an envelope marked "Super-gold" lying on the floor of the car between the two men in the front seat.

   The evidence that was available to the officer permitted him to draw an inference about which of the men possessed the marijuana. Did the evidence and the inference drawn from the evidence establish probable cause to arrest the driver? The two men in the front seat? Can it be inferred from the evidence that probable cause existed to arrest all four men? Explain. *New York v. Belton*, 453 U.S. 454, 101 S. Ct. 2860 (1981).

2. A guard at the state prison in Walpole, Massachusetts, heard loud voices coming from a walkway. The officer immediately opened the door to the walkway and saw "an inmate named Stephens bleeding from the mouth and suffering from a swollen eye. Dirt was strewn about the walkway, which the officer viewed to be further evidence of a scuffle." The officer saw three inmates, including an inmate named Hill, jogging away together down the walkway. There were no other inmates in the area, which was enclosed by a chain-link fence. The officer concluded that the three men acted as a group in assaulting Stephens. There was no evidence as to who actually beat Stephens. Was there sufficient evidence to punish Hill as one of the three men involved in the assault by taking away his good-time credits? Explain. *Superintendent, Mass. Correctional Institution, Walpole v. Hill*, 472 U.S. 445, 105 S. Ct. 2768, 37 CrL 3108 (1985).

3. Kent Hansen was sitting on a public park bench close to a man who was smoking a marijuana cigarette. When an officer in plain clothes saw the marijuana cigarette and smelled burning marijuana, he arrested both men. The officer did not see Hansen holding or smoking the marijuana cigarette. Could the officer properly infer from the information he had that Hansen was an active participant in the use or possession of the marijuana? Should Hansen's conviction be affirmed? Give reasons for your answer. *State of Arizona v. Hansen*, 573 P.2d 896 (Ariz. App. 1977).

4. An experienced law enforcement officer used the following incident as an example for classes. The officer's wife was babysitting their 3-year-old grandson while the parents were away. No one else was in the house when the grandmother put the child to bed for an afternoon nap. A short time later, while the grandmother was in the basement, she heard a crash and ran back upstairs. When she entered the child's room, she saw the window drapes lying across the bed and on the floor. Because the child had the means and opportunity of pulling the drapes down, the grandmother said to the child, "Why did you pull the drapes down?" The child looked his grandmother in the eye and replied, "You didn't see me do it, and you can't prove that I did it." List the evidence available to the grandmother that caused her to conclude that the child pulled the drapes down. Indicate whether this evidence was direct or circumstantial.

   If this situation was presented to a jury, would they be justified in drawing the same conclusion that the grandmother did? Would a jury's verdict of guilty be sustained by the trial court and the appellate court in that there was sufficient evidence to sustain the jury's finding?

5. A young woman wakes up in a bed in a hotel. Her state of dress appears to have been altered from that of the previous evening. The man who took her to the hotel had a bottle of Rohypnol, the "date rape" drug, in his possession. Experts testified that the woman had been drugged with Rohypnol. The woman has no memory of being raped, and there is no physical evidence of sexual intercourse. The man states that he simply watched the woman sleep. Is the evidence sufficient to convict the man of rape? If not, what other evidence might you look for? See *Sera v. Norris*, 400 F.3d 538 (8th Cir. 2005).

CASE ANALYSIS

Read Appendix B, Finding and Analyzing Cases (p. 499). With these guidelines in mind, please continue with the Case Analysis selections for Chapter 4.

1. Proving the sender of an e-mail message can be a problem. Rule 901 of the Federal Rules of Evidence requires that items like e-mails be authenticated, to show they are "what the proponent claims" they are. How is that to be done with an e-mail when no witnesses can testify they saw the e-mail sent? How does the e-mail get "authenticated? Compare the result in *United States v. Fluker*, 698 F.3d 988 (7th Cir. 2012) with *Devbrow v. Gallagos*, 735 F.3d 684 (7th Cir. 2013). What was different?

2. A similar problem can arise when the prosecution seeks to introduce posts to social media like a defendant's Facebook page. Social media posts can be falsified. How does the prosecution prove the posts it wants in as evidence were done by the defendant? Consider the "content rule," evidenced by *Parker v. State*, 85 A.3d 682 (Del. 2014), and the more restrictive requirement of documentation of the Internet history of the defendant's computer exemplified by *Griffin v. State*, 19 A.3d 415 (Md. 2011). Which is the better rule?

3. Many, perhaps most, murder convictions are based on circumstantial evidence. When an appeals court reviews a jury verdict of guilty, the "insufficient evidence" claim will almost always be part of the appeal. As we saw in this chapter, appellate courts do not easily overthrow a jury verdict based on the sufficiency of the evidence. Read the opinion in *State v. Carver*, 725 S.E.2nd 902 (N.C. App. 2014). What was the circumstantial evidence produced by the prosecution? Are you convinced? Do you think the "magic" of DNA evidence played a role in the verdict? Should it?

4. In many criminal prosecutions, convicting a defendant of the crime charged also entitles the prosecution to seize money used in or derived from the crime. What about seizing money before conviction, with the result the defendants can't afford to hire a lawyer? Is the grand jury's probable cause finding the money was connected to the crime enough to permit seizure? Should it be? The U.S. Supreme Court thinks so: *Kaley v. United States*, 134 S. Ct. 1090 (2014). Do you agree?

Notes

1. *In re Winship,* 397 U.S. 358, 364 (1970).
2. *Commonwealth v. Webster,* 59 Mass. 295, 320 (1850). In *Apodaca v. Oregon*, 406 U.S. 404, 412 (1972), the Supreme Court noted that following *Webster*, courts in the United States began using the "reasonable doubt" standard in criminal cases.
3. *In re Winship*, supra.
4. *Victor v. Nebraska*, 511 U.S. 1 (1994).
5. *Cage v. Louisiana*, 498 U.S. 39, 40 (1990).
6. *Sandoval v. California*, 511 U.S. 1, 6 (1994).
7. *Victor v. Nebraska*, *supra*, at 23 (Justice Ginsburg concurring).
8. Elisabeth Stoffelmayr and Shari S. Diamond, "The Conflict Between Precision and Flexibility in Explaining 'Beyond a Reasonable Doubt,'" 6 *Psychol. Pub. Pol'y & L.* 769 (2000).
9. Federal Judicial Center, *Pattern Criminal Jury Instructions* (1988), p. 21.
10. The Supreme Court of Louisiana pointed out that "[s]pecific intent to kill or inflict great bodily harm can easily be inferred where an individual discharges a firearm pointed directly at a victim from a short distance." *State v. Noble,* 425 So.2d 734 (La. 1983). The Supreme Court of Indiana approved of the following jury instruction in the case of *Henderson v. State*, 544 N.E.2d 507 (1989), where intent to steal had to be proved to convict Henderson of burglary:

[Y]ou may infer that a person is presumed to intend the natural and probable acts, unless the circumstances are such to indicate the absence of such intent. When an unlawful act, however, is proved to be knowingly done, no further proof is needed on the part of the state in the absence of justifying or excusing facts.

The Supreme Court of North Carolina affirmed the first-degree murder conviction of the defendant in the 1990 case of *State v. Porter* (391 S.E.2d 144). To prove intent to kill, the defendant's statement

"I meant to kill the s-of-a-b-." (direct evidence) was used, as was the fact that he "pumped three rounds into the body" of his girlfriend (circumstantial evidence of intent).

State of mind in attempted murder or assault in the first degree can be shown by circumstantial evidence, as was done in the 1991 case of *State v. Turner* (587 A.2d 1050), where the Connecticut Appellate Court held,

> The intent of the actor is a question for the trier of fact, and the conclusion of the trier in this regard should stand unless it is an unreasonable one." *State v. Avcollie*, 178 Conn. 450, 466, 423 A.2d 118 (1979), *cert. denied*, 444 U.S. 1015, 100 S. Ct. 667, 62 L.Ed.2d 645 (1980).

The jury was free to credit the testimony that the defendant pointed the loaded gun at Russell and pulled the trigger, and that the gun clicked but did not fire. Crediting this testimony, we cannot say that an inference that the defendant intended to inflict serious physical injury on Russell was either unreasonable or illogical. "It was within the province of the [trier] to draw reasonable and logical inferences from the facts proven." *State v. Avcollie, supra,* 178 Conn. at 470, 423 A.2d 118. Also, the jury can draw an inference from the facts they found as the result of other inferences. Thus, the evidence presented at trial amply supported the existence of the requisite intent.

In the 1991 case of *Commonwealth v. Chester* (587 A.2d 1367), the Supreme Court of Pennsylvania held that the slashing of a victim's throat was sufficient evidence to support a jury's finding that the killing was intentional.

The crime of theft requires proof of a specific intent to steal, which is almost always proven by inferences drawn from the defendant's conduct. In the case of *Morissette v. United States*, 72 S. Ct. 240 (1952), Morissette took rusted bomb casings that had been lying for years in a wooded area. For all his hard work, Morissette made $84. He was charged with theft and argued that he honestly believed the junk to be abandoned, unwanted, and of no value to the government. The trial judge instructed the jury that the government did not have to prove criminal intent for this crime and refused to allow Morissette's defense of honest mistake of fact. The U.S. Supreme Court reversed the trial judge, ruling that the specific intent to steal must be proven beyond a reasonable doubt and that juries must be properly instructed as to the law.

11. 626 A.2d 1238 (Pa. Super. 1993).
12. The inference that a person who has possession of recently stolen property is the thief is not used in many states. The validity of this inference, however, was tested in the U.S. Supreme Court in 1992. In the case of *Wright v. West* (112 S. Ct. 2482), the defendant was charged with grand larceny for the possession in his home of many household items stolen from another home two to four weeks earlier.

The defendant was convicted under a Virginia law that permits "an inference that a person who fails to explain, or falsely explains, his exclusive possession of recently stolen property is the thief." The court affirmed the defendant's conviction, holding that the evidence was sufficient to justify the conviction.

In the 1991 case of *Buchannon v. State*, 405 S.E.2d 583 (Ga. App.), the police stopped the defendant while he was driving a stolen car. The defendant and his passenger both gave false names to the police and had an explanation for the defendant's possession of the stolen car. The Georgia jury did not believe the defendant and convicted him of theft of the car.

Many prosecutors would not have charged theft in the *West* and *Buchannon* cases. Under the law of most states, crimes such as possession (receiving or concealing) of stolen property and operating a motor vehicle without the consent of the owner are charged because they are much easier to prove.

13. 966 F.2d 707 (1st Cir.).
14. 2011 WL 1076751 (E.D. Ca. 2011). The 9th Circuit Court of Appeals affirmed the trial court on appeal. That opinion appears at 475 Fed. Appx. 128 (9th Cir. 2012), *cert. denied* 133 S. Ct. 277 (2012). At times a Federal court of appeals may decide that an opinion in a case should not be published in the *Federal Reporter*, usually because the court believes the case has limited value as precedent. When that happens, the case is published in the *Federal Appendix*. Rule 32.1 (A) of the Federal Rules of Appellate Procedure, passed in 2007, states that all federal court decisions, published or unpublished, may be cited as authority in an appeals brief.
15. 348 U.S. 121, 139, 75 S. Ct. 127, 137.
16. 932 So.2d 736 (La. App. 2006), *rev. denied*, 957 So.2d 165 (La. 2007).
17. *See State v. Flynn*, 55 P.3d 324 (Kan. 2002).
18. See, for example, *Cantrell v. Commonwealth*, 329 S.E.2d 22 (Va. S.Ct. 1985).
19. *CHV v. Wisconsin*, 643 N.W.2d 878 (2002), *cert. denied,* 123 S. Ct. 443 (2002).
20. 524 A.2d 575 (R.I. S. Ct. 1987).
21. 2014 WL 1225113 (Ariz. App. 2014).
22. 590 N.E.2d 1177 (Mass. App 1992).
23. 38 A.3d 882 (Pa. Super. 2012), *rev. denied* 60 A.3d 535 (Pa. 2013).
24. *Review denied* 969 N.E.2d 718 (Mass. 2012).
25. *E.g., State v. McInnis*, 988 A.2d 999 (Me. 2010).
26. 546 A.2d at 419 (D.C. App.).

27. 2012 WL 5395345 (Neb. 2012).

28. 583 N.W.2d 680 (Mich. 1998).

29. P.L. 103-322.

30. Federal Rules of Evidence 413(a) and 414(a).

31. 2012 WL 4829813 (Ark. 2012).

32. 380 U.S. 609 (1965).

33. *Wainwright v. Greenfield*, 474 U.S. 284 (1986).

34. *Fletcher v. Weir*, 455 U.S. 603 (1982).

35. *Jenkins v. Anderson*, 447 U.S. 231 (1980).

36. *See United States v. Frazier*, 408 F.3d 1102 (8th Cir. 2005) (silence may be used in case-in-chief); *United States v. Velarde-Gomez*, 269 F.3d 1023 (9th Cir. 2001) (silence can't be used in case-in-chief). State courts are more in agreement: *Weitzel v. State*, 863 A.2d 999 (Md. 2004), and *State v. VanWinkle*, 273 P.3d 1148 (Az. 2012), are cases where courts found use of silence by the prosecution in its case-in-chief violated the Fifth Amendment.

37. *See United States v. Okatan*, 728 F.3d 111 (2nd Cir. 2013) (silence can't be used in case-in-chief) and cases discussed therein.

38. 582 A.2d 341.

39. 156 P.3d 1145 (Az. App. 2007).

40. 612 A.2d 1349, 52 CrL 1014.

41. 963 F.2d 708 (5th Cir. 1992).

42. The crime of transfer of an illegal drug also has a higher penalty than the crime of possession of the illegal drug. In the case of *Meek v. Mississippi*, 806 So.2d 236 (2002), *cert. denied*, U.S. Supreme Court, it was held that the inference that the defendant knew that marijuana was in a toilet kit he transferred was reasonable and proper. In the *Meek* case, the defendant was injured in a car crash. A passing motorist attempted to help the defendant, and in the course of doing so, the defendant handed the motorist a shaving kit and asked him to "get rid of it." When the police arrived, the motorist gave the kit to them. When the kit was discovered to contain marijuana, the defendant was charged with the crime of transfer of marijuana. The court held that the evidence was sufficient to prove the defendant knew the kit contained illegal drugs when he transferred it to the motorist.

43. 406 S.E.2d 833.

44. 923 F.2d 548 (7th Cir. 1991).

45. 747 F. Supp. 528 (N.D. Iowa 1989).

46. See 18 U.S.C. 1462.

47. 347 F.3d 893 (11th Cir. 2003).

48. 128 S. Ct. 1830 (2008).

49. 18 U.S.C. 2252(A)(a)(3)(B).

50. 563 A.2d 158.

51. 405 S.E.2d 1, 5 (Va. App.).

52. 597 So.2d 721 (Ala. 1991).

53. 807 P.2d 1009 (Cal. 1991).

54. See 23 CJS, *Criminal Law*, 917.

55. 393 S.E.2d 781.

56. 819 N.W.2d 521 (N.D. 2012).

57. 766 N.W.2d 442 (S.D. 2009).

58. 262 A.2d 331, 335 (Md. App. 1970).

59. *State v. Dyess*, 370 N.W.2d 222 (Wis. 1985).

60. *Commonwealth v. Vogel*, 268 A.2d 89, 102 (Pa. 1970).

61. *Sumpter v. State,* 261 Ind. 471, 306 N.E.2d 95 (1974).

62. 442 U.S. 510, 99 S. Ct. 2450 (1979).

Witnesses and the Testimony of Witnesses

AN ATTORNEY PRESENTS AN EXHIBIT TO A WITNESS

AP Images/Jack Kurtz

LEARNING OBJECTIVES

In this chapter we examine the role of witnesses in criminal trials. The learning objectives for this chapter are

List the general qualifications for being a witness.

List the special qualifications for child witnesses.

Identify the factors important in determining the credibility of a witness.

List the constitutional rights of a defendant related to witnesses.

State the difference between a lay witness and an expert witness.

Read and understand Rule 702 of the Federal Rules of Evidence.

List some objections that may be made to questions to a witness or answers by a witness.

he testimony of witnesses generally provides evidence of the disputed facts for resolution by the fact-finder; in criminal cases this is usually the jury. One of the functions delegated to the jury is the determination of the credibility (truthfulness) of a witness and the testimony given by the witness. It is up to the jury to decide who is telling the truth.

Assume you have been charged with filing a false income tax return, a federal crime. The prosecution plans to present three witnesses who will testify about your alleged fraudulent acts. You know this about the witnesses: Witness 1 entered into a "sham" marriage 25 years ago in order to gain entry into this country under immigration laws permitting such entry for persons married to U.S. citizens; Witness 2 has committed many acts of marital infidelity; Witness 3 has made a false statement in a letter to the U.S. Immigration office seeking a permit to travel abroad.

Would you like to cross-examine the witnesses and ask about these specific past acts? Why? Should you be permitted to do so? Consult Rule 608 (b) of the Federal Rules of Evidence (Appendix C of this book), and the case of *United States v. Ulloa*, 942 F. Supp.2d 202 (D.N.H. 2013).

QUALIFICATIONS NECESSARY TO BE A WITNESS

witness Person who appears and testifies under oath or affirmation before civil and criminal courts and other hearings.

Witnesses are essential in all cases. Without witnesses, neither civil nor criminal cases could commence.[1] In order to be a **witness**, a person must satisfy the following requirements:

Requirement of personal knowledge: The witness must have some personal knowledge of the matter before the court. The term "personal knowledge" is defined in Black's Law Dictionary (9th ed., 2009) as "knowledge gained through firsthand observation or experience, as distinguished from a belief based on what someone has said." Most lay witnesses give testimony about facts that can be perceived by the senses. As a result, their testimony is competent only if they have had an opportunity to observe the facts and actually did observe the facts. In the treatise McCormack, *Evidence* (Thomson, 6th ed., 2006), §10, a distinction is drawn between *incompetent witnesses* and *incompetent evidence*. That section states that a witness who has no personal knowledge of a fact is not a competent witness as to that fact, because the witness is guessing or speculating about the fact. A witness who testifies to information provided by another person is in theory a *competent witness* to the information, because the witness has personal knowledge of the information. However, "the evidence (hearsay) is inadmissible because the evidence is incompetent."

Requirement to declare that testimony is truthful: Most witnesses take an oath swearing that they will tell the truth. However, the Federal Rules of Evidence (Rule 602) and the Uniform Rules of Evidence also provide for an *affirmation*, which, like the oath, requires "every witness ... to declare that he will testify truthfully."

competency The fitness or ability of an individual to participate in legal proceedings.

Requirement of competency: In addition to competency as having personal knowledge, a witness most also demonstrate competency to function as a witness. The usual modern standard for determining the **competency** of a witness is that "Competency depends upon the witness' capacity to observe, remember and narrate as well as an understanding of the duty to tell the truth."[2]

The General Presumption That Adults Are Competent to Be Witnesses

Because the law presumes that adults are competent, most adult witnesses take the witness stand and testify without being challenged. The competency of a witness may be challenged based on the witness's inability to "perceive, remember, or narrate" the circumstances, or inability "to understand the duty to tell the truth."

Competency of witnesses can thus relate both to the ability of the witnesses to testify about the particular event when they witnessed the event, and to circumstances that cast doubt on the present ability to remember or narrate the event. Thus, a witness whose mental state renders her incapable of comprehending the event about which she seeks to testify can be judged incompetent. An example of this kind of incompetence is a witness who was so intoxicated at the time the witnessed event occurred that the witness lacked the capacity to properly observe and remember the event. Where the witness possessed the capacity to accurately observe the event but subsequently lost the mental faculties necessary to remember and testify about the event, the witness lacks the competence to testify. This could happen where the witness becomes mentally unstable or where some physical condition affects the memory of the witness.

The party contending the witness is incompetent has the burden of proving the witness completely lacks the ability to properly perceive or remember the circumstances in the testimony. In the case of an alleged mental illness of a witness a trial judge could order a psychiatric examination, but only if there is shown to be a "compelling need" for such an examination. See *Com. v. Boich*, 982 A2d 102 (Pa. Super. 2009), *appeal denied*, 3 A.3d 669 (Pa. 2010).

A witness is not normally judged incompetent based on circumstances that affect only the credibility of the witness. Thus, in *United States v. Bedonie*,[3] a witness was not found incompetent to testify simply because the witness had previously made several prior inconsistent statements. Also, in cases where the prosecutor presents testimony by paid informants, the fact that the informant was paid to testify does not usually render the witness incompetent (*United States v. Cresta*[4]). In these cases, the jury can decide what effect, if any, the circumstances should have on the credibility of the testimony given by the witness.

Children as Witnesses

If a young child is called as a witness, the trial judge first questions (voir dire—see below) the child to determine whether the child is competent to testify. The child must be able to remember what occurred, tell about the events, and know that he or she must be truthful. The trial judge then rules on the child's competence as a witness. The judge has broad discretion, and a court of appeals will not disturb the judge's ruling unless there was a clear abuse of that discretion.[5]

The Supreme Court of Arizona traced the history of child witnesses in the case of *State v. Schossow*,[6] where it was held that four children (aged 7 to 9) were competent to testify:

> At common law no child under fourteen years of age was eligible to testify as a witness. ... It was not until 1779 that the law renounced the rule of absolute disqualification. In *Rex v. Brasier*, 1 Leach 199, 168 Eng. Rep. 202 (1779), the court held that a child less than seven years old was competent to testify "*provided* such infant appears, *on strict examination by the court*, to possess a sufficient knowledge of the nature and consequences of an oath...." The United States Supreme Court followed the *Brasier*

rule in *Wheeler v. United States*, 159 U.S. 523, 16 S.Ct. 93, 40 L.Ed. 244 (1895), and held that a five-year-old child was competent to testify in a criminal trial for murder. The Court stated that the decision of this question rests primarily with the trial judge, who sees the proposed witness, notices his manner, his apparent possession or lack of intelligence, and *may resort to any examination* which will tend to disclose his capacity and intelligence.

The age of the child is important but not determinative. For example, in *Commonwealth v. Monzon*,[7] a 5-year-old child was judged competent to testify in a criminal case, but her 6-year-old sister was not. The older child told the judge she did not know the difference between telling the truth and lying, whereas the younger child was able to make that distinction.

Today most states and the federal government have statutes or court rules that enable children to appear as witnesses without specific age limitations. 18 U.S.C. §3509 (c) (2) (2009), which applies to children testifying as either victims of sexual abuse or as witnesses to a crime committed against another, states that "A child is presumed to be competent." A court will order a competency hearing only if "compelling reasons" for such an examination are shown. Furthermore, the only function of the examination is to determine if the child is capable of "understanding and answering simple questions." (§3509 (c) (8).

An example of guidelines used by courts when the competency of a child witness is challenged is the tests adopted by the Washington Supreme Court. In the 2011 case of *State v. Brousseau*[8] the court affirmed the trial court's holding that a 7-year-old child was competent to testify in the rape trial of her alleged assailant. Noting that under RCW 5.60.050 all persons, including children, are presumed to be competent to testify, the court stated factors a trial judge considering a challenge to a child witness should evaluate:

> (1) an understanding of the obligation to speak the truth on the witness stand; (2) the mental capacity at the time of the occurrence to receive an accurate impression of it; (3) a memory sufficient to retain an independent recollection of the occurrence; (4) the capacity to express his memory of the occurrence; and (5) the capacity to understand simple questions about it.

Voir Dire

voir dire The preliminary examination of a prospective juror or certain witnesses, such as an expert or a child witness, to determine qualifications.

The phrase **voir dire** comes from medieval French and roughly means "to speak the truth." The term describes the preliminary examination used to determine whether a witness or juror is competent or qualified.

Persons who are selected to serve on a jury are questioned before trial at a voir dire procedure. In some states the judge asks the questions; in others the lawyers for the prosecution and defense ask the questions. These questions help to provide a fair trial by excusing from the jury persons who for some reason would be unable or unwilling to deliver a fair, unbiased verdict.

In the case of expert witnesses, voir dire refers to the questions an opposing party asks when a proposed expert is called to testify by the other party. The party calling an expert witness must establish the witness's qualifications to give expert testimony. If the other party objects to the witness's qualifications, the other party may ask questions to support that objection. The trial judge then must decide if the witness is qualified to give expert testimony.

The voir dire of a young child whom one of the parties seeks to use as a witness is a series of questions to determine whether the child has the perception, memory, and ability to testify as a witness in that case.

CREDIBILITY OF WITNESSES

Methods Used to Keep Witnesses Honest

Witnesses have a serious responsibility to tell the truth. To encourage witnesses to tell the truth and to bring before the court and the jury the facts pertaining to the issues of the case, the following procedures are used:

- Witnesses must take an oath or affirmation that they will tell the truth.
- Witnesses must be personally present at the trial (the defendant's Sixth Amendment right to confront witnesses must be ensured).[9]
- Witnesses are subject to cross-examination.

In addition, witnesses who do not tell the truth run the risk of being charged with *perjury.* If they refuse to testify or refuse to answer questions that are not privileged, they could be found in *contempt of court* and punished.

Credibility and the Weight of Evidence

It is up to a judge or jury, as the trier of fact, to determine whether statements made by witnesses are to be believed and what weight to give them. In determining the **credibility** and the weight to be given to the testimony of witnesses, the following factors should be considered:

- *Perception:* Did the witness perceive (see, hear, smell, and so on) accurately? Did the witness have an opportunity to observe and perceive?
- *Memory:* Has the witness retained an accurate impression of what the witness saw, heard, smelled, and so on? Is the witness's memory of the events accurate?
- *Narration by the witness:* Do the testimony of the witness and the language used accurately describe the events?

In determining the weight and the credit to be given to the testimony of each witness, juries and judges as the triers of fact also use their knowledge and experience. Witness statements that are incredible or contrary to commonly known facts do not have to be accepted. The *incontrovertible physical facts rule* (also known as the *physical facts rule*) holds that the fact-finding body will give no weight to witness statements that are inherently incredible, unbelievable, and contrary to physical facts, known physical laws, general knowledge, or human experience.[10]

The reasonableness of witnesses' testimony, their interest or lack of interest in the results of the trial, their bias or prejudice (if any is shown), their clearness or lack of clearness of recollection, and the overall impression obtained by the jury are factors used in determining the weight and credit to be given to the testimony of a witness.

In a jury trial, the jury is the sole judge of the credibility of all witnesses, including the defendant if he or she takes the witness stand. The jury evaluates the weight and credibility of testimony, free from the influence of the trial judge.

PROTECTING AND HELPING CHILD VICTIMS AND WITNESSES

Being the victim of a crime is a terrible experience, but the crime itself may be just the beginning of the trauma. The child victim is often grilled repeatedly about the crime by a succession of total strangers (police officers, social workers, lawyers, and others). Court appearances could make the nightmare worse, especially for children who are victims of sex offenses. 18 U.S.C. § 3509, applicable in federal cases, permits as alternatives to live, in-court testimony by children, live testimony using closed-circuit television, or videotaped deposition testimony. If the child is threatened by the presence of the defendant, the defendant can be physically absent during the testimony, but must be permitted to view the child on a television monitor as the child testifies. To protect children and minimize emotional damage, states have enacted statutes to help children in the following ways:

- *Testimony by closed-circuit television:* In *Coy v. Iowa*, 487 U.S. 1012 (1988) the U S. Supreme Court held it was improper to place a screen between a child witness and the defendant without showing there was a need for such a screen. However, when a "child [is] suffering serious emotional distress," closed-circuit testimony was allowed by the U.S. Supreme Court in the 1990 case of *Maryland v. Craig* 497 U.S. 836, 842, 110 S. Ct. 3157, 3162, where this procedure was approved under a Maryland statute. The trial court found that the child witnesses were so traumatized that they could not "reasonably communicate." The Supreme Court held in *Craig* that the face-to-face right to confront an accusing witness is not absolute and "must occasionally give way to considerations of public policy and the necessities of the case." More than 30 states have statutes permitting this procedure when it is shown to be needed.
- *Videotaped testimony:* In criminal child abuse proceedings, videotapes are used in more than 35 states.
- *Statutes making it easier for children to be found competent to testify:* Such statutes have been enacted in all states to enable children as young as three years of age to appear as witnesses.
- *Special hearsay exceptions for child victims and child witnesses:* The Supreme Court's decision in *Washington v. Crawford*, discussed in Chapter 8 of this book, may limit the admissibility of some child hearsay. See Chapter 8 for a discussion of child hearsay exceptions.

Other statutes that seek to help and protect children include the following:

- *Use of anatomical dolls in criminal child abuse cases:* These dolls make it easier for child witnesses because they can point to body parts as they testify. Some states have statutes authorizing the practice, whereas others use the practice as part of accepted court procedure.
- *Closing the courtroom to all but necessary parties:* Having fewer people in the courtroom make a child victim or witness feel more comfortable while testifying. Many judges have this power; some states have statutes authorizing it.
- *Use of leading questions with child witnesses:* Most state judges can permit this, and a few states now have statutes authorizing it.
- *Limiting the length of time a child is on the witness stand:* A few states have statutes authorizing this, but judges in all states may limit cross-examination under their broad discretion in the conduct of criminal and civil trials.
- *Limiting the number of interviews with child victims:* In 1992 a California grand jury reported that some child victims were interviewed as many as 32 times. California and other states now have statutes limiting the number of interviews.
- *Statutes requiring speedy handling of cases involving child victims:* These have been enacted by more than half of the states.

FALSE MEMORY OR "TAINT"

When children testify as victims in criminal trials, particularly in sexual offenses, a defendant sometimes challenges the child's competency to testify based on a theory called "false memory" or "taint." (The related false memory syndrome is discussed in note 57 of this chapter.) The basis of a taint claim was stated by the Pennsylvania Supreme Court in *Commonwealth v. Delbridge* [855 A.2d 27, 35 (2003)] as follows:

> Taint is the implantation of false memories or the distortion of real memories caused by interview techniques of law enforcement, social service personnel, and other interested adults, that are so unduly suggestive and coercive as to infect the memory of the child, rendering that child incompetent to testify.

Defendants asserting the taint claim attempt to exclude a child's testimony based on these factors, claiming the taint results in the child testifying not to what actually happened but to what was suggested to the child. Some courts permit a defendant to subject a child witness to a competency hearing to explore the taint claim,[a] whereas others do not, on the theory that taint goes only to credibility, not competency.[b]

Where taint hearings are permitted, additional questions arise about the admissibility of expert testimony and about whether a child witness has or has not been "tainted" by interrogation techniques. Some courts exclude expert testimony on taint, finding that there is inadequate scientific foundation to support the theory (see Chapter 18). Other courts exclude it because the expert testimony improperly enhances the child's testimony or addresses the credibility of the testimony, which should be the function of the jury.

Finally, it is not clear if the defendant has a right to be present at a "taint" hearing. In *Kentucky v. Stincer*, 482 U.S. 730 (1987) the U.S. Supreme Court held that the Constitution does not require the presence of a defendant for a hearing to determine the competency of a child witness. However, many state courts disagree, and conclude that "taint" questioning goes well beyond simple questions about competency, and involves questions that go to the substance of the crimes charged. In such cases, the defendant has the right to be present at the "taint" hearing. (See *Woyak v. State*, 226 P.3d 841 (Wyo. 2010).)

[a]See, for example, *State v. Michaels*, 642 A.2d 1372 (N.J. 1992).
[b]For example, *Pendleton v. Kentucky*, 83 S.W.3d 522 (Ky. 2002).

Eyewitness Testimony

The testimony of an eyewitness to a crime is usually important to both the prosecution and the defendant. If the testimony is credible, the jury is likely to give it great weight. Because eyewitnesses can, and often do, make a mistaken identification (see Chapter 13) state and federal courts have developed standards for evaluating eyewitness testimony. The U.S. Supreme Court case of *Neil v. Biggers*,[11] discussed in Chapter 13, stated the test for evaluating eyewitness identifications. An eyewitness identification is unreliable, and thus inadmissible, if there is the likelihood of "irreparable misidentification." The *Neil* court said that factors to consider when evaluating the likelihood of misidentification are the opportunity of the witness to view the criminal at the time of the crime, the witness's degree of attention, the accuracy of the witness's prior description of the criminal, the witness's level of certainty, and the length of time between the identification and the crime.

Many states have adopted similar rules. For example, in *State v. Hollen*,[12] the Utah Supreme Court held that the eyewitness testimony of four victims of a robbery at an amusement park was reliable and admissible. The court stated that under the

Utah Constitution, unreliable eyewitness testimony is not admissible. The reliability of an eyewitness's identification depends on five factors, the court stated:

1. The opportunity of the witness to view the actor during the event
2. The witness's degree of attention to the actor at the time of the event
3. The witness's capacity to observe the event, including his or her physical and mental acuity
4. Whether the witness's identification was made spontaneously and remained consistent thereafter, or whether it was the product of suggestion
5. The nature of the event being observed and the likelihood that the witness would perceive, remember, and relate it correctly

Demeanor as Evidence in Determining Witness Credibility

Not only are the words of the witness evidence in a trial, but the demeanor of the witness also has been held to be evidence that may be used in determining credibility. In everyday life, we judge other people not only by what they say but also to some extent by their appearances and their conduct. Judge Learned Hand's ruling in the 1952 case of *Dyer v. MacDougall*[13] is sometimes quoted by other courts:

> It is true that the carriage, behavior, bearing, manner and appearance of a witness—in short, his "demeanor"—is a part of the evidence. The words used are by no means all that we rely on in making up our minds about the truth of a question that arises in our ordinary affairs, and it is abundantly settled that a jury is as little confined to them as we are. They may, and indeed they should, take into consideration the whole nexus of sense impressions which they get from a witness.

In the case of *Michigan v. Sammons*,[14] a Michigan court of appeals held that permitting an informant to wear a ski mask at a hearing on whether entrapment occurred violated the defendant's Sixth Amendment right to confront the witness. The court held that the mask prevented the judge from observing the informer's demeanor and adequately assessing his credibility. The U.S. Supreme Court denied review of the case.[15] In the 2004 Texas case of *Romero v. State*,[16] the court reversed a defendant's assault conviction because a key witness was permitted to testify with sunglasses, a baseball hat, and an upturned coat collar. The witness told prosecutors he was frightened to testify in the defendant's presence and would do so only if permitted to wear a disguise. The court of appeals held that the disguise attached improper drama and emphasis to the testimony and forced the defendant to ask the witness why he was wearing a disguise, thereby prejudicing the jury against the defendant.

In *State v. Hernandez*, 986 A.2d 480 (N.H. 2009) the court upheld the trial court's decision to let an undercover police officer testify wearing a ski mask, because it was necessary to keep the officer's identity a secret. The appeals court noted the decision in *Maryland v. Craig*, discussed previously, where the U.S. Supreme Court said that absolute "face-to-face" was not required where satisfactory reasons existed for more limited confrontation. The trial court gave a specific jury instruction that the use of the ski mask should not give the testimony either more or less weight or credibility.

WITNESSES AND THEIR TESTIMONY

In order to qualify as a witness, a person:
- Must have relevant information
- Must be competent
- Must declare that he or she will testify truthfully

To be competent, a witness:
- Must be able to remember and tell what happened
- Must be able to distinguish fact from fantasy
- Must know that he or she must tell the truth

In evaluating a witness's testimony, the fact finder should consider:
- Accuracy of perception
- Accuracy of memory and recall
- Accuracy of narration

American law seeks to keep witnesses honest by having them testify:
- Under oath or affirmation
- In the presence of the fact finder and the accused
- Subject to cross-examination
- Subject to possible perjury charges for failure to tell the truth

Methods used to help forgetful witnesses include:
- Jogging the memory by questions such as "What else happened at this point?"
- Handing reports, notes, files, and so on to the witness to refresh his or her memory
- Introducing the documents as evidence if refreshing memory does not work and documents exist

Vouching

All courts agree that it is the exclusive function of the jury (where, as is usually the case, the fact-finder is a jury, not the trial judge) to evaluate the credibility of a witness and the witness's testimony. One consequence of this rule is the prohibition of what courts call "vouching." Vouching occurs when the credibility of a witness is enhanced or detracted by statements made by other witnesses, or by comments made by an attorney in closing argument before the jury. For example, unless the other side has attacked the truthfulness of Witness A's testimony, it is improper and inadmissible for Witness B to testify "Witness A told the truth". Such testimony usurps the province of the jury; it is their task to determine who tells the truth. It is also improper for the prosecution to say in closing argument to the jury "I believe the state's witnesses are telling the truth." Such comments suggest to the jury that other evidence, not brought forward at the trial, supports the credibility of the witnesses.

In the following cases decide if the challenged testimony or comments constitute improper vouching:

- Two young girls testified about alleged sexual abuse. The prosecution introduced videos of the girls' interviews by counselors at an advocacy center.

The interviewer was called to lay a foundation for the interviews, and described the protocol for such interviews, stating the protocol "makes it very obvious when [the children] are being truthful." Should the trial judge have permitted this testimony? *Richardson v. State*, 43 A.3d 906 (Del. 2012).

- A victim of an assault testified that he identified the defendant as his assailant based on a photo array of six photographs, including a photo of the defendant. The victim had earlier helped to create a composite sketch of his assailant. No other evidence linked the defendant to the crime scene. The police detective who assembled the photo array testified, "[o]nce I received this photo, I saw how closely it resembled the sketch." Should this testimony have been permitted? *State v. Lazo*, 34 A.3d 1233 (N.J. 2012)

- The prosecution introduced a video of statements made by a defendant denying any role in a bank robbery. It then called as an expert witness an FBI agent to testify about the statements, based on the agent's training in "detecting deception in statements." The agent testified that based on his training the defendant's statements were not truthful. Admissible? *United States v. Hill*, 749 F.3d 1250 (10th Cir. 2014).

- At his trial on drug charges the defendant testified that contrary to testimony of the arresting police officer, there was not a "pervasive odor of marijuana" in his car. In closing argument the prosecutor stated that the officer had no incentive to give false testimony, because it would "violate his oath of office." Should the trial judge have permitted this argument? *United States v. Alexander*, 741 F.3d 866 (7th Cir. 2014).

subpoena An order compelling a person to appear as a witness; defense lawyers and prosecutors may have subpoenas issued for witnesses needed in either criminal or civil cases.

CONSTITUTIONAL RIGHTS OF DEFENDANTS REGARDING WITNESSES

The Right to Compel the Attendance of Witnesses

The Sixth Amendment to the U.S. Constitution provides that "In all criminal prosecutions, the accused shall enjoy the right to have compulsory process for obtaining witnesses in his favor." To ensure the attendance of a witness, a subpoena must be issued. A **subpoena** is a command to the person to whom it is directed to appear on a specified date at a given time and place for the purpose of testifying. In addition, the person may be required to bring documents or other materials that are expected to be useful in the proceedings. A **subpoena duces tecum** describes the material that the witness is to bring.

subpoena duces tecum A subpoena that not only requires the appearance of a witness but also requires the witness to bring relevant and competent documents or writings that may be in his or her possession.

The right to the compulsory process to obtain the attendance of witnesses does not mean that the defendant can subpoena anyone at all in order to delay the case and to make the trial a cumbersome process. Only competent witnesses who have a personal knowledge of facts relevant to the case may be subpoenaed.

The Right to Confront and Cross-Examine Witnesses

The Sixth Amendment also provides that "The accused shall enjoy the right … to be confronted with the witnesses against him." The witness not only testifies in open court in the presence of the accused but is also subject to cross-examination by the opposing party. The Confrontation Clause is discussed more fully in Chapter 8.

The U.S. Supreme Court has pointed out that for centuries cross-examination has been considered to be one of the safeguards of the accuracy and completeness of testimony by a witness. The Court held in the case of *Davis v. Alaska*[17] that

> Cross-examination is the principal means by which the believability of a witness and the truth of his testimony are tested. Subject always to the broad discretion of a trial judge to preclude repetitive and unduly harassing interrogation, the cross-examiner is not only permitted to delve into the witness' story to test the witness' perceptions and memory, but the cross-examiner has traditionally been allowed to impeach, i.e., discredit, the witness. One way of discrediting the witness is to introduce evidence of a prior criminal conviction of that witness. By so doing the cross-examiner intends to afford the jury a basis to infer that the witness' character is such that he would be less likely than the average trustworthy citizen to be truthful in his testimony. The introduction of evidence of a prior crime is thus a general attack on the credibility of the witness. A more particular attack on the witness' credibility is effected by means of cross-examination directed toward revealing possible biases, prejudices, or ulterior motives of the witness as they may relate directly to issues or personalities in the case at hand. The partiality of a witness is subject to exploration at trial. We have recognized that the exposure of a witness' motivation in testifying is a proper and important function of the constitutionally protected right of cross-examination.

There are situations where the right of cross-examination has been limited—for example, when the child victim of a sexual assault is called to testify, discussed earlier in this chapter. When a defendant has elected to exercise his Sixth Amendment right to represent himself in a criminal trial,[18] trial courts have sometimes limited his cross-examination rights.

The Defendant's Right to Testify in His or Her Defense

Defendants have a right to testify in their own behalf. As the U.S. Supreme Court stated in the case of *Rock v. Arkansas*,[19] this right is derived from the Sixth and Fourteenth Amendments. The Supreme Court held that the right "is essential to due process of law in a fair adversary process."

Under the common law, defendants in criminal cases were not considered competent to appear as witnesses in their own trial.[20] Today, all defendants are considered competent to take the witness stand in their own behalf.

However, defendants who take the witness stand to testify in their behalf waive their right to remain silent and must answer questions on cross-examination. Because of the danger of cross-examination and the risk of impeachment, defense lawyers in most instances strongly urge their clients not to risk testifying in their own defense, pointing out the additional danger that a defendant's testimony may "open the door to otherwise inadmissible evidence which is damaging to the case."[21]

In the case of *United States v. Dunnigan*,[22] the U.S. Supreme Court unanimously and bluntly held that "a defendant's right to testify does not include a right to commit perjury." It is not perjury for a defendant to enter a not guilty plea and then be found guilty. But it is perjury for a defendant to take the witness stand and lie in a material way. The Supreme Court stated in the *Dunnigan* case that a "defendant who commits a crime and perjures herself in an unlawful attempt to avoid responsibility is more threatening to society and less deserving of leniency than a defendant who does not defy the trial process."[23]

TYPES OF WITNESSES AND OPINION EVIDENCE

Ordinary Witnesses and Expert Witnesses

ordinary (lay) witnesses Witnesses who have firsthand information about a fact gained by personal observation.

Most witnesses are **ordinary (or lay) witnesses** who are called to testify about the firsthand information they have regarding the case before the court. Their testimony is typically limited to what they have seen, heard (although hearsay is in most instances excluded), smelled, felt, and, on rare occasions, tasted. Law enforcement officers appear in most instances as ordinary witnesses, although some officers also appear as expert witnesses when they qualify, testifying about fingerprinting, traffic matters, weapons, and so on.

expert witness A witness who has special knowledge or training in a specialized area.

An **expert witness** is a person who has had special training, education, or experience. Because of this experience and background, the expert witness may be able to assist the jury and the court in resolving the issues before them. The party that offers a witness as an expert must lay a foundation (that is, ask a series of questions) establishing the witness as an expert in the field in which the expert will testify and offer opinions.

Three questions are presented to a trial court when one of the parties seeks to introduce an expert witness:

- Is the subject on which the expert witness will testify one for which the court can receive the opinion of an expert?
- What qualifications are necessary to permit testimony of the witness as an expert?
- Does the witness meet these qualifications?

When there is a subject that is suitable for expert witness testimony, the trial judge has to determine whether the expert testimony is reliable enough to admit into evidence. The trial judge is given a great deal of latitude and discretion in determining whether a witness qualifies as an expert witness.

In recent years the U.S. Supreme Court has adopted new standards for use in federal courts for the admissibility of scientific evidence and supporting expert testimony. These standards are discussed extensively in Chapter 18 of this book.

To qualify as an expert in some fields (such as a medical expert) requires years of formal education, training, and a license. Other subjects, such as fingerprinting or handwriting analysis, require other qualifications. Rule 702 of the Federal Rules of Evidence provides:

> A witness who is qualified as an expert by knowledge, skill, experience, training, or education may testify in the form of an opinion or otherwise if: (a) the expert's scientific, technical, or other specialized knowledge will help the trier of fact to understand the evidence or to determine a fact in issue; (b) the testimony is based on sufficient facts or data; (c) the testimony is the product of reliable principles and methods; and (d) the expert has reliably applied the principles and methods to the facts of the case.[24]

In discussing the admissibility of handwriting analysis the court in the 2005 case of *United States v. Prime*[25] stated that the expert must be qualified based on experience, such as that held by the forensic document examiner from the U.S. Secret Service who testified in that case. The court also said the reliability of the handwriting expert's testimony must be based on empirical studies that show handwriting is "individualistic," that testimony was based on established methods of handwriting analysis, that there is a known rate of error (studies show handwriting experts are

Terry Joe Franklin, a forensic science supervisor for the Washington State Patrol Crime Lab in Tacoma, Washington, identified a .45 SIG Sauer pistol during his testimony as an expert witness in the penalty phase of the trial of convicted sniper John Allen Muhammad. Muhammad was convicted of capital murder for his role as organizer of a two-man sniper team that killed 10 people and terrorized the Washington, D.C., area.

accurate about 87% of the time), and that there is general acceptance of the analysis.

Expert testimony based on handwriting analysis is generally admissible in both federal and state courts under Federal Rule of Evidence 702 and similar state rules. In a few courts, handwriting experts are permitted to give testimony showing similarities between a defendant's handwriting and the "sample" related to the crime charged, such as a ransom note or threatening letter. However, in those courts the expert is not permitted to state an opinion on the author of the "sample." (See e.g., *United States v. Rutherford*, 104 F.Supp.2d 1190 (D. Neb. 2000).)

In the 1973 case of *Miller v. California*,[26] the U.S. Supreme Court held that a police officer qualified as an expert witness to "community standards" in an obscenity case, stating that

> The record simply does not support appellant's contention, belatedly raised on appeal, that the State's expert was unqualified to give evidence on California "community standards." The expert, a police officer with many years of specialization in obscenity offenses, had conducted an extensive statewide survey and had given expert evidence on 26 occasions in the year prior to this trial. Allowing such expert testimony was certainly not constitutional error.

It is not unusual for law enforcement officers to be called to testify as experts, based on their experience. For example, virtually all courts permit qualified police experts to testify about organized crime structures, narcotics operations, or gang cultures and rules in prosecutions of gang members. An example is the case of *People v. Hill*, 120 Cal. Rptr. 3d 251 (Cal. App. 2011). There, a San Francisco police officer who worked exclusively in gang-related investigations was permitted to testify about a murder suspect's motive in shooting an undercover police officer.

The defendant contended he acted in self-defense, and didn't know the victim was a police officer. The police officer testified that under gang culture, when a gang member from one gang (the defendant belonged to the "West Mob") entered the territory of a rival gang intending retribution (the intended victim was a member of the "Big Block"), he would have the intent to shoot somebody, even a police officer, if he did not find the intended victim.

Most courts limit police officers expert testimony to matters "beyond the ken" (understanding) of the average person. Thus, while a New York State Police Officer could give expert testimony about the practices of the infamous MS-13 gang, he could not testify, in an "expert" capacity, about facts that a juror could expect to grasp without expert help. In *United States v. Mejia*, 545 F.3d 179 (2nd Cir. 2008), the expert testified that in the five years prior to trial the Long Island branch of MS-13 committed 18 to 23 murders on Long Island. These facts, the court held, were facts the prosecution was required to prove by ordinary witnesses.

It is the fact finder (jury or judge) who determines the weight and credibility to be given to the testimony of both expert and ordinary witnesses.

Opinion Evidence by Ordinary Witnesses

An ordinary witness is qualified to testify because of firsthand knowledge of an issue before the court. The expert witness has something different to contribute in assisting the trier of fact. Neither type of witness is permitted to give an opinion as to whether the defendant is guilty or innocent. This determination is made by the fact finder, based on the evidence presented.

The testimony of ordinary witnesses usually consists of statements about the facts that have been observed firsthand (the "requirement of personal knowledge"). An ordinary witness may also include opinions and conclusions about common things that are within the knowledge of the average person. An opinion that the defendant was intoxicated or angry, for example, or as to the value of his property that was stolen or destroyed, would be allowed. Rule 701 of the Federal Rules of Evidence provides:

> If the witness is not testifying as an expert, his testimony in the form of opinions or inferences is limited to those opinions or inferences which are (a) rationally based on the perception of the witness and (b) helpful to a clear understanding of his testimony or the determination of a fact in issue.

A witness's prior knowledge of a defendant's apperance can support an opinion. In the 2008 case of *Dawson v. State*,[27] an ordinary witness was allowed to give his opinion about the identity of a suspected murderer captured on a video surveillance camera. Because the witness knew the defendant at the time the video was made, and because the defendant had changed his physical characteristics between that time and the time of trial, the witness was allowed to give his opinion that based on gestures and manner of speaking, the defendant was the person in the video. Similarly, if it is shown that an ordinary witness is well acquainted with a defendant's or another person's handwriting, that witness could be qualified to testify regarding the handwriting.[28]

Ordinary witnesses who are drug users, or who are well acquainted with drugs or guns, could be held qualified by a trial court to testify about the identity of drugs[29] or guns and ammunition.[30] Where there was sufficient foundation to justify a deputy sheriff's opinion about the cause of a snowmobile accident, the judgment in the civil case of *Cline v. Durden*[31] was affirmed in 1990.

The Federal Rules of Evidence provide that an ordinary witness may express an opinion that is "rationally based on the perception of the witness" (Rule 701). Under this type of rule, ordinary witnesses have expressed admissible opinions concerning insanity,[32] intoxication,[33] drug impairment,[34] the speed of a vehicle,[35] the time of death (testified to by a lieutenant in a fire department),[36] and the difficulty of interviewing a child witness (testified to by a police officer).[37]

When a witness testifies that the defendant was drunk, or looked surprised, or "seemed like he was trying to break my neck," the witness is using a "shorthand way" of collecting facts and expressing opinions about what the witness saw or experienced. Trial courts have considerable discretion and generally will permit such opinions.[38]

For example, in the case of *United States v. Bogan*,[39] the Seventh Circuit Court of Appeals permitted a lay witness to testify that based on his perception of the nature of an assault, he believed the defendants were trying to kill the victim. The defendants were convicted of assault with intent to commit serious bodily harm based on this and other evidence.

Here is another example of a court decision approving the use of opinion evidence by an ordinary witness.

Marks v. State Arkansas Supreme Court, 289 S.W.3d 923 (2008)	Defendant and two other men drove to the victim's house, and defendant started beating the victim. Defendant knocked the victim to the ground, and stated he would run over the victim. As he entered the car the other men ran away, and did not see what happened. The victim died from massive injuries, and the defendant was charged with capital murder by intentionally running over the victim with his car. At the trial one of the other men present testified that he saw the defendant get into the car, and then heard the car run over the victim. On cross-examination he stated he didn't actually see the car run over the victim, but did hear a noise—"bl-bloom, bl-bloom"—which he believed was the sound of the car running over the victim's body. The defendant objected to this as improper opinion evidence, but the testimony was admitted and the defendant was convicted of capital murder. On appeal the Arkansas Supreme Court held that the witness's opinion that the sound he heard was the sound of a car running over a body was admissible under the lay opinion rule. The Arkansas ordinary witness opinion rule, like Rule 701 of the Federal Rules of Evidence (see Appendix C) requires that the opinion be "rationally based on the witness's perception." The court said that the opinion the witness gave was one a "normal person would form on the basis of the facts he observed and what he heard." The murder conviction was affirmed.

DIRECT EXAMINATION OF WITNESSES

In criminal cases, the government has the burden of proving the charges made against the defendant beyond a reasonable doubt. The state also has the burden of coming forward first with evidence showing that the defendant committed the offenses with which she is charged. Therefore, the first witnesses to appear in criminal cases often are government witnesses called by the prosecutor to support the state's case.

You be the **JUDGE**

Police officers and federal agents testify frequently in criminal trials, either as ordinary fact witnesses (*e.g.,* "Where was the knife lying in relation to the body?") or as expert witnesses (*e.g.,* "Based on your experiences, officer, do the defendant's tattoos indicate membership in a street gang?"). Sometimes an officer who has not been qualified as an expert gives lay testimony that looks very much like expert testimony. When that happens, courts must determine if the testimony is "ordinary" opinion testimony (and admissible under rules like Federal Rule of Evidence 701), or expert opinion testimony, and inadmissible.

In the following cases, acting as the trial judge, determine if you should admit the testimony of a police officer or federal agent who has not been qualified as an expert:

- A DEA agent, qualified as a Spanish-language interpreter, is asked to testify that the Spanish-speaking voice on recorded phone conversations discussing drug deals was the voice of the defendant. The phone conversations have been admitted into evidence and heard by the jury. Admissible testimony under Rule 701? Does Fed. Rule of Evidence 901 have any bearing on the question? *See United States v. Mendiola,* 707 F.3d 735 (7th Cir. 2013).
- In a murder-for-hire trial, the jury heard 77 wiretapped telephone conversations, including the following phone conversation between two defendants: "Freeman: Everything good, man. Except for, you know … you know what I am talking about … just that one little thing. We ain't got the bonus dog. But, you know what I am saying, the situation is over with." An FBI agent, who monitored the phone wiretaps, proposes to testify that "the situation" referred to the murder of the victim. Should you let the agent testify about the meaning of this conversation? *See United States v. Freeman,* 730 F.3d 590 (6th Cir. 2013).
- A Jersey City police officer proposes to testify as a lay witness in a drug trial, based on observations by the officer of alleged drug transactions. The officer will testify as follows (if you let him): "No, I couldn't say for certain that heroin was inside the bag, but the packaging was consistent with the packaging of heroin." Admissible lay opinion testimony? *See State v. Turner,* 2013 WL 1798685 (N.J. A.D. 2013).
- An FBI agent proposes to testify about the meaning of recorded conversations, played for the jury, based on the agent's "knowledge of the entire investigation" of an alleged illegal drug ring. Admissible? *See United States v. Hampton,* 718 F.3d 978 (C.A.D.C. 2013).

In most instances, the government's case is presented by testimony about the chronological order of events as they occurred. Usually an attempt is made to let the witness tell his or her story first with as few interruptions as possible, by using such questions as the following:

- Where were you on the night of June 23?
- Will you tell the court and jury what you saw and heard at that time?

The question-and-answer method is used in American courtrooms so that the opposing lawyer may object to the question before the answer is in evidence. However, by the use of short general questions, such as What did you see?, What did

direct examination
Questioning of a witness by the lawyer who subpoenaed the witness.

you do?, and What happened next?, the witness is able to tell the story and at the same time is kept to the point. After the witness has presented a general account of the facts as known to the witness, through **direct examination**, the prosecutor may go back and fill in or emphasize details with more specific questions.

Cross-Examination of Witnesses

cross-examined When a witness is re-examined by the opposing attorney following the direct examination of the witness.

After the direct examination, the witness may be **cross-examined** by the opposing attorney. For centuries, cross-examination has been considered one of the essential safeguards of the accuracy and completeness of testimony given by a witness. The U.S. Supreme Court held in the 1974 case of *Davis v. Alaska*[40]:

> Cross-examination is the principal means by which the believability of a witness and the truth of his testimony are tested. Subject always to the broad discretion of a trial judge to preclude repetitive and unduly harassing interrogation, the cross-examiner is not only permitted to delve into the witness' story to test the witness' perceptions and memory, but the cross-examiner has traditionally been allowed to impeach, i.e., discredit, the witness.

The most effective defense to cross-examination is for a witness to testify truthfully and simply in answering all questions, even though the answers may sometimes be embarrassing or harmful. The purposes of cross-examination are the following:

- To test the "believability of a witness and the truth of his testimony" (the U.S. Supreme Court in *Davis v. Alaska*)
- To bring out facts that support the cross-examiner's case
- To impeach (discredit) the witness (which also is a means of testing the "believability of a witness and the truth of his testimony")

If a witness has not hurt the opposing party's case, there usually is no reason to cross-examine unless there is a possibility of bringing out facts that might help the case of the cross-examiner.

Cross-examination is often exploratory, and for that reason it is risky: Facts uncovered in cross-examination could hurt the cross-examiner's case. In the 1931 case of *Alford v. United States*,[41] the U.S. Supreme Court stated:

> Counsel often cannot know in advance what pertinent facts may be elicited on cross-examination. For that reason it is necessarily exploratory; and the rule that the examiner must indicate the purpose of his inquiry does not, in general, apply. It is the essence of a fair trial that reasonable latitude be given the cross-examiner, even though he is unable to state to the court what facts a reasonable cross-examination might develop. Prejudice ensues from a denial of the opportunity to place the witness in his proper setting and put the weight of his testimony and his credibility to a test, without which the jury cannot fairly appraise them.

impeachment Calling into question the truth or accuracy of direct testimony by cross-examination or introduction of contradictory evidence.

Impeachment is another aspect of cross-examination, and in criminal cases it is probably the most effective cross-examination technique. By using impeachment, "the cross-examiner intends to afford the jury a basis to infer that the witness's character is such that he would be less likely than the average trustworthy citizen to be truthful in his testimony."[42] Impeachment may be accomplished by cross-examination and also by the introduction of other evidence. The functions of impeachment may be classified as follows:

1. To attack the witness's credibility and qualifications to testify truthfully because of prior criminal conviction (and in some jurisdictions and some

instances, a showing of prior bad conduct). Rule 609 of the Federal Rules of Evidence limits evidence of prior criminal convictions to crimes with a penalty in excess of one year of imprisonment, or crimes involving dishonesty or false statement, regardless of the punishment.

Examples
- Evidence of a witness's conviction of assault was admissible to attack the witness's credibility, where the punishment was more than one year in prison.[43]
- Evidence of a witness's conviction of a misdemeanor offense of receiving stolen property was not admissible because the punishment was less than one year of imprisonment, and the crime of receiving stolen property does not automatically involve dishonesty or false statement.[44]

2. To attack the testimony given by the witness on direct examination by a showing of prior inconsistent statements.

Example
In a prosecution related to a defendant's alleged spousal abuse, prior inconsistent statements made by the witness (defendant's wife) about the nature of the abuse were admissible on the witness' credibility.[45]

3. To attack the witness's credibility by showing bias, prejudice, or ulterior motives of the witness.

Rule 611(a) of the Federal Rules of Evidence states that the "court shall exercise reasonable control over the mode and order of interrogating witnesses and presenting evidence so as to ... avoid needless consumption of time, and ... protect witnesses from harassment or undue embarrassment." In the 1988 case of *Olden v. Kentucky*,[46] the U.S. Supreme Court again pointed out that trial judges have "broad discretion ... to preclude repetitive and unduly harassing interrogation." In the 1987 case of *Kentucky v. Stincer*,[47] the Supreme Court held that the "Confrontation Clause guarantees only 'an *opportunity* for effective cross-examination, not cross-examination that is effective in whatever way, and to whatever extent, the defense might wish.'"

Objections to Questions

objections Formal statements made by attorneys during trials, objecting to the form or substance of a question or to the answer given by a witness to a question.

Under the adversary system, **objections** to questions are the first line of defense against statements the opposing party seeks to use. It is the lawyers who must object, not the judge. Failure to object, in most instances, waives the grounds for an appeal to a higher court.

The trial judge has considerable discretion in ruling on objections and in determining what is relevant, material, and competent. The trial judge will not be overruled by a higher court unless there is an abuse of discretion or plain error.

Objections are classified as follows:

- *Objections to the substance of the question:* These objections concern the answer called for by the question. Usual objections in this area are irrelevant, immaterial, incompetent, and hearsay.
- *Objections to the form of the question:* These objections concern the manner in which the question is worded. In most instances, the question may be rephrased and asked again in a form in which both the question and answer

PROCEDURES & PROCESSES

Objections to Questions

Objections to the Form of the Question
- Leading question (suggests the answer that is wanted)
- Calls for speculation
- Argumentative
- Misstates facts in evidence
- Assumes facts not in evidence
- Vague and ambiguous
- Repetitive or cumulative
- Misleading

Objections to the Substance of the Question
- Irrelevant
- Immaterial
- Incompetent
- Calls for hearsay
- Insufficient foundation
- Calls for inadmissible opinion answer
- Beyond the scope of the direct examination

Objections to the Answer
- Unresponsive
- Inadmissible opinion
- Inadmissible hearsay statement

are admissible. Usual objections to the form of a question are that the question is leading, argumentative, calls for speculation, or misstates a fact in evidence.

- *Objections to the answer:* If an attorney is slow in objecting, the attorney usually pays the penalty and is told to object faster. In this situation and others, a lawyer can object to an answer and ask that the answer be stricken from the record because: (1) the answer is unresponsive to the question (most often when the witness volunteers additional information beyond the scope of the question asked), (2) the answer contains an inadmissible opinion, or (3) the answer includes inadmissible hearsay statements.

THE REQUIREMENTS OF RELEVANCY, MATERIALITY, AND COMPETENCY

relevant, material, and competent
Evidence that will affect the result of a trial.

Criminal and civil trials would be much longer if there were no controls on the testimony and information allowed. Unrelated evidence would cause confusion and clutter the fact-finding process. To minimize confusion and to make trials manageable, all evidence must be **relevant, material, and competent**. Therefore, to introduce facts, testimony, or a physical object as evidence, it must be shown that

- The evidence addresses a material fact.
- The evidence is relevant to that fact.
- The evidence is able to affect the probable truth or falsity of that fact by being competent.

A fact is *material* if it will affect the result of a trial. For example, a defendant is charged with a crime committed in a tavern at ten o'clock at night. State witnesses testifying that they saw the defendant in a tavern at that time are relevant and material. Defense witnesses testifying that the defendant was at another place five miles away are also relevant and material to the fact in issue.

Evidence is *relevant* if it has a tendency to make a material fact more or less probable. Testimony by a witness that he saw the defendant in the tavern at ten o'clock is relevant evidence. However, testimony that the tavern was hit by lightning and burned down a week later is not relevant because the fire is not material to the case. These questions must be asked:

- Is the fact material to the dispute?
- If so, does the proposed evidence make the material evidence more or less probable (relevant)?

After our hypothetical witness has testified that the defendant was in the tavern at the time the crime was committed, the questioning continues:

Q: Were you in the tavern that night?

A: No, I wasn't.

Q: How do you know the defendant was in the tavern?

A: John told me.

The testimony is relevant to the material issue in dispute, but it is not *competent* because the personal knowledge foundation required by Federal Rule of Evidence 602 has not been satisfied. However, changing the example slightly makes the testimony competent:

Q: How do you know the defendant was in the tavern?

A: The defendant told me he was in the tavern.

Since the defendant is the opposing party in the criminal action, the matter about which the witness has personal knowledge is the defendant's incriminating admission. The testimony is now competent, relevant, and material. It is not forbidden by the hearsay rule.

REDIRECT EXAMINATION AND RECROSS-EXAMINATION

After the cross-examination, the lawyer who produced the witness may conduct a redirect examination of the witness. Questions on redirect examination are generally limited to new matters drawn out during cross-examination and in refuting and explaining impeachment issues. The purposes of redirect examination are as follows:

- To restore the credibility of a witness who has been impeached on cross-examination by explanations of matters on which the cross-examiner sought to impeach the witness. Questions such as these may be asked: Officer Smith, why did you ... ? and Officer Smith, what did you mean when you stated ... ?
- To restore the credibility of a witness by pointing out prior consistent statements when the impeachment was made by means of prior inconsistent statements.

During the redirect examination, additional witnesses may be used to rebut the cross-examination and assist in rehabilitation. New evidence may also be presented if the cross-examiner has opened the door to new matters.

Recross-examination is the fourth and usually the last stage of the examination of the witness. With many witnesses, the questioning is completed before reaching this stage. The recross-examination is usually confined to matters covered in the redirect examination.

THE ROLE OF THE TRIAL JUDGE

The trial judge manages the courtroom and the trial, and rules on questions of law. The judge also rules on motions and objections made by attorneys before and during a trial, and gives instructions to the jury when it starts deliberation on guilt or innocence. The trial judge has an obligation to safeguard both the rights of the accused and the interests of the public in the efficient and effective administration of criminal and civil justice.

In the great majority of jurisdictions in the United States, the trial judge may not comment on the weight of the evidence. Juries are usually instructed on the manner in which they may determine the weight of the evidence—that is, the credibility of witnesses and the weight that they may give to physical evidence. In only a very few jurisdictions in the United States may the trial judge comment on the weight of the evidence presented in a trial.

Virtually all states follow the procedure set forth in Federal Rule of Evidence 614(b). Rule 614(b) states that the *court* (the term as used here refers to the trial judge) "may interrogate witnesses, whether called by itself or by a party." In a few jurisdictions, jurors are permitted to question witnesses indirectly through the trial judge.

Because the trial judge must remain impartial, he or she must be careful in the use of leading questions in those jurisdictions that forbid the judge from commenting on the weight of the evidence. The improper use of leading questions could suggest to the jury that the judge believed the witness was lying, which violates the rule against commenting on the evidence. In the 1972 case of *Commonwealth v. Butler*,[48] the Supreme Court of Pennsylvania disapproved of a trial judge's practice of questioning only the witnesses he suspected of untruthfulness, while not questioning other witnesses. The court held:

> If a judge followed the practice which this judge advocated here, a practice of questioning every witness whom the judge did not believe to be telling the truth, while questioning no other witnesses, it would be tantamount to telling the jury his views of which witnesses were to be believed. Credibility is solely for the jury. Just as a trial judge is not permitted to indicate to the jury his views on the verdict that they should reach in a criminal case, ... similarly he is not permitted to indicate to a jury his views on whether particular witnesses are telling the truth.

Virtually all federal courts permit jurors to ask questions of witnesses by submitting the questions to the judge.[49] Many state courts also permit this practice,[50] and at least two states, Arizona and Florida, do so by statute.[51] As with questions posed by the judge, the parties may object to these questions on the same grounds as questions asked by one of the parties. However, the routine practice of allowing

You be the **APPEALS JUDGE**

As we saw in Chapter 3, appellate judges have a limited role when reviewing decisions of trial judges and juries. Appeals courts do not make fact findings, but instead defer to the findings of the jury. Appeals judges also generally defer to decisions of the trial judge on discretionary questions, such as determining the admissibility of evidence or the competency of a witness to testify.

As an appellate judge, how would you review the trial judge's decision in this situation: The defendant, who was charged with the crime of home invasion and assault, stated he had no memory of the crime, due to mental problems created by a self-inflicted gunshot wound to the head shortly after the crime was committed. The trial court found the defendant unfit to stand trial. The state has appealed, contending the defendant is fit to stand trial. What should you do? Does it affect your decision if medical evidence introduced was held by the trial judge to be sufficient to show the defendant had in fact lost his memory of the crime? If so, to what extent? *See People v. Stahl*, 10 N.E.3d 870 (Ill. 2014)

questions by jurors is generally discouraged. The court in *United States v. Collins*[52] suggested that juror questions be limited to cases where the trial is long and complicated, the parties are not properly questioning witnesses, or the witness becomes difficult or confused.

CAN A PERSON WHO HAS BEEN HYPNOTIZED TESTIFY AS A WITNESS?

Studies of hypnosis began more than 200 years ago, but to date there is no single explanation of the phenomenon that satisfies most scientists. Hundreds of cases involving hypnotized witnesses have come before American courts.[53] In the case of *Rock v. Arkansas*,[54] the U.S. Supreme Court identified the following three problems in the use of a witness whose testimony has been hypnotically refreshed:

> [T]he subject becomes "suggestible" and may try to please the hypnotist with answers the subject thinks will be met with approval; the subject is likely to "confabulate," that is, to fill in details from the imagination, in order to make an answer more coherent and complete; and, the subject experiences "memory hardening," which gives him great confidence in both true and false memories, making effective cross-examination more difficult.

Because of these and other problems, some states do not permit the use of hypnotically refreshed testimony as evidence. Other states have established guidelines for the use of hypnotically refreshed testimony, such as those in New Jersey[55] and New Mexico.[56] Such safeguards seek to ensure the accuracy and reliability of hypnotically refreshed testimony. The facts in the case of *Rock v. Arkansas* and the ruling of the U.S. Supreme Court follow.

Rock v. Arkansas

United States Supreme
Court, 483 U.S.44 (1987).

The defendant was charged with manslaughter in the killing of her husband during an argument. Because she could not remember precise details of the shooting, her attorney suggested hypnosis to refresh her memory. After the defendant underwent hypnosis, the trial court permitted her to testify only about what she had been able to remember before hypnosis.

After her conviction for manslaughter, she appealed to the U.S. Supreme Court on the issue that she had the constitutional right to testify in her own behalf. The Supreme Court vacated the conviction and ordered a new trial, stating that

> The more traditional means of assessing accuracy of testimony also remain applicable in the case of a previously hypnotized defendant. Certain information recalled as a result of hypnosis may be verified as highly accurate by corroborating evidence. Cross-examination, even in the face of a confident defendant, is an effective tool for revealing inconsistencies. Moreover, a jury can be educated to the risks of hypnosis through expert testimony and cautionary instructions. Indeed, it is probably to a defendant's advantage to establish carefully the extent of his memory prior to hypnosis, in order to minimize the decrease in credibility the procedure might introduce.
>
> … We are not now prepared to endorse without qualifications the use of hypnosis as an investigative tool; scientific understanding of the phenomenon and of the means to control the effects of hypnosis is still in its infancy. Arkansas, however, has not justified the exclusion of all of a defendant's testimony that the defendant is unable to prove to be the product of prehypnosis memory. A State's legitimate interest in barring unreliable evidence does not extend to per se exclusions that may be reliable in an individual case. Wholesale inadmissibility of a defendant's testimony is an arbitrary restriction on the right to testify in the absence of clear evidence by the State repudiating the validity of all posthypnosis recollections. The State would be well within its powers if it established guidelines to aid trial courts in the evaluation of posthypnosis testimony and it may be able to show that testimony in a particular case is so unreliable that exclusion is justified. But it has not shown that hypnotically enhanced testimony is always so untrustworthy and so immune to the traditional means of evaluating credibility that it should disable a defendant from presenting her version of the events for which she is on trial.

In the *Rock* case it was the defendant who wished to testify after hypnosis, and the Supreme Court held that the defendant had a constitutional right to testify on her own behalf. As a result, the Supreme Court held that the Arkansas *per se* inadmissibility rule was unconstitutional. Where a witness who is not a defendant wishes to testify after hypnosis, courts have held that a *per se* rule of inadmissibility is permitted.[57]

Another problem area commonly associated with hypnotically refreshed memory is "repressed memories." Accusations of sexual assaults that occurred years prior to the accusation could be based on a repressed memory that has been hypnotically or clinically refreshed.[58]

PROCEDURES & PROCESSES

The Functions of the Trial Judge and the Jury

The Trial Judge Determines

- Whether a witness is qualified
- The competence of a witness
- Questions of law:
  - Rules on motions
  - Rules on objections by attorneys
  - Instruction of the jury
  - Running the courtroom and trial
  - Safeguarding both the rights of the accused and the interests of the public in the administration of criminal justice

As Fact Finders, the Jury Alone

- Determines the credibility of the testimony of all witnesses. The fact finders may believe one witness as against many.
- Passes on and resolves conflicts in the testimony of witnesses.
- Determines the weight to be given all evidence (statements of witnesses, physical evidence, and so on).
- Determines whether sufficient evidence exists to justify a verdict of guilty. (A guilty verdict is subject to review by the trial judge and appellate courts, however, who determine as a matter of law whether sufficient evidence exists to sustain the guilty verdict.)

SUMMARY

1. **List the general qualifications for being a witness.**
    - To appear as a witness in a civil or criminal case, a person must have personal knowledge of an issue before the court. A witness must also be competent and declare (or swear) that he or she will testify truthfully.

2. **List the special qualifications for child witnesses.**
    - Today, many states do not have a minimum age for admitting testimony of child witnesses, so long as the child understands what it means to testify and tell the truth. Because of the trauma that a child victim or witness may experience when appearing as a witness, all the states and the federal courts have statutes and procedures that attempt to help child witnesses.

3. **Identify the factors important in determining the credibility of a witness.**
    - The perception (e.g., seeing, hearing, or smelling); memory (retaining an accurate impression of the facts perceived); and narration (giving an accurate description of the facts perceived) of the witness determine the credibility of the witness's testimony.

4. **List the constitutional rights of a defendant related to witnesses.**
    - Defendants have the right to compel witnesses to appear in court to testify for the defense. The Sixth Amendment right of a defendant to confront and cross-examine witnesses against the defendant is probably the most important tool of defense lawyers in defending their clients in criminal cases.

5. **State the difference between a lay (ordinary) witness and an expert witness.**
   - Witnesses may be either lay (ordinary) witnesses or expert witnesses. Lay witnesses mainly testify about facts they have personally perceived; expert witnesses may give opinions (e.g., that a particular gun fired a particular bullet) based on their knowledge and experience. Ordinary witnesses may sometimes give opinion evidence, but only within the rules of evidence of their state. (See Appendix C for Federal Rules of Evidence 701, 703, 704, and 705.)

6. **Read and understand Rule 702 of the Federal Rules of Evidence.**
   - The substance of Rule 702 of the Federal Rules of Evidence has been adopted by most states. Under that Rule, a witness can qualify as an expert based on "knowledge, skill, experience, or education" about facts or opinions that will help the jury understand the evidence or issues in the case. The testimony must be "reliable" in the sense that it is based on reliable principles and methods that were used by the witness to reach the expert opinion.

7. **List some objections that may be made to questions of a witness or answers by a witness.**
   - Some questions are objectionable because they have improper form: e.g., leading, argumentative, ambiguous. Some questions are objectionable because they have improper substance; e.g., calls for hearsay, irrelevant, insufficient foundation. Some answers are objectionable because they are improper; e.g., inadmissible hearsay, unresponsive, inadmissible opinion.

KEY TERMS

competency, 112	impeachment, 127	relevant, material,	subpoena duces tecum,
cross-examined, 127	objections, 128	and competent,	120
direct examination, 127	ordinary (or lay)	129	voir dire, 114
expert witness, 122	witnesses, 122	subpoena, 120	witness, 112

KEY CASES

Commonwealth v. Delbridge, 855 A2d. 27 (2003): Stated basis of claim that testimony of child was tainted.

Davis v. Alaska, 94 S. Ct. 1105 (1974): Described the role of cross-examination in criminal trials.

Kentucky v. Stincer, 482 U.S. 730 (1987): Held that defendant need not be present at witness competency hearing.

Marks v. State, 289 S.W.3d 923 (Ark. 2008): Stated when a lay witness may give opinion testimony.

Maryland v. Craig, 497 U.S. 836 (1990): Stated when protection for a child witness may include procedure other than face-to-face confrontation with the defendant.

Neil v. Biggers, 409 U.S. 188 (1972): States standards for evaluating eyewitness testimony.

People v. Hill, 120 Cal. Rptr. 2d 250 (Cal. App. 2011): States when a police officer may give expert testimony based on officer's experience.

State v. Hernandez, 986 A.2d 480 (N.H. 2009): States rules for when witness may wear a disguise while giving testimony.

United States v. Prime, 431 F.3d 1147 (9th Cir. 2005): States standards for qualifying handwriting experts.

PROBLEMS

1. Dunn is charged with battery after striking the victim outside a bar. Dunn admits striking the victim, but alleges he acted in self-defense. The prosecution seeks to introduce a voice mail left on the victim's cell phone message system by Dunn's girlfriend. The substance of the voice message is "I am sorry Dunn hit you. He is so jealous, without any reason." You may assume

the witness will testify that the voice mail message was in fact sent by her, and the voice in the voice mail is her voice. She is otherwise unwilling to confirm the voice mail, and indeed will testify she did not witness the fight. Is the voice mail admissible evidence? What must the prosecution establish before it can be admitted? How can it do this, given the girlfriend's reluctance? Would Rule 602 help the prosecution? See *Dunn v. State*, 919 N.E.2d 609 (Ind. App. 2010), *transfer denied*, 929 N.E.2d 790 (Ind. 2010).

2. As we saw in Chapter 2, evidence of past crimes is generally inadmissible, unless offered to prove some other material fact. Assume you are the prosecutor in a robbery/first-degree murder trial of a defendant charged with robbing and murdering a known drug dealer. You have reliable witnesses (FBI and DEA agents) who will testify the defendant is "deeply" involved in the local drug culture as a drug dealer. You anticipate the defense will object to this testimony as prejudicial and not relevant to any material fact. What argument will you make to the trial judge to get the testimony admitted? See *State v. Richmond*, 212 P.3d 165 (Kan. 2009).

3. A husband and wife are charged with sexual assault against a child. The husband pleads guilty, and agrees to testify against the wife. The prosecution wishes to introduce two photographs allegedly taken by the husband during or just before the sexual assault. One photograph shows the palm of a person's hand touching the child victim, and the prosecution will contend the palm in the photograph is the palm of the defendant. The other photograph is a nude picture of the defendant, allegedly taken just prior to the sexual assault.

   a. What must the prosecution do to get the palm photograph admitted? For now, do not consider the "reliability" of any expert testimony you believe necessary.

   b. Assuming the defendant does not contest that person in the nude photograph is her, can she object to its admissibility? Is it relevant evidence? (See *State v. Bickart*, 963 A.2d 183 (Me. 2009).) Be forewarned: In the opening sentence of the opinion the Maine Supreme Court advises that the circumstances of this crime are "particularly heinous and disturbing."

CASE ANALYSIS

Read Appendix B, Finding and Analyzing Cases (p. 499). With these guidelines in mind, please continue with the Case Analysis selections for Chapter 5.

1. Most states have adopted rules of evidence closely patterned after the Federal Rules of Evidence. That is the case in North Carolina. Under Rules 701 and 702, what must the prosecution produce to prove the "mental disability" element of a crime described as a sexual act with a mentally disabled person, with knowledge the person is mentally disabled? May the prosecution do so with lay witnesses, like social workers or special education teachers? Or must it produce expert witnesses like a psychologist or psychiatrist? *See State v. Hunt*, 722 S.E.2d 484 (N.C. 2012).

2. You are the defense attorney in a trial involving the alleged sale of illegal drugs by your client. In your state, the trial judge conducts the voir dire of prospective jury members, and you give

questions to the judge with a request the judge ask them of jury members. Would you like the judge to ask the prospective jurors these questions: (1) Have you or a family member ever been the victim of a crime? (2) Have you ever been employed by law enforcement? Why would you like these questions asked? If the judge refuses, and your client is convicted, do you have good grounds for an appeal? Consider the case of *Pearson v. State*, 86 A.3d 1232 (Md. App. 2014). What did the trial judge do wrong in that case?

3. You are the appeals judge in an illegal drugs and weapons case that has been appealed by the defendant to your court. At his trial, the defendant took the witness stand and confessed to all the crimes charged. At the trial's conclusion the trial judge instructed to jury to return a verdict of guilty, which it did. Should you reverse the conviction? On what grounds? *United States v. Salazar*, 751 F.3d 326 (5th Cir. 2014).

4. In a trial on charges of carjacking and robbery police detectives, who listened to and recorded phone conversations between the defendants, are listed as witnesses for the prosecution. They propose to testify about the meaning of certain "street terms" used by the defendants in the recorded conversations. Specifically, they will testify that the street word "gleezy" refers to a Glock gun, that "40" refers to a 40-caliber semiautomatic gun, and the term "bagged" refers to robbing someone and bagging the stolen property. Should they be permitted to testify? If so, must they be qualified as experts, or may they give lay testimony about these terms? *See King. United States*, 74 A.3d 678 (D.C.C.A. 2012).

Notes

1. Most witnesses will cooperate in performing their civic duty, but unfortunately some witnesses will not. The following reasons are commonly given for some witnesses not cooperating: (a) *Threats:* One experienced official estimated that half of all criminal cases dismissed are dropped because of witnesses' concerns for their safety. (b) *Financial losses:* Most states pay $30 or less per day as witness fees, which means that many witnesses lose money or have to take vacation time from their job to appear as a witness. (c) *Too many court delays and adjournments:* The National Advisory Committee on Criminal Justice Standards and Goals recognized that "delays are an accepted defense practice for wearing down the witness. Not infrequently, the financial and emotional costs become too much for the victim, and [he or] she asks to withdraw" (Report of the Task Force on Criminal Research and Development).

2. See *United States v. Benn*, 476 F.2d 1127 (D.C. Cir. 1972); *State v. Manning*, 291 A.2d 750 (Conn. 1972).

3. 913 F.2d 782 (10th Cir. 1990).

4. 825 F.2d 538 (1st Cir. 1987).

5. See 24A Corpus Juris Secundum 1869.

6. 703 P.2d 448.

7. 744 N.E.2d 1131 (Mass. App. Ct. 2001).

8. 259 P.3d 209 (Wash. 2011).

9. See Appendix A for the Sixth Amendment, which states in part: "In all criminal prosecutions, the accused shall enjoy the right ... to be confronted with the witnesses against him; to have compulsory process for obtaining witnesses in his favor ...."

10. See 32A Corpus Juris Secundum, Evidence 1031, and the case of *Chapman v. State* [230 N.W.2d 824 (Wis. 1975)]. In the *Chapman* case, a witness testified that the defendant stated that he participated in the crime charged and complained that he did not receive any of the proceeds of the joint criminal venture. The jury believed the testimony of the witness and convicted the defendant. The Wisconsin Supreme Court affirmed the conviction, holding: "This court will not upset a jury's determination of credibility ... unless the fact relied upon is inherently or patently incredible. To be incredible as a matter of law, evidence must be ... in conflict with the uniform course of nature or with fully established or conceded facts .... There is nothing inherently incredible about a participant in a crime telling others what he did. This is particularly so where his expressed complaint is that he received none of the proceeds of the joint criminal venture. The determination of this witness' credibility and the weight to be given his testimony was properly a function of the trier of facts."

11. 409 U.S. 188 (1972).

12. 44 P.3d 794, 798 (Utah 2002).

13. 201 F.2d 265 (2d Cir. 1952).

14. 478 N.W.2d 901 (1991), *review denied*, U.S. Supreme Court, 112 S. Ct. 3015 (1991).

15. 112 S. Ct. 3015.

16. 136 S.W.3d 680.

17. In the case of *Davis v. Alaska,* 94 S. Ct. 1105 (1974), the defendant was convicted of burglary and grand larceny. A crucial witness for the prosecution (Richard Green) was a 16-year-old who was on probation for burglarizing two cabins. The state obtained a protective order forbidding the disclosure of Green's juvenile record during his testimony in the trial of Davis. In reversing and remanding Davis's conviction for a new trial, the U.S. Supreme Court held: "The State's policy interest in protecting the confidentiality of a juvenile offender's record cannot require yielding of so vital a constitutional right as the effective cross-examination for bias of an adverse witness. The State could have protected Green from exposure of his juvenile adjudication in these circumstances by refraining from using him to make out its case; the State cannot, consistent with the right of confrontation, require the petitioner to bear the full burden of vindicating the State's interest in the secrecy of juvenile criminal records. The judgment affirming petitioner's convictions of burglary and grand larceny is reversed, and the case is remanded for further proceedings not inconsistent with this opinion."

18. See *Faretta v. California*, 422 U.S. 806 (1975).
19. 483 U.S. 44 (1987).
20. By the end of the nineteenth century every state had repealed the "incompetency" statutes that prevented a defendant from testifying in his own defense. Other limits on the right to testify have also been struck down. In *Brooks v. Tennessee* 406 U.S. 605 (1972) the U.S. Supreme Court held unconstitutional a Tennessee statute that required a defendant "to testify before any other testimony for the defense is heard by the court trying the case." In holding that the defendant "was deprived of his constitutional rights when the trial court excluded him from the stand for failing to testify first," the Supreme Court stated, "Although a defendant will usually have some idea of the strength of his evidence, he cannot be absolutely certain that his witnesses will testify as expected or that they will be effective on the stand. They may collapse under skillful and persistent cross-examination, and through no fault of their own they may fail to impress the jury as honest and reliable witnesses. In addition, a defendant is sometimes compelled to call a hostile prosecution witness as his own. Unless the State provides for discovery depositions of prosecution witnesses, which Tennessee apparently does not, the defendant is unlikely to know whether this testimony will prove entirely favorable."
21. *McGautha v. California*, 91 S. Ct. 1454 (1971).
22. 113 S. Ct. 1111 (1993).
23. The term *perjury trap* was defined as follows in the case of *United States v. Chen* [933 F.2d 793 (9th Cir. 1991)]: A "perjury trap is created when the government calls a witness before the grand jury for the primary purpose of obtaining testimony from him in order to prosecute him later for perjury. *United States v. Simone* [627 F.Supp. 1264, 1268 (D. N.J. 1986)] (perjury trap involves 'the deliberate use of a judicial proceeding to secure perjured testimony, a concept in itself abhorrent'). It involves the government's use of its investigatory powers to secure a perjury indictment on matters which are neither material nor germane to a legitimate ongoing investigation of the grand jury."

    Knowingly making a material false statement to a federal investigator can be charged as a crime under the federal False Statement Act. The U.S. Supreme Court affirmed a criminal conviction under this act in the 1998 case of *Brogan v. United States* [118 S. Ct. 805], when Brogan denied to federal investigators that he had received illegal cash or gifts in the incidents being investigated.
24. Rule 702 was amended in 2000 in response to the decisions of the U.S. Supreme Court in *Daubert v. Merrill Dow Pharmaceuticals Co.* [509 U.S. 579 (1993)] and *Kumho Tire Co. v. Carmichael* [119 S.

Ct. 1167 (1999)]. In those cases the Court established new standards for determining when a witness may be permitted to testify concerning scientific and technical knowledge. (*Daubert* and *Kumho*, and their influence on state court expert testimony rules, are discussed in more detail elsewhere in this book.)

Rule 702 and its counterparts in state evidence rules relate both to the qualification of a witness as an expert and to the nature of the testimony given by a witness, assuming he or she is an expert. As to the qualification aspect of Rule 702, a court usually looks at the witness's training, education, and experience to make the determination on the witness's qualification to be an expert. In the following cases, courts considered the qualifications necessary to give expert testimony.

In the 2001 case of *United States v. Watson* [260 F.3d 301 (3d Cir. 2001)], the Third Circuit Court of Appeals held that narcotics officers with extensive experience in narcotics trafficking could give expert testimony about the meaning of behavior of persons involved in illegal narcotics possession or distribution. There, the narcotics expert testified that the presence of crack cocaine, together with several hundred small plastic bags used by sellers of crack, was generally a sign that the holder of the crack was part of a distribution scheme, rather than holding the crack for personal use. The narcotics agent also testified, based on more than 200 arrests in bus stations, that bus trips between cities with brief layovers by persons in possession of crack and plastic bags were generally a sign of participation in a drug distribution system. The defendant, who was arrested on a bus trip to Philadelphia with a four-hour layover, had in his possession small amounts of crack cocaine and several hundred plastic bags of the type used in the sale of crack. He was convicted in the district court of possession with intent to distribute crack cocaine.

In the 2001 case of *United States v. Havvard* [260 F.3d 597 (7th Cir. 2001)], the Seventh Circuit Court of Appeals held that an FBI agent who had studied the success rates of fingerprint comparisons in numerous national cases, and who had a detailed process that he used to establish such comparisons, could give expert testimony that the latent fingerprint found on a firearm matched the fingerprint of the defendant. The defendant was found guilty of illegal possession of a firearm.

The second aspect of Rule 702 goes to the reliability of the testimony of the expert after the witness has been qualified as an expert. If the basis for the expert's opinion does not meet the Rule 702 and *Daubert* reliability tests, the expert may not testify. For example, in *United States v. Lea* [249 F.3d 632

(7th Cir. 2001)], a 2001 decision of the Seventh Circuit Court of Appeals, the defense sought to introduce evidence from a polygraph test administered by a Food and Drug Administration (FDA) agent to another person the defendant contended was the guilty party. Although the agent was qualified as an expert on administering and interpreting polygraph tests, he was not permitted to testify because his opinion that the person taking the test was not telling the truth was unreliable. The FDA agent could not say exactly which question was answered untruthfully and also had no statistical support for the accuracy of the testing methods used in the polygraph test administered. (The question of the reliability and admissibility of polygraph and voice spectrography is discussed more fully in Chapter 12.)

It is the fact finder (jury or judge) who determines the weight and credibility to be given to the testimony of both expert and ordinary witnesses. To promote this, most states have a rule similar to Federal Rule of Evidence 704(b), which states that in a criminal case an expert may not give an opinion that the defendant had or did not have the mental state constituting an element of the crime. That question must be decided by the jury. In *United States v. Watson*, discussed previously, even though the narcotics agents were qualified as experts, the trial court erred in permitting the agents to give their opinion that Watson, the defendant, had the intent to distribute the cocaine in his possession. The agents could testify generally about common behavior observed by them in drug distribution activities, but the jury must decide whether a given defendant exhibiting such behavior possesses the required intent to distribute. In *Watson*, the court of appeals reversed the defendant's conviction because of the expert's opinions on Watson's intent.

Effective December 1, 2011 Rule 702 was amended to change the way it is organized. However, the changes do not make significant changes in the substance of the Rule.

25. 431 F.3d 1147 (9th Cir. 2005).
26. 413 U.S. 15, 93 S. Ct. 2607, n.12.
27. 658 S.E.2d 755 (Ga. 2008).
28. *United States v. Tipton*, 964 F.2d 650 (7th Cir. 1992).
29. *United States v. Paiva*, 892 F.2d 148 (1st Cir. 1989).
30. *Waddell v. State*, 582 A.2d 260 (Md. App. 1990).
31. 803 P.2d 1077 (Mont.).
32. *United States v. Anthony*, 944 F.2d 780 (Okla. 1991).
33. *State v. Lamme*, 563 A.2d 1372 (Conn. App. 1989).
34. 1991 WL 263246.
35. *Commonwealth v. Cohen*, 605 A.2d 814 (Pa. Super. 1992).
36. *State v. Mallett*, 600 A.2d 273 (R.I. 1991).
37. *Kosbruk v. State*, 820 P.2d 1082 (Alaska App. 1991).
38. See the 1990 case of *Dysart v. State*, 581 So.2d 541 (Ala. Crim. App.).
39. 267 F.3d 614 (7th Cir. 2001).
40. 94 S. Ct. 1105.
41. 51 S. Ct. 218.
42. *Id.*
43. *Loehr v. Walton*, 242 F.3d 834 (8th Cir. 2001).
44. *United States v. Foster*, 227 F.3d 1096 (9th Cir. 2000).
45. *Udemba v. Nicoli*, 237 F.3d 8 (1st Cir. 2001).
46. 488 U.S. 277, 109 S. Ct. 480.
47. 482 U.S. 730, 107 S. Ct. 2658.
48. 291 A.2d 9 (Pa.).
49. *United States v. Richardson*, 233 F.3d 1285, 1288 (11th Cir. 2000).
50. *Id.*
51. Ariz. R. Ct. 39(b)(10); Fla. St. ch. 40.50(3).
52. 226 F.3d 457 (6th Cir. 2000).
53. Law enforcement officers have used hypnosis to assist an eyewitness in recalling a vehicle license plate number, the description of a fleeing offender, or a person seen in the vicinity of serious crime. Hypnosis was instrumental in apprehending offenders in the case of *State v. Joubert* [603 A.2d 861 (Me. 1992)] and in rescuing 26 children and their school bus driver in Chowchilla, California, when they were kidnapped in 1975. The school bus with all of its occupants had been buried in the ground to prevent the escape of the children and the bus driver.
54. 483 U.S. 44, 107 S. Ct. 2704.
55. *State v. Hurd*, 432 A.2d 86 (1989).
56. *State v. Varela*, 817 P.2d 731 (1991).
57. See *Stokes v. State*, 548 So.2d 188 (Fla. 1989).
58. More than 1,000 U.S. families belong to an organization known as the False Memory Syndrome Foundation. (The problem of false memories first became known more than 100 years ago when Sigmund Freud began treating patients. Freud was amazed at the number of hypnotized women who told of being raped by their fathers. Years later, Freud concluded that most of these women were fantasizing and that their memories were false. The problem of false memory syndrome is commonly associated with hypnotic therapy.) Most of these families struggle with the problem of a family member who has made accusations of sexual assault against another family member based on what might be a "false memory." Such accusations, whether true or false, affect whole families. The FMS Foundation (3401 Market Street, Philadelphia, PA 19104) tries to assist such families.

CHAPTER 6

Judicial Notice, Privileges of Witnesses, and Shield Laws

NEW YORK TIMES REPORTER, JUDITH MILLER.

Micah Walter/Reuters/Landov

LEARNING OBJECTIVES

In this chapter we discuss the practice of judicial notice in criminal trials and the privileges that may be used to exclude the testimony of some witnesses. The learning objectives for this chapter are

State the basis for and the limits of the judicial notice doctrine.

For at least three of the privileges discussed, state (1) the privilege, (2) the limits on the privilege, and (3) who may invoke the privilege.

State the difference between the spousal testimonial privilege and the marital communication privilege.

State the present status of the physician-patient privilege in federal courts.

State the present status of the journalist privilege.

List the "privileges" available to the government and government officers.

In late June of 2004 Donald Kasavich was found murdered in his mobile home. Some physical evidence pointed to Joseph Trzeciak as the perpetrator, and he was arrested and charged with first-degree murder. At his trial, his wife Laura Nilsen was called to testify by the prosecution. Over objection by defense counsel, Nilsen was allowed to give the following testimony, recounting statements she gave to police detectives on July 20, 2004: On April 4, 2004 the defendant beat her, tied her up, threw her in his truck, took a gun and drove to Kasavich's trailer. There the defendant threatened to "kill Kasavich and her, and then cut off Kasavich's dick and stick it in her mouth."

Trzeciak was found guilty of first-degree murder, but on appeal the Illinois Court of Appeals reversed the conviction, holding that the Illinois marital privilege statute prevented Nilsen from testifying about the defendant's murder threats.

The State appealed the Court of Appeals decision to the Illinois Supreme Court. The Illinois marital privilege statute states that marital communications are those that are made "in reliance on the confidence of the marital relationship." If you were sitting on the Illinois Supreme Court would you affirm or reverse the Court of Appeals decision? Why? *See People v. Trzeciak*, 5 N.E.3rd 141 (Ill. 2013)

JUDICIAL NOTICE IN GENERAL

If the parties to criminal and civil trials had to prove every fact of common knowledge and define every term they use, trials would be unreasonably long. Court calendars would back up, and delays in getting a case to trial would increase considerably.

judicial notice The doctrine that evidence of well-accepted facts may be introduced in court without proof; a judicial shortcut.

To avoid unnecessary delays, courts have developed the commonsense doctrine of **judicial notice**. This notice relieves parties in criminal and civil trials from the duty of introducing witnesses, documents, and other evidence to prove uncontroverted facts. For example, the California Supreme Court held that: "Judicial notice is a judicial short cut, a doing away … … with formal necessity of evidence because there is no real necessity for it."[1] The parties to trials also may use a device called a joint stipulation to stipulate to certain facts for trial purposes, making proof of such facts unnecessary.

All states have statutes or court rules that authorize the use of a judicial notice doctrine. Many state statutes that permit this use are similar to the Federal Rules of Evidence, Rule 201, found in Appendix C of this book. For example, Rule 201 of the New Hampshire Rules of Evidence states:

> [a] court may take judicial notice of a fact. A judicially noticed fact must be one not subject to reasonable dispute in that it is either (1) generally known within the territorial jurisdiction of the court or (2) capable of accurate and ready determination by resort to sources whose accuracy cannot reasonably be questioned.

Judicial Notice of Matters of General Knowledge

Judicial notice of matters generally known within the community or state is probably the oldest application of the doctrine of judicial notice.[2] This aspect of the doctrine permits judges and jurors to recognize facts commonly known to them without formal evidence proving those facts. In this way, judicial notice shortens and simplifies trials. The Supreme Court of California gave the following explanation of the "general knowledge" rule in a 1970 case:

> Judicial notice may not be taken of any matter unless authorized or required by law (Evid. Code, § 452). This court is compelled to take judicial notice only of facts and

propositions of generalized knowledge that are so universally known that they cannot reasonably be the subject of dispute (Evid. Code, § 451). If there is any doubt whatever either as to the fact itself or as to its being a matter of common knowledge, evidence should be required.[3]

The following are common examples of the use of judicial notice to prove matters of general knowledge:

- *Establishing the meaning of words, phrases, or abbreviations commonly used "on the street":* The street terms *fix* in drug cases and *turning a trick* in prostitution cases might be established by judicial notice. The parties may also establish the terms by asking a law enforcement witness to define them.
- *Establishing the sex of a witness or defendant:* For example, the Supreme Court of Indiana held that: "The sex of a human being is generally its most obvious characteristic. We can look at another human being and, with a very high degree of certainty, ascertain his or her sex. Therefore, why couldn't a presiding judge take judicial notice of a defendant's sex? We believe he can and should."[4]
- *Establishing the location of well-known sections of a city or well-known streets and buildings:* Another example is determining the distances to well-known cities and the interstates or highways used to drive to those cities.
- *Establishing well-known habits:* For example, in the case of *State v. Mundell,*[5] the Court of Appeals of Hawaii held: "We take judicial notice that drug dealers and traffickers rarely carry 'large' amounts of drugs on their person. Their supplies are generally secreted in their homes, in their luggage, or in other such places where they may be accessible for sale. Drug dealers often use other people to transport large quantities of drugs for them."

It has been held that courts should not take judicial notice of facts that are an element of the crime charged or serve as the basis for increased prison sentences. In *State v. Harvey*, 647 N.W.2d 489 (Wis. 2002) the court held that it was error for a judge to take judicial notice that a certain park was a "city park." The defendant was convicted of sales of illegal drugs, and under state law would receive an additional prison sentence if illegal drugs were sold within 1,000 feet of a "city park." The prosecution failed to offer any evidence that the park was a city park, but the trial judge took judicial notice of that fact. The Wisconsin Supreme Court stated that because under W.S.A.§ 902.01(7) the jury is instructed it must accept the fact as established, the judicial notice amounted to an unconstitutional mandatory presumption.

A court may not take judicial notice of a fact solely because the fact is well known to the trial judge. For example, in the 2002 case of *United States v. Mariscal*, 285 F.3d 1127, the Ninth Circuit Court of Appeals held that a trial judge could not take judicial notice of traffic conditions at a local intersection, when knowledge of those conditions arose only from the judge's personal driving experience. Narcotics agents made an investigative stop of a vehicle in which the defendant was present, and the prosecution attempted to justify the stop using evidence that the driver of the vehicle made an unsignaled right turn. This court ruled that an unsignaled turn is illegal only if traffic is present at the intersection where the turn occurred. The prosecution failed to offer evidence of such traffic, but the trial court filled that gap by taking judicial notice that the intersection was one of the busiest in the city. The court of appeals found the investigative stop unlawful because the agents had no reasonable belief that a law had been broken.

Judicial Notice of Facts Obtained from Sources, Such as Records, Books, and Newspapers

A court may properly take judicial notice of facts cited in recognized reports, learned treatises, or dictionaries, or simple data printed in newspapers, such as dates and temperatures. Such facts are not in controversy but may be very important to one of the parties in the trial.

The following examples illustrate the use of judicial notice in this area:

- In 1921, the U.S. Supreme Court held that judicial notice could be taken of the date on which a state ratified a proposed constitutional amendment, because this information could be easily obtained from records or books.[6]
- Courts could take judicial notice of dates, days, or time because this information is readily available in almanacs, newspapers, and the like (such as that the Fourth of July fell on a Friday in the year 2008, at what hour the sun set on a given day, or whether it rained or snowed on a given day).
- Courts may take notice of statutes of other states, court records of your state or other states, and ordinances of counties and cities within your state. In the 1992 case of *People v. Hardy,*[7] the Supreme Court of California pointed out that California Evidence Code, section 452, provides that "Judicial notice may be taken … (of the) records of … any court of record of the United States." As an example of when this may be used, in the 1991 case of *In the Matter of Breedlove*[8] the West Virginia Supreme Court held that it was proper to take judicial notice of a previous drunk-driving conviction in ordering a 10-year revocation of the driver's license.

Courts must be careful how they take judicial notice. In *State v. Gagnon,*[9] a defendant was convicted of negligent driving when he sped on the paved surface surrounding a fire station. The negligent driving statute applied to driving on a public "way," which under New Hampshire law means (a) a public road or (b) a private road maintained by the state through the use of state funds. The trial judge took judicial notice of the fact that the paved surface around the fire station was a "way," and the defendant was convicted. On appeal, the New Hampshire Supreme Court held that it was not "generally known" that public funds were appropriated for maintaining the fire station's paved surfaces, which made the first part of the New Hampshire judicial notice statute inapplicable. Because the trial court did not specify which source would provide the "accurate and ready determination" that state funds were so used, the court also held that the second part of the statute was not satisfied. The defendant's conviction was reversed.

Scientific and Technological Facts Recognized by Judicial Notice

Courts have long held that judicial notice may be taken of scientific theories that have been so established that they have "attained the status of scientific law," *United States v. Janis.*[10] Judicial notice also can be taken of a court ruling that a scientific technique is reliable; for example, after a state or federal court establishes that DNA fingerprinting is a reliable scientific technique, there is no need to bring in expert witnesses again and again in every case to prove that DNA fingerprinting is reliable and accurate. (This issue is discussed in more detail in Chapter 18.)

Examples
- In the case of *United States v. Jacobetz,*[11] DNA fingerprinting was used to identify the defendant as the man who abducted a woman in Vermont, repeatedly raped

her, and released her in New York. The court held that "in future cases with a similar evidentiary issue, a court could properly take judicial notice of the general acceptability of the general theory and the use of these specific techniques."

- An Ohio court of appeals held in the case of *State v. Brock*[12] that "courts may take judicial notice of any scientific fact that may be ascertained by reference to a standard dictionary or is of such general knowledge that it is known by any judicial officer. In the instant case, the trial court was correct in taking judicial notice of the fact that heroin is a narcotic drug and is habit forming."

THE PRIVILEGE AGAINST SELF-INCRIMINATION

In tracing the origins of the Fifth Amendment's right to remain silent, the U.S. Supreme Court pointed out in the case of *Miranda v. Arizona* that the privilege's "roots go back into ancient times" and probably has origins in the Bible.[13]

privilege A benefit or right enjoyed by a person; for example, the privilege of a witness not to answer a question might be based on the privilege against self-incrimination or the marital privilege.

The Fifth Amendment **privilege** against self-incrimination is the only privilege that has been incorporated into the U.S. Constitution and many state constitutions. All other privileges exist only in statutory or common law. The Fifth Amendment of the U.S. Constitution provides that: "No person ... shall be compelled in any criminal case to be a witness against himself."

This privilege "protects a person against being incriminated by his own compelled testimonial communications."[14] Because statements made by a person in any civil hearing or questioning might later be used against that person in a criminal proceeding, the U.S. Supreme Court has repeatedly held that the privilege can be asserted by a person to refuse to answer questions "in any proceeding, civil or criminal, formal or informal, where the answers might incriminate him in future criminal proceedings."[15] The privilege has thus been invoked, for example, in divorce and tax cases as well as in criminal cases and questioning by law enforcement officers.[16] In *Anton v. Prospect Café Milano, Inc.*, 233 F.R.D. 216 (D.D.C. 2006) the Fifth Amendment privilege was invoked by a café owner who was being sued for damages by the parents of a waitress who died after falling from a balcony at the owner's apartment. The owner refused to answer discovery questions asked by the parents because he feared his answers could be used by investigators to charge him with a crime. The court held the privilege applied, because even though no formal criminal charges had been brought against the owner, the possibility of such charges was enough to invoke the Fifth Amendment privilege.

The U.S. Supreme Court has held that the privilege against self-incrimination "reflects many of our fundamental values and noble aspirations."[17] Because this privilege is "the essential mainstay of our adversary system," the U.S. Constitution requires "that the government seeking to punish an individual produce the evidence against him by its own independent labor rather than by the cruel, simple expedient of compelling it from his own mouth."[18]

Areas Where the Fifth Amendment Privilege Against Self-Incrimination Does Not Apply

The U.S. Supreme Court has stated that while the Fifth Amendment privilege applies to documents and other material, that is so only if they are in the sole possession of the person invoking the privilege. *Crouch v. United States*, 409 U.S. 322, 331 (1973) ["possession bears the closest relationship to the personal compulsion forbidden by the Fifth Amendment."] In *In re Grand Jury Subpoena*, 584 F.3d 175 (4th Cir.

2009) the court held a U.S. Congressman could not invoke the Fifth Amendment privilege to prevent the prosecution from obtaining documents that belonged to him, but were in the possession of his chief of staff in her congressional office.

The Fifth Amendment privilege against self-incrimination applies only to evidence of a communicative or testimonial nature. It does not apply when only physical evidence is sought and obtained. Seizure of physical evidence is controlled by the Fourth Amendment to the U.S. Constitution. Thus, the privilege against self-incrimination does not extend to the following circumstances:

- Withdrawing blood and using it as evidence to show that the defendant was driving a vehicle while intoxicated (*Schmerber v. California*).[19]
- Using a handwriting exemplar (sample); held to be controlled by the Fourth Amendment, not the Fifth Amendment (*Gilbert v. California*).[20]
- Compelling the accused to exhibit his person for observation, as in a lineup or showup (*United States v. Wade*).[21]
- Making a voice exemplar (sample) (*United States v. Dionisio*).[22]
- Federal courts of appeals have held that no Fifth Amendment violation occurred when, for identification purposes, the defendant was compelled to wear a false goatee (*United States v. Hammond*),[23] to wear a wig (*United States v. Murray*),[24] to shave for identification purposes (*United States v. Valenzuela*),[25] to put on a stocking mask at trial to permit a witness to testify as to similarity to the masked robber (*United States v. Roberts*),[26] or to dye her or his hair to the color it was at the time of the offense (*United States v. Brown*).[27]
- Testimony of a witness that the defendant was compelled to put on a shirt, or other item of clothing, and that the item fit the defendant (*Holt v. United States*).[28]
- Where immunity has been granted and the person is compelled to testify or agrees to testify as part of a plea agreement. Immunity is of two kinds: use immunity, where the specific statements made by a witness may not be used in subsequent prosecutions, and transactional immunity, where the witness cannot be prosecuted for any crime related to the subject matter of the witness's testimony.
- The U.S. Supreme Court has repeatedly ruled that the Fifth Amendment privilege applies only to people and not to corporations, labor unions, and other organizations. Corporations and unincorporated unions and other organizations cannot claim the privilege against self-incrimination.[29]
- Where the incrimination is of others and is not self-incrimination.[30]
- Where the public interest in protecting children from abuse outweighs the Fifth Amendment privilege. After a small child had received numerous physical injuries and the child's mother was seen abusing the child, the mother was ordered to disclose the location of the child. The mother was jailed on contempt when she would not do so. The U.S. Supreme Court affirmed the contempt sentence in the 1990 case of *Baltimore Department of Social Services v. Bouknight*.[31]
- U.S. military personnel and law enforcement officers are obligated to report illegal conduct of their fellow officers and military associates. The U.S. Supreme Court upheld this service requirement as not being in violation of the Fifth Amendment privilege. It was held that the defense of fear of retaliation could not be used against the offense of failure to report the illegal conduct of others.[32] However, the Fifth Amendment privilege would apply if the military serviceperson or law enforcement officer had also been a party to the crime, such as drug use.[33]
- Where there has been a voluntary, intelligent waiver of the privilege.

WHEN AND WHERE THE FIFTH AMENDMENT PRIVILEGE AGAINST SELF-INCRIMINATION BECOMES APPLICABLE

The Fifth Amendment to the U.S. Constitution provides that "No person … shall be compelled in a criminal case to be a witness against himself." The Supreme Court held in 1976 that the Fifth Amendment "protects a person … against being incriminated by his own compelled testimonial communications." *Fisher v. United States*, 425 U.S. 391, 409 (1976). Therefore, the Fifth Amendment protection against self-incrimination becomes applicable when a person's statement or communication

1. Is "compelled." Only testimony or communications that a person is compelled to give are protected by the Fifth Amendment. Where statements or communications are given freely and voluntarily, without any compelling influence, there is no Fifth Amendment protection.
2. Is "testimonial." In *Doe v. United States*, 487 U.S. 201, 210, the Supreme Court held that " … in order to be testimonial, an accused's communication must of itself, explicitly or impliedly, relate a factual assertion or disclose information." Thus, as noted earlier in this chapter, neither blood or DNA samples, nor handwriting or voice samples, are testimonial. See Chapter 8 for more Supreme Court cases on the meaning of "testimonial."
3. Is "self-incriminating." The U.S. Supreme Court stated in the case of *Marchetti v. United States*, 390 U.S. 39, 53 (1968) that the privilege applies when a claimant is confronted by "substantial and 'real,' and not merely trifling or imaginary, hazards of incrimination." Incrimination of another person is not self-incrimination. Nor does the Fifth Amendment protect testimony that might become incriminating in the future. (See *United States v. Freed*, 401 U.S. 601 (1971).)
4. In "any criminal case." In the case of *Murphy v. Waterfront Comm.*, 378 U.S. 52 (1964) the U.S. Supreme Court held that the possibility of criminal prosecution by either the federal government or a state government made the Fifth Amendment privilege available. (See the case of *United States v. Balsys*, 524 U.S. 666 (1998) as to whether the possibility of criminal prosecution by a foreign government would make the privilege applicable.)

Examples Where the Fifth Amendment Privilege Against Self-Incrimination Does Apply

The Fifth Amendment privilege against self-incrimination has been found to apply in the circumstances of these recent cases:

- A witness may raise the Fifth Amendment privilege even where the witness insists she is innocent of any crime. In *Ohio v. Reiner*,[34] the U.S. Supreme Court held that a babysitter called to testify in the prosecution of a father for the death of his infant son could assert the privilege, even though she professed her complete innocence of any relation to the crime.
- A taxpayer may invoke the privilege to refuse to answer specific questions on a tax return but may not refuse to file a return altogether (*United States v. Sabino*).[35]
- The privilege is available when a person is questioned by a probation officer, so long as the officer makes it clear that answers to the question are mandatory, not optional. Answers could lead to violations of probation, which is a form of incrimination (*United States v. Davis*).[36]
- Where a defendant remains silent under questioning, the Fifth Amendment prohibits the prosecution from introducing evidence of that silence at trial. The fact that the defendant remained silent may lead one to conclude that the defendant admitted the accuracy of the questions, and the silence is thus incriminatory (*United States v. Velarde-Gomez*).[37]

THE ATTORNEY-CLIENT PRIVILEGE

attorney-client privilege The oldest of the privileges: protects communications between the client and the attorney.

As the U.S. Supreme Court pointed out in the 1981 case of *Upjohn Company et al. v. United States et al.*, "the attorney-client privilege is the oldest of the privileges for confidential communications known to the common law."[38] In that case the Supreme Court held that communications by Upjohn employees to corporate lawyers about illegal payments made to foreign government officials were covered by the **attorney-client privilege**. The Court stated that the purpose of the privilege was to encourage full and frank communication between attorneys and their clients and thereby promote broader public interests in the observance of law and administration

> to encourage full and frank communication between attorneys and their clients and thereby promote broader public interests in the observance of law and administration of justice. The privilege recognizes that sound legal advice or advocacy serves public ends and that such advice or advocacy depends upon the lawyer being fully informed by the client. As we stated last Term in *Trammel v. United States*, 445 U.S. 40, 51 (1980), "The attorney-client privilege rests on the need for the advocate and counselor to know all that relates to the client's reasons for seeking representation if the professional mission is to be carried out." … Admittedly complications in the application of the privilege arise when the client is a corporation, which in theory is an artificial creature of the law, and not an individual; but this Court has assumed that the privilege applies when the client is a corporation, and the Government does not contest the general proposition.

Many states have statutes regulating the attorney-client privilege. Other states, and the federal government, use the principles of common law. For example, Rule 501 of the Federal Rules of Evidence, as amended effective December 1, 2011, (see Appendix C) provides that the "common law as interpreted by United States courts in the light of reason and experience" is to be used for all of the communicative privileges.

Requirements of the Attorney-Client Privilege

For the attorney-client privilege to exist, both state and federal governments require that certain conditions be met. The client must seek the professional legal services of an attorney and have the intention of establishing an attorney-client relationship. Consulting with an attorney for non-legal services has been held not to fall within the privilege. Having conversations during which one informally seeks free legal advice from an attorney, such as at a chance meeting with the attorney, do not create the privilege. Additionally, it is generally held that the privilege applies only to confidential communications made within the attorney-client relationship.

The presence of a third party when statements are made by a client to an attorney usually causes the privilege to be waived, since the third person's presence normally destroys the client's expectation of confidentiality. However, the necessary presence of the attorney's secretary, law clerk, or other employee during a conference in the attorney's office would not cause a court to hold that the communications were not privileged. Such persons can be reasonably expected by the client to maintain confidentiality of statements made in their presence. The presence of a parent or spouse in a conference just before a trial or hearing is not uncommon, and there is every reason to believe that the privilege would apply to such communications.[39]

The Supreme Court has held that where the client is a corporation, not only are communications between officers of the corporation and corporate counsel privileged, but also communications of employees giving information to counsel at the request of their superiors.[40] Federal courts have reached different conclusions about

DOES THE ATTORNEY-CLIENT PRIVILEGE SURVIVE THE DEATH OF THE CLIENT?

An official in the Clinton administration was involved in the investigation of the White House Travel Office. He met with a private attorney to discuss the investigation, and seven days later committed suicide. Later, a federal grand jury subpoenaed the attorney's notes of the conversations with the official. The attorney moved to quash the subpoena, claiming the notes were privileged under the federal attorney-client privilege. The trial court agreed, and ordered the subpoena quashed. The court of appeals reversed, holding the privilege did not survive the death of the client.

The U.S. Supreme Court agreed with the trial judge, and held the privilege survived the death of the client. The court noted that the common law has long provided that the privilege survives death of the client. The court thought the knowledge of the privilege's survival would encourage a client to fully communicate with the attorney, which in the end is the main reason for the existence of the privilege, the court concluded. *Swidler & Berlin v. United States*, 524 U.S. 399 (1998).

whether the common-law attorney-client privilege applies to a government lawyer. Government lawyers frequently raise the attorney-client privilege when subpoenaed to testify before a federal grand jury. Some courts have held that the privilege may not be asserted by a government lawyer.[41] In a 2005 case, the Second Circuit Court of Appeals held that the privilege could be asserted by a government lawyer. In *In re Grand Jury Investigation (United States v. Doe)*,[42] a federal grand jury was investigating alleged corruption in the office of John Rowland, the governor of Connecticut. The federal prosecutors called an attorney who worked in the governor's office before the grand jury and asked her questions pertaining to the alleged corruption. She asserted the attorney-client privilege on behalf of her client, the governor, stating that she advised the governor on matters involved in the investigation. The district court ordered her to testify, but the court of appeals reversed, stating that the same purposes served when the privilege is asserted by private individuals, required the privilege to be available to a lawyer whose client is the government. The court also specifically noted that the **crime-fraud exception** would apply to government lawyers who became involved in any illegal conduct with their client.

crime-fraud exception
The exception made to attorney-client privilege when a client consults with an attorney for the purpose of committing a future crime such as perjury; communication and documents relating to this fraud are not protected.

Limits of the Attorney–Client Privilege

The U.S. Supreme Court pointed out in the 1989 case of *United States v. Zolin*[43] that since "the privilege has the effect of withholding relevant information from the fact finder, it applies only where necessary to achieve its purpose." There are therefore limits to the attorney-client privilege:

- The client must have a "reasonable expectation" of confidentiality of communications with an attorney before the privilege applies. In *Mueller Industries v. Beckman*, 927 N.E.2d 794 (Ill. App. 2010) the court held that where an attorney represented both a corporation and the president of the corporation at various times, the president could not have a reasonable expectation his communications with the attorney would be confidential in a subsequent lawsuit between the corporation and the president.
- The privilege applies when a client discloses past wrongdoing to the attorney, or when a client asks an attorney if contemplated future actions would be

PROCEDURES & PROCESSES

Raising the Crime Fraud Exception

The attorney-client privilege belongs to the client, but it is often the attorney who first invokes the privilege. For example, when a federal grand jury is convened to investigate the possible criminal activity of a person or organization, attorneys who have represented the client being investigated might be called to testify before the grand jury. As would be expected, the attorney will often refuse to testify about any communications between the client and the attorney, based on the privilege. What happens then, if the prosecution believes the crime-fraud exception applies? A 2014 Third Circuit Court of Appeals case shows how one court proceeds.

Federal prosecutors convened a grand jury to investigate whether a consulting firm violated the Foreign Corrupt Practices Act (FCPA) in its dealings with a financial institution located in the United Kingdom. They subpoenaed the consulting firm's former counsel to testify before the grand jury, and in anticipation of the attorney or client invoking the privilege, filed a motion in federal district court to compel compliance with the subpoena. The client intervened, and sought to quash the subpoena. The district judge, following the procedure established by the Supreme Court in the *Zolin* case discussed above, questioned the attorney *in camera* (without the prosecution or the client) to determine if the crime-fraud exception applied. The district court concluded the client approached the attorney for the purpose of acquiring information to be used to further the alleged crimes. Specifically, the court concluded reasonable grounds existed to believe the client intended to violate the FCPA, and was seeking ways to accomplish the crime. For example, the business dealings earned the client over $8 million in broker fees, and shortly after receiving the fees the client paid $3.5 million dollars to the sister of a bank official who approved the underlying transactions that earned the client the fees. The district court therefore refused to quash the subpoena, and ordered the attorney to testify before the grand jury. On appeal, the court of appeals affirmed the district court's decision. *In re Grand Jury Subpoena*, 745 F.3d 681 (3rd Cir. 2014).

legal. The privilege does not protect disclosures about present or future wrong-doing that the client intends. This is called the "crime-fraud exception." Moreover, an attorney becomes part of a criminal conspiracy when he or she advises a client on how to best commit a crime or fraud. Quoting a lower court, the Supreme Court ruled in the *Zolin* case that

> It is the purpose of the crime-fraud exception to assure that "the seal of secrecy" between lawyer and client does not extend to communications "made for the purpose of getting advice for commission of a fraud" or crime.

- Most courts hold that an attorney has a legal and ethical obligation to deliver physical evidence of a crime to the police. The Maryland Court of Appeals (the highest court of Maryland) reviewed cases from other state courts addressing this question in the case of *Rubin v. State*,[44] stating that

> ("[D]efense counsel may not retain physical evidence pertaining to the crime charged."); *Commonwealth v. Stenhach*, 356 Pa. Super. 5, 16, 514 A.2d 114, 119 (1986), *appeal denied*, 517 Pa. 589, 534 A.2d 769 (1987) ("[T]he overwhelming majority of states …

hold that physical evidence of crime in the possession of a criminal defense attorney is not subject to a privilege but must be delivered to the prosecution.").

- The general rule is that the attorney-client privilege does not protect the name and identity of a client or the amount of the attorney fee.[45] This rule was stated as follows by the Fourth Circuit Court of Appeals:

> [T]he identity of a client is a matter not normally within the privilege nor are matters involving the receipt of fees from a client usually privileged. *United States v. (Under Seal)*, 774 F.2d 624, 628 (4th Cir. 1985), *review denied*, 475 U.S. 1108, 106 S. Ct. 1514 (1986).

THE HUSBAND-WIFE PRIVILEGE

To foster marital harmony and to encourage a bond of confidentiality between wife and husband, English courts began in the early 1600s to use the rule that a spouse could not be forced to testify against the other spouse. Today, all states and the federal government use the husband-wife privilege (also known as the *marital privilege*), which originated before the United States became a nation.

The U.S. Supreme Court pointed out in the 1980 case of *Trammel v. United States*[46] that when the husband-wife privilege came into use, women were "regarded as chattel or demeaned by denial of a separate legal identity and dignity associated with recognition as a whole human being." The Supreme Court stated that because the "ancient foundations for so sweeping a privilege have long since disappeared," many changes have been made in the laws of states regarding the privilege. The Court noted that in more recent years the marital privilege has been divided into the "spousal testimonial privilege," and the "marital communication" privilege, with only a few states permitting one spouse to prevent the other spouse from giving any testimony whatsoever. Moreover, in states that retain the testimonial privilege, the privilege ends with the marriage. (See Problem 1 at the end of this chapter). Marital communications, on the other hand, are privileged even if the marriage is subsequently dissolved. Thus, the testimonial privilege generally belongs exclusively to each spouse, and only that spouse may decide to testify or not against the other spouse. The Court in *Trammel* held that the federal marital privilege permitted a spouse to exclude only confidential communications between spouses, and that the decision to testify about other facts belonged only to each spouse.

The requirements that must exist under Rule 501 of the Federal Rules of Evidence to use the privilege in federal courts are stated in the 1992 case of *United States v. Evans*:[47]

1. ... The marital confidential communications privilege prohibits testimony regarding private intra-spousal communications. The privilege extends only to words or acts that are intended as a communication to the other spouse. Thus, while a spouse may refuse to testify at all against a defendant spouse, the defendant spouse may only invoke the privilege to prevent testimony of a confidential communication when the other spouse is willing to testify.
2. ... The communication must also occur during a time when the marriage is valid under state law and the couple is not permanently separated.[48]
3. ... Finally, the communication must be made in confidence; in other words, it cannot be made in the presence of a third party, and the communicating spouse cannot intend for it to be passed on to others. Once these three prerequisites are met, a defendant may invoke the privilege to prevent his

spouse from testifying as to the content of the protected communication. (See 2 *Weinstein's Evidence* § 505[04] (1991).) This privilege continues even after the marriage has ended.

In most states the marital privilege statute is directed only at "testimony" of one spouse against the other about confidential communications. For example, the Ohio statute, Ohio R. C. § 2945.42, reads, "Husband or wife shall not testify concerning a communication by one to the other, or act done by either in the presence of the other, during coverture (marriage), unless the communication was made or act done in the known presence or hearing of a third person competent to be a witness." The Ohio Supreme Court has interpreted this statute to preclude only actual testimony by a spouse; *State v. Perez*, 920 N.E.2d 104 (Ohio 2009). In that case police persuaded a wife to make a tape recording of her conversations with her husband concerning his role in a robbery/murder. At his trial the wife testified, but not about the content of the tape recordings. Rather, the prosecution introduced the tape recordings as evidence over the objection of marital privilege by the defendant. The husband was convicted of murder. On appeal, the Ohio Supreme Court held the marital privilege did not apply to the tape recordings, but only the wife's actual testimony. While court decisions prohibiting admission of tape recordings made by a spouse can be found—see *People v. Dubanowski*, 394 N.E.2d 605 (Ill. App. 1979)—the Ohio position appears to be in the majority.

Courts have held a third party may testify about statements made by a defendant's spouse, even though the marital privilege would prevent the spouse from giving such testimony. Thus, where the defendant's spouse told a friend that her husband admitted murdering a woman, the friend could testify about those statements and the marital privilege would not apply.[49] Of course, such testimony is hearsay, and to be admitted must qualify as a hearsay exception and satisfy the Confrontation Clause of the U.S. Constitution (see Chapter 8 of this text).

Partner-in-Crime Exception to the Husband-Wife Privilege

partner-in-crime exception The exception to the marital privilege if a husband and wife commit a crime together.

The husband-wife privilege does not extend to situations where the wife and the husband are committing a crime (or crimes) together. Examples of the **partner-in-crime exception** or the *joint-criminal-participation exception* to the husband-wife privilege follow:

- Both the wife and the husband were involved in growing marijuana. In holding that the marital privilege did not apply, the U.S. Court of Appeals held that "the interests of justice outweigh the goal of fostering marital harmony."[50]
- The husband-wife privilege was held not to apply where both spouses were involved in trafficking cocaine.[51]
- When the husband ran off with his secretary, the angry wife provided the Internal Revenue Service with information of criminal tax evasion. The husband argued the marital privilege when the wife appeared as a prosecution witness against him at his criminal trial. The court held that the privilege would ordinarily be available to prevent the wife's testimony, but that in this case the wife was also guilty of the criminal conduct and the partnership-in-crime exception applied. It did not matter, the court held, that the wife was not prosecuted in return for her cooperation. The husband's conviction based on the testimony of his ex-wife was affirmed.

The husband-wife privilege is directed at privileged communications, but not necessarily at the fact that a communication occurred, as illustrated in the 2008 case of *Humphrey v. State.*[52] There, a husband was charged with murder. The state offered as evidence cell phone records obtained from the husband's cell phone provider. These records showed numerous calls between the defendant and his wife, which identified the time of each call and the location of the cell phone when the call was made. These records placed the cell phone outside the victim's workplace in the hours preceding the murder, and also at the murder scene at about the time the murder occurred. The trial court admitted the records over the husband's privilege claim, and the husband was convicted of murder. On appeal, the court upheld the trial court's decision admitting the cell phone records, stating that the husband-wife privilege went only to the contents of the conversations between the husband and wife, not the fact that such conversations occurred. The murder conviction was affirmed.

When One Spouse Commits Crimes Against the Other Spouse or Children

If a husband were to beat his wife or children and his wife could not testify against him in a criminal case because of the marital privilege, the law would not make sense. To avoid this result, the federal and every state marital privilege statute provide an exception to the marital privilege to permit one spouse to testify in criminal cases about beatings and other violence by the other spouse against either the spouse or their children.[53]

However, some states limit this exception to personal violence committed against the victim spouse. In the case of *State v. Webb,*[54] the husband destroyed his wife's property, and the wife could not testify against her husband because the crime was not a crime of personal violence against her. But in the case of *State v. Delaney,*[55] the defendant's ex-wife was permitted to testify about the husband's sexual assaults against their child and the wife's two younger sisters, which occurred during the marriage.

In the 2014 case of *United States v. Breton*[56] the First Circuit Court of Appeals held that the federal marital privilege "offense against spouse" exception included offenses against the spouse's child. The court noted that the great majority of state and federal courts that have faced the issue have held the privilege inapplicable.

At least one state has held that the violence against spouse exception also applies to persons outside the immediate family of the accused. In *Lynch v. Com.,*[57] the court held that the Kentucky exception to the marital privilege for harm to a person who was a "resident" of the household of the accused, Kentucky Rule of Evidence 504 (c), applied to a third person living with the husband who invoked the privilege. The defendant and his wife were having marital problems, mainly due to the husband's jealousy of his wife's earlier romantic arrangement with a former boyfriend, the eventual murder victim, and his wife moved out of the house. "Oddly enough," the court observed, the former boyfriend moved in with the husband after the wife left. The husband then murdered the former boyfriend as he slept one evening, and subsequently confessed the killing to his wife. The state called her as a witness, and the husband moved to exclude her testimony about his confession under the marital privilege statute. The trial court held that the former boyfriend qualified as a "person residing" in the defendant's household, and as a result the marital privilege did not extend to the wife's testimony about harm done to the former boyfriend. The defendant's murder conviction was affirmed.

THE PHYSICIAN-PATIENT PRIVILEGE

physician-patient privilege The privilege created, not by common law, but by state law for state courts; belongs to the patient and may be waived by the patient.

The **physician-patient privilege** did not exist at common law and therefore exists only in states that have created such a privilege by statute. Under Rule 501 of the Federal Rules of Evidence, the U.S. Supreme Court and other federal courts are charged with developing privilege law. As of 2014, the U.S. Supreme Court has not recognized a general physician-patient privilege. (See the case of *Jaffee v. Redmond*, discussed below, on a limited privilege.)

The various state statutes define the extent and the limitations of the privilege. Thus, the relevant state statute determines if the privilege protects communications to a nurse, a dentist, a druggist, an orthopedist, a chiropractor, a Christian Science practitioner, or a veterinary surgeon. In most states medical staff, such as physician's assistants and nurses, are covered by the doctor-patient privilege, at least for communications made in the course of treatment and pursuant to a doctor's orders. However, some state statutes have been construed as making the privilege not applicable to communications to emergency medical technicians (EMTs). (See *Rogers v. State*, 255 P.3d 1264 (Nev. 2011) [admission to ambulance EMT that patient smoked marijuana before car accident not protected by privilege].) All these professions, however, have codes of ethics, and members would ordinarily be reluctant to reveal information obtained in a professional relationship unless compelled to do so.[58]

Because state statutes control the privilege, if it does exist, physicians have to comply with the statutory requirements of their state. If the statutes of the state require that physicians report persons treated for gunshot wounds, physicians must comply with this requirement. If the statutes require physicians to report persons treated for venereal disease, this requirement must also be met.

Requirements of the Physician-Patient Privilege

For the physician-patient privilege to exist, the patient must have consulted the physician for treatment or diagnosis for possible treatment. Where such conditions exist, it is immaterial who employs or pays the physician. If the physician under these circumstances calls in other medical doctors to aid in the treatment or diagnosis, any disclosures made to any of the physicians are also privileged.

The scope of the privilege varies among the states. In some states the only communications protected are those made by a patient and relating to diagnosis or treatment of his medical conditions. (See e.g., Ohio R.C. Ann. § 2317.02(B)(1).) In others virtually all statements made to a doctor during treatment are protected. (See e.g., F.S.A. § 456.057(8), construed in *State v. Sun*, 82 So.3d 866 (Fla. App. 2011).

The general rule is that a physician-patient privilege does not exist when a suspect or a defendant is being examined at the request of a court, a law enforcement agency, or a prosecutor. Such examinations may be requested or ordered when a court or prosecutor wants to determine whether a defendant is competent to stand trial or whether commitment proceedings should be commenced instead of filing criminal charges. When probable cause exists to believe a person has been driving a vehicle under the influence, a law enforcement agency might request medical testing to determine whether a crime has been committed. The results of such tests are normally excluded from the physician-patient privilege. Most states have "implied consent" statutes under which drivers give their implied consent to these medical tests, such as section 905.04(4)(d) of the Wisconsin statutes.

The physician-patient privilege is considered a very limited privilege, subject to the interpretation of the statutes of each state. The privilege, where it does exist, is for the protection of the patient, not the physician. Where the privilege does exist, it may be waived by the patient or a representative of the patient. Whether the privilege exists after the death of the patient depends on each state's laws and court rulings. The attending physician must file a death certificate, however, and all states have laws that permit public officials with statutory authority to order autopsies and coroner's inquests.

THE PSYCHOTHERAPIST-PATIENT PRIVILEGE

psychotherapist-patient privilege A privilege created by statute in many states.

Although no **psychotherapist-patient privilege** existed at common law, all 50 states have created this privilege by statute. For a patient to qualify for this privilege, the patient must seek the treatment or diagnosis of a licensed psychotherapist for treatment of mental or emotional conditions, including drug addiction. Those professionals defined as psychotherapists ordinarily include licensed physicians and psychologists, or persons reasonably believed by the patient to be so licensed. The conditions and limitations of this privilege are ordinarily similar to those of the physician-patient privilege.

Under Rule 501 of the Federal Rules of Evidence, U.S. courts are responsible for formulating privileges. The federal courts have generally recognized those privileges that are available in state courts. In *Jaffee v. Redmond,*[59] the U.S. Supreme Court recognized the psychotherapist-patient privilege: "confidential communications between a licensed psychotherapist and his or her patients in the course of diagnosis and treatment are protected from compelled disclosure under Rule 501 of the Federal Rules of Evidence." The *Jaffee* court observed that all 50 states had enacted some form of psychotherapist privilege.

The psychotherapist privilege can be avoided in some kinds of cases. For example, in *United States v. Butrum,*[60] the court held that the privilege was not available where the patient was charged with child sexual abuse. The court permitted evidence of communications and records of psychiatric treatment the defendant received following the sexual abuse incidents.

The Dangerous Patient Exception to the Psychotherapist-Patient Privilege

Beginning with the landmark 1976 case of *Tarasoff v. Regents of the University of California,*[61] states began adopting a "duty to protect" rule. Under this rule, once a psychotherapist discovers that a patient poses a serious threat to a third person, the psychotherapist must exercise reasonable efforts to protect that person. Many states have codified this duty. (See, e.g., Tenn. Code Ann. 33-10-302.) California has adopted as part of its Evidence Code an exception to the psychotherapist-patient privilege that communications by a dangerous patient are not privileged. (See West's Cal. Evid. Code 1024.)

One federal court has adopted a "dangerous patient" exception to the psychotherapist privilege. In *United States v. Glass,*[62] the court held that a psychotherapist could testify in a criminal case about otherwise privileged communications only if no other alternative to disclosure of threats made by the patient against a third party existed to avert harm to that person. The defendant was charged with threats to kill the president of the United States, a federal crime. Testimony of the psychotherapist to whom the threats were made was the only evidence of the threats, upon which the defendant's conditional guilty plea was based. Although the *Glass* court found that the evidence did not support the government's position that disclosure by the psychotherapist was the only way to protect the president, and therefore vacated the guilty plea, it found that under the proper circumstances the privilege could be lost. The *Glass* court based its decision on a footnote in *Jaffee*, where the Supreme Court said, "[W]e do not doubt that there are situations in which the privilege must give way, for example, if a serious threat of harm to the patient or to others can be averted only by means of a disclosure by a therapist."[63]

One other federal court has refused to adopt the dangerous patient exception. In *United States v. Hayes,*[64] the court held that grafting such an exception onto the psychotherapist privilege would have a serious chilling effect on patients' willingness to seek treatment. It concluded that while the "duty to protect" might permit a psychotherapist to inform authorities about a patient's threats, that duty did not require that the psychotherapist be compelled or permitted over the patient's objection to testify at a criminal trial based on those threats.

In the 2008 case of *United States v. Auster,*[65] the Fifth Circuit Court of Appeals refused to follow the *Hayes* decision. The *Auster* court observed that it was now common practice for psychotherapists to inform dangerous patients in advance that a *Tarasoff* letter would be sent to persons threatened by the patient during a psychotherapy session. As a result, the patient would know in advance that not all his communications would be confidential. The *Auster* court thus concluded that the

 ## You be the **JUDGE**

All the states have procedures for the commitment of persons who are shown to be Sexually Violent Predators ("SVP"). SVP statutes, such as California Welfare and Institutions Code § 6600, provide for indeterminate commitment for persons who have been convicted of a sexually violent offense, and are believed to constitute a danger to society because they are likely to commit future sexually violent crimes. Often, these procedures are invoked after a SVP has been released from prison on parole, and has violated that parole in some manner related to possible victims of sexually violent crimes. This was the case in the 2013 California case of *People v. Gonzales*, 296 P.3d 945 (Cal. 2013).

Gonzales was convicted of sexual offenses against a child in 1994, and sentenced to 11 years in prison. As a condition of his release on parole in 2004, Gonzales was required to participate in counseling sessions with a psychologist at an outpatient counseling center. After numerous parole violations, including some that involved contact with minor children, California commenced SVP commitment proceedings against Gonzales. At the commitment trial it was the prosecution's burden to show Gonzales had a mental disorder that predisposed him to commit sexually violent crimes, and that he presented a high risk of doing so. To satisfy this burden, the prosecution proposed to introduce the records of the counseling sessions Gonzales attended as part of his parole, and testimony of the treating psychologist.

Defense attorneys have moved to exclude this evidence, claiming the psychotherapist-patient privilege. The prosecution argues the privilege does not apply to sessions with a psychotherapist ordered as a condition of parole, and even if it does, the dangerous patient exception should be applied. You are the judge. What do you rule?

negative impact on the patient's willingness to confide in the psychotherapist would be minimal if the psychotherapist was compelled to testify about the threats, and the court held that the privilege did not apply.

THE SEXUAL ASSAULT COUNSELOR'S PRIVILEGE AND PRIVILEGES COVERING OTHER COUNSELORS

Victims of sexual assaults and other crimes of violence often need and are provided with counseling. Drug and alcohol rehabilitation counseling is also available in all states. Counselors are available in schools at all levels of education. Families under stress often receive counseling.

Many states have statutes that protect the private communications of persons receiving counseling. In the case of *Commonwealth v. Wilson,*[66] the Supreme Court of Pennsylvania held that the Pennsylvania sexual assault privilege statute provided an absolute privilege protecting not only testimony but also the production of documents covering the history of persons protected by the privilege. The defendants in this case were charged with sex crimes and sought records of their victims in the files of the sexual assault counselor to use in their defense. The court held that the **sexual assault counselor's privilege** prevented the production of the counselor's files.

sexual assault counselor's privilege

The privilege for counselors of victims of sexual assault and crimes of violence; also applies to records and testimony by counselors without the consent of the victim or patient.

Other states have similar statutes, often called "victim advocate" statutes. These statutes, such as Ind. Code § 35-37-6-9(a), apply the privilege to communications made by a sexual assault or domestic violence victim to a "victim services advocate." These include advocates at rape crisis centers, family violence shelters, or battered women's shelters. Moreover, while in most states these victim advocates have a duty to report information they acquire through confidential communications about sexual assaults and child abuse to authorities, they do not lose their privileged status as a result of such reports. *In re Crisis Connections, Inc.*[67]

Many states, either as part of the psychotherapist-patient privilege or as a broader general privilege, have by statute made privileged confidential communications to "professional counselors," usually defined to include persons licensed by the state to engage in personal or family counseling. The privilege would thus normally apply to confidential communications with persons licensed to give counseling, such as a counseling clinic. However, most states also limit this privilege, in particular when the counseling involves child abuse. Where the counselor is given confidential information that the patient has been involved in child abuse or child sexual abuse, the counselor must inform authorities. (See e.g., Conn. Gen. Stat. § 17a-101.) Moreover, the counselor may testify concerning the communications or disclose records and the privilege does not apply to such testimony or disclosure. *State v. Mark R.*[68]

THE CLERGY-PENITENT PRIVILEGE

About two-thirds of the states have statutes defining the clergy-penitent privilege, with a few other states recognizing the privilege by court decisions. No clear-cut privilege emerged from the old common law protecting confidential communications with clergy.

Statutes ordinarily define clergy as a minister, priest, rabbi, or other similar functionary of a religious organization, or a person reasonably believed to be so by the penitent consulting him or her. A clergyperson does not have to be engaged full time in the profession, but the definitions are not so broad as to include all self-denominated "ministers."

Because of moral and ethical reasons, ministers, priests, and rabbis would not ordinarily reveal confessions and confidential disclosures made to them. The privilege establishes a legal protection against clergypersons being forced to testify on a witness stand about confidential disclosures made to them.

THE NEWS REPORTER'S PRIVILEGE NOT TO REVEAL THE SOURCE OF THE INFORMATION

Common law did not generally recognize a journalist privilege, but most states have enacted a news reporter shield law or have established protections for news reporters.[69] About 30 states have done so by statute, and most others have court decisions finding some form of journalist privilege under state common law or state constitution. (See, e.g., *State v. Salsbury,* 924 P.2d 208 (Idaho 1996).) These laws generally have exceptions, such as when a life is at risk or in a situation that concerns an emergency within the community such as a terrorist attack. The smorgasbord of different laws sometimes leaves journalists uncertain about the legal protections they can rely on.

Many states make the privilege "qualified," meaning a journalist can refuse to disclose sources, but must make available other information acquired through reporting activities. An example of a qualified privilege is Florida's shield law, FSA § 90.5015. That statute, like those in many other states, permits the privilege to be overcome if it can be shown that the information cannot be obtained from an alternative source, and a "compelling" reason exists for disclosing the information. A few states view the journalist privilege as "absolute" (see *Too Much Media LLC v. Hale,* 20 A.3d 364 (N.J. 2011); *Castellani v. Scranton Times LP,* 956 A.2d 937 (Pa. 2007)).

The privilege can be claimed only by professional journalists in most states, that is, persons who are employed in some fashion as journalists. While this includes traditional print journalists, like newspapers and magazines, the explosion of Internet news services has seen the journalist privilege invoked by persons posting information on websites that do not fit the traditional print media model. Generally, courts will make the journalist privilege available to Internet websites that purport to investigate stories and inform the public of the results. (See e.g., *TheStreet.com Inc. v. Carroll,* 20 So.3d 947 (Fla. App. 2009), *review denied* 39 So.3d 1264 (Fla. 2010).) On the other hand, at least one court has held that simply posting a story in an open forum website does not qualify for the privilege, and the person posting the story may be compelled to disclose sources. *Too Much Media LLC v. Hale, supra.*

Does the Constitution Give News Reporters a Privilege Not to Reveal the Source of Their Information?

We have all read stories about the newsperson who is sent to jail for contempt of court for refusing to disclose the source of a story or article. The newsperson usually contends that the **news reporter's privilege**, based on the First Amendment, provides a privilege against such disclosure. Does such a right exist? In the 1972 case of *Branzburg v. Hayes,*[70] the U.S. Supreme Court held it did not:

news reporter's privilege A privilege that does not exist in common law; created by statutes in many states.

> [T]he great weight of authority is that newsmen are not exempt from the normal
> duty of appearing before a grand jury and answering questions relevant to a criminal

investigation. At common law, courts consistently refused to recognize the existence of any privilege authorizing a newsman to refuse to reveal confidential information to a grand jury.

Unless a state has a statute creating the privilege, news reporters have no general absolute First Amendment privilege and right not to reveal sources of news articles when ordered by a court.[71] In the 2005 case of *In re Grand Jury Investigation—Judith Miller,*[72] the court of appeals held that the First Amendment does not create a privilege for a reporter to refuse to divulge the identity of a confidential source. It also stated that if there were a federal common-law privilege, it did not apply to grand jury proceedings involved in that case.

A number of federal courts of appeal and district courts have concluded there is a qualified journalist privilege under the First Amendment in civil cases, but most have concluded that there is no privilege in criminal cases. Cases are collected in the article *The Underprivileged Profession: The Case for Supreme Court Recognition of the Journalist Privilege*, 154 UPALR 201 (2005).

In 2007 the House of Representatives passed a media shield bill. Several versions of that bill were introduced in the Senate following adoption by the House, but none advanced to a floor vote. The current Senate version, called the Free Flow of Information Act, had not been enacted as of August 2014.

The Problem of Leaking Government Information to the Press, or Should Leaking Be Encouraged?

Newspeople and other media representatives frequently contend that they need to rely on government employees as sources for information about things like fraud and corruption in federal, state, and local governments. They argue that newsperson shield laws are very important in helping them obtain information that governments might otherwise seek to hide.

This is particularly important in the case of the federal government, which because of its greater size and more tax money to spend, has power and influence in many different areas, which can increase the need for outside inspection.

Two recent examples illustrate the importance of leaks by federal government employees to news organizations:

- In 2013 Edward Snowden, a computer contractor working for the National Security Agency (NSA) released thousands of classified documents he acquired as part of his work for the NSA. These documents revealed that the NSA, together with other government agencies, conducted a massive global surveillance program of telephone and other private communications. While some call Snowden a traitor, and others a patriot, his leaks have caused intensive inquiries into the need for, and wisdom of, such widespread surveillance programs.
- In 2010 Chelsea Manning, a U.S. Army intelligence analyst stationed in Iraq, leaked thousands of military documents (later called the "Iraq War Log" and the "Afghan War Log") and diplomatic cables to Wikileaks, which published the leaks. Manning was convicted of violation of the Espionage Act in 2013, and sentenced to 35 years in prison.

Former CIA analyst Valerie Plame is sworn in on Capitol Hill in Washington, Friday, March 16, 2007, prior to testifying before the House Oversight and Government Reform Committee. Plame resigned after her identity as a classified, covert CIA operative was compromised when Washington Post columnist Robert Novak named her as "an agency operative on weapons of mass destruction."

AP Images/Dennis Cook

IS THERE A PARENT-CHILD PRIVILEGE?

Can a parent be compelled to testify against a child? Could a child be compelled to testify against a parent? Or could either voluntarily testify in a criminal case against the other?

The question of whether a privilege exists based solely on the parent-child relationship has come before many courts in recent years, particularly in those states where courts have the power to interpret the common law to recognize privileges. Only one federal district court and one state appellate court have recognized some type of parent-child privilege in the absence of a statute creating the privilege.[73] Most courts that have considered the question have refused to recognize a parent-child privilege under the common law, but have referred the question to their state's legislature, as happened in the case below.

In Re Grand Jury Subpoena Supreme Judicial Court of Massachusetts 722 N.E.2d 450 (Mass. 2000)	Two 14-year-old juveniles were charged in a Massachusetts district court with raping a young girl. The parents of the boys were given subpoenas to testify at the boys' trial concerning statements the boys made to their parents about the alleged rape. The parents moved to quash the subpoenas, claiming a "common law" parent-child privilege that prohibited the prosecution from compelling their testimony. They based their claim on the Massachusetts legislature's adoption of MGLA 233 §20, which provides that a minor child cannot be compelled to testify against the child's parents. The parents argued this statute demonstrated that the common law of Massachusetts was intended to make communications between a parent and a minor child privileged. The Supreme Judicial Court disagreed. It held that the creation of a testimonial privilege in favor of parents to prevent their compelled testimony against a minor child should come from the legislature, not the courts. It refused to quash the subpoena. The Massachusetts legislature has not, as of 2014, enacted such a privilege.

Three states have adopted a parent-child testimonial privilege, though they differ in scope and application. Connecticut General Statute §46(b)-138a recognizes a limited privilege in proceedings in juvenile court under which either the juvenile or the parents may refuse to testify. Minnesota Statutes § 595.02 states that neither a parent nor a minor child can be examined about any confidential communication made to the parent. Idaho Rules of Evidence § 514 provides that a parent cannot be compelled to disclose confidential communications made by a minor child in any criminal action against the child. All these statutes provide exceptions where the criminal case involves injury or abuse between parent and child.

Moreover, as with other privileges, even if a parent-child privilege is recognized, it is limited to the use of testimony in judicial proceedings. In *United States v. Davies and Kaprelian*, 768 F.2d 893 (7th Cir. 1985), *cert. denied*, 474 U.S. 1008 (1986), FBI agents investigating an interstate felony jewelry theft put a house under surveillance. When a teenaged girl came out of the house one of the agents asked to talk to her. Although the girl was not required to talk to the agent, she did, telling them she was the daughter of Kaprelian, the suspect in the theft, and that a woman (Davies) was living with Kaprelian. She also gave the FBI agents her father's telephone number, which the agents used to develop evidence to arrest and convict the suspects. In rejecting Kaprelian's claim of parent-child privilege, the court said,

> Even were there some substantial support for the defendant's proposition that there is a parent-child privilege, this case would not be one in which it could be applied. Privileges apply only to prevent the use of testimony in a judicial proceeding. Kaprelian's daughter gave the F.B.I. agent his telephone number during the F.B.I.'s investigation of the jewelry robbery. As the Supreme Court has noted, "… [neither the husband-wife privilege] nor any other privilege, prevents the Government from enlisting one spouse to give information concerning the other to aid in the other's apprehension." *Trammel*, 445 U.S. at 52 n. 12, 100 S. Ct. at 913 n. 12. Kaprelian makes no assertion that the government ever intended to call his daughter at the trial; his assertions of privilege are based solely on her questioning during the investigation. Thus neither the phone number nor any other evidence obtained through this critical investigative lead are subject to suppression by the district court.

THE PRIVILEGE CONCERNING THE IDENTITY OF INFORMANTS

informants Persons
who provide information
to law officers.

Law enforcement agencies and government have always realized that information from private citizens and paid **informants** is needed for effective law enforcement. When a major crime occurs, law enforcement agencies often need information to head their investigations in the right direction. Most information that law officers receive from private citizens and informers is of little value in solving major crimes, but some information identifies wrongdoers or provides important clues about crimes.

To encourage people to provide information, governments must be able to assure those people that their identity will not be disclosed, whether they are private citizens voluntarily providing the information or individuals who provide information for money or other consideration.

Common law has always recognized the informant's privilege as an essential aid to law enforcement. Today, many states have enacted statutes defining the privilege, while other states and the federal government use the privilege in its common-law form.

In the 1957 case of *Roviaro v. United States,*[74] the U.S. Supreme Court commented as follows regarding the informant's privilege:

> What is usually referred to as the informer's privilege is in reality the Government's privilege to withhold from disclosure the identity of persons who furnish information of violations of law to officers charged with the enforcement of that law. The purpose of the privilege is the furtherance and protection of the public interest in effective law enforcement.

The Limits to the Informant's Privilege

The informant's privilege is not an absolute privilege and must give way when there is a compelling need to protect the rights of the accused. In the *Roviaro* case,[75] the Supreme Court held that the limits of the privilege arise from

> fundamental requirements of fairness. Where the disclosure of an informer's identity, or of the contents of his communication, is relevant and helpful to the defense of the accused, or is essential to the fair determination of a cause, the privilege must give way. In these situations the trial court may require disclosure.

Defendants in criminal trials have the right to know the names of people who were at the scene of the alleged crime or persons who were participants in the crime that is alleged. These people could be important material witnesses for the defense, and their testimony could be relevant. The courts have held that defense lawyers should have access to these people as potential witnesses. If the informant was at the scene of the crime or participated in the crime, courts hold that the informant's identity must be disclosed to the defense lawyer.

It is unlikely that a court will order the disclosure of the identity of an informant unless the informant was present at the scene of the crime charged, participated in the crime charged, or was at the scene of the arrest. Because the informant could be an undercover police officer, informants should be kept away from the scene of a crime or an arrest, if possible.

The question of an informant's identity is frequently raised in drug prosecutions. Search warrants used to search for illegal drugs are often based on tips from confidential informants. When drugs are found and the defendants charged, the name of the informant may be demanded by the defendant, to better judge the accuracy of the search warrant. Since the informant does not testify at the trial and has no direct evidence of the crime, his or her identity is not "material to the determination of the case," and the privilege applies.[76]

When a suspect could be charged for multiple drug transactions, prosecutors can avoid problems by not charging crimes where an informant was present at the scene of the crime or participated in the crime. If the court orders the identity of an informant, two options are available:

1. Drop the criminal charge against the defendant, which means that the defense has won its case, because this is what the defense lawyer seeks.
2. Disclose the identity of the informant, if this is practical, and go to trial, possibly using the informant as a witness.

THE GOVERNMENT'S PRIVILEGE NOT TO REVEAL GOVERNMENT SECRETS

The Privilege Not to Disclose Military or Diplomatic Secrets Vital to National Security

The U.S. Congress enacted the Classified Information Procedures Act (18 U.S.C.A. App. 1), which recognizes the power of the executive branch of the federal government to determine whether classified information should be disclosed in criminal or civil trials.

The use of the government's privilege was before the U.S. Supreme Court in the case of *United States v. Reynolds*.[77] Widows of civilians killed in the crash of a U.S. Air Force plane attempted to obtain the accident report for use in their civil lawsuit. The secretary of the Air Force wrote to the trial judge stating that the report contained information on secret electronic devices, so it was against the public interest to make the accident report public. In holding that the government had a privilege not to reveal such information, the Supreme Court held:

> In the instant case we cannot escape judicial notice that this is a time of vigorous preparation for national defense. Experience in the past war has made it common knowledge that air power is one of the most potent weapons in our scheme of defense, and that newly developing electronic devices have greatly enhanced the effective use of air power. It is equally apparent that these electronic devices must be kept secret if their full military advantage is to be exploited in the national interests. On the record before the trial court it appeared that this accident occurred to a military plane which had gone aloft to test secret electronic equipment. Certainly there was a reasonable danger that the accident investigation report would contain references to the secret electronic equipment which was the primary concern of the mission.
>
> [W]hen the formal claim of privilege was filed by the Secretary of the Air Force, under circumstances indicating a reasonable possibility that military secrets were involved, there was certainly a sufficient showing of privilege to cut off further demand for the document on the showing of necessity for its compulsion that had then been made.

The President's Privilege of Confidentiality

In holding that the president of the United States has a privilege of confidentiality of his conversations and correspondence, the U.S. Supreme Court held in the 1974 case of *United States v. Nixon*[78] that

> There is nothing novel about governmental confidentiality. The meetings of the Constitutional Convention in 1787 were conducted in complete privacy. Moreover, all records

of those meetings were sealed for more than 30 years after the Convention. Most of the Framers acknowledge that without secrecy no constitution of the kind that was developed could have been written. 418 U.S. at 705, 94 S. Ct. at 3106, n.15.

The Supreme Court gave these reasons for the privilege that protects confidential communications between the president and the president's immediate advisors:

> A President and those who assist him must be free to explore alternatives in the process of shaping policies and making decisions and to do so in a way many would be unwilling to express except privately. These are the considerations justifying a presumptive privilege for Presidential communications. The privilege is fundamental to the operation of Government and inextricably rooted in the separation of powers under the Constitution. 418 U.S. at 708, 94 S. Ct. at 3107.

The Court held, however, that the privilege is a qualified privilege and would give way should a party to a legal action show a great need for relevant evidence that is protected by the privilege.[79]

In 2012 President Obama invoked executive privilege to refuse a request by Congress for the release of "internal deliberation" documents surrounding the controversial "Fast and Furious" program. In that program federal Alcohol, Tobacco and Firearm agents purposely permitted buyers of 2,000 weapons in Arizona to illegally take the weapons into Mexico. ATF agents hoped to follow the weapons to

WITNESS PRIVILEGES, SHIELD LAWS, AND IMMUNITY

The following summarizes some of the privileges and immunity rules discussed in this chapter, as well as related topics.

Witness privileges
- Only one, the privilege against self-incrimination, is constitutional. All others are created by statute or common law.
- The privilege in most cases belongs to the client, patient, or other defendant.
- The privilege applies only to testimony in court, judicial proceedings, or testimony before legislative bodies.

Shield laws
- Rape shield laws in most states prohibit evidence in sexual assault trials that is believed to be prejudicial or harassing to the victim in the case.
- Journalist shield laws give news reporters the privilege to protect a news source. The privilege is not a constitutional right, and therefore the desire for a free press must be balanced with the need of government to uncover information of criminal activity.

Immunity laws, granting civil and criminal immunity
- Witness immunity may be granted to key witnesses, and they may then be compelled under power of contempt to testify.
- Government officials have immunity where provided by statute. Under 42 U.S.C.A. § 1983, federal officers are immune from lawsuits based on actions taken within their authority. Most states have similar laws. Judges and prosecutors have absolute immunity for actions done in the performance of their duties [see *Mireles v. Waco*, 502 U.S. 9 (1991)]. Law enforcement officers, corrections officers, and most other public officials are entitled to only qualified immunity under section 1983 [see *Harlow v. Fitzgerald*, 457 U.S. 800 (1982)].
- Heads of state have sovereign immunity, which under international law provides that they are not subject to the jurisdiction of foreign courts [see *United States v. Noriega*, 117 F.3d 1206 (11th Cir. 1997), *cert. denied*, 118 S. Ct. 1389 (1998)].

drug cartel members, but lost track of them. Many of the weapons later appeared at illegal drug crime scenes, including one involving the death of a U.S. Border Patrol officer.

The Secrecy of Grand Jury Proceedings as a Privilege

The federal government and some states use grand juries to criminally indict, or charge, persons. The federal government and many states also use grand juries to investigate situations where criminal activities may be occurring.

The use of grand juries goes back in English history more than a hundred years before the American Revolution. The framers of the Constitution included in the Fifth Amendment the requirement that the federal government use a grand jury of private citizens for indicting persons suspected of federal felonies (see Appendix A). States do not have to follow this requirement.

Citizens who serve on a grand jury are required to take an ancient oath that binds them to keep secret "the King's counsel, your fellows', and your own." The Federal Rules of Criminal Procedure forbid disclosure of "matters occurring before [a] grand jury" and provide that violations can be punished as contempt of court [Rule 6(e)].

grand jury secrecy requirements The mandate that persons serving on grand juries will not disclose "matters occurring before" the grand jury on which they serve.

According to the **grand jury secrecy requirements**, people who serve on a grand jury, therefore, cannot disclose proceedings and deliberations by that body. They have a privilege not to answer questions requiring disclosure of such matters unless they fall within exceptions listed in Federal Rule of Criminal Procedure 6(e).

Some of the reasons for the historic use of secrecy regarding deliberations and evidence considered by grand juries are to encourage and protect the independence and freedom of grand jury deliberations, to protect the reputations of people who are not indicted for criminal offenses but were considered, to prevent people who will be indicted from fleeing because they had information of the coming criminal charges, to encourage witnesses to testify freely, and to encourage members of the grand jury to deliberate freely, knowing that what is said will not be made public.

SUMMARY

1. **State the basis for and the limits of the judicial notice doctrine.**

   - The judicial notice doctrine helps to avoid unnecessary delays in courts. Trial judges may take judicial notice of facts known to the community that are not subject to reasonable dispute and to other information listed in the statutes of the state. This saves time and effort in helping to move both criminal and civil cases along. Judges may not take judicial notice of disputed facts or knowledge, or of knowledge possessed by the judge but not the community generally.

2. **For at least three of the major privileges discussed, state (1) the privilege, (2) the limits of the privilege, and (3) who may invoke the privilege.**

   - The privilege against self-incrimination applies to communicative or testimonial evidence. It does not apply to other physical evidence, or communications in the possession of another person. Only the person whose testimony is sought to be compelled may assert the privilege. The attorney-client privilege protects communications between a client and an attorney that are intended to be confidential. It does not permit an attorney to refuse to produce physical evidence, nor does it protect statements made about present intent to commit a crime. The privilege may be invoked by an attorney on behalf of the client, but the privilege belongs to the client and may be waived by the client. The spousal testimonial privilege permits one spouse to prohibit the other spouse from testifying in any manner against the spouse. It is lost when the marriage ends. The spousal communication privilege applies to all confidential communications between spouses. It does not cover tape recordings of conversations made by a spouse, and those recordings may be admitted as evidence. The privilege may be invoked by either spouse, and does not end with the dissolution of the marriage.

3. **State the difference between the spousal testimonial privilege and the marital communication privilege.**
   - The spousal testimonial privilege permits one spouse to prevent another from giving any testimony. The marital communication prevents only testimony concerning privileged communications.

4. **State the present status of the physician-patient privilege in federal courts.**
   - The U.S. Supreme Court and lower federal courts are charged under Rule 501 of the Federal Rules of Evidence with determining what privileges are applicable in federal courts. The Supreme Court has held that a psychotherapist-patient privilege exists, but has not recognized a general physician-patient privilege.

5. **State the present status of the journalist privilege.**
   - Most states have some form of a journalist privilege, though in some the privilege can be overcome if the prosecution can show the information claimed as privilege cannot be obtained from any other source, and there exists a "compelling" reason for its discovery. The U.S. Supreme Court has not recognized a journalist privilege under the First Amendment, but a few lower federal courts have done so in civil cases.

6. **List the "privileges" available to the government and government officers.**
   - Law enforcement officers may refuse to disclose the name of a confidential informant, though the privilege is limited and can be overcome by due process claims by a defendant. Governments may refuse to reveal military or diplomatic secrets, and the president may refuse to reveal confidential communications or correspondence. The proceedings of grand juries are secret.

KEY TERMS

attorney-client privilege, 148
crime-fraud exception, 149
grand jury secrecy requirements, 165

informants, 162
judicial notice, 142
news reporter's privilege, 158
partner-in-crime exception, 152

physician-patient privilege, 154
privilege, 145
psychotherapist-patient privilege, 155

sexual assault counselor's privilege, 157

KEY CASES

Branzburg v. Hayes, 408 U.S. 665 (1972): Held no journalist privilege under First Amendment in federal courts.

Barreiro v. State Bar of California, 471 P.2d 992 (Cal. 1970): States elements of judicial notice doctrine.

Crouch v. United States, 409 U.S. 322, 331 (1973): Held documents and other materials must be in sole possession of person invoking Fifth Amendment privilege.

Jaffee v. Redmond, 518 U.S. 1 (1996): Recognized psychotherapist-patient privilege in federal courts.

Kastigar v. United States, 406 U.S. 441, 444 (1972): Held that Fifth Amendment privilege may be invoked in any proceeding where self-incrimination might be possible.

State v. Perez, 920 N.E.2d 104 (Ohio 2009): Held that spousal privilege did not apply to permit one

spouse to invoke privilege against the use of tape recordings of confidential communications made by the other spouse.

TheStreet.com Inc. v. Carroll, 20 So.3d 947 (Fla. App. 2009): Determined when persons posting on Internet websites could claim journalist privilege.

PROBLEMS

1. The defendant, charged with murder, asks his wife to tell police he arrived home on the night of the murder at 7:30 P.M., about an hour before the victim was killed. Initially the wife did as requested. However, she subsequently changed her mind, and told police her husband came home at 9:05. At the husband's trial for murder the prosecution wishes to have the wife testify that her husband "asked me to lie to give a false alibi." Is her testimony admissible? Consider these variables:
   A. Your state has a "testimonial privilege" that permits a spouse to prevent the other spouse from testifying, but the husband and wife are divorced before the murder trial begins.
   B. Your state has only a "marital communication" privilege. Is the statement by the husband to the wife (i.e., lie to the police about when he got home), a confidential communication? If so, does it survive the marriage? (See *Winstead v. Com.*, 327 S.W.3d 386 (Ky. 2010).)

2. A defendant charged with murder is held in a jail pending trial. Also in that jail, on unrelated charges, is a prosecution witness in the murder trial. The defendant (client) is represented by a public defender, who learns the client has

intimidated the witness into signing a written document recanting the witness's prior statements to the prosecution. That document has been sent to the attorney.
   A. Must the attorney give the document to the prosecution when they issue a subpoena to the attorney demanding the production of the document?
   B. If you answered no, what additional facts would make the crime-fraud exception applicable? (See *In re Public Defender Services*, 831 A.2d 890 D.C. 2003).)

3. Police investigations often rely on information supplied by confidential informants (CIs). The privilege given to the police to refuse to divulge the identity of a CI is limited, usually based on whether the CI was involved in the crime or a witness to the crime. Courts often say the identity of a mere "tipster" CI need not be disclosed to the defense. This issue arises frequently in drug cases, where the use of CIs is common. When does a CI who has seen drug transactions take place in a defendant's apartment cease to be a "tipster," and become a witness? (See *State v. Ostein*, 293 S.W.3d 519 (Tenn. 2009).)

CASE ANALYSIS

Read Appendix B, Finding and Analyzing Cases (p. 499). With these guidelines in mind, please continue with the Case Analysis selections for Chapter 6.

1. As this chapter notes, federal courts are split about whether government officials could invoke the attorney-client privilege for communications with government lawyers. In the 2014 case of *In re 33rd Statewide Investigating Grand Jury*, 86 A.3d 204, the Pennsylvania Supreme Court held

that a state agency under investigation by the state attorney general could not invoke the privilege to prevent the agency's general counsel from giving information to the attorney general. What was the court's reason for its decision? Who is the "client" in these cases?

2. Kentucky retains a "spousal testimony" privilege as well as a "marital communication privilege." KRE Rule 504. The spousal

testimony rule permits one spouse to prevent the other spouse from testifying against the spouse about events occurring during the marriage. It also has the "offense against the other spouse" exception. In *Meyers v. Commonwealth*, 381 S.W.3d 280 (Ky. 2012) a husband was charged (among other crimes) with being a felon in possession of a weapon. To prove the charge, the prosecution proposed to call the wife to the stand, to testify the husband had the weapon and pointed it at her. Should the wife be permitted to testify over the husband's invocation of the privilege? Does the "offense against the spouse" exception apply? Why or why not?

3. Assume you dictated a letter to your secretary to be mailed to your spouse. Are the contents of this letter, assuming they would otherwise constitute marital communications, subject to the marital communication privilege? If not, what about the contents of an e-mail sent on a work e-mail account? Does it matter what the employer tells the employee about use of the e-mail account? *See United States v. Hamilton*, 701 F.3d 404 (4th Cir. 2012), *cert. denied* 133 S. Ct. 1838 (2013).

4. Some states have what is usually called a "public ignominy" statute, which permits a witness to refuse to give testimony that will expose the witness to public ignominy. Nebraska has such a statute, Neb. Rev. Stat. § 25-1210. Assume a young adult woman, married with small children, is called to testify in a criminal trial about alleged sexual assaults committed by her stepfather when she was 7 years old. She states she won't testify, because she does not want to relive the experiences and suffer the embarrassment of publicly revealing the details of the sexual assaults. She therefore invokes the "privilege" of section 25-1210. The trial judge orders her to testify, and she refuses, resulting in a contempt order against her. On appeal, should the Nebraska Supreme Court affirm the contempt order? *State v. Riensche*, 812 N.W.2d 293 (Neb. 2012).

Notes

1. *Varcoe v. Lee*, 181, P. 223, 226 (Cal. 1919).
2. Either party to a civil or criminal action may challenge a ruling by a judge who takes judicial notice of a fact. Many states have statutes similar to Federal Rule of Evidence 201(b), which provides that a "judicially noticed fact must be one not subject to reasonable dispute." In the case of *Palmer v. Mitchell*, 206 N.E.2d 776 (Ill. App. 1965)], a finding of judicial notice was reversed because the information was within the personal knowledge of the judge but was not a matter of common and general knowledge of the community.
3. *Barreiro v. State Bar of California*, 88 Cal. Rptr. 192, 471 P.2d 992 (1970).
4. *Sumpter v. State*, 306 N.E.2d 95 (1974).
5. 822 P.2d 23 (Haw. 1991).
6. *Dillon v. Gloss*, 256 U.S. 368, 41 S. Ct. 510.
7. 825 P.2d 781.
8. 412 S.E.2d 473.
9. 924 A.2d 384 (N.H. 2007).
10. 387 F.3d 682 (8th Cir. 2004).
11. 955 F.2d. 786 (2d Cir. 1993).
12. 296 N.E.2d 837 (1973).
13. Footnote 27 of the *Miranda* decision (384 U.S. at 458, 86 S. Ct. 1619) states, "Thirteenth-century commentators found an analogue to the privilege grounded in the Bible. 'To sum up the matter, the principle that no man is to be declared guilty on his own admission is a divine decree.'"
14. Maimonides, *Mishneh Torah (Code of Jewish Law)*, Book of Judges, Laws of the Sanhedrin, c. 18, 6. III Yale Judaica Series 52-53. See also Lamm, *The Fifth Amendment and Its Equivalent in the Halakhah*, 5 Judaism 53 (Winter 1956).
15. *Minnesota v. Murphy*, 465 U.S. 420, 426 (1984).
16. *Kastigar v. United States*, 406 U.S. 441, 444, 92 S. Ct. 1653, 1656 (1972).

  The problem of determining whether a person is properly using the privilege against self-incrimination and whether the person's answer will subject the person to criminal prosecution is complex. The U.S. Supreme Court stated in the 1953 case of *United States v. Reynolds* (73 S. Ct. 528) that

  Too much judicial inquiry into the claim of privilege would force disclosure of the thing the privilege was meant to protect, while a complete abandonment of judicial control would lead to intolerable abuses. Indeed, in the earlier stages of judicial experience with the problem, both extremes were advocated, some saying that the bare assertion by the witness must be taken as conclusive, and others saying that the witness should be required to reveal the matter behind his claim of privilege to the judge for verification. Neither extreme prevailed, and a sound formula of compromise was developed. This formula received authoritative expression in this country as early as the Burr trial. There are differences in phraseology, but in substance it is agreed that the court must be satisfied from all the evidence and circumstances, and "from the implications of the question, in the setting in which it is asked, that a responsive answer to the question or an explanation of why it cannot be answered might be dangerous because injurious exposure could result." *Hoffman v. United States*, 341 U.S. 479, 486487, 71 S. Ct. 814, 818 (1951). If the court is so satisfied, the claim of the privilege will be accepted without requiring further disclosure.

17. *Murphy v. Waterfront Comm.*, 378 U.S. 52, 55, 84 S. Ct. 1594, 1596 (1964).

18. *Miranda v. Arizona*, 384 U.S. 436, 460, 86 S. Ct. 1602, 1620 (1966).

19. *Schmerber v. California*, 384 U.S. 757, 86 S. Ct. 1826 (1966).

20. *Gilbert v. California*, 388 U.S. 263, 87 S. Ct. 1951 (1967).

21. *United States v. Wade*, 388 U.S. 218, 87 S. Ct 1926 (1967).

22. *United States v. Dionisio*, 410 U.S. 1, 93 S. Ct. 764 (1973).

23. *United States v. Hammond*, 419 F.2d 166, 168 (4th Cir. 1969), *cert. denied*, 397 U.S. 1068, 90 S. Ct. 1508 (1970).

24. *United States v. Murray*, 523 F.2d 489, 492 (8th Cir. 1975).

25. *United States v. Valenzuela*, 722 F.2d 1431, 1433 (9th Cir. 1983).

26. *United States v. Roberts*, 481 F.2d 892 (5th Cir. 1973).

27. *United States v. Brown*, 920 F.2d 1212 (5th Cir. 1991).

28. *Holt v. United States*, 218 U.S. 245, 31 S. Ct. 2 (1910).

29. *George Campbell Painting Corp. v. Reid*, 392 U.S. 286, 88 S. Ct. 1978 (1968); *United States v. Doe*, 465 U.S. 605, 104 S. Ct. 1237 (1984); *United States v. White*, 322 U.S. 694, 64 S. Ct. 1248 (1944).

30. *Bursey v. United States*, 466 F.2d 1059 (9th Cir. 1972).

31. The U.S. Supreme Court held in the *Bouknight* case that

> In *New York v. Quarles*, 467 US 649... (1984), we recognized a public safety exception to the usual Fifth Amendment rights afforded by *Miranda v. Arizona*, 384 US 436 ... (1966), so that police

could recover a firearm which otherwise would have remained in a public area. In the present case, a citation for civil contempt in order to obtain the production of a child such as Maurice M., or knowledge about his whereabouts, is not essentially criminal in nature and aims primarily to securing the safety of the child. Protecting infants from child abuse seems to me to rank in order of social importance with the regulation and prevention of traffic accidents.

32. *United States v. Medley*, 33 M.J. 75 (1991), *review denied*, U.S. Supreme Court, 112 S. Ct. 1473, 50 CrL 3199 (1992).

33. *United States v. Heyward*, 22 M.J. 35 (C.M.A. 1986).

34. 532 U.S. 17 (2001).

35. 274 F.3d 1053 (6th Cir. 2001).

36. 242 F.3d 49 (1st Cir. 2001).

37. 269 F.3d 1023 (9th Cir. 2001).

38. The "work-product" doctrine is closely related to the attorney-client privilege. The U.S. Supreme Court stated in *Upjohn Co. v. United States*, 449 U.S. 383, 101 S. Ct. 677 (1981)]:

> This doctrine was announced by the Court over 30 years ago in *Hickman v. Taylor*, 329 U.S. 495 (1947). In that case the Court rejected "an attempt, without purported necessity or justification, to secure written statements, private memoranda, and personal recollections prepared or formed by an adverse party's counsel in the course of his legal duties." *Id.*, at 510. The Court noted that "it is essential that a lawyer work with a certain degree of privacy" and reasoned that if discovery of the material sought were permitted, "much of what is now put down in writing would remain unwritten. An attorney's thoughts, heretofore inviolate, would not be his own. Inefficiency, unfairness, and sharp practices would inevitably develop in the giving of legal advice and in the preparation of cases for trial. The effect on the legal profession would be demoralizing. And the interests of the clients and the cause of justice would be poorly served." *Id.*, at 511.

39. *See e.g. State v. Sucharew*, 66 P.3d 59 (Az. App. 2003) (presence of juvenile defendant's parents at attorney-client conferences did not waive privilege).

40. *Upjohn Co. v. United States*, 449 U.S. 383 (1981).

41. *In re: A Witness Before the Special Grand Jury*, 288 F.3d 289 (7th Cir. 2002).

42. 399 F.3d 527.

43. 109 S. Ct. 2619.

44. 602 A.2d 677, 687 (Md. 1992).

45. Many courts have adopted what is called the *last link doctrine* or *legal advice rule*:

> Where a client goes to an attorney for legal advice and where revealing the client's identity would

be the last link in information needed to convict the client of a crime, the client's name is privileged. Here are examples of such rare situations where the last link doctrine apply: (a) In 1960 the Internal Revenue Service received a letter from an attorney stating that a check enclosed of $12,706.85 was forwarded for additional taxes owed by undisclosed taxpayers. The attorney refused to disclose any names, citing the attorney-client privilege. When the matter was appealed, the U.S. Court of Appeals, applying California law, upheld the privilege, holding that disclosing the clients' names would amount to an acknowledgement of guilt by the clients of the very matter for which legal advice was sought, *Baird v. Koerner*, 279 F.2d 623 (9th Cir. 1960). (b) In a federal drug conspiracy prosecution, prosecutors sought to compel the defense lawyer to disclose the name of the unknown person who paid the defense lawyer's fees. Claiming his client was also involved in the drug conspiracy and that disclosing his client's name would disclose a confidential communication, the defense lawyer was successful in asserting the attorney-client privilege. See *Matter of Grand Jury Proceeding*, 898 F.2d 565 (7th Cir. 1990).

    The last link or legal advice rule is not applicable if a lawyer is hired to further illegal activity. For example, this could occur where legal advice is sought for the operation of an illegal drug operation or to provide tax advice for illegal activities. See *In re Grand Jury Investigation*, 723 F.2d 447 (6th Cir. 1983), *review denied*, U.S. Supreme Court, 467 U.S. 1246, 104 S. Ct. 3524 (1984).

46. 445 U.S. 40, 100 S. Ct. 906.
47. 966 F.2d 398 (8th Cir.).
48. See 260 F.3d 1295 (11th Cir. 2001). Probably no state extends the husband-wife privilege to people living together but not married. See the 1991 case of *Montanez v. State*, 592 So.2d 650 (Ala. Crim. App.), where the court held that the defendant's communications with his "paramour" were not protected by the marital communications privilege. In that case, the woman was granted use immunity and testified against the defendant. In addition, she was a joint participant in the drug trafficking and came under the partners-in-crime exception.

    Most states have abolished common-law marriages, but the husband-wife privilege may generally be invoked not only in states that recognize common-law marriages but also in other states where common-law married couples have moved. See the 1998 case of *People v. Schmidt* (1998 WL 101837), where Michigan extended the privilege to a couple who had entered into a valid common-law marriage in Alabama and then moved to Michigan.

49. *State v. Jones*, 984 N.E.2d 948 (Ohio 2012).
50. *United States v. Evans*, 966 F.2d 398 (8th Cir. 1992).
51. *United States v. Hill*, 967 F.2d 902 (3d Cir. 1992).
52. 979 So.2d 283 (Fla. App. 2008).
53. *United States v. Marashi*, 913 F.2d 724 (9th Cir. 1990). Va. Code Ann. 19.2-271.2 is an example of a state marital privilege statute that contains this exception.
54. 824 P.2d 1257 (Wash. App.).
55. 417 S.E.2d 903 (W. Va. 1992).
56. 740 F.3d 1 (1st Cir. 2014).
57. 74 S.W.3d 711 (Ky. 2002).
58. For an extensive discussion of the physician-patient relationship, see Chapter 12 of *McCormick on Evidence*, 4th ed. (West Publishing, 1992).
59. 518 U.S. 1, 15 (1996).
60. 17 F.3d 1299 (10th Cir. 1993), *review denied*, 513 U.S. 863.
61. 551 P.2d 334 (Cal. 1976).
62. 133 F.3d 1356 (10th Cir. 1998).
63. 518 U.S. 1, 18.
64. 227 F.3d 578 (6th Cir. 2000).
65. 517 F.3d 312 (5th Cir.).
66. 602 A.2d 1290 (Pa. 1992).
67. 949 N.E.2d 789 (Ind. 2011)
68. 17 A.3d 1 (Conn. 2011).
69. See, e.g., Neb. Rev. Stat. § 20-146 (reissue 2007).
70. 408 U.S. 665 (1972).
71. If the general public is excluded from a crime scene or an area where a disaster has occurred, do newspersons have rights and privileges that the general public does not have? The U.S. Supreme Court addressed this question in the 1972 case of *Branzburg v. Hayes* (92 S. Ct. 2646), stating "Newsmen have no constitutional right of access to the scenes of crime or disaster when the general public is excluded, and they may be prohibited from attending or publishing information about trials if such restrictions are necessary to assure a defendant a fair trial before an impartial tribunal.... " In 1989 a Milwaukee news reporter refused to leave the scene of the crash of a commercial airline. The site was sealed off so that emergency equipment and personnel could assist the injured and dying. The newsman was arrested because he insisted that he had a right to photograph and view the scene. The Wisconsin Supreme Court affirmed his conviction for disorderly conduct in *City of Oak Creek v. King* (436 N.W.2d 285).
72. 397 F.3d 964 (D.C. Cir. 2005), *cert. denied*, 125 S. Ct. 2977 (2005).
73. The courts and cases holding that a parent-child privilege exists are *In re Agosto*, 553 F.Supp. 1298 (D. Nev. 1983), and *In re Application of A & M*, 403 N.Y.S.2d 375 (App. Div. 1975).

74. 353 U.S. 53, 77 S. Ct. 623.
75. 353 U.S. 60, 77 S. Ct. 628.
76. See *United States v. Hollis*, 245 F.3d 671 (8th Cir. 2001).
77. 345 U.S. 1 (1953).
78. 418 U.S. 683, 94 S. Ct. 3090.
79. Members of the U.S. Congress also have a privilege referred to as a "nondisclosure privilege." In 2006 search warrants were issued to obtain criminal evidence in the investigation of Congressman William Jefferson, who was later charged with 16 counts of money laundering and other offenses. Jefferson filed motions to have the evidence seized from his congressional office returned to him, claiming the information was privileged. In *United States v. Rayburn House Office Building, Room 2113,* 497 F.3d 654 (D.C. Cir. 2007), *cert. denied,* 128 S. Ct. 1738 (2008), the court of appeals held that all privileged evidence must be returned to Jefferson under the Speech or Debate Clause of ARTICLE I of the U.S. Constitution. That clause provides that the speech of a member of Congress "shall not be questioned in any other place for any speech or debate in either House."

The Use of Hearsay in the Courtroom

SIR WALTER RALEIGH

© Georgios Kollidas/Shutterstock.com

LEARNING OBJECTIVES

In this chapter we define hearsay and examine its boundaries. The learning objectives for this chapter are

Define *hearsay*.

List the questions that should be asked to determine if a statement is hearsay.

State why hearsay raises questions of reliability.

Define an *assertive statement*.

Explain why the statement "He said he would kill me" might not be hearsay.

State the co-conspirator rule.

Identify when a prior statement by a witness is not hearsay.

t is often important in a criminal trial for the prosecution to offer evidence explaining why police officers acted as they did, or why they were present in a particular place at a particular time. This kind of "background" information is not intended to prove any part of the prosecution's case, but rather to aid the jury in understanding the circumstances of an arrest or seizure. Thus, a police officer could testify in response to the question "Why were you in the alley?" that "a 911 operator told me he took a call from a person who said she saw a body lying in the alley." Neither the statement by the 911 operator nor the statement by the caller would be hearsay, because they were not offered to prove the truth of the statements.

If you were the judge, would you permit an officer, as "background information," to testify that a 911 operator told him an anonymous caller told the operator, "A black man with a "poofy" Afro wearing a green shirt and riding a bicycle was openly carrying a gun"? And that based on that information the officer found the defendant, who matched that description, and saw him throw something in a bush, which later turned out to be a gun? Is that a hearsay problem? *See United States v. Nelson*, 725 F.3d 615 (6th Cir. 2013).

WITNESSES AND THE HEARSAY RULE

Central to the nature of criminal prosecutions in the United States is the role of witnesses. It is through the testimony of witnesses that the facts are presented to the jury and upon which the guilt or innocence of the accused is determined.

When witnesses give their testimony, the subject matter is typically some event that they observed in some manner, and that they subsequently recollect by testimony in the courtroom. This testimony generally presents four risks relative to its truthfulness: the accuracy of the witness's perception, the memory of the witness, the meaning of the testimony, and the sincerity of the witness.

The principal means courts use to guard against these risks are the requirements that the witness testify under oath, which helps ensure sincerity, and that the witness be available for cross-examination, which can be used to test recollection, narration, and perception.

Imagine that a witness in an arson trial gives this testimony: "I saw the defendant throw something through the window of the building, and then the building caught fire." The truth of this statement carries the risks identified above: Is the witness sincere? Is his memory of the event clear? Were his perceptions of the event accurate? Did the event mean what he said it meant?

These risks can be tested by cross-examination, where the witness is available to explain his perceptions or demonstrate the clarity of his memory. Questions about the witness's eyesight, the time of day or night, his distance from the defendant, and so forth can test the accuracy of his perceptions. Similar questions can assess his memory and narration of the event.

But what if the witness testifies: "Fred told me he saw the defendant throw something through the window of the building, and then the building caught fire." It is possible, but very unlikely, that the witness may have questioned Fred to determine the accuracy of this statement. If not, the defendant will not be able to do so, because Fred is not at the trial.

The witness's statement about what Fred said is, of course, hearsay and in most federal and state criminal proceedings is inadmissible under the relevant hearsay rule. Unfortunately, identifying what is and is not hearsay is considerably more complex than this simple example. Moreover, even if something is hearsay, the rule excluding its admissibility is subject to numerous exceptions: The hearsay rule in the

Federal Rules of Evidence has two exemptions and twenty-eight exceptions. Finally, in criminal trials, the Confrontation Clause of the Sixth Amendment to the U.S. Constitution imposes a constitutional restriction on out-of-court testimony by witnesses.

In this chapter we explore the basic elements of hearsay evidence, giving examples of what is and is not hearsay. In Chapter 8 we discuss the Confrontation Clause and the exceptions to the hearsay rule.

THE HISTORY OF THE HEARSAY RULE

As we observed in Chapter 1, as far back as the thirteenth century, hearsay evidence was regarded as unreliable. Yet, between the thirteenth and seventeenth centuries, English criminal courts continued to convict defendants based on "anonymous accusers and absentee witnesses."[1]

While English common law in criminal cases was based on an accusatorial principle—that is, live testimony by witnesses in open court—during this period English courts adopted some procedures from the European inquisitorial civil law system, discussed in Chapter 2. Among these practices was the private examination of witnesses by justices of the peace or other government officials, with the testimony used in a subsequent criminal trial.

This practice was particularly prevalent in the infamous Star Chamber trials of the Elizabethan period in England, during the reign of Queen Elizabeth I (1558–1603) and her successor, King James I (1603–1625). The monarch used the Star Chamber, consisting of royal officers, to control political enemies. Such persons were often charged with treason and tried in the Star Chamber rather than in the usual courts. In such trials the evidence frequently consisted of testimonial statements made by witnesses to court or government officers and then read into the record at the trial. The witnesses were not available for cross-examination by the accused.

These abuses were condemned by many of Elizabeth's subjects, among them William Shakespeare. In his play *Richard II*, written in 1595, Shakespeare's fictional king sets the following procedure for trial—so unlike the standard the actual sovereign, Queen Elizabeth, was using: "Then call them into our presence—face to face, and frowning brow to brow, ourselves will hear the accuser and the accused freely speak …" (Act I, Scene I).

The 1603 Trial of Sir Walter Raleigh

More than any other case, the trial of Sir Walter Raleigh in 1603 illustrates the abuses that occurred in English criminal trials before hearsay rules were introduced. As a soldier and explorer, Sir Walter Raleigh was a colorful member of the English court of Queen Elizabeth.[2] Raleigh enjoyed the patronage and protection of Queen Elizabeth during her lifetime, but he had powerful enemies in the English court.

Upon Queen Elizabeth's death in 1603, the new king, James I, feared Raleigh and had him seized and thrown into the Tower of London in July 1603. In November 1603, Raleigh was tried for treason against the king. He was convicted based on statements made before the Privy Council by his alleged accomplice, Lord Cobham, who did not appear as a witness at the trial. These statements implicated Raleigh in a **conspiracy** to commit treason and, along with a letter Cobham wrote to officials, were read to the jury.

conspiracy An agreement by two or more people to commit an illegal act.

In the years following the trial of Sir Walter Raleigh, the English courts began to develop hearsay rules, and by 1690, it is reported that English courts were using hearsay rules to prevent the kind of abuses that occurred during that period.

After the 1670 trial of William Penn, the historic development of the concept of an impartial jury continued along with the development of the hearsay rule. Wigmore (5 Wigmore, *Evidence,* Sec. 1364) called the hearsay rule "the greatest contribution of the [English] legal system ... next to the jury trial."

Hearsay Rules and the Use of Independent Juries in the American Colonies/States

English settlers brought the concepts of impartial, independent juries and hearsay rules to the American colonies as part of the English common-law system.

However, trials in admiralty courts followed the civil law methods of private judicial examinations of witnesses. The infamous English Stamp Act, which was one of the English actions found most objectionable by the American colonies, was used to expand the jurisdiction of the admiralty courts and was strongly contested on that basis.

After the American Revolutionary War, both the right to an impartial jury and the use of hearsay rules were made part of the American legal system. The former colonists were determined that the new federal government would not resort to the same civil-law procedures that the English Crown had attempted to use in America. The result was the adoption of the Sixth Amendment's Confrontation Clause, which was made part of the American Bill of Rights in 1791: "In all criminal prosecutions, the accused shall enjoy the right ... to be confronted with witnesses against him."[3]

The U.S. Supreme Court has observed that the rule against hearsay is closely related to the constitutional right of confrontation, as both "stem from the same roots" and that "... hearsay rules and the Confrontation Clause are generally designed to protect similar values...."[4]

WHAT IS HEARSAY?

hearsay Secondhand testimony; reports by one person about what another person said.

Rule 801(c) of the Federal Rules of Evidence defines **hearsay**: "'Hearsay' is a statement, other than one made by the declarant while testifying at the trial or hearing, offered in evidence to prove the truth of the matter asserted."

The Rule 801(c) elements of hearsay are thus:

1. A *statement*, which can be verbal, written, or assertive conduct;
2. Made by an out-of-court *declarant*;
3. Offered to prove the truth of the matter asserted.

declarant A person who makes a statement, either in or out of court.

The **declarant** is the person who makes the statement. To be hearsay, that statement must be offered into evidence by some other person, usually one to whom the declarant made the statement or who overheard (or observed[5]) the statement.

What Is an Assertive Statement?

assertive statement A statement by which a person intends to communicate a thought or belief.

To fall within the hearsay rule, a declarant's statement must be an **assertive statement** offered as proof that the subject matter of the statement is true.[6] An assertive statement is one in which the declarant intends to communicate his or her thoughts or beliefs.

Examples
- Witness *W* testifies: "My brother (*X*) told me that he shot my dad because he thought my dad was planning to kill him." This is hearsay and not admissible because it is an assertive statement. There is no opportunity to test the accuracy of this statement by cross-examination unless the brother is brought into court. If the brother were the defendant in this trial, however, this would be an incriminating statement that would be admissible under Federal Rule of Evidence 801(d)(2) (see Appendix C).
- Witness *W* testifies: "I heard my brother (*X*) mutter 'I killed my dad' in his sleep." This is not hearsay because *X*, while sleeping, did not intend to communicate a thought or belief.[7]

Nonverbal Communications Can Be Assertive

nonverbal communication Acts that do not involve words or speech but that may be assertive and therefore hearsay.

Nonverbal acts can be used to communicate. If the purpose of the nonverbal act is to communicate and the communication is assertive, it is hearsay.

Examples
- The witness testifies that when she asked *X* where his drug dealer lived, *X* pointed to the defendant's house. This is hearsay because it is an assertion that cannot be tested by cross-examination. *X* should be brought in as a witness if he is available.
- The witness testifies that she requested the victim of a mugging to draw a sketch of the mugger. This is hearsay because it is assertive conduct that cannot be tested by cross-examination. The victim must be brought in as a witness.
- The conduct that is the subject of the witness's testimony must have been undertaken for the purpose of asserting some relevant fact. If a witness testifies that a captain, to prove his boat was seaworthy, took his family for a cruise, the captain's conduct is "assertive" because the conduct was intended to show the boat was seaworthy. However, if the fact of the family cruise is offered only because it shows the likely belief of the captain, it is admissible circumstantial evidence.

Conduct That Is Not Meant to Communicate

If a person were engaging in conduct that was not meant to communicate, this would generally not be treated as hearsay because there is no attempt to be assertive.[8]

Examples
- A police officer testifies: "I showed Ms. (rape victim) a display of seven photographs. When she saw the picture of *X* (the defendant), she gasped and began to cry." This is not hearsay because the rape victim's conduct is not meant as a communication, even though it creates the indirect inference that she believes the defendant was the person who raped her.[9]
- Questions are not hearsay. Thus, a police officer may testify that, while the officer was in a defendant's home, an unknown party asked the defendant if he had "any stuff." The person asking the question was not intending to assert anything.

The Hearsay Rule Forbids Only Statements Offered to Prove the Truth of That Statement

truth of the matter asserted The subject to be proved in an assertive statement.

If an attorney can convince a judge that a statement offered for use in evidence is meant to prove something other than the truth of that statement, the judge will rule that it is admissible for evidence. The hearsay rule forbids only statements offered to prove the **truth of the matter asserted**. The hearsay rule does not forbid evidence offered to prove something other than the truth of that statement.

McCormick on Evidence[10] points out that there are "an almost infinite variety of other purposes" to take a statement out of the hearsay rule and permit it to be used as evidence. The following examples illustrate only a few of the numerous other purposes that take an out-of-court statement out of the hearsay classification:

- *Knowledge:* William Witness testifies that Fred Firebug told him that a can of gasoline was in the attic of the house the day before the fire occurred. Witness's testimony would *not* be admissible to prove that there was gasoline in the attic the day before the fire. It would be admissible to show that Firebug *knew* that there was gasoline in the attic before the fire.

- *Feelings or state of mind:* William Witness testifies that Fred Firebug had said, "Bobby Burnout took my money, stole my girl, and wrecked my car on the night of the senior prom." This testimony would not be admissible to show that Burnout had taken Firebug's money, or stolen his girlfriend, or wrecked his car. It would be admissible to demonstrate Firebug's feelings or state of mind about Burnout.

- *Insanity:* William Witness testifies that Charles Crazy had said, "I am Napoleon Bonaparte, Emperor of all France." Witness's testimony would not be admissible to show that Crazy was in fact a person named Napoleon Bonaparte. It would, however, be admissible to show circumstantially that Crazy was insane.

- *Effect on hearer:* William Witness testifies that he heard Bill Bully say to Tom Timid, "No one better mess with me. I am carrying a loaded .38." The testimony would not be admissible to show that Bully was carrying a gun. It would be admissible to show the effect on Timid's state of mind.

- *Independent rational significance:* A witness testifies that an elderly victim said, following a sexual assault, "The man drove off in a new Ford; it still had the dealer sticker in the window." The statement would not be admissible to prove the attacker drove a Ford; it would be admissible to prove the victim was mentally competent after the attack.

The trial judge should instruct the jury that it must consider the evidence only for the allowable purpose. This would work well in the above Charles Crazy example. The jury would view the statement as bearing on Crazy's state of mind and would not conclude that Crazy might indeed be Napoleon Bonaparte.

But as Professor McCormick points out, "such ... instructions may not always be effective," and there are situations in which juries misuse the evidence or become unduly confused by the judge's instructions.

Statements that would otherwise be testimonial and require that the defendant have the right of cross-examination under the rule of *Crawford v. Washington*[11] (discussed in Chapter 8) can be admitted without such right of cross-examination if they are not intended to prove the truth of their contents. An example of this principle is the 2004 decision of the California Supreme Court in *People v. Combs*.[12]

California's evidence code has a provision called "adoptive admissions." Under this rule, an out-of-court statement is not hearsay if the defendant has manifested "by words or other conduct" that he or she adopts the truth of those statements. In *Combs*, the defendant and an accomplice reenacted the killing of a victim. The police filmed the reenactment. In the video, the accomplice made statements that were damaging to the defendant. The video captured the defendant's expressions while these statements were made, and he made no effort to object to the statements when they were made. When the video was offered in evidence, the defendant objected, alleging the statements were testimonial hearsay and inadmissible under *Crawford*. The California Supreme Court held that the video was offered not to prove the truth of the statements but to show that the defendant had adopted those statements. As a result, the statements were not hearsay and were admissible.

WHAT IS NOT HEARSAY? FEDERAL RULES OF EVIDENCE 801(D)(1), 801(D)(2), AND 801(D)(2)(E)

Besides being limited to assertions offered to establish proof of the assertion, the hearsay rule does not apply to various out-of-court statements that would otherwise literally fall within the definition of hearsay. These statements are described in Rules 801(d)(1) and (2) of the Federal Rules of Evidence.

Prior Statement by a Witness

Rule 801(d)(1) lists three circumstances where a prior, out-of-court statement is not classified as hearsay. All three require that the person making the prior statement (the declarant) be present in court and subject to cross-examination about the prior statement. If a witness testifies at a trial and can be cross-examined concerning an earlier statement made by the witness, the statement is not hearsay if

1. 801(d)(1)(A). The statement is inconsistent with the present testimony of the witness and was given under oath at a previous trial, hearing, or deposition.

    Example
    At D's murder trial, W testifies that he did not see D in the victim's car on the night the victim was killed. W, at an earlier preliminary hearing where D's attorney was present and able to cross-examine him, had stated that D was in the victim's car. W's earlier statement is not hearsay. However, if the witness is not present to testify at the trial, the prior statement is hearsay, and can be admitted only if one of the hearsay exceptions applies, such as the "former testimony" exception in Rule 804(b). (See Chapter 8 for discussion of the hearsay exceptions.)

2. 801(d)(1)(B). The statement is consistent and is offered to rebut a charge that the witness's present testimony is a recent fabrication or stems from an improper motive.

    Example
    The witness, who is the defendant's employee, testifies that he saw the defendant in Cleveland on the date a robbery occurred in Denver. On cross-examination, the prosecutor suggests the witness's motive is to protect his employer. A similar, consistent statement made by the witness to a police officer investigating the robbery, made before the witness was employed by the defendant, is not hearsay.

3. 801(d)(1)(C). The statement is one of identification of a person made after perceiving that person.

    Examples
    A witness testifies at defendant's murder trial and at that time identifies the defendant as the murderer. The prosecutor asks the witness if prior to the trial he attended a lineup and identified the defendant there. The witness may answer the question because his earlier identification is not hearsay.

A police officer testifies that a bartender who was given counterfeit $20 bills identified the defendant from a photograph display. The bartender testifies he remembers making an identification, but does not remember if it was the defendant he identified. The earlier identification statement is not hearsay. However, the procedures used to make the photographic identification must meet constitutional standards. (See Chapter 13.)

Admission by a Party-Opponent

Where the statement sought to be admitted is an out-of-court statement made by the defendant (a "party" in the trial) or someone acting on his or her behalf, Federal Rule of Evidence 801(d)(2) provides that the statement is not hearsay.[13]

Different reasons are given as the basis for the rule; perhaps the most common justification is that statements against the interest of the person making the statement are inherently reliable, because people don't usually say things against their interest if they are not true. The problem with hearsay evidence is that while the witness who testifies about the out-of-court statement can be questioned to determine how reliable his testimony is about hearing the statement, the reliability of the person who made the statement (the declarant) cannot be tested at the trial. But if the witness, after examination, is believed to be accurate about what he heard the declarant say, a statement against interest carries its own indicia of reliability. In any case, as Professor McCormick points out, the hearsay rule never forbids admissions by a party-opponent (the defendant in a criminal case).

Examples

- Witness W testifies in D's trial for possession of stolen property that shortly after a burglary D stated, "I have the jewels stolen from the Johnson house." The statement is not hearsay.
- Witness W testifies at D's trial for assault against V that, in the presence of D, V stated, "Last night after work, D beat me up," and D said nothing. D's silence can be seen as adoption or belief in the statement and prevents the statement from being hearsay.
- Witness W testifies at D's trial for illegal bookmaking that E, a person who worked for D by picking up betting slips, stated, "These are markers in D's sports book." The statement is not hearsay because it was made by a person employed by D and concerns a matter within the scope of that employment.
- Same facts as above, except that W testifies that E told W that D had illegal firearms at his bookmaking office. E's statement is hearsay, because having illegal firearms is not a matter within the scope of his employment with D.

The Co-Conspirator Rule

Federal Rule of Evidence 801(d)(2)(E) provides that statements made by a coconspirator during and in furtherance of the conspiracy are not hearsay.[14] The justification for this rule is that parties in a conspiracy are essentially partners, and an admission by one partner is fairly attributable to the other partners. The U.S. Supreme Court has said that statements by a co-conspirator "provide evidence of the conspiracy's context that cannot be replicated, even if the [co-conspirator] testifies to the same matters in court." The Court also noted that "simply calling the [co-conspirator] in hopes of having him repeat his prior out-of-court statements is a poor substitute for the full ... significance that flow[s] from statements made when the conspiracy is operating in full force"[15] (co-conspirator rule).

Most courts have held that statements by co-conspirators are not "testimonial," and thus are not subject to the Confrontation Clause's requirement that the defendant have an opportunity to confront and cross-examine the person who made the statement. Courts denying claims that the Confrontation Clause applies to co-conspirator statements reason that such statements are not made for the purpose of establishing or preserving the contents of the statement. The meaning of "testimonial" for Confrontation Clause purposes is discussed in Chapter 8.

Example
A and *B* are engaged in a conspiracy to import and sell illegal drugs. While acting in furtherance of the conspiracy, *A* states to *C*, "*B* sold the cocaine from the last shipment." *A*'s statement is not hearsay as an admission of a co-conspirator and is admissible in *B*'s prosecution.

SUMMARY

1. **Define *hearsay*.**
   - Hearsay is an out-of-court statement (oral, written, or an action) that is assertive and offered into evidence to prove the truth of the subject matter of the statement. A statement is assertive if it is intended to communicate a thought or belief.

2. **List the questions that should be asked to determine if a statement is hearsay.**
   - When a witness at a criminal trial is asked to repeat in court a statement made out of court, the following questions should be asked to determine whether that testimony is inadmissible hearsay:
     a. Is the statement (verbal or nonverbal conduct) an assertion?
     b. Is the statement offered to prove the truth of the assertion?
     c. Was the statement made under oath and subject to cross-examination at a prior trial, hearing, or deposition?
     d. Was the admission (or statement) made by a party-opponent in a civil case or a defendant in a criminal case?

3. **State why hearsay raises questions of reliability.**
   - Hearsay is offered to prove the truth of the content of the statement. Because the person making the statement (the declarant) is not present in court, the tests, mainly cross-examination, to determine the accuracy and truth of the statement cannot be used. Thus, while the reliability of the witness repeating the statement in court can be tested, the reliability of the person who made the statement cannot.

4. **Define an *assertive statement*.**
   - An assertive statement, whether it is an oral statement, a written statement, or some action by the declarant, is one that is intended by the declarant to communicate something the declarant believes or is thinking.

5. **Explain why the statement "he said he would kill me" might not be hearsay.**
   - The statement would be hearsay if offered into evidence to prove the declarant's intent to commit a crime. It would not be hearsay if offered only to prove the state of mind of the witness, or to prove the effect the statement had on the witness.

6. **State the co-conspirator rule.**
   - Statements made by a co-conspirator made during the course of the conspiracy and in furtherance of the conspiracy are not hearsay.

7. **Identify when a prior statement by a witness is not hearsay.**
   - If a witness is at the trial and testifies, prior statements made by the witness are not hearsay if: a) they were inconsistent with the testimony, and were made under oath at a prior hearing; b) they were consistent with the testimony, and are offered to rebut a claim that the witness's testimony is fabricated or the result of improper influence or motive; c) they were made as a prior identification of a person after perceiving that person.

KEY TERMS

assertive statement, 176

conspiracy, 175

declarant, 176

hearsay, 176

nonverbal communication, 177

truth of the matter asserted, 177

PROBLEMS

1. Police officers use information from confidential informants ("CI") for many reasons. One common reason is to supply the officer with a basis for stopping or arresting a person believed to be committing a crime. For example, assume a CI tells a detective that "John Smith is selling heroin." In a criminal prosecution against Smith, may the officer testify that the CI "told me John Smith was selling illegal drugs"? May the officer testify that the CI "told me people were selling drugs on the corner of 1st and Main Street"? May the officer testify the CI told him "an individual wearing jeans and a blue hoodie is selling heroin on the corner of 1st and Main Street"? Which of these statements is hearsay, and which not? (See *Parker v. State*, 970 A.2d 320 (Md. 2009).)

2. So-called "double hearsay" involves situations like this: A testifies that B told her that C said the defendant stole her money. If that testimony is intended to prove the defendant stole C's money, it is double hearsay: B's statement to A is hearsay, and C's statement to B is hearsay. Is it double hearsay if a police officer testifies that C, an assault victim who did not speak English, told B, an interpreter, that the defendant assaulted her, which the interpreter then told the detective in English? Is the "statement" by the interpreter an "assertive" statement? (See *State v. Rodriguez-Castillo*, 188 P.3d 268 (Or. 2008).)

3. As the text states, courts routinely hold that questions are not assertive statements. Thus, when police are searching a house believed to be used for drug transactions, an officer who answers a telephone at that house may testify at a subsequent prosecution of the house's owner for sale of illegal drugs that the caller said, "Are you holding?" Why would the prosecution want to introduce the caller's words? Does that reason suggest there might be a good argument that the caller's words should be treated as hearsay? What if the caller said "Hey man, the weed you got me yesterday was great. Got any more?" (See *People v. Morgan*, 23 Cal. Rptr. 3d 224 (Cal. App. 2005).)

CASE ANALYSIS

Read Appendix B, Finding and Analyzing Cases (p. 499). With these guidelines in mind, please continue with the Case Analysis selections for Chapter 7.

In this chapter we distinguished between hearsay statements and statements that are not offered to prove the truth of the statement. Applying this distinction to statements offered at trial may be difficult, as can be seen in the first two cases described next.

1. An injured man is brought to an emergency room in an ambulance. The EMT transporting the man also brought various articles to the trauma room, including a backpack. An emergency room nurse inventoried the articles, including the backpack, where she discovered illegal drugs. Later, two women came to the emergency room and said to the injured man, "Where is your backpack?" The women then took the backpack and left the emergency room. May the nurse who overheard the women's questions testify to what the women said? *State v. Palmer*, 270 P.3d 891 (Az. App. 2012).

2. A defendant is charged with illegal trespass on a neighbor's property. Trespass is a crime that requires proof the defendant had no reasonable belief that he was permitted to be on the property. The defendant seeks to testify that a co-owner of the property, who is not present and can't testify, told him "you can stay here tonight." Is the testimony hearsay? *State v. McCave*, 805 N.W.2d 290 (Neb. 2011). What is the "verbal acts" rule, and why aren't verbal acts hearsay?

3. When informants give police a tip about an investigation, police officers may be asked to testify about the nature and content of the tip at a subsequent criminal trial. If the testimony is given to show the "course of the investigation" it is not hearsay because it is not introduced to prove the truth of the facts in the tip, but only to show how the officers conducted their investigation. However, if the officer's testimony is used as part of the prosecution's case against the defendant, it is hearsay, because in such a case it is offered to prove the truth of the statement. How does a court tell the difference? Consider this testimony by an investigating officer at the murder trial of Jones: "The informant told me his brother James Parks told him he, Aaron, and Jones committed the murders, and that's why we focused on Jones." Course of investigation, or hearsay? Double hearsay? Would it affect your answer if the prosecution introduced evidence intended to show the informant was reliable? *Jones v. Basinger*, 635 F.3d 1030 (7th Cir. 2011).

4. The U.S. Supreme Court is responsible for making recommendations to Congress on changes to the Federal Rules of Evidence. In April 2014 the Court recommended that the "prior consistent statement" hearsay rule, Fed. R. Evid. 801 (d)(1)(B), be expanded to include more such statements when offered to rehabilitate a witness, as well as to rebut accusations that the witness recently fabricated the statements. The Court also recommended that such statements be admitted as "substantive evidence." How would that recommendation change the existing rule? Do you think it is a good suggestion?

Notes

1. See Chapter 8 (pp. 186–206) for a discussion of the development of Confrontation Clause law.
2. Sir Walter Raleigh established a reputation as a ruthless fighter and is said to have come to the attention of Queen Elizabeth by spreading his coat over a mud puddle so that the queen could walk on his coat. Raleigh's later conviction for treason put him in the Tower of London for 12 years, where he lived comfortably with his family and servants. Upon his release, he violated the king's order not to invade Spanish territory in South America and was sentenced to death.
3. Justices Thomas and Scalia state in the 1992 case of *White v. Illinois* (502 U.S. 346, 112 S. Ct. 736, 744, 50 CrL 2036) that there "is virtually no evidence of what the drafters of the Confrontation Clause intended it to mean." They quote Justice Harlan's concurring opinion in the 1970 case of *Dutton v. Evans* (400 U.S. 74, 94, 91 S. Ct. 210, 222): "From the scant information available it may tentatively be concluded that the Confrontation Clause was meant to constitutionalize a barrier against flagrant abuses, trials by anonymous accusers, and absentee witnesses."

    The famous English judge Sir James Stephens stated in his 1883 book, *A History of the Criminal Law of England* (Macmillan, 1883), that early English judges questioned the prisoner, accomplices, and others prior to criminal trials and that the "prisoner had no right to be, and probably never was, present." At the trial itself, "proof was usually given by reading depositions, confession of accomplices, letters, and the like; and this occasioned frequent demands by the prisoner to have his 'accusers' (i.e., the witnesses against him), brought before him face to face" (vol. 1, p. 326, *A History of the Criminal Law of England*).

4. *Dutton v. Evans*, 400 U.S. 74, 86, 91 S. Ct. 210, 218 (1970).
5. A statement need not be verbal. It can be in writing, or it can be a nonverbal act intended as an assertion. (See Federal Rule of Evidence 801(a).)
6. (See *Martinez v. McCaughtry*, 951 F.2d 130 (7th Cir. 1991).) Statements by the declarant that "you're a dead man" made to the accused are not hearsay because they are not assertions. Many courts use the kind of sentence made by the declarant as a guide to whether the statement is assertive. Sentences that are questions (interrogative) or commands (imperative) are not assertions. Only indicative or declaratory sentences can be assertions. (See, for example, *Holland v. State*, 713 A.2d 364 (Md. App. 1998).)
7. (See, for example, *State v. Tate*, 817 S.W.2d 578 (Mo. App. 1991).)
8. The Advisory Committee on Rules of Evidence, which drafted Rule 801 of the Federal Rules, made this comment about nonassertive conduct: Subdivision (a). The definition of "statement" assumes importance because the term is used in the definition of hearsay in subdivision (c). The effect of the definition of "statement" is to exclude from the operation of the hearsay rule all evidence of conduct, verbal or nonverbal, not intended as an assertion. The key to the definition is that nothing is an assertion unless intended to be one.

Cited in *People v. Jones*, 579 N.W.2d 82, 92 (Mich. App. 1998).

9. Federal Rule of Evidence 801(d)(1)(C) also permits prior out-of-court identifications by a witness available for cross-examination at the trial. See *Gilbert v. California* 388 U.S. 263 (1967).

10. *McCormick on Evidence*, 4th ed. (West, 1992).

11. 541 U.S. 36 (2004).

12. 22 Cal. Rptr. 3d 61.

13. However, under the *Bruton* rule (see Chapter 12), the confession of an accomplice may not ordinarily be introduced at a joint trial of persons who commit a crime together if the confession incriminates the other defendant or defendants. Such a confession could be admissible, however, (a) if the person making the confession takes the witness stand, (b) if the confession does not incriminate other defendants, or (c) if all defendants confess and the confessions are significantly interlocking to rebut the presumption of unreliability.

14. Federal Rule of Evidence 801(d)(2)(E) provides that the co-conspirator's statement, while relevant to the question, cannot alone establish that the person against whom the statement is offered was a party to the conspiracy. Most courts require some independent proof of that fact, and if such proof is not available, the co-conspirator's statement is inadmissible. (See *United States v. Tellier*, 83 F.3d 578 (2d Cir. 1996), *cert. denied,* 117 S. Ct. 373 (1996).)

15. 475 U.S. 307 (1985).

The Confrontation Clause and Exceptions to the Hearsay Rule

A 911 OPERATOR

AP Images/Kelley McCall

LEARNING OBJECTIVES

In this chapter we consider exceptions to the hearsay rule and the role of the Confrontation Clause in admitting hearsay evidence. The learning objectives for this chapter are

State the *pre-Crawford* test for admissibility of hearsay evidence.

State the rule of *Crawford v. Washington*.

Define a *testimonial statement*.

State when hearsay exceptions may be used as the basis for admission of out-of-court statements.

Give the justification for the recognition of the "firmly rooted" exceptions to the hearsay rule.

State the rule for the admissibility of nontestimonial statements.

Identify hearsay exceptions in child sexual abuse cases.

One of the most difficult evidentiary issues American criminal courts face is the admissibility of out-of-court statements made by young children in child abuse prosecutions. Courts considering the admissibility of such evidence must balance society's desire to protect young children against the rights of those accused of crimes. This difficulty is even more acute after the U.S. Supreme Court's opinion in the *Crawford* case, discussed in this chapter, which construed the Confrontation Clause to require the opportunity of cross-examination for all "testimonial" statements.

Consider the problem that confronted the Ohio Supreme Court in the case of *State v. Clark*, 999 N.E.2d 592 (2013). A 3-year-old child arrived at a preschool class with whip-like marks on his face. The teacher asked the child "Who did this?" and the child gave the name of the defendant. Under Ohio law, the teacher was required to report the suspected child abuse to police, which the teacher did. The defendant was charged with child abuse, and at his trial the teacher was asked to testify about the child's answers to the teacher's questions (the child was found incompetent to testify, and was thus "unavailable"). Should the teacher be allowed to testify? As you read this first part of the chapter, what does your intuition suggest the answer should be? After you have studied the cases on the Confrontation Clause, consider your answer again. Now you can better appreciate the problem courts have in this area. The U.S. Supreme Court granted review of *State v. Clark* in October of 2014.

HEARSAY AND THE CONFRONTATION CLAUSE

Confrontation Clause

The clause in the U.S. Constitution that entitles a defendant in a criminal case to demand witnesses to testify against him in his presence.

In criminal trials, the admission of out-of-court statements presents not only issues under relevant hearsay rules but also potential conflict with the Sixth Amendment's **Confrontation Clause**. That clause states, "In all criminal prosecutions, the accused shall enjoy the right ... to be confronted with the witnesses against him...." This includes the right to confront adverse witnesses, and the right to be present at any stage of a trial to effectively cross-examine adverse witnesses. The Confrontation Clause seeks to "ensure the reliability of the evidence against a defendant by subjecting it (the evidence) to rigorous testing." *Maryland v. Craig,* 497 U.S. 836 (1990).

The policy behind the Confrontation Clause is to guarantee that a criminal defendant has the opportunity to confront and examine witnesses to test the truthfulness, accuracy, and reliability of their testimony. The implications of hearsay evidence for the Confrontation Clause are clear: If an out-of-court statement is admitted as evidence against the accused, the person making that statement is a "witness"[1] who is not "confronting" the accused.

Hearsay rules (and their exceptions) were used in trials hundreds of years before the Sixth Amendment was adopted in 1791 as part of the Bill of Rights. The Sixth Amendment applies only in criminal cases, and is available only to criminal defendants; neither the prosecution in criminal cases nor parties to civil cases may invoke the Sixth Amendment.

Prior to 1965 few cases discussed the relationships among the hearsay rule, hearsay exceptions, and the Confrontation Clause. This was because the Confrontation Clause had not been extended to state criminal cases and applied only to federal criminal trials. In those trials, admissibility tended to be determined by reference only to federal evidentiary rules.[2]

In the 1965 case of *Pointer v. Texas,*[3] the U.S. Supreme Court held that the Fourteenth Amendment Due Process Clause made the Confrontation Clause binding in state criminal trials. Because state evidentiary rules differed widely from federal evidence rules and from one another, the Supreme Court considered the admissibility of hearsay evidence as a Confrontation Clause problem. A state might, for example, have an evidentiary rule that permits admissibility of hearsay evidence in criminal cases for reasons unique to that state's evidentiary system. In such a case, the state's justification for admission of the hearsay evidence must pass the Confrontation Clause test.

In the 1970 case of *California v. Green* the Supreme Court noted that "hearsay rules and the Confrontation Clause are generally designed to protect similar values."[4] They both recognize the importance of face-to-face contact between witness and accused and the crucial role of cross-examination, "the greatest legal engine ever invented for the discovery of truth."[5] Although the Court had always been careful not to equate the Confrontation Clause with the hearsay rule,[6] the early Confrontation Clause cases looked to the hearsay exceptions as appropriate **"indicia of reliability"** for admission in criminal trials of out-of-court statements. In essence, these cases stood for the proposition that the "indicia of reliability" inherent in most hearsay exceptions provided an adequate substitute for confrontation and cross-examination of a live witness. *Ohio v. Roberts*, 448 U.S. 56 (1980) was the leading case for this approach to the Confrontation Clause.

indicia of reliability
Characteristics of a statement, otherwise inadmissible as hearsay, which courts believe sufficiently establish the statement's reliability that cross-examination is not required.

A GUIDE TO HEARSAY/CONFRONTATION CLAUSE SOLUTIONS

When a witness is called to testify in a criminal trial, and is asked to repeat before the jury an out-of-court statement made to the witness by a person not present at the trial, asking (and answering) the following questions will help lead one to the "correct" solution about the statement's admissibility. As you study the materials in this chapter, keep this guide in mind:

1. **Is the statement hearsay?** Is it being offered into evidence to prove the subject of the statement, or for some other purpose? This was what we studied in Chapter 7.
2. **If it is hearsay, is it "testimonial"?** *Crawford* and the cases that came after it will help you distinguish testimonial statements from non-testimonial ones, but generally you should look to the primary purpose of the questions asked by, and the out-of-court answers given to, the person now seeking to testify about the statement.
3. **If an out-of-court statement is testimonial, the Confrontation Clause requires the person who made the statement be in court and available for cross-examination.** The point of *Crawford* was to eliminate any question about the "reliability" of out-of-court statements that are testimonial. The person who made the statement must be available for cross-examination, or else the statement is inadmissible under the Sixth Amendment.
4. **If an out-of-court statement is not testimonial, no Confrontation Clause issue arises.** Non-testimonial hearsay, such as a statement made during an ongoing emergency, is not subject to the Confrontation Clause because it was not made to provide evidence of a past crime or identify the perpetrator of the crime.
5. **Does the forfeiture by wrongdoing rule apply?** Even if hearsay is testimonial, if the defendant has wrongfully made the person who made the out-of-court statement unavailable, the Confrontation Clause right is forfeited.
6. **If the hearsay statement is not testimonial, does one of the hearsay exceptions apply to make it admissible?** Even if the Confrontation Clause does not bar admission of non-testimonial hearsay statements, state and federal rules of evidence require a showing of the applicability of a hearsay exception for the statements admissibility.

THE CONFRONTATION CLAUSE AFTER *CRAWFORD*

The U.S. Supreme Court's 2004 decision in *Crawford v. Washington,* discussed more fully below, specifically overruled the key "indicia of reliability" case, *Ohio v. Roberts.* The Court held in *Crawford* that it is no longer enough that out-of-court statements have some "guarantee of trustworthiness," such as a recognized hearsay exception. Rather, the Court held, the "guarantee" of the Confrontation Clause was the defendant's right to confront and cross-examine those "who bear testimony" against him. A witness's "testimonial" statement is thus inadmissible unless (1) the witness is available to testify and appears at trial, or (2) the witness is unavailable but the defendant had an earlier opportunity for cross-examination of the witness.

After *Crawford,* if the out-of-court statement of a person is "testimonial" and is offered as evidence against a defendant in a criminal trial, it can be admitted only if the person is present at the trial to be cross-examined about the statement, or if unavailable, was subject to cross-examination about the statement in a prior proceeding. The fact that the statement meets the requirements of some well-recognized hearsay exception does not serve as an alternative basis for the statement's admission.

Most testimonial statements are statements made by a witness in court, while under oath, and subject to cross-examination. If the witness is testifying to events that the witness saw or knew from firsthand experience, then the testimony is not hearsay. If the witness is not testifying from firsthand knowledge, however, the testimony is generally hearsay and inadmissible unless an exception to the hearsay rule applies. (See the discussion of the hearsay exceptions later in this chapter.)

In the 2004 landmark case of *Crawford v. Washington,*[7] the U.S. Supreme Court adopted a new "bright-line" rule for the introduction of "testimonial" evidence. The Court held that the Sixth Amendment Confrontation Clause guarantees a defendant in a criminal case the opportunity to cross-examine the person who gives testimony, and if that person is unavailable to testify at the trial, a statement made by that person is inadmissible unless the defendant had an earlier opportunity to cross-examine the person. This is true, the Court held, even if the statement meets the indicia of reliability requirement established in *Ohio v. Roberts* or is covered by a "firmly rooted" exception to the hearsay rule.

Crawford v. Washington

United States Supreme Court, 541 U.S. 36 (2004)

Hours after her husband had been arrested for stabbing another man, Sylvia Crawford was in police custody, and was given *Miranda* warnings as a possible suspect. She was questioned at a police station house, and was calmly answering the interrogating officers. Her answers were recorded and the police took notes during the examination.

Her husband, Michael Crawford, claimed self-defense against the stabbing-assault charge filed against him. Crawford alleged the victim had a weapon that the victim threatened to use against him. Because some of Sylvia's statements to police during her interrogation cast doubt on Crawford's self-defense claim, Crawford invoked the "marital privilege" and Sylvia was prevented from testifying at his trial.

At Crawford's trial, the judge permitted the prosecution to introduce a tape recording of answers given by Sylvia to police officers shortly after the stabbing occurred. The prosecution successfully argued in the trial court that because Sylvia had facilitated the assault and had her own criminal responsibility, at the time she made her statements they were "against her penal interests" and admissible under that exception to the hearsay rule. The trial court ruled that Sylvia's statements were "against her penal interests" and admissible under that exception to the hearsay rule. Crawford was convicted, and appealed. The Washington Court of Appeals reversed his conviction, but the Washington Supreme Court held that the statements were admissible and reversed the appeals court.

The U.S. Supreme Court reversed the Washington Supreme Court, holding that where "testimonial" hearsay is offered and the person who made the statement is unavailable to testify, the Confrontation Clause prohibits the introduction of the statement unless the defendant has an opportunity to cross-examine the person who made the statement. It held Sylvia's statements were "testimonial" because "interrogations by law enforcement officers fall squarely within the class of" testimonial statements:

> … interrogation (was) solely directed at establishing the facts of a past crime, in order to identify (or provide evidence to convict) the perpetrator. The product of such interrogation, whether reduced to a writing signed by the declarant or embedded in the memory (and perhaps notes) of the interrogating officer, is testimonial.[8]

Because Sylvia was "unavailable" to testify and thus could not be cross-examined, her "testimonial" hearsay statements were inadmissible.

A difficult question left open in *Crawford* was the meaning of "testimonial" statements. On this issue the Court said: "We leave for another day any effort to spell out a comprehensive definition of "testimonial." The Court did list some examples of statements that are "testimonial": "Whatever else that term covers, it applies at a minimum to prior testimony at a preliminary hearing, before a grand jury, or at a former trial; and to police interrogations."[9]

The Meaning of "Testimonial"

Any out-of-court "statement" (which can be a verbal or written statement or an assertive act) by a person that is offered as evidence in a criminal trial without the opportunity of cross-examination of that person can be challenged under the Confrontation Clause. If that statement is "testimonial" it is inadmissible. If it is "non-testimonial," the Confrontation Clause does not prevent its admissibility, though the hearsay rule might. The difficulty is determining when a statement is "testimonial."

The hearsay rules and the Sixth Amendment right to confront and cross-examine adverse witnesses often become applicable to evidence produced as the result of police interrogation. Police officers respond to disturbance and trouble calls on a daily basis on streets and in homes or apartments. When they respond, the police take statements from victims and witnesses, both to deal with the problem and to collect evidence. In circumstances like the following example, the "reliability" test and the new test after *Crawford* yield different results.

Example

Officer Able responded to a domestic disturbance call and came upon a woman with bruising, torn clothing, and a bloody mouth. Able asks, "Who did this to you?" The woman answers, "My husband, Bill Brute." Brute is arrested and charged with assault. At his trial his wife does not appear to testify. The prosecution calls Officer Able to testify. Able's testimony about what he saw and did is not hearsay, and thus admissible. However, his testimony about what the wife said to him when he arrived on the scene would be hearsay.

Under the old "reliability" test: Officer Able's testimony would likely be admitted because of one of the hearsay exceptions, since under the old rule the inherent reliability of those exceptions was enough to satisfy the Confrontation Clause.

Under the new rule: Officer Able's testimony would not be admitted, because the wife's statements were "testimonial," and the defendant never had an opportunity to cross-examine the wife. If the statements were admitted it would violate the defendant's Sixth Amendment right to confront the witness against him, here his wife. Thus, the "indicia of reliability" justifying the hearsay exception can no longer satisfy the Sixth Amendment rights of a criminal defendant.

Police Interrogations and 911 Calls One of the "core" situations identified in *Crawford* to which the Confrontation Clause applied was "police interrogations." Like the facts in *Crawford*, police interrogations in response to domestic disturbances can result in both "testimonial" and "non-testimonial" statements from victims and witnesses. In the three U.S. Supreme Court cases that follow, the Court addressed the question of the distinction between testimonial and non-testimonial statements. Two were domestic disturbance cases that were combined for decision; in *Hammon v. Indiana* and *Davis v. Washington*, 547 U.S. 813 (2006), the Supreme Court addressed the question left open in *Crawford:* What is "testimonial" in the context of police interrogations, and what is "non-testimonial?" In the third case the Supreme Court discussed the difference between statements made during an "on-going emergency" and those made to "establish facts" for future prosecutions.

Davis v. Washington

United States Supreme
Court, 547 U.S. 813 (2006)

In *Davis* the defendant was charged with a domestic battery offense in which his former girlfriend, Michelle, was the victim. She did not appear to testify at the defendant's trial, so the prosecution introduced a 911 tape that included Michelle's statements describing the domestic abuse, and naming the defendant as the person who abused her.

The police arrived within four minutes of the 911 call, and stated they observed Michelle in a shaken state, "with fresh injuries to her forearm and face" and that she used "frantic efforts to gather her belongings and her children so that they could leave the residence."

Davis was charged with felony violation of a domestic no-contact order, but at his trial Michelle did not appear to testify. The state's only witnesses were the police officers, who testified as to what they observed. Over the defendant's objections the trial judge admitted portions of the tape of the 911 call, and the jury convicted the defendant.

The state appellate courts affirmed the conviction, holding that the portion of the 911 tape in which Michelle identified Davis as the assailant was not "testimonial." The U.S. Supreme Court agreed, and affirmed the conviction. It stated:

> Statements are nontestimonial when made in the course of police interrogation under circumstances objectively indicating that the primary purpose of the interrogation is to enable police assistance to meet an ongoing emergency. They are testimonial when the circumstances objectively indicate that there is no such ongoing emergency, and that the primary purpose of the interrogation is to establish or prove past events potentially relevant to later criminal prosecution.[10]

Hammon v. Indiana

United States Supreme
Court, 547 U.S. 813 (2006)

In *Hammon* the defendant was charged with a domestic violence offense in which his wife was the victim. Police responding late at night to a "domestic disturbance" call arrived to find Amy Hammon, the defendant's wife, alone on the front porch. She appeared "somewhat frightened," but told the officers "nothing was the matter." She gave the police permission to enter the house, where an officer saw "a gas heating unit in the corner of the living room" that had "flames coming out of the … partial glass front. There were pieces of glass on the ground in front of it and there was flame emitting from the front of the unit."

The husband, Herchel, was in the kitchen and told the police "he and his wife" had "been in an argument" but that "everything was fine now." He said the argument "never became physical." Another officer then talked with Amy in the living room, asking her "what had occurred." After hearing Amy's account, the officer stated he "had her fill out and sign a battery affidavit." Amy handwrote: "Broke our furnace & shoved me down on the floor into the broken glass. Hit me on the chest and threw me down. Broke our lamps and phone. Tore up my van where I couldn't leave the house. Attacked my daughter."

The husband was charged with domestic battery, and also with parole violation. Amy was subpoenaed but did not appear to testify at the trial. The State called the officer who questioned Amy and asked him to recount what Amy said, and to authenticate the affidavit. The defense lawyer objected to the admission of the officer's testimony recounting Amy's statements and the affidavit because "there was no opportunity to cross-examine the person who allegedly drafted it."

The trial court admitted the affidavit as a "present sense impression" and Amy's statements as "excited utterances" that "are expressly permitted in these kinds of cases even if the declarant is unavailable to testify." The trial judge found the defendant guilty, and on appeal the Indiana Court of Appeals affirmed the conviction. The Indiana Supreme Court held that the statements by Amy were non-testimonial and admissible under the state law hearsay exception for excited utterances. The Indiana Court held that the affidavit was testimonial and should not have been admitted, but that the admission was harmless error beyond a reasonable doubt, largely because it was a bench trial.

The U.S. Supreme Court reversed, holding that

> It is entirely clear from the circumstances that the interrogation was part of an investigation into possible criminal past conduct … There was no emergency in progress; the interrogating officer testified that he heard no arguments or crashing and saw no one throw or break anything. When the officers first arrived, Amy told them that things were fine and that there was no immediate threat to her person. When the officer questioned Amy for the second time, and elicited the challenged statements, he was not seeking to determine (as in Davis) "what is happening" but rather "what happened."[11]

In *Davis*, the questions asked and answered during the 911 call, the Court said, were clearly intended to deal with the domestic crisis that was occurring during the call. As a result, the statements made by the victim were more in the nature of an excited utterance. Since the statements were not testimonial under the rule just announced, the Court stated that the Confrontation Clause did not apply to the statements.

Conversely, the statements made by the victim in *Hammon* to the officer who came to the scene were made after the emergency was over and were specifically obtained by the officer, as he testified, to establish events that have occurred previously. As a result, they were testimonial, and the Confrontation Clause requirements were applicable.

The Court was careful to limit the breadth of its holding in *Davis*. The Court stated:

> Although we necessarily reject the Indiana Supreme Court's implication that virtually any "initial inquiries" at the crime scene will not be testimonial, (citation omitted) we do not hold the opposite—that no questions at the scene will yield nontestimonial answers.[12]

Furthermore, the Court said,

> This is not to say that a conversation which begins as an interrogation to determine the need for emergency assistance cannot, as the Indiana Supreme Court put it, "evolve into testimonial statements (citation omitted), once that purpose has been achieved."[13]

> Finally, in both *Davis* and *Hammon* the state argued that domestic abuse cases needed a relaxed Confrontation Clause analysis, because the defendants in such cases have considerable power over their victims, and can often prevent them from testifying through threats of future harm. The Court rejected that argument, stating that in cases where the state could prove such intimidation, the common-law rule of "forfeiture by wrongdoing" (discussed below) could be used to find a waiver of Confrontation Clause rights.

Michigan v. Bryant

United States Supreme Court, 131 S. Ct. 1143 (2011)

Police were dispatched to investigate a report a man had been shot. When they arrived at the scene at 3:25 A.M., they found the victim lying on the ground with a severe abdominal gunshot wound. The police officers testified they asked the victim "[w]hat had happened, who had shot him, and where the shooting had occurred." The victim stated "Rick" (Bryant) shot him at about 3:00 A.M., and that he recognized Bryant's voice through the door of Bryant's house, where the victim was shot as he turned away from the door. The victim died after medical services arrived on the scene a few minutes after he made these statements. This testimony was admitted over the objection of Bryant, and the jury convicted him of murder. The Michigan Supreme Court reversed the conviction, holding the victim's statement was "testimonial," and inadmissible under the *Crawford* rule. That court concluded there was no "ongoing emergency" when the victim answered the officers' questions, and that the "primary purpose" of the statements was to establish the facts of the event.

The U.S. Supreme Court disagreed. It first said this about the holding in *Davis*:

> The existence of an ongoing emergency is relevant to determining the primary purpose of the interrogation because an emergency focuses the participants on something other than "prov[ing] past events potentially relevant to later criminal prosecutions." … Rather, it focuses them on "end[ing] a threatening situation." … Implicit in *Davis* is the idea that because the prospect of fabrication in statements given for the primary purpose of resolving that emergency is presumably significantly

diminished, the Confrontation Clause does not require such statements to be subject to the crucible of cross-examination.[14]

The Court then concluded an ongoing emergency was occurring, and that the primary purpose of the statements was to resolve that emergency, and not to establish facts for future prosecution. The factors the Court found important were (1) the informal, "disorganized" nature of the questioning; (2) it occurred in a public parking lot, not in the station house as in *Crawford;* (3) a gun was involved, and the whereabouts of the shooter was unknown; and (4) the victim was mortally wounded. The Court concluded that looking at the purpose of the questioning and the answers given from both the perspective of the victim and the police, the statements were made to resolve the emergency, and thus non-testimonial. The Court reversed the Michigan Supreme Court. (The Michigan Supreme Court made no ruling on the applicability of the "dying declarations" hearsay exception; as a result, the U.S. Supreme Court stated it did not consider that exception in its decision.)

After the decisions in *Davis*, *Hammon*, and *Bryant*, statements made as a result of interrogation by officers will be considered testimonial unless they were made in response to questions that were asked only to identify and control an emergency. Even interrogations begun as such can develop another purpose, the preservation of statements for subsequent use, and when they do, the statements become testimonial and the Confrontation Clause requirements must be met.

In *Michigan v. Bryant* the Supreme Court concluded that the "testimonial" vs. "non-testimonial" distinction in police interrogations was heavily dependent on the circumstances of the interrogations, as relevant to a determination of the purpose of the interrogation. The Court urged lower courts and the police to carefully consider "statements and actions of ... the parties (to) provide the most accurate assessment(s) of the purpose(s) of ... police interrogation(s)." 131 S. Ct. at 1162. The following circumstances were identified by the Supreme Court as contributing to the different assessments of the purpose of the interrogations in *Crawford, Hammon,* and *Davis*:

- "A 911 call ... is ordinarily not designed primarily to 'establish or prove' some past fact, but to describe current circumstances requiring police assistance." 547 U.S. at 827.
- "In *Davis,* (Michelle) McCottrey was speaking about events *as they were actually happening,* rather than 'describing past events' ... Sylvia Crawford's interrogation, on the other hand, took place hours after the events she described had occurred." *Id.*
- "The statements in *Davis* were taken when McCottry was alone, not only not protected by police (as Amy Hammon was protected) but apparently in immediate danger from Davis. She was seeking aid, not telling a story about the past ... (in *Hammon*) Amy's narrative of past events was delivered at some remove in time from the danger she described. And after Amy answered the officer's questions, he had her execute an affidavit, in order, he testified, "to establish events that have occurred previously." *Id.* at 831.
- "McCottrey (unlike Sylvia Crawford) was facing an ongoing emergency. Although one *might* call 911 to provide a narrative report of a crime absent an imminent danger, McCottrey's 911 call was plainly a call for help against a bona fide physical threat." *Id.*

- "The nature of what was asked and answered (by Michelle) in *Davis* ... was such that the elicited statements were necessary to *resolve* the present emergency, rather than simply to learn (as in *Crawford*) what had happened in the past." *Id.*
- "And finally, the difference in the level of formality between the two interviews is striking. Crawford was responding calmly, at the station house, to a series of questions, with the officer-interrogator taping and making notes of her answers; McCottrey's frantic answers were provided over the phone, in an environment that was not tranquil, or even ... safe." *Id.*
- "'[P]olice officers can and will distinguish almost instinctively between questions necessary to secure their own safety or the safety of the public and questions designed solely to elicit testimonial evidence from a subject.'" (Citation omitted). 547 U.S. at 829.
- "We conclude that the circumstances of McCottrey's interrogation objectively indicate its primary purpose was to enable police assistance to meet an ongoing emergency. She simply was not acting as a *witness;* she was not *testifying.* What she said was not 'a weaker substitute for live testimony' at trial." *Id.* at 828.

 ## EXAMPLES OF NON-TESTIMONIAL HEARSAY AFTER *CRAWFORD*

While the Supreme Court in *Crawford* gave lower courts guidelines for distinguishing testimonial from non-testimonial hearsay, there is no clear "bright-line" rule for those courts to apply. The following cases are examples of courts concluding hearsay evidence was non-testimonial:

1. **Breathalyzer calibration records**. Machines that measure the blood alcohol content of a suspected drunk driver must be shown to be reliable and properly calibrated. The documents introduced to show that reliability—records of maintenance tests to determine accuracy—are hearsay. Most courts have concluded the records are non-testimonial, because the records are not "case specific," that is, they aren't used to prove any particular defendant was guilty of a crime. *People v. Pealer*, 985 N.E.2d 903 (N.Y. 2013).
2. **Statements made to victim's lawyer**. In a murder trial, statements made to the victim's divorce lawyer incriminating the defendant, the victim's husband, were non-testimonial. The court reasoned the statements were not made with "an eye for a criminal prosecution," and were not made to a government agent. *Hughes v. State*, 815 N.W.2d 602 (Minn. 2012).
3. **Drug slang meaning**. The testimony of a federal drug agent in a conspiracy trial about the meaning of coded slang terms in statements made by third parties was non-testimonial. The federal agent was not simply repeating the statements, which would be testimonial, but was testifying what his experience told him the terms meant in the illegal drug trade. *United States v. Akins*, 746 F.3d 590 (5th Cir. 2014).
4. **Tip to 911 operator**. Statements made by an anonymous tipster to a 911 operator identifying the defendant as a drug dealer who hid illegal drugs in the side panel of a car identified by the tipster were non-testimonial. The questions asked by the 911 operator were not intended to prove past events for later criminal prosecution, but to give police information to deal with ongoing criminal activity. *United States v. Polidore*, 690 F.3d 705 (5th Cir. 2012).
5. **Certificate of nationality**. In a prosecution for drug trafficking on international waters, a U.S. State Department certificate stating the defendant's vessel was not registered in the country claimed by the defendant was non-testimonial. While the certificate was used to prove the vessel was "stateless" and thus subject to the jurisdiction of the United States, it was not used to prove the element of the offense, and thus no Confrontation Clause right existed. *United States v. Campbell*, 743 F.3d 802 (11th Cir. 2014).

Forensic Analysts' Reports There are many situations beyond the "core" testimonial situations identified in *Crawford* where out-of-court statements are introduced as evidence in criminal trials. One such situation involves reports by forensic analysis labs to police investigators on subjects like identification of suspected illegal drugs, or results of blood or DNA tests. It had been the practice in many criminal cases to admit the reports generated by such analysis without the live testimony of the person who conducted the tests. Courts usually concluded the reports had "reliability" because of the neutral content of the scientific tests used to generate the report.

In *Melendez-Diaz v. Massachusetts*,[15] the U.S Supreme Court ended that practice. There, police officers found baggies holding suspected illegal drugs in the possession of the defendant. The baggies were sent to a state laboratory for a chemical analysis. The lab reported that the substance was cocaine. At the defendant's trial the report was entered into evidence without the testimony of the lab analyst who conducted the tests. The state appellate courts held the report was non-testimonial under *Crawford*, and affirmed the defendant's conviction.

The Supreme Court held that the reports were testimonial and inadmissible, and reversed the convictions. The basis for that conclusion was threefold: (1) the analysts formally swore to the test reports before a notary public, and thus the reports were in essence affidavits, which the Court said were classic examples of testimonial evidence; (2) the lab analysts knew the reports would be used as evidence in a criminal trial; and (3) the primary purpose of the reports was to establish a fact to be used in a criminal trial.

In the 2011 case of *Bullcoming v. New Mexico*[16] the U.S. Supreme Court reached a similar conclusion in a case involving a report certifying the result of a gas chromatograph machine. This machine is used to determine the blood/alcohol content (BAC) in DUI prosecutions. The defendant was charged with aggravated DUI, and at his trial the certified result of the BAC test was entered into evidence. An analyst from the testing lab appeared at the trial and identified the report, but it was not the analyst who actually did the test. The Court held that the purpose of the report was to establish a fact that would be used at a criminal trial, and was thus testimonial evidence under *Melendez-Diaz*. The Court held that the person who did the testing and certified the report must appear at trial to be cross-examined about the report.

Many states have statutes that require defendants to give the prosecution notice before trial if they wish to cross-examine an analyst who conducted forensic tests. (See, e.g., V.C.A. §19.2-187.1.) These statutes provide that if the defendant fails to give the required notice, the test results are admissible without the live testimony of the analyst who did the test. In a 2010 *per curiam* order in *Briscoe v. Virginia*[17] the U.S. Supreme Court reversed a decision of the Virginia Supreme Court that upheld the waiver provision of the Virginia statute. The Court remanded the case to the Virginia Supreme Court for action "not inconsistent" with the decision in *Melendez-Diaz*. On remand in *Cypress v. Comm.*,[18] the Virginia Supreme Court held that the waiver provision did not satisfy the Confrontation Clause requirements.

Expert Testimony Interpreting Forensic Reports One area left undecided by *Mendez-Diaz* and *Bullcoming* is the testimony of expert witnesses who interpret or otherwise comment on forensic reports, without actually performing the tests contained in the report. This is common in cases where DNA evidence is introduced, since DNA tests are complex and expensive and are often conducted by nationally accredited testing labs like the Cellmark laboratory in Maryland. The U.S. Supreme Court considered the Confrontation Clause problems in this area in the 2012 case of *Williams v. United States*.[19] The Court split three ways on the Confrontation Clause issue; the divided majority opinion held the expert testimony was admissible, but for different reasons. Four justices dissented.

In *Williams* a woman was sexually assaulted by a stranger. An examination of the woman disclosed semen in her body, and the police sent the semen to Cellmark for DNA analysis. Later, the defendant was arrested on an unrelated charge, and a blood sample was taken; its DNA results were entered into the Illinois State Police DNA database. An Illinois forensic analyst used the DNA profile created by the Cellmark lab to make a comparison to the defendant's DNA profile in the database. The defendant was then charged with sexual assault and kidnapping.

At the trial the Illinois forensic expert testified that in her expert opinion the DNA profile from the Cellmark tests matched the DNA profile from the tests done by analysts of the defendant's blood sample. In doing so she identified the Cellmark report, and stated she relied on that report for her opinion. The defendant objected to admission of the expert's testimony, because the person who did the tests at Cellmark did not testify, as required by *Melendez-Diaz*. The expert was allowed to testify, and the defendant was convicted.

On appeal, the Illinois Supreme Court affirmed. It held the Cellmark report was not introduced to prove any facts, but rather only to show how the expert reached her opinion: "The evidence was (the expert's) opinion, not Cellmark's report...."[20] As such it was not introduced to prove the truth of the report, and wasn't hearsay. As the *Crawford* Court said, the Confrontation Clause does not bar the introduction of statements, including testimonial statements, if not offered to prove the truth of the statement.[21]

The U.S. Supreme Court affirmed the Illinois Supreme Court, but in a manner that shows a continued division in the Court on the fundamentals of Confrontation Clause jurisprudence. Four judges agreed that the Cellmark report was not offered to prove the truth of the statements in the report, and thus was not hearsay: "An expert witness referred to the report not to prove the truth of the matter asserted in the report, i.e., that the report contained an accurate profile of the perpetrator's DNA, but only to establish that the report contained a DNA profile that matched the DNA profile deduced from petitioner's blood."[22] Other circumstantial evidence was then used to show the relevance of the match, the Court concluded. The plurality justices also agreed that even if the report was hearsay, it was non-testimonial, because when it was made the police had no suspect in mind. Justice Thomas agreed the report was admissible, but only because he believes the Confrontation Clause excludes only formal documents, like signed affidavits, from admission in criminal trials. The four dissenting justices believed the analyst who generated the report was a witness, and must be available for cross-examination. Those justices believed the "primary purpose" test should be applied to such forensic reports.

Forfeiture by Wrongdoing

forfeiture by wrongdoing A rule permitting the admission of hearsay evidence as a penalty against a defendant who wrongfully made the declarant unavailable; often used in murder cases.

In addition to the hearsay exceptions, most states have adopted some form of a doctrine called **forfeiture by wrongdoing**, under which out-of-court statements may be admitted without live testimony. This doctrine was specifically accepted by the Supreme Court in *Crawford v. Washington*.[23] Under this doctrine, a person who has wrongfully made the declarant unavailable for the purpose of preventing his or her testimony has waived the right to object to the declarant's out-of-court statements as hearsay. However, courts often disagreed on what must be proved to invoke the doctrine.

ARE AUTOPSY REPORTS TESTIMONIAL HEARSAY?

An example of the uncertainty that remains after the *Williams* decision can be seen in the admissibility of autopsy reports. If the medical examiner who performed the autopsy on a possible homicide victim is unavailable to testify at a resulting criminal trial (which is not uncommon in "cold case" investigations), courts differ on the admissibility of the report made by the examiner. Some courts have concluded autopsy reports are always testimonial. The West Virginia Supreme Court held that because the statute requiring autopsies states they are for "the formulation of conclusions, opinions or testimony in judicial proceedings," the primary purpose test makes autopsy reports testimonial. *State v. Kennedy*, 735 S.E.2d 905 (W.Va. 2012).

Other courts rely on the presence of other purposes for autopsy reports. In *State v. Maxwell*, 9 N.E.3d 930 (Ohio 2014), the Ohio Supreme Court held that because autopsy reports are generally prepared for public records and public health concerns, their primary purpose is not to preserve evidence of criminal wrongdoing, and thus they are non-testimonial.

In the 2004 case of *State v. Meeks*,[24] the Kansas Supreme Court held that the defendant waived his Confrontation Clause right to object to the victim's statements by murdering the victim and thus making him unavailable to testify. Other courts have held that more is required. In the 2005 case of *United States v. Jordan*,[25] a Colorado district court said that the forfeiture by wrongdoing doctrine requires an intent to make the declarant unavailable to testify, not just acts that in fact have that result. Thus, the court held that a defendant accused of murdering the declarant did not forfeit his confrontation rights by killing the declarant.

In 2008 the Supreme Court settled any questions about the required relationship between a "forfeiture by wrongdoing" rule and the Confrontation Clause. In *Giles v. California*,[26] the Court held that in order for the doctrine to be used to obviate the need for Confrontation Clause protections, the state must show that the defendant committed the acts that prevented the victim from testifying with the intent to make the witness unavailable. It rejected the California court's holding that a defendant who murdered his girlfriend forfeited his Confrontation Clause right concerning earlier statements the victim made to a police officer, even if it was not his purpose in murdering the victim to keep her from testifying.

Relying on the *Giles* decision, the Michigan Supreme Court reversed a sexual offense conviction based on the trial court's finding that the defendant forfeited his Confrontation Clause rights. In *People v. Burns*, 832 N.W.2d 738 (Mich. 2013) the four-year-old daughter of the defendant told investigators the defendant sexually abused her. The daughter refused to testify at the defendants trial. As the basis for a finding of foreefiture by wrongdoing the prosecution introduced statements by the daughter that the defendant "told her not to tell" and that "she would get in trouble" if she told. The Michigan Supreme Court held that since these statements were made at the time of the alleged abuse, and before there was any pending criminal prosecution, the state failed to prove the statements were made with the intent to prevent the daughter from testifying. (Hearsay and child sexual abuse cases are discussed later in this chapter.)

"FIRMLY ROOTED" EXCEPTIONS TO THE HEARSAY RULE

The hearsay exceptions, reliable or not, can no longer be used as a substitute for cross-examination under the Confrontation Clause for "testimonial" statements. However, where the statements are not testimonial, or not hearsay because they were not offered to prove the truth of the matter asserted, the Confrontation Clause has no application. In those cases, whether or not the evidence comes in is purely a matter of state or federal rules of evidence.[27] Many of the hearsay exceptions discussed below involve out-of-court statements that would not be "testimonial" under the *Crawford* rule. Excited utterances, state of mind, medical diagnosis, marriage and birth certificates, many documents and public records, and business records are subjects of hearsay exceptions. Courts since *Crawford* have found such statements to be non-testimonial, and not subject to the Confrontation Clause.

Hearsay that is "non-testimonial" under the *Crawford* rules discussed above should not present a Confrontation Clause problem. In *Crawford* the Supreme Court said that

> Where nontestimonial hearsay is at issue, it is wholly consistent with the Framers' design to afford the States flexibility in their development of hearsay law as does *Roberts,* and as would an approach that exempted such statements from Confrontation Clause scrutiny altogether.[28]

Whether or not such hearsay statements are admitted in a criminal case will thus normally be determined under state or federal evidence rules, without any Confrontation Clause implication. That suggests that the reliability test of *Roberts* is not needed. In 2007 the Supreme Court said in *Whorten v. Bockting* that under *Roberts* both testimonial and non-testimonial hearsay statements could not be admitted without a determination of reliability; however, after *Crawford* for non-testimonial hearsay "… the Confrontation Clause has no application to such statements and therefore permits their admission even if they lack indicia of reliability."[29]

For non-testimonial hearsay the "reliability" test from *Ohio v. Roberts* may yet have importance. Some courts have held that the *Roberts* "reliability" test has no further role in admissibility of non-testimonial hearsay: All the prosecution must show is that any hearsay fits within one of that jurisdiction's exceptions to the hearsay rule.[30] Other courts continue to apply the "reliability" test to nontestimonial hearsay, although it is not clear exactly what the test controls.[31] The U.S. Supreme Court's statements in the most recent Confrontation Clause cases will likely result in the great majority of courts dropping any reference to "indicia of reliability" and the Confrontation Clause when considering the admissibility of non-testimonial hearsay. It is possible that courts might use the "reliability" test as a supplement or addition to one of the recognized hearsay exceptions.

Hearsay Exceptions Independent of the Confrontation Clause, to be admitted at a criminal trial evidence must still be reliable; as we saw in Chapter Seven, the hearsay rule excluding hearsay evidence is based on the questionable reliability of out-of-court statements. Exceptions to the hearsay rule for admissibility of nontestimonial hearsay should be permitted only when reliability of the out-of-court statements can be assumed. Fortunately, most states have hearsay rules and exceptions similar to the Federal Rules of Evidence, which are commonly identified as the "firmly rooted" exceptions to the hearsay rule.

Hearsay is not admissible as evidence unless there is a showing of substantial reliability for the statement. One of the ways reliability is shown in criminal trials is by reference to exceptions to the hearsay rule developed in the common law. If there is a long-recognized exception to the hearsay rule, courts feel confident in concluding that the hearsay statements possess the required reliability.

The following materials discuss some of the major exceptions to the hearsay rule. Each exception has conditions and circumstances that the courts and legislative bodies have determined create sufficient reliability and trustworthiness to allow the hearsay statements to be used as evidence. In many of the hearsay exceptions, such as the twenty-three listed in Rule 803 of the Federal Rules of Evidence, the availability to testify of the person who made the statement is immaterial. For others, such as those listed in Rule 804 of the Federal Rules of Evidence, state or federal law requires a showing that the declarant (the speaker) is unavailable as a witness at the trial. If the state or federal law requires a showing of "unavailability" for an exception, then this burden must be carried before the statement (or statements) can be used as evidence.

The hearsay rule and its exceptions developed over a 300-year history in English and American law. The rule developed by English and American courts has now been made a part of federal and state law. The present Federal Rules of Evidence, which most states follow, list twenty-seven specific, "firmly rooted" exceptions, plus a "forfeiture by wrongdoing" section and a "residual exception" section.

In enacting these exceptions into statutory law, the U.S. Congress and state legislatures have concluded that these exceptions have sufficient guarantees of reliability to be classified as "firmly rooted" hearsay exceptions. Some of the most widely used exceptions, which are part of federal law and the laws of most states, are described in the remaining sections of this chapter.

Excited Utterance Exception[32]

Federal Rule of Evidence 803(2), excited utterance: "A statement relating to a startling event or condition made while the declarant was under the stress of excitement caused by the event or condition."

Reason for the Exception Many crimes are "startling events" that cause victims and witnesses to make excited statements during or immediately after the event. If such statements are in response to the startling event, the trustworthiness of such statements comes from the fact that the victim or witness had no time to reflect and possibly fabricate the statements.

Examples
- Statements by witnesses and victims during or immediately after shootings, stabbings, or robberies made "under the stress of excitement" caused by the startling event of the crime of violence.[33]
- Statements of rape victims immediately after the crime.[34]
- Recorded 911 calls and other telephone calls where courts held that the caller was speaking under the stress of excitement and permitted the recording to be used as evidence.[35]
- Many courts hold that there can be more of a time lapse between the startling event and statements when crimes such as sex crimes are reported by children or mentally retarded persons.[36]

Then Existing Mental, Emotional, or Physical Condition Exception

then existing mental, emotional, or physical condition The exception defined by Rule 803(3); for example, testimony that the victim stated that she was going to visit her boyfriend is admissible under this exception to show intent.

Federal Rule of Evidence 803(3), **then existing mental, emotional, or physical condition**: "A statement of the declarant's then existing state of mind, emotion, sensation, or physical condition (such as intent, plan, motive, design, mental feeling, pain, and bodily health)."

Reason for the Exception   Hearsay is defined by statute as a statement "offered in evidence to prove the truth of the matter asserted." If a statement is not offered to prove the truth of the matter asserted, courts almost always hold that the statement is not hearsay and is admissible as evidence.

Examples
- *Motive of the offender can be shown:* Prior to death, murder victims sometimes make statements to other persons about why they are afraid of the killer. The statement is offered not to show that the defendant committed the murder but instead to show motive or state of mind. In the 1990 case of *State v. Alvarez,*[37] the victim owed the defendant money for cocaine; in the 1992 case of *Parker v. State,*[38] a woman victim was afraid of the defendant because she had been with another man.
- *Intent can be shown:* In a murder case, the victim had stated to a friend that she was going to visit the defendant (her boyfriend) and then go skating. The victim was then found strangled and beaten to death. The state-of-mind statement was allowed in evidence to show the victim's present purpose and intent at the time the statement was made.[39]
- *Insanity or mental illness can be shown:* Witness A testifies that X repeatedly said that he heard voices and that he believed he was Napoleon. The testimony is offered not to prove that X was Napoleon but to prove that X had serious mental problems.
- *State of mind can be shown:* In 1962 a bigamy case, *People v. Marsh,*[40] came before the Supreme Court of California. The defendant was charged with being married to two women at the same time. It was held that statements supporting the defendant's defense of his reasonable belief that he was free to remarry were admissible to prove his state of mind at that time. The following case discusses the "state of mind" exception after *Crawford:*

Horton v. Allen

First Circuit Court of Appeals, 370 F.3d 75 (2004), *cert. denied,* 125 S. Ct. 971 (2005).

The defendant, Horton, was convicted of robbery and murder in a Massachusetts state court. At his trial, the out-of-court statements of another participant in the robbery, Christian, were admitted over Horton's objection. A witness testified that on the day of the robbery Christian told him that he needed money for drugs, that a drug dealer named Desir would not give him drugs on credit, and that he knew Desir carried a sizable amount of money. Desir was subsequently robbed, and persons with him were murdered.

After the Massachusetts appellate court upheld Horton's conviction, he filed a writ of habeas corpus in federal district court. He alleged that admission of Christian's hearsay statements violated his Confrontation Clause right. The district court denied his petition, and he appealed to the U.S. Court of Appeals. While his appeal was pending, the U.S. Supreme Court decided the *Crawford* case (discussed previously). The Court of Appeals affirmed the District Court. It held that the statements made by Christian were admitted only to show Christian's state of mind, and thus were admissible under the Massachusetts state-of-mind exception to the hearsay rule:

> Under Massachusetts law, the state-of-mind exception permits the admission of statements that demonstrate the declarant's intent to perform some future act. (Citation omitted.) The [Massachusetts Appellate Court] determined that Christian's statements that he needed money and that Desir would not give him drugs on credit suggested his intent to subsequently rob Desir, and the statements were admissible to show this intent.[41]

> The court concluded that Christian's statements were not "testimonial" because they were made to a casual acquaintance, not to someone who would be expected to use the statements in a criminal trial. As a result, the court held that *Crawford* did not apply, and the statements were properly admitted pursuant to a "firmly rooted" hearsay exception.

Statements for Purposes of Medical Diagnosis or Treatment Exception

statements for purposes of medical diagnosis or treatment exception The exception defined by Rule 803(4); for example, statements by doctors and nurses are admissible in child abuse cases.

Federal Rule of Evidence 8.03 (4): Statements for medical diagnosis or treatment, such as descriptions of past medical treatment or past or present symptoms.

Reason for the Exception The statements were made as part of the medical treatment, and patients have a strong motivation to be truthful when their own health and well-being is at stake. Thus, the statements can be assumed to be trustworthy.

Use of the Exception in Criminal Trials Because the physician-patient privilege forbids medical doctors from disclosing information regarding their patients, few cases involve adult defendants. Most of the cases concern child victims of sexual abuse. If the child reasonably understands the need to be truthful to his or her physician and the identification of the assailant is reasonably necessary to his or her medical diagnosis and treatment, the exception would apply and the physician could testify about statements the child made under such circumstances.

Example
In the 2013 case of *McLaury v. State*[42] testimony of a sexual assault nurse examiner ("SANE") about statements made to her by the victim were held to be admissible under the medical diagnosis exception. The SANE nurse stated she asked questions about the assault not to gather evidence but to help her to determine what parts of the victim to examine to find and treat injuries.[43]

Regularly Kept Records Exception

regularly kept records exception The exception defined by Rule 803, which allows the use of regularly kept business records and public, religious, and family records.

Regularly kept business records, public records, records of religious organizations, and family records are admissible under certain federal rules (**regularly kept records exception**).

The following records are admissible under Rule 803 of the Federal Rules of Evidence:

- 803(6) Records of regularly conducted (business) activity
- 803(8) Public records and reports

- 803(9) Records of vital statistics
- 803(11) Records of religious organizations (marriage, baptism, and so on)
- 803(13) Family records (personal and family history)
- 803(16) Statements in ancient documents (more than 20 years old)
- 803(18) Learned treatises (history, medicine, or other science established as a reliable authority)

Reason for the Exception The regularly kept records exception (shop books) goes back to the 1600s in England and was adopted by the American states. The exception refers to usually accurate records that can be attacked by the opposing party. The fact finder (jury or judge) always determines the credibility and weight to be given to such evidence. Today, courts that conclude a record is "non-testimonial," as some have done for autopsy reports, generally allow such reports to be admitted under the business records exception.

Dying Declaration Exception[44]

dying declaration exception The exception defined by Rule 804(b)(2), making admissible statements made by a victim or other person under the belief of impending death.

Federal Rule of Evidence 804(b)(2) concerns a statement made under belief of impending death (**dying declaration**). "In a prosecution for homicide or in a civil action or proceeding, a statement made by a declarant while believing that the declarant's death was imminent, concerning the cause or circumstances of what the declarant believed to be impending death."

Reason for the Exception The use of dying declarations as evidence goes back to the 1500s in England. The practice became an exception to the hearsay rules by the 1700s. In the 1789 King's Bench case of *Rex v. Woodcock,*[45] the English court stated the reason for the exception:

> [T]hey are declarations made in extremity, when the party is at the point of death, and when every hope of this world is gone, when every motive to falsehood is silenced, and the mind is induced by the most powerful considerations to speak the truth. A situation so solemn and so awful is considered by the law as creating an obligation equal to that which is imposed by an oath administered in court. *Woodcock's Case*, I Leach, 502.

In the 1990 case of *State v. Weir,*[46] the Florida Appellate Court held:

> Admission of dying declarations is justified on the grounds of public necessity, manifest justice and the sense that impending death makes a false statement by the decedent improbable. § 90.804, Law Revision Council Note—1976.

The U.S. Supreme stated in *Crawford* that the "dying declaration" exception may well have been intended by the Framers to be an exception to the Confrontation Clause requirements. The Court noted that the dying declaration exception was well known at the time the Bill of Rights was adopted, and the drafters may have intended the exception to apply to the Confrontation Clause. The Supreme Court has not yet directly decided this question, though some lower federal courts seem willing to read the dying declaration exception into the Confrontation Clause. In many situations the Confrontation Clause issue does not arise because the dying declaration is treated as "non-testimonial" hearsay. It is common for such declarations to be made to family members, or witnesses who aren't part of a police investigation. In such a case it could be held that the statement is not made with the intent to preserve evidence for a trial, and thus not testimonial.

Examples

- To use a dying declaration as evidence, the person must have died or otherwise become unavailable (lacking memory or in a coma, for example). The Supreme Court of Minnesota stated the requirement for use of the exception in the 1990 case of *State v. Bergeron:*[47]

  > To make a dying declaration admissible, something more is required than that declarant realize the seriousness of his condition and the possibility of death. The testimony offered as a dying declaration ... must have been spoken without hope of recovery and in the shadow of impending death. This state of mind must be exhibited in the evidence and not left to conjecture.

- The Supreme Court of Florida held in the 1991 case of *Henry v. State*[48] that it is not required that the declarant make "express utterances ... that he knew he was going to die, or could not live, or would never recover." *Lester v. State,* 37 Fla. 382, 385, 20 So. 232, 233 (1896). Rather, the court should satisfy itself, on the totality of the circumstances, "that the deceased knew and appreciated his condition as being that of an approach to certain and immediate death." *Id.,* 20 So. at 233.

Because killings are startling events, statements made immediately after a fatal shooting or knifing could be found to be admissible under both the excited utterance exception and the dying declaration exception to the hearsay rule. Two cases where statements were admissible under both exceptions are *Lyons v. United States*[49] and *State v. Griffin.*[50]

Statement Against Penal Interest Exception

statement against penal interest exception The exception defined by Rule 804(b)(3) that makes admissible a statement that exposes the speaker to criminal liability.

Federal Rule of Evidence 804(b)(3) defines a **statement against penal interest** thus: "A statement which was at the time of its making so far contrary to the declarant's pecuniary or proprietary interest or so far tended to subject the declarant to civil or criminal liability ... that a reasonable person in the declarant's position would not have made the statement unless believing it to be true."

Reason for the Exception Persons who admit they have committed a crime or were involved in criminal activity are making a statement against penal interest. Such incriminating admissions or confessions ordinarily are considered to have a reliable basis. The U.S. Supreme Court pointed out in the 1971 case of *United States v. Harris*[51] that "People do not lightly admit a crime and place critical evidence in the hands of the police in the form of their own admissions."

In the *Harris* case, the statement against penal interest was made by a known informant. The Supreme Court held that the statement against penal interest plus other evidence established the trustworthiness of the informant's statement.

Examples

- In the U.S. Supreme Court case of *Chambers v. Mississippi,*[52] the defendant was charged with a murder, but another person had admitted to committing that murder and had signed a number of confessions. Mississippi's hearsay rules prevented Chambers from introducing any of the confessions or statements into evidence in his defense. The Supreme Court held that a state may not use the hearsay rule to deprive defendants in criminal cases of reliable and important evidence.

- In the *Chambers* case, there was sufficient corroborating evidence that "clearly" supported the "trustworthiness of the statement [confession]." Two cases in which trial courts held there was insufficient evidence to support the trustworthiness of confessions are *State v. Rosado*[53] and *Lee v. McCaughtry*.[54] In these cases, the defendants were convicted (one of murder and the other of drug trafficking) when evidence that other people had confessed to the crimes was not allowed because of a lack of supporting evidence.[55]

THE FRESH COMPLAINT AND THE OUTCRY RULE

Hundreds of years ago, the victim of a crime was expected to raise an immediate *hue and cry,* or *outcry.* The failure to do so frequently resulted in the victim losing the right to charge the perpetrator with the crime in a later trial. The requirement of raising the outcry was imposed as a method of marshaling the neighborhood defenses to catch the assailant. It also served to negate the inference that the victim somehow was in complicity with the defendant. The requirement that one make an outcry was dropped from the law many years ago, but a vestige of the requirement survives in sexual assault cases under the "fresh complaint" and "outcry" rules.

In the nineteenth century and well into the twentieth century, the common law assumed that only those victims who immediately complained of rape were actually raped; the silence of other rape victims was seen as proof they "consented" to the sexual assault. To combat the inference that an alleged sexual assault was a consensual encounter, courts began permitting the prosecution to introduce "fresh complaint" statements made by the victim to others about the assault, even though those statements would normally be inadmissible hearsay.

Today, modern courts reject the concept that there was no rape if there was no immediate, or fresh, complaint. As a result, in many jurisdictions the "fresh complaint" rule has been abolished, or in others modified to permit evidence of fresh complaints, but only for non-hearsay purposes. However, a long delay in reporting a sexual assault could be a factor considered by a jury in determining whether there was consent to the sexual act. Delay could also cause the loss of important physical evidence of the crime of sexual assault.

Some states continue to use the "fresh complaint" as an exception to the hearsay rule. In 1990 the Maryland Court of Special Appeals pointed out that a victim's timely complaint of a sexual assault to a person who repeats the statement as a witness is admissible hearsay as follows:

> In prosecution for sex offenses, evidence of the victim's complaint, coupled with the circumstances of the complaint is admissible as part of the prosecution's case if the complaint was made in a recent period of time after the offense.[56]

Among the states that use the fresh complaint rule are California,[57] New Jersey,[58] Oregon,[59] Maryland,[60] Massachusetts,[61] and Florida.[62] Texas uses the outcry rule.[63] In the 2013 case of *Bays v. State*, 396 S.W.3d 580 (Tex. Crim. App. 2013) the court held the Texas outcry statute only applied to permit live testimony of the first adult to whom the child made statements about a recent sexual assault. The statute did not permit admission of a video recording of such statements made to the person making the video.

In other states, the excited reporting of a rape or other crimes, which are startling events, while under the stress of excitement could be admissible under the excited utterance exception to the hearsay rule.

THE DEFENSE THAT SOMEONE ELSE COMMITTED THE CRIME

When the state has a strong case against a defendant, the defense that someone else committed the crime is sometimes offered as evidence, usually through testimony of persons to whom incriminating statements were made by a third party. These statements of the third party are admissible as "statements against interest" under Federal Rule of Evidence 804(b)(3), but only if it can be shown that "corroborating circumstances clearly indicate the trustworthiness of the statement" (Federal Rule of Evidence 804(b)(3)).

Example
In *Guinn v. Kemna*, 489 F.3d 351 (8th Cir. 2007), *cert. denied,* 128 S. Ct. 1716 (2008), a defendant accused of assault attempted to introduce testimony of witnesses who claimed that a third person had told them he committed the assault for which the defendant was being tried. The trial court refused to permit the testimony, and on appeal the court of appeals upheld the trial court's decision. The court stated that the witnesses' proposed testimony lacked sufficient trustworthiness to be admitted as a statement against the interest of the third person. Among other problems with the proposed hearsay testimony, the court stated that the witnesses who proposed to testify that they heard the third-party confession were not people to whom such a confession might be made, that the alleged confession was made in response to a specific question by one of the witnesses, and that no corroborating evidence was offered to show a connection between the third party and the crime.

MODERN HEARSAY EXCEPTIONS IN CHILD SEXUAL ABUSE CASES

Out-of-court statements by children reporting crimes, especially sexual assault crimes, historically have been treated differently from hearsay statements made by adults. First, children often lack the vocabulary or knowledge to fabricate sexual assaults, and thus they generally are truthful when they relate such situations. Second, because children do not have fully formed memory skills, their testimony at a trial may be less reliable than statements made shortly after an event. Moreover, the stress of testifying itself can affect a child's memory.

For these reasons, child hearsay evidence was often admitted under the accepted hearsay exceptions, such as "excited utterance" or statements made to physicians for diagnosis or treatment. These and other exceptions are often relaxed for children so that juries and judges may determine the reliability and weight that should be given to such evidence in child sexual abuse cases.

The U.S. Supreme Court has in the past recognized that child hearsay presents a unique problem. The Court held in the 1992 case of *White v. Illinois* and the 1990 case of *Idaho v. Wright*[64] that for a child's out-of-court statement to be admissible, the child's truthfulness must be "so clear from the surrounding circumstances that the test of cross-examination would be of marginal utility." In *Wright* the Supreme Court listed the following factors that it thought "properly relate to whether hearsay statements made by a child witness in child sexual abuse cases are reliable:"[65]

1. "spontaneity and consistent repetition"[66]
2. "mental state of the declarant [child]"[67]
3. "use of terminology unexpected of a child of similar age"[68]
4. "lack of motive to fabricate"[69]

The Court added that these "factors are ... not exclusive, and courts have considerable leeway in their consideration of appropriate factors."[70]

The U.S. Supreme Court has not ruled expressly on the effect of *Crawford* and *Davis* on the holdings in *White* and *Wright*. However, some conclusions may be drawn. First, the various procedural protections created for children (see Chapter 5), such as closed-circuit testimony or videotaped testimony, are probably not affected by *Crawford,* because the defendant is able to view the child's testimony and submit questions. Second, many statements by a child victim to a parent, a family friend, or physician, are "non-testimonial" under *Davis,* because they are not made for the purpose of establishing facts for use at a criminal trial. Thus, such statements would be admissible under state hearsay exceptions, with or without the right of the defendant to confront and cross-examine the child. Most courts deciding the question after *Davis* have reached that result.[71]

Statements by a child to the police, or to a specialist hired by the police to question the child, would likely be classified "testimonial" under *Crawford* and *Davis*.[72] The purpose of questioning the child is to gain information for possible criminal prosecution, and the Confrontation Clause requires the right to cross-examination. The court in *In re S.R.* held that statements by a child to her mother were non-testimonial, but statements to a child specialist working with the police were testimonial, and inadmissible.[73]

It is thus not clear what effect, if any, Confrontation Clause cases after *Crawford* will have on state child hearsay laws, which generally permit more out-of-court statements by children to be used as evidence in child sexual abuse cases. However, the different results in the 2012 case of *United States v. DeLeon*[74] and the 2013 case of *State v. Maguire*[75] show the likely approach courts will take on the testimonial-non-testimonial distinction. In *Maguire* the Connecticut Supreme Court concluded a "forensic" interview of a child was conducted not for the purpose of obtaining medical treatment of the child, but for the preservation of evidence for later use in a criminal trial. The court thus found the statements testimonial, and not admissible under *Crawford*. Conversely, in *DeLeon* the social worker interviewing the child asked questions in order to develop a treatment plan for the child. Moreover, unlike in *Maguire*, where it appeared the interviewer was acting by request of law enforcement officers, in *DeLeon* the social worker had no contact with law enforcement before conducting the interview of the child. The Fourth Circuit Court of Appeals thus held the statements were non-testimonial under *Crawford*.

SUMMARY

1. **State the *pre-Crawford* test for the admissibility of hearsay testimony.**
   - If the out-of-court statements had "indicia of reliability," such as the reliability that exists in the "firmly rooted hearsay exceptions," the statements were admissible without the opportunity for cross-examination.

2. **State the rule of *Crawford v. Washington.***
   - Out-of-court statements that are testimonial may be admitted only if the witness is available to testify and be cross-examined, or if unavailable was subject to cross-examination at an earlier hearing.

3. **Define *testimonial statement.***
   - A statement is testimonial if it was made outside an ongoing emergency and for the purpose of establishing facts for use in a subsequent prosecution, or given as a response to questions where the person making the statement should know the answers would be used for such a purpose.

4. **State when a testimonial out-of-court statement may be admitted as evidence.**
   - A testimonial out-of-court statement may only be admitted into evidence if the witness testifies and the defendant has the opportunity to cross-examine the witness. If the witness is not available to testify, the statement is not admissible unless the defendant had an opportunity to cross-examine the witness at an earlier hearing. It is possible "dying declarations," but only "dying declarations," may be an exception to this rule.

5. **State the rule for admissibility of non-testimonial statements.**
   - The Confrontation Clause does not apply to non-testimonial out-of-court statements. The admissibility of these statements is determined by state or federal hearsay rules and exceptions.

6. **Identify hearsay exceptions in child sexual cases.**
   - The "excited utterance" or "tender years statutes" exceptions to the hearsay rule are commonly use in child sexual abuse cases to permit parents, friends, and physicians to testify about out-of-court statements made by a child. Many states have statutes that define "unavailable" as including emotional stress placed on a child by giving live testimony.

KEY TERMS

KEY CASES

***Briscoe v. Virginia,* 130 S. Ct. 1316 (2010):** State waiver statutes that require a defendant to give notice of intent to cross-examine forensic analysts must comply with *Melendez-Diaz.*

***Bullcoming v. New Mexico,* 131 S. Ct. 2705 (2011):** The analyst who performed a forensic test and authored a report must be the person who testifies about the result of the forensic test, not simply someone who is familiar with the tests.

***Crawford v. Washington,* 541 U.S. 36 (2004):** Testimonial out-of-court statements are admissible in criminal trials only if the witness testifies at the trial, or if unavailable, the defendant had an opportunity to cross-examine the witness at an earlier hearing.

***Davis v. Washington,* 547 U.S. 56 (1980):** Statements made during police interrogations are testimonial if the purpose of the statement was to establish existing facts for later use in a criminal prosecution, or if the person making the statement knew or should know the statement would likely be used in a criminal prosecution.

***Giles v. California,* 554 U.S. 353 (2008):** The Supreme Court stated the forfeiture by wrongdoing doctrine was applicable in criminal prosecutions, but required showing the defendant had the intent to make a witness unavailable.

***Melendez-Diaz v. Massachusetts,* 129 S. Ct. 2527 (2009):** Reports of tests conducted by forensic analysts for use in criminal prosecutions are testimonial, and as a result the analyst must be present at trial to testify before test results may be admitted.

Michigan v. Bryant, 131 S. Ct. 1143 (2011): Statements made during an "ongoing emergency" are non-testimonial; whether an "ongoing" emergency exists is a fact question that needs to be resolved on a case-by-case basis.

Williams v. United States, 132 S. Ct. 2224 (2012): Testimony of expert witness that includes references to forensics report done by another expert is non-testimonial and admissible under the Confrontation Clause.

PROBLEMS

1. A defendant was charged with sexual assault of his minor daughters. His daughters and his wife testified at a preliminary hearing, where the defendant's attorney cross-examined the daughters about the sexual assault allegations. The case was bound over for trial. Before trial on the sexual assault charges, defendant's wife and daughters were murdered. The defendant was charged with and tried for capital murder. At his trial, the prosecution introduced transcripts from the preliminary hearing containing the daughters' testimony about the sexual assaults. The defendant objected, stating the Confrontation Clause precluded admission of the preliminary hearing testimony. Is the daughters' prior testimony hearsay? Is that testimony "testimonial"? Does the *Crawford* rule bar its admission? Would the "forfeiture by wrongdoing" exception apply to permit the daughters' testimony? Is it relevant to that question for which crime, sexual assault or murder, the defendant intended to make his daughters "unavailable"? See *Commonwealth v Wholaver,* 989 A.2d 883 (Pa. 2010).

2. A few months before her death, the defendant's girlfriend called 911, and reported that the defendant had beaten her. The tape included statements that the victim was afraid of the defendant, but also detailed statements about the beating, its motive, and when it occurred. The defendant was arrested and charged with assault. Before trial on that charge the victim was found murdered, with multiple knife wounds. The defendant was arrested and charged with murder. He pled self-defense. At his trial the 911 tapes were offered by the prosecution. Are the 911 tapes hearsay? If so, should they be admitted? Why did the prosecution want to admit the 911 tapes? Does that purpose have a bearing on whether or not the tapes are "testimonial" under the reasoning of

the *Davis* case? Finally, why weren't the tapes admissible under the forfeiture by wrongdoing doctrine? See *Hunt v. State,* 218 P.3d 516 (Okla. Crim. App. 2009).

3. Statements made by a victim during police interrogations after an "ongoing emergency" has terminated are testimonial and inadmissible if offered to prove the truth of facts in the statement. This is true even though the circumstances under which the statements are made otherwise qualified it as an exception to the hearsay rule. What about statements made to persons asking questions not as police officers, but for other purposes? Are statements to a social welfare caseworker by a victim of domestic violence testimonial? Statements to a physician during treatment of an injury that was caused by domestic violence? Does it matter that the caseworker was a state employee, and who as part of her job sent her report to the police? Does it matter if a physician treating a victim is required by law to give information learned from his examination of the victim to the police? See *State v. Bella,* 220 P.3d 128 (Or. App. 2009).

4. The hearsay rule does not apply only to the prosecution's case. Sometimes the rule can keep out evidence offered by the defendant, such as alibi evidence based on out-of-court statements. Where a defendant offers hearsay, there is no Confrontation Clause issue. However, the offered evidence must satisfy the state's hearsay exceptions. One area where this issue is controversial is the "against penal interest" exception, which permits the introduction of a hearsay statement made by a person that "so subjects that person to criminal liability" that it is presumed the statement would not be made if not true.

   When a defendant tries to introduce a statement against interest of a third person in order to exculpate the defendant, Rule 804(b)(3) of the

Federal Rules of Evidence, and most state rules, have the additional requirement that the defendant produce evidence corroborating the trustworthiness of the statement. Why is this required? Would it help to know that over 200 people confessed to the famous Lindbergh baby murder? How "inculpating" must the statement be? Would a statement by a person that "I might have done it" be admissible? What if the mother of a baby exhibiting the "shaken baby syndrome" symptoms stated "he (the defendant) didn't do it," and "I don't want him to take the fall?" In what sense are these statements against the mother's penal interest? Would it help to know who was watching the baby when the injuries occurred? Finally, what amount of corroborating evidence is required? Enough to prove the defendant didn't commit the crime? See *State v. Paredes,* 775 N.W.2d 554 (Iowa 2009).

CASE ANALYSIS

Read Appendix B, Finding and Analyzing Cases (p. 499). With these guidelines in mind, please continue with the Case Analysis selections for Chapter 8.

1. Are fingerprint cards, prepared by a police officer when the defendant was booked at the station using an alias, hearsay when offered at a later criminal trial to prove the defendant was the person who used the alias? If so, are the fingerprint cards testimonial evidence under *Crawford? United States v. Williams,* 720 F.3d 674 (8th Cir. 2013).

2. The key to the admissibility of testimonial hearsay is the opportunity the defendant has to cross-examine the person who made the statement. If that occurs at the criminal trial, presumably the Confrontation Clause has been satisfied under *Crawford.* What if the person making the statement is not available at the criminal trial, but was subjected to cross-examination by the defendant at a preliminary hearing? Does that satisfy *Crawford?* How did the Illinois Supreme Court handle this issue in *People v. Torres,* 962 N.E.2d 919 (Ill. 2012)? What did the court see as the problem?

3. Can hearsay, testimonial or non-testimonial, be admitted at the sentencing phase of a trial? Does the Confrontation Clause apply to sentencing hearings? Should the police be allowed to testify at a hearing to determine if a convicted murderer should be given the death sentence that "other gang members told us the defendant has committed other murders for the gang"? Why or why not? *United States v. Umana,* 750 F.3d 320 (4th Cir. 2014).

4. If the state charges a defendant with driving under a suspended driver's license, the prosecution must prove as an element of the offense that the defendant's license has been suspended or revoked. Can it do so by introducing an affidavit prepared by the director of the state motor vehicle department that certifies the department has notified the defendant his license has been suspended? Is the affidavit hearsay? If so, is it testimonial hearsay? Does it matter when the affidavit was prepared? *See State v. Kennedy,* 846 N.W.2d 517 (Iowa 2014).

Notes

1. Some have contended that the term *witness* in the Confrontation Clause was originally intended to refer only to out-of-court statements directed solely at inculpating the defendant, such as affidavits, depositions, and confessions. Those were "particular abuses common in sixteenth- and seventeenth-century England: prosecuting a defendant through the presentation of ex parte affidavits without the affiants ever being produced at trial" *White v. Illinois,* 502 U.S. 346, 352 (1992). The federal government—and Justice Thomas, concurring in *White v. Illinois*—argued that the Confrontation Clause "extends to any witness who actually testifies at trial, but the Confrontation Clause is implicated by extrajudicial statements only insofar as they are contained in formalized testimonial materials, such as affidavits, depositions, prior testimony, or confessions" *White,* 502 U.S. 365 (J. Thomas, concurring) (1992).

The majority in *White* rejected this argument: "We think that the argument presented by the Government comes too late in the day to warrant reexamination of this approach" (*White*, 502 U.S. 353). In *Lilly v. Virginia*, 527 U.S. 116 (1999), the Court again rejected this argument. (See 119 S. Ct. at 1894.) However, the decision in *Davis* comes close to taking this approach.

2. See Friedman, *Confrontation: The Search for Basic Principles,* 86 Geo. L.J. 1011, 1014 (1998).

3. 380 U.S. 400.

4. *California v. Green,* 399 U.S. 149, 155 (1970).

5. 399 U.S. at 158.

6. *Idaho v. Wright,* 497 U.S. 805 (1990).

7. *Crawford v. Washington,* 541 U.S. 36, at 62. (2004).

8. *Davis v. California,* 547 U.S., at 826, citing *Crawford,* 541 U.S., at 53.

9. 541 U.S. at 68.

10. 547 U.S 813, 822 (2006).

11. Id, at 832.

12. Id, at 832.

13. Id, at 828.

14. 131 S. Ct. at 1157.

15. 129 S. Ct. 2527 (2009).

16. 131 S. Ct. 2705 (2011).

17. 130 S. Ct. 1316 (2010).

18. 699 S.E.2d 206 (Va. 2010).

19. 132 S. Ct. 2224 (2012).

20. 939 N.E.2d, at 279.

21. 541 U.S., at 59, n. 9.

22. 132 S. Ct. 2224, 2241.

23. 541 U.S. at 62.

24. 88 P.3d 789 (Kan. 2004).

25. 2005 WL 513501 (D. Colo. 2005).

26. 554 U.S. 353 (2008).

27. In *Montana v. Egelhoff,* 518 U.S. 37 (1996), the Court held that while a state's evidentiary rules may be so unreasonable so as to present a due process problem, such a determination is "fact intensive," and does not admit to a general rule. 376 P.2d 300.

28. 541 U.S. at 68. 370 F.3d at 84.

29. 549 U.S. 406, 420. The *Bockting* court also held that the *Crawford* rule was not retroactive for purposes of collateral attacks on convictions entered prior to *Crawford.* 502 U.S. 346, 112 S. Ct. 736.

30. See, for example, *United States v. Williams,* 506 F.3d 151(2d Cir. 2007), *cert. denied,* 128 S. Ct. 1329 (2008).

31. See, for example, *United States v. Thomas,* 453 F.3d 838 (7th Cir. 2006).

32. Many years ago the excited utterance exception was lumped with other exceptions under a broad category known as the "*res gestae* exception" to the hearsay rule. A few states continue to use the *res gestae* exception.

Federal Rule of Evidence 803(1) states the hearsay exception called "present sense impression," which in some states is called the "spontaneous statement exception." The unexcited statement exception of present sense impressions is made part of the laws of many states. Rule 803(1) provides, *"Present sense impression:* A statement describing or explaining an event or condition made while the declarant was perceiving the event or condition, or immediately thereafter."

33. *Webb v. Lane,* 922 F.2d 390 (7th Cir. 1991); *State v. Farmer,* 408 S.E.2d 458 (W. Va. 1991); *State v. Anaya,* 799 P.2d 876 (1990); *State v. Baker,* 582 So.2d 1320 (La. App. 1991); *State v. Gibson,* 413 S.E.2d 120 (W. Va. 1991); *Russell v. State,* 815 S.W.2d 929 (Ark. 1991); *Royal v. Commonwealth,* 407 S.E.2d 346 (W. Va. 1991).

34. *State v. Reaves,* 596 So.2d 650 (La. App. 1990); *State v. Ferguson,* 540 So.2d 1116 (La. App.; *Cole v. State,* 818 S.W.2d 573 (Ark. 1991).

35. *Ware v. State,* 596 So.2d 1200 (Fla. App. 1992); *State v. Edwards,* 485 N.W.2d 911 (Minn. 1992); *State v. Guizzotti,* 803 P.2d 808 (Wash. App. 1991).

36. *State v. Fox,* 585 N.E.2d 561 (Ohio 1990); *People v. Garcia,* 826 P.2d 1259 (Colo. 1992); *People v. Houghteling,* 455 N.W.2d 440 (Mich. App.); *Cole v. State,* 818 S.W.2d 573 (Ark.); *State v. Hy,* 458 N.W.2d 609 (Iowa 1990); *State v. Murphy,* 462 N.W.2d 715 (Iowa App.); *Commonwealth v. Sanford,* 580 A.2d 784 (Pa. Super. 1990); *State v. Bryant,* 828 P.2d 1121 (Wash. App. 1992); *People v. Enoch,* 545 N.E.2d 429, 45 CrL 1059 (Ill. 1989).

37. 579 A.2d 515 (Conn.).

38. 403 U.S. 573, 91 S. Ct. 2075.

39. *State v. MacDonald,* 598 A.2d 1134 (Del. Super.).

40. 376 P.2d 300.

41. 370 F.3d at 84.

42. 305 P.3d 1144 (Wyo. 2013).

43. Of course, a preliminary question—is the testimony testimonial?—must be answered under *Crawford.*

44. The U.S. Supreme Court has previously held that the use of a dying declaration as evidence does not violate a defendant's Sixth Amendment right to confrontation and cross-examination. See *Mattox v. United States,* 156 U.S. 237, 15 S. Ct. 337 (1895). The continued viability of the *Mattox* case is brought into question by the Court's decision in *Crawford.*

45. 168 Eng. Rep. 352.

46. 569 So.2d 897.

47. 452 N.W.2d 918, 922.

48. 586 So.2d 1033.

49. 606 A.2d 1354 (D.C. App. 1992).

50. 540 So.2d 1144 (La. App. 1989).

51. 403 U.S. 573 (1971).

52. 410 U.S. 284.

53. 588 A.2d 1066 (Conn. 1991).

54. 933 F.2d 536 (7th Cir. 1991).

55. There is some disagreement about the amount of corroboration needed for the admissibility of statements by people who assert they committed the crime being charged. More corroboration seems to be required for out-of-court confessions than for in-court confessions. For a discussion of some of the cases, see *McCormick on Evidence,* 4th ed. (West, 1992), vol. 2, pp. 340–43.

56. *Cole v. State,* 574 A.2d 326, 330 (Md. App. 1990).

57. *People v. Burton,* 359 P.2d 433 (1961); *but see People v. Brown,* 883 P.2d 949 (Cal. 1994), where the Court stated the fresh complaint rule was not abolished, but was modified to permit the admission of the fresh complaint for limited purposes.

58. *State v. Hill,* 578 A.2d 370 (1990). The criminal proceedings in the *McMartin* case went on for more than five years, with the preliminary hearing alone lasting a year and a half. The trial and proceedings received national attention. All of the national talk shows covered the trial, in which there were many criminal charges of bizarre sex acts and naked children. Civil lawsuits by former defendants are discussed in *Satz v. Supreme Court (McMartin),* 275 Cal. Rptr. 710 (1990), and *McMartin v. Children's Institute International,* 261 Cal. Rptr. 437 (1989), *review denied,* 494 U.S. 1057, 110 S. Ct. 1526 (1990).

59. *State v. Campbell,* 705 P.2d 694 (1985). The Supreme Court of Nevada noted that the *Felix* case (849 P.2d 220) was "the most extensive and costly criminal investigation and prosecution in Carson City [Nevada] history." It was alleged that as many as nineteen children had been sexually assaulted.

60. *Cole v. State,* 574 A.2d 326 (App. 1990).

61. *Commonwealth v. Licata,* 591 N.E.2d 672 (1992).

62. *McDonald v. State,* 578 So.2d 371 (1991).

63. *Anderson v. State,* 831 S.W.2d 50 (App. 1992).

64. 497 U.S. 805, 806, *White v. Illinois,* 502 U.S. 346.

65. 497 U.S. 805, 821.

66. *State v. Robinson,* 735 P.2d 801 (Ariz. 1987).

67. *Morgan v. Foretich,* 846 F.2d 941 (4th Cir. 1988).

68. *State v. Sorenson,* 421 N.W.2d 77 (Wis. 1988).

69. *State v. Kuone,* 757 P.2d 289 (Kans. 1988).

70. 497 U.S. 822.

71. See e.g., *People v. Duhs,* 922 N.Y.S.2d 843 (N.Y. 2011); statement by 3-year-old child to emergency room pediatrician that defendant would not "let me out of the bathtub" which was full of scalding hot water held to be non-testimonial.

72. *State v. Arnold,* 933 N.E.2d 775 (Ohio 2010); statements made by child to Child Advocacy Center workers that were intended to obtain information for police were testimonial; statements made to same workers that related to medical treatment were non-testimonial.

73. 920 A.2d 1262 (Pa. Super. 2007). Appeal was granted in this case (941 A.2d 671), but the record does not contain any decision in the case.

74. 678 F.3d 317 (4th Cir. 2012), *vacated on other grounds,* 133 S. Ct. 2850 (2013).

75. 78 A.3d 828 (Conn. 2013).

The Exclusionary Rule

SHERIFF OFFICERS PREPARE FOR FORCED ENTRY

Mikael Karlsson/Alamy

LEARNING OBJECTIVES

In this chapter we examine the scope of the exclusionary rule, a court-created rule that, when invoked, results in the suppression of otherwise admissible evidence based on improper police conduct. The learning objectives for this chapter are

State the origin of the exclusionary rule.

Define the *derivative evidence rule*.

List the exceptions to the exclusionary rule and what they entail.

State the role of the exclusionary rule for evidence obtained by an improper search.

State the role of the exclusionary rule for evidence obtained as a result of a violation of the *Miranda* rule.

State the role of the exclusionary rule for incriminating statements procured in violation of the Due Process Clause.

Police believed Calvin Henderson was involved in a rape and kidnapping crime. Detectives Johnson and Evans, members of the police sex assault squad, worked on the investigation. Detective Johnson gathered evidence and obtained a warrant authorizing police to take a DNA sample from Henderson. Tests showed his DNA profile matched that of DNA found on the persons of the victims. Based on this evidence, Henderson was charged with rape and kidnapping. Prior to trial, Henderson filed a motion to suppress the DNA evidence, based on his claim the search warrant used to obtain the DNA sample lacked the required probable cause. Faced with this claim, prosecutors had Detective Evans prepare a new request for a second warrant, and when it was granted, obtained a new DNA sample for tests.

Henderson has now moved to suppress the results of both DNA tests, contending the second test was the "fruit of the poisonous tree," the first test. You are the judge, and agree the first search warrant lacked sufficient probable cause. The test results from the DNA taken under the first warrant must be suppressed, you conclude. You conclude, however, that the second warrant was supported by the requisite probable cause. Is the second warrant the "fruit" of the first, illegal search warrant? Or was it gathered from an "independent source," Detective Evans? In what sense must Detective Johnson and Detective Evans be acting independently of each other to avoid the "fruit of the poisonous tree" connection? *See Com. v. Henderson*, 47 A.3d 797 (Pa. 2012).

THE EXCLUSIONARY RULE (OR THE RULE OF THE EXCLUSION OF EVIDENCE)

The United States has more than 17,000 police and sheriff's departments, employing over 600,000 full-time officers with general arrest powers. Although these officers are charged with the responsibility of performing their duties within the limitations set by statutes, state constitutions, and the U.S. Constitution, they do not always do so. When that happens, the criminal justice system "polices the police."[1]

exclusionary rule A judicial rule that makes evidence obtained in violation of the U.S. Constitution, state or federal laws, or court rules inadmissible.

Just as football teams are penalized 5 or 10 yards for a rule violation by an individual player, the **exclusionary rule** excludes (keeps out) evidence that was improperly or illegally obtained (see Figure 9.1). Like a football penalty, the exclusionary rule seeks to discourage improper or illegal investigative procedures by law enforcement officers.

Investigative conduct by law enforcement officers (both state and federal officers) can be improper for many reasons. Conduct might violate a police department rule, an FBI procedures handbook, or even a police union rule. These violations, which may have no real impact on a defendant, can be dealt with by internal police procedures.

Some law enforcement conduct is improper because it adversely affects a criminal defendant's statutory or constitutional rights. The principal U.S. constitutional rights threatened by police misconduct are the Fifth Amendment's privilege against self-incrimination[2] and the Fourth Amendment's protection against unreasonable searches and seizures.[3] Other constitutional protections are secured for both federal and state defendants under the Due Process Clauses of the Fifth and Fourteenth Amendments.[4]

Origin of the Exclusionary Rule

For much of U.S. history, relevant and reliable evidence was admissible in criminal prosecutions even if it was obtained illegally. This practice began its evolution to the present status of the exclusionary rule in a meandering process, initially through

Purpose	Enforcement	Violation
The exclusionary rule seeks to deter and discourage police • Violations of constitutional rights of defendants • Violations of statutory rights of defendants • Violations of court rules	"The rule is calculated to prevent . . . its purpose is to deter-to compel respect for the constitutional guarantees." *Elkins v. United States*, 364 U.S. 206 (1960). "To trigger the exclusionary rule, police conduct must be sufficiently deliberate . . . and sufficiently culpable that such deterrence is worth the price paid by the justice system . . . [t]he exclusionary rule serves to deter deliberate, reckless, or grossly negligent conduct, or in some circumstances recurring, or systemic negligence . . . " *Herring v. United States*, 555 U.S. 135 (2009).[a]	In interpreting their own state constitutions, state courts may set higher, but not lower, standards than those set by the U.S. Supreme Court for violations of the U.S. Constitution.[b] The U.S. Supreme Court has held that "Inadmissibility (exclusion of evidence) has not been automatic, therefore, we have instead applied an exclusionary-rule balancing test." *Kansas v. Ventris*, 129 S.Ct. 1841, 1845 (2009).

[a]In *United States v. Herring*, cited above, a county clerk advised a police officer that an arrest warrant was on file against the defendant. The officer arrested the defendant, and a search found illegal drugs and weapons in his possession. In fact, the arrest warrant had been cancelled five months earlier, but the county failed to record the cancellation. The U.S. Supreme Court affirmed the convictions for the drug and weapon offenses, holding that even though the arrest violated the Fourth Amendment, the exclusionary rule should not apply. The Court said the officers acted in good faith reliance on the information provided to them, and their conduct did not rise to the level to which the exclusionary rule applied.

[b]All states have court rulings governing "knock-and-announce" rules in the execution of search warrants. In addition, execution of search warrants can be governed by state laws, police regulations, and the judge issuing the search warrant. Complaints about a search may be filed with the law enforcement agency involved, a police or fire commission, or the local prosecutor.

Figure 9.1 | The Function of the Exclusionary Rule

the doctrine called "selective incorporation," and more recently through decisions of the U. S. Supreme Court defining the scope of the rule.

Early in our nation's history, in 1833, the U. S. Supreme Court held that the Bill of Rights, the first ten amendments to the Constitution, applied only to the federal government.[5] Though ratified by the states, the amendments were not directly binding upon them. As a result, decisions of the Supreme Court interpreting the Bill of Rights initially bound only federal officers and courts.

In 1914 the Supreme Court decided to abandon the common-law practice of admitting illegally obtained evidence in federal criminal trials. In *Weeks v. United States*[6] the Court concluded that in order to protect the citizens' Fourth Amendment right to be free from unreasonable searches and seizures, illegally seized evidence must be excluded in federal criminal trials. This decision did not apply to state courts, which could continue, if they wished, to admit such evidence in state criminal trials.

This distinction between federal and state criminal trials resulted in the so-called (and much-maligned) "silver platter" doctrine. In several cases during the Prohibition years, the Supreme Court held that federal courts could admit evidence obtained by state officers under circumstances that would violate the Fourth Amendment if obtained by federal officers, when that evidence was turned over to federal officers by state officers for use in federal prosecutions. Such evidence, it was said, came to the federal officers on a "silver platter."

In 1949 in *Wolf v. Colorado*[7] the Supreme Court held that the Fourteenth Amendment's guarantee that "no state" shall deprive a person of life or liberty without "Due Process of law" incorporated the rights protected by the Fourth Amendment into the Due Process clause, and made them binding in state criminal prosecutions. This marked the beginning of the "selective incorporation" doctrine in the Supreme Court. It is called "selective" because the Court then, and now, has refused to hold that **every** right or provision in the Bill of Rights was automatically incorporated into the Fourteenth Amendment.[8]

However, the Court in *Wolf* refused to include incorporation of the federal exclusionary rule in its decision. It held that states should be free to consider other solutions to the problem of the admission of illegally obtained evidence. Many states quickly developed their own exclusionary rules, and by 1960 it was clear the "silver platter" doctrine was out of step with history.[9]

In 1961 the Supreme Court held in *Mapp v. Ohio* that the Due Process Clause requires that the exclusionary rule must apply to all criminal prosecutions, including those in state courts.[10] The Court concluded in *Mapp* that the only effective way to protect the people's rights to be free of illegal searches and seizures was through the exclusionary rule.

The U.S. Supreme Court has also used the exclusionary rule for violations of court-fashioned rules, like the famous *Miranda*[11] rule. In the *Miranda* case, the Supreme Court adopted a court rule[12] for determining the minimum safeguards that must be followed by police before obtaining a confession or other incriminating statements. If these safeguards are not followed, any resulting confession or incriminating statement is inadmissible.

The use of exclusionary rules to suppress otherwise reliable, relevant evidence has a cost to society: In the famous words of New York State Judge (later U. S. Supreme Court Justice) Cardozo, "The criminal is to go free because the constable has blundered."[13] Defenders of the exclusionary rule argue in response that such rules are necessary to deter official police misconduct and are the only practical alternatives available to achieve that deterrence. Striking a balance between these competing goals—admitting reliable evidence and deterring police misconduct—has long occupied the interest of the U.S. Supreme Court, as the case of *Hudson v. Michigan* shows.

Hudson v. Michigan

United States Supreme Court, 547 U.S. 586 (2006)

Defendants in criminal cases who move to suppress evidence obtained by improper police conduct do so by invoking the exclusionary rule, contending that the improper police conduct violated their constitutional rights (and in some instances statutory rights) and therefore the evidence must be suppressed. Logically, two questions are posed by such a contention: (1) Did the police conduct violate the defendant's rights? (2) If so, is the suppression of the evidence obtained the appropriate remedy?

Although defendants might argue that an affirmative answer to the first question inevitably leads to the same answer to the second, the U.S. Supreme Court has long refused to accept such a broad reading of the rule. In *United States v. Leon*,[14] the Court said, "whether the exclusion sanction is appropriately imposed in a particular case ... is an 'issue separate from the question whether the Fourth Amendment rights of the party seeking to invoke the rule were violated by police conduct.'"

In *Hudson v. Michigan* the Court reiterated that approach, and affirmed a Michigan appellate court's refusal to suppress evidence obtained after a violation of a "knock-and-announce" warrant.

The defendant was arrested and charged with possession of unlawful drugs and firearms under Michigan state law. At his trial, the prosecution sought to introduce evidence obtained when police searched the defendant's residence pursuant to a valid search warrant. When the police arrived at the defendant's residence, they knocked at his door, announced their presence, and after a three- to five-second wait opened the door and conducted a search. The search uncovered unlawful drugs and firearms.

The defendant moved to suppress the evidence based on his claim that the police failed to wait a sufficient time after announcing their presence. The trial court initially ordered the evidence suppressed, but after a Michigan appellate court reversed that decision, the evidence was admitted and the defendant was convicted. He appealed to the Michigan Court of Appeals, which affirmed his conviction, and the Michigan Supreme Court refused review. The U.S. Supreme Court granted certiorari and affirmed the conviction.

The Supreme Court first noted that the only issue presented on appeal was the appropriateness of the exclusionary sanction. The State of Michigan conceded that the police violated the defendant's rights by failing to wait a sufficient time after announcing their presence.[15]

The Court then stated that under *Wilson v. Arkansas,*[16] announcing police presence is part of the Fourth Amendment requirements for a reasonable search, unless the police have some basis for believing that announcing would (1) allow evidence to be destroyed, (2) create a threat of violence against the officers about to enter the residence, or (3) be futile. The *Hudson* Court stressed, however, that in *Wilson* the Court specifically refused to determine whether the exclusionary rule applied to a knock-and-announce violation.[17]

The Court stated that the exclusionary rule is most appropriate in the case of warrantless searches because the Fourth Amendment clearly operates to protect citizens' right to "shield their persons, houses, papers and effects" from warrantless searches.[18] When there is no valid warrant, a citizen is entitled to keep his personal effects free from police inspection, and the exclusionary rule is appropriate to make sure that happens, the Court concluded.

When a valid warrant has been issued, it is inevitable that the citizen's right to keep his effects private will be lost because the police will, sooner or later, be able to inspect the private dwelling as provided in the search warrant. Thus, the Court reasoned, the real question was what interests were protected by the knock-and-announce requirement. It concluded that the primary interests were the avoidance of a potential violent reaction to a surprise entrance, the protection against property damage occasioned by a forceful police entry, and the right of the citizen to prepare for police entry by getting dressed, getting out of bed, or arranging one's appearance. Beyond that, the Court said,

> What the knock-and-announce rule has never protected, however, is one's interest in preventing the government from seeing or taking evidence described in a warrant. Since the interests that were violated in this case have nothing to do with the seizure of the evidence, the exclusionary rule is inapplicable. *Id.* at 594.

Thus, the Court reasoned, unlike cases where a search was invalid because the police did not have a valid warrant, here the questioned evidence was not discovered as a result of the violation. Whether or not the police properly announced their presence, they were going to discover the evidence. Although a defendant might suggest that a longer announcement period would have enabled him to hide the evidence, the defendant has no right to do so, the Court said. This eliminated the "but-for" causation that exists in warrantless searches, because there, "but for" the violation, the police would not have discovered the evidence.

Moreover, the Court stated, in knock-and-announce cases application of the exclusionary rule would turn on an extremely fine determinations of how long the police should have waited before entering under a valid search warrant. This makes the deterrent effect of the rule difficult to evaluate. Also, the Court said, professional police departments that obtain valid search warrants can be expected to follow reasonable rules about announcing their presence. For these additional reasons, the Court concluded, the exclusionary rule is inappropriate for knock-and-announce violations.

THE FRUIT OF THE POISONOUS TREE DOCTRINE (OR THE DERIVATIVE EVIDENCE RULE)

derivative evidence rule Another term for the fruit of the poisonous tree doctrine.

fruit of the poisonous tree rule Evidence obtained legally through the use of evidence obtained illegally.

The exclusionary rule applies not only to evidence obtained directly as a result of improper police conduct but also to evidence obtained indirectly from that improper conduct. The doctrine that provides for the exclusion of evidence derived from initial improper conduct is called the **derivative evidence rule**, also known as the **fruit of the poisonous tree rule**. In *Murray v. United States*, discussed later in this chapter, the U.S. Supreme Court described the scope of the exclusionary rule and its application to indirect evidence:

> The exclusionary rule prohibits introduction into evidence of tangible materials seized during an unlawful search, ... and of testimony concerning knowledge acquired during an unlawful search ... Beyond that, the exclusionary rule also prohibits the introduction of derivative evidence, both tangible and testimonial, that is the product of the primary evidence, or that is otherwise acquired as an indirect result of the unlawful search, up to the point at which the connection with the unlawful search becomes "so attenuated as to dissipate the taint."[19]

Examples
- If the police wrongfully enter a house and find a key to a storage locker, the key is a direct result of the wrongful entry and is inadmissible. If the police then use the key to unlock the storage locker and find illegal drugs, the drugs are excluded as fruit of the initial wrongful search.
- If a search of a house is illegal, and police seize notes that lead them to a witness who gives testimony that implicates the defendant in the crime that was the reason for the invalid search, the testimony is excluded as fruit of the illegal search.

The fruit of the poisonous tree doctrine is applicable if improperly or illegally obtained evidence is the basis for the discovery of

- Other evidence that otherwise would not have been found
- A witness who otherwise might not have been found
- A confession or incriminating admission that would not have been made if the suspect or defendant had not been confronted with the tainted (soiled) evidence

A police officer searches a car door for evidence of criminal activity. Evidence that she finds will be admissible only if the initial stop was made legally and if her search techniques follow legal procedures.

Syracuse Newspapers/Peter Chen/The Image Works

The U.S. Supreme Court case *Fahy v. Connecticut* illustrates why the derivative evidence rule is needed:

Fahy v. Connecticut

Supreme Court of the United States, 375 U.S. 85, 84 S. Ct. 229 (1963)

A police officer saw a car driving slowly in downtown Norwalk, Connecticut, at about 4:40 in the morning. The police officer lawfully stopped the car and questioned the two men in the car. In checking the car for weapons, the officer found a can of black paint and a paintbrush under the front seat. Fahy (the driver of the car) then drove his car home. A short time later, the police officer found that someone had painted swastikas on a Jewish synagogue a short distance from where he had stopped Fahy's car.

The officer went to Fahy's home and, without a search warrant or consent from Fahy, entered Fahy's garage and removed the paint and brush from Fahy's car. After determining that the paint and brush fit the markings on the synagogue, the officer obtained an arrest warrant. When arrested, Fahy made incriminating statements, and later, at the police station, Fahy made a full confession. All the evidence was used in obtaining a conviction of Fahy and his companion. The physical evidence, the paint and the paintbrush, clearly would be excluded as the direct result of the illegal search of Fahy's garage. The incriminating statement, if derived from the evidence obtained in the illegal search, should have been excluded as the "fruit" of that "poisonous tree," the illegal search. In reversing Fahy's conviction, the U.S. Supreme Court held that

[P]etitioner (Fahy) should have had a chance to show that his admissions were induced by being confronted with the illegally seized evidence.

Nor can we ignore the cumulative prejudicial effect of this evidence upon the conduct of the defense at trial. It was only after admission of the paint and brush and only after their subsequent use to corroborate other state's evidence and only after introduction of the confession that the defendants took the stand, admitted their acts, and tried to establish that the nature of those acts was not within the scope of the felony statute under which the defendants had been charged. We do not mean to suggest that petitioner has presented any valid claim based on the privilege against self-incrimination. We merely note this course of events as another indication of the prejudicial effect of erroneously admitted evidence.

EXCEPTIONS TO THE FRUIT OF THE POISONOUS TREE DOCTRINE

The *derivative evidence rule*, as the name suggests, applies only if the challenged evidence is directly and exclusively derived from improper police conduct. The U.S. Supreme Court has developed the following three exceptions to the doctrine in those situations where the police misconduct has not irrevocably "tainted" the challenged evidence.

The Independent Source Doctrine

Improper police conduct may lead to the discovery of evidence, while at the same time another proper source leads to the same evidence. If the second, proper source of the evidence is independent—that is, not tainted by the improper conduct—the evidence is admissible.[20]

Murray v. United States

United States Supreme Court, 487 U.S. 533 (1988)

Federal agents made an unlawful entry into a warehouse where they saw bales of marijuana. The federal agents later applied for a search warrant without making reference to the unlawful entry. The U.S. Supreme Court sent the case back to the trial court "for determination whether the [search authorized by the warrant] was an independent source of the challenged evidence...," stating

> Knowledge that the marijuana was in the warehouse was assuredly acquired at the time of the unlawful entry. But it was also acquired at the time of entry pursuant to the warrant, and if that later acquisition was not the result of the earlier entry there is no reason why the independent source doctrine should not apply. Invoking the exclusionary rule would put the police (and society) not in the same position they would have occupied if no violation occurred, but in a *worse* one ...

You be the JUDGE

You are the trial judge in the criminal trial of a defendant, Benny Jones, who is accused of burglarizing a local jewelry store. Police investigators initially had a witness tell them they saw a person leave the store premises about the time of the burglary, but could not identify the person beyond stating he wore a "bright green" jacket. Benny Jones, believed by the police to be a professional thief, is also known to regularly wear his bright green, trademark jacket with "Benny and the Jets" written on the back.

Later, a police officer noticed Benny leaving a car, and looked in the car windows. The officer spotted Benny's green jacket, opened the car door, and took it out. The officer brought the jacket to investigators, who found some jewels in the jacket pocket, as well as Benny's address book. The address book had the names and addresses of "Clyde; usually gives top dollar on hot jewelry" and "Sharon: Clyde's girl?"

The investigators interviewed Clyde, who reluctantly agreed to testify that Benny sold some stolen jewels to him, and Sharon, who stated she no longer dated Clyde, but saw Benny deliver some jewels to Clyde.

The prosecution wants to introduce the jacket, the jewels found in the jacket, and the address book. It also wants to put Clyde and Sharon on the stand to testify against Benny. You have (rightly) concluded the search of the car was illegal. What, if any, of the evidence presented by the prosecution will you exclude as derived from that illegal search? The U.S. Supreme Court's opinion in *United States v. Ceccolini*, 435 U.S. 268 (1978), might help you make your decision.

The Inevitable Discovery Rule

inevitable discovery rule An exception to the exclusionary rule where illegally discovered evidence would certainly have been discovered legally.

If police error or police misconduct has tainted some evidence, then that evidence and also derivative evidence can be suppressed and not used in a criminal trial. If it can be shown that the challenged derivative evidence would certainly have been discovered by legitimate police efforts, however, it is admissible under the **inevitable discovery rule**. The U.S. Supreme Court adopted the inevitable discovery rule in the *Nix v. Williams* case and explained its relationship to the independent source test.

Nix v. Williams

United States Supreme Court, 467 U.S. 431 (1984)

A 10-year-old Iowa girl was reported missing, and a massive search involving hundreds of police officers and volunteers was organized. During the search, Williams was arrested, based on reports that he had been seen carrying a small girl near the place and at the time she was reported missing. During questioning, the police violated the *Massiah* rule[21] by questioning Williams about the location of the girl's body without the consent or presence of his attorney. Based on Williams's statements, the girl's body was found and the search suspended.

Williams's statements to police were declared inadmissible, but the prosecution sought to introduce evidence of the condition of the body, articles of clothing found, and results of medical tests on the body. The defense contended that this evidence was the "fruit" of the "poisonous" questioning. In upholding the admissibility of this evidence, the Supreme Court concluded that the inevitable discovery rule has the same justification as the independent source rule:

> [The] core rationale consistently advanced by this Court for extending the Exclusionary Rule to evidence that is the fruit of unlawful police conduct has been that this admittedly drastic and socially costly course is needed to deter police from violations of constitutional and statutory protections. [On] this rationale, the prosecution is not to be put in a better position than it would have been in if no illegality had transpired.
>
> By contrast, the derivative evidence analysis ensures that the prosecution is not put in a worse position simply because of some earlier police error or misconduct. The independent source doctrine allows admission of evidence that has been discovered by means wholly independent of any constitutional violation. That doctrine, although closely related to the inevitable discovery doctrine, does not apply here: Williams' statements to Learning [police officer] indeed led police to the child's body, but that is not the whole story. The independent source doctrine teaches us that the interest of society in deterring unlawful police conduct and the public interest in having juries receive all probative evidence of a crime are properly balanced by putting the police in the same, not a worse, position than they would have been in if no police error or misconduct had occurred. When the challenged evidence has an independent source, exclusion of such evidence would put the police in a worse position than they would have been in absent any error or violation. There is a functional similarity between these two doctrines in that exclusion of evidence that would inevitably have been discovered would also put the government in a worse position, because the police would have obtained that evidence if no misconduct had taken place. Thus, while the independent source exception would not justify admission of evidence in this case, its rationale is wholly consistent with and justifies our adoption of the ultimate or inevitable discovery exception to the Exclusionary Rule.

The U.S. Supreme Court concluded that the search parties, which were systematically searching the area where the body was found, would have found the body in a short time without Williams's directions, and thus the evidence found on or near the body would have been found at the same time.

As the Supreme Court noted in *Nix*, there are similarities between the Independent Source Doctrine and the Inevitable Discovery Doctrine. In both cases, it can be said that the illegal search does not pass the "but-for" test; that is, but for the illegal search, the evidence would not have been discovered. Rather, the evidence found after the illegal search would have been found without the knowledge gained in the illegal search. If a distinction between the two doctrines must be drawn, it can be seen as the difference between something that **did** happen that led to the new evidence (the Independent Source Doctrine), and something that hypothetically **would** have happened that would have led to the new evidence (the Inevitable Discovery Doctrine).

The Attenuation, or Passage of Time, Rule

passage of time rule (attenuation) An exception to the exclusionary rule where the "taint" from the improper conduct is dissipated over a significant period of time after the improper conduct.

Where improper police conduct occurs and shortly thereafter that conduct leads to the discovery of other evidence, the fruit of the poisonous tree doctrine reasonably concludes that a connection exists between the improper conduct and the other evidence. Where, however, a significant period of time goes by between the improper conduct and the new evidence, the U.S. Supreme Court has long held that the "taint" from the improper conduct can be dissipated. This is termed the **passage of time rule,** or **attenuation**.

Wong Sun v. United States

United States Supreme Court, 371 U.S. 471 (1963)

Federal narcotics agents illegally broke into Wong Sun's laundry and pressured him to make statements that led to the arrest of Wong Sun on narcotics charges. After his arrest, Wong Sun was arraigned and released on his own recognizance. Several days later, Wong Sun voluntarily appeared at the San Francisco Narcotics Bureau and confessed to the illegal transportation and concealment of heroin.

At his trial, Wong Sun sought to exclude his confession as the fruit of the illegal entry. The Supreme Court found the evidence admissible because the connection between Wong Sun's illegal arrest and his confession "had become so attenuated as to dissipate the taint."

THE *MIRANDA* RULE, CONFESSIONS, AND THE FRUIT OF THE POISONOUS TREE DOCTRINE

The fruit of the poisonous tree doctrine places emphasis on the "poisonous tree"—that is, the improper police conduct. Where the initial improper conduct is an illegal search and seizure, the doctrine is justified by the reasons for having an exclusionary rule at all: The improper police conduct must be deterred in order to accomplish the purpose of the Fourth Amendment. In cases of Fourth Amendment violations (subject to the limitations set forth in *Hudson* and *Herring, supra*), courts will normally exclude any evidence that is the "fruit" of the violation, unless one of the recognized exceptions discussed above is applicable. Application of the fruit of the poisonous tree rule is more complicated where the improper police conduct is other than a Fourth Amendment violation.

TYPES OF EVIDENCE CONTROLLED BY THE EXCLUSIONARY RULE

Type of Evidence	U.S. Constitutional Amendment That Controls the Evidence	Test of Admissibility for Use of Evidence
Physical evidence (drugs, weapons, contraband, clothing, fingerprints, etc.)	Fourth Amendment: "The right of the people to be secure … against unreasonable searches and seizures shall not be violated."	The Fourth Amendment requires a search warrant if a right of privacy is involved. If a warrant is not used, the burden is on the officer to show that the search was authorized by one of the well-recognized exceptions to the requirement of a search warrant. (See Chapters 14 and 15.)
Confessions, incriminating admissions, and statements	Fifth Amendment: "No person … shall be compelled … to be a witness against himself." Sixth Amendment: "In all criminal prosecutions, the accused shall enjoy the right … to have the assistance of counsel for his defense."	The voluntariness test applies to the use of all statements as evidence. The following tests may be applicable depending on the circumstances: *Miranda* requirements and test, *Massiah* test, and *Bruton* requirements. (See Chapter 12.)
Eyewitness and voice identification	Fifth and Fourteenth Amendments: "No person shall be … deprived of life, liberty, or property, without due process of law." Sixth Amendment: "In all criminal prosecutions, the accused shall enjoy the right … to have the assistance of counsel for his defense."	Were the procedures used so unnecessarily suggestive and conducive to irreparable mistaken identification as to be a denial of due process of law? (See Chapter 13.) Was the accused denied the assistance of counsel during the criminal proceedings? See *Kirby v. Illinois,* 406 U.S. 682, 92 S. Ct. 1877 (1972).
Evidence obtained as a result of wiretapping and electronic surveillance	Wiretapping and electronic surveillances are searches controlled by the Fourth Amendment. Wiretapping is also controlled by Title III, Federal Omnibus Crime Control and Safe Streets Act, and applicable statutes in every state.	18 U.S.C.A. § 2515, the Federal Wiretap statute, states that "… no part of the contents of [an illegal wiretap] communication and no evidence derived therefrom maybe received in evidence in any trial…" In *United States v. Donovan,* 429 U.S. 413, 432 (1977) the Court said "The availability of the suppression remedy for these statutory, as opposed to constitutional, violations … turns on the provisions of Title III rather than on the judicially fashioned exclusionary rule."

Miranda and the Poisonous Tree Rule

Where the improper police conduct involves the Fifth Amendment's protection against self-incrimination, such as a failure to give a *Miranda* warning (see Chapter 12), courts have been less consistent in applying the poisonous tree doctrine. An example of that difference is the decision and resulting review by the U.S. Supreme Court of the Wisconsin case of *State v. Knapp.*[22]

There, a suspect in a murder case permitted a police officer into his home to wait while he got dressed to go to the police station and answer questions. Without giving a *Miranda* warning, the officer asked the defendant what he was wearing the night before, the night of the murder. The defendant pointed to a sweatshirt, and the officer seized it. Subsequent DNA tests established the presence of the victim's blood on the sweatshirt.

Based on that and other evidence, the defendant was charged with murder. He moved to suppress both his pre-*Miranda* warning statements made to the officer and the physical evidence (the sweatshirt) seized as a result of those statements. The prosecution conceded that the statements must be excluded but argued that the physical evidence was admissible.

The Wisconsin Supreme Court held that the physical evidence must be excluded as the fruit of a poisonous tree. The "poisonous tree" was the intentional failure to give the defendant *Miranda* warnings. Since the violation was intentional, the court concluded that the deterrent effect of the exclusionary rule required suppression of the evidence. Other courts have decided this issue differently. For example, in *United States v. Sterling*,[23] the Fourth Circuit Court of Appeals upheld the admission of a gun found as a result of statements made by the defendant without a *Miranda* warning. That court concluded that, so long as the statement was voluntary, physical evidence can never be the fruit of the poisonous tree of a *Miranda* violation.

In the case of *United States v. Patane*,[24] the Tenth Circuit Court of Appeals went even further than did the Wisconsin court in the *Knapp* case. It held that physical evidence obtained by the police as a result not of an intentional but a negligent failure to give a defendant his *Miranda* warnings must be suppressed. In that case the police lawfully arrested the defendant at his residence for violation of a restraining order. Before the officers finished giving the defendant the *Miranda* warning the defendant stated, "he knew his rights." The officers did not finish the warning, and asked questions that led to the discovery of an illegal firearm in the defendant's bedroom. The prosecution conceded the defendant's statements were inadmissible because of the failure to give the complete *Miranda* warning, but contended the firearm should not be suppressed. The Circuit Court held the firearm must be suppressed as the "fruit" of the illegal questioning.

The U.S. Supreme Court combined the two cases and granted certiorari in *Knapp* and *Patane*.[25] In 2004 in *United States v. Patane*,[26] the Court reversed the Tenth Circuit Court of Appeals, holding that the Fifth Amendment's Self-Incrimination Clause does not require the exclusion of physical evidence obtained as a result of a voluntary statement made without a *Miranda* warning:

> [T]he *Miranda* rule is a prophylactic employed to protect against violations of the Self-Incrimination Clause. The Self-Incrimination Clause, however, is not implicated by the admission into evidence of the physical fruit of a voluntary statement. The *Miranda* rule is not a code of police conduct, and police do not violate the Constitution (or even the *Miranda* rule, for that matter) by mere failure to warn. For this reason, the exclusionary rule articulated in cases such as *Wong Sun* does not apply.[27]

The Court stated that the Self-Incrimination Clause has only one, specific goal: to protect against compelled, self-incriminating statements. As a result, the Court said, the only exclusionary rule necessitated by the Fifth Amendment is the exclusion of unwarned statements:

> It follows that police do not violate a suspect's constitutional rights (or the *Miranda* rule) by negligent or even deliberate failures to provide the suspect with the full panoply of warnings prescribed by *Miranda*. Potential violations occur, if at all, only upon the admission of unwarned statements into evidence at trial. And, at that point, "[t]he exclusion of unwarned statements … is a complete and sufficient remedy" for any perceived *Miranda* violation. (Citation omitted.)
>
> Thus, unlike unreasonable searches under the Fourth Amendment or actual violations of the Due Process Clause or the Self-Incrimination Clause, there is, with respect to a mere failure to warn, nothing to deter. There is therefore no reason to apply the 'fruit of the poisonous tree' doctrine of *Wong Sun*. (Citation omitted.)

Because it was the companion case to *Patane,* the U.S. Supreme Court vacated the decision of the Wisconsin Supreme Court in *Knapp*, and the case was remanded to the Wisconsin Supreme Court. In 2005, that court on remand held that the physical evidence must be excluded under the Wisconsin State Constitution, Article I, Section 8, because it was the result of intentional police conduct.[28] Massachusetts and Vermont courts have reached similar conclusions.[29]

Patane by its terms applies only to physical evidence obtained as a result of a voluntary but unwarned statement made after a defendant is lawfully arrested. Though the statement is inadmissible because of the failure to give the *Miranda* warning, evidence derived from the voluntary statement is not excluded. However, if the arrest itself is unlawful, and thus an "unreasonable seizure" under the Fourth Amendment, subsequent statements leading to physical evidence may well invoke the poisonous tree doctrine. (See the box below.)

Involuntary Statements, Due Process, and the Poisonous Tree Rule

The Supreme Court's holding in *Patane* does not apply if the statements made by the defendant are involuntary, that is, because the police have improperly coerced the defendant into making the statements that led to the physical evidence. In cases like *Michigan v. Tucker*[30] the U.S. Supreme Court has held that involuntary or coerced statements violate the Due Process Clause, and both the statements and physical or testimonial evidence derived from the statements must be suppressed.

Courts have continued this practice after the *Patane* decision. In the 2010 case of *United States v. Lall*,[31] the federal court of appeals found that a defendant's incriminating statements were involuntary because the police told him his answers would not be used to bring charges against him. (The tests for involuntary confessions are discussed in Chapter 12.) Based on that assurance, the defendant showed the officers equipment used to commit identity theft crimes. The defendant was then charged with identity theft, and moved to suppress both his statements and the physical evidence that was derived from those statements. The court of appeals concluded his incriminating statements were made involuntarily, and ordered suppression of the statements and the physical evidence as "fruits" of the involuntary statements. The court said,

While a confession obtained in violation of *Miranda* is inadmissible, the physical evidence derived from such a confession is not subject to the *Miranda* exclusionary rule, assuming the predicate for its admissibility can be satisfied without resort to the confession. (Citations omitted.) The rule is otherwise for evidence derived from an involuntary confession obtained in violation of the Due Process Clause. In this case, we have found Lall's confession involuntary—a conclusion that compels the suppression of any physical evidence derived from it. The record is clear that the physical evidence seized from Lall's bedroom was the fruit of the coerced confession.[32]

PROCEDURES & PROCESSES

"Knock–and-Talk" and the Fruit of the Poisonous Tree Rule

The U.S. Supreme Court has often held that "Mere police questioning does not constitute a seizure," *Florida v. Bostick*, 501 U.S. 429, 434 (1991), whether or not the officer doing the questioning has any basis for suspecting an individual of criminal activity. As a result, police officers may go to a person's front door and "knock-and-talk" to the person. If incriminating statements are made or evidence discovered from such consensual talks, the statements or evidence may be used in criminal prosecutions.

Knock-and talk sessions can become "custodial," if the questioning changes from consensual to interrogation, and may result in constitutional violations. If the circumstances surrounding the knock-and-talk are such that the person does not feel free to leave and stop answering questions, the questioning becomes "custodial" and the person is "seized" under the Fourth Amendment. If that seizure is unlawful, because police don't have reasonable grounds for placing the person in custody, any statements made after the "seizure" could be suppressed under the fruit of the poisonous tree rule.

In *United States v. Villa-Gonzalez*[33] the Court held that a knock-and-talk session between the police and two suspects became "custodial" when police surrounded the suspects, told them they were suspected drug dealers, and asked them questions about their alien status. Because the police had no reasonable grounds for taking the suspects into custody, doing so was an illegal "seizure" under the Fourth Amendment. No *Miranda* warnings were given. The officers used statements made by the defendants after that point to obtain a search warrant and searched the suspects' residence. Illegal drugs and weapons were found in that search, and the defendants were charged with crimes relating to the illegal drugs and weapons.

The prosecution conceded the statements made without *Miranda* warnings must be suppressed. However, in reliance on the *Patane* decision it contended the physical evidence obtained in the search was admissible. The court of appeals held *Patane* did not apply, and that the physical evidence must be suppressed under the fruit of the poisonous tree rule:

> Although *Patane*, like this case, involved a *Miranda* violation, the similarities end there. In *Patane*, the unwarned statements were made after a lawful arrest.... In this case, by contrast, Trinidad's unwarned statements to Becker were themselves fruits of an illegal seizure. Applying *Patane's* rule in this context would swallow up the entirety of the fruit of the poisonous tree doctrine. Here, like in *Wong Sun*, the initial constitutional violation was a Fourth Amendment violation.[34]

From the above it is reasonable to say that there are four constitutional violations that can lead to incriminating statements and the discovery of physical evidence: (1) unlawful searches or seizures in violation of the Fourth Amendment, (2) involuntary confessions or statements that violate the Due Process Clause, (3) violations of the Sixth Amendment (see Chapter 12), and (4) violations of the *Miranda* rule. It is only *Miranda* violations that do not bring the fruit of the poisonous tree rule into play. Any of the other constitutional violations that yield physical evidence may require suppression of that physical evidence, though, as shown above, application of the exclusionary rule is not automatic. Moreover, either the "inevitable discovery" or "attenuation" exceptions might apply to avoid exclusion of the evidence.

MANY STATES HAVE TWO SETS OF EXCLUSIONARY RULES

The federal exclusionary rule has become very complex since the 1961 *Mapp v. Ohio* case.[35] All states must follow the federal *Mapp* rule in determining the admissibility of evidence. However, it is not uncommon for state courts to impose additional requirements in interpreting that state's constitution or statutes. State statutes, by themselves, may alter the federal *Mapp* rule and impose a stricter standard in a given area of the law.

An example of such an alteration is in *State v. Eckel,*[36] where the New Jersey Supreme Court joined several other states that had rejected the U.S. Supreme Court's pre-2009 rule that the Fourth Amendment permits police to routinely search the passenger compartment of a vehicle incident to the arrest of a recent occupant. (See *New York v. Belton,*[37] discussed in Chapter 14.) The New Jersey court held that under the New Jersey Constitution police cannot search a passenger compartment of a vehicle without a warrant after the occupant has been removed from the vehicle, handcuffed, and placed in the police vehicle.

Therefore, many states have two sets of exclusionary rules. The federal rule is defined by the U.S. Supreme Court and other federal courts, whereas the state exclusionary rule is defined and required by the state supreme court (and sometimes by state statutes). State law enforcement officers are required to comply with the state requirements, which may be more stringent than those required by the federal *Mapp* rule. However, evidence that is to be used in criminal cases in federal courts in all states is judged by the federal *Mapp* rule. Because most crimes are violations of state criminal codes, however, most criminal cases go to state criminal courts.

Some states have simplified this situation by eliminating, to a large extent, their state exclusionary rule. California and Florida are among the states that have added sections to their state constitutions requiring state courts to determine the admissibility of evidence "in conformity with the 4th Amendment … as interpreted by the U.S. Supreme Court" (Florida Constitution). (For the California change, see *In re Lance W.*[38])

THE FUTURE OF THE EXCLUSIONARY RULE

The exclusionary rule was 100 years old in 2014. Throughout the history of the rule there has been concern in the United States about the cost to society when otherwise reliable evidence is suppressed and apparently guilty persons go free. Most other countries do not have an exclusionary rule triggered by police misconduct. (See the *New York Times* article, "U.S. Stands Alone in Rejecting All Evidence When Police Err," published July 19, 2008.)

Cases in the U.S. Supreme Court involving the exclusionary rule are followed closely by the American public: the front page of the January 31, 2009 *New York Times* carried the headline "Supreme Court Edging Closer to Repeal of Evidence Ruling." If, as appears to be the case, there is a growing sentiment in both the public and the U.S. Supreme Court in favor of some change in the exclusionary rule, what are the limits of such a change?

First, an "exclusionary rule" may be used to address different kinds of violations of individual rights. In the case of statutory violations, such as violations of the federal wiretap laws, the exclusionary rule is controlled by the legislature that created the rule. In the case of rights guaranteed by the various state constitutions, state statutes or court opinions will determine the scope of an exclusionary rule.

Where police misconduct violates an individual right protected by the U.S. Constitution, the applicability of an exclusionary rule (and a court's ability to change the rule) can depend on the constitutional right violated. In *Kansas v. Ventris* the U.S. Supreme Court stated that the exclusionary rule "...depends on the nature of the constitutional guarantee that is violated. Sometimes (the U.S. Constitution) mandates exclusion from trial and sometimes it does not ..."[39] The Court briefly identified the following "constitutional mandates" and their relationship to the exclusionary rule:

Constitutional Mandate	Does the Constitution Mandate Exclusion
The Fifth Amendment guarantees that "no person ... shall be compelled in any criminal case to be a witness against himself ..."	**Yes**. The constitutional right is directly violated "whenever a truly coerced confession is introduced at trial ..." 129 S. Ct., at 1845.
The Fourth Amendment guarantees that persons shall be free of "unreasonable searches and seizures."	**No**. The Fourth Amendment "says nothing about excluding their fruits from evidence ... Inadmissibility has not been automatic, therefore, we have instead applied an exclusionary-rule balancing test." *Id*
The Sixth Amendment guarantees that in all criminal proceedings the accused ... "shall enjoy the right ... to have the Assistance of Counsel for his defence."	**Yes**. "... once formal criminal proceedings begin, the Sixth Amendment renders inadmissible in the prosecutions case in chief statements 'deliberately elicited' from a defendant without an express waiver of the right to counsel."[40]
The "... Fifth and Sixth Amendment prophylactic rules against forbidding certain pretrial police conduct."	**No**. Statements made in violation of the Sixth Amendment may be used for impeachment purposes: "It is one thing to say the Government cannot make an affirmative use of evidence unlawfully obtained. It is quite another to say the defendant can ... provide himself a shield against contradiction of his untruth." 129 S. Ct., at 1846.

As can be seen from the Supreme Court's opinion discussed above, the American exclusionary rule may not be completely abolished by either the U.S. Supreme Court or Congress. The Fifth and Sixth Amendments make it clear that the introduction of evidence obtained in violation of those amendments is itself the constitutional violation. In other cases, such as violations of the Fourth Amendment, the exclusionary rule operates as a remedy for a constitutional violation that has occurred in the past; the admission of evidence acquired in a violation of the Fourth Amendment is not itself a violation of that Amendment. The exclusion of such evidence is thus not constitutionally mandated, and the exclusionary rule as a remedy may be changed over time.

There are many exceptions to the exclusionary rule. This chapter contains the three major exceptions to the rule, and Chapter 10 discusses the many areas exempted from operation of the rule. It is likely the U.S. Supreme Court will in the future hear cases where the full extent of the exclusionary rule is at issue. As discussed above, the Supreme Court has said the rule cannot be abolished altogether; it also likely that a majority of the nine judges of the Supreme Court would not rule for dramatic changes in the rule.

SUMMARY

1. **State the origin of the exclusionary rule.**
   - The exclusionary rule was created by the U.S. Supreme Court as a means of deterring violations by police officers of constitutional and statutory rights, primarily violations of the Fourth Amendment.

2. **Define the *derivative evidence rule*.**
   - The derivative evidence rule provides for exclusion of evidence obtained indirectly by police by using information obtained in an illegal search or seizure, or by using information obtained from unlawful incriminating statements.

3. **List the exceptions to the exclusionary rule, and what they entail.**
   - The "inevitable discovery" doctrine requires police to show the evidence they obtained by using illegally obtained evidence or statements would certainly have been discovered by the police in an investigation that did not rely on the illegal evidence or statements.

   - The "independent source" doctrine requires the police to show the challenged evidence was in fact discovered by an alternate source or investigation, and neither the source nor the investigation used any part of the illegally obtained evidence or statements.

   - The "attenuation" doctrine requires a showing that the time between the improper police conduct and the subsequently discovered evidence was sufficiently lengthy to dissipate the "taint" of the illegal conduct.

4. **State the role of the exclusionary rule for evidence obtained in an improper search.**
   - If a search is made without a search warrant and in violation of the Fourth Amendment, all evidence derived from the search, including derivative evidence, must be suppressed. If the search was made under a search warrant, but the terms of the search warrant were not followed exactly, evidence discovered in the search may not be subject to exclusion if the police error did not affect the privacy rights of the defendant.

5. **State the role of the exclusionary rule for evidence obtained as a result of a violation of the *Miranda* rule.**
   - Statements made without a proper *Miranda* warning must be suppressed. Evidence, including physical evidence, obtained from voluntary, unwarned, statements is not excluded.

6. **State the role of the exclusionary rule for incriminating statements procured in violation of the Due Process Clause.**
   - If involuntary statements are obtained by police, the Due Process Clause is violated, and the statements and any derivative evidence obtained from information in the involuntary statements is excluded.

KEY TERMS

derivative evidence rule, 218

exclusionary rule, 214

fruit of the poisonous tree rule, 218

inevitable discovery rule, 221

passage of time rule, or attenuation, 222

KEY CASES

Hudson v. Michigan, 547 U.S. 586 (2006): Held exclusionary rule did not apply where evidence was seized under search warrant, but police failed to "knock and announce" their presence.

Michigan v. Tucker, 417 U.S. 433 (1974): Held involuntary incriminating statements and evidence derived from those statements obtained in violation of Due Process Clause were subject to exclusionary rule.

Murray v. United States, 487 U.S. 533 (1988): Evidence discovered by independent source should not be excluded because it was discovered as a result of improper police conduct.

Nix v. Williams, 467 U.S. 431 (1984): Adopted the inevitable discovery rule as an exception to the exclusionary rule.

United States v. Herring, 555 U.S. 135 (2009): Held exclusionary rule was not appropriate where police misconduct resulting in an unlawful arrest and search was only negligent, and based on incorrect information supplied by a county clerk.

United States v. Patane, 124 S. Ct. 2620 (2004): Held that violations of *Miranda* rule did not make exclusionary rule applicable to physical evidence obtained from voluntary statements made without the *Miranda* warning.

Wong Sun v. United States, 371 U.S. 471 (1963): Held that if sufficient time passes after an illegal search or seizure to break the connection between the illegal acts and evidence obtained, the evidence is cleared of the "taint" of the illegal acts and can be admitted.

PROBLEMS

1. Police suspected the defendant was operating a house of prostitution. After investigation, the police developed enough evidence for the probable cause needed to obtain a search warrant. While officers were obtaining the search warrant, other officers went to the location and "detained" the house. The owner was prevented from entering the house during this detention. Ultimately, the search warrant was not obtained until 26 hours after the initial detention of the house. The search warrant yielded evidence of prostitution. The defendant moved to suppress all the evidence obtained under the search warrant. Should it be suppressed? Does the "fruit of the poisonous tree" rule apply to that evidence? If not, why not? Should *Herring* apply to make the exclusionary rule inappropriate? If not, why not? [See *United States v. Song Ja Cha,* 597 F.3d 995 (9th Cir. 2010).]

2. Texas police obtained a proper search warrant to search defendant's house to look for evidence of check forgery, including equipment purchased with forged checks. The warrant

identified various purchased property to look for, including a safe, but did not include the safe in the list of property to be seized. Police found two safes, and took the back to the stationhouse for a locksmith to open. Inside the safes they found illegal drugs, and the defendant was charged with a drug offense. The defendant moved to suppress the illegal drugs, claiming they were "seized" in violation of the Fourth Amendment and must be suppressed. Assuming the "seizure" of the safes was not properly identified in the warrant and thus was unlawful, should the evidence inside the safes be suppressed? Does the *Hudson* case provide an answer? (See *State v. Powell,* 306 S.W.3d 761 (Tex. Crim. App. 2010).)

3. Amtrak police officers believed the defendant fit the drug courier profile, in part because he purchased a train ticket for cash the day before his trip. When the defendant arrived at the train station, the defendant and a briefcase he was carrying were "detained" by the officers, who called for a drug-detecting dog to sniff the

briefcase. Before the dog arrived the officers opened the briefcase, which had over $100,000 inside. The officers closed the briefcase, and the dog arrived and "alerted" to drugs in the briefcase. Assuming the officers had reasonable suspicion to hold the briefcase for further investigation (see Chapter 14), was the search of the briefcase before the dog arrived lawful? If not, should the evidence inside the briefcase be suppressed? [See *United States v. Marrocco*, 578 F.3d 627 (7th Cir. 2009).] (The case involved a forfeiture action by the government, but the court held the usual rules about exclusion of evidence applied to the result.)

CASE ANALYSIS

Read Appendix B, Finding and Analyzing Cases (p. 499). With these guidelines in mind, please continue with the Case Analysis selections for Chapter 9.

1. Assume police officers conducted an illegal search of defendant's apartment. In the process they discovered the identity of two victims of sexual assaults by the defendant. The police interviewed the victims, and they agreed to testify against the defendant. At his trial, the defendant moved to suppress the victim's testimony, invoking the "fruit of the poisonous tree" argument. Should the testimony be suppressed? What factors did the Maine Supreme Judicial Court consider important on this question? *State v. Bailey*, 41 A.3d 535 (Me. 2012).

2. F.B.I. officers in California learned that the defendant drove from New Mexico to California to meet a teenager with whom the defendant had had sexually explicit online conversations on the Internet. The agents also had evidence that the defendant and the teenager drove back to New Mexico together. The agents informed New Mexico police, who sent an officer to observe defendant's home. Seeing the teenager inside in a state of undress, the officer entered the home and arrested the defendant. In a search accompanying the arrest the officer found evidence of child pornography. Defendant was charged with bringing a minor across state lines for sexual purposes, and possession of child

4. Not all state courts have been willing to follow the Supreme Court's lead in the *Herring* decision. Some courts, like the Wisconsin Supreme Court, have reached different results by application of a state constitutional provision and exclusionary rule. In a situation similar to the facts in Herring the Wisconsin Supreme Court thought application of the exclusionary rule was appropriate. What interest did the Court believe would be furthered by exclusion of evidence obtained under an invalid warrant? Do you agree? [See *State v. Hess*, 785 N.W.2d 568 (Wis. 2010).]

pornography. Defendant moved to suppress all the evidence gathered from the search of his home, which the prosecution conceded was illegal. Should the evidence be suppressed? Does the Independent Source Doctrine help the prosecution? The Inevitable Discovery Doctrine? Must the prosecution show there was an independent investigation underway that would have uncovered the same evidence? *United States v. Christy*, 739 F.3d 534 (10th Cir. 2014).

3. As we noted in this chapter, many states have exclusionary rules more rigorous than the federal rule. How does the Hawaii state rule differ from the federal rule in the following situation: Police arrested defendant on an outstanding warrant, and after doing so made him empty his pockets, discovering a stash of illegal drugs. The defendant was then taken to the police station, and ultimately charged with possession of illegal drugs. At his trial, the judge agreed the search was illegal, and ordered the drugs found on the defendant to be suppressed under the state exclusionary rule. On appeal, the state argued the inevitable discovery rule applied, because had the illegal search not occurred the drugs would have been lawfully discovered during an inventory search held at the police station. The Hawaii Supreme rejected that argument. Why did it do so? *State v. Rodrigues*, 286 P.3d 809 (Hawaii 2012).

4. Police officers conducted an investigation of a murder, and believed the defendant was involved in the murder. The defendant came to the police station for questioning, but early on said he needed to talk to his attorney. Officers continued to question him, and he subsequently said he hid the knife used in the killing, and showed them where the knife was hidden. At his trial, the defendant moved to suppress the statements made to the police, and the knife found as a result of those statements. It is clear the officers should not have continued to question the defendant after he invoked his right to a lawyer (see Chapter 12). Should this result in the exclusion of all the statements and physical evidence derived from the statements? Or, like the decision in the *Patane* case discussed in this chapter, is such exclusion improper? *See State v. Venegas*, 79 So.3d 912 (Fla. App. 2012).

Notes

1. Former Chief Justice of the U.S. Supreme Court Warren Burger raised the question in his 1964 article, *Who Will Watch the Watchman?* (14 Am. U. L. Rev. 1), before he was appointed to the Court.
2. See Chapter 12 for material on Fifth Amendment rights.
3. See Chapter 14 for material on Fourth Amendment rights.
4. Early Supreme Court cases seem to have tied inadmissibility of involuntary confessions to the Fifth Amendment's privilege against self-incrimination. (See *Bram v. United States*, 68 U.S. 532 (1897).) Since *Brown v. Mississippi*, 297 U.S. 278 (1936), the Due Process Clause has been regarded as the basis for the requirement that confession be voluntary.
5. *Barron v. Baltimore*, 32 U.S. 243 (1833).
6. The federal *Weeks* rule is named after the 1914 case of *Weeks v. United States* (34 S. Ct. 341), in which federal agents entered Weeks's home without consent and without a search warrant or any other authority. The agents seized evidence in Weeks's home, which was used to obtain Weeks's criminal conviction.
7. 338 U.S. 25 (1949).
8. Since *Wolf* was decided most of the rights in the Bill of Rights have been incorporated into the Due Process Clause of the Fourteenth Amendment. In subsequent chapters of this book we will discuss many of those rights.
9. In *Elkins v. United States*, 364 U.S. 206 (1960) the Supreme Court held that evidence obtained by state officers in violation of the Fourth Amendment could not be used in federal prosecutions.
10. In *Mapp v. Ohio*, 81 S. Ct. 1684 (1961), police officers forced their way into Ms. Mapp's home without probable cause, consent, a search warrant, or any other authority. The officers suspected that a fugitive was hiding in the house. When they did not find a fugitive, they searched through drawers and boxes until they found evidence of pornography, which they used to convict Mapp of the crime of possession of pornography.
11. *Miranda v. Arizona*, 384 U.S. 436 (1966). The *Miranda* rule is discussed more fully in Chapter 12.
12. The *Miranda* warnings are that (a) the suspect has the right to remain silent, (b) any statements made can be used against the suspect, (c) the suspect has the right to have an attorney present, and (d) an attorney will be appointed if the suspect cannot afford one. In *Dickerson v. United States,* 530 U.S. 428 (2000), the Court stated the *Miranda* rule was of "constitutional dimension" and could not be overturned by Congress.
13. *People v. Defoe*, 150 N.E. 585, 587 (N.Y. 1926).
14. 468 U.S. 897, 906 (1984).
15. 547 U.S. at 590.
16. 514 U.S. 927 (1995).
17. 547 U.S. at 590.
18. *Id.* at 593.
19. 487 U.S. 533, 536–537 (1988) [Citations omitted].
20. See *Silverthorne Lumber Co. v. United States*, 251 U.S. 385 (1920), and *Nardone v. United States*, 308 U.S. 338 (1939). *Nardone* was the first case to use the fruit of the poisonous tree analogy.
21. See *Massiah v. United States*, 377 U.S. 201 (1964), discussed in Chapter 12. The rescue exception or the public safety exception to the *Miranda* rule might reasonably be applied to the *Massiah* doctrine in cases like *Williams*.
22. 666 N.W.2d 881 (2003).
23. 283 F.3d 216 (4th Cir. 2002), *cert. denied,* 536 U.S. 931 (2002).
24. 304 F.3d 1013 (10th Cir. 2002).
25. 123 S. Ct. 1788 (2003).
26. 542 U.S. 630 (2004).
27. 542 U.S. at 636.
28. *State v. Knapp,* 700 N.W.2d 899 (Wis. 2005).
29. *Comm. v. Martin*, 827 N.E.2d 198 (Mass. 2005); *State v. Peterson*, 923 A.2d 585 (Vt. 2007).
30. 417 U.S. 433 (1974).

31. 607 F.3d 1277 (11th Cir. 2010).
32. 607 F.3d at 1291.
33. 623 F.3d 526 (8th Cir. 2010).
34. *Id.* at 535.
35. See note 6 for a summary of *Mapp v. Ohio.*
36. 888 A.2d 1266 (N.J. 2006).

37. 453 U.S. 454 (1981). In *Arizona v. Gant*, 556 U.S. 332 (2009), discussed in Chapter 14, the Supreme Court limited searches of automobiles after arrests.
38. Cal. Rptr. 631, 694 P.2d 744 (1985).
39. 129 U.S. at 1845.
40. *Michigan v. Harvey*, 494 U.S. 344, 348 (1990).

CHAPTER 10

Where the Exclusionary Rule Does Not Apply

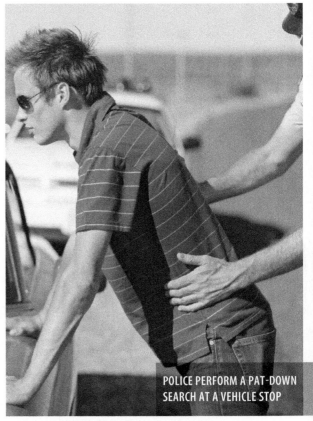

POLICE PERFORM A PAT-DOWN SEARCH AT A VEHICLE STOP

Stockbyte/Stockbyte/Getty Images

LEARNING OBJECTIVES

In this chapter we present some of the accepted situations where the exclusionary rule does not apply. The learning objectives for this chapter are

Define *standing* for Fourth Amendment purposes.

Explain the role of "consent" in searches of persons or residences.

State when property is abandoned for Fourth Amendment purposes.

List the factors to be considered when the good faith test from *Leon* is applied to a search warrant or an arrest.

Distinguish "good faith" from "honest mistake."

As we state in this chapter, the U.S. Supreme Court has held that a person who places trash bags or trash receptacles on the curb for pickup by the trash collector has no expectation of privacy in the contents of the trash bags or receptacles. As a result, if police without probable cause look inside the trash containers and find evidence of criminal activity, the evidence will not be subject to the exclusionary rule.

Exactly what actions of the homeowners cause them to lose their expectation of privacy? Putting trash in the trash containers? Placing the containers on the house's driveway? Placing the containers on the curb? Not surprisingly, courts differ on the answers to these questions. In *Commonwealth v. Ousley*, 393 S.W.3d 15 (Ky. 2013), police officers without probable cause searched the defendant's trash container sitting outside his townhome, in the open, but near his driveway. Based on evidence found there police obtained a search warrant, searched the defendant's townhome, and found illegal drugs. Should the evidence discovered in the trash container be suppressed under the exclusionary rule? (Doing so would likely render the resulting search warrant also excludable under the "fruit of the poisonous tree" rule.) Are these facts relevant: The police search occurred at night; one search was on a Monday, and trash pickup is on Fridays; the trash containers were between the cars parked in the driveway and the front of the townhouse? Why or why not? Compare this case to the opinion of the court in *United States v. Jackson*, 728 F.3d 367 (4th Cir. 2013), *cert. denied* 134 S. Ct. 1347 (2014). Are the cases different on an important fact?

THE LIMITS OF THE EXCLUSIONARY RULE

The exclusionary rule and its applications (discussed in Chapter 9) have been the subject of extensive criticism. The principal argument against the rule is that society pays a high cost to secure its benefits. The goal of the exclusionary rule is to deter improper police conduct, which in theory benefits all citizens, but in most cases the direct beneficiary of the rule is someone who would be convicted if the evidence were not excluded. The rule can thus result in dangerous criminals going free.

Mindful of this cost, the U.S. Supreme Court has repeatedly held that "the [exclusionary] rule has been [and is] restricted to those areas where its remedial objectives are thought most efficaciously served."

In the previous chapter we introduced the exclusionary rule as it has been applied to situations where state or federal officers acted in violation of a person's constitutional rights. The "remedial objective" in those situations is to deter illegal police conduct. In this chapter we define the scope and extent of the exclusionary rule by examining its borders, that is, situations where evidence has been discovered without a clear violation by police of some person's rights. In what areas of conduct, even improper or illegal conduct, should the exclusionary rule be inapplicable?

THE EXCLUSIONARY RULE DOES NOT APPLY TO EVIDENCE OBTAINED IN A PRIVATE SEARCH BY A PRIVATE PERSON

The Fourth Amendment to the U.S. Constitution prohibits unreasonable searches and seizures. Evidence obtained in violation of the Fourth Amendment is generally inadmissible under the exclusionary rule.[1] This prohibition applies to mistakes or misconduct by the police and other officials in the executive branch of government. The exclusionary rule does not apply to private persons. Evidence obtained by private persons, even if obtained illegally, is not subject to the exclusionary rule, as the Supreme Court held in the following case.

Burdeau v. McDowell

United States Supreme
Court, 256 U.S. 465 (1921)

An unknown person or persons burglarized the defendant's office, breaking into his desk and private safe. The burglars took files and papers that implicated the defendant in criminal activity. These papers and files ended up in the possession of federal prosecutors, who showed "clean hands" and then used them in the indictment and conviction of the defendant.

The defendant argued that the evidence should have been excluded because it was obtained by an unlawful search and seizure. The Supreme Court rejected that argument, holding "the record clearly shows that no official of the federal government had anything to do with the wrongful seizure of the petitioner's property, or had any knowledge thereof until several months after the property had been taken from him."

In refusing to make the Fourth Amendment applicable to purely private conduct, the Supreme Court observed that the origin and history of that amendment "clearly shows that it was intended as a restraint upon the activities of sovereign authority and was not intended to be a limitation upon other than government agencies."[2]

A private search can be transformed into a government search if the government participates in the search, as the California case of *People v. Wilkinson*[3] illustrates. There, the defendant was charged with burglary when he entered the bedroom of a co-occupant of his residence and downloaded images from her computer showing her engaged in sexual acts with her boyfriend. At his trial, the defendant moved to suppress the computer discs he had made and kept in his room because the discs were taken from his room by the boyfriend in cooperation with police. The trial court denied his motion, and he was convicted of burglary. On appeal, the court of appeals reversed, holding that while the boyfriend's original entry into the defendant's room to find the discs was a purely private search, because the police only "passively" acquiesced in the search, after the police viewed the discs and urged the boyfriend to find some with more explicit sexual images, the search was "instigated" by the police and lost its private status. The evidence was suppressed.

Searches by private security guards in the course of their employment are generally not Fourth Amendment violations. This is true even if the guards are licensed by the state, subject to state regulations, and have the power to arrest persons who commit crimes. In *United States v. Day*, 591 F.3d 679 (4th Cir. 2010), the court held that a search of a defendant's person by "armed security officers" was a private search, even though under Virginia state law the officers were given power to make arrests.

THE EXCLUSIONARY RULE APPLIES ONLY IN CRIMINAL CASES

The exclusionary rule forbids the use of evidence tainted or soiled by improper or illegal police conduct in criminal cases. Such evidence, however, can be used in civil cases. For example, after O. J. Simpson was found not guilty of murder charges in 1995, a civil lawsuit was brought against him by the estates of the two homicide victims. Evidence that had been suppressed in Simpson's murder case was used against him in the civil lawsuit, which resulted in jury awards of more than $34 million against Simpson.

In the case of *United States v. Janis*,[4] evidence that had been suppressed in a criminal action against Janis for illegal wagering was turned over to the Internal Revenue Service. The evidence was used against Janis to obtain a civil judgment

PROCEDURES & PROCESSES

When Is a Search Private?

If a search is **private** (conducted solely by a private person), the exclusionary rule does not apply. Courts have adopted the following requirements to determine whether a search is purely private:

	Held Private	**Held Not Private**
The evidence was obtained by a private person acting in a private capacity.[a]	*Armstrong v. State*, 46 So.3d 589 (Fla. App. 2010): Search of package mistakenly delivered to F.B.I. agent named Armstrong was private search.	*State v. Smith*, 782 N.W.2d 913 (Neb. 2010): An off-duty uniformed police officer employed by bar told bar patron to keep his hands up while private security guard searched the patron.
The idea or initiative to obtain the evidence originated with the private person.	*Limpuangthip v. United States*, 932 A.2d 1137 (D.C. 2007): Search in college dorm room initiated by private college administrator and accompanied by state-authorized university police officers was private search.	*State v. Madson*, 760 N.W.2d 370 (S.D. 2009): Private security guards at Indian casino forced their way into guest room based on reports of marijuana odor at room door. Held not private search.
The police or government agent did not participate in obtaining the evidence.	*Dawson v. State* 106 S.W.3d 388 (Tex. App. 2003): Motel manager suspected motel guest was smoking marijuana, and opened door in presence of police officer. Held private search.	*United States v. Booker*, 728 F.3d 535 (6th Cir. 2013): Police took suspect to emergency room where private doctor performed rectal search of suspect, finding rock cocaine. Held search was not private.

[a]State courts differ as to whether an off-duty police officer is a private person, though most hold that a police officer in uniform is acting in an official capacity even if off duty.

private search A search by a private person that is not subject to the exclusionary rule.

of tax fraud. The U.S. Supreme Court affirmed the judgment against Janis, holding that:

> Jurists and scholars uniformly have recognized that the exclusionary rule imposes a substantial cost on the societal interest in law enforcement by its proscription of what concededly is relevant evidence.... And alternatives that would be less costly to societal interests have been the subject of extensive discussion and exploration....
>
> We conclude that exclusion from federal civil proceedings of evidence unlawfully seized by a state criminal enforcement officer has not been shown to have a sufficient likelihood of deterring the conduct of the state police so that it outweighs the societal costs imposed by the exclusion. This Court, therefore, is not justified in so extending the exclusionary rule.

THE EXCLUSIONARY RULE DOES NOT APPLY TO EVIDENCE OBTAINED IN A CONSENT SEARCH

The U.S. Supreme Court has long held that a warrantless search of premises is permissible if undertaken with the valid consent of the person who occupies the premises.[5] As a July 2008 article in the *FBI Law Enforcement Bulletin* pointed out, "consent is a well-known and lawful tool police officers often rely on to conduct searches and seizures in a wide variety of situations and circumstances." In *United States v. Drayton,*[6] the Court said,

> police officers act in full accordance with the law when they ask citizens for consent. It reinforces the rule of law for the citizen to advise the police of his or her own wishes and for the police to act in reliance on that understanding. When this exchange takes place, it dispels inferences of coercion.

Admissibility of evidence obtained in a consent search has two requirements:

1. *Proof that consent was given voluntarily:* Law officers must prove that consent to enter premises or consent to search a person was given voluntarily and was not the product of duress or coercion. Whether consent is voluntary is a question of fact to be determined by the totality of the circumstances.[7] Factors to consider under this test are the age of the person giving consent (very young or very old); the vulnerability of that person based on mental impairment, lack of education, intoxication, or other similar causes; and the use of threats, promises, deception, or trickery to obtain consent. Courts have held that consent is not necessarily rendered involuntary under the following circumstances:

   a. The person is not advised of the right to refuse to give consent. This advice is not required, but some officers give it.[8]
   b. Consent is given by a handcuffed person while officers have their weapons drawn.[9]
   c. Consent is given while a person is under the influence of drugs.[10]

2. *Proof that consent was obtained from a person with "actual or apparent authority" to grant the consent:* The person granting consent to search premises or a vehicle need not be the owner of the property. It is enough if the person giving consent has actual authority (authority to consent to the search is actually possessed by the consenting person) or apparent authority (authority that a reasonable person would believe the consenting person possesses). The driver of a car or a tenant in an apartment building could have actual or apparent authority to consent to a search. However, a co-tenant of an apartment may not give consent over the objection of the other co-tenant (see *Georgia v. Randolph* below), nor can a landlord or motel manager consent to a search of rented space.

The person giving consent may limit the search area or, after giving consent, may revoke the consent. If the revocation is clear and specific, it is effective if done prior to the discovery of contraband evidence, even if in plain view. Revocation of consent is not permitted in two situations: (1) persons who present themselves and their belongings for security screening at airports, and (2) persons visiting prisons. Such persons give their consent by entering restricted areas, and that consent may not be withdrawn.[11]

Finally, consent is not needed to enter premises if exigent circumstances require police officers to enter. Screams for help, fire, and gunshots are examples of circumstances that justify officers entering premises without first obtaining consent.

LEGAL CASES

The "Consent-Once-Removed" Doctrine and Civil Liability of Police Officers for Illegal Searches

The question of police officer liability for civil damages based on an illegal search was raised in the case of *Callahan v. Millard City*, 494 F.3d 891 (10th Cir. 2007). In a "drug buy and bust" operation an undercover informant entered a home after receiving consent from the occupant. After making a purchase of illegal drugs the informant communicated consent to the backup officers waiting outside to enter the premises. The backup officers entered the home, arrested the drug dealer, and seized illegal drugs as evidence. The officers were relying on the "consent-once-removed" doctrine as a justification for entering the home without a search warrant. At the time, several state and federal courts had held that consent given to an undercover police officer allowed the officer to give consent to other officers to enter premises. (See e.g., *United States v. Pollard*, 215 F.3d 643 (6th Cir. 2000); *State v. Johnston*, 518 N.W.2d 759 (Wis. 1994).) A few courts made the doctrine applicable where the initial consent was given to an undercover informant. (*United States v. Paul*, 808 F.2d 645 (7th Cir. 1996).)

In *Callahan* the occupant was convicted on illegal drug charges, based on the drugs seized by police who entered his house. A state appeals court vacated the conviction, holding the seizure violated the Fourth Amendment. The defendant then brought an action in federal court for civil damages against the police officers who entered his house, under the authority of *Bivens v. Six Unknown Fed. Narcotics Agents*, 403 U.S. 388 (1971), which held law enforcement officers can be liable for violations of the Fourth Amendment. In *Callahan v. Millard City, supra,* the Tenth Circuit Court of Appeals held the officers could be sued for damages because the "consent-once-removed" doctrine did not apply where an informant was given the initial consent.

The case ultimately came before the U.S. Supreme Court in *Pearson v. Callahan*, 555 U.S. 223 (2009). The Court held that while (1) the officers had no warrant to enter, (2) the occupant had not given the police consent to enter, and (3) there was no exigency justifying their entry, the officers were not liable for civil damages. The Supreme Court declined to rule on the constitutionality of the consent-once-removed doctrine, but held that whether or not the entry violated the Fourth Amendment, the officers' entry under the "consent-once-removed" doctrine "did not violate clearly established law." The Court said that at the time of the entry many courts had adopted the "consent-once-removed" doctrine, and the officers acted reasonably in relying on those cases. As a result, the officers were entitled to qualified immunity from civil actions for damages. In a similar 2012 case, *Messerschmidt v. Millender*, 132 S. Ct. 1235 (2012), the Supreme Court held officers were entitled to immunity based on their reasonable reliance on a search warrant later found to be invalid.

Georgia v. Randolph

United States Supreme Court, 547 U.S. 103 (2006)

In *United States v. Matlock*,[12] the U.S. Supreme Court held that consent to search under the Fourth Amendment may be given by a person other than the defendant, if that person has "common authority" over the area searched. "Common authority," the *Matlock* Court said, is authority that rests on "mutual use of the property by persons generally having joint access or control for most purposes."[13] The *Matlock* Court then held that "the consent of one who possesses common authority over premises or effects is valid as against the absent, nonconsenting person with whom the authority is shared."[14]

The holding in *Matlock* was interpreted differently in lower courts presented with third-party consent cases. Some courts held that consent by one cohabitant was valid even if the other cohabitant was present and objected to a search. Others held that the risk assumed by choosing to live with another person is limited to the risk that person might give permission to search the residence in the other person's absence. In *Georgia v. Randolph,* the Supreme Court held that if a cohabitant is present when the other cohabitant gives consent to search, but objects to the search, the search is no longer consensual.

In *Randolph,* the defendant's estranged wife gave police permission to search their home for illegal drugs. The defendant was present when this occurred and unequivocally refused to give his consent to the search. The search proceeded, illegal drugs were found, and the defendant was convicted on drug charges. The Georgia Supreme Court reversed the conviction, holding that the drugs should have been suppressed because the search lacked a valid warrant or consent. The state appealed to the U.S. Supreme Court, which affirmed the Georgia Supreme Court.

The U.S. Supreme Court said that the basis of third-party consent in *Matlock* was the reasonable expectation one cohabitant should have about the authority of another cohabitant to use the common premises. The Court concluded that there exists a common understanding that one cohabitant has the authority to, among other things, invite persons into the premises. However, the Court concluded that there is no common understanding that "one co-tenant generally has a right or authority to prevail over the express wishes of another, whether the issue is the color of the curtains or invitations to outsiders." As a result, the objection by the defendant meant the police officer had no more reason to assume entry was permitted than the officer would have had if there had been no consent at all, the Court held.

The *Randolph* Court noted that the line being drawn was very "fine." If the cohabitant is not asked for consent, even if present, and remains silent, then the consent remains valid, reaffirming the holding in *Illinois v. Rodriguez.*[15] Moreover, the Court refused to require police who have obtained consent from one cohabitant to take affirmative steps to obtain the other cohabitant's consent, so long as they did not remove the cohabitant from the premises for the purpose of obtaining the other's consent.

The response to *Randolph* has been to regard its holding as limited to the "fine line" drawn. For example, in *United States v. Groves,*[16] the Seventh Circuit Court of Appeals upheld the validity of a search under the consent of one cohabitant, even though police officers planned to arrive at the shared residence at a time the officers knew the defendant would be away from home. However, courts have also held under the rule in *Randolph* that an objection to a search by a temporary resident of a home, even though consent was given by the principal resident in the home, makes a resulting search unlawful. *United States v. Johnson,* 656 F.3d 275 (6th Cir. 2011).

In the 2014 case of *Fernandez v. California,* 134 S. Ct. 1126, the U.S. Supreme Court made it clear *Randolph* was a limited exception to the consent rule. In *Fernandez* a female resident of an apartment, showing signs of domestic abuse, gave consent to police to enter the apartment. However, before they could do so, the male resident clearly objected to their entry. The police arrested the male resident based on their belief he abused the female resident, and took him to jail. The female resident again gave consent to enter and search the apartment, where police found evidence linking the male resident to a recent robbery. Lower courts refused to suppress the evidence found in the search, and the male resident was convicted of robbery and domestic abuse. The Supreme Court affirmed the conviction, holding that *Randolph* applied only if the co-resident was present and objected at the time the other resident gave consent to search. Even though the co-resident was absent because the police lawfully removed him, the Court said the "narrow exception" in *Randolph* no longer applied, and the other resident had power to give consent.

THE EXCLUSIONARY RULE DOES NOT APPLY IF THE DEFENDANT DOES NOT HAVE STANDING OR IF NO RIGHT OF PRIVACY OF THE DEFENDANT HAS BEEN VIOLATED

standing Possession of the necessary relationship to an issue to be permitted to raise that issue in a court of law.

Evidence may be excluded under the exclusionary rule when the defendant makes a motion to suppress that evidence. To succeed in this motion, however, the defendant must show that his or her own rights were violated, not the rights of some other person. This concept is called **standing**, which means that the defendant is the proper person to challenge the police conduct because it violated the defendant's rights.

PROCEDURES & PROCESSES

The Scope and Duration of Consent to Search

The nature and extent of a consensual search is determined by the consent given. *Florida v. Jimeno*, 500 U.S. 248 (1991). Courts therefore hold that a consent search cannot exceed the consent given, and once consent is revoked the search must end. (See *Gates v. Tex. Dept. of Prot. and Reg. Services*, 537 F.3d 404 (5th Cir. 2008).) The following cases illustrate some applications of the consent rules:

Search Was Within Scope and Duration

Consent to search room in house included consent to search briefcase where object of search might be found. *United States v. Stierhoff*, 549 F.3d 19 (1st Cir. 2008).

Consent to search passenger compartment of truck included taking the screws out of stereo speakers in the dash, where officers noticed recent tool marks on the screws holding the speakers. *United States v. Garcia*, 604 F.3d 186 (5th Cir. 2010).

Consent to search house included consent for officers to use device to unlock doors to house. *United States v. Pikyavit*, 527 F.3d 1126 (10th Cir. 2008).

General consent to search house "and personal property" included computers, and also included consent to remove computer hard drives from house for more investigation. *State v. Ramage*, 784 N.W.2d 746 (Wis. App. 2010), *rev. denied*, 791 N.W.2d 66 (Wis. 2010).

Search Was Outside Scope and Duration

Federal marshals seeking fugitive exceeded consent to enter defendant's residence when marshals exited house to apprehend fugitive, but then reentered and discovered evidence used to convict defendant of illegal firearm crime. *United States v. McMullin*, 576 F.3d 810 (8th Cir. 2009).

Consent to search computer for suspected computer virus did not include use of device to scan pornographic images on computer. *People v. Prinzing*, 907 N.E.2d 87 (Ill. App. 2009).

Consent to "look in car" did not include search of undercarriage and gas tank. *State v. Troxell*, 78 S.W. 3d 866 (Tenn. 2002).

Consent to examine computer to see if any "unauthorized access" by third parties had occurred did not give officers consent to look inside computer files for child pornography images. *State v. Bailey*, 989 A.2d 716 (Me. 2010).

In Fourth Amendment cases, standing is mainly based on the existence of a "reasonable expectation of privacy" in the place where a search or seizure occurred. Those with such an expectation have standing; those without do not. The definition of the "right or expectation of privacy" for these purposes has been developed over the years by the U.S. Supreme Court and other courts.

The Definition of the Expectation of Privacy

The Fourth Amendment protects the right of privacy of persons. The U.S. Supreme Court held in the case of *Katz v. United States* 88 S. Ct. 507 (1967) that:

> The Fourth Amendment protects people, not places. What a person knowingly exposes to the public, even in his own home or office, is not a subject of Fourth Amendment protection.... But what he seeks to preserve as private, may be constitutionally protected.

A reasonable expectation of privacy exists *only* if

- An individual actually expects privacy.
- His (or her) expectation is reasonable.

A police search is an intrusion into a right of privacy. The U.S. Supreme Court stated in *United States v. Jacobson,* 104 S. Ct. 1654 (1984), that "a search occurs when an expectation of privacy that society is prepared to consider reasonable is infringed." If the officer can show authority to make the search, the intrusion into privacy is lawful.

In *Mancusi v. DeForte* 392 U.S. 364 (1968), the U.S. Supreme Court held that employees have a reasonable expectation of privacy in the workplace. The *Katz* principle stated above means that anything knowingly exposed to fellow workers or supervisors is not protected. However, an employee is protected in areas of the workplace used for the employee's private purposes. In the 2005 case of *People v. Galvadon,* 103 P.3rd 923, the Colorado Supreme Court held that a night manager of a liquor store had a reasonable expectation of privacy in the store's back room, which he used for his work and which was not open to the public, even though the store owner used video cameras to monitor the back room. The court held that knowledge of the video cameras was not the kind of "knowing exposure" contemplated by *Katz.*

Persons renting hotel rooms, storage lockers, or rental vehicles can have a reasonable expectation of privacy in the rented areas or vehicles; the U.S. Supreme Court has held that the prohibition of the Fourth Amendment is not limited to permanent residences. *Stone v. California,* 376 U.S. 483 (1964) However, the expectation of privacy can terminate, as when the hotel check-out time passes without extension, *United States v. Lanier,* 636 F.3d 228 (6th Cir. 2011), or when a tenant is served with an eviction notice, *United States v. Curlin,* 638 F.3d 562 (4th Cir. 2011). Courts also hold that one does not have a reasonable expectation of privacy in another person's hotel room, even if that person is absent from the room. *United States v. Wells,* 739 F.3d 511 (10th Cir. 2014).

Persons who are overnight guests in another person's home have a reasonable expectation of privacy, *Minnesota v. Olson,* 495 U.S. 91 (1980), but those present for only a short time do not have a reasonable expectation of privacy. *Minnesota v. Carter,* 525 U.S. 83 (1998).

It is generally held that persons who rent hotel rooms or storage lockers using an alias or under the name on a stolen credit card have no expectation of privacy in the room or storage locker; *United States v. Johnson*, 584 F.3d 995 (10th Cir. 2009). The same is true for drivers of a rental car not authorized in the rental agreement, even if driving with the permission of the person who rented the car. *United States v. Kennedy*, 638 F.3d 159 (3d Cir. 2011).

While owners of a vehicle have a reasonable expectation of privacy in the vehicle, passengers in the vehicle do not; *Rakas v. Illinois*, 439 U.S. 128 (1978). There is no reasonable expectation of privacy even if the passenger is in the vehicle for an extended road trip, courts have held. *United States v. Symonevich*, 688 F.3d 12 (1st Cir. 2012) (One must distinguish for Fourth Amendment purposes between a search of a vehicle in which a passenger is present, and a seizure of that passenger after a vehicle stop. See *Arizona v. Johnson*, discussed in Chapter 14.)

EVIDENCE OBTAINED FROM ABANDONED PROPERTY WILL NOT BE SUPPRESSED

abandoned property
Property that a person has deserted or thrown away and thereby disclaims interest in it; may be used as evidence against the former owner.

If by conduct or words the defendant shows that he or she has relinquished the expectation of privacy in property, the object may be used as evidence. This legal concept of **abandoned property** was defined in the 1989 case of *United States v. Thomas*[17] as follows:

> The test for abandonment in the search and seizure context is distinct from the property notion of abandonment: it is possible for a person to retain a property interest in an item, but nonetheless to relinquish his or her reasonable expectation of privacy in the object.

The following sections present different forms of abandonment.

Throwaway as a Form of Abandonment

Persons who flee the police with illegal drugs or other contraband on their person often throw away what can be very incriminating evidence. If the throwaway is a voluntary abandonment of the object, courts allow the object to be used as evidence against the person. But if the throwaway is the direct or indirect product of an illegal police stop or other improper police conduct, courts generally forbid the use of the throwaway item as evidence. The following U.S. Supreme Court cases are examples of this kind of abandonment:

California v. Hodari

United States Supreme Court, 499 U.S. 621, 111 S. Ct. 1547 (1991)

Police officers on patrol in an unmarked police car observed four or five youths huddled around a car parked at a curb. All the young men began to run at the approach of the officers' car, so one of the officers chased them on foot. The officer caught up with Hodari and tackled him. Just before he was tackled, Hodari threw to the ground what turned out to be crack cocaine. In holding that the cocaine could be used as evidence against Hodari, the Supreme Court held that:

> [A]ssuming that Pertoso's [policeman] pursuit in the present case constituted a "show of authority" enjoining Hodari to halt, since Hodari did not comply with that injunction he was not seized until he was tackled. The cocaine abandoned while he was running was in this case not the fruit of a seizure, and his motion to exclude evidence of it was properly denied.

Michigan v. Chesternut United States Supreme Court, 486 U.S. 567, 108 S. Ct. 1975 (1988)	Chesternut was standing on a street corner in Detroit, and when he saw a police car approaching the corner, he began to run. The police, on routine patrol, followed Chesternut in their car "to see where he was going." As he ran, Chesternut began throwing objects away. A police officer picked up the packets and found they contained pills. Based on the officer's experience as a paramedic, he believed that the pills contained codeine. Chesternut was arrested, and in the search incident to the arrest, heroin and a hypodermic needle were found. The Supreme Court held that the defendant "was not unlawfully seized during the initial police pursuit" and affirmed the use of the pills, heroin, and needle as evidence, holding that:

> [T]he police conduct here—a brief acceleration to catch up with respondent, followed by a short drive alongside him—was not "so intimidating" that respondent could reasonably have believed that he was not free to disregard the police presence and go about his business. The police therefore were not required to have "a particularized and objective basis for suspecting [respondent] of criminal activity," in order to pursue him.[18]

Denial of Ownership as a Form of Abandonment

Persons who deny ownership of property to a law enforcement officer relinquish their right of privacy in the property and do not later have standing to challenge the use of evidence obtained from the property. The following are a few of the hundreds of denial cases that have come before criminal courts in recent years:

- Travelers' denial of ownership of luggage at airports. Because of their denials, the defendants could not later challenge searches of their luggage by law officers. Illegal drugs and other contraband found in the luggage were used as evidence against the defendants.[19]
- Train passenger's denial of a garment bag under his feet.[20]
- Denial of luggage in the trunk of the car.[21]
- Denial of a satchel that the defendant hid after a car accident.[22]
- Denial of ownership of an apartment.[23]

Abandoned Real Estate

If a real estate structure has been abandoned by its owners or other users, those persons can have no reasonable expectation of privacy in the structure. Unlike other abandoned property, where the fact that it is discarded is proof of abandonment, real estate structures are not similarly discarded. Indeed, for purposes of real estate law, real estate cannot ever be abandoned in the literal sense.

Courts have found that real estate can be abandoned for Fourth Amendment purposes. To prove a structure has been abandoned, police must produce evidence that would lead a reasonable person to believe the structure has been abandoned. For example, in *United States v. Harrison*, 689 F.3d 301 (3rd Cir. 2012), *cert. denied* 133 S. Ct. 1616 (2013), police entered a building they believed to be abandoned, because they found a stolen motorcycle outside the building. In fact the building had been rented to the defendant, whom police discovered was in possession of illegal drugs. At his trial the defendant moved to suppress the evidence acquired when police entered the building, claiming they had no probable cause to enter the building without a search warrant. The trial court denied the motion and on appeal the Court of Appeals affirmed the decision. The court said that while the deteriorated condition of a building is not enough by itself to support the reasonable inference it has been abandoned, here other evidence of abandonment existed. The building had been boarded up for months, and police had previously entered the house and observed that it was empty, had no bathroom or running water, and appeared essentially uninhabitable. This was enough, the court said, to make the belief that the property was abandoned reasonable.[24]

Evidence Obtained from Garbage or Trash

The owners of trash receptacles kept in a home or a garage have Fourth Amendment constitutional protection while the receptacles are located in such places. Evidence obtained from these places without valid consent or a search warrant is suppressed and may not be used, even if it is proven that the trash was abandoned.

In *California v. Greenwood*[25] police asked the regular trash collector to turn trash collected at the curb in front of the Greenwood home over to them without commingling it with trash from other homes. Inspection of the Greenwood trash revealed evidence of drugs, which was used to obtain a search warrant of the Greenwood home. Greenwood was then charged and convicted of felony drug use. In affirming the drug convictions, the U.S. Supreme Court held that the defendants "could have no reasonable expectation of privacy in ... the plastic garbage bags left on or at the side of the public street."[26]

A few state courts, however, impose stricter standards, including New Jersey, Washington, and Vermont.[27] In the 2005 case of *Litchfield v. State*,[28] the Indiana Supreme Court held that the Indiana Constitution requires police to have an "articulable individualized suspicion" that a crime occurred, similar to that required for a *Terry* stop (see Chapter 14), before trash left outside a defendant's home for regular pickup can be searched.

Abandoned Motor Vehicles

Abandoned and stolen vehicles are a problem in every American city and state. Many states have statutes that define when a vehicle is legally abandoned. For example, Section 342.40(i) of the Wisconsin Statutes provides that if a vehicle is left unattended on a public highway or on private or public property "under such circumstances as to cause the vehicle to reasonably appear to have been abandoned" for more than 48 hours, "the vehicle is deemed abandoned and constitutes a public nuisance."

A similar provision in the North Dakota Highway Patrol Police Manual was invoked in the case of *United States v. Duong*.[29] In that case the defendant's rental car left a highway and overturned in the highway ditch. A state patrol officer discovered the car, and attempted without success to identify and locate the owner. The officer called for a tow truck, treating the vehicle as abandoned under the Police Manual, because the owner could not be located and the vehicle "constituted a hazard." The officer then conducted an inventory search of the vehicle, finding hundreds of pounds of marijuana. At the trial of the defendants for illegal drug crimes the court refused to suppress the evidence, holding that the vehicle was abandoned, and that as a result the person listed as the driver in the vehicle rental agreement had no reasonable expectation of privacy in the vehicle.

EVIDENCE DISCOVERED IN OPEN FIELDS WILL NOT BE SUPPRESSED

curtilage The area close to a home where persons have a right of privacy.

Curtilage is that area close to a home where persons assert a right of privacy. The protection of the Fourth Amendment extends to the home and to the curtilage. The U.S. Supreme Court defined *curtilage* as follows in 1984:[30]

> At common law, the curtilage is the area to which extends the intimate activity associated with the "sanctity of a man's home and the privacies of life," *Boyd v. United States,* 116 U.S. 616, 630, 6 S. Ct. 524, 532, 29 L.Ed. 746 (1886), and therefore has been considered part of the home itself for Fourth Amendment purposes. Thus, courts have extended Fourth Amendment protection to the curtilage; and they have defined the curtilage, as did the common law, by reference to the factors that determine whether an individual reasonably may expect that an area immediately adjacent to the home will remain private.

In 1987 in *United States v. Dunn,*[31] the U.S. Supreme Court held that curtilage questions should be resolved with particular reference to four factors:

1. The proximity to the home of the area claimed to be curtilage.
2. Whether the area is included within an enclosure surrounding the home.
3. The nature of the uses to which the area is put.
4. The steps taken by the resident to protect the area from observation by people passing by.

There is a high degree of privacy in the curtilage, or backyard, of a one-family dwelling that is fenced in so as to be protected from observation by people passing. The degree of privacy is much lower, however, in the curtilage of a fifty-unit apartment building because all occupants of the building can use the common area available to them. In the 2011 case of *United States v. Maestas*[32] the court held that a guest staying in a triplex apartment building had no expectation of privacy in an enclosed garbage storage area adjacent to the apartment building. The court said that even if the guest had an expectation of privacy in the apartment itself, that expectation did not carry over to the storage area because all the other tenants in the building used the storage area, and could thus view the garbage stored there. The defendant's conviction for drug and illegal weapons charges was affirmed.

One frequent question raised about the extent of the curtilage involves driveways and walkways on the edge of a defendant's property. The following case is an example of a court applying the four factors identified by the Supreme Court, and discussed above, to such situations (see also Figure 10.1):

United States v. French

Seventh Circuit Court of Appeals, 291 F.3d 945 (2002)

The defendant was charged with various counts of attempting to manufacture methamphetamine and possession of a firearm in furtherance of a drug offense, based on evidence obtained by officers after a search of the defendant's property. The search was conducted under a search warrant obtained after a probation officer observed evidence of suspected illegal drug manufacture while standing on a walkway located on the defendant's property. The defendant moved to suppress the evidence obtained in the search on the theory that the warrant was itself based on evidence gained by the probation officer's unlawful entry onto the curtilage of the property. The trial court held that the curtilage did not extend to that part of the walkway upon which the officer was standing when he observed the illegal activity, and it refused to suppress the evidence seized. The defendant then pled guilty to one count of illegal drug manufacture and one count of illegal firearm possession, subject to appellate review of the curtilage claim.

On appeal, the U.S. Court of Appeals affirmed the conviction. It applied the four factors from *Dunn*[33] and concluded that the walkway was not in the curtilage. It concluded that although the spot where the officer was standing when he observed the illegal activity was within 20 feet of the defendant's residence, that fact alone did not make the walkway part of the curtilage. More significant, the court found, were the facts that no attempt was made to erect an enclosure around the walkway or the area near it, that no evidence of "intimate use" of the area by the defendant existed, that no "keep out" or "no trespassing" signs had been posted, and that clutter and debris in the area indicated the public was free to and often did use the walkway for various purposes. These facts, the court concluded, indicated that the defendant did not use the property for personal, private uses, and the surrounding area was not part of the curtilage. The defendant's conviction was affirmed.

Should Fourth Amendment protection extend beyond the curtilage to open fields? The U.S. Supreme Court in the case of *Hester v. United States*[34] refused to extend the Fourth Amendment to sights seen in open fields. In the *Hester* case, government agents were trespassing on the defendant's land when they observed the defendant running away from them and throwing contraband to the ground in open fields. In holding that the contraband could be used as evidence to obtain a conviction against the defendant, the U.S. Supreme Court ruled:

> The special protection accorded by the Fourth Amendment to the people in their "persons, houses, papers and effects," is not extended to the open fields. The distinction between the latter and the house is as old as the common law.[35]

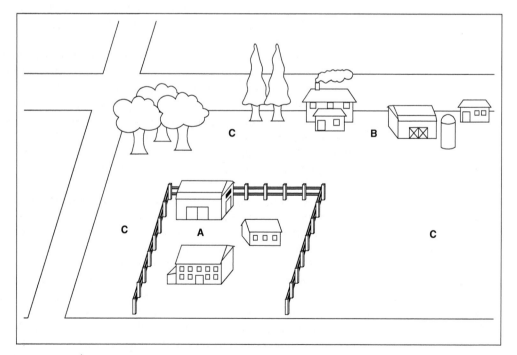

Figure 10.1 | Persons Living in Single-Family Homes Have a Greater Expectation of Privacy in their Curtilage (A and B) than do those Living in a Large Apartment Building. Owners or Other Persons have no Privacy Rights in Open Fields (C).

PROCEDURES & PROCESSES

The Plain View or Open View Doctrine[a]

If a law enforcement officer is where he or she has a right to be and sees contraband or evidence of a crime in plain view, the evidence may be seized and will be admissible at a trial.

plain view or **open view doctrine** The principle that if a law officer is where he or she has a right to be and sees evidence or contraband in plain view, then the evidence may be seized and used in a criminal trial.

The **plain view** or **open view doctrine** was stated as follows in the case of *Texas v. Brown* [103 S. Ct. 1535 (1983)]:

First, the police officer must lawfully make an "initial intrusion" or otherwise properly be in a position from which he can view a particular area.

Second, the officer must discover incriminating evidence "inadvertently," which is to say, he may not "know in advance the location of …evidence and intend to seize it," relying on the plain-view doctrine only as a pretext.

Finally, it must be "immediately apparent" to the police that the items they observe may be evidence of a crime, contraband, or otherwise subject to seizure.

Plain View and the Five Human Senses

Most plain view cases occur when an officer, who is where he or she has a right to be, sees contraband or evidence of a crime. However, plain view is not limited to visual observations. Any of the five human senses may provide information that makes it "immediately apparent" to the police that the object is evidence of a crime.

- *Plain smell:* In 1948, the U.S. Supreme Court in *Johnson v. United States* (333 U.S. 10, 13, 68 S. Ct. 367, 368) held that odors may be "found to be evidence of the most persuasive character." However, odor alone has been found to be not enough to support a search without a warrant. For example, in *People v. Michigan* [564 N.W.2d 24 (1997)], the Michigan Supreme Court held that evidence seized from an automobile after a police officer smelled marijuana in the vehicle was inadmissible. The court stated that smell differed from "plain view" and "plain touch" because odor alone does not both identify the illegal contraband and show its location, as plain view and plain touch do.
- *Plain hearing:* The "naked ear" or plain hearing rule applies to sounds that are heard without the use of any electronic or mechanical devices.[b]
- *Plain touch:* If police officers have made a lawful *Terry* stop (see Chapter 14) because a suspect has exhibited suspicious behavior, they may "pat down" the suspect to determine whether the suspect is armed. The purpose of the pat-down is not to search the suspect but to protect the officers. In *Minnesota v. Dickerson* [508 U.S. 366 (1993)] (also discussed in Chapter 14), the U.S. Supreme Court held that if the officers doing the pat-down discover an article whose nature is "immediately apparent from its tactile impression," the officers may seize the article without a search warrant. In *Dickerson* the officer conducting the pat-down felt a small object in the suspect's pocket and, by manipulating the object, concluded that it was crack cocaine. The Court held that the seizure violated the Fourth Amendment and the drugs were inadmissible because their identity as contraband was discernible only after the pat-down had already determined that the suspect was not

armed. If the initial pat-down had made the drug's identity "immediately apparent," the seizure would have been lawful, the Court held.

• *Plain taste:* The sense of taste is rarely used to provide information to a law enforcement officer. No reported decisions can be found on this point.

[a]See the U.S. Supreme Court case of *Coolidge v. New Hampshire* 91 S. Ct. 2022 (1971), where one justice stated that the terms *plain view* and *open view* differ. This distinction, however, has not been followed. *Plain view* is now the term used broadly without any distinction from *open view*.

[b]See *United States v. Agapito*, 620 F.2d 324 (2d Cir. 1980); *United States v. Mankani*, 738 F.2d 538 (2d Cir. 1984); *United States v. Lopez*, 475 F.2d 537 (7th Cir. 1973); and *United States v. Fisch*, 474 F.2d 1071 (9th Cir. 1973)].

open field An unoccupied or undeveloped area outside of the curtilage; objects found there may be used as evidence.

In *Oliver v. United States,*[36] the Supreme Court defined "open fields":

Open fields include any unoccupied or undeveloped area outside of the curtilage. An open field need be neither "open" nor a "field" as those terms are used in common speech.

An **open field** can consist of woods, swamps, meadows, or fields of farm crops.

EVIDENCE DISCOVERED IN GOOD FAITH OR BY HONEST MISTAKE WILL NOT BE SUPPRESSED

The Good Faith Exception

In the 1984 U.S. Supreme Court case of *United States v. Leon,*[37] police officers executed a search warrant that they believed to be valid but was defective. The evidence obtained under the defective warrant was ruled to be admissible because the police believed in good faith that the search warrant was valid. In holding that the evidence could be used, the Court held that "the exclusionary rule is designed to deter police misconduct rather than punish the errors of judges and magistrates."

good faith exception
The exception that makes admissible evidence that is obtained under a search warrant that has a technical error unknown to the law officers executing the warrant.

The *Leon* **good faith exception** permits the use of evidence obtained through the use of a search warrant containing a technical error that does not violate a fundamental constitutional right of a suspect.[38] However, the warrant and affidavits given to obtain it must be sufficient so that an "objectively reasonable" officer would rely on the warrant that was issued. The *Laughton* case is an example of a search warrant that did not satisfy this requirement.

State v. Laughton

Sixth Circuit Court of Appeals, 409 F.3d 744 (2005)

Following a tip from a confidential informant, police officers staked out and observed the informant making "controlled" purchases of illegal drugs from the defendant at his home. Based on these purchases, one of the officers prepared an affidavit seeking a search warrant for the defendant's residence. The warrant was issued even though the affidavit submitted did not state all the facts of the controlled purchases as they actually occurred and were known to the officer preparing the affidavit. As a result, the search warrant was a "bare bones" warrant and did not satisfy the probable cause requirement. The police argued that the good faith exception of *Leon* was applicable and justified the search because the officer who obtained the warrant had actual knowledge that probable cause existed, even though the affidavit and the warrant did not recite this knowledge.

The U.S. Court of Appeals held the good faith exception inapplicable. It stated that even though the officer who obtained the warrant possessed enough knowledge to support probable cause, neither the warrant nor the affidavit submitted to obtain it contained sufficient information to lead an "objectively reasonable" officer to believe the search was proper. If the personal knowledge of the officer who obtained the search warrant were relevant, the court said, every suppression hearing on a search warrant would require an inquiry into what the officer knew and when he knew it. This kind of subjectivity, the court reasoned, had consistently been rejected by the Supreme Court.

One area where courts disagree on the application of the good faith doctrine is illustrated by the case of *United States v. McClain.*[39] In that case, police conducted a warrantless search of premises that appeared to be vacant and discovered a marijuana growing operation in the basement. They informed drug investigators, who conducted surveillance of the house and connected the defendant to the house. Using the information given them by the officers who first entered the house, the drug investigators obtained a warrant to search the house, and found evidence used to charge the defendant with illegal drug crimes.

The defendant moved to suppress the evidence, contending that the initial entry into the house was a violation of the Fourth Amendment because the officers lacked probable cause to enter under the "exigent circumstances" exception to the warrant requirement. The trial court suppressed the evidence, but on appeal the court of appeals held that the good faith exception from *Leon* applied, even though in this case the warrant was not technically invalid because of a magistrate mistake, as was the case in *Leon,* but was itself the "fruit of the poisonous tree." The court agreed that the initial search was invalid but not so unreasonable that the officers who obtained the search warrant based on that illegal entry should clearly have known it was invalid. As a result, the court concluded that those officers could objectively and reasonably have believed the search warrant was valid, thus invoking the good faith exception. The court noted that other circuits had reached the opposite result.[40]

Not all states have adopted a good faith exception that permits the use of evidence because of a mistake by a judge, prosecutor, police dispatcher, or computer. For example, in the 2014 case of *Commonwealth v. Johnson*[41] the Pennsylvania Supreme Court held that the federal "good faith" exception to the exclusionary rule was not applicable under the Pennsylvania constitution to arrests made under an expired arrest warrant, or searches conducted under a defective search warrant.

Good Faith and Changes in the Law

The good faith exception to the exclusionary rule is based in part on the notion that if police officers act in good faith to make an arrest or conduct a search, the fact that a search or arrest warrant is technically defective should not result in exclusion of evidence found in the arrest or search. The rule exists to deter wrongful police conduct, but there is little to deter if the police are acting in good faith.

Police compliance with Fourth Amendment requirements is perhaps more difficult and complex than any other area of the criminal law. The difficulty is exacerbated by court decisions, mainly those of the U.S. Supreme Court, that change the rules under which the police operate. Actions thought to be in compliance with the

LEGAL CASES

Invalid Searches or Arrests to Which the "Good Faith" Exception has been Applied

In *United States v. Leon*, discussed above, the Supreme Court adopted the "good faith" exception to the exclusionary rule because the police officers in that case were not responsible for the mistake that made a search warrant invalid. The mistake was made by a judicial officer; the Supreme Court said the Fourth Amendment was not aimed at judicial officers, and that suppression of evidence was not likely to have any deterrent effect. Since the purpose of the exclusionary rule was to deter misconduct by law enforcement officers, the Supreme Court held that purpose was not present when the police conduct was not the reason a search or seizure violated the Fourth Amendment. Since *Leon*, the Supreme Court has gradually expanded the kind of errors to which the "good faith" exception applies:

- *Illinois v. Krull*, 480 U.S. 340, 350 (1987); Exception applied where police "objectively" reasonably relied on a state statute that authorized a warrantless search, but was subsequently found to violate the Fourth Amendment. Like *Leon*, the problem was not misconduct by the police officers, but error by the legislature: "Penalizing the officer for the (legislature's) error, rather than his own, cannot logically contribute to the deterrence of Fourth Amendment violations."
- *Arizona v. Evans*, 514 U.S. 1, 14 (1995); Exception applied where police relied on incorrect information on an arrest warrant in a database maintained by a judicial officer. "Finally, and most important, there is no basis for believing that application of the exclusionary rule in these circumstances will have a significant effect on court employees responsible for informing the police a warrant has been quashed."
- *Herring v. United States*, 555 U.S. 135, 147 (2009); Exception applied when police officer relied on incorrect information on an arrest warrant in a database maintained by law enforcement employees. "...[w]e conclude that when police mistakes are the result of negligence... rather than systemic error or reckless disregard of constitutional requirements, any marginal deterrence does not 'pay its way.'"

Davis v. United States, 131 S. Ct. 2419, 2428–29 (2011); Exception applied where police conducted search of automobile after arrest of the driver in accordance with what was at that time "binding judicial precedent" (see the discussion of *Arizona v. Gant* in Chapter 14). "The officers who conducted the search did not violate Davis's Fourth Amendment rights deliberately, recklessly, or with gross negligence.... The police acted in strict compliance with binding precedent, and their behavior was not wrongful. Unless the exclusionary rule is to become a strict-liability regime, it can have no application in this case."

Fourth Amendment suddenly are in violation of that Amendment. The good faith exception can be used to solve this dilemma for the police, as the two following cases illustrate:

- *United States v. Pineda-Moreno*, 688 F.3d 1087 (9th Cir. 2012). Prior to the U.S. Supreme Court's decision in *United States v. Jones* (discussed in Chapter 15 of this book), which held that attaching a GPS tracking device to a vehicle was a search, many courts held the opposite. Based on such a holding in the Ninth Circuit, federal agents without a search warrant attached a GPS tracking device to a suspect's vehicle; the device then connected the suspect to a marijuana field. At his trial on illegal drugs charges, the defendant moved to suppress the evidence obtained from the GPS tracking device, but the trial court refused to do so and the defendant was convicted. During the appeal process the U.S. Supreme Court decided *Jones*, which made the warrantless use of the GPS tracking device invalid. The Ninth Circuit Court nonetheless refused to apply the exclusionary rule to exclude the evidence obtained by the federal agents, since their actions were at the time based on their good faith belief that attaching a GPS tracking device was not a search covered by the Fourth Amendment.

- Other courts have reached the opposite result, holding the good faith exception inapplicable to warrantless use of GPS tracking devices before *Jones* was decided: *See United States v. Katzin*, 732 F.3d 187 (3rd Cir. 2013); however, the Third Circuit granted *en banc* review of that decision in December of 2013. 2013 WL 7033666 (3rd Cir. 2013).

- *State v. Scull*, 843 N.W.2d 859 (Wis. App. 2014). Based on an "alert" at a suspect's house by a drug-sniffing police dog, police obtained a search warrant to search the house, where they discovered illegal drugs. At his trial the defendant moved to suppress the evidence, arguing the dog sniff lacked probable cause. The motion was denied, and the defendant was convicted. During the appeal process the U.S. Supreme Court decided *Florida v. Jardines* (discussed in Chapter 15 of this book), which held that a dog sniff at a private residence was a search. The Wisconsin Court of Appeals affirmed the trial court's decision refusing to exclude the evidence obtained by the search warrant, which after *Jardines* was invalid. The court said the officers and magistrate that issued the warrant did so in the good faith belief that dog sniffs were not searches under the Fourth Amendment.

The Honest Mistake Rule

After an armed robbery, California police had probable cause to arrest an individual named Hill for the robbery. They obtained Hill's home address and his description. A man who "exactly fit [Hill's] description" answered the door to Hill's home but denied that he was Hill. Nevertheless, the police arrested the man, believing that he was Hill. In the search incident to the arrest of the man, the police found and seized evidence that incriminated Hill. The police later became aware that they had arrested the wrong man. They released the man and within a short time arrested Hill.

Because probable cause existed to arrest the man in Hill's home, the U.S. Supreme Court held in the 1971 case of *Hill v. California*[42] that the "arrest (of the wrong man) and subsequent search were reasonable and valid under the Fourth Amendment" and therefore the evidence could be used in the trial and conviction of Hill.

In the 1987 U.S. Supreme Court case of *Maryland v. Garrison*,[43] a search warrant was issued to search a third-floor apartment. The police reasonably believed that only one apartment was on the third floor of the building and did not become aware of the second apartment, which belonged to Garrison, until after they found heroin, cash, and drug paraphernalia there. In holding that the evidence could be used to convict Garrison of drug violations, the Supreme Court pointed out that the Court has "recognized the need to allow some latitude for honest mistakes that are made by officers in the dangerous and difficult process of making arrests and executing search warrants." The result in *Garrison* would likely have been different had the police realized during their search that the dwelling contained a second apartment. The *Ritter* case illustrates this limitation on the **honest mistake rule**.

honest mistake rule
The U.S. Supreme Court's ruling that courts must "allow some latitude for honest mistakes that are made by officers in the dangerous and difficult process of making arrests and executing search warrants."

United States v. Ritter

Third Circuit Court of
Appeals, 416 F.3d 256
(3rd Cir. 2005)

Based on aerial photographs of the defendants' property as well as on an informant's statements, federal officers obtained a search warrant to search that property. The warrant and supporting affidavits identified only one address as the property to be searched. When officers arrived at the property and entered a "common area" located on the property, they realized that more than one dwelling was located on the property shown in the aerial photographs and identified by the informant. The defendants resided in only one of the dwellings. The police searched all the buildings on the property and found illegal drugs. The defendants moved to suppress the evidence seized in the search, contending that the inaccurate description of the property as containing only one property rendered the search warrant invalid.

On appeal, the court of appeals held that the search warrant was not rendered invalid by the mistake and that any evidence found by the officers in the common area was admissible. After the officers discovered that more than one dwelling was located on the property, however, they were required to stop the search. The honest mistake rule did not apply to any evidence seized after the officers knew of the mistake, the court held. Because it was not clear when the illegal drugs were found, the case was remanded for a determination of this question.

Mistake of Law   The honest mistake cases discussed above involved mistakes of fact made by police officers. Does the honest mistake rule apply to mistakes of law? In *Heien v. North Carolina*, 737 S.E. 2d 351 (N.C. 2012), the court said it did. There, an officer stopped a car with one brake light working; the officer believed North Carolina law required two working brake lights, and that as a result the driver of the car was violating that law. A search subsequent to the stop uncovered illegal drugs, and the driver was convicted of various drug offenses. On appeal the defendant contended all the drug evidence should be suppressed because the initial traffic stop violated the Fourth Amendment because the police officer did not have individualized suspicion the defendant was breaking the law. In fact, North Carolina law requires only one working brake light. The North Carolina Supreme Court held that the honest mistake of law by the officer satisfied the requirement of individualized suspicion, because the officer reasonably believed the defendant was breaking the traffic laws. On December 15, 2014, the U.S. Supreme Court agreed, holding that individualized suspicion for a traffic stop satisfies the Fourth Amendment even if the officer is mistaken about the law the officer believes was violated, so long as the mistake was reasonable. Here, the Court said, the North Carolina "stop lamp" law could easily be misunderstood by a reasonable police officer charged with its enforcement.

OTHER AREAS WHERE THE EXCLUSIONARY RULE DOES NOT APPLY

Source of Evidence or Use of Evidence	Court Rulings
Common carriers (airlines, parcel services, truckers, railroads, and so on)	"Common carriers have a common-law right to inspect packages they accept for shipment, based on their duty to restrain from carrying contraband."[44]
U.S. Customs Service	"The U.S. Government has the undoubted right to inspect all incoming goods at a port of entry it would be impossible for customs officers to inspect every package."[45] [but like the common carriers]

Source of Evidence or Use of Evidence	Court Rulings
Grand jury proceedings	"… [I]t is unrealistic to assume that application of the rule of grand jury proceedings would significantly further [the] goal of deterrence of police misconduct. The grand jury's investigative power must be broad if its public responsibility is adequately to be discharged."[46]
Probation or parole revocation	"…[T]he overwhelming number of reported hearings cases have held that the Fourth Amendment's 'exclusionary rule' was not applicable under the circumstances to probation revocation proceedings or qualitatively comparable proceedings to revoke parole. The only reservation expressed by several courts in denying application of the 'exclusionary rule' to a revocation proceeding might occur in situations where police harassment of probationers is demonstrated."[47] In 1998 the U.S. Supreme Court followed the ruling of a state court in a parole revocation case.[48]
Searches by probation or parole officers	"[A] probation agent who reasonably believes that a probationer is violating the terms of probation may conduct a warrantless search of a probationer's residence. A probation agent has a duty to see that a probationer is complying with the terms of his probation."[49] In 1987 the U.S. Supreme Court affirmed the conviction of a probationer, Griffin, for possession of a handgun discovered by a warrantless search of Griffin's home. The Court held that the "search of Griffin's home satisfied the demands of the Fourth Amendment because it was carried out pursuant to a regulation that itself satisfies the Fourth Amendment reasonableness requirement."[50] The U.S. Supreme Court affirmed another probation search in 2001 in *United States v. Knights*.[51] Knights was on probation and had signed a consent to search agreement to obtain the benefits of probation. Detectives had reasonable suspicion that Knights had started an arson fire. Without a search warrant, the detectives searched Knights' apartment, relying on the probation consent to search. The U.S. Supreme Court affirmed the use of the evidence obtained.
Eyewitness testimony of witness to robbery	Despite a mistake by police in showing a picture to the witness, the U.S. Supreme Court affirmed the use of in-court witness.[52]
Evidence obtained in foreign countries by foreign officials	Such evidence is admissible unless the product of inhumane or outrages means, or if there was substantial cooperation by American officials.[53]

Source of Evidence or Use of Evidence	Court Rulings
Evidence obtained during "community caretaking" functions,[54] military discharge proceedings, child protection proceedings, civil tax and civil deportation proceedings, and sentencing proceedings after a criminal conviction.	Held exclusionary rule not applicable in these proceedings.

SUMMARY

1. **Define *standing* for Fourth Amendment purposes.**
   - Only persons who have a reasonable expectation of privacy in a person, a dwelling, a vehicle, a storage area, container, or other area or article subjected to a search or seizure by government officers may claim a Fourth Amendment violation.

2. **Explain the role of "consent" in searches of persons or residences.**
   - Consent to a search of a person must be voluntarily given by that person. Consent to search a dwelling, if voluntary, may be given by any person who inhabits the dwelling, unless a co-inhabitant objects to the search to the police. Consent may be limited in scope and time, and may be revoked.

3. **State when property is abandoned for Fourth Amendment purposes.**
   - Property is abandoned when the owner of the property relinquishes possession of the property with no intent to reclaim it, or disclaims any ownership interest in the property. For some kinds of property, such as vehicles on highways, a vehicle is deemed abandoned when it is left unattended for a period of time (often 48 hours) under circumstances where it constitutes a hazard to other motorists.

4. **List the factors to be considered when the good faith test from *Leon* is applied to a search warrant or an arrest.**
   - A clerical mistake in a search warrant does not make a search invalid if the officers executing the warrant had a good faith belief in the accuracy of the warrant. An arrest based on incorrect information in an arrest-warrant database does not violate the Fourth Amendment if the officers had good faith belief in the validity of the arrest warrant. A search after arrest conducted according the then-binding judicial precedent is made in good faith and does not violate the Fourth Amendment.

5. **Distinguish "good faith" from "honest mistake."**
   - If an honest mistake about the area to be searched is made by officers executing a valid search warrant, or if officers make an honest mistake executing a valid arrest warrant, evidence discovered as a result of the honest mistake is not subject to the exclusionary rule.

CROSS-REFERENCES TO OTHER CHAPTERS

The exclusionary rule is most often encountered where alleged violations of the Fourth Amendment have occurred, though it also applies in other circumstances. The following chapters discuss aspects of the exclusionary rule in a variety of settings where police officers improperly or illegally:

- Obtain physical and other evidence (Chapter 14)
- Obtain confessions and statements to be used as evidence (Chapter 12)
- Obtain evidence by use of search warrants, wiretapping, or trained dogs (Chapter 15)
- Obtain identification evidence (Chapter 13)

- Obtain fingerprints and DNA evidence (Chapters 16 and 18)
- Obtain evidence from the crime scene (Chapter 16)

- Obtain scientific evidence (Chapter 18)
- Obtain videotapes, photographs, documents, or writings for use as evidence (Chapter 17)

KEY TERMS

abandoned property, 244

curtilage, 247

good faith exception, 250

honest mistake rule, 253

open field, 250

plain view or open view doctrine, 249

private search, 238

standing, 242

KEY CASES

Bourdeau v. McDowell, 256 U.S. 465 (1921): Fourth Amendment does not apply to private searches.

Davis v. United States, 131 S. Ct. 2419 (2011): "Good faith" exception applies where police conduct search in reliance on existing binding precedent.

Herring v. United States, 555 U.S. 135 (2009): Isolated, non-recurring negligence by police maintaining warrant database lacks culpability for applying exclusionary rule.

Fernandez v. California, 134 S. Ct. 1126 (2014): Objection by co-resident cancels consent by the other resident only if objecting resident is present when the other resident grants consent to enter the shared premises.

Georgia v. Randolph, 547 U.S. 103 (2006): Objection to search by co-inhabitant makes search non-consensual, even though the other inhabitant gave consent to search.

Maryland v. Garrison, 480 U.S. 79 (1987): Evidence obtained under "honest mistake" by police will not be excluded.

Oliver v. United States, 466 U.S. 170 (1984): A legitimate expectation of privacy extends to the curtilage of a residence.

Rakus v. Illinois, 439 U.S. 128 (1978): Only persons with a legitimate expectation of privacy may object to an unlawful search.

Stone v. California, 376 U.S. 483 (1984): A person's expectation of privacy is not limited to permanent residences, but includes rental homes and automobiles.

Texas v. Brown, 460 U.S. 730 (1983): Objects in plain view of police may lawfully be seized.

United States v. Dayton, 536 U.S. 194 (2002): Voluntary consent to search given by a person lawfully inhabiting a house or apartment does not violate the Fourth Amendment.

United States v. Janis, 428 U.S. 433 (1978): The Fourth Amendment exclusionary rule does not apply in civil cases.

United States v. Leon, 468 U.S. 897 (1984): Evidence obtained in "good faith" reliance on search warrant by police officers will not be excluded.

PROBLEMS

1. How does the "plain view" doctrine apply to computer searches? If law enforcement officers have a valid warrant to search a computer for evidence of a specific crime, when, if ever, do other computer files come under their "plain view"? See *United States v. Stabile*, 633 F.3d 219 (3rd Cir. 2011).

2. Consent searches are lawful; what limits are placed on how the police obtain that consent? If consent must be voluntary, may the police use

trickery or deception to obtain that consent? *United States v. Harrison*, 639 F.3d 1273 (10th Cir. 2011).

3. Private searches are not subject to the exclusionary rule in part because no government agents are involved with the search. What happens when government employees conduct searches for personal reasons, but find evidence of crimes, which they then turn over to law

enforcement officers? See *United States v. Inman*, 558 F.3d 742 (8th Cir. 2009).

4. Consider the issues presented by the following fact situation. A person regularly spent time at his girlfriend's apartment, often staying for weekends. He left a box with the girlfriend, telling her not to "mess with" the box. Based on information from another person, police came to the girlfriend's apartment and asked her to give them the box, which she did. The police searched the box, and found evidence used to convict the owner of fraud crimes. (A) Was the search of the box lawful? Did it violate the Fourth Amendment? (B) Would it change your answer if the girlfriend, notwithstanding the owner's instructions to not "mess with" the box, looked inside the box? Why or why not? (C) Does it matter if the girlfriend told the police officers to whom she gave the box that she had already looked at the contents? See *United States v. Oliver*, 630 F.3d 397 (5th Cir. 2011).

CASE ANALYSIS

Read Appendix B, Finding and Analyzing Cases (p. 499). With these guidelines in mind, please continue with the Case Analysis selections for Chapter 10.

1. Do you have a "reasonable expectation of privacy" in the text messages you send from your cell phone? As we will see later in this book, the U.S. Supreme Court held in *Riley v. California*, 134 S. Ct. 2473 (2014), that police could not make a warrantless search of an arrested person's cell phone. But what about someone else's cell phone? Are the text messages sent by you and stored there protected by the Fourth Amendment? In *State v. Patino*, 93 A.3d 40 (R.I. 2014), a defendant was charged with first-degree murder of his girlfriend's child, based on text messages found on the girlfriend's cell phone. The defendant moved to suppress the text messages, claiming they were "seized" in violation of his Fourth Amendment rights. Should his motion be granted or denied? Why?

2. We now know police may not, without a search warrant, attach a GPS tracking device to our vehicles to follow us as we drive the vehicle. Can they follow us by "pinging" our cell phone, and use the "pings" to follow us from one cell tower to another? In *United States v. Skinner*, 690 F.3d 772 (6th Cir. 2013), *cert. denied* 133 S. Ct. 2851 (2013), federal agents followed the progress of a suspected drug runner by "pinging" his cell phone, which ultimately led them to a motorhome, where a dog trained to find drugs alerted on the vehicle. Agents found illegal drugs in the vehicle. The defendant moved to suppress the illegal drugs found in the motorhome, claiming they were the product of an illegal search because of the "pinging" of his cell phone. Should his motion be granted? What is the issue?

3. Assume that a defendant's wife opened a compressed file on the defendant's computer, and saw a child pornographic image. The wife copied the file to a disc, and brought the disc to the police, who opened it and found other pornographic images, as well as photographs of the defendant sexually assaulting children. Are all the photographs admissible, or did the police conduct an illegal search of the computer disc? *Rann v. Atchison*, 689 F.3d 832 (7th Cir. 2012), *cert. denied*, 133 S. Ct. 672 (2012).

4. Passengers in a vehicle do not ordinarily have a reasonable expectation of privacy in the vehicle. Thus, if the passengers have hidden illegal drugs in the trunk of the car, police can search the trunk without probable cause, and the illegal drugs will not be excluded. On the other hand, if a person borrows another's vehicle, possession of the vehicle creates a reasonable expectation of privacy, most courts have held. What about when the owner of a vehicle is a passenger, and another person is driving the car? Does the driver of the car now have a reasonable expectation of privacy? *United States v. Almeida*, 748 F.3d 41 (1st Cir. 2014).

Notes

1. The exclusionary rule under the Fourth Amendment is discussed in greater detail in Chapter 14 of this book.
2. Virtually all states follow the *Burdeau* rule. See N. Lafave, *Search and Seizure: A Treatise on the Fourth Amendment,* 3d ed. (West, 1996), sec. 1.8, note 16.
3. 78 Cal. Rptr. 3d 501 (Cal. 2008).
4. 428 U.S. 433.
5. See *Schneckloth v. Bustamonte,* 412 U.S. 218 (1973).
6. 536 U.S. 194 (2002).
7. *Schneckloth,* 412 U.S. at 227.
8. 412 U.S. at 227.
9. *United States v. Wilkenson,* 926 F.2d 22 (1st Cir. 1991), *cert. denied,* 501 U.S. 1211 (1991).
10. Id.
11. See "Revoking Consent to Search," *FBI Law Enforcement Bulletin* (February 2005).
12. 415 U.S. 164 (1974).
13. 415 U.S. at 171, fn.7.
14. *Id.* at 171.
15. 497 U.S. 177 (1990).
16. 530 F.3d 506 (7th Cir. 2008).
17. 864 F.2d 843 (D.C. Cir.).
18. *United States v. Cortez,* 449 U.S. 411.
19. *United States v. Tolbert,* 692 F.2d 1041 (6th Cir. 1982); *United States v. Sanders,* 719 F.2d 882 (6th Cir. 1983); *United States v. Roman,* 849 F.2d 920 (5th Cir. 1988).
20. *United States v. Carrasquillo,* 877 F.2d 73 (D.C. Cir. 1989).
21. *United States v. McBean,* 861 F.2d 1570 (11th Cir. 1988).
22. *Commonwealth v. Anderl,* 477 A.2d 1356 (Pa. Super. 1984).
23. *Hayes v. State,* 158 N.W.2d 545 (Wis. 1968).
24. The Court did not decide if the prior entries by the police were themselves violations of the Fourth Amendment, and thus inadmissible evidence to support the abandonment claim, because the defendant failed to object to that evidence at trial.
25. 486 U.S. 35 (1988).
26. In the 1998 case of *Redmon v. United States* (138 F.3d 1109), the city of Urbana, Illinois, forbade leaving trash at the curb, so Redmon placed his cans for collection at the top of his 28-foot-long driveway. The cans were outside the attached two-car townhouse garage that Redmon shared with another townhouse. To reach the only approach to the front door of the townhouses, visitors had to walk up the driveway to a walkway that ran along the side of the garage. Walkways to and from a front door, though on private property, are generally regarded as open to the public. Because Redmon had no control over visitors to his neighbor's townhouse, the court pointed out that the area was open to the public. Drug enforcement agents had Redmon under surveillance and searched the garbage cans outside his garage, where they found evidence of cocaine that enabled the DEA agents to obtain a search warrant. The search of Redmon's townhouse resulted in additional evidence. On appeal to the Seventh Circuit Court of Appeals, the conviction was upheld in an eight-to-five vote.
27. New Jersey: *State v. Hempele,* 576 A.2d 793 (1990); Washington: *State v. Boland,* 48 CrL 1205 (1990); Vermont: *State v. Morris,* 1996 WL 135179 (1996).
28. 824 N.E.2d 356.
29. 336 F. Supp. 2d 967 (D. N.D. 2004).
30. *Oliver v. United States,* 466 U.S. 170, 104 S. Ct. 1735 (1984).
31. *United States v. Dunn,* 480 U.S. 294, 107 S. Ct. 1134 (1987), where the four factors were used to determine that the defendant's barn lay outside the curtilage of his ranch house.
32. 639 F.3d 1032 (10th Cir. 2011). In the case of *United States v. Acosta* [1992 WL 109641 (1992)], the Third Circuit Court of Appeals held that occupants of a three-story apartment building did not have any legitimate expectation of privacy in the back yard of the apartment building. Therefore, the defendant did not have standing and could not challenge the use of evidence thrown out of his bathroom window and picked up by law officers in the back yard of the apartment building.
33. *Id.*
34. 265 U.S. 57 (1924).
35. *Id.*
36. 466 U.S. 170, 180, 104 S. Ct. 1735, 1742 n. 11 (1984).
37. 104 S. Ct. 3405.
38. The U.S. Supreme Court followed the *Leon* case in the 1995 case of *Arizona v. Evans* (115 S. Ct. 1185). Evans was stopped by Arizona police for a traffic violation. The officers checked their in-car computer and received information that there was an outstanding arrest warrant for Evans. The police then arrested Evans and, in the search incident to Evans's arrest, found marijuana. This evidence was used to convict Evans for the possession of marijuana. The use of the

evidence was challenged because the warrant had been canceled 17 days before Evans's arrest. The incorrect information was in the computer due to an error by a court clerk. Following *Leon,* the U.S. Supreme Court held that the evidence of the marijuana could be used because there had been good-faith reliance by the police on the incorrect information.

39. 444 F.3d 556 (6th Cir. 2005), *cert. denied,* 127 S. Ct. 580 (2006).

40. See, for example, *United States v. McGough,* 412 F.3d 1232 (11th Cir. 2005).

41. 86 A.3d 182 (Pa. 2014).

42. 91 S. Ct. 1106.

43. 107 S. Ct. 1013.

44. *Illinois v. Andreas,* 463 U.S. 765, 769 n.1, 103 S. Ct. 3319, 3323 n. 1 (1983).

45. Id.

46. *United States v. Calandra,* 414 U.S. 338, 94 S. Ct. 613 (1974).

47. Supreme Court of Illinois in *People v. Dowery,* 340 N.E.2d 529 (Ill. 1975).

48. *Pennsylvania Board of Probation and Parole v. Scott,* 118 S. Ct. 2014.

49. *Wisconsin v. Griffin,* 107 S. Ct. 3164 (1987).

50. *Wisconsin v. Griffin,* 107 S. Ct. 3164, 3168.

51. 534 U.S. 112, and also see 483 U.S. 868.

52. *United States v.* Crews, 100 S. Ct. 1244 (1980).

53. *United States v. Verdugo-Urquidez,* 112 S. Ct. 2986 (1992); *United States v. Alvarez-Machain,* 112 S. Ct. 2188 (1992).

54. *Cady v. Dombrowski,* 93 S. Ct. 2523 (1971).

"Special Needs" and Administrative Searches

THE LATEST TECHNOLOGY IN AIRPORT SECURITY SCANNING

Ethan Miller/Getty Images

LEARNING OBJECTIVES

In this chapter we identify various governmental administrative functions that have "special needs" and, as a result, fewer limits on searches and seizures. The learning objectives for this chapter are

In your own words, state the concept called "special needs."

List some activities in which drug testing may be required without probable cause.

State when roadblocks may not be justified under the "special needs" doctrine.

What are the limits, if any, on the right of a border guard or customs agent to search the person or belongings of a person entering this country?

State the limits, if any, on a state's right to search a person on parole or probation.

In *Samson v. California*, discussed in this chapter, the U. S. Supreme Court held that a person on parole could be searched with or without cause or suspicion, because a parolee has a "diminished" expectation of privacy. The Court also said that a parolee has a lower expectation of privacy than a person on probation; a probationer, in turn, has a lower expectation of privacy than a "regular" citizen. What does that mean for a person on probation? May police search a probationer without probable cause (as they could not search a "regular" citizen)? Without any suspicion of criminal conduct whatsoever (as they could search a parolee)? Should it matter that the probationer, as a condition of probation, was required to sign a consent form agreeing to a warrantless search of his person or premises "with or without probable cause" by any peace or probation officer? See *United States v. King*, 736 F.3d 805 (9th Cir. 2013); what is the dissent's disagreement with the majority? Do you agree with the majority or the dissent?

SPECIAL NEEDS AND THE FOURTH AMENDMENT

The Fourth Amendment generally requires law enforcement officers to conduct searches only if they have a search warrant, probable cause, or voluntary consent to search. However, where the purpose of a search (which includes actions like blood or urine testing) is not law enforcement but some other legitimate governmental interest, the Fourth Amendment requirements have been modified.

administrative functions Functions such as screening at airports and courthouses and many fire, health, housing, and school services.

In 1989, the U.S. Supreme Court identified "special needs" governments may have which require searches for purposes unrelated to law enforcement. In such situations, the Court held that "the probable cause standard is peculiarly related to criminal investigations" and "may be unhelpful in analyzing the reasonableness of routine administrative functions."[1]

Thousands of administrative searches and functions are conducted every day by local, state, and federal employees. The majority of these employees are not law enforcement officers. They are not conducting criminal investigations but are conducting **administrative functions** that are related to the **"special needs" of government** and the community.

"special needs" of government The basic government requirements of safety, health, education, and concern for the well-being of the society as a whole.

The U.S. Supreme Court and hundreds of lower courts have held that neither probable cause nor search warrants are required to carry out most of these routine administrative functions. Evidence obtained as a result of the administrative function is admissible if the function is performed within the guidelines established by law.

SECURITY SCREENING AT AIRPORTS, COURTHOUSES, AND OTHER PUBLIC BUILDINGS AND PLACES

At U.S. airports alone, more than one billion security screenings of persons and personal belongings occur each year. Since 9/11, security screening has been extended to courthouses, public buildings, sporting events, rock concerts, and other public functions.

Thousands of illegal weapons and other illegal objects are confiscated as a result of these administrative security screenings. Many of the seized items are then used as evidence in U.S. courts. The U.S. Supreme Court has not expressly held such airport screenings do not violate the Fourth Amendment. However, in ruling that the objects are admissible evidence, most courts hold that security screenings are administrative searches under the special government need for security. Other courts hold that such evidence is admissible because once individuals present their person and their property to a security checkpoint for screening, they have consented to the screening, and that consent cannot be withdrawn during the screening process.[2]

However, such evidence may be held inadmissible if a defense lawyer can establish that the "security officers looked to considerations other than safety in conducting the screening, such as when they are on the lookout for evidence of drug trafficking, the search loses its protective character."[3] In *United States v. Fofana*,[4] the court held a search of closed envelopes in a passenger's carry-on bag violated the Fourth Amendment. Although the administrative "screening" purpose justified the search of the bag, the TSA officer conducting the search stated she looked inside the envelope because she believed it contained a large quantity of cash, which was evidence of criminal activity. The court held that because the purpose of airport screening searches was to look for weapons or explosives, any search that had another purpose violated the Fourth Amendment.

Courts have held that a random search of checked luggage at an airport does not violate the Fourth Amendment, as a proper administrative search. However, since the search is directed at discovering threats to the safety of the airplane and passengers, like explosives, the search must be limited. If in the course of such a limited search the TSA officer sees evidence of other crimes, the evidence is not subject to suppression.[5]

FIRE, HEALTH, AND HOUSING INSPECTIONS

All large cities have valid concerns for health and fire safety within their community. Health and fire concerns are even greater in areas of cities where buildings are crowded, old, and decaying. Efforts are always made to prevent fires, the collapse of buildings, and the infestation of rodents or insects, and to preserve the community in a safe and healthful condition. The U.S. Supreme Court held that fire, health, and housing inspection programs "touch at most upon the periphery of the important interests safeguarded by the Fourteenth Amendment's protection against official intrusion."[6]

Most property owners consent to inspections by health, fire, and housing inspectors. If a homeowner or the owner of commercial property refuses to allow an inspection, however, a search warrant must be obtained, and the owner of the property cannot be punished for refusal to consent to a search.

The U.S. Supreme Court set a much lower standard for obtaining a fire, health, or housing inspection search warrant in the case of *Camara v. Municipal Court*,[7] holding that:

> The warrant procedure is designed to guarantee that a decision to search private property is justified by a reasonable governmental interest. But reasonableness is still the ultimate standard. If a valid public interest justifies the intrusion contemplated, then there is probable cause to issue a suitably restricted search warrant.

Some states have passed laws or have established procedures where area search warrants may be issued when health and sanitation risks exist. For example, if an area of a city is infested with rats, an area search warrant could be issued to find the source (or sources) of the problem and eliminate the health risk.

In the case of *See v. City of Seattle*[8], the U.S. Supreme Court made it clear that a search warrant was not needed in an emergency situation such as seizure of contaminated food, compulsory smallpox vaccinations, health quarantines, or destruction of tubercular cattle.

SCHOOL SEARCHES ON REASONABLE SUSPICION

The U.S. Supreme Court held in *New Jersey v. T.L.O.* that "the (search) warrant requirement … is unsuitable to the school environment and requiring a teacher to obtain a warrant before searching a child suspected of infraction of school rules (or the criminal code) would unduly interfere with maintenance of the swift and informal disciplinary procedures needed in the schools." The Court thus held that the public interests would be "best served by a Fourth Amendment standard of reasonableness that stops short of probable cause."[9]

The general rule in the United States is to permit school officials in school and quasi-school settings to conduct searches of students on reasonable suspicion. In *Vernonia School District v. Acton*[10] (which approved suspicionless drug testing of student-athletes, see page 266), the Court stated that three factors must be considered when determining whether a search is reasonable:

1. The students' legitimate expectations of privacy
2. The intrusiveness of the search
3. The importance of the school's needs that serve as the basis for the search

In the 2009 case of *Safford Unified Public School District v. Redding*,[11] the U.S. Supreme Court held that a strip search of a 13-year-old female student violated the

 ## SCHOOL SEARCHES OF BACKPACKS, CELL PHONES, AND LOCKERS

Courts require that a warrantless search of a student at school pass a two-pronged test: (1) The initial search must be "justified at its inception"; the *T.L.O.* case discussed above permits schools to search students and their possessions on "reasonable suspicion" the student has violated school or criminal laws, or poses the threat of injury to the student or others. (2) The actual search must be reasonably related in scope to the basis of the suspicion in the first place: *Redding* requires that a search based only on suspicion must not be too "intrusive." What does that mean for a student's backpack and cell phone, two pieces of personal property virtually every student brings to school? What about a student's locker? Here are some responses to claims by students that searches of the above violated the Fourth Amendment:

*   *State v. Meneese*, 282 P.3d 83 (Wash. 2012): Search of student's backpack by uniformed police officer acting as "school resource officer" was unreasonable. Officer was looking for evidence of criminal activity, not implementing school policy for student discipline or safety.
*   *State v. A.J.C.*, 326 P.3d 1195 (Ore. 2014): Statement by other student that A.J.C. told her he would bring a gun to school justified school administrator's search of backpack.
*   *G.C. v. Owensboro Public Schools*, 711 F.3d 623 (6th Cir. 2013): School principal who searched cell phone text messages of student who texted in class in violation of school policy lacked reasonable grounds for suspecting the search would turn up evidence indicating the student violated school rules or criminal laws.
*   *Burlison v. Springfield Public Schools*, 708 F.3d 1034 (8th Cir. 2013), *cert. denied* 134 S. Ct. 151 (2013): School policy of using police dog sniffs of student backpacks was reasonable in light of school drug problem, and was minimally intrusive.
*   *In re S.M.C.*, 338 S.W.3d 16 (Tex. App. 2011): Random search of school lockers upheld because (in part) the locker was school property controlled by school, and student had no reasonable expectation of privacy in the locker.

Fourth Amendment. The school had reasonable grounds, based on statements made by other students to school officials, to believe the student had given other students over-the-counter pain relief drugs, the Court said, and that justified the school's search of the student's backpack and her outer clothing. However, the Court said, the strip search was improper because " ... the content of the suspicion failed to match the degree of intrusion." The school knew the drugs did not present a threat of serious danger, and also had no reason to suspect the student was hiding the drugs in her underwear. As a result, the Court said, the search of the student's "intimate parts" was unreasonable.

DRUG TESTING WITHOUT PROBABLE CAUSE OR A SEARCH WARRANT

Drug Testing of Law Officers and Other Persons in Critical Occupations

Private businesses may conduct drug testing of employees without fear of Fourth Amendment rights because the Fourth Amendment does not apply to searches by private persons. However, the Fourth Amendment does apply to government drug testing.

In 1989, the U.S. Supreme Court decided two cases involving drug testing of government employees. In the case of *National Treasury Employees Union v. Von Raab*,[12] the Supreme Court sustained a U.S. Customs requirement that employees seeking transfers or promotions must submit to a urinalysis. In *Skinner v. Railway Labor Executives' Association*,[13] a similar requirement was approved for workers involved in certain train accidents or incidents. In these kinds of cases, the Supreme Court stated,

> ... where a Fourth Amendment intrusion serves special governmental needs, beyond the normal need for law enforcement, it is necessary to balance the individual's privacy expectations against the Government's interests to determine whether it is impractical to require a (search) warrant or some level of individualized suspicion in the particular context.[14]

The U.S. Supreme Court identified three governmental interests that are sufficiently compelling to justify drug testing where there is no information causing suspicion of drug abuse:

1. Ensuring that certain employees "have unimpeachable integrity and judgment."[15]
2. Enhancing public safety.[16]
3. "Protecting truly sensitive information."[17]

Many federal, state, and local governmental agencies now require suspicionless drug testing of employees who have secret and top secret security clearance, detectives, police officers, guards, firefighters, fire protection specialists, nurses, employees who handle or inspect hazardous wastes, motor vehicle operators, heavy equipment operators, locomotive operators, brake-switching employees, employees required to carry firearms, and other employees with duties "fraught with such risks of injury to others that even a momentary lapse of attention can have disastrous consequences."[18] The courts have sustained random drug testing of persons within these groups by virtue of their being employed in a "heavily regulated industry."[19]

Drug Testing on Reasonable Suspicion

The Supreme Court of Hawaii pointed out that law officers have a diminished expectation of privacy because of their employment and "must always be mentally and physically alert while driving motor vehicles, and must exercise good judgment in the use of guns."[20] In the following cases, drug testing was held to be constitutionally based on reasonable suspicion:

- There was reasonable suspicion to believe that a police officer was using drugs.[21]
- An anonymous telephone call that an airman in Air Force Flight Operations had recently used marijuana was held to provide reasonable suspicion for a drug test.[22]

Random Drug Testing of Student Athletes

In the 1995 case of *Vernonia School District v. Acton,*[23] the U.S. Supreme Court upheld the random, suspicionless urine testing of public school students participating in interscholastic sports. The school district had required this testing in its custodial capacity to combat growing drug use by students and to protect the health and safety of student athletes.

The U.S. Supreme Court held that the procedure was not an unreasonable search, citing "special needs, beyond the normal need for law enforcement (making) the warrant and probable cause requirement (of the Fourth Amendment) impractical." The Supreme Court listed the following considerations in approving the reasonableness of the procedure:

- Student athletes have a reduced expectation of privacy.
- The intrusion on the student athletes' privacy by urine collection was "negligible."
- The government (school authorities) had an important and compelling interest in curbing drug use by student athletes as part of the effort to curb drug use.

Random Drug Testing of Students Participating in Extracurricular Activities

The U.S. Supreme Court stated in the 1969 case of *Tinker v. Des Moines Independent School District*[24] that "children do not shed their constitutional rights ... at the schoolhouse gate." That statement remains true today, but under the "special needs" of government doctrine, elected school boards may, if they deem necessary, require random drug tests of not only student athletes but also students participating in any extracurricular activities. The Supreme Court concluded in the 2002 case of *Board of Education of Pottawatomie County v. Earls* (discussed below), "We find that testing students who participate in extracurricular activities is a reasonably effective means of addressing the school district's legitimate concerns in preventing, deterring and detecting drug use."

Board of Education of Pottawatomie County v. Earls

United States Supreme Court, 122 S. Ct. 2559 (2002)

Petitioners were students at a public high school run by the respondent board of education. The board passed a rule that required all students participating in extracurricular activities to submit to a urinalysis test for illegal drugs and to submit to random testing during that participation. The petitioners objected to the drug testing rule, contending that it violated their Fourth Amendment rights because the tests were given without any level of "individualized suspicion." In rejecting that contention, the

Supreme Court described the "special needs" exception to the "particularized suspicion" usually required by the Fourth Amendment in normal criminal investigations:

> It is true that we generally determine the reasonableness of a search by balancing the nature of the intrusion on the individual's privacy against the promotion of legitimate governmental interests. But we have long held that "the Fourth Amendment imposes no irreducible requirement of [individualized] suspicion." "[I]n certain limited circumstances, the Government's need to discover such latent or hidden conditions, or to prevent their development, is sufficiently compelling to justify the intrusion on privacy entailed by conducting such searches without any measure of individualized suspicion." 122 S. Ct. at 2563–2564.

 ## COLLECTING DNA SAMPLES

Both the federal government and most states have established DNA databases, in which DNA samples are analyzed and stored. (See Chapter 18 for a detailed discussion of DNA analysis.) Under the statutes creating these databases, certain persons must submit to procedures necessary to collect DNA, such as a blood sample, or more commonly by "buccal swabs," which are cotton swabs designed to collect interior cheek cells. The list of persons required to give a DNA sample depends on the statute. All 50 states, and the federal government (42 U.S.C. § 14135(a)) require persons convicted of "any felony" to give a DNA sample.

Twenty-eight states and the federal government require persons arrested on probable cause and charged with a crime (in many states limited to a "serious" crime of violence) to submit to DNA sampling when booked at the police station. This is virtually always done by using the buccal swab procedure. In *Maryland v. King*, 133 S. Ct. 1958 (2013), the U.S. Supreme Court held that collecting DNA under these circumstances is not a violation of the Fourth Amendment.

The Supreme Court agreed, as Courts have universally held, that taking DNA samples constitutes a search. Moreover, because samples are required of all designated persons, they are "suspicionless searches," which are generally prohibited by the Fourth Amendment.

For convicted felons, courts virtually always have upheld mandatory, suspicionless DNA samples, either under the "special needs" doctrine, or the "totality of the circumstances" test: *United States v. Amerson*, 483 F.3d 73 (2nd Cir. 2007), *cert denied*, 552 U.S. 1042 (2007) [special need to maintain identification system for convicted felons justified suspicionless search; purpose of collection was not directed at solving particular crime, so special needs doctrine applied]; *United States v. Conley*, 453 F.3d 674 (6th Cir. 2006) [totality of circumstances justified suspicionless search].

In *Maryland v. King* the Supreme Court concluded that obtaining a DNA sample by use of the buccal swab was similar to "routine administrative steps incident to an arrest, i.e. book[ing], photograph[ing], and fingerprint[ing]". [25] Like those procedures, collecting the DNA sample is necessary to "fully identify" the person arrested for a variety of legitimate police purposes beyond seeking evidence of a crime, the Court concluded. Moreover, taking a DNA sample is minimally intrusive, the Court said, and that has a bearing on the reasonableness of the practice. As a result, taking a DNA sample without suspicion is not a violation of the Fourth Amendment, it concluded.

Four Justices dissented. They noted that the DNA sample taken in the case before the court was not tested until over 4 months after the arrest, when the defendant was already out on bail. For the dissent, it was clear that identification was not the reason for taking the DNA sample; rather, it was to see if the sample matched any of the DNA samples indexed in the federal CODIS system, which it did, and which led to the defendant's conviction of rape. This, they said, is exactly the practice the Fourth Amendment prohibits without at least suspicion, if not actual probable cause.

SEARCHES WITHOUT PROBABLE CAUSE OR SEARCH WARRANTS OF CLOSELY REGULATED BUSINESSES

closely regulated businesses Businesses that are subject to careful oversight by laws and codes, such as liquor stores, firearms dealers, coal mines, and pharmacies.

The U.S. Supreme Court held that a "businessman, like the occupant of a residence, has a constitutional right to go about his business free from unreasonable official entries upon his private commercial property."[26] Search warrants, therefore, are generally required for the administrative searches of commercial properties.

Search warrants are not required for searches of **closely regulated businesses**, however, where courts have held that the owner's privacy interests are adequately protected by detailed state or federal laws that authorize inspections (searches) without warrants. The U.S. Supreme Court held in 1978 that "the closely regulated industry … is the exception," and "when an entrepreneur embarks upon such a business, he has voluntarily chosen to subject himself to a full arsenal of governmental regulation."[27]

> States and the federal government can address major social problems both by way of an administrative scheme and through penal sanctions.… An administrative statute establishes how a particular business in a "closely regulated" industry should be operated, setting forth rules to guide an operator's conduct of the business and allowing government officials (sometimes the police) to ensure that these rules are followed. Such a regulatory approach contrasts with that of the (criminal) laws, a major emphasis of which is the punishment of individuals for specific acts of behavior. (The U.S. Supreme Court in the 1987 case of *New York v. Burger,* 482 U.S. 691, 107 S. Ct. 2636.)

In the *Burger* case, the U.S. Supreme Court established three requirements for authorizing inspections without search warrants of closely regulated businesses:

1. There must be a "substantial" government interest that informs the business operator of the "regulatory scheme" to which the inspection is to be made. For example, in the *Burger* case, the closely regulated industry was the junkyard business. These businesses are regulated because of the serious problem of stolen cars and stolen vehicle parts. Five police officers entered Burger's junkyard to inspect the junkyard as permitted by New York law. Burger stated that he did not have a license or records of vehicles he was required to have. The officers then found stolen cars and stolen vehicle parts. Burger was charged with the possession of stolen property. The New York law was found constitutional by the U.S. Supreme Court.
2. The inspection without a search warrant must be "necessary to further the regulatory scheme."
3. The regulatory law must perform the two basic functions of a search warrant:
   a. It must advise the business owner that a search is to be made pursuant to the law.
   b. It must limit the discretion of the inspecting officers.

Examples of industries that have "such a history of government oversight that no reasonable expectation of privacy could exist for proprietors over the stock of such an enterprise"[28] include liquor,[29] firearms,[30] coal mines,[31] pharmacies,[32] horse racing,[33] taverns,[34] common carriers in the trucking industry,[35] and other businesses and industries regulated by specific state or federal statutes.

WORK-RELATED SEARCHES IN GOVERNMENT OFFICES (THE *ORTEGA* RULE)

work-related searches
A search of a worker's desk and workstation for necessary records or equipment so that another employee can fill in for the absent worker or the employer can check for theft or fraud.

Private employers may make **work-related searches** of employees' desks, files, and company-owned computers as they wish. This could be done if an employee is sick and another person is filling in for the absent employee. Or, an employer could suspect that theft fraud, or other employee misconduct is occurring.

Should government employers have the same ability? In *O'Connor v. Ortega,* the U.S. Supreme Court held that to require "the Government to procure a warrant for every work-related intrusion would conflict with 'the common-sense realization' that government offices could not function if every decision became a constitutional matter."[36] Thus, though public employees have Fourth Amendment rights in the workplace ("Individuals do not lose Fourth Amendment rights merely because they work for the government instead of a private employer."), it is reasonable for public employers, like private employers, to search the workplace for suspected evidence or work-related misconduct.

Public supervisors have wide latitude to search public employees' offices, desks, and files without search warrants or probable cause to believe that the search will uncover evidence of wrongdoing. The Supreme Court held the search must be justified at its inception, meaning that the employer must have a reasonable belief the search is needed to discover evidence of improper work-related conduct. The scope of the search must not be unnecessarily intrusive. In this regard, the Court noted that it would require greater justification to search personal items such as "a piece of closed personal luggage, a handbag or a briefcase that happens to be within the employer's business address."

The U.S. Supreme Court considered the application of the *Ortega* rules in the 2010 case of *City of Ontario v. Quon,* 130 S. Ct. 2619. There, the police department issued pagers to SWAT team members, so the SWAT team members could easily communicate with each other during emergencies by sending text messages. However, officers using the text message feature exceeded the character limit set by the company providing the pager service, requiring the officers to compensate the department for the overage charges. The police department obtained access to transcripts of text messages sent and received by SWAT team members, to see if the officers needed greater text-messaging service, and determined the use of the pagers violated department policy. One of the officers, Quon, was disciplined. He brought an action against the city, alleging the search of the text messages violated his Fourth Amendment rights. The circuit court of appeals held that the officer had a reasonable expectation of privacy in the text messages, and that the search by the department was not reasonable.

The U.S. Supreme Court disagreed and reversed the decision of the court of appeals. The Court accepted for purposes of this decision the claim the officers had reasonable expectations of privacy in the text messages. It concluded that under *Ortega* the department was reasonable in viewing transcripts of text messages because the purpose of doing so was a non-investigative, work-related purpose. The search was thus "justified at its inception," and was not overly intrusive.

ROADBLOCKS OR VEHICLE CHECKPOINT STOPS

Highway checkpoints are used in the United States for many reasons. Checkpoints are used to weigh and inspect trucks,[37] to detect illegal aliens,[38] to check driver's licenses,[39] to look for drunk drivers,[40] and for other public safety reasons.

Under the "special needs" rule, police can use roadblocks to stop vehicles for certain purposes, such as finding drunk drivers or illegal aliens.

MICHAEL NELSON/EPA/LANDOV

The U.S. Supreme Court affirmed the conviction and the use of evidence obtained in the drunk driver case of *Michigan State Police v. Sitz*,[41] holding that a "special government need" existed because "drunk drivers cause an annual death toll of over 25,000 and nearly one million personal injuries and more than $5 billion in property damage."

In the case of a roadblock to check driver's licenses (*Texas v. Brown*),[42] the officer shined a flashlight into Brown's car and bent down at an angle where the officer saw loose white powder in small plastic vials and a green party balloon with white powder. The U.S. Supreme Court affirmed the admission into evidence of the white powder, heroin, as evidence obtained in a plain view seizure and affirmed Brown's illegal drug conviction.

However, in the 2000 case of *City of Indianapolis v. Edmonds*,[43] the U.S. Supreme Court held that law officers may not simply set up roadblocks in high-crime neighborhoods as general crime-fighting procedures but must have an "immediate vehicle-bound threat to life and limb." The Supreme Court held that the stops, made without "individualized suspicion," were unconstitutional. The purpose of the checkpoint was not to deal with some special need like a particular hazard related to the checkpoint, such as drunk driving in the *Sitz* case, but rather the police's "general interest in crime control." The Court reasoned that if such checkpoints were permitted, then the police could set up a checkpoint to see if motorists were violating any criminal law.

In the 2004 case of *Illinois v. Lidster*,[44] the Court upheld a roadblock established by police to obtain information about a hit-and-run accident that occurred at the location where the roadblock was set up. The Court said the *Edmonds* rule did not apply where the purpose of the roadblock was not to check for criminal activity by the occupants of vehicles stopped, but only to acquire information from those occupants. It therefore upheld the conviction for drunk driving of a motorist stopped at this roadblock. A similar result occurred where National Park rangers established a roadblock to the entrance of a national park to deter illegal poaching

IDENTIFICATION CHECKPOINTS IN PUBLIC HOUSING PROJECTS

Public housing projects in large cities have often been plagued by excessive illegal drug use and associated violence. More than any others, it is the law-abiding residents of the housing projects who suffer the consequences. In recent years, in an attempt to combat this problem, city governments have adopted programs that turn over the supervision of streets within the housing projects to the housing authority, which then employs officers to patrol the streets. These officers have the status of police officers. Many housing authorities set up an "identification checkpoint" at an entrance to the housing project. Housing authorities believe they can reduce drug crimes and violence by excluding persons who have no lawful purpose for entering the housing project's grounds. To accomplish this, the housing authorities issue identification badges to residents, and when persons entering the premises fail to produce a badge, checkpoint officers inquire into that person's reasons for entering the housing project's grounds.

Are these checkpoints lawful? If officers stop a person entering the housing project for this identification check and then discover illegal drugs or other crimes, can the evidence discovered be used in the prosecution of that person?

In *State v. Hayes*, 88 S.W.3d 505 (Tenn. 2006), the Tennessee Supreme Court joined a growing number of courts that hold that such checkpoints violate the Fourth Amendment. In *Hayes* a housing authority officer stopped a motorist as he turned onto a street leading into the project. The officer had no suspicion of criminal activity. When the officer asked for identification, the motorist showed him an expired driver's license, for which the motorist was subsequently charged under Tennessee's motor vehicle laws. The motorist moved to suppress the evidence seized at the checkpoint, contending that the checkpoint was unconstitutional under *Indianapolis v. Edmond*. The Tennessee Supreme Court agreed.

The housing authority sought to distinguish *Edmund* by arguing that the problem with the checkpoint in *Edmund* was that its only purpose was the "general interest in crime control" and it was aimed at identifying those already involved in illegal activity. Here, the authority contended, the purpose was to prevent illegal activity.

The Tennessee Supreme Court rejected that contention, holding that a purpose of preventing crime is nonetheless only a general interest in crime control, and no different than the situation in *Edmund*. Other courts have agreed with this conclusion. (See, for example, *People v. Pope*, 738 N.Y.S.2d 543 (N.Y. Sup. Ct. 2002), *appeal denied*, 793 N.E.2d 421 (N.Y. 2003).) In *Mills v. District of Columbia*, 571 F.3d 1304 (D.C. Cir. 2009) the Court held that police establishment of checkpoints in a high-crime area of Washington, D.C., that required all motorists entering the neighborhood to give identification and explain their reasons for entering violated the Fourth Amendment.

---

of park animals. In *United States v. Fraire*, 575 F.3d 929 (9th Cir. 2009), the court held that the purpose of the roadblock was not general crime control, but to protect an important government interest, the safety of park animals.

The Supreme Court has identified some circumstances where "special needs" justify suspicionless highway stops:

- Detecting drunk drivers
- Verifying driver's licenses and vehicle registration
- Intercepting illegal aliens on border highways
- Apprehending fleeing criminals
- Thwarting terrorist activity or attack

Border Searches

Thousands of vehicles crossing U.S. borders are searched every day. Often the reason a particular vehicle is searched is the instincts and experience of the border agent responsible for the border checkpoint. As a result, a line of cases had developed in which the Fourth Amendment's reasonableness requirement was determined by the routine or nonroutine character of the search.

In the 2004 case of *United States v. Flores-Montano*,[45] however, the U.S. Supreme Court rejected a balancing test based on the routine or nonroutine nature of the search. The Court said that the reasonableness requirement does not require border agents to have any "particularized suspicion" before searching a vehicle. In *Flores-Montano,* agents removed and disassembled a vehicle's fuel tank looking for illegal drugs. The Court upheld the agents' actions, stating that the test for determining whether a search was unreasonable should be the "intrusiveness" of the search, not its routine or nonroutine character. The Court did state that a search of a vehicle could be so "destructive" that it becomes unreasonable.

In *United States v. Cortez-Rocha*,[46] the court upheld a border search of the spare tire in a vehicle attempting to cross the border at a checkpoint. Agents suspected that the tire on the vehicle might contain illegal drugs, and agents slashed the tire, finding 42 kilograms of marijuana. The court held that the tire slashing was not so "destructive" that the search was unreasonable because it did not hinder the operation of the vehicle or prevent the occupants from continuing their travels.

Following these decisions, most courts have held that the "border search" doctrine means that any search at a border can be made without suspicion, unless the search is unusually excessive and destructive. In the 2008 case of *United States v. Arnold*,[47] the Ninth Circuit Court of Appeals held that federal border agents did not need any "particularized suspicion" to view the files on a laptop computer brought into this country by a passenger on an international flight. The border agents required the passenger to turn on the laptop, and then the agents browsed through the files, finally discovering child pornography photographs. At the trial on child pornography charges, the district court suppressed the laptop photographs, and the government appealed. The court of appeals reversed. It said a "quick look" at the computer was appropriate at the border.

In the 2013 case of *United States v. Cotterman*[48] the Ninth Circuit placed a limit on the extent border agents may examine a computer at the border. There, the border agents didn't simply take a "quick look" at computer files, but put a laptop computer through a "comprehensive forensic examination" of the computer's hard drive using sophisticated forensic software. The court held that such an intrusive search required individualized suspicion before the border agents could conduct the search.

Searches of persons or vehicles conducted after a border has been crossed and the persons are in the United States have a higher requirement than border searches. So-called "extended border" searches generally require that officers have reasonable suspicion that the person or vehicle searched recently came through a border, and reasonable suspicion that the person or vehicle was engaged in criminal activity. *United States v. Guzman-Padilla*, 573 F.3d 865 (9th Cir. 2009), *cert denied* 131 S. Ct. 67 (2010). However, the simple fact the search occurred at a place removed from the border does not always trigger the "extended border search" rule. In the 2013 case of *United States v. Stewart*, 729 F.3d 517 (6th Cir. 2013), *cert denied*

134 S. Ct. 1044 (2014) the court held that federal agents were still conducting a border search of a laptop when they took the laptop to their office to "power it up" and view the images on the lap top. Since it wasn't an "extended" border search, the court said, the agents did not need a search warrant or individualized suspicion.

Sham Roadblocks

After the decision in *Indianapolis v. Edmonds,* police cannot set up roadblocks and stop vehicles for the purpose of searching them for illegal drugs or evidence of other criminal activity. May police set up so-called sham roadblocks by posting signs on a highway that there is a drug checkpoint ahead, in the belief that motorists who are carrying drugs will respond to the fake notice by discarding those drugs. In *United States v. Flynn*[49] and *People v. Roth,*[50] the courts upheld such sham roadblocks. In both cases, police erected signs on a highway stating that a drug checkpoint was set up ahead on the highway. In fact, no such checkpoint existed. After passing the signs, a motorist in each case was observed throwing something out of the vehicle by police. The vehicles were then stopped and searched, and illegal drugs were found. The subsequent convictions were upheld by both courts. The Tenth Circuit Court of Appeals in *Flynn* held that posting a fake sign was not illegal, and that the resulting actions by the motorist gave the police the necessary "particularized suspicion" to stop the vehicle. However, other courts have held that the simple act of exiting a highway after encountering a sham roadblock sign did not provide the reasonable suspicion needed for an investigative stop. *United States v. Yousif*, 308 F.3d 820 (8th Cir. 2002), *State v. Rademaker*, 813 N.W.2d 174 (S.D. 2012).

CORRECTIONAL PROGRAMS, HEARINGS, OR REQUIREMENTS THAT MAY CAUSE A PRISON INMATE TO INCRIMINATE HIMSELF

In 2002 the U.S. Supreme Court wrote about the seriousness of sexual assaults in the United States:

> In 1995 an estimated 355,000 rapes and sexual assaults occurred nationwide. Between 1980 and 1994, the population of imprisoned sex offenders increased at a faster rate than for any other category of violent crime. (The) victims of sexual assault are most often juveniles. (N)early 4 in 10 violent sex offenders said their victims were 12 or younger.
>
> When convicted sex offenders reenter society they are much more likely than any other type of offender to be rearrested for a new rape or sexual assault.[51]

Because of the seriousness of this problem, sexual abuse treatment programs (SATP) are in place in state and federal prisons. In these programs inmates must disclose and accept responsibility for "the crimes for which they have been sentenced" and also "all prior sexual activities," whether lawful or whether "the activities constitute uncharged criminal offenses." Inmates have challenged various aspects of these programs, contending that participation in the programs is in essence mandatory, and that participation requires the inmate to abandon constitutional rights like the right to remain silent. The states' response to these challenges has been to contend that the "special needs" doctrine justifies their actions. The following SATP cases have come before the U.S. Supreme Court:

Case	Hearing Requirements and Consequences, Including Punishment If Inmate Refused to Disclose Uncharged Crimes	Court Ruling
McKune v. Lile, 536 U.S. 24 (2002)	Lile was convicted of the rape and sexual assault of a high school student. As an inmate in a Kansas prison, he challenged the Kansas SATP. Punishment for failure to comply in Kansas would be reduction and curtailment of visitation rights, earnings, work opportunity, access to television, sending money to family, and purchases in the canteen. Lile would also be transferred to a potentially more dangerous maximum-security unit	"Acceptance of responsibility is the beginning of rehabilitation." "The Kansas SATP represents a sensible approach to reducing the serious danger that repeat offenders pose to many innocent persons, most often children." (The fact that Kansas does not offer legal immunity from prosecution for disclosures does not render the Kansas SATP invalid.)
Minnesota v. Murphy, 104 S. Ct. 1136 (1984)	As a condition of probation, the defendant agreed to be truthful with his probation officer in all matters. Because the defendant feared being returned to prison for 16 months if he remained silent, he confessed to a rape and murder. Murphy was tried and convicted for these crimes.	Murphy obtained probation from prison by agreeing in writing to be truthful with his probation officer. Convictions for rape and murder were affirmed.
Ohio Adult Parole Authority v. Woodard, 118 S. Ct. 1244 (1998)	A death row inmate at his voluntary clemency interview chose to incriminate himself rather than be silent and cause "the clemency board (to) construe that silence against him."	The defendant faced "a choice quite similar to the sorts of choices that a criminal defendant must make in the course of criminal proceedings, none of which has ever been held to violate the Fifth Amendment." The Court held it was not an unconstitutional compulsion.
Baxter v. Palmigiano, 96 S. Ct. 1551 (1976)	A state prisoner objected to the fact that his silence at a prison disciplinary hearing would be held against him. The prisoner faced 30 days in punitive segregation. The Supreme Court held that the disciplinary board could draw an inference of guilt from the prisoner's silence.	Prison disciplinary hearings "involve the correctional process and important state interests" and are unlike a criminal trial where a jury is forbidden from drawing an inference of guilt from a defendant's failure to testify.

Do Inmates on Parole Have Privacy Expectations Protected by the Fourth Amendment?

At various times the U.S. Supreme Court has addressed the question of whether a person who in some way is under the jurisdiction of a prison authority has the expectation of privacy protected by the Fourth Amendment. The privacy expectation varies because the extent of the prison authority's control differs for an inmate incarcerated in a prison population and for an inmate released on parole or probation. In the following case the Supreme Court discussed the relationship of the Fourth Amendment to prisoners and their expectations of privacy. It should be noted that, in reaching its decision, the Court was careful to state that it was not reaching that decision solely under the "special needs" doctrine.

Samson v. California

United States Supreme Court, 547 U.S. 843 (2006)

In *United States v. Knights*,[52] the Supreme Court held that a person on probation had a "diminished privacy" interest that justified an officer to stop and search that person based only on "reasonable suspicion" that the person was engaged in criminal activity. The Court also noted that as a condition of probation in *Knights*, the probationer had to submit to a search at any time, with or without reasonable suspicion. The state has a legitimate interest in closely monitoring those on probation, the Court said, both to reintegrate the probationer into society and to prevent recidivism. Viewing these factors together, the Court said the search was reasonable in *Knights*. The Court specifically declined to answer the question "whether the search would have been reasonable under the Fourth Amendment had it been solely predicated upon the condition of probation."[53] *Samson* directly presented that question, the Court in that case stated, "albeit in the context of a parolee search."[54]

In concluding that the search was reasonable under general Fourth Amendment principles, the Court first placed parole on a "continuum of state-imposed punishments" that resulted in fewer expectations of privacy than in the case of persons on probation. Parole, the Court said, is closely akin to being a prisoner, since under California law a parolee remains under the legal custody of the Department of Corrections and must comply with all the conditions of parole. The totality of these conditions, the Court said, " …demonstrate that parolees like petitioner have severely diminished expectations of privacy by virtue of their status alone."[55]

Moreover, the Court noted, as in *Knights*, that parolees must sign an order in which they must submit to suspicionless searches by officers at any time. The Court held:

> Examining the totality of the circumstances pertaining to petitioner's status as a parolee, "an established variation on imprisonment," *Morrissey*, 408 U.S. at 477, 92 S. Ct. 2593, including the plain terms of the parole search condition, we conclude that petitioner did not have an expectation of privacy that society would recognize as legitimate. *Id*.

By comparison, the state's interest in searches of parolees is substantial, the Court said. It noted that in 2005 California had more than 130,000 released prisoners on parole, and that the parolee population has a 68 to 70 percent recidivism rate.[56] Closely monitoring parolees is clearly in the state's interest, the Court concluded, and suspicionless searches serve the state's interest in reducing recidivism.[57]

Judging suspicionless searches under these circumstances, the Court held that "the Fourth Amendment does not prohibit a police officer from conducting a suspicionless search of a parolee."[58]

The Court was careful to make it clear that its decision was based solely on "general Fourth Amendment" principles, and as a result it did not reach the issue of whether acceptance of the search condition constituted "consent" and thus operated as a complete waiver of Fourth Amendment rights. Nor, the Court said, did it base its decision on "special needs" rules.[59] Finally, the Court said its decision did not equate parolees with prisoners, who have no Fourth Amendment rights, as was held in *Hudson v. Palmer*.[60]

OTHER SPECIAL GOVERNMENT NEEDS WHERE NEITHER PROBABLE CAUSE NOR SEARCH WARRANTS ARE NEEDED

The need to supervise persons on probation and parole closely: *Griffin v. Wisconsin*: 483 U.S. 868, 107 S. Ct. 3164 (1987)

The U.S. Supreme Court upheld the search by a probation officer under a Wisconsin statute that authorized such searches on the basis of reasonable suspicion. The Supreme Court held that the "special needs of the probation system requires the need to supervise persons on probation and parole closely."

Not only do many states have such statutes but it is also a common practice to include consent to search sections in parole and probation agreements. Persons being placed on parole or probation must sign these agreements to receive such status.

Illegal aliens: *United States v. Martinez-Fuerte*: 428 U.S. 543 96 S. Ct. 3078 (1976)

In permitting checkpoints for illegal aliens the U.S. Supreme Court held that "requiring particularized suspicion before routine stops on major highways near the Mexican border would be impractical because the flow of traffic tends to be too heavy to allow the particularized study of a given car that would enable it to be identified as a possible carrier of illegal aliens."[61]

Safety in jails and prisons: *Bell v. Wolfish*, 441 U.S. 520 99 S. Ct. 1861 (1979)

Since persons in jails and prisons have a reduced right to privacy they are subject to random searches for weapons and contraband without any showing of suspicion. The U.S. Supreme Court held that visual body cavity searches may be made of inmates to find weapons and drugs and to maintain safety in jails and prisons.

Blanket Strip Searches of All Arrestees, Including Those Arrested for Minor Offenses: *Florence v. Board of Freeholders of County of Burlingham*, 132 S. Ct. 1510 (2012)

The court held that any person arrested and brought into the general population of a jail may be subjected to a strip search. The jail's interest in discovering hidden contraband or weapons justified the intrusion of the strip search.

 PROCEDURES & PROCESSES

Obtaining Evidence in Foreign Countries

Sometimes evidence of serious crimes about to be committed (or being committed) in the United States becomes available in foreign countries (including Mexico or Canada). The following general rules for the admissibility of such evidence in U.S. courts are presented in an article in the *FBI Law Enforcement Bulletin* (July 2002), available at http://www.fbi.gov, entitled "Investigating International Terrorism Overseas: Constitutional Considerations":

- When law officers in the foreign country acting alone and independently obtain evidence, "Generally, American legal standards do not apply to the seizure of evidence ... where a foreign country is conducting the investigation independently and seizes evidence that is later introduced into an American court."[a]

- "If American investigators are acting alone in seeking to obtain evidence in a foreign country, they should always comply with the laws of that country and should conduct their investigation as if they were operating in the United States."
- "When American investigators are working jointly with foreign officials, they should remember that searches or interrogations ... will invoke (American) constitutional protections on the part of the subject (of the search or interrogation)."

Another way of obtaining evidence from foreign countries is through the use of Mutual Legal Assistance Treaties (MLAT), which the United States has signed with thirty-four countries including Canada and Mexico. If an MLAT does not exist, authority may be requested from a federal court to ask officials in a foreign country to obtain evidence. This is called a "letter rogatory." Subpoenas may also be issued on persons or corporations in the United States who have constructive possession of evidence located in foreign countries.

[a]American courts would refuse to use evidence obtained by foreign government officials if the conduct of the foreign officials in obtaining the evidence shocked the conscience of the U.S. court. See the case of *United States v. Callaway*, 446 F.2d 753 (3d Cir. 1971), where Canadian police who were not acting in connection or cooperation with American law enforcement officials obtained criminal evidence that was used to convict Callaway in a New Jersey court. Because the actions of the Canadian police were not so outrageous as to shock the conscience of the trial court, the evidence was admitted, and Callaway's conviction was affirmed.

SUMMARY

1. **In your own words, state the concept called "special needs."**
   - Where government actions have as their purpose some legitimate government goal, such as administrative functions or public safety, rather than general crime protection, the probable cause requirement in the Fourth Amendment does not apply to any search or seizure that occurs in compliance with the government function. As a result, evidence of crimes discovered during these functions is admissible in prosecutions for those crimes.

2. **List some activities in which drug testing may be required without probable cause.**
   - Private employers may conduct drug testing without any need for a showing of probable cause. Governments may conduct drug testing without probable cause for many kinds of employment, such as police officers,

   firefighters, doctors or nurses, or others whose duties involve risk to themselves or others, or who have access to governmental secrets. In addition, students involved in interscholastic athletics may be randomly tested for illegal drugs. Inmates in a jail or prison may be tested for drugs without probable cause.

3. **State when roadblocks may not be justified under the "special needs" doctrine.**
   - Roadblocks are not justified when the purpose of the roadblock is "general crime prevention or investigation." Roadblocks are justified only when the purpose of the roadblock is to protect some other governmental interest, such as highway safety. So-called "sham" roadblocks are not by themselves illegal, but police may not use the simple fact a vehicle exits a highway after encountering the sham roadblock sign as a sufficient reason to search the vehicle.

4. **What are the limits, if any, on the right of a border guard or customs agent to search a person or belongings of a person entering this country?**
   - Any person, including his or her belongings, entering this country may be searched at a border crossing without individualized suspicion. However, searches that are highly "intrusive" to the person or "destructive" of a vehicle or belongings require reasonable suspicion. Once a person has left the border and entered this country, "extended border searches" require officials to have reasonable suspicion for a search.

5. **State the limits, if any, on a state's right to search a person on parole or probation.**
   - Inmates in a jail or prison have greatly diminished expectations of privacy, and as a result have almost no Fourth Amendment rights. Persons on parole have a reduced expectation of privacy, because they continue to be under the jurisdiction of the state corrections department. Police may conduct a suspicionless search of a parolee. Persons on probation have a higher expectation of privacy, although state's continuing interest in monitoring the progress of probationers justifies searches based only on reasonable suspicion.

KEY TERMS

administrative functions, 262

closely regulated businesses, 268

"special needs" of government, 262

work-related searches, 269

KEY CASES

City of Indianapolis v. Edmunds, 541 U.S. 32 (2000): Police may not establish highway roadblocks for the purpose of general law enforcement or investigation.

Florence v. Board of Freeholders of County of Burlingham, 132 S. Ct. 1510 (2012): States may conduct strip searches of all persons lawfully arrested, even for minor offenses.

Maryland v. King, 133 S. Ct. 1958 (2013): States and the federal government may collect DNA samples from all persons arrested and charged with crimes through use of the non-intrusive buccal swab method.

Michigan State Police v. Sitz, 496 U.S. 444 (1990): Police may establish roadblocks where purpose is highway safety, rather than general law enforcement.

National Treasury Employees v. Von Raab, 489 U.S. 656 (1989): Established special needs doctrine for permitting searches without probable cause where governments have a legitimate public purpose other than general law enforcement for the searches.

New York v. Burger, 482 U.S. 691 (1987): Closely regulated businesses may be subjected to administrative searches without a search warrant under governmental regulations authorizing such searches.

Samson v. California, 547 U.S. 843 (2006): Parolees have a diminished expectation of privacy and can be subjected to searches without particularized suspicion.

United States v. Florez-Montano, 541 U.S. 149 (2000): Border searches do not require individualized suspicion, and all persons and their belongings entering this country at a border crossing are subject to searches.

PROBLEMS

1. How far does the "workplace" extend so as to apply the rules in *O'Conner v. Ortega*? May prison officials search the vehicles owned by prison employees parked in the prison parking lot? Do they need "probable cause" and a search warrant, or reasonable suspicion? If the latter, what is sufficient "suspicion"? (See *Wiley v. Department of Justice,* 328 F.3d 1346 (C.A. Fed. 2003).)

2. In *Michigan State Police v. Sitz,* the Supreme Court held sobriety checkpoints constitutional in part because they differed from "roving-patrol" stops of motorists because the checkpoints were

established by police supervisors. Why does that matter? May field officers make their own independent decision to set up a sobriety roadblock? Compare *State v. Varner*, 160 S.W.3d 535 (Tenn. App. 2004) with *Gonzales v. State*, 657 S.E.2d 617 (Ga. App. 2008).

3. As we saw in this chapter, cases like *New Jersey v. T.L.O.* require "reasonable suspicion" for searches of school children on school property. However, cases like *Vernonia School District v. Acton* and *Board of Education of Pottawatomie County v. Earls* permit random, suspicionless searches of students engaged in interscholastic activities. Keeping in mind that drug testing constitutes a search, can these decisions be reconciled? Are you persuaded by the Supreme Court's justification of random drug testing of student athletes? Should states adopt different standards under state constitutions? (See *York v. Wahkiakum School District No. 200*, 178 P.3d 995 (Wash. 2008).)

4. The U. S. Supreme Court has held parolees have a limited expectation of privacy in their persons and their homes, such that police can make a warrantless, suspicionless search of those places. Does that mean the police can conduct a similar search of every place a parolee visits or stays for a period of time? What should the rule be? *See United States v. Grandberry*, 730 F.3d 968 (9th Cir. 2013).

CASE ANALYSIS

Read Appendix B, Finding and Analyzing Cases (p. 499). With these guidelines in mind, please continue with the Case Analysis selections for Chapter 11.

1. Under the school search rules, can the principal of a high school go out in the parking lot and search the vehicles of students he suspects are using illegal drugs? What about student cars parked across the street from the high school? *See J.P. v. Millard Public Schools*, 830 N.W.2d 453 (Neb. 2013).

2. The city council passed a law that required every vehicle owned by a city resident to have a city sticker displayed on the vehicle's license plate. The purpose of the law was to collect the $10 sticker fee. May the city police set up a "sticker checkpoint" to stop vehicles to see if they have the required sticker? Can they then check the drivers to see, among other things, if they are intoxicated, or have drugs in the vehicle? *Singleton v. Commonwealth*, 364 S.W.3d 97 (Ky. 2012).

3. Assume a police officer in a valid traffic stop of a vehicle learns a passenger in the vehicle is on parole. The officer orders both the passenger and the driver out of the car, searches it thoroughly, and finds evidence the driver of the car had illegal drugs in the car. Assuming the search of the vehicle would not be lawful but for the presence of the parolee in the vehicle (it wouldn't; see Chapter 14), can the driver successfully argue the evidence of the illegal drugs should be suppressed? Why or why not? *See People v. Schmitz*, 288 P.3d 1259 (Cal. 2012), *cert denied*, 133 S. Ct. 2740 (2013).

4. Can police take a DNA sample from the saliva left on a straw used by a probationer who is required to take routine sobriety tests as part of his probation for a DUI conviction? Can they then see if it matches the DNA left at the scene of a homicide? What do you see as the issue presented by these facts? *See Corbin v. State*, 52 A.3d 946 (Md. 2012).

Notes

1. *National Treasury Employee Union v. Von Raab*, 489 U.S. 656, 668; *Colorado v. Bertine*, 479 U.S. 367, 371.
2. *People v. Heimel*, 812 P.2d 1177 (1991). For similar rulings, see *State v. Plante*, 594 A.2d 165 (N.H. 1991), and *United States v. Vigil*, 989 F.2d 337 (9th Cir. 1993).
3. *Klarfeld v. United States*, 962 F.2d 866 (9th Cir. 1992).
4. 620 F. Supp. 2d 857 (S.D. Ohio 2009). On appeal, the Circuit Court of Appeals agreed the envelopes and their contents were not admissible as evidence of bank fraud. However, the court held, the information in the envelopes, a fraudulent passport, could be sued by the government to explain and make relevant bank records already in the possession of the government.

5. *Higerd v. State*, 54 So.3d 513 (Fla. App. 2011), *cert denied*, 132 S. Ct. 521 (2011). TSA officer, while swabbing contents of checked luggage for explosive trace elements, saw child pornography photos; held admissible as discovered by proper administrative search.

6. *Frank v. Maryland*, 359 U.S. 360.

7. *Camara v. Municipal Court*, 387 U.S. 523 (1967).

8. 387 U.S. 541 (1967).

9. 469 U.S. 325, at 340–341 (1985).

10. 515 U.S. 646 (1995).

11. 402 F.3d 598 (6th Cir. 2005).

12. 489 U.S. 656.

13. 489 U.S. 602.

14. *Von Raab*, 489 U.S. at 665; *Skinner*, 489 U.S. at 617–18.

15. 489 U.S. at 670.

16. 489 U.S. at 628.

17. 489 U.S. at 676.

18. 109 S. Ct. at 1419.

19. *Policemen's Benevolent Ass'n v. Township of Washington*, 850 F.2d 133 (3d Cir. 1988), *review denied*, 490 U.S. 1004, 109 S. Ct. 1637, 45 CrL 4002 (1989). Not all courts go along with the reasoning in the U.S. Supreme Court's *Von Raab* decision. In the 1991 case of *Guiney v. Police Commissioner of Boston*, 582 N.E.2d 523, the Massachusetts Supreme Judicial Court held that "unannounced, warrantless, suspicionless, random" urinalysis testing of Boston police officers violated the Massachusetts Constitution even if permitted under the U.S. Constitution.

20. *McCloskey v. Honolulu Police Department*, 799 P.2d 953 (1990).

21. *Copeland v. Philadelphia Police Department*, 840 F.2d 1139 (3d Cir. 1988), *review denied*, 490 U.S. 1004, 109 S. Ct. 1636, 45 CrL 4001 (1989).

22. *United States v. Blair*, 32 M.J. 404 (1991), *review denied*, U.S. Supreme Court, 112 S. Ct. 438, 50 CrL, 3077 (1991).

23. 115 S. Ct. 2386 (1995).

24. 393 U.S. 503 (1969).

25. 133 S. Ct. 1977.

26. *See v. City of Seattle*, 387 U.S. 541, 543, 87 S. Ct. 1737, 1739 (1967).

27. Marshall v. Barlow's Inc., 436 U.S. 307 (1978).

28. *Marshall v. Barlow's Inc.*, 436 U.S. at 313, 98 S. Ct. at 1821.

29. *Colonnade Catering Corp. v. United States*, 397 U.S. 72, 90 S. Ct. 774 (1970).

30. *United States v. Biswell*, 406 U.S. 311, 92 S. Ct. 1593 (1972).

31. *Donovan v. Dewey*, 452 U.S. 594, 101 S. Ct. 2534 (1981).

32. *State v. Del City*, 947 F.2d 432 (10th Cir. 1991).

33. *State v. Williams*, 417 A.2d 1046 (N.J. 1980).

34. *State v. Rednor*, 497 A.2d 544 (N.J. 1985).

35. *United States v. Dominguez-Prieto*, 923 F.2d 464 (6th Cir. 1991).

36. 480 U.S. 709 (1987).

37. *Delaware v. Prouse*, 440 U.S. 648, 663 n. 26, 99 S. Ct. 1391, 1401 n. 26 (1979).

38. *United States v. Martinez-Fuerte*, 428 U.S. 543, 96 S. Ct. 3074 (1976).

39. *Texas v. Brown*, 460 U.S. 730, 103 S. Ct. 1535 (1983).

40. *Michigan State Police v. Sitz*, 496 U.S. 444, 110 S. Ct. 2481 (1990).

41. *Id.*

42. 460 U.S. 730 (1983).

43. 531 U.S. 32 (2000).

44. 540 U.S. 419 (2004).

45. 541 U.S. 149.

46. 383 F.3d 1093 (9th Cir. 2004).

47. 523 F.3d 941 (9th Cir. 2008), *rehearing denied*, 2008 WL 2675794.

48. 709 F.3d 952 (9th Cir. 2013), *cert denied* 134 S. Ct. 899 (2014).

49. 309 F.3d 736 (10th Cir. 2002).

50. 85 P.3d 571 (Colo. 2003).

51. *McKune v. Lile*, 536 U.S. 24 at 32, 33.

52. 534 U.S. 112 (2002).

53. 547 U.S. at 850.

54. *Id.*

55. *Id.* at 852.

56. *Id.* at 853.

57. *Id.* at 854.

58. *Id.* at 857.

59. *Id.* at 852, fn. 3.

60. 468 U.S. 517 (1984). *Id.* at 850, fn. 2.

61. 428 U.S. at 557, 96 S. Ct. at 3082, and 489 U.S. at 668, 109 S. Ct. at 1392.

CHAPTER 12

Obtaining Statements and Confessions for Use as Evidence

NON-CUSTODIAL, ON-THE-SCENE QUESTIONING BY AN OFFICER

Mikael Karlsson/Alamy

LEARNING OBJECTIVES

In this chapter we focus on the use of confessions and other incriminating statements in criminal trials. The learning objectives for this chapter are

State the factors to be considered in the "totality of the circumstances" test.

List the *Miranda* requirements for information that must be communicated to a suspect in custody before questioning.

Identify when a person is in "custody" for purposes of *Miranda*.

List some exceptions to the *Miranda* rule.

State the *Massiah* rule and compare it to the *Miranda* rule.

State the role of a confession under the *Bruton* rule, where there are multiple defendants.

I n this chapter we learn that "involuntary" confessions are not admissible in a criminal trial, because they amount to "compelling" a suspect to be a "witness against himself" in violation of the Fifth Amendment and the Due Process Clause of the Fourteenth Amendment. Some kinds of involuntary confessions are clear: Beating a suspect until he confesses is obviously a violation. But other situations are not so clear.

What should happen in this case? A 16-year-old girl, after spending 55 hours in a police station without access to a lawyer and limited assistance from her father (her mother was in jail) confessed to murdering her roommate. While at the police station she was not given clean clothes or allowed to shower, and slept on a bench in the station house. She changed her story several times, and after being given her *Miranda* warnings she agreed to take a polygraph test. After a pretest interview, detectives told her that they thought she was not telling the truth; she then changed her story again. Ultimately, she told investigators she killed the victim.

What are some factors that might lead a court to question whether the confession was involuntary? How persuasive are they? *See Carter v. Thompson*, 690 F.3d 837 (2012), *cert. denied*, 133 S. Ct. 887 (2013). How important was it, if at all, that this case was before the Court of Appeals as a habeas corpus case?

CONFESSIONS

A confession is like no other evidence. Indeed, the defendant's own confession is probably the most probative and damaging evidence that can be admitted against him. [T]he admissions of a defendant come from the actor himself, the most knowledgeable and unimpeachable source of information about his past conduct.[1]

These words by U.S. Supreme Court Justice White underscore both the evidentiary value and the risk associated with confessions and incriminating statements. A **confession** is generally viewed as the same as a guilty plea in open court. An **incriminating statement** differs from a confession in that a confession directly acknowledges guilt, whereas an incriminating statement "is any statement or conduct from which guilt of the crime can be inferred."[2] Sometimes even silence can constitute an incriminating statement. In *Key-el v. State*,[3] the prosecution introduced evidence that the defendant had remained silent when his wife, in the presence of a police officer, accused him of battering. The evidence was held properly admissible under the tacit admission rule, and the defendant's conviction was affirmed.

If true, confessions are the best evidence of guilt. On the other hand, if untrue and given by the defendant because of coercion or pressure, confessions carry a high risk of misleading the jury. For those and other reasons, the law governing the use of confessions and incriminating statements in criminal trials has a long and complex history. In many respects, it is still developing. In this chapter we explore some of those developments.

confession A direct acknowledgment of guilt; generally viewed the same as a guilty plea in open court.

incriminating statement "Any statement or conduct from which guilt of the crime can be inferred" [*People v. Stanton*, 158 N.E.2d 47 (Ill. 1959)].

CAN A CONFESSION ALONE SUSTAIN A CRIMINAL CONVICTION?
The Corpus Delicti Rule

Frank Connelly approached a police officer on a Denver street and confessed to a murder.[4] If the police could find no other evidence of the murder, could Connelly be charged and convicted of a murder solely on the basis of his confession? The answer is "no," because a confession alone will not sustain a conviction.

When a confession is used as evidence, corroborating evidence must also be provided to prove corpus delicti (that the crime was committed). This requirement originated in England in the notorious 1660 *Perry's Case*,[5] where a defendant was convicted of murder and executed solely on the basis of a confession, only to have the murder "victim" subsequently appear alive. As the Supreme Court of California pointed out in *People v. Jennings*, the rule was used "to protect the defendant against the possibility of fabricated testimony which might wrongfully establish the crime and the perpetrator."[6]

In *People v. Jennings*, the defendant bragged to others about how he picked up prostitutes, paid them for sex, and then later killed them and took their money before burying the bodies. The State of California produced evidence corroborating the confessions to three murders and other felonies such as kidnapping and robberies of the women. In affirming the convictions and death penalty in the *Jennings* case, the Supreme Court of California quoted another court in sustaining the corpus delicti rule, holding

> As one court explained, "Today's judicial retention of the rule reflects the continued fear that confessions may be the result of either improper police activity or the mental instability of the accused, and the recognition that juries are likely to accept confessions uncritically." [*Jones v. Superior Court*, (1979) 96 Cal. App. 3d 390, 397, 157 Cal. Rptr. 809.]
>
> Viewed with this in mind, the low threshold that must be met before a defendant's own statements can be admitted against him makes sense; so long as there is some indication that the charged crime actually happened, we are satisfied that the accused is not admitting to a crime that never occurred.

The federal courts and the courts of some states use a modified version of the corpus delicti rule called the "trustworthiness doctrine" first announced by the U.S. Supreme Court in *Opper v. United States*.[7] Under this rule, although an uncorroborated confession is not by itself sufficient to convict a defendant, the corroborating evidence need not independently establish an element of the commission of the crime. Rather, the corroborating evidence must establish the "trustworthiness" of the confession. However, many courts that have adopted this rule continue to require "some independent evidence of a criminal act."[8]

Some states that retain the corpus delicti rule have adopted exceptions for specific crimes, usually relating to sexual assaults. For example, Florida's law, F.S.A. § 92.565, permits conviction based on a confession if the state is unable to

MAKING SENSE OF THE CORPUS DELICTI RULE

One area where it can be difficult to obtain independent, corroborating evidence of a crime is sexual assaults of children, which (sadly) happen all too often. In many cases, the child is simply too young or immature to give corroborating evidence of a sexual assault. That is perhaps why, as noted above, some states have abandoned the full corpus delicti rule in such prosecutions.

Those states that have not faced difficult applications of the corpus delicti rule in child sexual assault cases, as two cases decided by the Illinois Supreme Court illustrate. In both cases, the defendant was charged with predatory criminal sexual assault of a child (PCSA), which differs from the lesser offense of aggravated criminal sexual assault of a child (ACSA) because PCSA requires proof of penetration of the child's private parts. In both cases, the defendant confessed to such penetration, but only limited corroborating evidence from the victims was available. In *People v. Sargent*, 940 N.E.2d 1045 (Ill. 2010), the court reversed the PCSA convictions under the corpus delicti rule because of the lack of corroborating evidence. Two years later, in *People v. Lara*, 983 N.W.2d 959 (Ill. 2012), PCSA convictions under similar circumstances were affirmed. How were these cases different, and does the corpus delicti rule make sense as applied in those cases? Or, is the concurring judge in *Lara* correct in believing *Sargent* has effectively been overruled?

prove each element of the offense because of factors such as the victim's age, mental state, or physical incapacitation. The court must find that the confession is trustworthy. In *Hobbs v. State*,[9] the Florida Supreme Court held that the fact a victim recanted earlier testimony could be used as a factor in determining if the state was unable to prove the elements of the crime charged, and make a confession sufficient proof to support a guilty verdict.

THE REQUIREMENT THAT CONFESSIONS AND INCRIMINATING STATEMENTS BE VOLUNTARY

In fifteenth-century England, courts and law officers often obtained confessions to crimes by torture and violence. These abuses led the English courts to create the concept that "no man is bound to accuse himself" *(nemo tenetur seipsum accusare)* and ultimately led to Parliament's abolition of the infamous Star Chamber. English courts used this maxim to hold that persons ought not to be put on trial for a crime and compelled to answer incriminating questions until after they had been properly accused by a grand jury.

voluntariness test The requirement that confessions, incriminating statements, and consent be voluntary and freely given and not obtained by means that overwhelmed the will of the accused or another person.

To protect against the historic abuses that occurred in England, Europe, and Colonial America, the Fifth Amendment of the U.S. Constitution, adopted in 1791, requires that no person "… shall be compelled in a criminal case to be a witness against himself, nor be deprived of life, liberty, or property, without due process of law."

It has never been held that interrogations by police are *per se* unconstitutional. However, the **voluntariness test** used today requires that confessions and admissions by a suspect must be voluntarily and freely given. If the police or a prosecutor obtains a confession or an incriminating admission by means that overbear the will of the accused, that statement or confession cannot be used as evidence, on the grounds that it is a denial of the Fifth and Fourteenth Amendment requirements of due process of law.

Using Violence to Obtain Confessions

Until 1936, each state established its own voluntariness test and determined for itself what "due process of law" meant within that state. In the following important U.S. Supreme Court case, the Court reversed murder convictions in the state of Mississippi and, in a strongly worded decision, held that the confessions used as evidence were involuntarily obtained.[10]

Brown v. Mississippi

United States Supreme Court, 297 U.S. 278, 56 S. Ct. 461 (1936)

When a murder occurred in Mississippi in 1934, the defendants, three black men, were taken into custody by law enforcement officers. By means of whippings, beatings, and the actual hanging of one of the defendants by a rope to the limb of a tree, confessions to the murder were obtained from the defendants. With practically no other evidence and with the rope mark "plainly visible" on the neck of the defendant who was hanged, the criminal trial charging the defendants with murder began. The defendants were convicted despite the fact that a state witness (a deputy sheriff) admitted that brutality and violence were used to obtain the confessions.

In reversing the convictions, the U.S. Supreme Court held:

The question in this case is whether convictions, which rest solely upon confessions shown to have been extorted by officers of the state by brutality and violence, are consistent with the due process of law required by the Fourteenth Amendment of the Constitution of the United States.

...The rack and torture chamber may not be substituted for the witness stand. In the instant case, the trial court was fully advised by the undisputed evidence of the way in which the confessions had been procured. The trial court knew that there was no other evidence upon which conviction and sentence could be based. Yet it proceeded to permit conviction and to pronounce sentence. The conviction and sentence were void for want of the essential elements of due process, and the proceeding thus vitiated could be challenged in any appropriate manner.

The Totality of the Circumstances Test to Determine Whether a Confession or Statement Is Voluntary

totality of the circumstances test
The test that looks at the whole picture and all factors—in determining whether a confession, incriminating statement, or consent was freely and voluntarily given.

Confessions and statements can be involuntarily obtained from a suspect not only by torture and violence but also by many other means. For example, if a confession were obtained by withholding food, heat, clothing, or other essentials of life from a prisoner, courts would refuse to allow the confession to be used as evidence because it was involuntarily induced and was a violation of due process.

Defendants in criminal cases can be convicted only on reliable, relevant evidence. To be admissible as evidence, confessions and statements must be made voluntarily and freely. If the police obtain a confession or admission by means that overbear the will of the accused, the statement or confession will not be admitted for use as evidence, on the grounds that a denial of due process of law occurred.

In determining whether a confession or statement may be used as evidence, courts use the **totality of the circumstances test**. When a court looks at the whole picture (totality of the circumstances), it considers all of the following factors:

- *Suspect vulnerabilities:* Age (very young or very old), education, mental impairment, or physical condition that could make the suspect vulnerable. Was the suspect an alcoholic or a drug addict, a chain smoker, someone in need of a drink, a fix, or a cigarette?
- *Interrogating factors:* Length of questioning; number of officers; time of day or night; denial of food, water, heat, sleep, or other basic necessities. Did the questioning overbear the will of the accused?
- *Place of questioning:* Was questioning done in an isolated area of a police station, or did it occur in the suspect's home or office or in a public place?
- *Other factors:* Were any threats, promises, deception, lies, or trickery used?

Hundreds of state and federal court cases address the question of when lies, threats, promises, deceits, or trickery could cause a confession to be held to be involuntary. Courts generally hold that deception or lies used to promote a confession do not automatically make the confession involuntary, but are merely factors in the totality of circumstances test. For example, in the case of *Lincoln v State*,[11] a confession was held to be given voluntarily even though the police showed the defendant fabricated documents that incriminated him in a murder.

Explicit promises of leniency in exchange for a confession generally result in the confession being treated as involuntary. Although it is permissible to offer "limited assurances" of lighter punishment if a defendant cooperates with investigators, more specific references to lighter punishment if a defendant confesses to a crime are commonly viewed as being unduly coercive. For example, in the case of *United States v. Lopez*,[12] the court held that a confession was given involuntarily where the investigators interrogating the defendant placed two slips of paper before him, one that said "mistake—6" and one that said "murder—60." The numbers were

You be the JUDGE: CONFESSIONS

Before you, the trial judge, are motions to suppress as involuntary confessions made by the defendants in the following cases:

1. A police detective told the defendant he would get "shorter time in county lockup" rather than a "longer stint in state prison" if he took a one-time offer and confessed to the crime charged. Should you permit the confession to be admitted? *State v. Wiley*, 61 A.3d 750 (Me. 2013)
2. A police detective told a defendant that a refusal to confess would lead to a longer sentence and prevent him from spending "crucial years" with his elderly father. Is the confession admissible or involuntary? *United States v. Jacques*, 744 F.3d 804 (1st Cir. 2014)
3. A police detective advised a suspect to "come clean" to a child sex abuse charge so investigators could "keep [his] name out of the newspapers." Is the resulting confession admissible? *State v. Madsen*, 813 N.W.2d 714 (Iowa 2012) [Note: Does Iowa have a rule different from the usual "totality of the circumstances" rule?]
4. In the course of interrogation of the father of a child who had been critically injured by abuse, investigators told the defendant they would arrest his wife and remove her from the dying boy's bedside if he didn't confess. They also told the defendant the circumstances of the abuse were essential to the doctors trying to save the boy's life. Is the resulting confession admissible? *People v. Thomas*, 8 N.E.3d 308 (N.Y. 2014)

the likely years in prison for a confession that a killing was the result of a mistake and a conviction for murder.

Courts also look very closely at confessions given after interrogators make threats to arrest family members of the person who confesses, or remove children from the custody of the person who confesses or others. In *Lynumn v. Illinois*, 372 U.S. 528 (1963), the U.S. Supreme Court held that the threat of removal of a suspect's children "distorted the suspect's rational choice" to confess or not. (See also *Brisbon v. United States*, 957 A.2d 931 (D.C. 2008) [police statement that grandmother would be arrested improper]; *People v. Medina*, 25 P.3d 126 (Colo. 2001) [threat that suspect's children would be taken from mother if he didn't confess to child abuse crime].) However, where police have probable cause to arrest a family member of the person interrogated, use of that threat to obtain a confession has been held not to make the confession involuntary. *State v. Perez*, 920 N.E.2d 104 (Ohio 2009).

THE *MIRANDA* REQUIREMENTS

For many years, the voluntariness requirement was the only test used to determine the admissibility of confessions and statements as evidence. In 1966, the U.S. Supreme Court added an additional requirement.

In the landmark case of *Miranda v. Arizona*,[13] the U.S. Supreme Court made the admissibility of confessions and statements turn not only on a finding of voluntariness but also on proof that confessions or incriminating statements were

APPLICATIONS OF THE TOTALITY OF THE CIRCUMSTANCES TEST IN JUVENILE CASES

When juveniles are questioned by police about crimes they might have committed, the totality of the circumstances test is used to determine whether the juveniles made their statements voluntarily and whether they voluntarily waived their rights under the Self-Incrimination Clause following a *Miranda* warning. The presence or absence of the juveniles' parents during questioning is often an issue in these determinations. In *Fare v. Michael C.* [442 U.S. 707 (1979)], the U.S. Supreme Court held that the age and experience of the juvenile must be considered in reaching that decision, but that the denial of a juvenile's request to talk to his parents would not in every case make the resulting statements inadmissible. The following cases illustrate the totality of the circumstances test in juvenile cases:

- *In re Jerrell, C.J.*, 699 N.W.2d 110 (2005): The Wisconsin Supreme Court held that the denial by police of a 14-year-old boy's repeated requests to call his parents during a five-hour interrogation made his waiver of his *Miranda* rights involuntary. The totality of the circumstances test applied by the court included the age of the boy, his low IQ, and his limited previous contacts with the police. The court also held that the denial of a juvenile's request to speak to his parents would be "strong evidence of coercive tactics" by the police. The court also in this case exercised its supervisory power over lower courts in Wisconsin to adopt a requirement that all interrogations of juveniles must be videotaped. Such a videotape would be extremely useful in making the totality of the circumstances determination, the court decided.
- *In re J.F.*, 987 A.2d 1168 (D.C. Cir. 2010): Police questioned a 14-year-old boy for 11 hours without adult present, and told the boy he couldn't leave until he told detectives "who assaulted your sister"; boy denied assault 63 times before confessing; most details in the confession of the assault were adopted from detectives' suggestions. The appeals court held the confession involuntary.

given only after interrogators complied with certain procedural safeguards. The Court held:

> The prosecution may not use statements, whether exculpatory or inculpatory, stemming from custodial interrogation of the defendant unless it demonstrates the use of procedural safeguards effective to secure the privilege against self-incrimination.

Miranda requirements
The procedural safeguards established by the U.S. Supreme Court in 1966.

The well-known **Miranda requirements** were established by the U.S. Supreme Court as part of the procedural safeguards. There are four *Miranda* requirements:

1. The suspect must be told of his right to remain silent.
2. Anything he says may be used against him in a court of law.
3. He is entitled to the presence of an attorney.
4. If he cannot afford an attorney, one will be appointed to represent him.

The *Miranda* requirements do not have to be complied with unless the following two conditions exist:

- The suspect must be in custody (custody is defined as "the functional equivalent of formal arrest"). In *Thompson v. Keohane*, 516 U.S. 99 (1995) the U.S. Supreme Court held that whether or not a person is in "custody" is determined by an objective test. The test requires consideration of the circumstances surrounding questioning (e.g., at the police station compared to on a city street), as well as whether a reasonable person would believe he was free to leave the interrogation or was in the equivalent of under arrest. In the 2011 case of *J.D.B. v. North Carolina*, 131 S. Ct. 94, the U.S. Supreme Court held that the young age

In 1963 Ernest Miranda (shown here) was charged with rape and armed robbery. (He was not charged and convicted of kidnapping, although he should have been because he transported the victim some distance.) He confessed to the crimes during a police interrogation in which he was not informed that he had a right to have an attorney present or that anything he said could be used against him in court. Although subsequently convicted, he successfully appealed to the U.S. Supreme Court, which overturned his conviction and established the *Miranda* warning to guard a citizen's right to protection against self-incrimination.

Bettmann/Corbis

of a suspect, if known to the officer conducting the questioning, must be considered as a factor in determining if the suspect could believe he was free to leave.

- A government official (police, sheriff, and so on) is seeking to interrogate the suspect about his or her suspected criminal conduct ("questioning initiated by a law enforcement officer after a person has been taken into custody or otherwise deprived of his freedom of action in any significant way").

When a prosecutor seeks to use statements that are the product of custodial interrogation as evidence, the prosecutor must demonstrate the following procedural safeguards:

- Sufficient and adequate warnings were given to the suspect.
- The suspect understood the warnings.
- The suspect waived his or her rights to remain silent and to have an attorney present during the questioning.

Persons in Custody Must Clearly and Unambiguously Invoke Their Fifth Amendment Rights

After giving the *Miranda* warnings to persons lawfully in custody, the police may begin questioning them. However, if the person invokes the right to remain silent or to have an attorney present, police must stop questioning at once. When has a person in custody done so? The U.S. Supreme Court held in the 2010 case of *Berghuis v. Thompkins*, 130 S. Ct. 2250, that simply remaining silent is not enough; the person must affirmatively invoke those rights.

In *Berghuis*, the defendant Thompkins remained silent for almost three hours after being taken into custody and given his *Miranda* warnings. Had he said,

"I want to remain silent," "I want a lawyer," or other unambiguous language invoking his rights, the police would have been required to cease interrogating him.

Thompkins did not do so. He remained silent and sat "tacit and uncommunicative" through almost three hours of police interrogation. After about 2 hours and 45 minutes of questioning Thompkins was asked,

> "Do you believe in God"? ... Thompkins made eye contact with Helgert (police officer) and said "Yes" as his eyes well(ed) up with tears ... Helgert asked "Do you pray to God?" Thompkins said "Yes" ... Helgert asked "Do you pray to God to forgive you for shooting that boy down?" Thompkins answered "Yes" and looked away. Thompson refused to make a written confession, and the interrogation ended about 15 minutes later. 130 S. Ct. at 1257.

The U.S. Supreme Court affirmed the use of Thompkins' answers as evidence against him in his criminal trial, holding that his conduct indicated a waiver of his right to remain silent, and that there was no evidence his statements were coerced. The Court first rejected Thompkins' contention that the police were required to obtain a waiver from him before starting interrogations:

> Thus, after giving a *Miranda* warning, police may interrogate a suspect who has neither invoked nor waived his or her *Miranda* rights. On these premises, it follows the police were not required to obtain a waiver of Thompkins' *Miranda* rights before commencing the interrogation. 130 S. Ct. at 2264.

The Court also stated the following about Thompkins' conduct that resulted in the waiver of his *Miranda* rights:

> In sum, a suspect who has received and understood the *Miranda* warnings, and has not invoked his *Miranda* rights, waives the right to remain silent by making an uncoerced statement to the police. Thompkins did not invoke his right to remain silent and stop the questioning. Understanding his rights in full, he waived his right to remain silent by making a voluntary statement to the police. The police, moreover, were not required to obtain a waiver of Thompkins' right to remain silent. *Id.*

Under the reasoning of *Berghuis*, statements like "maybe I should talk to a lawyer," "Do you think I need a lawyer?" or "I was going to get a lawyer" are not unambiguous invocations of Fifth Amendment rights. In *United States v. Pugh*, 648 F.3d 118 (2nd Cir. 2010), *cert. denied* 132 S. Ct. 1610 (2012), the court held that simple refusal to sign a *Miranda* waiver form was insufficient to constitute an unambiguous invocation of rights.

On the other hand, if an invocation is ambiguous because of some police actions or statements, the result may be different. In *United States v. Scott*, 693 F.3d 715 (6th Cir. 2012), a defendant wrote "no" in a *Miranda* waiver form as his answer to the question "Do you wish to talk to us now?" The police later questioned the defendant, who then confessed to several robberies. The state argued that the "no" answer was ambiguous, because the question only asked if the defendant wanted to talk "now," not later. The court held the subsequent statements should be excluded, because the defendant's invocation of his Firth Amendment rights was unambiguous.

When *Miranda* Warnings Are Not Required

1. *Miranda* warnings are not required if the person is not in custody, or if a suspect is in custody and there is no intention or effort by a law officer to interrogate the suspect about the crime for which the suspect has been arrested. Some

THE HISTORY AND REASON FOR THE "14-DAY RULE" AFTER THERE HAS BEEN A BREAK IN CUSTODY UNDER *MIRANDA*: 1966–2010

Once a person has been placed in custody and given the *Miranda* warnings, and asserts either the right to remain silent or the right to a lawyer, all efforts by the police to interrogate the person must stop, unless the person's lawyer is present.

The person detained may at this point be released from custody and permitted to leave, or, if a suspect in a crime, charged with that crime. Whether the person originally in custody is simply allowed to go home, released on bail, or held in custody awaiting trial, law officers may not approach the person, give another *Miranda* warning, and attempt to obtain a waiver of rights and initiate further questioning until there has been a "break" in the custody during which the initial *Miranda* warnings were given. In 2010 the U.S. Supreme Court held that this "break" in custody must be at least 14 days from the initial custody where the *Miranda* warnings were given.

The history and reasoning for this "break-in-custody" rule began with the 1966 *Miranda* case, which was followed by the U.S. Supreme Court case of *Edwards v. Arizona* in 1981. The "14-day" part of the rule came out of the 2010 U.S. Supreme Court case of *Maryland v. Shatzer*. A brief presentation of the history and origin of the rule follows:

The *Miranda* rule established in 1966	Prior to 1966, British police were required to "caution" persons held in custody as to their rights before British police could question them. Citing this British practice, the U.S. Supreme Court created a set of measures to protect a defendant's Fifth Amendment privilege against compelled self-incrimination. The Court reasoned this right could be seriously jeopardized by the "inherently compelling pressures"[1] and the "police-dominated atmosphere"[2] of police custodial interrogation. "To protect against this danger, the *Miranda* rule creates a presumption of coercion (that) in the absence of specific warnings (the presumption) is generally irrebuttable for the purposes of the prosecution's case in chief."[3]
The 1981 *Edwards* rule, also known as the second layer of protection after *Miranda*	The *Edwards* rule, from *Edwards v. Arizona*, 451 U.S. 477 (1981), creates a presumption that once a person invokes the rights protected in *Miranda* (the first layer of protection), any subsequent waiver of those rights in response to attempts by police to initiate interrogation is presumed involuntary. The Supreme Court said "[a]ny subsequent waiver that comes (at police/prosecutor's) bequest, and not at the suspect's own instigation is itself the product of the "inherently compelling pressures," and not the purely voluntary choice of the suspect."[4]
	The U.S. Supreme Court stated in *Michigan v. Harvey*[5] that the purpose of the *Edwards* rule was to "prevent police from badgering (a suspect) into waiving his previously asserted *Miranda* rights."
	The rule in *Miranda* and *Edwards* is not "crime specific" and applies to any attempts to interrogate a suspect, including in the investigation of other crimes, after the suspect has invoked the *Miranda* rights. *Arizona v. Roberson*.[6] (This contrasts with the Sixth Amendment right to counsel, discussed in this chapter, which is "crime specific.")
The 14-day rule after a break in *Miranda* custody	The *Edwards* prohibition against police-initiated questioning does not last forever. Lower courts uniformly held in the years after *Edwards* that the protection afforded in *Edwards* ended with a break in *Miranda* custody, sometimes for only a few hours when the suspect was released and returned home, and then was later interrogated by police.
	The U.S. Supreme Court accepted the "break in *Miranda* custody" limit on the *Edwards* rule in the 2010 case of *Maryland v. Shatzer*.[7] The Supreme Court added a "bright line" rule that the *Edwards* prohibition stays in place for 14 days after a suspect has been released from custody. It stated that 14 days "… is plenty of time for the suspect to get reacclimated to his normal life, to consult with friends and counsel, and to shake off any residual coercive effects of the prior custody."[8]

In the *Shatzer* case the suspect, Shatzer, was in a state prison for a prior conviction. While in prison, Shatzer was brought in for questioning relating to another crime, and Shatzer invoked his *Miranda* rights. He was released back to the general prison population. Two years later, another detective investigating the other crime came to the prison to question Shatzer again. This time, Shatzer waived his *Miranda* rights, and made incriminating statements. The U.S. Supreme Court held that returning Shatzer to the general prison population constituted a break in *Miranda* custody that ended the presumption of involuntariness established in *Edwards*.

[1]*Miranda v. Arizona*, 384 U.S. 436, 467 (1966).
[2]*Id*, 384 U.S. at 445.
[3]*United States v. Patane*, 542 U.S. 630, 639 (2004).
[4]*Arizona v. Roberson*, 486 U.S. 675 (1988).
[5]494 U.S. 344, 350 (1990).
[6]486 U.S. 675 (1988).
[7]130 S. Ct. 1213 (2010).
[8]*Id.*, at 1223.

police and sheriff departments require that *Miranda* warnings be given after every arrest. This, then, would be a requirement of that department or within that state, but the U.S. Supreme Court does not require *Miranda* warnings under these circumstances.

2. *Miranda* warnings are not required when a person volunteers information. The U.S. Supreme Court held that "There is no requirement that police stop a person who enters a police station and states that he wishes to confess to a crime, or a person who calls the police to offer a confession or any other statement he desires to make. Volunteered statements of any kind are not barred by the Fifth Amendment and their admissibility is not affected by our holding today."[14]
As an example, a deputy sheriff asked a prisoner awaiting trial, "How's it going, Ashford?" Ashford answered with a statement that incriminated himself. The court held that the deputy could testify about Ashford's incriminating statement.[15]

Other examples of volunteered statements include cases in which the defendant surprised everyone by admitting while he was on the witness stand that he killed the victim;[16] the defendant walked into a police station and told the police that he had shot his wife;[17] and the defendant voluntarily stated that he had a gun under the front seat of his automobile.[18]

The Maryland Court of Appeals pointed out that there is no privilege against inadvertent self-incrimination, or even stupid self-incrimination, but only against self-incrimination.[19] In that case, the defendant blurted out he had a lot of illegal drugs in his car.

3. *"General on-the-scene questioning* as to facts surrounding a crime or other general questioning of citizens in the fact-finding process is not affected by our holding. It is an act of responsible citizenship for individuals to give whatever information they may have to aid in law enforcement. In such situations the compelling atmosphere inherent in the process of in-custody interrogation is not necessarily present."[20] Consider the following examples:

- When a deputy sheriff working in a jail saw one of two men held in a drunk tank lying on the floor in a pool of blood, he asked the other man sleeping on a wall bench, "What happened?" The man answered, "I killed the son of a bitch last night; he would not shut up." The Supreme Court of Utah held that the defendant's response was properly admitted in evidence.[21]

- Minutes after a shooting occurred on a street, a police officer arrived at the scene. A young boy at the scene told the officer that the assailant had run away between two houses. The officer proceeded in that direction and saw a man step out of a doorway. The officer, who had his revolver out, asked the man if he had been involved in the shooting. The man answered, "Yeah, I shot him." After the man was arrested, the murder weapon was found in his pocket. The statement of the defendant and the weapon were held to be properly admitted in evidence by the Wisconsin Supreme Court.[22]

- In investigating crimes, police officers are required to ask questions and talk to persons who are *material witnesses* to crimes. In some instances, the investigation could reveal that a material witness is the person who committed the crime. In the 1991 case of *Wallace v. State*,[23] it was held that an officer called to a store to investigate a forged check was not obligated to give *Miranda* warnings to Wallace, who was viewed as a material witness when questioned.

4. Miranda warnings are not required for investigative detentions (stop and inquire) based on reasonable suspicion to believe that the person is committing, has committed, or is about to commit a crime. In the 1984 case *of Berkemer v. McCarty*,[24] the U.S. Supreme Court stated this rule as follows:

> Under the Fourth Amendment, we have held, a policeman who lacks probable cause but whose "observations lead him reasonably to suspect" that a particular person has committed, is committing, or is about to commit a crime, may detain that person briefly in order to "investigate the circumstances that provoke suspicion." *United States v. Brignoni-Ponce*, 422 U.S. 873, 881, 45 L.Ed.2d 607, 95 S. Ct. 2574 (1975). "[T]he stop and inquiry must be 'reasonably related in scope to the justification for their initiation.'" *Ibid.* [quoting *Terry v. Ohio, supra*, at 29, 20 L.Ed.2d 889, 88 S. Ct. 1868]. Typically, this means that the officer may ask the detainee a moderate number of questions to determine his identity and to try to obtain information confirming or dispelling the officer's suspicions. But the detainee is not obliged to respond. And, unless the detainee's answers provide the officer with probable cause to arrest him, he must then be released. The comparatively non-threatening character of detentions of this sort explains the absence of any suggestion in our opinions that Terry stops are subject to the dictates of *Miranda*.

5. *Miranda* warnings are not required in "ordinary traffic stops." The U.S. Supreme Court also ruled in *Berkemer v. McCarty*[25] that an investigative stop and a traffic stop are similar in that both have "noncoercive aspect(s)," with traffic stops usually being temporary, brief, and public. The Court ruled that "persons temporarily detained pursuant to (traffic) stops are not 'in custody' for the purposes of *Miranda*." The reasons for this ruling were explained as follows by the U.S. Supreme Court:

> Two features of an ordinary traffic stop mitigate the danger that a person questioned will be induced "to speak where he would not otherwise do so freely," *Miranda v. Arizona*. First, detention of a motorist pursuant to a traffic stop is presumptively temporary and brief. The vast majority of roadside detentions last only a few minutes. A motorist's expectations, when he sees a policeman's light flashing behind him, are that he will be obliged to spend a short period of time answering questions and waiting while the officer checks his license and registration, that he

may then be given a citation, but that in the end he most likely will be allowed to continue on his way. In this respect, questioning incident to an ordinary traffic stop is quite different from stationhouse interrogation, which frequently is prolonged, and in which the detainee often is aware that questioning will continue until he provides his interrogators the answers they seek.

Second, circumstances associated with the typical traffic stop are not such that the motorist feels completely at the mercy of the police. To be sure, the aura of authority surrounding an armed, uniformed officer and the knowledge that the officer has some discretion in deciding whether to issue a citation, in combination, exert some pressure on the detainee to respond to questions. But other aspects of the situation substantially offset these forces. Perhaps most importantly, the typical traffic stop is public, at least to some degree. Passersby, on foot or in other cars, witness the interaction of officer and motorist. This exposure to public view both reduces the ability of an unscrupulous policeman to use illegitimate means to elicit self-incriminating statements and diminishes the motorist's fear that, if he does not cooperate, he will be subjected to abuse. The fact that the detained motorist typically is confronted by only one or at most two policemen further mutes his sense of vulnerability. In short, the atmosphere surrounding an ordinary traffic stop is substantially less "police dominated" than that surrounding the kinds of interrogation at issue in *Miranda* itself, and in the subsequent cases in which we have applied *Miranda*.468 U.S., at 437–438.

If a motorist (or a passenger in a vehicle) is arrested or taken into custody, however, *Miranda* becomes applicable. In the *Berkemer v. McCarty* case, for example, any incriminating statements made by the defendant after his arrest for drunk driving would be inadmissible if the *Miranda* warnings had not been given. In that case, however, the prosecution did not attempt to introduce any post-arrest statements, but only those made prior to the arrest.

6. Routine booking questions are exempt from *Miranda*'s coverage. In the 1990 case of *Pennsylvania v. Muniz*,[26] the U.S. Supreme Court held that questions and answers as to "name, address, height, weight, eye color, date of birth, and current age—did not constitute custodial interrogation ... (and) fall within a *routine booking question exception*, which exempts from *Miranda*'s coverage questions to secure the 'biographical data necessary to complete booking or pretrial service' 873 F.2d 180, 181 n.2." The U.S. Supreme Court pointed out with approval that the trial court in the *Muniz* case held that these questions were "requested for recordkeeping purposes only" and therefore "appear reasonably related to the police's administrative concerns."

Booking questions about employment are also routinely asked and were sustained in the 1991 case of *People v. Abdelmassih*.[27] In the 1991 case of *State v. Mallozzi*,[28] the defendant made incriminating statements during the booking process after an FBI agent informed him of the charges against him. Because no questions other than routine booking questions were asked, the defendant's statements were admissible in evidence against him.

7. The *Miranda* warnings are not imposed on private persons who ask questions. For example, a family member may ask, "Why did you do it, Joe?" Or an employer or other private person may ask questions that could produce incriminating answers. Because *Miranda* is not required of private persons, any incriminating statement could be admitted as evidence in both civil and criminal cases. The following cases further illustrate:

- A shoplifter made incriminating statements in response to questions from a store clerk. The Georgia Court of Appeals held that *Miranda* is applicable only to law enforcement officers; the store clerk was not required to give the *Miranda* warnings before questioning.[29]

- A journalist gathering material for a book visited John Joubert in a Nebraska prison where Joubert was sentenced to death. Joubert made statements incriminating himself in the death of an 11-year-old boy in Maine. The Supreme Court of Maine held that the admissions were admissible because the journalist was not acting as an agent of the police. No *Miranda* warnings were given or required.[30]

- Most courts hold that private security officers do not come under the *Miranda* requirements. New York state courts held:

  To hold that the conduct of [a] private store detective was governed by *Miranda* would be an extravagant expansion of the intended scope of that decision, and would constitute an unnecessary and unauthorized interference with the right of a merchant to protect his property by lawful means. *Id.* at 287, 480 N.W.2d at 1068, 491 N.Y.S.2d at 285. The duty of giving "*Miranda* warnings" is limited to employees of governmental agencies whose function is to enforce the law, or to those acting for such law enforcement agencies by direction of the agencies...

- In also holding that *Miranda* does not apply to private security persons, the Virginia Court of Appeals reviewed state court cases with similar rulings in the 1991 case of *Mier v. Commonwealth.*[31]

8. *Miranda* warnings are not required when border agents question aliens seeking admission into this country. Even if aliens being questioned at a border about their admission into this country are in "custody," most courts have held that official, routine questioning of an alien does not require a *Miranda* warning, even if that questioning results in incriminating statements from the alien.[32] In the 2006 case of *United States v. Kiam,*[33] the Third Circuit Court of Appeals concluded that the exception should be expanded beyond "routine" questioning and held that any questioning of aliens related to their admissibility did not require a *Miranda* warning. However, the court stated that when questioning is directed solely at a potential criminal investigation, the warning must be given. In *United States v. FNU LNU,* 653 F.3d 144 (2d Cir. 2011), the court held that the test for border questioning should continue to focus on whether the person was in "custody," not the nature of the questions asked as bearing on the person's suitability for entering the country. However, the court said the question of custody must be decided taking into account the fact that the person was detained at a border crossing, something the court said most people would consider "par for the course" when seeking to enter this country.

9. The *Miranda* requirements have been held *not* to be applicable in the following cases:

- Offenders (sexual and other offenses) who are required by conditions of their probation or parole to participate in treatment programs and be truthful "in all matters" or risk revocation of their parole or probation do not have to get *Miranda* warnings. In the 1984 case of *Minnesota v. Murphy,*[34] Murphy was in such a program and confessed to an unsolved rape and murder. The U.S. Supreme Court held his admissions could be used to sustain his conviction.

- Undercover officers conducting investigations while not disclosing their true identity do not have to give *Miranda* warnings and do not have to identify themselves. See the 1990 case of *Illinois v. Perkins*,[35] where an undercover officer went into a prison cell, and the 1966 case of *Hoffa v. United States*,[36] where an undercover agent was obtaining information against former Teamsters Union President James Hoffa.
- When a probation or parole officer is doing a presentence interview on behalf of the trial court, it has been repeatedly held that *Miranda* is not applicable.[37]

The Public Safety Exception to *Miranda* Requirements

The *Miranda* warnings must be given before police may question a suspect. Thus, if police question a suspect while in custody but without the *Miranda* warnings, the answers may not be used in a subsequent criminal trial. An important and well-recognized exception permits police questioning before *Miranda* warnings are given when the safety of the police or the public is potentially threatened.

The Public Safety Exception The U.S. Supreme Court established the *public safety exception* in the 1984 case of *New York v. Quarles*.[38] In that case, an armed rapist was fleeing police in New York City. The man fled to an A&P supermarket, carrying a gun. He hid the gun somewhere in the store before being captured by police officers. After the man was handcuffed, he was asked where the gun was without being given the *Miranda* warnings. The suspect (Quarles) nodded in the direction of some empty cartons and answered, "The gun is over there." In addition to rape, Quarles was convicted of criminal possession of a weapon. The weapon and the statement by Quarles were used as evidence against him. In affirming the convictions and creating the public safety exception to *Miranda*, the U.S. Supreme Court held:

> The exception will not be difficult for police officers to apply because in each case it will be circumscribed by the exigency which justifies it. We think police officers can and will distinguish almost instinctively between questions necessary to secure their own safety or the safety of the public and questions designed solely to elicit testimonial evidence from a suspect.
>
> The facts of this case clearly demonstrate that distinction and an officer's ability to recognize it. Officer Kraft asked only the question necessary to locate the missing gun before advising respondent of his rights. It was only after securing the loaded revolver and giving the warnings that he continued with investigatory questions about the ownership and place of purchase of the gun. The exception which we recognize today, far from complicating the thought processes and the on-the-scene judgments of police officers, will simply free them to follow their legitimate instincts when confronting situations presenting a danger to the public safety.

The following cases are examples of courts that upheld pre-*Miranda* questioning by police of a suspect in custody based on the public safety exception:

- *United States v. Hernandez*, 751 F.3d 538 (7th Cir. 2014): Police saw a man running down an alley carrying a red bag. They approached the man, who dropped the bag and said, "I just have some dope". He showed the officers four packets of what later turned out to be heroin. The officers arrested the man, and before giving the *Miranda* warnings asked him, "What is in the bag?" He answered he had "ripped the guys around the corner for dope and a

CHALLENGES TO *MIRANDA*

Can the U.S. Congress Overturn *Miranda*?

Two years after the *Miranda* decision, opponents to the *Miranda* rule attached a provision to a bill that overturned *Miranda* when it became law. The 1968 enactment provided that if a confession or incriminating statement was voluntary, then the confession or statement should be admitted as evidence in federal criminal cases whether *Miranda* had been complied with or not.

U.S. presidents for more than 30 years instructed the Justice Department to ignore this law [18 U.S.C. section 3501] until 1999, when a federal appeals court in Richmond, Virginia, ruled in the case of *Dickerson v. United States* that the U.S. Congress was free to overturn *Miranda* and had done so in section 3501.

In the *Dickerson* case, Dickerson's incriminating statements about his involvement in a bank robbery were suppressed because he had not received a *Miranda* warning. The U.S. Court of Appeals in Virginia ruled that because the statements were voluntary, they were admissible under section 3501. The U.S. Supreme Court reversed in *Dickerson v. United States* [530 U.S. 428 (2000)], holding that the statements were not admissible and that the *Miranda* doctrine could not be overruled by the U.S. Congress:

> *Miranda* has become embedded in routine police practices [in the United States] to the point where the warnings have become part of our national culture…we conclude that *Miranda* announced a constitutional rule that Congress may not supersede legislatively.

Is a Question First/Warn Later Procedure Permissible Under *Miranda*?

In the 1985 case of *Oregon v. Elstad*, 470 U.S. 298, police inadvertently failed to give the *Miranda* warnings. After the defendant confessed the police complied with the *Miranda* rule, and the defendant confessed again. The U.S. Supreme Court held that because both confessions were made voluntarily, the second confession was admissible as evidence and affirmed the defendant's conviction.

In the 2004 case of *Missouri v. Seibert* [542 U.S. 600, 124 S. Ct. 2601], the U.S. Supreme Court held that the police's deliberate failure to give the *Miranda* warnings to a woman suspected of arson before questioning her made the resulting confession inadmissible. After Seibert confessed to the arson, the police turned on a tape recorder and complied with the *Miranda* rule, reminding the defendant of her incriminating statements.

Because the police admitted to routinely using this two-step interrogation technique in an effort to obtain confessions and incriminating statements, the Missouri Supreme Court reversed Seibert's conviction, calling the procedure an "end run" around *Miranda*.

The U.S. Supreme Court agreed and affirmed the Missouri Supreme Court, stating,

> Strategists dedicated to draining the substance out of *Miranda* cannot accomplish by training instructions what *Dickerson* held Congress could not do by statute. Because the question-first tactic effectively threatens to thwart *Miranda's* purpose of reducing the risk that a coerced confession would be admitted, and because the facts here do not reasonably support a conclusion that the warnings given could have served their purpose, Seibert's post-warning statements are inadmissible. 124 S. Ct. at 2613.
>
> In the 2006 case of *United States v. Gonzalez-Lauren* [437 F.3d 1128 (11th Cir. 2006), *cert. denied*, 127 S. Ct. 146], the court held that investigators did not violate a defendant's Fifth Amendment rights when they intentionally delayed giving the *Miranda* warnings until they had shown the defendant all the evidence they had gathered connecting him to a murder. The investigators did not ask the defendant any questions designed to elicit incriminating statements, the court noted, which made the case different from *Missouri v. Seibert*. The defendant's subsequent waiver of his rights and confession after the *Miranda* warning were upheld.

gun." Officers found a gun in the bag. The court upheld his conviction for illegal possession of a firearm. The pre-*Miranda* questions were justifiable to protect the officers and the public, the court held.

- *United States v. Ferguson*, 702 F.3d 89 (2nd Cir. 2012), *cert. denied* 134 S. Ct. 56 (2013): After a 911 caller told police the defendant had fired shots outside an apartment building, police located the defendant near a park and playground and arrested him. One hour later, at the police station, police questioned the defendant about the location of the gun. An officer testified they did not give the *Miranda* warnings because they were afraid the defendant would cease answering questions, leaving the gun hidden where a child might find it. The court affirmed the defendant's conviction for a gun violation, holding that the police only asked questions aimed at locating the gun, which clearly presented a potential danger to the public if gone unfound. The one-hour delay, the court said, was not determinative of the reasonableness of the police's actions.

- *United States v. Hodge*, 714 F.3d 380 (6th Cir. 2013), *cert. denied* 134 S. Ct. 286 (2013): Police were about to search defendant's house under a search warrant directed at a meth operation. While in control of the premises and before giving the *Miranda* warnings, police asked the defendant if anything dangerous was in the house. He answered "there is a bomb inside". Police shut down the search, and used a robot device to find the pipe-bomb in the house. The court affirmed the defendant's conviction for illegal possession of an unregistered destructive device (the pipe bomb). It rejected his claim that because the police had secured the area the public could not gain access to the bomb, making the public safety exception inapplicable. It said it was enough that the police would be concerned about the safety of officers searching the house if a bomb was hidden in the house.

- *People v. Doll*, 998 N.E.2d 384 (N.Y. 2013), *cert. denied* 134 S. Ct. 1552 (2014): Police officers saw a man walking on a road wearing a coat that appeared to have blood on it. They stopped him, took him to the vehicle he said he was driving before the walk, and saw blood in the interior. They then took him into custody, and without giving the *Miranda* warnings asked him where the blood came from. The man refused to answer, so officers took him to the station house because they were afraid someone had been injured. There they continued questioning, and ultimately heard the defendant implicate himself in the death of his business partner earlier that evening. The court affirmed the defendant's conviction for second-degree murder, holding that statements and evidence gained from the pre-*Miranda* warnings questions was justified under the public safety exception. The court said the questions were directed only to determine if someone needed emergency assistance.

SILENCE, *MIRANDA*, AND IMPEACHMENT

Assume the jury in a criminal trial is told the defendant remained silent in the face of questions by police about the crime charged. It is possible, perhaps even probable, that the jury could draw an inference of guilt from the defendant's silence. When, if at all, should the prosecution be permitted to bring evidence of a defendant's silence before the jury? The answer depends on whether the defendant

PROCEDURES & PROCESSES

When Does a Person Have a Right to an Attorney?

A person may hire an attorney at any time, and generally may have that attorney present when dealing with law enforcement officers. There are only two situations in which the government may not proceed unless a person either has an attorney or elects to waive the right to have an attorney present. Those two situations are listed below. In those situations, if the person is indigent and lacks the resources to hire a lawyer, the government must provide a lawyer at the government's expense. Some situations where an attorney may be present, though not required, are also listed.

A Person Has a Right to an Attorney

1. During a custodial interrogation, when a person is in custody and a government official seeks to question the person regarding a crime, the right to an attorney is guaranteed by the Fifth and Sixth Amendments.

    (Note that if the person is not in custody and is free to leave the police presence, or if the person is in custody but there is no attempt to interrogate the person, there is no right to an attorney. See *Miranda v. Arizona*, 384 U.S. 436 (1966).)

2. "[O]nce a criminal prosecution is commenced … whether by formal charge, indictment, preliminary hearing, or arraignment," the defendant has a right to an attorney under the Sixth Amendment. (See *Rothgery v. Gillespie County*, 128 S. Ct. 2578 (2008), discussed below.)

No Right to an Attorney Exists, Although One May Be Present

During voluntary conversations between a law officer and a private citizen.

During a traffic stop (speeding, for example).

During an investigative detention based on reasonable suspicion or probable cause.

During identification proceedings (showups or photo viewing).

During routine booking procedures after arrest.

During appearances before a prosecuting attorney.

During an appearance before a grand jury or a "John Doe" jury.

When a person who has not been charged with a crime is ordered by either the police or the prosecutor to appear in the office of the prosecutor. (In many of these situations there is a high likelihood that the prosecutor will seek criminal charges.)

When Does a Criminal Prosecution Commence?

The right to counsel guaranteed by the Sixth Amendment applies in any "criminal prosecution." If the defendant cannot afford counsel, the government must appoint counsel once a criminal prosecution is commenced. The U.S. Supreme Court has said that a criminal prosecution is commenced by the initiation of adversary criminal proceedings, whether by formal charge, indictment, preliminary hearing, or arraignment. It is at that point, the Court stated, that the state has committed itself to prosecuting an arrestee, and the person is "immersed in the intricacies of substantive and procedural criminal law."[39]

The Supreme Court held in *Rothgery v. Gillespie* (cited above) that the government has "committed" itself to prosecution whenever the accusations against a defendant prompt an appearance before a judicial officer, and restraints are placed on the defendant's liberty. Thus, where the defendant has been brought before a magistrate to determine if probable cause exists for an arrest, the case has "commenced," even if the prosecutor did not appear at the hearing, and had made no decision to prosecute at that time. The Supreme Court noted that this is the procedure in the majority of states, and that forty-three states appointed counsel after the initial hearing, with or without the filing of formal charges.[40]

was in "custody" when the questioning occurred, and whether the silence is used in the prosecution's case-in-chief or to impeach the trial testimony of the defendant. The following chart shows the U. S. Supreme Court's answer to the use of silence in various settings:

Defendant was in custody when questioned

A. A defendant's silence in the face of questions asked **before** the *Miranda* warnings were given cannot be used by the prosecution in its case-in-chief. That is the point of *Miranda*.

B. A defendant's complete silence in the face of questions asked after the *Miranda* warnings may not be used for any purpose, including for purposes of impeachment if the defendant testifies at the resulting trial. In *Doyle v. Ohio*,[42] the U.S. Supreme Court held that such use would violate the Due Process Clause.

C. If a defendant makes a voluntary statement after Miranda warnings, and later gives conflicting testimony at trial, the fact that the defendant was "silent" about the parts of the trial testimony that were new or different from the prior statement can be used by the prosecution to impeach the trial testimony. *Anderson v. Charles*[43] **Example:** Defendant made a voluntary statement after Miranda warnings were given that he saw "another guy running away" from the scene of a crime. At his trial, defendant testifies in greater detail about the identity of the alleged "other guy." Prosecutors may ask the defendant why he didn't give these details in the earlier statement.

Defendant was not in custody when questioned

A. If a defendant remains silent during pre-custody, pre-*Miranda* questioning, but later testifies at trial, the defendant's silence to earlier questions can be used for impeachment purposes. *Jenkins v. Anderson*[41]

B. If a defendant remains silent during pre-custody, pre-*Miranda* questioning but **does not expressly** invoke the Fifth Amendment privilege, the prosecution may use the defendant's silence in its case-in-chief, even if the defendant does not testify at the resulting trial. *Salinas v. Texas*, 133 S. Ct. 2174 (2013). **Example:** When asked by police if shotgun shells found at a crime scene would match the defendant's shotgun, defendant stopped talking with police and "looked down at the floor, and shuffled his feet." At his subsequent murder trial officers would be permitted to testify about the defendant's silence, even if the defendant did not testify at his trial. Under the holding in *Salinas* the defendant's failure to invoke expressly his Fifth Amendment privilege meant his rights were not prejudiced by use of his silence.

C. If a defendant remains silent during pre-custody, pre-*Miranda* questioning and **expressly does** invoke the Fifth Amendment privilege it is uncertain if the prosecution can use that silence in its case-in-chief. The Supreme Court in *Salinas* noted that there is a clear split among lower courts on the question. However, the Court said "But because [defendant] did not invoke the privilege during his interview [with the police], we find it unnecessary to reach that question."[44]

EVIDENCE OBTAINED BY THREATS OF LOSS OF A JOB OR LICENSE

When complaints are filed against a law enforcement officer, lawyer, teacher, doctor, or other person holding a state-required license, it is common practice for investigators to request that a written response to the complaint be submitted; such a response, if given, could implicate the person in criminal proceedings. May investigators threaten the person being investigated with loss of job or license if that person refuses to answer based on the Fifth Amendment?

In *Garrity v. State of New Jersey*[45] the U. S. Supreme Court said no. There, police officers were told they must answer questions, and if they invoked their right to remain silent they would be fired. Subsequently, prosecutors used the answers given in criminal cases against the officers. The Supreme Court reversed the officers' convictions, holding they were compelled to give testimony against themselves by the threat of losing their jobs. Similarly, in *Spevack v. Klein*[46] the Supreme Court held that disbarment by a state bar association of an attorney because he invoked his Fifth Amendment rights to refuse to answer investigator's questions was a violation.

However, if a person voluntarily answers questions during an investigation, the answers may be used in subsequent criminal prosecutions.[47] Also, courts uniformly hold that if the investigators agree that any answers made to their questions cannot be used in a subsequent criminal prosecution, the person being investigated must answer the questions. Since the answers cannot be used in a criminal case, the person is not being "compelled" to be "a witness against himself."

LEGAL CASES

Can the Failure to Give *Miranda* Warnings Be the Basis for a Civil Lawsuit?

The 2003 Case of *Chavez v. Martinez*, 123 S. Ct. 1994

Two police officers stopped Martinez while he was riding his bicycle at night. During a subsequent search, a struggle ensued. One officer shouted, "He's got my gun," and the other officer shot Martinez several times. Martinez was brought to a hospital, and, while he was receiving emergency treatment, a police supervisor, Chavez, questioned him about the altercation, including questions that related to criminal actions Martinez may have taken. Martinez was not given his *Miranda* warnings.

No criminal charges were brought against Martinez, and his statements made to Chavez were never used in any prosecution against him. Martinez brought a civil action against Chavez under federal civil rights laws, alleging that Chavez violated his Fifth Amendment rights by questioning him without *Miranda* warnings. The Ninth Circuit Court of Appeals held that Martinez's Fifth Amendment rights had been violated.

The U.S. Supreme Court reversed, holding that no Fifth Amendment rights had been violated because the statements were never used in a criminal case brought against Martinez. Noting that the Fifth Amendment provides that "No person shall be compelled in any criminal case" to be a witness against himself, the Court concluded that in the absence of such a criminal case, the Fifth Amendment did not apply. Thus, the police interrogation violated neither the *Miranda* rule nor the Fifth Amendment. The Court also noted that if the police use torture or other abuse in questioning a suspect but never attempt to use the resulting statements in a criminal case, the Fourteenth Amendment would provide a remedy for the torture or other abuse inflicted on the suspect.

■ WHEN DOES A CONVERSATION WITH A DEFENDANT BECOME "INTERROGATION"?

In *Rhode Island v. Innis*, 446 U.S. 291, 300–301 (1980), the U.S. Supreme Court stated: "We conclude the *Miranda* safeguards come into play whenever a person in custody is subjected to either express questioning or its functional equivalent." Functional equivalent means any " … words or actions on the part of the police … that the police should know are reasonably likely to elicit an incriminating response from the suspect." For example, if the police minimize the seriousness of the crime, or "blame" the victim, in conversations with the suspect, this is the functional equivalent of interrogation because the police know, and perhaps intend, that doing so is likely to encourage the suspect to make incriminating statements.

It can sometimes be difficult to determine whether conversations with a defendant in custody constitute "interrogation" requiring a *Miranda* warning, or whether conversations after a suspect has invoked his right to remain silent constitute interrogation. For example, in *Drury v. State*, 793 A.2d 567 (Md. Ct. App. 2002), police took a defendant to the police station for questioning concerning a burglary. The door of a store was pried open with a tire iron, which was found near the crime scene. Before the defendant was advised of his *Miranda* rights, police showed the defendant the tire iron and some other articles found near the crime scene and told the defendant the items were to be sent out for fingerprints. The defendant then made incriminating statements, which were used against him at his trial. On appeal, the court held that showing the defendant the evidence found near the crime scene was the functional equivalent of interrogation, since the police should have known that it would evoke an incriminating response from the defendant.

Other courts have reached the opposite result. In *United States v. Allen*, 247 F.3d 741 (8th Cir. 2001), the court held that it was not interrogation to inform the defendant in custody that three of four witnesses identified the defendant as present at the scene of a crime; the court said that information was merely describing the state of the investigation.

THE SIXTH AMENDMENT RIGHT TO COUNSEL AND THE *MASSIAH* LIMITATION

Until a person is formally charged with a crime, the only criteria used to determine whether a confession or incriminating statements can be used are the voluntariness test and the *Miranda* requirements. After a suspect is formally charged with a crime, it is "entirely proper [for law officers] to continue an investigation of the … criminal activities of the defendant and his alleged confederates."[48] However, law enforcement officers must remember that "once adversary proceedings have commenced against an individual, he has a right to legal representation when the government interrogates him."[49] This is the **Massiah limitation.**

Massiah limitation
The holding that after a person has been charged with a crime, law officers cannot question the person or otherwise obtain incriminating statements regarding that crime without the person's attorney present.

The rights to counsel under the Fifth and Sixth Amendments are similar but not identical. The Fifth Amendment and *Miranda* require police to inform a suspect in custody of his rights before interrogation begins. They must stop interrogation once a suspect in custody has been informed of his rights and invokes his right to remain silent or have the assistance of counsel. However, that does not mean the suspect will obtain a lawyer, since the police can simply cease interrogation, or release the suspect from custody without further interrogation. Moreover, the police may, if custody of a suspect has been terminated for a suitable time, initiate interrogation and obtain a waiver of Fifth Amendment rights.

Under the Sixth Amendment, once "adversarial judicial proceedings have commenced" against a defendant, the right to counsel attaches, and if the defendant requests counsel he is entitled to have one appointed if necessary. As a result, after adversarial proceedings have commenced, unless the defendant has made a voluntary waiver of the right to an attorney the police may not interrogate the defendant without an attorney present, or employ other investigative procedures involving the defendant such as lineups, without the presence of his attorney. That includes situations where police, without the presence of his attorney, obtain a waiver of the right to counsel from the defendant *after* the defendant has requested an attorney.

Questioning of the defendant by law enforcement officers or eliciting incriminating statements from the defendant without the attorney present may violate the Sixth Amendment, as the following two Supreme Court cases held:

Massiah v. United States

United States Supreme Court, 377 U.S. 201, 84 S. Ct. 1199 (1964)

The defendant (a merchant seaman) and a man named Colson were charged with importing, concealing, and facilitating the sale of cocaine. The defendants were indicted for these offenses and released on bail. A few days later, and without Massiah's knowledge, Colson agreed to cooperate with the federal agents and permitted a radio transmitter to be installed under the front seat of his automobile. Then, according to a prearranged plan, Colson carried on a lengthy conversation with Massiah while federal agents listened in another car a short distance away. At Massiah's trial, one of the federal agents testified as to the incriminating statements he overheard by means of the radio transmitter. Although this investigative technique and procedure is a permissible means of obtaining evidence before suspects are indicted or charged, the U.S. Supreme Court held that Massiah's Sixth Amendment rights were violated because he had already been indicted and was awaiting trial. In reversing Massiah's conviction, the Court held:

> [T]he [defendant] was denied the basic protection of [the Sixth Amendment] when there was used against him at his trial evidence of his own incriminating words, which federal agents had deliberately elicited from him after he had been indicted and in the absence of his counsel.

Brewer v. Williams

United States Supreme Court, 430 U.S. 387, 97 S. Ct. 1232 (1977)

Williams was arrested and charged in Davenport, Iowa, for the abduction of a 10-year-old girl. Because the crime was committed in Des Moines, Iowa, Williams had to be transported 160 miles back to Des Moines.

The police officers driving Williams to Des Moines were told by the lawyer appointed to represent Williams that they were not to question Williams without his presence. Williams had stated to the officers, "When I get to Des Moines … I will tell you the whole story." The officers, however, believed that the little girl was dead, and one of the officers persuaded Williams to tell the officers where he had buried the girl's body.

The trial court allowed all the evidence obtained during the automobile trip, holding that Williams had waived his Sixth Amendment right to an attorney. The U.S. Supreme Court held that it was error to use the evidence of how the girl's body was recovered. In ordering a new trial, the Supreme Court held:

> [T]he clear rule of *Massiah* is that once adversary proceedings have commenced against an individual, he has a right to legal representation when the government interrogates him. It thus requires no wooden or technical application of the *Massiah* doctrine to conclude that Williams was entitled to the assistance of counsel guaranteed to him by the Sixth and Fourteenth Amendments.

The Sixth Amendment right to an attorney is "offense specific." That is, once a suspect has been charged with a specific crime, and has requested an attorney, no further questions *about that crime* may be asked without an attorney present.

However, police may continue to ask questions, assuming *Miranda* is satisfied, about other crimes under investigation. The following case illustrates the "offense specific" limit on the right to an attorney:

Texas v. Cobb

United States Supreme Court, 121 S. Ct. 1335 (2001)

While Cobb was under arrest for an unrelated offense, he confessed to a home burglary. But Cobb denied knowledge of the disappearance of a woman and a child from the home. He was indicted for the burglary, and a lawyer was appointed to represent him. Cobb later confessed to his father that he killed the woman and child. His father contacted the police, and the police questioned Cobb without the presence of his attorney but after obtaining a waiver of Cobb's *Miranda* rights. Cobb confessed to the double murder and was convicted of capital murder and was sentenced to death.

On appeal, Cobb contended that his Sixth Amendment rights were violated because his lawyer was not present during the police interrogation that led to his confession to the double murders.

The U.S. Supreme Court held that the Sixth Amendment right to counsel is "offense specific" (limited here to the burglary Cobb was charged with) and was not "factually related" (to the two murders related to the burglary). The Court ruled "burglary and capital murder are not the same offense. The Sixth Amendment right to counsel did not bar police from interrogating (Cobb) regarding the murders, and (Cobb's) confession was therefore admissible."

Police may not make an "end-run" around the Sixth Amendment by taking actions intended to elicit incriminating information from a defendant who has not waived his right to counsel. Even though the police are not asking direct questions about the crime charged, if the purpose was to gain incriminating information about that crime the Sixth Amendment is violated, as the *Fellers* case held:

Fellers v. United States

United States Supreme Court, 540 U.S. 519 (2004)

In this case the Supreme Court held that once the Sixth Amendment's right to counsel attached, statements made by the defendant must be excluded if police "deliberately elicit" incriminating information from the defendant. After the defendant was indicted on drug charges, but had not waived his right to counsel, police went to his house and mentioned the names of other people named in the indictment. The defendant then stated that he had used drugs with those people. The defendant later executed a valid rights waiver. The Supreme Court held that because the police admittedly went to the defendant's house to "discuss" the indictment, they violated the "deliberate elicitation" rule, and the statements had to be excluded under the Sixth Amendment.

Just as a defendant may make a voluntary waiver of Fifth Amendment rights after a *Miranda* warning has been given, so too can a defendant make a voluntary waiver of the right to counsel. Once a defendant has requested an attorney, any subsequent waiver of the right to counsel made *without* an attorney present is presumed to be involuntary. In the following case the Supreme Court considered the implications of this rule:

Montejo v. Louisiana

United States Supreme Court, 129 S. Ct. 2079 (2009)

The defendant was charged with capital murder, and at his arraignment the trial court stated an attorney would be appointed to represent him. The defendant did not expressly request an attorney. Subsequently, police officers read the defendant his *Miranda* rights, and the defendant agreed to accompany the police to locate the murder weapon. During the course of doing so, the defendant wrote a letter of apology to the victim's widow, which implicated the defendant in the killing. This letter was introduced into evidence at his trial for murder over the defendant's objection that it must be suppressed under the rule of *Michigan v. Jackson*, 475 U.S. 625 (1986). In that case the Supreme Court held that once a defendant had requested counsel at an arraignment or similar hearing any subsequent interrogation by police where the defendant waived his right to counsel was presumed to be involuntary.

The U.S. Supreme Court concluded that because the defendant had not requested an attorney to represent him, it was not necessary to assume that any waiver of the right to counsel given by the defendant in subsequent interrogations was involuntary. It overruled *Michigan v. Jackson*, and remanded the case to the state court to determine if the incriminating statements should be suppressed under the rule of *Edwards v. Arizona, supra*, which held police must stop interrogation once a defendant has invoked the right to counsel. If the defendant had done so, then the subsequent interrogation by the police was prohibited, and any waiver by the defendant would be presumed to be invalid.

THE *BRUTON* RULE

Major crimes are often committed by more than one person. For example, three men commit an armed robbery. One of the men, X, is apprehended and makes statements incriminating himself and the other two men (Y and Z). On the basis of this information, arrest warrants and/or search warrants are obtained, and Y and Z are taken into custody.

If the victim and witnesses can identify all three men, the state now has a good case to go to trial. But if witnesses can identify only X and the state cannot otherwise incriminate Y and Z, a *Bruton* problem is going to occur when X's lawyer becomes aware of the situation.

X's confession and incriminating statements can be used as evidence against X but cannot be used against Y unless X takes the witness stand and incriminates Y. Y has a Sixth Amendment right to be confronted with the witness against him or her.

But X does not have to take the witness stand and cannot be forced to incriminate himself and his friend. His confession can be used only against him unless X takes the witness stand. This is where the bargaining begins. To get around this **Bruton rule**, the prosecutor ordinarily has two options available:

Bruton rule The rule that a criminal trial may not hear a confession or incriminating statement against a defendant that was made by another party to the crime without producing the speaker.

1. Make concessions to X (lower or drop criminal charges or sentence concessions) to get him to become a state witness and incriminate himself and Y and Z.
2. If X will not cooperate or if it is decided that concessions should not be made, drop the criminal charges against Y and Z and proceed to trial against X (failure to cooperate could result in a greater sentence).

In situations where there is sufficient evidence to go to trial against Y and Z, two additional options are available:

1. Try the defendants in two trials, which would permit using X's confession in the trial against him.[50]
2. Redact (reduce or edit) X's statements to eliminate any references to Y and Z and use the statements in a joint trial.[51]

The 1968 *Bruton* case, which established this rule of law, follows.

DOES A SIXTH AMENDMENT VIOLATION PROHIBIT USE OF INCRIMINATING STATEMENTS FOR IMPEACHMENT PURPOSES?

In the *Massiah* case the Supreme Court held that statements made by a defendant awaiting trial to an undercover informant could not be introduced at the defendant's trial because doing so would violate the defendant's Sixth Amendment right to counsel. May such incriminating statements, admittedly obtained in violation of the Sixth Amendment, be introduced to impeach a defendant's trial testimony? In *Kansas v. Ventris*, 129 S. Ct. 1841 (2009), the U.S. Supreme Court answered "yes" to that question.

The defendant was charged with murder and robbery, and while in jail awaiting trial police placed a "jailhouse informant" in his cell. The informant told police the defendant confessed to the murder in a conversation with the informant, which under *Massiah* would not be admissible in the prosecution's case-in-chief. However, when the defendant took the stand and testified that another person committed the murder, the prosecution was permitted to introduce the informant's testimony to rebut the defendant's testimony. The defendant was convicted of robbery, but on appeal the Kansas Supreme Court reversed the conviction, holding that statements obtained in violation of the Sixth Amendment may not be used at trial for any purpose.

The U.S. Supreme Court reversed, holding that the statements were properly admitted for impeachment purposes. The Court specifically held that for Sixth Amendment purposes, "The constitutional violation occurs when the uncounselled interrogation is conducted." As a result, the question of the use of incriminating statements obtained in violation of the Sixth Amendment was "not the prevention of a constitutional violation, but rather the scope of the remedy for a violation that has already occurred." The Court concluded that while the remedy of suppression of the statements for use in the prosecution's case was necessary, the same remedy was not appropriate when the statements were used to impeach a defendant's inconsistent testimony at his trial: "We have held in every other context that tainted evidence—evidence whose very introduction does not constitute the constitutional violation, but whose obtaining was constitutionally invalid—is admissible for impeachment.... We see no distinction that would alter the balance here." 129 S. Ct. at 1847.

Bruton v. United States

United States Supreme Court, 391 U.S. 123, 88 S. Ct. 1620 (1968)

The defendant (Bruton) and a co-defendant (Evans) were tried together and convicted of armed postal robbery. Evans had confessed and admitted that he had an accomplice whom he would not name. The confession was used as evidence against Evans, and the trial judge "instructed the jury that although Evans' confession was competent evidence against Evans it was inadmissible hearsay against petitioner (Bruton) and therefore had to be disregarded in determining petitioner's (Bruton's) guilt or innocence."

In reversing Bruton's conviction, the Supreme Court held:

Here the introduction of Evans' confession posed a substantial threat to petitioner's right to confront the witnesses against him, and this is a hazard we cannot ignore. Despite the concededly clear instructions to the jury to disregard Evans' inadmissible hearsay evidence inculpating petitioner, in the context of a joint trial we cannot accept limiting instructions as an adequate substitute for petitioner's constitutional right of cross-examination. The effect is the same as if there had been no instruction at all.

QUESTIONING PEOPLE IN JAIL OR PRISON, INCLUDING USING INFORMANTS AND UNDERCOVER AGENTS

There are more than two million inmates in U.S. prisons and jails. The presence of a career or violent criminal in a jail or prison presents an opportunity for law officers to investigate and attempt to obtain evidence about unsolved crimes or additional evidence about crimes for which the person is incarcerated. There now is a substantial body of federal and state case law detailing the application of the four major tests (discussed in the box on page 308) for evidence obtained from prisoners.

An article entitled "Constitutional Rights to Counsel During Interrogation" in the September 2002 *FBI Law Enforcement Bulletin* points out the similarity between questioning by an undercover law enforcement officer and questioning by a cellmate informant or an undercover law officer posing as a prisoner. *Miranda* warnings are not required in either situation because, as the article points out, "(as) the subjects of the questioning do not know that the government is interrogating them, they cannot feel the coerciveness *Miranda* was designed to protect against. Consequently, the practice of using cellmate informants does not contravene the *Miranda* rule." Thus, while the Sixth Amendment prohibits police from using jailhouse informants to obtain incriminating statements from a defendant charged with a crime and awaiting trial, the Fifth Amendment does not have such a prohibition.

The following U.S. Supreme Court decisions are applications of this principle in cases involving informants, cellmates, and other prison questioning tactics.

Case	Type of Questioning	Ruling
Kuhlmann v. Wilson, 477 U.S. 436, 106 S. Ct. 2616 (1986)	An informant was placed in Wilson's jail cell and told only to listen and not to ask any questions. The informant complied with these directions.	"[T]he defendant must demonstrate that the police took some action, beyond merely listening, that was designed deliberately to elicit incriminating remarks."
United States v. Henry, 447 U.S. 264, 100 S. Ct. 2183 (1980)	Henry's cellmate deliberately elicited information about the bank robbery that Henry was charged with and for which he was awaiting trial.	The conviction was reversed because the testimony of the cellmate violated Henry's Sixth Amendment right to counsel (*Massiah* violation).
Illinois v. Perkins, 496 U.S. 292, 110 S. Ct. 2394 (1990)	Perkins was in prison for assault. An undercover agent was placed in his cell to gain information about an unsolved murder. Perkins bragged about committing the murder when asked if he had ever "done" anyone. It was held that *Miranda* warnings were not required.	The Court held: "The use of undercover agents is a recognized law enforcement technique, often employed in the prison context to detect violence against correctional officials or inmates, as well as for the purposes served here. The interests protected by *Miranda* are not implicated in these cases, and the warnings are not required to safeguard the constitutional rights of inmates who make voluntary statements."
Arizona v. Fulminante, 499 U.S. 279, 111 S. Ct. 1246 (1991)	A paid informant promised to protect the defendant from other inmates in the prison if he confessed to a murder. The defendant admitted he killed his 11-year-old stepdaughter.	It was held that the confession was coerced because there was a threat of physical violence unless the defendant confessed. However, because of the amount of other incriminating evidence in the case, the use of the confession, even if improper, might have been harmless error.

Case	Type of Questioning	Ruling
Maine v. Moulton, 106 S. Ct. 477 (1985)	Moulton was in jail for burglary and theft. Incriminating statements of these crimes were obtained by recording his conversations with an undercover cellmate.	The state could intercept conversations about other uncharged offenses but not about the crime the defendant was in jail for because of Sixth Amendment violation of right to an attorney.
Bradley v. Ohio, 541 N.E.2d 78 (Ohio 1989), review denied, 497 U.S. 1011, 110 S. Ct. 3258 (1990)	After the murder of a prison employee, a strip search of inmates in the area began. Blood was seen on the defendant's clothes; he was questioned and admitted that he committed the murder. No *Miranda* warnings were given.	Ohio courts held that it was "on-the-scene questioning," and this ruling was let stand by the U.S. Supreme Court.
Howes v. Fields, 2012 WL 538280 (S. Ct. 2012)	Prisoner was questioned about out-of-prison conduct by state police, who told prisoner he was free to return to cell at any time. No Miranda warning given.	Supreme Court held prisoner was not in custody because he was "free to leave," so no Miranda warning was necessary. The Court rejected a "categorical" rule that any removal from the general population involved custody.

POLYGRAPH TEST RESULTS AS EVIDENCE

Persons charged or suspected of a crime cannot be ordered to take a polygraph (lie detector) test because such compulsion would violate their Fifth Amendment privilege against self-incrimination.[52] Nor does a defendant charged with a crime have a right to take a polygraph test to prove his or her innocence.[53]

It is reported that more than a million polygraph tests are given each year in the United States, however. Many of these tests are given by private companies, and some are administered within the criminal justice system. Prosecutors or a law enforcement agency might ask persons to voluntarily take a lie detector test to affirm statements they have made or to demonstrate their innocence.

In 1998 the U.S. Supreme Court noted that "(m)ost states maintain *per se* rules excluding polygraph evidence" and pointed out that "New Mexico is unique in making polygraph evidence generally admissible without prior stipulation of the parties and without significant restriction."[54] The reasons generally given by states for forbidding polygraph evidence entirely, or for placing severe restrictions on the use of polygraph evidence in criminal or civil trials, are as follows:

- A belief that polygraph results are not sufficiently reliable and trustworthy.
- The tendency of juries to rely too heavily on the report of polygraph examiners who appear as "expert" witnesses in criminal or civil cases and testify whether persons taking lie detector tests were truthful or not truthful.
- The inability of trial courts to judge the competency of polygraph examiners.

The Controversy over Polygraph Testing

Polygraph testing is very controversial.[55] Persons who oppose the use of lie detector tests refer to them as degrading and humiliating. The late U.S. Senator Sam Ervin called the tests "twentieth-century witchcraft." On the other hand, defense lawyer

PROCEDURES & PROCESSES

The Four Major Tests Controlling the Use of Confessions

1. The *voluntariness test*, which the Due Process Clause makes applicable at all times during the criminal proceeding, requires that confessions be freely and voluntarily given. Violations occur when the government obtains a confession by means that overbear the will of the accused. The resulting confession would be excluded as evidence on the grounds that there was denial of due process law.

2. The *Miranda test* is required when (a) a suspect is in custody and (b) a law officer seeks to obtain incriminating information through questioning. *Miranda* must be complied with if answers are to be used as evidence. *Miranda* requires that

   - Warnings (cautions) must be given.
   - Suspect states or acknowledges that he or she understands the warnings.
   - Suspect waives rights and answers some or all questions.

3. After a suspect is formally charged with a crime, his Sixth Amendment right to an attorney must be observed. A *Massiah* violation would occur if a defendant who has already been charged with a crime and has not waived his right to counsel is questioned in regard to that crime without an attorney present. (See the U.S. Supreme Court cases of *Massiah v. United States* and *Brewer v. Williams* discussed above.)

4. A confession by one suspect cannot be used against another suspect unless the second suspect has an opportunity to cross-examine the source of the accusation against him or her. A *Bruton violation* could occur unless

   - The first suspect agrees to take the witness stand and testify.
   - The suspects are tried in separate trials.
   - The suspects are tried in one trial with reference to the second suspect taken out of the confession.
   - If all else fails, charges against the second suspect are dropped.

F. Lee Bailey testified before the U.S. Congress in 1986 that polygraph tests are "useful investigative tools" and that when "properly run in good hands, it is a good test."

After it was discovered in 2001 that a high-ranking FBI agent (Robert Hanssen) had been selling secret information to Russia for more than 15 years, the FBI was criticized for not giving more lie detector tests to key FBI agents.

In 2002, however, a panel of leading scientists confirmed a U.S. congressional study done in 1983, with both studies reporting that lie detector tests do a poor job of identifying spies or other national security risks and are likely in security screenings to produce false accusations about innocent people. The 1983 congressional report stated that spies "may well be the most motivated and perhaps the best trained to avoid detection" by developing skills necessary to deceive polygraph machines and operators.

The 2002 panel of scientists acknowledged that their report would cause much debate and would probably reduce some of the tens of thousands of security lie detector tests that were being given yearly. The panel noted, however, that there is a place for polygraphs in the investigation of specific crimes.

Most states have refused to permit polygraph evidence under the rule announced in *Daubert v. Merrill Dow Pharmaceuticals Inc.*,[56] discussed in Chapter 18.

These states conclude that the scientific reliability of polygraph tests has not been adequately established. At least one state, New Mexico, permits the use of polygraph results in criminal cases by statute.[57] In the 2004 case of *Lee v. Martinez*,[58] the New Mexico Supreme Court held that polygraph results using the "control method" of questioning were sufficiently reliable to be admitted in criminal trials. Under the "control method," the examiner asks the examinee questions designed to generate psychological and physical responses, which then can be used to compare responses to questions involving the criminal conduct in question.

Polygraph Testing in the American Criminal Justice System

Polygraph testing is occasionally used by law enforcement agencies from the FBI to local police and sheriff departments, primarily for investigative and advisory purposes. Some defense lawyers also use lie detector tests in efforts to establish defense positions or arguments for their clients. Most states forbid the use of lie detector evidence in civil and criminal trials, but some states allow such evidence upon prior stipulation of both parties. The following cases and material illustrate some of the other uses of polygraph testing:

- While working undercover for the U.S. Air Force, Scheffer was required to periodically take drug tests and polygraph tests. When a drug test revealed the presence of an illegal drug in the airman's urine, a polygraph test was given, and it supported Scheffer's statement that he did not knowingly take the illegal drug. At Scheffer's trial for wrongfully using methamphetamine, the trial court excluded the evidence of the polygraph test because the military has a *pro se* ban on the use of polygraph evidence. The U.S. Supreme Court affirmed the ban on evidence of polygraph testing imposed on military courts, holding that "(s)tate and federal governments ... have a legitimate interest in ensuring that reliable evidence is presented to the trier of fact in criminal trials."[59]

- In the 1995 case of *Wood v. Bartholomew*,[60] the U.S. Supreme Court sustained the state of Washington's ban on the use of polygraph evidence even for impeachment purposes. In that case, a prosecutor failed to disclose that a witness had failed a polygraph test. The Court held that this failure did not deprive the defendant of "material" evidence under the *Brady* rule.

- In the 1991 case of *People v. Suly*,[61] the Supreme Court of California approved the use of a required lie detector test in a plea-bargain agreement. The defendant in this case was convicted of six murders and sentenced to death. His alleged accomplice who testified against him was required by the plea agreement to pass a lie detector test showing that she had not herself committed any of the murders.

- Several states have established polygraph testing as a condition of probation. In agreeing to the conditions of probation, defendants would agree to periodic polygraph examinations. In *Commonwealth v. A.R.*, 80 A.3d 1180 (Pa. 2013) the court upheld the introduction of a polygraph test at a revocation hearing.

LEGAL CASES

Other U.S. Supreme Court Cases on the Law of Confessions

Miranda

- The U.S. Supreme Court has "never insisted that *Miranda* warnings be given in the exact form described ..." [*Duckworth v. Eagan*, 492 U.S. 195, 109 S. Ct. 2875 (1989), and *California v. Prysock*, 453 U.S. 355, 101 S. Ct. 2806 (1981)].
- A defendant who states that he or she is willing to make an oral statement but is unwilling to make a written statement without his attorney has waived the rights stated in the *Miranda* warnings [*Connecticut v. Barrett*, 479 U.S. 523, 107 S. Ct. 828 (1987)].
- Undercover law enforcement officers do not have to give *Miranda* warnings and do not have to disclose their true identity [an undercover officer was placed in Perkins's prison cell block: *Illinois v. Perkins*, 110 S. Ct. 2394 (1990); an undercover officer pretended to be a friend of James Hoffa: *Hoffa v. United States*, 385 U.S. 293, 87 S. Ct. 408 (1966)].
- Police do not have to tell a suspect being interrogated that a lawyer hired by someone else has agreed to represent the suspect and has offered to be present [the suspect was about to confess to the brutal slaying of a young woman: *Moran v. Burbine*, 475 U.S. 412, 106 S. Ct. 1135 (1986)].
- Police do not trick a suspect when they fail to inform him as to all the crimes he may be questioned about [instead of questioning about only stolen firearms, ATF agents also questioned Spring about a murder to which he confessed: *Colorado v. Spring*, 479 U.S. 564, 107 S. Ct. 851 (1987)].
- Custody for *Miranda*'s purposes is based on facts and circumstances known to the suspect and not on the uncommunicated suspicions of the police [*Stansbury v. California*, 114 S. Ct. 1526 (1994)].
- "Interrogation" by police is not limited to express questioning; the term also includes "any words or actions on the part of the police ... that the police should know are reasonably likely to elicit an incriminating response from the suspect" [*Rhode Island v. Innis*, 446 U.S. 291 (1980)].
- A person may assert his constitutional rights at any time; he may answer questions if he wishes, but he may stop at any time [*Miranda v. Arizona*, 384 U.S. 436, 86 S. Ct. 1602, 16 L.Ed.2d 694 (1966)].
- In *Florida v.* Powell, 130 S. Ct. 1195 (2010), the Supreme Court reversed a decision of the Florida Supreme Court that held a *Miranda* warning defective because it didn't expressly inform the defendant he could ask for a lawyer during questioning. The U.S. Supreme Court said that the warning given was adequate because the parts of the warning taken together informed the suspect that a lawyer could be demanded at any time;:"This Court has never indicated the rigidity of *Miranda* extends to the precise formulation of the warnings given a criminal defendant." 130 S. Ct. at 1204. After remand, the Florida Supreme Court held the warning satisfied the Florida State constitution as well. *State v. Powell*, 66 So.3d 905 (Fla. 2011).
- Additional Warning to a Non-Citizen. Article 36 of the Vienna Convention on Consulate Relations requires that a non-citizen in police custody be informed of the citizen's right to speak with a consular official from the person's home country. American law officers generally comply with this requirement but in the case of *Saanchez-Llamas v. Oregon*, 126 S. Ct. 2669 (2006), the defendant, a Mexican citizen who wounded an officer in a gunfight, was given *Miranda* warnings in both English and Spanish, but not the Vienna Convention warning. The U.S. Supreme Court refused to suppress the numerous incriminating statements made by the defendant, holding that "suppression would be a vastly disproportionate remedy for an Article 6 violation."

- After a suspect lets the "cat out of the bag" and admits his guilt, *Miranda* warnings may be given (if they were not already given) and a second admission of guilt taken: "The relevant inquiry is whether, in fact, the second statement was also voluntarily made" [*Oregon v. Elstad*, 470 U.S. 298, 105 S. Ct. 1285 (1985)].
- Juveniles have the same rights as adults and should be given *Miranda* warnings prior to interrogation while in custody [*Fare v. Michael C.*, 442 U.S. 707, 99 S. Ct. 2560 (1979)].

Involuntary Confessions

A federal court reviewing the use of a confession in a state court is not bound by a state court's finding and has a "duty to make an independent evaluation of the record" [*Mincey v. Arizona*, 437 U.S. 385, 98 S. Ct. 2408 (1978); *Miller v. Fenton*, 474 U.S. 104, 106 S. Ct. 445 (1985)].

The defendant was required to complete a sex offender treatment program as part of his probation. He was discharged from the program before completion. Polygraph test results were admitted at the revocation hearing because they were introduced only to show why the treatment administrators believed the defendant was dishonest in his treatment program, not that the defendant didn't tell the truth.

VOICE SPECTROGRAPHY EVIDENCE

There have been many attempts to use voiceprints (spectrographic voice identification) as evidence over the years. Most courts that use the old *Frye* test (see Chapter 18 for a discussion of the *Frye* test) have held that spectrographic voice identification was inadmissible. The stricter and higher standards for the admission of scientific evidence established by the U.S. Supreme Court in the 1993 *Daubert* case (see Chapter 18 on scientific evidence) make it more difficult to use voiceprints as evidence unless dramatic improvements are made in voiceprints.

In seeking to use voiceprints as evidence, a lawyer is attempting to identify a speaker on a tape or wiretap recording. The technique could be used to evaluate the voice (or voices) heard on taped conversations and compare the results to other taped conversations of an identified person.

Some courts have admitted voice spectrography evidence—for example, *United States v. Smith*[62] and *United States v. Love*.[63] Those decisions were reached before the *Daubert* decision and may not accurately represent the current approach to voice spectrography. In a 2000 decision, the Eighth Circuit Court of Appeals excluded voice spectrography evidence offered by a defendant to prove that his voice was not the voice heard on a federal wiretap. The court found that the expert testimony did not meet the *Daubert* standards for reliability.[64]

SUMMARY

1. **State the factors to be considered in the "totality of the circumstances" test.**
   - "Suspect vulnerability," which includes the mental and physical condition of the suspect, and the age of the suspect.

2. **List the *Miranda* requirements for information that must be communicated to a suspect in custody before questioning.**
   - The suspect must be told he has the right to remain silent and not answer questions, that

anything he says may be used against him in a court of law, that he has a right to the presence of an attorney at all times during questioning, and that if he cannot afford to hire an attorney one will be appointed to represent him.

3. **Identify when a person is in "custody" for purposes of *Miranda*.**
   - Using an objective test that factors in the circumstances surrounding the questioning, a person is in custody when a reasonable person would not feel free to leave the place where the questioning occurs.

4. **List some exceptions to the *Miranda* requirement.**
   - The *Miranda* warnings are not required if a person is not in custody, volunteers information to police, or answers only general questions in a fact-finding process such as at a crime scene. Brief stops by police of persons suspected of committing a crime, such as vehicle stops, with questions directed at the circumstances that provided the suspicion that a crime might be occurring do not require the warning. However, longer detentions with or without arrest require the warnings. In cases where public safety is at risk an officer may ask questions related to the public safety risk without giving the warnings. Warnings are not required for questioning persons at border

crossings, at least when the questions go to factors that are relevant to a person's suitability for entering this country.

5. **State the *Massiah* rule, and compare it with *Miranda*.**
   - Under the Sixth Amendment right to counsel, once a suspect has been charged with a crime and has requested an attorney, police may not initiate interrogation about the crime charged without the presence of the attorney. The police are also prohibited from conducting other kinds of investigation procedures, such as a lineup, without the presence of counsel. Any waiver by the suspect of Sixth Amendment rights after a request for counsel is deemed involuntary. By contrast, even if a suspect invokes his *Miranda* rights, the police may initiate questioning after a break in custody, and if the suspect waives his rights and has not requested counsel the waiver is effective.

6. **State the role of a confession under the *Bruton* rule, where there are multiple defendants.**
   - A confession or incriminating statement that could be used at trial against one defendant (because it was voluntary and made in compliance with *Miranda* requirements) is not admissible if it incriminates other defendants, unless the defendant making the confession testifies at the trial and can be cross-examined.

KEY TERMS

Bruton rule, 304
confession, 282
incriminating
   statement, 282

Massiah limitation,
   301
Miranda requirements,
   287

totality of the
   circumstances test, 285
voluntariness test, 284

KEY CASES

Berghuis v. Thompkins, 130 S. Ct. 2250 (2010): A suspect must unequivocally invoke his *Miranda* rights, and waiver of *Miranda* rights can be implied if a suspect answers questions without coercion after being given a clear warning that was understood.

Brown v. Mississippi, 297 U.S. 278 (1936): Confessions must be made voluntarily, and any violence, threats of violence, or other coercive tactics make the confession inadmissible.

Bruton v. United States, 391 U.S. 123 (1968): In cases of multiple defendants, a confession by one that implicates the others is inadmissible unless the defendant making the confession testifies at trial and is subject to cross-examination.

Dickinson v. United States, 530 U.S. 428 (2000): The *Miranda* rule is constitutional, and cannot be abrogated by Congress.

Edwards v. Arizona, 451 U.S. 477 (1981): Police may not initiate questioning of a suspect after invocation of *Miranda* rights, and any subsequent waiver by the suspect is deemed involuntary. (See *Maryland v. Shatzer, infra,* on break in custody and its effect on this rule.)

Florida v. Powell, 130 S. Ct. 1195 (2010): The exact formulation of the *Miranda* warnings is not rigid, so long as the warnings given effectively inform the suspect of his Fifth Amendment rights.

Kansas v. Ventris, 129 S. Ct. 1841 (2009): The prosecution may use incriminating statements obtained in violation of the Sixth Amendment to impeach testimony given by the defendant who made the statements.

Maryland v. Shatzer, 130 S. Ct. 1213 (2010): Police may reinstitute questioning of a suspect who invoked the *Miranda* rights after a break in custody (at least 14 days), and if the suspect waives his *Miranda* rights and has not requested counsel the waiver is valid.

Massiah v. United States, 377 U.S. 201 (1964): The Sixth Amendment right to counsel prohibits police from questioning or eliciting incriminating statements from a defendant related to the crime charged after the defendant has requested counsel.

Miranda v. Arizona, 384 U.S. 436 (1966): Police may not question a suspect in custody without first informing the suspect of his right to remain silent, his right to an attorney, that an attorney would be appointed to represent him if needed, and that any statements made could be used against him in a court of law.

Montejo v. Louisiana, 129 S. Ct. 2079 (2009): Overruled *Michigan v. Jackson*, 475 U.S. 625 (1986), which had held under the Sixth Amendment that any interrogation initiated by police after a defendant was charged with a crime was prohibited and any subsequent waiver of the right to counsel was presumed to be invalid. Instead, police may initiate questioning of a defendant even after he has been charged with the crime and entitled to counsel, unless the defendant requests assistance of counsel. A voluntary and knowing waiver of the Sixth Amendment right is valid if made before the request for assistance of counsel.

Opper v. United States, 348 U.S. 147 (1954): Confessions and incriminating statements cannot alone prove *corpus delicti*, but corroborating evidence need only prove the trustworthiness of the confession or statement; it need not produce independent evidence of the crime.

Rothgery v. Gillispie County, 128 S. Ct. 2578 (2008): A criminal trial commences for purposes of the Sixth Amendment when a defendant appears before a magistrate and constraints are placed on his liberty.

Salinas v. Texas, 133 S. Ct. 2174 (2013): If a defendant has not invoked his Fifth Amendment right to remain silent, his pre-custodial, pre-*Miranda* silence can be introduced by the prosecution in its case in chief.

Thompson v. Keohane, 516 U.S. 99 (1995): Whether a person is "in custody" for interrogation purposes is determined on an objective basis under all the circumstances. If a reasonable person would not feel free to leave and end the interrogation the interrogation is custodial.

PROBLEMS

1. The police arrested a defendant in connection with a murder by gunshot in which another person was also involved. After giving the defendant the *Miranda* warnings, the defendant requested an attorney. The police ceased interrogation, and placed the defendant in a cell. A few minutes later the lead investigator went to the cell and read the defendant the statement of charges, which included a summary of the third person's allegation that the defendant shot the victim. Another officer said, "I bet you want to talk now," but was told by the lead investigator to refrain from making such statements. A few minutes after that, when the lead investigator brought some clothes to the defendant, the defendant said "Can I still talk to you?" After giving him the *Miranda* warnings again, the defendant made incriminating statements. Can these statements be used against him at his trial for murder? Was there one potential violation of *Miranda* or two? Is it a problem that the police gave two *Miranda* warnings within the span of

a few hours? (See *United States v. Blake*, 571 F.3d 331 (4th Cir. 2009).) How did this criminal case end up in the federal courts?

2. Most courts continue to hold that the results of polygraph tests are not admissible in criminal trials, mainly because the science behind polygraph tests has not been shown to be "reliable." (See the discussion of scientific evidence in Chapter 18.) In *United States v. Allard*, 464 F.3d 529 (5th Cir. 2006), a Secret Service agent investigating the crime of consumer product tampering administered a polygraph test to the defendant suspected of committing the crime. At her subsequent trial for consumer tampering, the agent was permitted to testify about the polygraph test and events surrounding the time when it was taken by the defendant. Why was the agent permitted to give this testimony? Under the reasoning of the court, what could the agent testify? What could he not testify?

3. Police were called to a crime scene at night, where a woman had been killed by being struck in the head with a blunt object. While canvassing the vicinity of the crime scene the police encountered the defendant, who fit the description of two men observed kicking the victim. The police officer cuffed the defendant, and walked him toward the crime scene to explain why he had been stopped. In the process the officer shined his flashlight on the defendant's shoes, which had blood on the tips. Without any statement by the officer the defendant said, "I kicked some lady back there. She pulled my hair." Can this statement be used against the defendant in his trial for second-degree murder? What is the best argument for the defendant? (See *Johnson v. Haviland*, 2011 WL 855832 (N.D. Cal. 2011).)

4. As stated in this chapter, the right to counsel under the Sixth Amendment is "charge specific," meaning that the right attaches only to interaction with police relating to the charges against the defendant. As a result, police may question a defendant charged with one crime about another crime, without the presence of the defendant's attorney. The *Miranda* rules, of course, apply to such interrogation.

Assume a defendant is charged with capital murder. While awaiting trial, and after counsel had been appointed to represent the defendant, police discover the defendant has been attempting to hire someone to murder the prosecution's main witness. The police send an undercover informant to question the defendant about the murder plot, and obtain tape recordings of that conversation that include incriminating statements about the murder charge as well as the plot to murder the witness. Are the tapes admissible in the murder trial? Would they be admissible if the defendant was charged with conspiracy to murder the witness? Does use of the undercover informant violate *Miranda*? May the prosecution use the tapes in the sentencing stage, after the defendant has been convicted of murder? (See *Thompson v. State*, 93 S.W.3d 16 (Tex. Crim. App. 2001).)

CASE ANALYSIS

Read Appendix B, Finding and Analyzing Cases (p. 499). With these guidelines in mind, please continue with the Case Analysis selections for Chapter 12.

1. A 15-year-old boy confessed to the homicide of a man during a "crack" cocaine transaction. After giving him his *Miranda* warning, detectives questioned the boy for 11 hours, with a few breaks between sessions, and the boy ultimately confessed. After unsuccessfully trying to suppress the confession, the boy pled guilty to reckless homicide. On appeal, the Wisconsin Court of appeals affirmed the conviction, finding the confession "voluntary". Based on the tests the court used, do you agree the boy confessed voluntarily? *See State v. Moore*, 846 N.W.2d 18 (Wis. App. 2014). The Wisconsin Supreme Court agreed in May 2014 to review the case. What do you think will be the result?

2. The U. S. Supreme Court has held that police may not circumvent the Sixth Amendment by using informants, like fellow prison inmates or friends of a defendant, to conduct interrogations for the police. On the other hand, there appears no reason to suppress a statement made to an informant voluntarily by a defendant with no

attempt by the informant to induce the statement. Deciding between those two results can be difficult. Why did the court permit the use of statements made by the defendant to a "friend" who secretly recorded the conversations for the FBI in the case of *United States v. Jacques*, 684 F.3d 324 (2nd Cir. 2012), *cert. denied* 133 S. Ct. 324 (2012)? Does the "offense-specific" rule have any role in the court's decision?

3. The "question first, warn later" procedure condemned in *Missouri v. Seibert* (discussed in this chapter) involved a police department that used the procedure in a deliberate attempt to circumvent *Miranda*. Should police be permitted to use the tactic if they have a reason for doing so, other than to get incriminating statements from the suspect? If so, what should the police be required to show about their motivation? See *United States v. Williams*, 682 F.3d 35 (2nd Cir. 2012).

4. It is sometimes said that "custody" for *Miranda* purposes occurs when a person believes he is not "free to leave" when police interrogate him. As we will see in Chapter 14, a person is "seized" under the Fourth Amendment when he believes he is not "free to leave." Are they the same tests? Should they be? In *People v. Begay*, 325 P.3d 1026 (Colo. 2014) police stopped a man walking on a bridge who resembled the description of a man who earlier in the evening had assaulted two people in a nearby park. The officers told the man to sit down while the officers gathered a witness for a "showup" (in effect, a one-person lineup) to see if the witness could identify the man as the assailant. While he sat there, police asked the man questions, to which he gave incriminating responses. After the witness showed up and identified the man as the assailant, police arrested him and gave him his *Miranda* warnings. At his trial, the defendant moved to suppress all his statements made prior to being given the *Miranda* warnings, claiming he was in custody when those questions were asked? Was he in custody? Was he free to leave? If not, does that require the conclusion he was in custody?

Notes

1. *Arizona v. Fulminante*, 499 U.S. 279 (1991).
2. *People v. Stanton*, 158 N.E.2d 47 (Ill. 1959).
3. 709 A.2d 1305 (Md. 1999).
4. This occurred in the U.S. Supreme Court case of *Colorado v. Connelly*, 479 U.S. 157, 107 S. Ct. 515 (1986). In the *Connelly* case, the defense lawyer argued that Connelly was suffering from a psychosis that prevented Connelly from understanding his rights and motivated his confession. Because the confession had been corroborated, it was held to be admissible evidence, and Connelly's conviction was affirmed.
5. 14 How. St. Tr. 1311 (1660).
6. *People v. Jennings*, 807 P.2d 1009.
7. 348 U.S. 147 (1954).
8. *State v. Wilson*, 248 P.3d 315, 341 (N.M. 2010).
9. 999 So.2d 1025 (Fla. 2008).
10. In the 1953 case of *Stein v. New York* (346 U.S. 156, 73 S. Ct. 1077), the U.S. Supreme Court pointed out why confessions obtained by physical violence are considered involuntary and unreliable:

    Physical violence or threat of it by the custodian of a prisoner during detention serves no lawful purpose, invalidates confessions that otherwise would be convincing, and is universally condemned by the law. When present, there is no need to weigh or measure its effects on the will of the individual victim. The tendency of the innocent, as well as the guilty, to risk remote results of a false confession rather than suffer immediate pain is so strong that judges long ago found it necessary to guard against miscarriages of justice by treating any confession made concurrently with torture or threat of brutality as too untrustworthy to be received as evidence of guilt. *Stein*, 346 U.S. at 182, 73 S. Ct. at 1091.

11. 882 A.2d 944 (Md. App.).
12. 437 F.3d 1059 (10th Cir.).
13. 384 U.S. 436 (1966).
14. *Miranda v. Arizona*, 384 U.S. 436, 86 S.Ct. 1602 (1966).
15. *People v. Ashford*, 71 Cal. Rptr. 619 (Cal. App. 1968).
16. *People v. Gonzales*, 554 N.E.2d 1269 (N.Y. 1990).
17. *State v. Jackson*, 600 So.2d 739 (La. App. 1992).
18. *Commonwealth v. Daniels*, 590 A.2d 778 (Pa. Super. 1991).
19. *Ciriago v. State*, 471 A.2d 320 (1984).
20. *Miranda v. Arizona*, 384 U.S. 477, 86 S. Ct. 1629 (1966).
21. *State v. Bennett*, 517 P.2d 1029 (Utah 1973).
22. *Britton v. State*, 170 N.W.2d 785 (Wis. 1969).

23. 813 S.W.2d 748 (Tex. App.).
24. 468 U.S. 420, 104 S. Ct. 3138 (1984).
25. *Id.*
26. 496 U.S. 582, 110 S. Ct. 2638.
27. 577 N.E.2d 861 (Ill. App.).
28. 588 A.2d 389 (N.J. Super.).
29. *Glean v. State*, 397 S.E.2d 459 (Ga. App. 1990).
30. *State of Maine v. Joubert*, 603 A.2d 861 (1992).
31. 407 S.E.2d 342.
32. See *United States v. Gupta*, 183 F.3d 615 (7th Cir. 1999).
33. 432 F.3d 524 (3d Cir. 2006), *cert. denied*, 546 U.S. 1223.
34. 465 U.S. 420, 104 S. Ct. 1136.
35. 496 U.S. 292, 110 S. Ct. 2394.
36. 385 U.S. 293, 87 S. Ct. 408.
37. *United States v. Rosengard*, 949 F.2d 905 (7th Cir. 1991); *United States v. Cortes*, 922 F.2d 123 (2d Cir. 1990).
38. 467 U.S. 649, 104 S. Ct. 2626.
39. *McNeil v. Wisconsin*, 501 U.S. 171 (1991).
40. 128 S. Ct. at 2587.
41. 87 S. Ct. 616 (1967).
42. 87 S. Ct. 625 (1967).
43. 447 U.S. 404 (1980).
44. 133 S. Ct., at 2179.
45. 87 S. Ct. 616 (1967).
46. 87 S. Ct. 625 (1967).
47. *United States v. Kordel*, 397 U.S. 1 (1970).
48. *Massiah v. United States*, 377 U.S. 201, 84 S. Ct. 1199 (1964).
49. *Brewer v. Williams*, 430 U.S. 387, 97 S. Ct. 1232 (1977).
50. This case was before the U.S. Supreme Court again in 1984 under the title of *Nix v. Williams*, 467 U.S. 431, 104 S. Ct. 2501 (1984), discussed in Chapter 9.
51. The U.S. Supreme Court has decided two redacting cases. In *Richardson v. Marsh,* 481 U.S. 200 (1987), the Court upheld a conviction in a joint murder trial of two defendants. One defendant, Williams, made a confession implicating the codefendant, Marsh. This confession was introduced at Marsh and Williams's joint trial but was redacted to omit any reference to Marsh and also any reference to Marsh's existence. The Supreme Court held that this redaction took the case outside the *Bruton* rule. In *Gray v. Maryland,* 523 U.S. 185, 118 S. Ct. 1151 (1998), Bell and Gray were jointly tried for murder. Bell confessed, and this confession was introduced in the joint trial. It was redacted to delete any reference to Gray, but where Gray's name appeared in the confession the police

officer reading the confession in court said, "deleted." For example, the confession read "Question: Who was in the group that beat Stacey?" Answer: "Me, deleted, deleted, and a few other guys." The Supreme Court said keeping the "deleted" spaces in the confession invited the jury to tie the confession to Gray and held the *Bruton* rule applicable.
52. See the 1992 case of *Melvin v. State*, 606 A.2d 69, 50 CrL 1575 (Del.), where the State of Delaware produced evidence during the trial showing that the defendant was in possession of cocaine. After the evidence was presented, the trial judge stated that he was "going to give this (juvenile) an opportunity to prove me wrong" by taking a polygraph test about whether the cocaine belonged to the defendant. When the defendant refused to take the test, the judge found him guilty, stating, "I gave him an opportunity to clear himself."

    The Supreme Court of Delaware reversed the conviction and ordered a new trial for the violation of the Fifth Amendment privilege against self-incrimination.
53. In the 1977 case of *Sandlin v. Oregon Women's Correctional Center*, 28 Or. App. 519, 559 P.2d 1308, the defendant argued that she had a right to a polygraph test. However, a test was not given to her. In affirming the defendant's conviction, the court held that due process did not require the state to grant the defendant's request for a polygraph test.
54. *United States v. Scheffer*, 118 S. Ct. 1265 (1998).
55. After holding public hearings on the use of polygraph testing, the U.S. Congress enacted the Employee Polygraph Protection Act, which generally forbids employers engaged in interstate commerce from using lie detector tests either for employment screening (i.e., as part of a job application procedure) or during employment with certain exceptions. One of the exceptions permits polygraph testing when an investigation into a money loss or other theft is being conducted.
56. 509 U.S. 579 (1993).
57. See N.M.R. Evid. 11-707.
58. 96 P.3d 291 (2004).
59. *United States v. Scheffer*, 118 S. Ct. 1261 (1998).
60. 116 S. Ct. 7.
61. 812 P.2d 163.
62. 869 F.2d 348 (7th Cir. 1989).
63. 767 F.2d 1052 (4th Cir. 1985), *cert. denied*, 474 U.S. 1081 (1986).
64. *United States v. Bahena*, 223 F.3d 797 (8th Cir. 2000).

CHAPTER 13

The Law Governing Identification Evidence

SUBJECTS IN A POLICE LINEUP

Rich Legg/Getty Images

LEARNING OBJECTIVES

In this chapter we discuss some of the ways evidence that is intended to identify an offender is gathered and admitted in criminal trials. The learning objectives for this chapter are

List some of the reasons for mistaken eyewitness identification.

State the differences between a lineup and a showup.

State the requirements for a non-suggestive photo array.

Define *sequential lineup*.

Discuss when a single photograph may be used to identify a suspect.

List the factors established by *Neil v. Biggers* for testing the reliability of eyewitness identifications.

yewitness identifications are one of the most powerful evidentiary tools available to the prosecution. At the same time, such identifications possess one of the highest possibilities of error. It is, after all, a human witness who makes the identification; and unlike DNA or fingerprint evidence, humans are not infallible. It is for this reason the criminal law has tried to develop sensible methods to help increase the likelihood of accurate eyewitness identifications.

For most of the time before 1983, so-called "reliability" tests, coupled with courtroom cross-examination of an eyewitness, have been the principal methods of judging eyewitness identifications. They continue to be important today. And, throughout that period, very few courts permitted expert scientific testimony on the nature, and limits, of eyewitness identifications. That is changing.

Beginning in 1983 with a decision of the Arizona Supreme Court permitting such expert testimony, the approach to eyewitness testimony has dramatically changed. This change is illustrated by the 2014 decision of the Pennsylvania Supreme Court in *Commonwealth v. Walker*[1], where the court reversed its 30-year rule excluding expert testimony on the science of eyewitness reliability, and gave trial courts the discretion to admit such testimony. The *Walker* court noted that every state but Kansas and Louisiana, and every Federal Circuit Court, now permit such use of expert testimony.

EVIDENCE NEEDED FOR A CRIMINAL CONVICTION

To convict a person of a crime, the government must prove

1.   That the crime charged did occur (proof of corpus delicti)
2.   That the defendant committed or was a party to the crime charged

In all criminal cases, the defendant must be identified as the person who committed or was a party to the crime. This can be done by direct or circumstantial evidence, or a combination of both direct and circumstantial evidence. Identification evidence may consist of one or more of the following:

- Identification by the victim of the crime
- Identification by an eyewitness to the crime (In a July 2002 release, *NCJ* reported that bystanders are present in 70 percent of simple and aggravated assaults, 52 percent of robberies, and 29 percent of rapes/sexual assaults. See *NCJ* 189100.)
- Confessions, admissions, or incriminating statements by the defendant or his associates showing that the defendant committed the crime or was a party to the crime
- DNA fingerprints, regular fingerprints, tire tracks, and the like, which place the defendant at the scene of the crime
- Other physical evidence left at the scene of the crime or obtained later by the police that implicates the defendant as the perpetrator of the crime (for example, the gun that killed the victim is found in the defendant's possession the day after the crime was committed)
- Photos or videos from a surveillance camera or handheld video taken as the defendant committed the crime
- Voice identification or, if admissible, voiceprint (spectrographic) evidence that identifies the defendant as the perpetrator of the crime or as a party to the crime

It is the trier of the facts (the jury or the judge) who determines whether the identification evidence is sufficient to carry the burden of proof beyond reasonable doubt. In jury trials, it is primarily the responsibility of the jury to determine the accuracy of identification evidence. In the case of eyewitness identifications, the Due Process Clause of the U.S. Constitution requires courts to make an initial determination of the reliability of any identification that occurred under impermissibly suggestive circumstances. If the identification evidence cannot be shown to be reliable, it is not admitted for submission to the jury.

Examples of cases with unusual identification evidence include *People v. Sutterland*,[2] where a shoeprint, found on the victim's back, and tire tracks were held to be sufficient evidence to sustain charges of kidnapping, sexual assault, and murder of a 10-year-old girl; *Culbreath v. State*,[3] where the victim's caller ID was used as evidence to sustain a stalking prosecution; *People v. Campbell*,[4] where clear and unique shoeprints plus flight from an officer three days after the crime were held to be sufficient; *Spence v. State*,[5] where bite mark evidence on the body of the victim was used to link the defendant to the crime; *State v. Faircloth*,[6] where hair evidence (most often used in rape and murder cases) was used in identifying the offender (the court pointed out that although hair—unlike DNA—cannot positively identify an offender, it can be relevant evidence for identification purposes); and *State v. Jells*,[7] where footprints (as distinguished from shoeprints) were used as evidence for a murder conviction and the use of the death penalty.

THE PROBLEM OF MISTAKEN EYEWITNESS IDENTIFICATION

In the 1960s, the International Association of Chiefs of Police recognized that eyewitness "identification and description is regarded as a most unreliable form of evidence and causes more miscarriages of justice than any other method of proof."[8] In a 2008 article that reviewed studies of the reliability of eyewitness testimony, the author concluded that more than 40 percent of wrongful convictions were the result of mistaken identifications, with the highest percentage attributable to "showup identifications."[9]

Mistaken eyewitness identification may lead to the accusation or conviction of an innocent person, and it may allow a guilty person to avoid identification and conviction. In the 30 years following the U.S. Supreme Court's decisions in *Neil v. Biggers* and *Manson v. Brathwaite*, discussed later in this chapter, significant scientific research on misidentification has been conducted. (For an exhaustive review of this research see the text of the "Special Master" Report, discussed in the box on page 328 of this chapter, at www.judiciary.state.nj.us).

Based on this research, experts agree that certain specific variables contribute greatly to eyewitness misidentification, and to the extent they can be, these variables should be controlled. The research divides these variables into "system variables" and "estimator variables." System variables are factors that are controlled by law enforcement, mainly in live or photographic lineup procedures, whereas estimator variables include factors related to the witness, the event, or the perpetrator. Estimator variables cannot be controlled by the legal system, but nonetheless contribute to misidentifications; experts agree their existence must be recognized and integrated into eyewitness identifications and assessments of their reliability.

Some examples of system variables and methods used to control them in lineup procedures are the following:

1. **"Double-blind" administration.** Fewer instances of misidentification occur where neither the investigator administering the lineup nor the witness know the suspect's identity. Research shows that where the police officer conducting a lineup knows which person is the suspect the witness is more likely to identify that person.

2. **Instructions to witnesses.** Witnesses should be told that the lineup may not include the suspect. Where that instruction is given, only about one-third of witnesses identified "fillers" (i.e., non-suspects in the lineup). Without that instruction, about three-fourths of the witnesses identified fillers.

3. **Lineup array.** All experts agree the lineup, whether live or photographic, must not be administered so that the suspect stands out from the others. Moreover, a lineup should not include more than one suspect, to avoid the "lucky" guess by a witness.

4. **Multiple lineup procedures.** A witness should not view multiple lineups with the same suspect, since the "memory" from seeing the suspect in a prior lineup may be mistaken by the witness as a "memory" of the event.

5. **Feedback to witness.** "Feedback" by the lineup administrator, such as a nod or a smile when the suspect is picked, serves to cement the opinion of the witness that the identification is certain. This is wrong, because "certainty" of the witness is one of the factors used by courts to judge the reliability of the witness's identification.

6. **Simultaneous versus sequential lineups.** Showing the witness a lineup one person or one photograph at a time yields more accurate identifications than simultaneous lineups.

7. **Composite procedures.** All experts agree identifications made by police-created composite pictures of a suspect are unreliable.

Some examples of estimator variables include

1. **Stress.** A person under high stress has a greatly reduced ability to remember the stressful event.

2. **Witness focus on weapon.** Where a weapon is used in a crime, witnesses tend to focus their attention on the weapon, not the person brandishing the weapon.

3. **Duration of event.** The longer a witness observes an event, the greater the accuracy of the witness's memory. Since witnesses to crimes frequently have a short time to observe the perpetrators, their memory is less accurate.

4. **Distance and lighting.** These two factors, which often require expert testimony to establish, significantly affect the accuracy of what a witness sees or hears.

5. **Witness character.** Age, emotional condition, presence of drugs or alcohol, and other personal characteristics of a witness affect the accuracy of the witness's observations and memory.

6. **Memory decay.** Memory decays rapidly. The more removed the witness is from the event when an identification is made, the less likely the identification is accurate.

7. **Cross-racial bias.** The chance of a misidentification is 1.56 times more likely where the witness and the suspect are members of a different race.

Determining the actual incidence of misidentifications is difficult, because studies examining past crimes, called "archival studies," are not common. That is because discovery of misidentifications in most criminal convictions does not often occur. Those archival studies that have been made conclude that misidentifications lead to the conviction of innocent persons about one-third of the time.

The 2008 Study of Innocent Persons Mistakenly Incarcerated

In April 2007 DNA evidence was used to clear the 200th innocent person mistakenly convicted of a crime. These innocent persons served an average of 12 years in prison for crimes they had not committed. A study of the circumstances surrounding the convictions of these 200 people was published in the 2008 issue of *Columbia Law Review* and titled "Judging Innocence." The results revealed that:

- The leading cause of the wrongful convictions was erroneous identification by eyewitnesses; this occurred in 79 percent of the cases.
- Faulty forensic evidence was used in 55 percent of the cases. This included undue weight placed on evidence of limited value, such as the fact that the defendant's blood type matched the blood found at the crime scene. The faulty evidence also included exaggerated or mistaken testimony of expert witnesses for the prosecution, often involving the analysis of blood or semen. Forty-two cases had expert testimony about hair characteristics, forensic evidence the author called "notoriously unreliable."
- In 18 percent of the cases police informants testified against the defendants. Not only was the informant's testimony unreliable, but also in three of the cases DNA evidence showed that the informants themselves were guilty of the crime they sought to attribute to the defendant.
- False confessions were admitted in evidence in 16 percent of the cases. Two-thirds of the defendants who gave false confessions were juveniles, mentally retarded, or both.
- More than 90 percent of the persons exonerated by DNA evidence were convicted of rape, murder, or both. DNA evidence is often available in these crimes of violence unless the perpetrator takes measures to remove all hair, semen, blood, and other bodily fluids from the crime scene.
- DNA testing and evidence are available in fewer than 10 percent of violent crimes, typically rape and murder cases, where it is more likely the offender will leave skin tissue or bodily fluids that will yield DNA.

In a May 13, 2010, report, the Innocence Project organization stated that as of the date of the report, of the 254 persons wrongly convicted but ultimately exonerated by use of DNA evidence, 75 percent were the subject of erroneous eyewitness identifications. For a summary of this report see http://www.innocenceproject.org.

The conclusions in the *Columbia Law Review* study were based on violent crimes where DNA evidence was available. Because DNA evidence is not available in 90 percent of the violent crimes committed each year in this country, however, it is difficult to estimate how many innocent persons are wrongly convicted each year. The National Institute of Justice estimates that more than 75,000 persons a year are brought to trial in this country on criminal charges based primarily on eyewitness identification. How many of these persons will be wrongly convicted?

What Is Being Done About the Problem of Convicting Innocent Persons?

Not only is the conviction of innocent persons shocking, but it also means the guilty person is free to commit other crimes. For years, courts have been aware of the unreliability of eyewitness testimony used in criminal convictions, which has contributed greatly to wrongful convictions. In the case of *United States v. Wade,*[10] the U.S. Supreme Court stated,

> The vagaries of eyewitness identification are well known: the annals of criminal law are rife with instances of mistaken identification. Mr. Justice Frankfurter once said: "What is the worth of identification testimony even when uncontradicted? The identity of strangers is proverbially untrustworthy. The hazards of such testimony are established by a formidable number of instances in the records of English and American trials"[11]

Because it is inevitable, and perhaps necessary, that eyewitness identifications will continue to be used as evidence in criminal prosecutions in the United States, many steps have been taken to lessen the likelihood of conviction of innocent persons. Some of those steps are listed here:

- Throughout the United States, judges, prosecutors, defense lawyers, and law enforcement officers are being made aware of, and instructed in, the hazards inherent in collecting, processing, and using eyewitness testimony in criminal prosecutions. Prosecutors are advised to screen cases more thoroughly when eyewitness identification is a principal part of the prosecution's case. At the same time, judges are more demanding about reliability issues, and defense attorneys are urged to cross-examine witnesses more vigorously. Judges, prosecutors, and juries are more skeptical and demand higher burdens of proof in cases where eyewitness identification is a major part of the prosecution's case. Juries are cautioned more extensively by both defense attorneys and prosecuting attorneys about the risks of eyewitness identifications in closing arguments, and judges are giving jury instructions to the same effect.[12]
- It is likely that courts will permit more expert testimony on the hazards of eyewitness identifications. In eyewitness identification cases, particularly where no corroborating evidence is available, courts are increasingly willing to permit expert testimony about the unreliability of eyewitness identifications.[13]
- Corroborating evidence is important in eyewitness identification cases, and law enforcement officers are working harder to obtain evidence bearing on the reliability (or unreliability) of eyewitness testimony. For example, in the 2006 case of *State v. Williams,*[14] the defendants were convicted after eyewitness identifications by the victims of a robbery. The appeals court upheld the convictions, noting that the eyewitnesses stated that one of the robbers was on crutches, one was wearing an Orlando Magic jacket, and one was wearing a dark sweatshirt, which was true in each case. Also, a gold necklace owned by one of the victims was found in the backseat of the cruiser in which one of the defendants was transported to police headquarters.

PROCEDURES & PROCESSES

Some Procedures, and Their Limitations, Used In Pretrial Identifications

More than 75,000 persons each year are charged with crimes based on eyewitness identification. These identifications result from a variety of identification procedures or situations. Listed here are some of the procedures and situations that result in identifications as well as the problems associated with those procedures.

When the Person Who Committed the Crime Is Unknown

Composite sketches can be used to identify the suspect.	Research has shown that none of the existing methods used to produce a composite sketch are reliable in real-world settings. The Wisconsin Department of Justice has observed that "... an inaccurate composite might taint an eyewitness's memory and lead to a misidentification.... Composite sketches can alter witnesses' memory and lead witnesses to pick out suspects who resemble the sketch rather than the actual perpetrator."

When the Police Lack Probable Cause for an Arrest or Exigent Circumstances Are Present

In a showup, a victim or witness is permitted to view a suspect detained by police singly rather than as part of a group.

Evidence obtained from an out-of-court showup is admissible if the procedure was necessary. A showup was necessary if the police lacked probable cause to make an arrest or, as a result of other exigent circumstances, could not have conducted a lineup or photo array. If the showup was not necessary, courts use that as an important factor in determining whether the identification is admissible.

When a Suspect Is in Custody or Has Been Charged with a Crime

Lineups are used to minimize suggestiveness and to increase the reliability of identification evidence.

In order to minimize suggestiveness, courts prohibit police from telling victims and witnesses that police have made an arrest and having the suspect appear as the only person shown in a lineup. Courts also require that only one person in a lineup be highlighted at a time, to only one witness at a time, by an officer who does not know the real suspect.

When Police Have Photographs of a Suspect or in Lineups

Photo arrays, consisting of several photographs of different people including a suspect, and lineups can be shown to witnesses.

Generally, the same requirements apply to both photo arrays and lineups: (1) six or more persons or photographs must be shown; (2) each person or photograph of a person must be alike in age, size, color, and dress, and none (other than the suspect) can be known to the witness; (3) the persons or photographs must be shown one at a time by an officer who does not know who the real suspect is; and (4) persons in lineups can be required to speak certain words or phrases or put on specific clothing, such as a hat, jacket, or gloves.

Other Circumstances Where Identification Might Occur

Inadvertent confrontations by a witness or the victim can lead to an identification of a suspect.

Where without police involvement a witness or victim encounters a suspect and identifies him or her, the identification can be admitted as evidence so long as the encounter was really inadvertent. However, this issue was brought before the U.S. Supreme Court in 2011 in the case of *Perry v. New Hampshire*, discussed later in this chapter.

In-court identifications as part of a criminal trial are permitted.

These identifications continue to be used, even though they are the most suggestive type of showup possible. Because the in-court identification is made in the presence of the judge and jury, and is subject to immediate cross-examination, its reliability can be tested in the presence of the jury. If the in-court identification is the product of an invalid pretrial identification, however, it can be excluded.

- Witnesses to crimes are often separated and interviewed alone by officers who are skilled in obtaining details about the crime the witnesses observed, thus avoiding suggestive questions or coaching in any way. The resulting independent descriptions of the offender or offenders can then be compared to determine whether the identification is accurate and dependable. If independent, uncontaminated descriptions by different witnesses match in sufficient detail, the investigating officer can testify at the trial as to the similarity of the identifications and their match of the defendant charged with the crime.

U.S. SUPREME COURT CASES ON SHOWUPS

showups An identification procedure in which only one subject is shown to witnesses or the victim of a crime.

Showups differ from lineups; in showups law enforcement officers permit witnesses or the victim of a crime to view a person being detained singly instead of as part of a group. In 1967 the U.S. Supreme Court stated that "(t)he practice of showing suspects singly to persons for the purposes of identification and not as part of a lineup, has been widely condemned."[15]

Showups are highly suggestive, and courts generally hold that law enforcement officers should not use them unless they are necessary under the circumstances. However, suggestiveness alone would not justify a ruling by a court that there has been a violation of the defendant's due process rights. To rule that the defendant's due process rights have been violated, there must have been impermissible suggestiveness to such a degree as to make the identification unreliable as a matter of law and resulting in a possible miscarriage of justice.

The U.S. Supreme Court has repeatedly held that whether there has been a violation of the defendant's due process rights must be determined "on the totality of the circumstances."[16] In using the totality of the circumstances test, the Supreme Court and other courts have held that showups do not violate the due process rights of defendants under the following circumstances:

- *The showup is necessary, and police lack probable cause.* This kind of showup is most often held a short time after the crime was committed, in a scene of-the-crime, on-the-spot, or short-detour confrontation and viewing. Courts have approved such showups because the memory of the witness is fresh, and officers can immediately determine whether they have taken the right person into custody.

  Example
  A woman's purse is snatched. Witnesses to the incident chase the purse-snatcher, a man, and after several blocks catch him. A police officer is summoned and places the man under investigative detention. The victim is brought to the spot where the man was stopped, and asked to identify him as the purse-snatcher. If not, he may be immediately released; if the victim identifies him, the police have probable cause for an arrest, and he can then be searched for property of the victim.

- *Necessary and exigent circumstances are present.* Although showups are generally held a short time after the crime and are generally held at or near the crime scene, they have also been approved by the U.S. Supreme Court when the victim or witness was in critical condition and could die at any time. In the case of *Stovall v. Denno,*[17] one of the victims of a criminal attack was dead, and his wife was in critical condition because of eleven stab wounds. Two days after the crime, Stovall was taken in handcuffs to the victim's hospital room, where she identified him as the perpetrator of the crime. In affirming Stovall's convictions and the use of this procedure, the U.S. Supreme Court quoted a lower court, holding,

  Here was the only person in the world who could possibly exonerate Stovall. Her words and only her words, "He is not the man," could have resulted in freedom for Stovall.

- A *suspect is in possession of property recently stolen from the victim.* The defendant in the case of *Kirby v. Illinois*[18] was arrested in downtown Chicago with traveler's checks and a Social Security card taken from a man who had been robbed the day before. The holdup victim was driven to the police station, where he identified Kirby as one of the holdup men. In affirming Kirby's conviction and in holding that there is no right to an attorney during showups, the U.S. Supreme Court stated:

> In this case we are asked to import into a routine police investigation an absolute constitutional guarantee historically and rationally applicable only after the onset of formal prosecutorial proceedings. We decline to do so.

It should be noted that many states would hold that the showup used in *Kirby* was improper because the police had probable cause and could have used a lineup or photo array. Indeed, it is likely that had the defense in *Kirby* argued against the showup rather than the right to an attorney, it would have succeeded.

- *The showup does not create a substantial likelihood of irreparable misidentification, and the suspect is in custody for another crime.* If the victim or witness knows the offender or has seen the offender on previous occasions, but the police are not sure they have the right person in custody, a showup to identify the person is permissible. Or, if the victim or witnesses to the crime give the police such a *specific* or unique description of the suspect that it clearly distinguishes the offender from other persons, then a showup is permissible, as occurred in the following U.S. Supreme Court case.

Neil v. Biggers

United States Supreme Court, 409 U.S. 188, 93 S. Ct. 375 (1972)

A nurse was assaulted in her home and then taken outside, where she was raped. The incident lasted between 15 and 30 minutes on a bright moonlit night. The victim gave the police a very specific description of her assailant. In the months that followed, she viewed many lineups and photo arrays but made no identification.

Seven months after the rape, the defendant was taken into police custody for another offense. When the police noticed the similarity of the defendant to the description given by the rape victim, the police attempted to make up a lineup but could find no one fitting the defendant's "unusual physical description."

When the rape victim arrived at the police station, a showup was used. After hearing the defendant repeat, "Shut up or I'll kill you," the victim identified the defendant as her assailant. The defendant appealed his rape conviction, arguing that the identification evidence obtained in the station house showup was so "suggestive" that it violated due process. The Supreme Court held that the fact the showup itself was suggestive did not by itself make the identification inadmissible under the Due Process Clause: "It is, first of all, apparent that the primary evil to be avoided is 'a very substantial likelihood of irreparable misidentification.'" An identification made under suggestive circumstances may be admitted consistent with due process if other factors indicate the identification was reliable, the Court held. The Supreme Court then held the identification evidence was properly admitted, ruling, "Weighing all the factors, we find no substantial likelihood of misidentification. The evidence was properly allowed to go to the jury."

DETERMINING THE RELIABILITY OF IDENTIFICATION EVIDENCE: THE *NEIL V. BIGGERS* GUIDELINES

The U.S. Supreme Court has stated, "It is the reliability of identification evidence that primarily determines its admissibility [as evidence in a trial]." While the ability to "both cross-examine the identification witness and argue in summation as to the factors causing doubts as to the accuracy of the identification"[19] is useful, the

Supreme Court has also held that if a pretrial identification occurred under impermissibly "suggestive" circumstances, the Due Process Clause requires courts to make a determination of the reliability of the identification. An eyewitness identification made under suggestive circumstances can give rise to a very "substantial likelihood" of misidentification: "It is the likelihood of misidentification that violates a defendant's right to due process...."[20]

The guidelines for determining the reliability of identification evidence were established by the U.S. Supreme Court in the case of *Neil v. Biggers,* discussed above. The Supreme Court held that the fact that a pretrial identification by a witness was obtained under "suggestive" circumstances does not automatically mean that identification is inadmissible, nor does it require that a subsequent in-court identification by the same witness must be excluded. However, the Due Process Clause requires that only reliable evidence be admitted in a criminal trial. To minimize the possibility that an innocent person will be identified as a criminal and sent to prison, the Supreme Court said the following factors should be used to determine whether the evidence is sufficiently accurate and reliable to present to a jury for their deliberation:[21]

- What opportunity did the witness have to observe the criminal at the time of the crime? Relevant factors are length of time of the encounter, distance between the witness and the suspect, lighting conditions, whether the witness's view was unobstructed, and the witness's state of mind at the time.
- Was the witness a casual observer, or did the witness show a high degree of attention? A witness who observed someone hurry down a hall or a street might be a very casual observer and may not be able to accurately describe or identify that person a short time later. On the other hand, the victim of a rape or a robbery ordinarily has a very high degree of attention, which could result in a more accurate and more reliable identification of the perpetrator of the crime.
- How accurate was the witness's prior description of the criminal? How accurate was the description recorded by the investigating officers? Did the description include unusual features, such as scars, moles, birthmarks, tattoos, or distinctive clothing, which could establish an independent basis of identification and make the identification highly reliable? How well did the testimony of the witness in court stand up under cross-examination? Was the witness able to explain why she identified the defendant as the person who committed the crime? Any discrepancies between the prior identification and the actual appearance of the defendant is ordinarily brought out in cross-examination.
- What level of certainty did the witness demonstrate at the confrontation? Did the witness immediately identify the suspect? Was there hesitancy? Was there a misidentification?
- How much time elapsed between the commission of the crime and the identification of the suspect as the perpetrator of the crime? Did the identification occur 10 minutes after the crime or 10 hours, 10 days, or 10 months? This factor, when combined with the other factors, would determine the reliability of the identification, which is the basis for the decision by the trial judge as to whether to submit the identification evidence to a jury.

Most states have adopted these guidelines from the *Neil* decision, although some states have added modifications, such as those used by the Utah Supreme

PROCEDURES & PROCESSES

The Importance of Obtaining Prior Descriptions of Offenders

After separating witnesses and interviewing them away from other persons, investigating officers should have witnesses provide as detailed a description of the offender as possible soon after the crime is reported. Officers should assist the victim and the witness in searching their memories (without being in any way suggestive) for details of physical appearances and clothing, no matter how insignificant such details may seem. Such prior descriptions are important for several reasons:

- They will authorize stops in the neighborhood and elsewhere for investigative detentions of persons who reasonably match these descriptions.
- The descriptions may be compared to descriptions given by victims and witnesses of other crimes and further aid in the apprehension of the offender.
- Detailed descriptions that match the defendants can significantly increase the reliability of identifications made later by victims and witnesses.
- Testimony by the investigating officers in court concerning prior descriptions is important evidence for juries and judges in determining the issue of guilt or innocence.

Court in *State v. Hollen.*[22] In *State v. Hunt,*[23] the Kansas Supreme Court adopted the Utah guidelines for eyewitness identification evidence.

One area where courts have differed on application of the *Neil v. Biggers* guidelines involves the origin of a "suggestive" pretrial identification. Courts agree that where a witness makes an out-of-court identification under suggestive circumstances caused by the government, the witness's out-of-court identification, or subsequent in-court identification, must be shown to be reliable. The due process clause requires the trial court to make a determination of reliability using the *Biggers* tests. However, federal and state courts have disagreed about the need for a *Biggers* reliability determination where the suggestive circumstances were not caused by the government. For example, in *United States v. Bouthot,* 878 F.2d 1506 (1st Cir. 1989) the court held that a trial court must hold a reliability hearing even though the suggestive circumstances were not caused by law enforcement officers.

Some state courts have reached the opposite conclusion. In *State v. Addison,* 8 A.3d 118 (N.H. 2010), the New Hampshire Supreme Court held that where the suggestive circumstances surrounding an out-of-court identification were not caused by state action, the trial court need not conduct a *Biggers* analysis of the reliability of the identification: "Accordingly, we do not engage in any further analysis of the out-of-court identification testimony." 8 A.3d125.

The opinion in *Addison* appears to be the majority view. In *Perry v. New Hampshire,* 132 S. Ct. 716 (2012), the U.S. Supreme Court reached the same conclusion, and overruled *United States v. Bouthot* and similar federal cases that had adopted the contrary view. In *Perry* police were called to an apartment house by a resident, and found Perry in the parking lot holding two car speakers. Officers asked Perry to stay in the parking lot, and went into the house to talk to the complaining witness. When asked to describe the person she saw breaking into cars in the lot, the witness pointed out the window to the parking lot and said "he is standing there," meaning Perry.

 RETHINKING THE *BIGGERS/BRAITHWAITE* RELIABILITY TESTS

The U.S. Supreme Court's decisions over 30 years ago in *Neil v. Biggers* and *Manson v. Brathwaite*, discussed in this chapter, established factors courts should consider when testing the reliability of identifications made under impermissible suggestive circumstances. The reliability test, the Supreme Court held, was required by the Due Process Clause of the U.S. Constitution. The Supreme Court did not address the *Biggers* factors in *Perry v. New Hampshire*, discussed above, since the Court concluded no reliability inquiry was required in that case.

Research since *Biggers* was decided has convinced some courts to modify, explain, or expand the factors identified by the U.S. Supreme Court. In what may become a leading case under state law on admissibility of eyewitness identifications, in 2011 the New Jersey Supreme Court announced its decision in the case of *State v. Henderson*.[a] There, the Court appointed a "special master" to review and report on the content and conclusions of the extensive scientific research on eyewitness identifications. (The Internet location where this report can be found is cited earlier in this chapter.) The Court concluded based on the report that the *Biggers/Manson* test rested on three assumptions that research has proved to be false. The *Biggers/Manson* test fails because "it does not provide a sufficient measure for reliability, it does not deter, and it overstates the jury's innate ability to evaluate eyewitness testimony."[b] The New Jersey Court then established procedures to be followed at a pretrial hearing to determine if eyewitness identifications are admissible. They are the following:

1. The defendant must introduce some evidence of suggestiveness to obtain a pretrial hearing, focusing on "system" variables rather than "estimator" variables. The defendant need not prove the higher burden of "impermissible" suggestiveness that is required under the current tests.
2. If suggestiveness is shown, the prosecution must offer evidence to prove the identification was reliable.
3. It remains the defendant's burden to prove the ultimate question: was there a "very substantial likelihood of irreparable misidentification"?
4. If identification evidence is admitted, the jury must be given instructions on the effect of "system" and "estimator" variables on the accuracy of an identification.

The New Jersey Supreme Court also suggested the police adopt as guidelines many of the "system" variable control procedures discussed earlier in this chapter. The Court did not, however, make them mandatory, and specifically refused to require sequential rather than simultaneous lineups.

Examples of other courts ordering changes in a state's eyewitness identification rules include

- *State v. Guilbert*, 49 A.3d 705 (Conn. 2012): Held expert testimony about eyewitness reliability should be permitted, and that existing jury instructions about evaluating such testimony are not effective and must be made more specific.
- *State v. Cabagbag*, 277 P.3d 1027 (Hawaii 2012): Jury instructions must separately list as cautionary factors the specific weaknesses of eyewitness testimony identified by recent studies.
- *State v. Mitchell*, 275 P.3d 905 (Kan. 2012): It was error to instruct the jury to give weight to the expressed certainty of the witness making the eyewitness identification.
- *State v. Lawson*, 291 P.3d 673 (Ore. 2012): If facts show an identification might have been the result of suggestive factors, the prosecution now has the burden to show the identification was based on a permissible basis.

[a]27 A.3d 872 (N.J. 2011)
[b]27 A.3d at 918.

At his trial on theft charges, Perry contended the trial court had to hold a reliability hearing because of the suggestive circumstances (what amounted to a "one-person showup") that surrounded the eyewitness identification. The trial court refused, and Perry was convicted. The New Hampshire Supreme Court affirmed the conviction, stating that because the police had nothing to do with creating the suggestive circumstances no pretrial screening hearing was required.

The U.S. Supreme Court agreed. It refused to extend the pretrial reliability hearing to eyewitness identifications that occurred under suggestive circumstances that were not created by the police:

> ... [w]e hold that the Due Process Clause does not require a preliminary judicial inquiry into the reliability of an eyewitness identification when the identification was not procured under unnecessarily suggestive circumstances arranged by law enforcement.[24]

Perry contended that a trial that involves the admission of unreliable eyewitness testimony violates the Due Process Clause, relying on the statement in *Manson v. Brathwaite* (discussed in this chapter) that "reliability is the lynchpin in determining the admissibility of identification evidence." The Supreme Court said that statement in *Brathwaite* applied only where it had first been determined that law enforcement officers arranged the suggestive circumstances. It said,

> ....The fallibility of eyewitness evidence does not, without the taint of improper state conduct, warrant a due process rule requiring a trial court to screen such evidence for reliability before allowing the jury to assess its creditworthiness. [25]

The Supreme Court did note that courts have other methods of dealing with the problem of eyewitness testimony under suggestive circumstances, such as specific jury instructions on the effect of suggestive circumstances, and expert testimony on the hazards of such eyewitness testimony. *Id.*

THE USE OF POLICE LINEUPS: CHANGES FROM THE 1960S TO THE PRESENT

lineups An identification procedure in which six or more persons are shown to witnesses or the victim of a crime.

Lineups should be used whenever practical and must be used in situations where show-ups would not be authorized. Lineups properly run not only minimize suggestiveness but also increase the reliability of the identification evidence.

The procedures that state and local law enforcement agencies follow in police lineups historically have varied greatly from state to state. Recognizing that mistaken identifications in lineups often lead to mistaken in-court identifications and wrongful convictions, in the 1960s the U.S. Supreme Court decided several cases where lineup procedures were called into question.

The following Supreme Court cases reflect lineup problems that existed during that period, and the Court's response to those problems.

United States v. Wade

United States Supreme Court, 388 U.S. 218 (1967)

Wade was arrested for robbing a bank in Texas, and was indicted on the charge of bank robbery. A lineup was conducted in the courtroom of a local courthouse without first informing Wade's attorney, where a witness identified Wade as the robber. Subsequently, the witness identified Wade in court at the criminal trial, and Wade was convicted. On appeal, the U.S. Supreme Court held that a post-indictment lineup was a "critical stage" of the prosecution where a defendant is entitled to have an attorney present. The Supreme Court vacated the Court of Appeals decision ordering a new trial, and remanded the case for a hearing to determine if the in-court identification was tainted by the earlier lineup identification. At the hearing, the government was given an opportunity to establish by clear and convincing evidence that the in-court identifications were based on observations of the suspect other than the lineup identification.

Gilbert v. California

United States Supreme Court, 388 U.S. 263 (1967)

Gilbert was arrested for robbing a savings and loan association and murdering a police officer during the robbery. Gilbert was also charged with other robberies. A lineup was held without notifying Gilbert's lawyer. The lineup was held on a stage with "upwards of 100 persons in the audience," each an eyewitness to one of the robberies charged to Gilbert. Bright lights prevented the persons in the lineup from seeing the audience. Persons in the audience would call out the number of the man they could identify in the lineup. It is not known whether audience members talked to one another during the lineup, but they did talk to one another after the lineup. In holding that the lineup was illegal, the Court stated:

> The admission of the in-court identifications without first determining that they were not tainted by the illegal lineup but were of independent origin was constitutional error. *United States v. Wade, supra.* We there held that a post-indictment pretrial lineup at which the accused is exhibited to identifying witnesses is a critical stage of the criminal prosecution; that police conduct of such a lineup without notice to and in the absence of his counsel denies the accused his Sixth Amendment right to counsel and calls in question the admissibility at trial of the in-court identifications of the accused by witnesses who attended the lineup.

Foster v. California

United States Supreme Court, 394 U.S. 440 (1969)

The defendant was a suspect in a robbery. He was brought to the police station and placed in a lineup with five other persons, each of whom was shorter than he was. The robbery victim viewed the lineup but could not identify the suspect. Subsequently, a second lineup was held, and the defendant was the only person from the first lineup who appeared in the second lineup. The victim identified the defendant as the robber and subsequently made an in-court identification of him. The defendant was convicted of robbery. On appeal, the Supreme Court held that the procedures followed in the two lineups made them so suggestive of the defendant's guilt that he was denied due process. The convictions were reversed.

Because so many wrongful convictions can be tied to misidentifications by eyewitnesses viewing lineups, states have considered modifications of the classic police lineup. Two procedures that have been recommended, and adopted in some states, are (1) the sequential lineup, in which a witness is shown one person at a time rather than all at once, and (2) the double-blind administrator, where the officer conducting the lineup has no involvement in the underlying case and no knowledge of which person in the lineup is the suspect.

Lineups should be conducted to test recognition in a manner that avoids suggestiveness. The National Council of Judges provides the following rules for the lineup procedure:[26]

- Reasonable notice of the proposed lineup shall be given to the suspect and his counsel, and both shall be informed that the suspect may have his attorney present at the lineup. If the suspect is not represented by counsel, he shall be advised of his right to have counsel assigned without charge. He may waive in writing the presence of his attorney.[27]

- The lineup should consist of at least six persons, approximately alike in age, size, color, and dress; and none of them, other than possibly the suspect, shall be known to the witness.
- Persons in the lineup may be requested to speak certain words, identical for each person, for purposes of voice identification.
- Neither directly nor indirectly shall any police officer indicate or allow anyone but the witness to indicate in any way any person in the lineup as the suspect or defendant. Any instructions shall be given to all as a group, not individually.
- The lineup shall be viewed by only one witness at a time, others being excluded from the room and not permitted to discuss the lineup or descriptions of the suspect.

USING PHOTOGRAPHS TO OBTAIN IDENTIFICATION EVIDENCE

Photographs are often used for identification purposes in criminal investigations. The Metropolitan Police Department of the District of Columbia (Washington, DC) issued the following instructions concerning the use of photographs and the **photographic array**:

photographic array A group of photographs shown to witnesses or the victim of a crime for identification purposes.

1. The use of photographs for identification purposes prior to an arrest is permissible provided the suspect's photograph is grouped with at least eight[28] other photographs of the same general description.[29]
2. Adequate records of the photographs shown to each witness must be kept so that the exact group of photographs from which an identification is made can be presented in court at a later date to counteract any claim of undue suggestion and enhance the reliability of the in-court identification. This information shall be recorded in the statement of facts of the case.
3. Each witness shall view the photographs independently, out of the immediate presence of the other witnesses.

As in the case of lineups, some states require that photographs be shown one at a time instead of all together, and that the person showing the photographs have no knowledge of which (if any) is the photograph of a suspect.

Failure to preserve the photographs used to make an identification creates serious problems. The court cannot then determine whether law officers complied with due process and whether identification was made without excessive suggestiveness. In the 1980 case of *Branch v. Estelle,* the Fifth Circuit Court of Appeals held that "in situations where the police fail to preserve the photographic array, there shall exist a presumption that the array is impermissibly suggestive."[30]

Using a Single Photograph for Identification

In the case of *People v. Kelly,* the Illinois Court of Appeals pointed out that as "a rule, the use of a single-photograph display is unduly suggestive and gives rise to a substantial likelihood of irreparable misidentification if the totality of the circumstances surrounding the identification renders it unreliable."[31]

Single-photograph showings are suggestive; however, a prosecutor and the police could attempt to show by testimony or other evidence that the identification is sufficiently reliable. Reliability is determined by the factors established in the U.S. Supreme Court case of *Neil v. Biggers* (discussed above).

The following single-photograph case was decided by the U.S. Supreme Court in 1977:

Manson v. Brathwaite U.S. Supreme Court, 432 U.S. 98 (1977)	Connecticut State Trooper Glover was working as an undercover officer in narcotics. He and an informer went to an apartment building in Hartford, where Glover knocked on the door of one of the apartments. A man (the defendant in this case) opened the door and in a 5- to 7-minute period sold $20 worth of heroin to Glover. Glover had never seen the defendant before and did not know the defendant's proper name. Upon leaving the building, Glover described the man to Officer D'Onofrio, who had been backing him up outside the building. From the description, D'Onofrio suspected that the seller was the defendant. D'Onofrio obtained a single photograph of the defendant and left the picture at Glover's office. Two days later, Glover viewed the single picture and identified the defendant as the man who sold him the heroin. Based on this information, the defendant was arrested. With no objection by the defense, the picture was used as evidence, and Glover made a positive in-court identification of the defendant. Using the *Neil v. Biggers* factors, the Supreme Court affirmed the criminal conviction, holding that even though using only one photograph was suggestive, the identification evidence was sufficiently reliable and did not cause a substantial likelihood of irreparable misidentification.

OBTAINING IDENTIFICATION EVIDENCE BY OTHER MEANS

Other means of obtaining identification evidence include those listed here:

- *Surveillance cameras, cell phone cameras, and camcorders:* These devices seem to be everywhere. Many businesses, apartment buildings, schools, parking lots, and public places have surveillance cameras. Private citizens have ready access to cell phone cameras and camcorders, with almost instantaneous ability to record images. As a result, it is no longer unusual to have crime-scene photographs as evidence. In the case of *United States v. Gray,*[32] bank surveillance photographs and descriptions of the offender from bank employees led to Gray's arrest two weeks after he robbed a bank. In affirming his conviction, the court pointed out that "the reliability of these identification procedures is obvious."

- *Fingerprint and DNA banks:* Both the federal government and many states maintain these data banks, which store crime-scene evidence such as semen, saliva, and hair particles. Comparisons between a sample taken from a suspect and evidence maintained by these data banks can assist in the identification of criminals. Such evidence has also proved important in preventing wrongful convictions of innocent persons.

- *AMBER Alert Program:* This is a notification system to provide immediate information to the public about suspected child abductions. It is named after Amber Hagerman, a 9-year-old child who was abducted and murdered in Texas in 1996. More than 43 states use the system, which has been credited with the recovery of many children and the apprehension of offenders.

The U.S. Department of Justice AMBER Alert report for 2007 states that 316 AMBER Alerts were issued in 2006, and 214 resulted in the recovery of the child. Nine children were found deceased. In AMBER Alerts, highway signs and television and radio broadcasts flash a description of the child, the possible abductor, and the license plates of any suspected vehicle in which the child might be held. Within a short time, thousands of persons are alerted to look for the abducted child or a suspect's vehicle.

composite sketches
Drawings made by an artist or with an Identi-Kit for use in identification.

- *Composite Sketches:* **Composite sketches** can be made by an artist or with an Identi-Kit with the assistance of one witness or the input of a number of witnesses. "Wanted" posters may be made from a sketch, or the sketch may be published in newspapers or shown on television. The Identi-Kit, invented by a police officer, has hundreds of facial components (noses, eyes, chins, hairlines, hair, and so on) that can be combined into the likeness of a person.[33]

  The admissibility of composite sketches has sometimes been at issue. Prosecutors are aware that in-court identifications are frequently viewed with skepticism by the jury because the defendant is sitting apart from others in the courtroom, charged with the crime. As a result, prosecutors usually ask the witness who has made an in-court identification whether the witness has made a previous identification, such as in a lineup. Assuming the prior identification was made consistent with the defendant's due process rights, the prior identification is admissible. Initially, many courts excluded composite sketches as hearsay, but most now permit the witness to testify to a prior identification through a composite sketch for purposes of corroborating an in-court identification. Federal Rule of Evidence 801(d)(1) provides that prior statements of the witness that are identification of a person are not hearsay. Some courts permit the introduction of a composite sketch as substantive evidence of identification.[34]

- *Unusual features:* A description of such features as tattoos, scars, gold teeth or other dental features, hair, weight, and size can increase the reliability of an identification. Such unusual features can be exhibited in a courtroom as identification evidence.

- *Clothing:* Clothing is often included in descriptions given by victims or witnesses. Sometimes in rape cases an offender's clothing becomes torn, dirty, or stained in his struggle with the victim. Hats or other items of clothing are sometimes left behind or dropped in a hasty exit. Knowledgeable suspects sometimes change their clothing with others in an effort to avoid identification through a hat or jacket.

  The Supreme Court of California held that a defendant's refusal to don a jacket and cap during a showup at a police station can be used as evidence in the trial of the defendant,[35] as can a defendant's refusal to participate in a lineup.[36] Such evidence is not protected by the Fifth Amendment privilege against self-incrimination and can be compelled, with refusal by the defendants used as evidence against them.

  The robbery victim's identification of the defendant's hat and jacket was used as evidence to convict the defendant in the case of *Johnson v. Ross.*[37] The suspect's voice and clothes were used as aids in identification in the case of *State v. Holloman.*[38] The gun carried by one of the defendants was used in identification in the case of *Turner v. State.*[39] In the case of *Holder v. State,*[40] the defendant was required to stand in court and put on a jacket, mask, and cap worn by the robber and to say words spoken by the robber. To mitigate such evidence, the defense lawyer also put on the cap and the bandana, but the jury's finding of guilt was sustained by the appellate court.

- *Voice identification:* Voice identification has been admissible as evidence for years in the United States. In some cases, the victim has had previous contact with the defendant and recognizes the voice. In other cases, the offender is unknown to the victim, but the victim or other persons recall features of the offender's voice. A recording of the offender's voice may be available from a message-recording machine, voice mail, or other means. The defendant can be required to give a voice sample at trial, so that the victim can determine whether the voice matches that of the assailant.

  In the 2004 case of *Hubanks v. Frank,*[41] the defendant in a sexual assault case was ordered at his trial to speak the words the assailant used to determine whether the victim could recognize the voice. The defendant refused to speak. The trial judge subsequently instructed the jury that it could consider the fact that the defendant refused to give the voice sample in deciding his guilt. The defendant was convicted and appealed, contending that his Fifth Amendment rights were violated by the trial judge's order to speak and instructions to the jury. The court of appeals rejected these contentions, holding that because giving a voice sample is not testimonial, the Fifth Amendment does not apply, and the trial court was correct in ordering the sample and in instructing the jury about the consequences of the defendant's refusal to give the sample.

  In crimes such as rape and robbery, most victims not only see the offenders but also hear their voices. In cases of telephone threats, telephone harassment, and stalking, however, voice identification alone can be used as evidence if the victim can identify the voice.[42] Victims can ordinarily testify that the voice "sounds like" the voice of the offender. The Supreme Court of Minnesota stated the rule of law for the admissibility of voice identification evidence:

  > It is the rule in this state that the foundation for admission of testimony as to the identity of the voice of a telephone caller is sufficient when it appears that the witness to whom the telephone call is made testifies that he is reasonably certain as to the voice of such caller and can identify it.[43]

spectrograms or **voiceprints** Voice graphs made on a spectrograph, which analyzes voice recordings based on intensity, frequency, and time gaps.

- *Spectrograms or voiceprints:* If voice recordings become available in such crimes as kidnapping, murder plots, bomb threats, or false alarms, **spectrograms** or **voiceprints** may be made in an effort to identify offenders. If a match is made with the voiceprint of a suspect, some state courts permit the spectrograms to be used as evidence in criminal trials. The highest court in Maryland described the operation of a spectrograph in the case of *Reed v. State:*[44]

  > The process involves the use of a machine known as a spectrograph. This machine analyzes the acoustic energy of the human voice into three components—time, frequency, and intensity—and graphically displays these components by generating, through an electric stylus, a series of closely spaced light and dark lines, varying in position, on a sheet of electrically sensitive paper. The resulting graphic representation is what is called a spectrogram or "voiceprint." It reveals certain patterns or "formals" which correspond to the sounds that are analyzed.

  Many courts have rejected the scientific reliability of voice spectrographic evidence and have refused to permit such evidence in criminal trials. For example, in *United States v. Angleton*,[45] a defendant charged with commissioning a murder for hire sought to introduce expert testimony based on a voice spectrograph to identify the speaker on a wiretap recording. The trial court refused to admit the expert testimony, finding that the science of voice spectrography lacked reliability and thus was inadmissible under Rule 702 of the Federal Rules of Evidence (see Chapter 18). A few courts have admitted expert testimony based on voice spectrograph tests. In *State v. Coon*, 974 P.2d 386 (Alaska 1999) the court applied the *Daubert* test (see Chapter 18) and concluded voice spectrographs possessed adequate scientific validity and were admissible.

COURTROOM IDENTIFICATION OF A DEFENDANT

In criminal trials the state must carry the burden of identifying the defendant beyond a reasonable doubt as the person who committed the crime or as an aider and abettor or a conspirator to the crime. This task can be accomplished through any of the means discussed in this chapter.

During criminal trials, defendants may be required to try on such items as jackets, hats, and glasses to show whether such items fit the defendant. Defendants may also be required to speak or to display tattoos, scars, or a gold tooth.

Eyewitnesses or earwitnesses are asked by the prosecutor to describe the person who committed the crime or who was seen fleeing from the crime scene. The witness is then asked whether that person is in the courtroom. When the witness answers yes, the witness is asked to point out the person.

Because the defendant is ordinarily seated next to his or her attorney at the defense table,[46] the witness points the person out to the court and the jury. To clearly establish that the witness has identified the defendant as the person who committed the crime, the witness is then ordinarily requested to further identify the defendant by one or more of the following methods:

- Asking the witness to describe what the defendant is wearing in court and to specifically describe where that person is sitting
- Asking the defendant to stand and asking the witness whether this is the person who committed the crime or was seen fleeing from the crime scene
- Requesting the witness to step down from the stand and to point to or to touch the person who committed the crime or who was seen fleeing from the crime scene

The prosecutor then requests that the court record show that the witness has identified the defendant as the person who was seen committing the crime or was seen fleeing from the crime scene.

courtroom identification A prescribed series of steps used during a trial to identify the defendant as the person who committed the crime or was a party to the crime charged.

Because many jurisdictions permit testimony by eyewitnesses regarding prior out-of-court identification, witnesses may then be asked whether they had previously identified the defendant as the person who assaulted them or committed the crime being charged. Such testimony can be technically considered hearsay, but it is important and meaningful because it gives the jury and judge a full picture of the identification process that was used. Such testimony also buttresses the ritualized **courtroom identification** against possible attack in cross-examination and shows to the jury and the judge the extent of the investigation and deliberation before the decision was made to bring the defendant to trial.

USING BIOMETRICS FOR IDENTIFICATION AND AUTHENTICATION

It is important that persons who enter security areas or cross borders into the United States be accurately identified. Unfortunately, cleverly forged identification documents are available in many parts of the world, including the United States. Because of this, accurate, on-the-scene identification is needed not only in the areas just mentioned but also for cashing checks, collecting welfare benefits, using automatic teller machines (ATMs) as well as other crime prevention purposes.

One response to this need is called biometric identification, which is identification not from documents but instead by biological reference systems. Fingerprints and DNA analysis continue to be used at crime scenes in efforts to determine the identity of the person who committed the crime, and then later to identify with certainty the persons who have been arrested and charged with the crime. In the June 2000 issue of the *FBI Law Enforcement Bulletin,* the article entitled "Biometrics: Solving Cases of Mistaken Identity and More" identifies the following biometric systems:

- Iris-based systems, which in the future may equal or exceed fingerprint evidence in accuracy.
- Hand-geometry systems, which have better access and control and can be vital in prisons and jails where high levels of accuracy and security are required.
- Voice recognition, which is the least accurate but the most available way to verify identity over a telephone.
- Facial-recognition systems, which present opportunities to identify people unobtrusively and without their cooperation in video surveillance and other means.

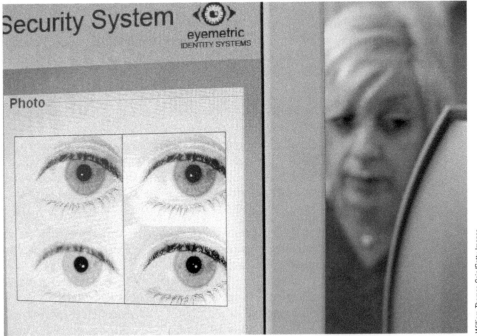

William Thomas Cain/Getty Images

Teaching assistant Joann Lamaruggine has her iris recorded into the iris recognition system at Park Avenue Elementary School in Freehold, New Jersey. Iris recognition systems use a video camera to record the colored ring around the eye's pupil, matching the unique markings in the iris that identify each person.

TESTS THAT DETERMINE THE ADMISSIBILITY OF EYEWITNESS IDENTIFICATION EVIDENCE

- Were the defendant's Fifth Amendment due process rights violated by identification procedures that were so unnecessarily suggestive as to cause "a very substantial likelihood of irreparable misidentification?" *Simmons v. United States,* 390 U.S. 377, 384, 88 S. Ct. 967, 974 (1968).
- Was the defendant's Sixth Amendment right to an attorney observed during identification proceedings after the defendant was charged or indicted?

The One-on-One Showup

- Showups are suggestive but not necessarily in violation of the Fifth Amendment due process requirement.
- The propriety of a showup is determined by the "totality of the circumstances surrounding" the identification (U.S. Supreme Court in *Stovall v. Denno*).
- The suggestiveness inherent in the one-to-one showup can be outweighed by the following policy considerations:
    - The reliability due to the nearness in time of the identification to the crime committed and the need for immediate release of a person who is innocent.
    - The reliability of a witness, as demonstrated in *Neil v. Biggers,* in which the U.S. Supreme Court stated, "Her record for reliability was thus a good one, as she had previously resisted whatever suggestiveness inheres in a showup."
    - An emergency condition, such as in *Stovall v. Denno,* in which two days after a murder, the only witness was in critical condition in a hospital. The U.S. Supreme Court held that an "immediate hospital confrontation was imperative."

Photographic Identification

- The propriety of pretrial photographic identification is determined by the "totality of the circumstances surrounding" the identification and will be set aside "only if the photographic identification was so impermissibly suggestive as to give rise to a very substantial likelihood of irreparable misidentification" *Simmons v. United States,* 390 U.S. 377, 88 S. Ct. 967 (1968).
- The suspect's photograph should be grouped with a sufficient number of other photographs of the same general description and shown to witnesses separately. The exact group of photographs should be preserved so it may be presented to the court at a later date to counteract any claim of undue suggestiveness and to enhance the reliability of the in-court identification.
- A suspect has no right to have an attorney present during a photographic identification proceeding, *United States v. Ash,* 413 U.S. 300, 93 S. Ct. 2568 (1973), unless the state courts have held otherwise.
- A single-photograph identification procedure is suggestive but may not be impermissibly suggestive. The burden is on the state to show that the identification was sufficiently reliable to be used as evidence in view of the "totality of the circumstances surrounding" the identification procedure used.

SUMMARY

1. **List some of the reasons for mistaken eyewitness identifications.**
   - Mistaken identifications can be caused by the suggestive circumstances under which an out-of-court identification occurs. Faulty lineups, insufficient photographic arrays, and impermissible coaching of a witness are examples of "system variables" that can influence a witness to make a misidentification. Also, the circumstances surrounding the event

witnessed, the lighting, the distance of the witness, and the race of the witness or suspect are "estimator" variables that can adversely affect the accuracy of an identification.

2. **State the difference between a lineup and a showup.**
   - Lineups are composed of multiple individuals, usually five or more, who have relatively common physical characteristics. A showup is a procedure where a witness views a suspect singly, without other individuals presented to the witness.

3. **State the requirements for a nonsuggestive photo array.**
   - A photo array must include multiple photographs, usually six or eight, showing a person of the same general description. The photos are usually shown one at a time, and all photos must be preserved so that the full array can be presented in a criminal trial where the identification is used.

4. **Define *sequential lineup*.**
   - In a sequential lineup each person in the lineup is viewed by the witness independently from other persons in the lineup.

5. **When may a single photograph be used to identify a suspect?**
   - Although single photographs are highly suggestive, use of a single photograph to identify a suspect is permitted when other evidence establishes the reliability of the identification.

6. **List the factors established by *Neil v. Biggers* for testing the reliability of eyewitness identifications.**
   - The opportunity of the witness to observe the suspect, the characteristics of the witness, the accuracy of any prior description of the suspect, the level of certainty of the witness in the identification, and the time between the event and the identification are factors to be used in determining reliability.

KEY TERMS

KEY CASES

Foster v. California, 394 U.S. 440 (1969): Admission in criminal trial of identifications made under unduly suggestive circumstances violates due process.

Manson v. Brathwaite, 432 U.S. 98 (1977): Use of a single photograph to identify a suspect does not prohibit the admission of the identification if evidence shows the evidence was reliable.

Neil v. Biggers, 409 U.S. 188 (1972): Established the factors courts are to use in determining if an eyewitness identification made under suggestive circumstances must be excluded under the Due Process Clause. Many state courts have adopted

those factors, but some have modified or changed the factors to be used under state laws.

Simmons v. United States, 390 U.S. 377 (1968): The reliability of a photo identification must be determined under the "totality of the circumstances" under which the identification was made.

State v. Henderson, 27 A.3d 872 (N.J. 2011): Leading case among state courts questioning the continued use of the *Neil v. Biggers* guidelines for admissibility of eyewitness identifications made under suggestive circumstances.

PROBLEMS

1. The police arrest a suspect in a murder/robbery case. They bring the suspect to police headquarters for a lineup where three witnesses to the crime would view the suspect. In order to fill the lineup, the police place Raheem, who was being held in connection with an unrelated

crime, in the lineup with the suspect and three other persons. Of the five, only Raheem wears a coat, a black jacket. The witnesses identify Raheem as the person who committed the murder/robbery. In earlier statements to police describing the person witnessed by them they had all noted he was wearing a black jacket. Is the lineup so suggestive the identification evidence should be excluded? Does it matter that the police picked what they thought were "fillers" in order to match the physical characteristics of the person they suspected? (See *Raheem v. Kelly*, 257 F.3d 122 (2d Cir. 2001).)

2. This actually happened; you be the judge. Police arranged a lineup for a witness to view so he could identify the person who robbed him. Because the police could not get the witness on the phone, they left a message with his mother asking her to tell the witness to be at police headquarters at a certain time "for a lineup." The witness, thinking he was a suspect in a crime, came to police headquarters, stating he was to be in a lineup. He was given shield number 4, and was placed in a lineup with the actual suspect, who wore shield number 6. Investigators waited for the witness to come to the viewing area, but were puzzled by his absence. Suddenly, the witness standing in the lineup shouted, "Shield number 6 is the robber!" If you were the judge, would you permit this identification to be admitted at the trial of the suspect in the robbery? What are the factors you should consider?

3. All courts state that one-person showups are not the best practice, and present greater risks of misidentification than lineups. However, most courts also permit the use of showup identification evidence, if the showup was tied to "exigent circumstances." In the following case from Massachusetts, two levels of appellate courts disagreed about the trial court's decision to permit introduction of a showup identification. In the end, suggestive identifications violate due process if they create the "substantial likelihood of misidentification." One court said the showup created that likelihood; the other said it did not. Which court do you think was correct? (See *Massachusetts v. Martin*, 827 N.E.2d 1263 (Mass. App. 2005), *reversed*, 850 N.E.2d 555 (Mass. 2006).)

4. In *Tillman v. State*, 2011 WL 4577675 (Tex. Crim. App. 2011) the court reversed a trial court's decision in a murder trial to exclude evidence of an expert witness called by the defendant to give an opinion on eyewitness identification reliability. The court referenced the New Jersey Supreme Court's extensive discussion of scientific research in eyewitness identification in *State v. Henderson*, discussed in this chapter. What reasons did the trial court give for excluding the testimony of the expert? What would the expert testify about if he were permitted to testify? Finally, what did the appeals court think was the "relevance" of the expert's testimony?

CASE ANALYSIS

Read Appendix B, Finding and Analyzing Cases (p. 499). With these guidelines in mind, please continue with the Case Analysis selections for Chapter 13.

1. Assume a witness observed a man, who fit the description of a man involved in a shooting, exiting a white car that was involved in the shooting. A few minutes later, police brought the man, wearing handcuffs, to the witness for a "showup," telling the witness the man had thrown away a brown shirt, part of the description given for the man involved in the shooting. The witness identified the man as the person he saw exiting the white car, and later made the same identification at the defendant's murder trial. Should the identification be excluded based on a "suggestive" showup? Would it matter if the witness was a police officer? *State v. Taylor*, 842 N.W.2d 771 (Neb. 2014).

2. A witness to a shooting is brought to the police stationhouse for a photographic array in an attempt to identify the shooter. The witness is shown six photographs simultaneously, grouped in two rows of three. The witness identifies the defendant as the shooter, and

does so again at trial. Is there a problem with this procedure? What should police tell a witness before showing the witness a photographic array? *State v. Gallop*, 89 A.3d 795 (R.I. 2014).

3. Assume a witness to a shooting is shown a photo lineup with six persons, each standing next to a ruler that measures height. One person, the defendant, is 5 feet 6 inches tall; the other persons shown vary from 5 feet 11 to 6 feet 4. Other witnesses had told police the shooter was a short man. Is this photo lineup unduly suggestive? Does it matter if the witness said he did not notice the height ruler? If the photo lineup is unduly suggestive, does that

mean an identification of the defendant by the witness at the trial must be excluded? *Butler v. State*, 102 So.3d 260 (Miss. 2012).

4. What happens when an identification of a defendant made by a witness at a pre-trial lineup was done under circumstances that an appeals court concludes rendered the subsequent identification by the witness at the defendant's trial inadmissible? If the prosecution decides to retry the defendant, can they show the witness a new, proper, lineup that includes the defendant, and then have the witness identify the defendant at the trial? *Young v. Conner*, 698 F.3d 69 (2nd Cir. 2012), *cert. denied* 134 S. Ct. 20 (2013).

Notes

1. 92 A.3d 766.
2. 610 N.E.2d 1 (Ill. App. 1993).
3. 667 So.2d 156 (Ala. Crim. App. 1995).
4. 586 N.E.2d 1261 (App. 1992).
5. CrL 1252 (Tex. Crim. App. 1990).
6. 394 S.E.2d 198 (N.C. App. 1990).
7. 559 N.E.2d 464 (Ohio 1990).
8. IACP Training Key #67 entitled "Witness Perception."
9. 86 Neb. L. Rev. 515 (2008).
10. 388 U.S. 218 (1967).
11. 388 U.S. at 228.
12. See generally *Eyewitness Identification: Science and Reform*, 29 Apr. Champ. 12 (2005).
13. See, for example, *State v. Palmer*, 715 N.W.2d 767 (Iowa App. 2007).
14. 2006 WL 337085 (Cal. App. 2006).
15. *Stovall v. Denno*, 388 U.S. 293, 87 S. Ct. 1967 (1967).
16. *Stovall v. Denno; Neil v. Biggers*, 409 U.S. 188, 93 S. Ct. 375 (1972).
17. 87 S. Ct. 1967 (1967).
18. 92 S. Ct. 1877 (1972).
19. *Watkins v. Sowders*, 449 U.S. 341 (1981).
20. *Neil v. Biggers*, 409 U.S. 188, 198 (1972).
21. These guidelines and factors for determining the accuracy and reliability of eyewitness identification established by the U.S. Supreme Court in the case of *Neil v. Biggers* are similar to those in Model Jury Instruction 52.20. This Model Jury Instruction can be found in *State v. Willis*, 731 P.2d 287 (Kans. 1987).
22. 44 P.3d 794 (2002).
23. 69 P.3d 571 (2003).
24. 132 S. Ct. at 730.
25. 132 S. Ct. at 728.
26. "Procedures for Obtaining Pretrial Eyewitness Identification," Series 304, No. 7.
27. In the 1992 case of *State v. Hoyte* (413 S.E.2d 806), the Supreme Court of South Carolina reversed the defendant's crack cocaine conviction because a showup without the defendant's attorney present was held five and a half months after the last drug sale and after the defendant's arrest. The court held that "there was no lineup; it was a one-man showup without notice to appointed counsel. While showups have been upheld by [this] Court, these situations usually involve either extenuating circumstances or are very close in time to the crime."
28. Courts have held that in view of the totality of circumstances less than eight photographs are sufficient. The Supreme Court of Nebraska held that five photographs constituted "a fair and adequate array when attempting to identify a single perpetrator." *State v. Gibbs*, 470 N.W.2d 558 (Neb. 1991). In the case of *United States v. Sanchez*, 24 F.3d 1259 (10th Cir. 1994), it was held that six photos were not impermissibly suggestive when there was only a minor difference between the photos. In the *Sanchez* case, the defendant's photo was the only photo depicting a person with his eyes closed. A major difference could consist of using photos depicting persons of different appearances (such as weight, lack of hair, age, sex, color, and dress) than the defendant.
29. Law enforcement agencies keep mug shots not only for citizen identification purposes but also to acquaint law enforcement officers with known suspects and persons who have criminal records. Mug shots should not be used as evidence, however, because they could

easily cause jury members to believe that the defendant had a prior criminal record or prior trouble with the law; this could deny the defendant the right to a fair trial. Evidence of other offenses and prior trouble with the law is inadmissible as part of the government's case against a defendant. (See *Michelson v. United States,* 335 U.S. 469, 69 S. Ct. 213 (1948).)

30. 631 F.2d 1229 (5th Cir.).

31. Cases in which courts held that misidentification in single-photograph showings was a remote possibility due to "the totality of the circumstances" include *People v. Kelly,* 540 N.E.2d 1125 (1989), in which the victims were 5- and 7-year-old children; *United States v. Dring,* 930 F.2d 687 (9th Cir. 1991); *State v. Barnett,* 588 N.E.2d 887 (Ohio App. 1990), in which the showing of only one photo was held to be "unnecessarily suggestive" but not "impermissibly suggestive"; and *State v. James,* 592 So.2d 867 (La. App. 1991), which held that an independent basis for identification existed in view of the *Manson* factors.

    In the 1992 case of *State v. Martin,* 595 So.2d 592, the Supreme Court of Louisiana held that a single-photograph showing was made under circumstances that resulted in substantial likelihood of irreparable misidentification and that there was no independent basis for the undercover police officer's in-court identification of the defendant. Another case in which a criminal conviction was reversed for a new trial was *Commonwealth v. Jarecki,* 1992 WL 104524 (Pa. Super. 1992), where a police officer permitted four witnesses to a store robbery to view a photographic array at the same time and talk among themselves in attempting to select the picture of the robber. In the 1991 case of *Hull v. State,* 581 So.2d 1202, the Alabama Appellate Court reversed the conviction of Hull for a new trial because, in a photographic array of five pictures, only the defendant's picture was in black and white, whereas the other four photos were in color.

    The court held that the in-court identification by a witness was not independently reliable.

32. 958 F.2d 9 (1st Cir. 1992).

33. In the 1992 case of *Sanders v. English et al.,* 950 F.2d 1152 (5th Cir.), Sanders was arrested as the result of a composite sketch of the "bicycle bandit" who repeatedly robbed at gunpoint. After Sanders was held in custody for 50 days, a grand jury refused to indict him after concluding that probable cause did not exist. In a civil lawsuit against the police officers involved, Sanders lost on the false arrest claims but was able to sue for the 50 days of illegal detention and malicious prosecution.

34. See, for example, *Commonwealth v. Weichell,* 453 N.E.2d 1038 (Mass. Sup. Jud. Ct. 1983).

35. *People v. Smith,* 91 Cal. Rptr. 786 (1970).

36. *People v. Johnson,* 842 P.2d 1 (Calif. 1992).

37. 955 F.2d 178 (2d Cir. 1992).

38. 837 P.2d 826 (Kan. App. 1992).

39. 803 P.2d 1152 (Okla. Crim. App. 1990).

40. 837 S.W.2d 802 (Tex. App. 1992).

41. 392 F.3d 926 (7th Cir. 2004).

42. It is a common practice to have persons in a lineup say words and sentences or to try on hats or clothing. Voice-only lineups could be held by having six or more persons repeat sentences or by tape-recording the voices stating the sentence or phrase for replay when necessary. Defense lawyers requested this procedure in the case *Evans v. Superior Court,* 522 P.2d 681 (Calif. 1974). California trial judges have the authority to order voice-only lineups just as they have the authority to order physical lineups. (See *Garcia v. San Joaquin Superior Court,* 50 CrL 1312 (Calif. App. 1991).)

    On-the-street and stationhouse voice identifications in rape cases were held not to be impermissibly suggestive in the cases of *State v. Jones,* 587 N.E.2d 886 (Ohio App. 1990), and *Jefferson v. State,* 425 S. E.2d 915 (Ga. App. 1992).

    Voice exemplars, or recorded voice samples, were approved for use as evidence by the U.S. Supreme Court; see *United States v. Wade,* 87 S. Ct. 1926 (1967) and *United States v. Dionisio,* 93 S. Ct. 764 (1973). Compelling a defendant or suspect to speak for the purposes of identification does not violate a suspect's Fifth Amendment privilege against self-incrimination.

43. *City of St. Paul v. Caulfield,* 94 N.W.2d 263 (Minn. 1959).

44. 391 A.2d 364 (1978).

45. 269 F.Supp.2d 892 (S.D. Tex. 2003).

46. In a few instances, defense lawyers have had persons who look similar to the defendant sit next to them at the defense table with the defendant sitting elsewhere in the courtroom during the trial. If the court is not informed of this situation, both the defense attorney and the look-alike could be charged with contempt. In the 1973 case of *Duke v. State,* 298 N.E.2d 453 (Ind.), the decoy sitting next to the defense lawyer was convicted and temporarily jailed in place of the defendant.

    Other cases where defense lawyers were found in direct criminal contempt of court for not informing the trial court that the person sitting next to them was not the defendant include *United States v. Thoreen,* 653 F.2d 1332 (9th Cir. 1981); *People v. Simac,* 603 N.E.2d 97, 52 CrL 1260 (Ill. App. 1992); and *Miskovsky v. State ex rel. Jones,* 586 P.2d 1104 (Okla. Crim. App. 1978).

Obtaining Physical and Other Evidence

A POLICE IMPOUND LOT

JIM WEBER/The Commercial Appeal/Landov

LEARNING OBJECTIVES

In this chapter we focus on the methods employed to obtain physical evidence in the investigation of crimes. The learning objectives for this chapter are

Describe the level of evidence needed for an investigative detention.

List searches that may be made without a search warrant.

State what actions police may take in a routine traffic stop.

State the *Arizona v. Gant* rule for searches of a vehicle incident to an arrest.

Explain the "automobile exception" and how it differs from a search of a residence.

Define *exigent circumstance* as an exception to the search warrant requirement.

343

Beginning in 2004 the New York City Police Department (NYPD) began a controversial "stop and frisk" policy under which NYPD officers, often without probable cause or even reasonable suspicion of a crime being committed, stopped persons on the streets of New York, questioned them, and in some cases frisked them. This happened about 4.4 million times between January 2004 and June 2012, when several New York residents filed federal lawsuits seeking to enjoin the practice.[1] About 80 per cent of the persons stopped were black or Hispanic.

A New York federal district judge initially ordered the city to cease the stop and frisk practice, as well as ordering other remedies. However, on appeal the Second Circuit Court of Appeals (1) issued a stay of the order pending appeal, and (2) disqualified the district judge from further involvement in the case.[2] In February 2014 the Second Circuit stayed pending appeals, and sent the cases back to U.S. District Court in the hopes the parties could resolve their differences by negotiation.[3] The newly elected mayor of New York, Bill deBlasio, and the Police Commissioner stated in January 2014 that the city would agree to have a court-appointed monitor supervise police reforms in the city's stop and frisk policy.

---

physical evidence (real evidence)
Physical objects, such as weapons, drugs, and clothing.

Physical evidence—or **real evidence**, as it is sometimes called—is important and even critical evidence in many criminal cases. Examples of physical evidence are weapons (guns, knives, and so on); illegal drugs; fingerprints; clothing; documents; footprints; hair; blood; grass marks or other stains on clothing; metal and wood fragments; and objects that were stolen, such as merchandise, money, and purses.

While the Fourth Amendment emphasizes the need for and importance of search warrants for searching our persons or places, in fact physical evidence is commonly (and properly) obtained by police in a variety of settings where warrants are neither used nor required. They include a public place in which a crime has been committed; from the person of a suspect or the suspect's motor vehicle; or even a residence or other private place. Real evidence might be obtained with lawful consent, observed in plain view, or obtained in a lawful arrest and search by a law enforcement officer.

In Chapters 9 and 10 we learned about the exclusionary rule, often (though not always) in the context of a Fourth Amendment violation. In Chapter 15 we will explore the role of search warrants in obtaining physical evidence, as well as the rules on obtaining non-physical evidence from computers. In this chapter we continue the study of the Fourth Amendment limits on searches and seizures by focusing on those activities in the absence of a warrant.

OBTAINING PHYSICAL EVIDENCE FROM THE PERSON OF A SUSPECT
Obtaining Evidence and Information by Means of Voluntary Conversations

Three types of encounters occur between citizens and law enforcement officers:

Terry stop An investigative street detention named after the 1968 U.S. Supreme Court case of *Terry v. Ohio.*

1. The voluntary encounter or voluntary conversation
2. The investigative stop, or **Terry stop**, where the officer has reasonable suspicion to believe "a crime is afoot" (i.e., that the suspect has committed, is committing, or is about to commit a crime)
3. An arrest that is justified by probable cause to believe that the person has committed a crime

All persons in a democracy have a fundamental right to move freely about without unnecessary interference by the government. The U.S. Supreme Court pointed out:

No right is held more sacred, or is more carefully guarded, by the common law, than the right of every individual to the possession and control of their own person, free from all restraint or interference of others, unless by clear and unquestionable authority of law.[4]

Law enforcement officers may attempt to engage a person in a voluntary conversation in a public place, such as on a sidewalk or in an airport or train station.[5] The U.S. Supreme Court pointed out that:

> [T]he person approached…need not answer any questions…indeed, he may decline to listen to the questions at all and may go on his way. He may not be detained even momentarily without reasonable objective grounds for doing so; and his refusal to listen, or answer does not, without more furnish these grounds.[6]

free-to-leave test The test used to determine whether a conversation between a person and a law officer is voluntary; a reasonable person must believe he is free to leave.

Most persons will engage in voluntary conversations with law enforcement officers. If at some point they wish to discontinue the conversation, they may do so.[7] The test used by American courts to determine whether such situations are voluntary is the **free-to-leave test**, which was defined this way by the U.S. Supreme Court: …[A] person has been "seized" within the meaning of the Fourth Amendment only if in view of all the circumstances surrounding the incident, a reasonable person would have believed that he was not free to leave.[8]

"Knock and Talk" as an Investigative Technique

"Knock and talk" is not a new concept. It has been used for years by law enforcement officers who knock on the door of a person's residence and talk to the residents about problems that might concern the community. Because it is a practical, efficient, and sensible way for law enforcement to confront problems, the technique is now widely used by overworked law officers. Use of the technique has been given general approval by courts in this country. The 2006 *FBI Law Enforcement Bulletin* article "Knock and Talk" cited dozens of state and federal court decisions upholding the technique, stating that:

> The general rule under federal law is that knock and talk is a lawful investigative technique that does not violate the Fourth Amendment. Many states' courts have taken the same position. (The complete text of the article may be found at http://www.fbi.gov.)

An officer knocking at a door may only be seeking information or responding to a neighborhood complaint. The officer could be acting on personal information or information from another officer; the officer could have reasonable suspicion sufficient to make an investigative detention of an occupant of the premises, or even probable cause to arrest an occupant or obtain a search warrant. Whatever the case, as the Wyoming Supreme Court stated,

> The prevailing rule is that, absent a clear expression by the owner to the contrary, police officers are permitted to approach a dwelling and seek permission to question an occupant in the course of their official business. (Citations omitted). There is no requirement that law enforcement have probable cause or reasonable suspicion before they may approach a home and ask for permission to enter.[10]

Although the term *knock and talk* is of recent vintage, the underlying rule that where the front door of a home is accessible to the public the police may approach it is longstanding. In the 1964 decision in *Davis v. United States*, 327 F.2d 301, 303, the court stated,

> Absent express orders from the person in possession against any possible trespass, there is no rule which makes it illegal per se, or a condemned invasion of the person's right

LEGAL CASES

The 2002 U.S. Supreme Court Case on "Free to Leave"

Facts in the Case

In the case of *United States v. Drayton*,[9] passengers on a Greyhound bus disembarked at a scheduled stop in Tallahassee, Florida, while the bus was refueled and cleaned. Shortly after the passengers re-boarded the bus, three plainclothes police officers boarded as part of a drug and weapons interdiction program. One officer knelt on the driver's seat facing the passengers, a second stood at the back of the bus, and the third walked down the aisle speaking with individual passengers, asking about their travel plans and trying to match them with luggage in the overhead bins. To avoid blocking the aisle, the officer stood next to, or behind, each passenger with whom he spoke. No general announcement was made about why the officers were on the bus, and the passengers were never told that they could refuse to consent to any search of their luggage.

An officer approached Drayton and his traveling companion, introduced himself, and told them he was looking for drugs and weapons. The officer asked whether the pair had any luggage. They responded that they shared a single bag located in the overhead bin. They gave the officer permission to search the bag, but no contraband was found. The officer then asked permission to frisk Drayton's traveling companion. He consented to the frisk, and drug packages were found strapped to his inner thighs. He was arrested and escorted off the bus. Drayton was then asked to consent to a pat-down search. Drayton also consented, and similar packages were found in his possession. Drayton and his companion were charged with conspiracy to distribute cocaine and possession with intent to distribute cocaine.

Questions Before the Courts

1. Should the evidence be suppressed because the passengers were not free to leave the bus?
2. Were the officers obligated to inform the passengers that they could refuse to give consent to search?

Rulings of the Courts

- *Trial court:* The defense motion to suppress the evidence (drug packages) was denied.
- *Court of appeals:* The evidence was suppressed because the officers were obligated to inform the passengers of their right to refuse to give consent to search.

After you have considered the facts and the rulings by the lower courts, read how the U.S. Supreme Court decided the case in note 75 of this chapter.

of privacy, for anyone openly and peacefully, at high noon, to walk up the steps and knock on the front door of any man's "castle" with the honest intent of asking questions of the occupant thereof—whether the questioner be a pollster, a salesman, or an officer of the law.

Many of the legal issues discussed in this text are related to knock and talk investigations. Questions as to whether the curtilage has been entered (where a front door is not readily accessible to the public), consent of the occupants of a residence (when an apartment is involved or the police have entered a residence), the plain view doctrine (when contraband is seen or smelled in the premises), protective measures such as frisks and protective sweeps, and exigent circumstances where persons flee the police or attempt to destroy evidence often relate to a knock and talk investigation.

City police officers question a man on a public sidewalk. Law enforcement officers may request a conversation with any person in a public place. The person can choose to respond or not.

Chris McGrath/Getty Images

In most "knock and talk" situations probable cause to arrest an occupant or obtain a search warrant does not exist. If probable cause does not exist, officers must terminate the knock and talk once the occupant indicates the conversation must cease, unless circumstances that provide an exception to the search warrant requirement are present. If probable cause does exist, officers would normally obtain arrest or search warrants before going further.

The case of *City of Sheboygan v. Cesar*, 796 N.W.2d 429 (Wis. App. 2011), *cert. denied* 132 S. Ct. 114 (2011) is a good illustration of how courts can distinguish a true "knock and talk," where no Fourth Amendment issues are involved, from a more intrusive action that does implicate the Fourth Amendment. There, the appeals court rejected a defendant's claim that a "knock and talk" violated his Fourth Amendment rights by "constructive entry" into his home. In that case, police received a report that a red pickup truck had struck a fire hydrant and left the scene. At 10 o'clock at night the police found the truck parked at the home of the registered owner of the truck. Two officers knocked at the front door, and one officer waited at the back door. After knocking at the door and windows for some time, the defendant, Cesar, came to a window.

In a "back-and-forth" conversation, Cesar told the officers he was not coming out of the house. The officers replied they would stay there until he came out or they obtained a search warrant. Cesar ultimately came out, and in conversations with the police admitted he had driven the truck after consuming Ambien and alcohol. Cesar was then arrested and convicted of driving under the influence of an intoxicant (OWI) and hit and run of property.

On appeal, Cesar contended the officers had made a "constructive entry" of his residence, which was unlawful under the Fourth Amendment because the officers did not have a search warrant. As a result, he argued, statements made to the officers came while he was unlawfully seized, and must be suppressed.

The appeals court rejected that argument and affirmed the convictions. The court stated that a person is "seized" when police have acted so that a reasonable person does not feel free to leave or terminate a conversation. If the person is at a location, such as a home, that he does not want to leave, the question becomes whether a reasonable person would believe he was free to terminate the encounter. The court agreed that "...a 'knock and talk' interview at a private residence that has lost its consensual nature and has effectively become an in-home seizure or 'constructive entry' may trigger Fourth Amendment scrutiny..." 796 N.W.2d, at 436.

The court concluded that under the circumstances of this case the police did not "constructively enter" the defendant's residence and unlawfully "seize" him. The court noted that the police did not threaten Cesar in order to make him exit the house, did not threaten to enter the house, and indeed did not even request permission to enter the house. Since the police had sufficient probable cause to obtain a search warrant, the statement by police that they would stay until they obtained a warrant was not a threat designed to force Cesar to exit the house. Throughout the encounter, Cesar appeared willing to engage in the conversation. The court therefore held that the police were not "overly intrusive or coercive in attempting to gain contact with Cesar. We conclude that once informed of his or her options, a reasonable person would have understood that he or she was free to terminate the encounter." 796 N.W.2d at 437, 438.

Authority Needed to Make an Investigative Detention (*Terry* Stop)

reasonable suspicion
The amount of evidence a law enforcement officer needs to make an investigative stop (a *Terry* stop); less than probable cause but more than a hunch or mere suspicion.

A *Terry* stop (from the U.S. Supreme Court case of *Terry v. Ohio,* discussed in this chapter), is the next step up from a knock and talk or voluntary encounter with police. To make a *Terry* stop, also called an investigative detention, police must have **reasonable suspicion** the person stopped is or has been involved in criminal activity. Reasonable suspicion is less than the probable cause needed to authorize an arrest, but more than a simple, unfounded suspicion. To make a temporary stop, the officer must be able to "point to specific and articulable facts which, taken together with rational inferences from those facts, reasonably warrant that intrusion."[11]

Reasonable suspicion is therefore more than a hunch, a gut reaction, or mere suspicion. Reasonable suspicion is that amount of evidence and facts that will cause a reasonable person to believe that the suspect has committed, is committing, or is about to commit a crime. In *United States v. Arvizu* the U.S. Supreme Court said, "Although an officer's reliance on a mere "hunch" is insufficient to justify a stop, the likelihood of criminal activity need not rise to the level required for probable cause, and it falls considerably short of satisfying a preponderance of the evidence standard."[12]

The totality of the circumstances test is used to determine whether reasonable suspicion exists. That is, reasonable suspicion is determined by looking at the whole picture and all of the circumstances that existed. The *Arvizu* Court stressed that actions that might be perfectly innocent in one context could, to a trained officer, arouse reasonable suspicion in another context. For example, in the case of *United States v. Bumper*, 705 F.3d 168 (4th Cir. 2013), *cert. denied* 134 S. Ct. 218 (2013), the court held that an officer's knowledge that a convenience store owner, because of instances of criminal activity near his store, had requested police to enforce "no trespassing" signs on the property was relevant to the reasonableness of his decision to stop a man standing on the property, far from the store entrance. While the U.S. Supreme Court has held that mere presence in a high-crime area is not enough to justify a *Terry* stop (*Illinois v. Wardlow*, 528 U.S. 119 (2000)), the *Bumper* court held that knowledge that persons trespassing on the property had in the past committed criminal acts was a "particularized suspicion" sufficient to justify a stop.

The reasonable suspicion requirement is usually satisfied by personal knowledge of the police officer making the stop. However, in the 2014 case of *Navarette v. California*[13] the U.S. Supreme Court made it clear such personal knowledge is not required. There, an anonymous 911 caller informed police that a driver had forced her vehicle off the road at a certain mile marker on a California highway. The caller described the car, and an officer soon found the car on the highway, stopped it, and discovered 30 pounds of marijuana in the trunk. The Supreme Court affirmed the conviction for illegal transportation of marijuana, holding that the anonymous call supported the officers' reasonable suspicion the identified car was being driven recklessly, and that the reason for doing so might be intoxication. It therefore upheld the traffic stop.

The issue of reasonable suspicion arises frequently in suspected drug trafficking cases, where law enforcement officers make investigative stops based on circumstances they believe indicate signs of such trafficking. These stops have often been found to lack reasonable suspicion. For example, in *Reid v. Georgia*,[14] the U.S. Supreme Court held that no reasonable suspicion existed to justify an investigative detention based on the facts that the defendant (1) arrived at the Fort Lauderdale airport very early in the morning, (2) appeared to conceal that he was traveling with a companion, and (3) failed to check any luggage.

State and lower federal courts have done the same. In the following situations courts found that the officers lacked reasonable suspicion to make an investigative stop:

- A young man was driving a late-model car on an interstate highway in Florida at 4:15 A.M. *State v. Johnson.*[15]
- A nervous driver of a car with several visible air fresheners avoided eye contact with police officers.[16]
- A car known to have been purchased from a car dealer suspected of drug trafficking was registered in a common drug smuggling area and had a two-way antenna protruding from the trunk.[17]
- A nervous Hispanic-looking man was driving a car with out-of-state license plates, looking for work, but had no luggage in the car.[18]
- A man arriving on an early flight from San Francisco to Kansas was the first person to deplane, carried no luggage except a garment bag, was wearing a gold chain, and had paid cash for his airline ticket.[19]

The Importance of "Stop and Identify" Laws

Many, but not all, states have statutes that require a person stopped to respond to an officer's request to identify himself or herself. In the 2004 case of *Hiibel v. Sixth Judicial District Court of Nevada*,[20] the U.S. Supreme Court considered the validity of these statutes.

PROCEDURES & PROCESSES

How Long Is Too Long for the Detention of Persons, Luggage, or Packages?

Most investigative detentions are supported by reasonable suspicion, and occur over a reasonable short period of time. There are limits to the length of time an officer may detain a person, and police are obligated to act diligently in questioning the person or investigating the suspicious circumstances that justified the detention. The police must continue to have reasonable suspicion throughout the detention. In *United States v. Sharpe*[a] the U.S. Supreme Court declined to adopt a court of appeals' "bright-line" rule that detentions lasting longer than 20 minutes were unreasonable: "Much as a "bright line" rule would be desirable, in evaluating whether an investigative detention is unreasonable, common sense and ordinary human experience must govern over rigid criteria." Thus, while the duration of a detention should be brief, the time reasonable necessary to effectuate the purpose of the investigative stop must be a factor.

In cases of luggage or packages, the U.S. Supreme Court held in *United States v. Place*[b] that luggage could be detained when reasonable suspicion existed to believe the luggage contained illegal drugs or other evidence of a crime. However, the 90-minute delay while police waited for a drug-detection dog to arrive, and the fact the police moved the luggage to a different location, caused the detention to become unreasonable, and an unlawful seizure. (See Chapter 15 for a discussion of *Place* and dog-sniff cases.)

In the 2008 case of *Farag v. United States*,[c] the court reviewed many of the leading cases on the permissible duration of investigative detentions. It noted that while detentions of 30, 45, and 70 minutes had been upheld, absent unusual circumstances courts have not upheld detentions longer than 90 minutes.

[a]470 U.S. 675, 685 (1985).
[b]462 U.S. 696 (1983).
[c]587 F.Supp.2d 436, 456 (E.D. N.Y. 2008).

In responding to a telephone call reporting an assault in a rural area, a Nevada deputy sheriff came upon a man, who appeared to be intoxicated, standing beside a truck on the side of a road. A young woman was sitting in the truck. The officer asked the man for identification, but the man refused to give any identification and instead asked why the officer wanted to see it. When the officer stated that he was conducting an investigation, the man became agitated and insisted he had done nothing wrong. The officer explained that he wanted to find out who the man was and what he was doing there. The officer asked for identification eleven times and was refused each time.

The man was then arrested under Nevada's "resisting, delaying, or obstructing a public officer" law in failing to disclose his identity. The law specifically requires that the "person so detained shall identify himself, but may not be compelled to answer any other inquiry of any peace officer."[21]

The U.S. Supreme Court had held in three earlier cases that "an individual's refusal to answer or give a name does not give rise in and of itself to a reasonable suspicion that criminal activity is afoot."[22] Simply refusing to identify oneself is thus not a crime unless, like Nevada, a state has a "stop and identify" law. The question in *Hiibel* was whether a state could constitutionally pass such a law.

The Supreme Court held the Nevada law constitutional, stating,

> Asking questions is an essential part of police investigations. In the ordinary course a police officer is free to ask a person for identification without implicating the Fourth Amendment. "Interrogation relating to one's identity or a request for identification by the police does not, by itself, constitute a Fourth Amendment seizure."[23]

A search incident to the arrest in cases such as *Hiibel* often reveals the identity of and other information about the person. If it does not, the person will not be released on bail but instead will be booked as a "John Doe" or an "unknown." Jailers delight in relating stories of conversations with lawyers who seek to see their client but either cannot or will not identify the client. Such persons are eventually identified through fingerprints or appearances before a very busy and impatient judge.

SEARCHES WITHOUT WARRANTS: DETENTIONS AND ARRESTS

We have seen that police may stop and briefly detain a person based on reasonable suspicion, but need probable cause to make an arrest. We also noted at the beginning of this chapter that the Fourth Amendment requires that searches of a person or place should normally be preceded by a search warrant. Assuming police have properly detained or arrested a person, when may they conduct a search without first getting a search warrant? The following materials discuss the recognized exceptions to the warrant requirement.

Searches That Can Be Justified During an Investigative Detention

Consent searches and protective searches (where the law officer has a valid safety concern) are the only searches that can be justified during an investigative detention.

Consent to search must be voluntarily and clearly given. Consent searches are then limited to the area or object consented to be searched. The consent to search could be of luggage, a parcel, a purse, a vehicle, or another object or place.

protective search A search limited to discovering threatening weapons.

A **protective search** can be made if an officer who has made a valid investigative stop has reasonable suspicion to believe that the suspect "may be armed and presently dangerous." The U.S. Supreme Court also pointed out that "it would be unreasonable to require that police officers take unnecessary risks in the performance of their duties. American criminals have a long tradition of armed violence, and every year in this country many law enforcement officers are killed in the line of duty and thousands more are wounded."[24]

The protective frisk is strictly limited to discovering threatening weapons. If the pat-down causes the officer to reasonably believe that an object detected in the frisk could be a weapon, the object may be removed and may be used as evidence if the object is a weapon or other illegal contraband.

You be the **JUDGE**

The quantity of suspicion of criminal activity required for judging police encounters with citizens runs from none in wholly voluntary encounters to the requirement of probable cause for an arrest. How police conduct an encounter carries the possibility that the encounter can evolve into something other than its initial status.

As the trial judge in the following situations, determine if evidence obtained by police in an encounter with the defendants should be suppressed because of a Fourth Amendment violation:

1. A police officer observed a car parked late at night in a parking lot. The officer pulled his cruiser behind the car to illuminate the interior. He approached the car, and after determining the occupants appeared to be under the age of 18, asked for identification. When a passenger opened the glove box to get his ID the officer observed bags of marijuana. The occupants were arrested and charged with possession of illegal drugs. They moved to suppress the marijuana found in the glove box, contending the encounter was a *Terry* stop and the officer lacked reasonable suspicion. Are they correct? *Commonwealth v. Au*, 42 A.3d 1002 (Md. 2012).

2. Responding to a call, a police officer was told by a store employee that a man matching defendant's description just tried to steal some goods from the store. The officer saw the defendant walking away from the store, and stopped him. The officer frisked him, and felt what he thought were batteries in the defendant's rear pocket. The officer asked: "Why do you have batteries?" When the defendant said they were shotgun shells, not batteries, the officer asked him if he had ever been to prison, and when the defendant said he had the officer arrested him for being a felon in possession of ammunition. The defendant moved to suppress the shotgun shells, contending the officer prolonged the *Terry* stop unreasonably by asking questions unrelated to the reason for the stop. Correct? *United States v. Griffin*, 696 F.3d 1354 (11th Cir. 2012), *cert. denied*, 134 S. Ct. 956 (2014).

3. Based on a 911 tip that the defendant was selling drugs, officers approached the defendant as he stood in a crowd of men near a convenience store. As they approached, the defendant walked away, refusing orders to stop. The officers then fired their Taser guns, striking the defendant in the back and immobilizing him. The officers next frisked the defendant, and found a gun. The defendant was charged with being a felon in possession of a gun. At his trial the defendant contended the officers lacked probable cause to arrest him, even if they had reasonable suspicion for a *Terry* stop, and as a result the evidence found after the Taser guns were used should be suppressed. Was this an arrest or a stop? *Reid v. State*, 51 A.3d 597 (Md. 2012).

In the U.S. Supreme Court case of *Minnesota v. Dickerson*,[25] a police officer making a lawful pat-down felt an object that he knew was not a weapon but suspected to be a lump of rock cocaine. The Supreme Court held that once it was immediately apparent that the object was not a weapon, no further search was permissible. If the nature of the unknown object is not immediately apparent and there is no probable cause to believe it is evidence of a crime, it cannot be seized and used as evidence.

Searches Incident to a Lawful Arrest

The Fourth Amendment of the U.S. Constitution requires that probable cause exist for either a law enforcement officer or a private citizen[26] to make an **arrest**. The U.S. Supreme Court pointed out that the "requirement of probable cause has roots that are deep in our history" and that "common rumor or report, suspicion, or even 'strong reason to suspect' was not adequate to support a warrant or arrest.[27]

The famous English lawyer and writer, Sir William Blackstone, defined the legal term "**arrest**" in his 1760 *Commentaries* as "the apprehending or restraining of one's person, in order to be forthcoming to answer an alleged or suspected crime."

arrest Defined in 1760 by Sir William Blackstone as "the apprehending or restraining of one's person, in order to be forthcoming to answer an alleged or suspected crime."

If probable cause to make an arrest exists, the U.S. Supreme Court held in *Chimel v. California*, then arresting officers may make a search "incident to the arrest."[28] Such a search is reasonable because of officer safety, and the possibility of the destruction of evidence related to the arrest. However, not every stop by a police officer is an arrest. The fifty states have all passed criminal laws, but cities and counties also have passed laws addressing violations of local ordinances. Many encounters between police and persons involve civil violations of municipal ordinances like traffic violations, usually punishable by fines. When a person is stopped for violations of these laws an arrest is not normally made.

In the case of *Knowles v. Iowa*,[29] the U.S. Supreme Court held that the Fourth Amendment does not permit searches without probable cause incident to a citation. In that case, Knowles was stopped for driving 43 mph in a 25 mph zone. The officer issued Knowles a citation, and then conducted a search of his car under an Iowa statute that authorized searches "incident to the citation." The officer found marijuana, and arrested Knowles. At the trial, the officer testified he had no basis for suspecting Knowles of any offense other than speeding. Knowles was convicted of possessing illegal drugs.

The U.S. Supreme Court reversed Knowles's conviction. It held that where an officer does not arrest a person stopped for a violation, but instead issues a citation, a search made solely as "incident" to the citation violated the Fourth Amendment. The Court said that the reasons for permitting a search incident to an arrest, officer safety and preservation of evidence, did not apply to citations: "The threat to officer safety from issuing a traffic citation, however, is a good deal less than in the case of a custodial arrest." And "...all the evidence necessary to prosecute the offense had been obtained." The Court thus concluded, "Here we are asked to extend (the search incident to arrest rule) to a situation where the concern for officer safety is not present to the same extent and the concern for the destruction or loss of evidence is not present at all. We decline to do so."[30]

The Scope and Extent of Searches Incident to an Arrest

As early as 1914 the U.S. Supreme Court acknowledged the right of the government to conduct a search of the person when an arrest is made.[31] However, those statements were dicta when made, and it wasn't until much later that the Court decided cases that fully explained the government's "right" to search a person as an incident to a lawful arrest. The following materials discuss those cases, including an important 2014 decision.

Searches of the Arrested Person and the Immediate Vicinity In the case of *Chimel v. California*, discussed above, the U.S. Supreme Court held that a search of the area within the "immediate control" of the arrested person for weapons and evidence of the crime may be made incident to arrest. The Supreme Court held that a search was justified without a warrant because of concern for the safety of the officer making the arrest, and preservation of the evidence. In *United States v. Robinson*[32] the Supreme Court held that in a valid arrest police may always search the person arrested, including in that case a cigarette pack found on the person.

As the U.S. Supreme Court noted in the 2014 case of *Riley v. California*[33] (discussed below), lower courts, in reliance on *Chimel* and *Robinson*, interpreted those decisions as authorizing police to search other kinds of personal effects found on an arrested person, such as wallets or purses.

Searches of Vehicles in Which the Arrested Person Was an Occupant   In the case of *New York v. Belton*, the Supreme Court held that when the arrested person is in a motor vehicle, the police "may, as a contemporaneous incident of that arrest, search the passenger compartment of that automobile," and the police "may also examine the contents of any containers found within the passenger compartment."[34]

After *Belton*, most courts interpreted that case to permit police officers to conduct a warrantless search of a vehicle incident to an arrest of a person who was a recent occupant of the vehicle. These courts did not require the police to show the person arrested either had access to the vehicle, or could regain access to the vehicle. As a result, most officers were trained to routinely conduct warrantless searches of vehicles in which the person arrested was an occupant. That changed with the 2009 case of *Arizona v. Gant*.[35]

In *Gant* the U.S. Supreme Court again considered the scope and extent of the exception to the warrant requirement in the Fourth Amendment for a search incident to a lawful arrest. The Court reiterated its holding in *Chimel*:

> In *Chimel*, we held that a search incident to an arrest may only include "the arrestee's person and the 'area within his immediate control'—construing that phrase to mean the area from which he might gain possession of a weapon or destructible evidence." That limitation, which continues to define the boundaries of the exception, ensures that the scope of a search incident to arrest is commensurate with its purpose of protecting officers and safeguarding any evidence of the offense of arrest that an arrestee might conceal or destroy.... If there is no possibility that an arrestee could reach into the area that law enforcement officers seek to search, both justifications for the search-incident-to-arrest exception are absent and the rule does not apply. 129 S. Ct. at 1716.

In *Gant* the police observed the defendant driving his vehicle to the scene of a drug bust. The police recognized the defendant as someone with a suspended driver's license, so they arrested him for that violation. They cuffed the defendant and placed him in the back seat of a patrol car. At that time, the police thus had all the evidence needed to convict Gant of the crime for which he was arrested, and there was no threat to their safety.

The officers then searched Gant's vehicle, where they found cocaine in a jacket pocket. He was convicted of drug offenses based on this evidence, but the Arizona Supreme Court reversed his conviction, concluding the search of the vehicle violated the Fourth Amendment.

The U.S. Supreme Court agreed. It rejected the view that every arrest of a person in a vehicle permits the arresting officers to search the vehicle for weapons or evidence of crimes. Rather, the Court said, "Accordingly, we reject this reading of *Belton*, and hold that the *Chimel* rationale authorizes police to search a vehicle incident to a recent occupant's arrest only when the arrestee is unsecured and within reaching distance of the passenger compartment at the time of the search."[36] The Court stated that "blind adherence to *Belton's* faulty assumptions" resulted in 28 years of "routine constitutional violations."

The Supreme Court also adopted the reasoning of a concurring opinion in *Thornton v. United States*, discussed later in this chapter, and held that "circumstances unique to the vehicle context" justified searches of a vehicle incident to an arrest if police officers have a reasonable belief that evidence of the crime for which the arrest was made may be found in the vehicle. Under this rule, the Court stated, the evidence searches in *Belton* and *Thornton* would be reasonable, but the search in *Gant* was not. Gant was charged with a driving offense, and the officers had no reason to believe any evidence of that offense would be found in the vehicle.

The Supreme Court also stated that because the "broad" reading of *Belton* had been widely accepted and made part of police training, officers making searches in reliance on that broad reading would be entitled to qualified immunity in civil rights actions brought against them arising out of such searches.

Searches of Cell Phones Carried by the Arrested Person In *Riley v. California* the U.S. Supreme Court separated cell phones (and presumably other forms of digital media) from other personal effects carried by the arrested person. Cell phones, the Court said, can contain vast amounts of information as to which people have a legitimate expectation of privacy. Once seized by police during an arrest, a cell phone presents no threat to the police, and the police can easily prevent any removal of evidence contained in the cell phone. As a result, the two reasons for upholding warrantless searches in *Chimel* and *Robinson* do not apply, the Court said. It thus held that police making a lawful arrest may not, as an incident of the arrest, search the contents of a cell phone found on the person arrested. Rather, the Court said "Our answer to what police must do to search a cell phone seized incident to an arrest is accordingly simple—get a warrant."[37]

protective sweep or safety check An investigation of a building or vehicle to determine whether other persons or weapons are present that could jeopardize safety.

"Protective Sweeps" Incident to an Arrest In *Maryland v. Buie*[38] the U.S. Supreme Court said:

> We [hold] that as an incident to the arrest the officers could, as a precautionary matter and without probable cause or reasonable suspicion, look in closets and other spaces immediately adjoining the place of arrest from which an attack could be immediately launched. Beyond that, however, we hold that there must be articulable facts which, taken together with the rational inferences from those facts, would warrant a reasonably prudent officer in believing that the area to be swept harbors an individual posing a danger to those on the arrest scene.

Courts are split on whether a protective sweep of premises is permitted if officers are present not to make an arrest, but solely with consent of a resident. Some federal courts permit protective sweeps in those circumstances; others do not.[39] Those courts that don't permit the sweep reason that officers who are lawfully in premises to accomplish a particular purpose, the arrest, must be permitted to make a protective sweep of the premises. But if the officers are in the premises only by consent, the protective sweep was done simply because the officers chose to enter the premises, not as part of the lawful purpose of making an arrest.[40]

PROCEDURES & PROCESSES

Obtaining Evidence from the Person of a Lawfully Arrested Suspect

In *United States v. Robinson*, 414 U.S. 218, 235 (1973), the U.S. Supreme Court held that in any lawful arrest police may conduct an immediate search of the person of the arrestee: "In the case of a lawful custodial arrest a full search of the person is not only an exception to the warrant requirement of the Fourth Amendment, but is also a 'reasonable' search under that amendment." The search of the person may be done at the scene of the arrest, or later, when the accused arrives at the place of detention.[a] Once the person has been brought to a police station, police may make an inventory search of personal effects such as clothes and containers in the arrestee's possession. (See the discussion in the next section of this chapter.)

A wide variety of evidence might be "on" or "in" an arrested person when arrested. While police may search every arrested person, the nature and extent of the search must still be reasonable. The columns below contain a list of some of the kinds of evidence related to the person of a suspect, and the reasons that would support a search of the person.

Type of Evidence	Authority That Must Exist and Means Used
"Non-intrusive" Evidence:	A. Authority must exist for search and seizure of the evidence under one of the following:
Fingerprints	1. Initial search at time of arrest.
Photographs	2. Obtained during booking process or inventory search.
Measurements	3. Consent given by the suspect.
Hand Swabbing	4. Exigent circumstances justified search and seizure.
Strip Searches[b]	B. The means used to obtain the evidence must not be so intrusive or onerous that they violate either the Fourth Amendment or the Due Process Clause.
Body Hair	C. There must be probable cause or "clear indication" that evidence is present.
Clothing of Suspect	D. Authority must exist for intrusion into the body of the suspect by showing that
Handwriting	
Fingernail Dirt	1. Exigent circumstances existed; in *Missouri v. McNeeley*, 133 S. Ct. 1552 (2013), the U.S. Supreme Court held that the simple fact that alcohol metabolizes in the bloodstream is not an "exigent circumstance" justifying a warrantless blood draw in a DUI arrest.
Use of Ultraviolet Light on Suspect	
Breath (under state implied consent laws for DUI cases)	
	2. A search warrant was obtained; or
"Intrusive" Evidence:	3. Consent of suspect was given.
	E. The means used to extract the evidence must not violate the Fourth Amendment or due process rights of the suspect.
Blood	
Bullets in Body	
Evidence in Stomach of Suspect[c]	
Evidence in Body Cavity	

Type of Evidence	Authority That Must Exist and Means Used
Dental Impressions of Suspect's Teeth Urine	1. A professionally trained person (doctor, nurse, dentist, etc.) obtained the evidence; and 2. Procedure was done under sanitary conditions and means. (Note: When evidence is removed by a doctor or other person law enforcement officers may obtain the evidence by (a) plain view, (b) abandonment, or (c) turnover by private person to the officer.)

[a]*United States v. Edwards*, 415 U.S. 800 (1974).

[b]Strip searches of school children were considered by the U.S. Supreme Court in *Safford Unified Public School District v. Redding*, discussed in Chapter 11 of this text. The Court affirmed the decision of the lower court in the case of *Florence v. Board of Freeholders*, 132 S. Ct. 1510 (2012), also discussed in Chapter 11, permitting searches of all persons jailed for minor, non-violent offenses, including those where no suspicion of drugs or weapons in a body cavity exists.

[c]Persons about to be arrested sometimes swallow evidence, such as illegal drugs. In that case, a medical emergency exists that requires immediate attention. Where the swallowed evidence cannot be recovered, such as when a suspect "eats" a forged check, the suspect could be charged with destruction of evidence.

Evidence Obtained During Inventory Searches

The U.S. Supreme Court listed the following reasons for inventorying property that is being held by the police:

1. Protection of the owner's property while it remains in police custody
2. Protection of the police against claims or disputes over lost or stolen property
3. Protection of the police from potential danger[41]

inventory search The procedure that law officers use to account for the property of people who are in their custody.

Inventory searches are therefore not searches for incriminating evidence. Rather, they are a common and sensible police procedure to determine the responsibility of the law enforcement agency. They are "not an independent legal concept but rather an incidental administrative step following arrest and preceding incarceration."[42]

In the U.S. Supreme Court case of *Illinois v. Lafayette*,[43] the defendant was arrested for fighting with a theater manager. At the police station, the defendant was told to empty his pockets and the purse-type shoulder bag he was carrying, as part of the established police inventory procedure being used. Ten amphetamine pills were found inside a cigarette package. In holding that the pills could be used as evidence, the Supreme Court stated that

> …it is not "unreasonable" for police, as part of the routine procedure incident to incarcerating an arrested person, to search any container or article in his possession, in accordance with established inventory procedure.

Probable Cause: Objective or Subjective Standard?

As stated earlier in this chapter, before making an arrest, the police must have probable cause to believe that a crime has been committed. If they do, they can make a search incident to that arrest. If physical evidence of criminal activity is found in that search, it is admissible in court.

The following cases illustrate two questions raised about the required probable cause. A common factor is whether the police officer's belief was judged on a subjective or objective basis.

- *May an arrest be upheld if it was made for commission of an offense that didn't exist, but a closely related offense did exist?* In *Devenpeck v. Alford*, 125 S. Ct. 588, 594 (2004), the U.S. Supreme Court held that the subjective intent of the arresting officer does not determine whether probable cause exists. In *Devenpeck*, the police arrested a man and charged him with unlawfully taping a conversation with the police. The police stopped to question the man because he appeared to be impersonating a police officer. They then discovered that the man was taping their conversation, which the officers thought was a criminal violation. The unlawful taping charge was subsequently dismissed because it was not a crime to make such a tape recording. However, probable cause existed to arrest the man for the crime of impersonating a police officer. The Ninth Circuit Court of Appeals held that the arrest was unlawful because probable cause to arrest the man for the "unrelated" offense of impersonating an officer did not cure the lack of probable cause to arrest him for taping the officers' conversation. In reversing the Ninth Circuit Court, the U.S. Supreme Court said that the rule is based on an objective standard; if a reasonable person viewing the facts and circumstances would conclude that probable cause existed to arrest the suspect for a crime, a subsequent arrest is lawful: "Subjective intent of the arresting officer...is simply no basis for invalidating an arrest. Those are lawfully arrested whom the facts known to the arresting officers gave probable cause to arrest." The Court therefore remanded the case to determine whether an objective basis for probable cause existed.

- *Must the police intend to make an arrest?* In a case decided after the U.S. Supreme Court's decision in *Devenpeck*, the Wisconsin Supreme Court held that if probable cause to make an arrest exists, judged on an objective basis, then a search conducted by the officers possessing that probable cause is a search incident to a lawful arrest, even if the officers initially had no intent to make an arrest when the search occurred. In *State v. Sykes*, 695 N.W.2d 277 (2005), the police were called by a landlord to the landlord's premises because persons had trespassed on his property. The police officer entered the premises and asked those within to identify themselves. The defendant told the officer his wallet was in his jacket, lying on the floor. The officer picked up the jacket, searched the pockets, and found the wallet. Inside the wallet was a bag of crack cocaine. A subsequent search of the apartment found more illegal drugs. The officer arrested the defendant and charged him with illegal drug possession. The defendant moved to suppress the evidence of illegal drug possession, contending that because the officer had no intent to arrest the defendant when he asked to see some identification, but was merely exercising the caretaking function, the search of the wallet could not be incident to a lawful arrest. The

LEGAL CASES

Terry Stops and the U.S. Supreme Court

Cases Where Reasonable Suspicion Authorized *Terry* Stops

Case	Facts That Authorized Terry Stop	Ruling
Terry v. Ohio, 88 S. Ct. 1868 (1968)	A veteran Cleveland detective observed two men who made a dozen trips past a store, looking in and then talking to each other. The officer suspected that the men were "casing" the store for a stickup. The officer approached the men, identified himself, and, because he feared for his safety, frisked them and seized two pistols.	In affirming the concealed weapons convictions, the Court held "that where the police officer observes unusual conduct which leads him reasonably to conclude in light of his experience that criminal activity may be afoot and that the persons with whom he is dealing may be armed and presently dangerous… the officer may take protective measures."
Adams v. Williams, 92 S. Ct. 1921 (1972)	A known informant told police that Williams was sitting in a car late at night in a public place and had narcotics and a gun on his person. The tip was corroborated when Williams was seen sitting in the parked car.	After seizing the gun, the police arrested Williams and, in the search incident to the arrest, found the drugs. The Court held: "The purpose of this limited search is not to discover evidence of crime, but to allow the officer to pursue his investigation without fear of violence." Conviction of two crimes was sustained.
Alabama v. White, 110 S. Ct. 2412 (1990)	An anonymous telephone caller told police that White would be driving a brown Plymouth station wagon with a broken right taillight, from her house to a named motel, carrying cocaine. After the tip was corroborated, when White arrived at the motel, a police *Terry* stop was made.	The Court held that there was sufficient indication of reliability to justify the stop based on reasonable suspicion after police corroborated the tip. White gave the police consent to search her attaché case and gave the police the combination to the lock.
United States v. Sokolow, 109 S. Ct. 1581 (1989)	The defendant bought airline tickets to travel from Honolulu to Miami (20 hours). He stayed in Miami for 48 hours and then returned to Honolulu. He paid $2,100 in cash for his airfare from a big roll of $20 bills and appeared nervous. A drug-detection dog led to the finding of cocaine in Sokolow's luggage.	The Court held that reasonable suspicion existed to make the stop, holding that: "Any one of these factors is not by itself proof of illegal conduct and is quite consistent with innocent travel. But we think that taken together, they amount to reasonable suspicion."

Note: Three additional U.S. Supreme Court cases in this area are described in the "Problems" section at the end of this chapter.

lower courts denied his motion to suppress, and the Wisconsin Supreme Court affirmed. The court held, based on the reasoning in *Devenpeck*, that since the officer clearly had probable cause to arrest the defendant for criminal trespass, and the defendant was subsequently arrested, the search was incident to a lawful arrest even though the arrest was for a crime other than the one for which probable cause existed and even though the subjective intent of the officer was not to arrest the defendant when the search took place.

OBTAINING EVIDENCE BY POLICE ENTRY INTO PRIVATE PREMISES

The Fourth Amendment to the U.S. Constitution protects the "right of the people to be secure in their persons, houses, papers, and effects." The U.S. Supreme Court has repeatedly said that "searches conducted outside the judicial process, without prior approval by judge or magistrate, are *per se* unreasonable under the Fourth Amendment-subject only to a few specifically established and well-delineated exceptions."[44] Indeed, the U.S. Supreme Court has stated that an illegal or improper police "physical entry of the home is the chief evil against which the wording of the Fourth Amendment is directed."[45]

The right of privacy in the home has deep roots in Anglo-Saxon law. The U.S. Supreme Court quoted the following statement attributed to William Pitt in 1763:

> The poorest man may in his cottage bid defiance to all the forces of the Crown. It may be frail—its roof may shake—the wind may blow through it—the storm may enter—the rain may enter—but the King of England cannot enter—all his force dares not cross the threshold of the ruined tenement![46]

As early as 1461, an English court held that it was unlawful for a sheriff to break down the door of a man's house to arrest him in a civil suit for debt or trespass. Sir William Blackstone wrote in 1822 in *4 Blackstone's Commentaries* that "the law of England has [such] ... regard to the immunity of a man's house, that it styles it his castle, and will never suffer it to be violated with impunity..." (p. 222).

The home of a person could be worth millions, or it could be a very poor and simple building. It could be an apartment in a large building, or it could be a motel or hotel room. A person could be living alone or with other persons. A tent pitched lawfully on public or private land was held to be a home in the cases of *United States v. Gooch*[47] and *LaDuke v. Nelson*.[48] In whatever form, a person's home is protected by the privacy clause of the Fourth Amendment of the U.S. Constitution.[49]

Authority Needed by Police Officers to Enter Private Premises

Probable cause alone does not authorize a law enforcement officer to enter private premises. The general rule is that a search warrant is required to enter and search a private residence. The fact alone that an officer has probable cause to believe evidence of a crime may be found in a home is not one of the "well-delineated" exceptions to the warrant requirement. In the following cases, the U.S. Supreme Court held that the evidence obtained by police officers who entered private premises with only probable cause could not be used in criminal trials.

Vale v. Louisiana United States Supreme Court, 90 S. Ct. 1969 (1970)	After arresting Vale on the front steps of his house, police had probable cause to believe illegal narcotics were in the house. The narcotics that police seized in the house could not be used as evidence and were suppressed.

THE FOURTH AMENDMENT

The Fourth Amendment to the U.S. Constitution consists of one long sentence with two clauses:

The Rights (or Privacy) Clause

The right of the people to be secure in their persons, houses, papers, and effects against unreasonable searches and seizures shall not be violated."

Regarding the Rights Clause, the U.S. Supreme Court Has Held

- The Fourth Amendment is not a guarantee against all searches and seizures, but only against *unreasonable* searches and seizures"[a]
- "The ultimate standard set forth in the Fourth Amendment is reasonableness"[b]
- The touchstone of the Court's analysis under the Fourth Amendment "is always the reasonableness in all the circumstances of the particular governmental invasion of a citizen's personal security"[c]

The Warrant Clause

"And no warrant shall issue, but upon probable cause, supported by oath or affirmation, and particularly describing the place to be searched and the persons or things to be seized."

Regarding the Warrant Clause, the U.S. Supreme Court Has Held

A basic principle of Fourth Amendment law is "that searches and seizures inside a home without a warrant are presumptively unreasonable."[d]

[a]*United States v. Hensley*, 469 U.S. 221, 105 S. Ct. 675 (1985).
[b]*Camara v. Municipal Court*, 387 U.S. 523, 87 S. Ct. 1727 (1967).
[c]*Terry v. Ohio*, 392 U.S. 1, 19, 88 S. Ct. 1868, 1878.
[d]*Payton v. New York*, 445 U.S. at 586, 100 S. Ct. at 1380.

Payton v. New York and Riddick v. New York

United States Supreme Court, 100 S. Ct. 1371 (1980)

The Supreme Court combined these cases where police entered private premises to arrest the two defendants without either arrest warrants or search warrants. Police had probable cause to arrest Payton for murder and Riddick for two armed robberies. The Court held that evidence obtained in both cases could not be used in the two criminal trials.

arrest warrant An order signed by a judge or magistrate authorizing the arrest of a named person or persons.

search warrant An order signed by a judge or magistrate authorizing the place identified to be searched and the persons or things to be seized.

Search warrants and arrest warrants authorize police entry into private premises. However, law enforcement officers who have valid warrants to enter private premises must comply with the rules described next.

An **arrest warrant** "carries with it the limited authority to enter a dwelling in which the suspect lives when there is reason to believe the suspect is within."[50] Police may enter with an arrest warrant under the following limitations:

- Entry is limited to a suspect's *own residence.*
- "There is reason to believe the suspect is within."[51]

If these conditions do not exist, law officers should obtain a **search warrant** in addition to the arrest warrant, or they could wait until the suspect appears in a public place to make an arrest.

Prior to entering private premises with either a search warrant or an arrest warrant, law enforcement officers are obligated to knock, identify themselves, state their purpose, and await a refusal or silence before entering. There are two reasons for imposing these requirements and forbidding unannounced police entries into private premises:

1. *Possibility of mistake:* "[C]ases of mistaken identity are surely not novel in the investigation of crime. The possibility is very real that the police may be misinformed as to the name or address of a suspect, or as to other material information.... Innocent citizens should not suffer the shock, fright or embarrassment attendant upon an unannounced police intrusion."[52]

2. *Protection of the officers:* "[It] is also a safeguard for the police themselves who might be mistaken for prowlers and be shot down by a fearful householder."[53]

Although knock-and-announce entries are the most usual type of police entry, a no-knock entry would be justified if one or more of the following conditions can be shown:

- Such notice would be likely to endanger the life or the safety of the officer or another person.
- Such notice would be likely to result in the evidence subject to seizure being easily and quickly destroyed or disposed of.[54]
- Such notice would be likely to enable the escape of a party to be arrested.
- Such notice would be a useless gesture.

In order to justify a no-knock entry when no prior notice was given, the officer would have to point to evidence that would give the officer the authority to enter without announcement. (See the discussion of *Hudson v. Michigan* in Chapter 9 on the applicability of the exclusionary rule for violations of a knock-and-announce warrant.)

Police may detain and prevent owners and occupants from entering private premises while the police are in the process of obtaining a search warrant for the premises. In the 2001 case of *Illinois v. McArthur*,[55] the U.S. Supreme Court held that the police lawfully denied the defendant access to the premises during the two hours that it took to obtain a search warrant, unless an officer accompanied the defendant into the building.

In *Michigan v. Summers*,[56] the Supreme Court held that officers executing a search warrant have the authority "to detain the occupants of the premises while a proper search is conducted." The Court noted that a reasonable detention was a "minimal intrusion" compared to the lawful search and served three legitimate law enforcement interests: (1) preventing flight of a suspect, (2) protecting the officers, and (3) facilitating an orderly completion of the search. In the following 2005 case, the Court considered the scope of the right to detain such occupants.

Muehler v. Mena

United States Supreme Court, 125 S. Ct. 1465 (2005)

In *Bivens v. Six Unknown Named Agents of the Federal Narcotics Bureau*,[57] the Supreme Court held that the Fourth Amendment created a civil cause of action for damages against police officers who conduct an unreasonable search and seizure. Such causes of action—so-called 1983 actions—are now brought under 42 U.S.C. section 1983, Because the basis of these lawsuits is the unreasonableness of a search and seizure, decisions in these civil cases are generally applicable to the same issue when it is raised in a criminal case. *Devenpeck*, discussed previously, is such a case. *Muehler v. Mena* is another one.

In *Muehler*, the police suspected that a known gang member was residing in Mena's home and that the suspect was armed and dangerous. They obtained a search warrant, and a SWAT team entered the house, woke up Mena, and brought her into the garage. There, they handcuffed her and detained her for two to three hours. In addition, an INS officer present during the detention asked her questions about her immigration status. After the search was completed, Mena was released. She sued the officers, contending that her detention was in violation of her Fourth Amendment rights and that the questioning by the INS officer was an unlawful seizure because the officer lacked any basis for reasonable suspicion that she was an illegal alien. The jury agreed and awarded her $10,000 in actual damages and $20,000 in punitive damages. The Ninth Circuit Court of Appeals affirmed the verdict.

The U.S. Supreme Court reversed, holding that under *Summers* the detention was permissible: "An officer's authority to detain incident to a search is categorical; it does not depend on the 'quantum of proof justifying detention or the extent of the intrusion to be imposed by the seizure.'" The Court also stated, "Inherent in *Summers's* authorization to detain an occupant of the place to be searched is the authority to use reasonable force to effectuate the detention." Finally, the Court held that the questioning by the INS officer was not an independent seizure requiring reasonable suspicion.

Lower courts have disagreed on the extent of the police's power under *Michigan v. Summers* to detain persons who are observed leaving private premises that are the subject of a search warrant. In *United States v. Bailey*, 133 S. Ct. 1031 (2013), the U.S. Supreme Court resolved that disagreement. It held that detention without probable cause or individualized suspicion was permitted so long as the person detained was leaving the premises and was still in the "immediate vicinity" of the premises to be searched. Once such a person has left the immediate vicinity, officers need probable cause or individualized suspicion (*i.e.* a *Terry* stop) to detain the person, the Court held.

Exceptions to the Warrant Requirement to Enter Private Premises

The Fourth Amendment of the U.S. Constitution forbids "unreasonable searches and seizures" and requires a search warrant unless the government can show that a court-recognized exception to the warrant requirement of the Fourth Amendment exists. Those exceptions are the following:

exigent circumstances
An exception to the warrant requirement of the Fourth Amendment based on emergency circumstances; authorizes entry by police officers, firefighters, or emergency medical personnel.

Consent Consent that is voluntarily given by a person who either has sole control of the property or has such mutual use of the premises to have joint access and control of the premises may authorize law enforcement officers to enter the premises.[58]

Exigent Circumstances The existence of **exigent circumstances**, also known as the *emergency aid doctrine*, also provides a court-recognized exception to the warrant requirement of the Fourth Amendment. It authorizes entry by not only law enforcement officers but also firefighters and emergency medical personnel.

Situations that fall under the exigency, or emergency, search doctrine may be classified as follows:

- When an officer has reason to believe that a life may be in jeopardy
- When an officer is in hot pursuit of a person who has committed a crime, or there is danger of escape by criminals
- Now-or-never situations in which evidence or contraband such as drugs will be destroyed or moved to another place before a search warrant can be obtained

If an entry into premises by a law enforcement officer is lawful and proper, the officer then has the right to be where he or she is. What the officer then sees in plain view (and unexpectedly) comes under the plain view doctrine and can be seized if there is reason to believe it is evidence of a crime.

Brigham City v. Stuart

U.S. Supreme Court, 126 S. Ct. 1943 (2006)

In *Brigham* police officers responding to a call about a loud party went to a residence, and heard what sounded like a fight inside the residence. They looked in the front window but saw nothing, so they went around to the back of the residence, where they saw two juveniles drinking in the backyard. Through a screened back door the officers saw four adults attempting to restrain a juvenile. The officers observed punches being thrown during the altercation. An officer went into the house and announced the police presence. Occupants of the residence were arrested for disorderly conduct, intoxication, and contributing to the delinquency of a minor. At the trial on these charges, the trial court suppressed evidence obtained by the police who entered the residence, and the Utah Supreme Court affirmed the trial court.

The U.S. Supreme Court reversed the Utah Supreme Court, disagreeing on the two reasons given by that court for suppression of the evidence. The first reason was that the police were motivated to enter the residence not to render emergency aid but to arrest the occupants. The Supreme Court held that as long as the officers' actions were objectively reasonable, the Fourth Amendment is not violated. The Court stated:

> It therefore does not matter here—even if [the officers'] motives could be so neatly unraveled—whether the officers entered the kitchen to arrest respondents and gather evidence against them or to assist the injured and prevent violence.

The second reason was that the defendants' conduct was not serious enough to justify the police entry into the residence. The Supreme Court held that the ongoing violence was serious enough to justify the police entry, stating that the test is whether entry into the residence was "plainly reasonable under the circumstances." The Court stated:

> Nothing in the Fourth Amendment required [the police] to wait until another blow rendered someone "unconscious" or "semi-conscious" or worse before entering. The role of the police officer includes preventing violence and restoring order, not simply rendering first aid to casualties; an officer is not like a boxing (or hockey) referee, poised to stop a bout only if it becomes one-sided.

In the 2009 case of *Michigan v. Fisher*, 130 S. Ct. 546, the Supreme Court reversed a Michigan state court's decision suppressing evidence obtained during a warrantless search based on the "emergency aid" exception. The Michigan court concluded the evidence of imminent injury to the occupants of the premises was not sufficiently serious to justify the warrantless entry. The U.S. Supreme Court disagreed. It said that the officers need not have "iron-clad" proof of serious, life-threatening injury to invoke the emergency aid exception. It was enough, the Court said, that the officers had a reasonable belief someone needed medical assistance, or was a threat to others in the house.

⚖ LEGAL CASES

The 2011 U.S. Supreme Court Test of the "Police-Created-Exigency" Doctrine

Following the recognition by the U.S. Supreme Court of the "exigent circumstances" exception for police entry into private premises, lower courts developed a doctrine known as the "police-created-exigency" doctrine. Under this doctrine, a warrantless search based on exigent circumstances was not permitted if the police "created" the exigency. In the 2011 case of *Kentucky v. King*,[a] the Supreme Court adopted a test for determining when exigent circumstances were wrongfully "created" by police.

In *King* police officers made a "controlled drug buy" from a suspected drug dealer. The suspect went into an apartment complex, and the police followed him to make an arrest. They did not see the suspect enter an apartment, but saw doors to two adjacent apartments, one of which had to have been entered by the suspect. The police knocked on the door of the apartment on the right, smelled marijuana, and announced "Police! Police!" The officers heard movement inside the apartment they believed could be the occupants destroying evidence, so they forced entry into the apartment. They discovered the occupants with illegal drugs, and arrested them. It was not the apartment entered by the suspected drug dealer, who police later found in the other apartment.

The occupants moved to suppress the illegal drugs, which the trial court and court of appeals rejected. However, the Kentucky Supreme Court reversed, holding that the police "created" the exigent circumstances, which made the entry a violation of the Fourth Amendment.

The U.S. Supreme Court reversed the Kentucky Supreme Court. It recognized that under some circumstances police could "create" exigent circumstances, but rejected the test used by the Kentucky Supreme Court to determine when that had happened. Kentucky, like many other courts, found exigent circumstances created by the police where the police had a "bad-faith" intent to avoid the warrant requirement, or where the police should reasonably foresee their actions would cause occupants in a house to take the very actions giving rise to the "exigency."

The Supreme Court said the "bad faith test" was inconsistent with its rejection of the subjective test of police officers' intent in Fourth Amendment cases in favor of the objective test of reasonable belief. It rejected the "reasonably foreseeable" test as unworkable. Instead, the Court held that "Where, as here, the police did not create the exigency by engaging or threatening to engage in conduct that violated the Fourth Amendment, warrantless entry to prevent the destruction of evidence is reasonable and thus allowed."[b]

The Supreme Court suggested in a footnote that exigent circumstances would not justify a warrantless search where police, with no "legally sound" basis for entry without a warrant, threatened to enter if permission to enter was not granted.[c]

[a]131 S. Ct. 1849 (2011).
[b]131 S. Ct., at 1858.
[c]*Id.*, fn. 4.

Community Caretaking Doctrine In *Cady v. Dombrowski*[59] the U.S. Supreme Court upheld a warrantless search of an automobile based on what it referred to as a "community caretaking function" of police investigating an automobile accident. The Court said that the police actions of entering vehicles involved in an accident are totally "divorced from crime detection," and thus reasonable under the Fourth Amendment.

While the Supreme Court has never identified a "community caretaking" exception to the warrant requirement, a very few lower courts have done so, upholding warrantless searches of residences under the doctrine.[60] Most courts agree with the holding of the New Jersey Supreme Court in the 2013 case of *State v. Vargas*[61] that the "community caretaking" doctrine is limited to automobile searches, and is not an independent exception for warrantless searches of private residences. If police decide to enter private premises, they must do so under either the exigent circumstances or consent exceptions to the warrant requirement, the court held.

OBTAINING EVIDENCE IN TRAFFIC STOPS AND VEHICLE SEARCHES

Studies show that motor vehicles are involved in more than 75 percent of the crimes committed every year in the United States. Vehicles are used as instrumentalities of most crimes, crimes are committed in vehicles, and motor vehicles are the object of criminal efforts because more than a million motor vehicles are stolen every year in the United States. Motor vehicles that are illegally driven cause thousands of deaths and hundreds of thousands of injuries every year.

May a Police Officer Stop a Motor Vehicle for No Reason?

A law enforcement officer may stop a vehicle for many valid reasons: The driver may be speeding or may have violated other sections of the traffic code; there may be an equipment violation, such as a headlight out; or there may be probable cause or reasonable suspicion to arrest or question the driver or a passenger in the vehicle.

But can a vehicle be stopped for no reason? That question was before the U.S. Supreme Court in *Delaware v. Prouse*.[62] In that case, the officer making the vehicle stop testified, "I saw the car in the area and wasn't answering any complaints, so I decided to pull them off." In holding that such stops are unreasonable under the Fourth Amendment, the Court ruled,

> [E]xcept in those situations in which there is at least articulable and reasonable suspicion that a motorist is unlicensed or that an automobile is not registered, or that either the vehicle or an occupant is otherwise subject to seizure for violation of law, stopping an automobile and detaining the driver in order to check his driver's license and the registration of the automobile are unreasonable under the Fourth Amendment.

A traffic stop significantly interferes with the freedom of movement of not only the vehicle driver but also the passengers, but, again, most traffic stops are temporary, brief, and public police stops. In *Berkemer v. McCarty*,[63] the U.S. Supreme Court pointed out the consequences to a motorist of failing to obey a law enforcement officer's signal to stop:

> It must be acknowledged at the outset that a traffic stop significantly curtails the "freedom of action" of the driver and the passengers, if any, of the detained vehicle. Under the law of most States, it is a crime either to ignore a policeman's signal to stop one's car or, once having stopped, to drive away without permission.
>
> …Certainly few motorists would feel free either to disobey a directive to pull over or to leave the scene of a traffic stop without being told they might do so. Partly for these reasons, we have long acknowledged that "stopping an automobile and detaining its occupants constitute a 'seizure' within the meaning of [the Fourth] Amendmen[t], even though the purpose of the stop is limited and the resulting detention quite brief."[64]

Using Pretextual Stops to Obtain Evidence

Thousands of vehicle stops are made every year in the United States. About one-half are made for speeding and about one-fourth for equipment violations. Some of these stops are called *pretextual stops:* On the surface the reason for the stop is some minor violation, but the underlying reason is to obtain evidence of more serious crimes. The officer in a pretextual stop usually suspects the driver (or a passenger) of having committed, or being in the process of committing, a serious crime.

Prior to 1996, a common defense to illegal drug charges and other serious offenses was that the traffic stop was a pretext, and that as a result the evidence obtained should be suppressed. However, in *Whren v. United States,*[65] the U.S. Supreme Court eliminated most of these defenses.

A unanimous court held in *Whren* that, if the traffic stop is objectively supported by probable cause to believe that a traffic violation has occurred, the traffic stop is reasonable under the Fourth Amendment even if the officer's motivation for making the traffic stop was different from enforcement of traffic laws. The Court pointed out that probable cause is an objective standard that is determined by the totality of the circumstances and not by the officer's subjective intent.

Obtaining Evidence During Routine Traffic Stops

On routine traffic stops, evidence of violations often becomes available as law enforcement officers carry out the following routine:

1. Officers may and do request a driver's license and other required documents.[66] Because operating a motor vehicle on public highways is a privilege rather than a right, it is constitutional to require a lawfully stopped driver to produce a driver's license upon request, the vehicle registration, and other documents required by statute. The information in these documents gives officers important facts to assist them in determining whether they are confronting innocent or criminal conduct. Inconsistencies between documents or between what is found in the documents and what the driver tells the officers may provide clues to criminal behavior that might otherwise be overlooked. Refusal to produce required documents almost universally constitutes criminal behavior under state statutes. Thus, demands for and examination of required documentation by police officers are sound early steps in investigating a stopped vehicle and its driver.

2. Officers may question the occupants of the vehicle. Police officers gathering information may briefly question a stopped car's driver and other occupants of the car where the car and occupants have been lawfully stopped.[67] The U.S. Supreme Court has made clear that such questioning may take place without any prior *Miranda*-type warnings, so long as the persons questioned have not been placed under arrest or subjected to arrest-type treatment.[68] This is true even where officers may have determined that they have lawful grounds for arrest and have decided to effect such an arrest. Even though no warnings are required, persons being questioned do enjoy a constitutional right not to respond, and although a failure to respond may be taken into consideration as officers assess whether probable cause exists to arrest or search, a person's failure to respond probably cannot constitute in itself a criminal offense, since the person is merely exercising a right guaranteed by the Constitution.

MOST TRAFFIC STOPS ARE TEMPORARY, BRIEF, AND PUBLIC

In pointing out that most traffic stops are temporary, brief, and public, the U.S. Supreme Court stated in footnote 26 of *Berkemer v. McCarty,* 104 S. Ct. 3138, 3149 (1984), that "no state requires that a detained motorist be arrested unless he is accused of a specified serious crime, refuses to promise to appear in court, or demands to be taken before a magistrate."

However, a motorist who fails to furnish satisfactory self-identification or an out-of-state motorist who is unable to post bail or to pay a traffic fine or a citation is likely to be detained until the matter is cleared.

3. Officers sometimes request consent to search. An officer who has lawfully stopped a car may request that the person in lawful control of the car (generally the driver) waive his or her Fourth Amendment rights and give consent to a search of the car.[69] If such a consent is obtained, the officer should be prepared to prove at a later time that the consent was voluntarily given, that the person giving the consent was in lawful control of the items searched, and that the search performed was within the scope of the consent that was given.

4. Officers may make plain-view observations of parts of the vehicle exposed to public view.[70] The Fourth Amendment does not require officers who approach a lawfully stopped car to wear blinders. The exterior of a car on a public highway is exposed to the public view, and it is unreasonable for a person to expect that a car's exterior appearance is therefore private. Consequently, an officer's visual inspection of the exterior of a stopped car does not constitute a search for Fourth Amendment purposes. Portions of the interior that are likewise exposed to the public view due to the placement of windows are also not private, and so an officer's visual examination of these areas from outside the car is not a Fourth Amendment search. As a result, officers approaching a lawfully stopped vehicle frequently are exposed to a wealth of information that they may lawfully use for investigative purposes.

What May Police Do in Routine Traffic Stops?

What are the rights of drivers and passengers when police stop a vehicle for a routine traffic violation? Do the limiting principles of a *Terry* stop apply to traffic stops? That is, does the reason for the traffic stop serve as a limitation on both the duration of the stop and the scope of the stop? In 2007 and 2008 the U.S. Supreme Court discussed two aspects of this question, and in a 2009 case the Court addressed the application of *Terry* to traffic stops.

In *Brendlin v. California,* 127 S. Ct. 2400 (2007), police officers stopped a vehicle based on an invalid registration sticker, even though in fact the sticker on the vehicle was in compliance with the law. The officers observed a passenger dropping something out of the passenger door, and after identifying the passenger as a person wanted on a parole violation, they arrested the passenger. A subsequent search by police of the passenger and the vehicle uncovered evidence of illegal drugs. The passenger moved to suppress the evidence, contending that the traffic stop was illegal and was an unlawful seizure of his person. The trial court and state appellate courts refused to suppress the evidence.

The U.S. Supreme Court reversed, and held that the passenger was "seized" by the traffic stop. The Court held that whether a passenger is seized when the driver of a vehicle is stopped depends on whether the passenger felt "free to leave":

> We resolve this question by asking whether a reasonable person in Brendlin's position when the car stopped would have believed himself free to "terminate the encounter" between the police and himself. (Citation omitted.) We think that in these circumstances any reasonable passenger would have understood the police officers to be exercising control to the point that no one in the car was free to depart without police permission. 127 S. Ct. at 2406.

In *Virginia v. Moore* 128 S. Ct. 1598 (2008), police stopped a driver who they knew was driving with a suspended license. Under Virginia state law the officers were authorized to issue a summons for that offense, but were not authorized to make an arrest. The officers nonetheless arrested the driver, and a subsequent search incident to the arrest uncovered crack cocaine on the driver's person. The defendant was convicted of a drug offense, and he appealed, contending that the unauthorized arrest made the resulting search a violation of the Fourth Amendment.

The U.S. Supreme Court disagreed. The Court held that because the officer had probable cause to arrest the defendant under Fourth Amendment standards, the resulting custodial search was valid, and the evidence of illegal drugs was properly admitted at his trial.

In *Arizona v. Johnson,* 555 U.S. 323 (2009), the Supreme Court reiterated rules on "pat-downs" in traffic stops, and announced a rule on the permissible scope of questioning after a traffic stop. There, officers stopped a vehicle for a traffic violation. Two officers dealt with the driver on the traffic violation. Another officer thought Johnson, a passenger in the vehicle, might be a member of a gang, so she asked him to exit the vehicle. Johnson did, and the officer patted him down, finding a weapon. Johnson was charged with illegal possession of a weapon.

The Arizona Supreme Court held the evidence of the weapon should be suppressed under the Fourth Amendment, because the pat-down that uncovered the weapon exceeded the scope of the permissible detention of the traffic stop. That court held that the officer's purpose in having Johnson exit the vehicle was not related to the traffic stop, but instead was to gain evidence of a different crime, gang membership. As a result, the court concluded the limitations in a *Terry* stop were exceeded.

The U.S. Supreme Court reversed, holding the evidence should not be suppressed. The Court first reiterated its conclusions from prior traffic stop cases that "[o]fficers who conduct 'routine traffic stops' may perform a pat-down of a driver and any passenger upon reasonable suspicion they may be armed and dangerous." *Id.,* 555 U.S. at 332.

The Supreme Court also rejected the Arizona Supreme Court's holding that because the pat-down came after the officer began investigating Johnson for criminal activity other than the reason for the traffic stop, the pat-down authority ceased to exist, absent reasonable suspicion about that criminal activity. The Supreme Court held that "An officer's inquiries into matters unrelated to the justification for the traffic stop, this Court has made plain, do not convert the encounter into something other than a lawful seizure, so long as those inquiries do not measurably extend the duration of the stop." *Id.,* 555 U.S. at 333.

Most courts have interpreted *Johnson* as meaning that officers may ask any questions during a traffic stop, including those related to investigation of crimes unrelated to the reason for the stop. The only limit on such questioning is the duration of the stop: they may not "measurably" extend the duration of the stop. Some courts continue to use the "scope" of a stop as part of a determination of the reasonableness of the stop. *See United States v. Digiovanni*, 650 F.3d 498 (4th Cir. 2011). However, a few courts have held that even if a traffic stop is based on reasonable suspicion, once that suspicion is eliminated the driver of the vehicle cannot be detained for additional questioning. *See People v. Cummings*, 6 N.E.3d 725 (Ill. 2014).

When is a Traffic Stop Too Long?

In *United States v. Rodriguez*, 741 F.3d 905 (8th Cir. 2013), an appeals court upheld the conviction of the driver of a car in which illegal drugs were discovered during a traffic stop. A state trooper stopped the vehicle after the trooper observed the vehicle swerve toward the shoulder of the road, and then quickly move back to the road. This was a valid stop under these circumstances. The trooper obtained the driver's license and registration, and for 21 minutes checked for outstanding warrants. At that time the trooper issued the driver a written warning. After handing the driver the warning, the trooper asked if he could use his drug dog, which was in the trooper's vehicle, to do a walk-around of the driver's vehicle. The driver refused consent. The trooper then called for backup and, when another officer appeared about 7 or 8 minutes later, conducted a dog sniff. The dog alerted to illegal drugs, and a search found illegal drugs.

The driver was charged with possession with intent to deliver illegal drugs. At his trial he moved to suppress the evidence obtained in the search of his vehicle, contending the search violated the Fourth Amendment. The trial court denied the motion and the court of appeals affirmed that denial. In October 2014 the U.S. Supreme Court granted the defendant's petition for certiorari. 2014 WL 1766135 (October 2014).

In previous cases, discussed in this chapter, we learned that it was permissible for police in a valid traffic stop to use that stop to conduct other investigations, like questioning the driver or having a dog sniff; the only limit was that the police do not unreasonable extend the duration of the traffic stop. Presumably the Supreme Court is interested in the duration of this traffic stop. What factors do you think the Court should consider when determining if the duration was unconstitutionally extended: The total time (about 28 minutes) of the stop? The reason for the stop? The presence of facts suggesting the vehicle held illegal drugs? Should it matter that the police dog was available for the sniff from the inception of the stop?

Obtaining Evidence in Searches of Vehicles, Drivers, and Passengers

The following two U.S. Supreme Court cases illustrate the protective measures law enforcement officers may take in traffic stops and while investigating an accident. The U.S. Supreme Court sustained the use of the evidence and affirmed the criminal convictions.

Pennsylvania v. Mimms United States Supreme Court, 98 S. Ct. 330 (1977)	Mimms's vehicle was stopped because of an expired license plate. Mimms was asked to step out of the car, and as he did the officer noticed a bulge under his sport coat. The officer reached under the coat and removed a revolver from Mimms's waistband. The Supreme Court sustained the use of the evidence, holding that "In these circumstances, any man of 'reasonable caution' would have conducted the 'pat-down.'"

Chapter 14 Obtaining Physical and Other Evidence **371**

Michigan v. Long

United States Supreme
Court, 103 S. Ct. 3469 (1983)

Long, the driver, lost control of a speeding car late at night on a country road and crashed in a ditch. Long was the only occupant of the car and appeared to be under the influence of something when officers saw him standing at the rear of the car. When he was asked to show his driver's license, Long began to return to the open door of the car. Before allowing Long into the car, the officers checked the interior of the car for weapons. They found a large hunting knife on the floor of the driver's side of the car. Marijuana was then found in the car, and Long was arrested. The Supreme Court held that officers may make a limited search of the interior of vehicles to locate and control weapons when officers reasonably suspect the presence of weapons.

In the 2004 case of *Thornton v. United* States,[71] the Supreme Court held that a warrantless search of the passenger compartment of a vehicle is a lawful search incident to an arrest, even if the police first initiated contact with the passenger after the passenger had exited the vehicle. (The decision in *Gant* requires the police to reasonably believe evidence of the crime may be found in the vehicle. See the discussion of *Gant* earlier in this chapter.) The *Thornton* Court rejected the so-called "contact initiation" rule followed in some jurisdictions, which limits a search of the passenger compartment to cases where contact with the passenger is initiated when the passenger is still inside the vehicle. Stating that such a rule would require arresting officers to make the subjective determination of when they first confronted the suspect, the Court stated,

> This determination would be inherently subjective and highly fact specific, and would require precisely the sort of ad hoc determination on the part of officers in the field and reviewing courts that *Belton* sought to avoid.… Experience has shown that such a rule is impracticable, and we refuse to adopt it. So long as an arrestee is the sort of "recent occupant" of a vehicle such as petitioner was here, officers may search that vehicle incident to the arrest.[72]

PROCEDURES & PROCESSES

Obtaining Evidence from Motor Vehicles (Including Aircraft, Watercraft, Snowmobiles, Trucks, Buses, and Others)

Authority	Requirements
Plain view observations and smells of vehicles exposed to public view	• The officer is where she or he has a right to be; if the police stop the vehicle, the stop must be lawful. • The contraband is in plain view, and it is "immediately apparent" that the item may be evidence of a crime. • The officer may seize the contraband if the officer has a lawful right of access to the object.
Consent to search	The officer must show that the consent was voluntarily given and that the person giving consent had actual or apparent authority to grant consent.

Authority	Requirements
Reasonable suspicion, which justifies • An investigative stop • A frisk or search for weapons if there was justifiable concern for safety • A search of the passenger compartment of a vehicle for weapons	To make a *Terry stop*, the officer "must have a particularized and objective basis for suspecting the particular person stopped of criminal activity." The officer has reasonable suspicion that "the suspect is dangerous and the suspect may gain immediate control of weapons" *Michigan v. Long*, 463 U.S. 1032, 103 S. Ct. 3469 (1983).
Searches incident to an arrest under the *Chimel v. California* "immediate control" test	The search "may only include the arrestee's person and the area within his immediate control" for weapons and evidence of the crime. Police may also search containers and other items found on the arrestee's person, but the search may not be unreasonably intrusive, such as surgically removing a bullet from the arrestee's body. (See *Winston v. Lee,* 470 U.S. 753 (1985).)
Search incident to the arrest of a recent occupant of a vehicle	In the 2009 case of *Arizona v. Gant,* the U.S. Supreme Court imposed the following new rule on searches of vehicles following arrest of a recent occupant of that vehicle: "Police may search the vehicle • "only if the arrestee is within reaching distance of the passenger's compartment at the time of the search," • "or it is reasonable to believe the vehicle contains evidence of the offense of the arrest."
The automobile exception (or the *Carroll* rule, or probable cause rule)	There is probable cause to believe that a vehicle contains evidence of a crime. A search of "a lawfully stopped vehicle" can then be made. The search can be "of every part of the vehicle and its contents that may conceal the object of the search" U.S. Supreme Court in *United States v. Ross* (discussed later).
Community caretaking function	A community caretaking function is a task or job that has to be done or that should be done in the best interests of the community. The officer is not looking for evidence of a crime but, while he is performing the community caretaking function, comes upon evidence of a crime. For example, an accident blocks traffic lanes on a busy street. To open the street to traffic, an officer gets into one of the cars and moves it to the curb. While in the vehicle, the officer sees contraband. See the U.S. Supreme Court case of Cady v. Dombrowski, 93 S. Ct. 2523 (1973).

Permissible Searches Under the Motor Vehicle Exception

During the years since motor vehicles were first used as a means of transportation, the courts have consistently noted the constitutional difference between motor vehicles and fixed structures such as homes and other types of buildings.

In the case of *South Dakota v. Opperman*,[73] the U.S. Supreme Court stated:

> This Court has traditionally drawn a distinction between automobiles and homes or offices in relation to the Fourth Amendment. Although automobiles are "effects" and thus within the reach of the Fourth Amendment, warrantless examinations of automobiles have been upheld in circumstances in which a search of a home or office would not.

The automobile or motor vehicle exception (or the *Carroll* rule, or probable cause rule) is simple. It authorizes a law enforcement officer who has probable cause to believe that a vehicle contains evidence of a crime to search the vehicle and to seize the evidence. Probable cause alone will not get a law enforcement officer into a home to make an arrest or a search for evidence. However, probable cause alone will authorize entry into a vehicle to seize evidence.

The scope of the search of a vehicle is limited by the nature of the probable cause that justified the search. If the search is for a small item, such as a small amount of illegal drugs, the entire vehicle can be searched. If the search is for a large item, like a stolen lawn mower or a large bicycle, only parts of the vehicle where such an item could be located may be searched.

The automobile exception is not limited to ordinary automobiles. In the case of *California v. Carney*,[74] the U.S. Supreme Court held that a movable motor home, because of its ease of movement, created a lesser expectation of privacy than a regular home or office and was thus subject to the motor vehicle exception:

> Among the factors that might be relevant in determining whether a [search] warrant would be required in such a circumstance is its location, whether the vehicle is readily mobile or instead, for instance, elevated on blocks, whether the vehicle is licensed, whether it is connected to utilities, and whether it has convenient access to a public road.

In an article in the *FBI Law Enforcement Bulletin* of August 2005, entitled "The Motor Vehicle Exception," the author cites cases where the rule has been applied to "trucks, trailers pulled by trucks, boats, house boats, airplanes, and even the sleeping compartments of trains." The following cases are examples of the automobile exception, which originated in the *Carroll* case:

 PROCEDURES & PROCESSES

Exceptions to the Fourth Amendment's Search Warrant Requirement Recognized by the U.S. Supreme Court

Exception	Reason for Exception	Requirement of Exception	Other Limitations
Search incident to custodial arrest	1. To protect officers and others 2. To prevent escape 3. To prevent destruction of evidence	1. There must be lawful, custodial arrest. 2. Search must be made at the time and place of arrest or at later time. 3. Search can be made only of the area of the arrestee's "immediate presence."	The law of state or state court decision may limit any of the listed exceptions.

Exception	Reason for Exception	Requirement of Exception	Other Limitations
Automobile exception(includes motor vehicles, watercraft, and aircraft)	The reduced (lesser) right of privacy in these means of transportation as distinguished from homes	There must be probable cause to believe that the vehicle held evidence of crime or an object that may be seized by law enforcement officer.	If probable cause justifies the search of lawfully stopped vehicle, every part of the vehicle that may conceal the object of the search can be searched.
Consent to search	Person may waive his or her right of privacy in home, vehicle, or object and may waive the Fourth Amendment requirement of probable cause	1. Consent must be given voluntarily and intelligently. 2. It must be shown that the person giving consent had actual or apparent authority to grant consent.	Neither written consent nor *Miranda-type* warnings are required under the federal rule. (However, either or both are helpful in showing that the consent was voluntarily given.)
Protective safety measures • Frisks during investigative stops, and so on • Frisks during execution of search warrants	Evidence must show that it is for the safety of law officers or the safety of other persons and that it would be "unreasonable to require unnecessary risks"	1. The officer is where he or she has right to be. 2. Reasonable suspicion or more exists for the *Terry* stop. 3. Reasonable suspicion or more exists to fear for personal safety or safety of others.	Officer must be able to state justification for his or her action.
Exigency (emergency) searches • Where there is reason to believe that a life is in danger • Where there is "hot pursuit" • "Now-or-never" situations to prevent the loss or destruction of evidence of crime	1. Need to protect or preserve life 2. Need to act immediately to • Prevent escape • Prevent loss or destruction of evidence of crime	Reasonable grounds to believe that: • A life is endangered • A fleeing felon will escape and may harm himself or herself, or may destroy evidence • Action must be taken to prevent the loss or destruction of evidence	

Carroll v. United States

United States Supreme Court, 45 S. Ct. 280 (1925)

Officers had probable cause to believe that Carroll's roadster had gin and whiskey in it, in violation of the National Prohibition Act. The evidence found in the car was held to be lawfully obtained and could be used to sustain Carroll's conviction.[75]

Chambers v. Maroney

United States Supreme
Court, 90 S. Ct. 1975 (1970)

Four armed robbers were arrested late at night. After the suspects were confined in a jail cell, officers went out to the robbers' vehicle, which had been moved to the police station, and obtained incriminating evidence that the police had probable cause to believe was in the vehicle. The Supreme Court sustained the use of the evidence, holding that a "careful search [at the place of the arrest] was impractical and perhaps not safe for the officers."

United States v. Ross

United States Supreme
Court, 102 S. Ct. 2157 (1982)

Police had probable cause to believe that Ross was selling heroin out of the trunk of his car in Washington, D.C. After stopping the defendant, the police found a pistol in the glove compartment. The police arrested Ross and took his keys to open the car trunk. They opened a brown paper bag in the trunk and found glassine bags containing white powder. They then took Ross and his car to a police station, where it was determined that the white powder was heroin. A further search of the trunk produced additional evidence. In sustaining the convictions and the use of the evidence, the Supreme Court held: "If probable cause justifies the search of a lawfully stopped vehicle, it justifies the search of every part of the vehicle and its contents that may conceal the object of the search."

Wyoming v. Houghton

United States Supreme
Court, 526 U.S. 295, 302 (1999)

Police had probable cause to believe that an automobile contained illegal drugs, after seeing a hypodermic syringe in the driver's pocket and being told by the driver that he used the syringe to take drugs. The police searched the automobile and found a black container in the backseat that, when opened, was found to contain illegal drugs. The container belonged to Houghton, a passenger in the car. At her trial on the charge of possession of a controlled substance, Houghton argued that the search of her property violated the Fourth Amendment. The Supreme Court held it did not:

> When there is probable cause to search for contraband in a car, it is reasonable for police officers—like customs officials in the Founding era—to examine packages and containers without a showing of individualized probable cause for each one. A passenger's personal belongings, just like the driver's belongings or containers attached to the car like a glove compartment, are "in" the car, and the officer has probable cause to search for contraband *in* the car.

SUMMARY

1. **Describe the level of evidence needed for an investigative detention.**
   - Police must have a reasonable suspicion based on "articulable" facts that a person has committed a crime or is about to commit a crime. It is less than probable cause, but more than a mere hunch.

2. **List searches that may be made without a search warrant.**
   - Any search without a warrant must fit within an established exception. Exceptions include consent, exigency, incident to a lawful arrest, inventory searches, and protective sweeps.

3. **State what actions police may take in a routine traffic stop.**
   - Police may always require production of a valid driver's license. Officers may question occupants, and ask occupants to exit the vehicle. If officers reasonably believe an occupant has a weapon on his person, the officer can "pat down" the occupant. If officers make a lawful custodial arrest during the stop they may, in compliance with *Gant*, make a search incident to arrest.

4. **State the *Arizona v. Gant* rule for searches of a vehicle incident to arrest.**
   - Police may search a vehicle after a lawful arrest only if the person arrested is within reaching distance of the passenger compartment of the vehicle, or the officers reasonably believe the vehicle holds evidence related to the offense of the arrest.

5. **Explain the "automobile exception" and how it differs from a search of a residence.**
   - Police officers may search an automobile if they have probable cause to believe it contains evidence of a crime, and seize any evidence found. No search warrant is required. A search of a residence based only on probable cause is not permitted.

6. **Define "exigent circumstances" as an exception to the search warrant requirement.**
   - Police may enter a residence if they reasonable believe someone inside the residence is injured and needs help, someone is threatening injury to another person in the house, a suspect fleeing from a crime is in the residence, or officers reasonable believe entry is necessary to prevent the destruction of evidence of a crime.

KEY TERMS

arrest, 353
arrest warrant, 361
exigent circumstances, 363

free-to-leave test, 345
inventory searches, 357
physical evidence (real evidence), 344

protective search, 351
protective sweep or safety check, 355

reasonable suspicion, 348
search warrant, 361
Terry stop, 344

KEY CASES

Arizona v. Gant, 129 S. Ct. 1710 (2009): States the rule for permissible searches of vehicles after lawful arrest.

Arizona v. Johnson, 555 U.S. 323 (2009): Police may question occupants of vehicle during lawful stop, and if they have reasonable cause to believe an occupant is armed they may "pat down" the occupant.

Bailey v. United States, 133 S. Ct. 103 (2013): Police may detain person seen leaving premises named in search warrant only if person is in the immediate vicinity of the premises when stopped by the police.

Brendlin v. California, 127 S. Ct. 2400 (2007): Passengers are "seized" for purpose of the Fourth Amendment in traffic stops.

Carroll v. United States, 45 S. Ct. 280 (1925): Established the "automobile exception" for searches of vehicles based only on probable cause.

Chimel v. California, 395 U.S. 752 (1969): Police may search vehicle during lawful arrest for the purpose of officer safety and preservation of evidence.

Devenpeck v. Alford, 125 S. Ct. 588 (2004): Probable cause is determined by objective standard of a reasonable person, not subjective belief of police officer.

Michigan v. Fisher, 130 S. Ct. 546 (2009): Officers need only reasonable belief that an occupant of a house needs emergency aid because of injury or threat of harm by another.

Missouri v. McNeeley, 133 S. Ct. 1552 (2013): Fact that alcohol metabolizes in the blood over time is not exigent circumstance justifying warrantless blood draw.

Navarette v. California, 134 S. Ct. 1683 (2014): Anonymous 911 caller provided officers with reasonable suspicion to stop driver caller said ran her off the road.

Terry v. Ohio, 88 S. Ct. 1868 (1968): Police may make an investigative stop and brief detention if they have a reasonable suspicion of criminal activity based on articulable facts.

United States v. Place, 462 U.S. 696 (1983): Police may detain luggage or containers in a public place based on reasonable suspicion they contain evidence of a crime.

PROBLEMS

1. Detectives first noticed the defendant at a ticket counter in the Miami airport. Their attention was drawn to the defendant because he and his two companions behaved in an unusual manner as they left the counter. The other two men talked to each other but not to the defendant. When one of the men saw the detectives who were following the three men, he turned and talked to one of his companions. When the second man saw the detectives as the men were getting off an escalator, he turned to the defendant and said, "Let's get out of here." He repeated in a lower voice, "Get out of here." The defendant then saw the detectives. A detective testified that the defendant attempted to move away, but his "legs were pumping up and down very fast and not covering much ground, but his legs were as if the person were running in place." Finding that he was not leaving the presence of the detectives, the defendant turned to a detective and uttered a vulgar expression.

   A detective then showed his badge to the defendant and asked if they might talk. The defendant agreed, and the detective suggested they move a short distance to where the other two men and the other detective stood. Both detectives had identified themselves to all of the men, and as they stood in the public area of the airport, the defendant was asked for identification and if he had an airline ticket. When one of the other men produced a ticket, the officers asked for consent to search the defendant's luggage. The defendant handed the officer a key to the luggage, and three bags of cocaine were found in a suit bag.

   Was the procedure used by the officers proper and lawful? Explain. Can the evidence obtained be used in the trial of the three men? Should they be charged with possession with intent to deliver? *Florida v. Rodriguez*, 469 U.S. 1 (1984)

2. Portland, Oregon, police officers were investigating the strangulation murder of the defendant's wife in her home. The defendant was not living with his wife and voluntarily came into the police station with an attorney for questioning. The defendant was not arrested, but probable cause to arrest him existed on the following facts:

   - The fact that there were no signs of a struggle, break-in, or robbery at the scene of the crime "tended to indicate a killer known to the victim rather than a burglar or other stranger."
   - "The decedent's son, the only other person in the house that night, did not have fingernails which could have made the lacerations observed on the victim's throat."
   - "The defendant and his deceased wife had a stormy marriage and did not get along well."
   - The defendant admitted being at the home of his wife on the night of the murder but claimed that he drove back to central Oregon without entering the house or seeing his wife.
   - The defendant "volunteered a great deal of information without being asked, yet expressed no concern or curiosity about his wife."
   - While the defendant and his attorney were in the police station, officers noticed dark spots on the defendant's finger and under his fingernails. The police asked Murphy if they could take a sample of scraping from under his fingernails. Murphy refused, put his hands in his pockets, and was attempting to clean his nails with objects in his pockets. Was there any way that the police could get samples of scrapings from under Murphy's nails before he destroyed what might be important evidence of the murder? Explain. *Cupp v. Murphy*, 412 U.S. 291 (1973).

3. After overhearing from a public telephone what appeared to be arrangements for a drug transaction, a Florida police officer followed the defendant's car. When Jimeno committed a traffic violation, the officer stopped his car. The officer told Jimeno that he believed that Jimeno was carrying narcotics in is car, and asked for consent to search the car. After Jimeno said he had nothing to hide, he gave consent. The officer opened a door on the passenger side and saw a folded brown paper bag on the floor of the car. He opened the bag and found cocaine inside. Did his consent give authority to open the bag? (See *Florida v. Jimeno*, 111 S. Ct. 1801 (1991).)

4. Assume a police officer, after making a lawful stop, conducts an invalid search of a vehicle under the *Gant* rule. The search uncovered illegal drugs and weapons, and the driver was arrested. The car was impounded and brought to a police impound lot. The driver was charged with possession of illegal drugs and weapons. Should the evidence obtained in the invalid search be suppressed? Does your answer depend on why the driver was arrested? (See *United States v. Ruckes*, 586 F.3d 713 (9th Cir. 2009), *cert. denied*, 130 S. Ct. 2132 (2010).)

CASE ANALYSIS

Read Appendix B, Finding and Analyzing Cases (p. 499). With these guidelines in mind, please continue with the Case Analysis selections for Chapter 14.

1. Assume an officer stopped a car with only one working brake light, because the officer believed having only one working brake light was a violation. The officer asked for consent to search the car, which was given. The search turned up illegal drugs, and the owner of the car was convicted of transportation of illegal drugs. The defendant argued in the trial court that the initial stop lacked reasonable suspicion, because under state law it is not illegal to have only one working brake light. What should happen on appeal? *See State v. Heien*, 741 S.E.2d 1 (N.C. App. 2013). The U.S. Supreme Court has granted certiorari, 134 S. Ct. 1872 (2014). What do you think the Court finds interesting in this case?

2. A police officer received a complaint about defendant's loud car, and went to defendant's residence to talk about the problem. At the door the officer smelled what he thought might be marijuana. He knocked at the door, and covered the peephole so the occupant could not see who was knocking. When the defendant answered the door the officer saw a gun in his hand, and the officer pushed into the room. There he saw illegal drugs, and arrested the defendant. At his trial on drug charges the

defendant moved to suppress the illegal drugs found in his home, contending any exigent circumstances that existed because of the handgun were created by the officer's own actions. Should the evidence be suppressed? *State v. Campbell*, 300 P.3d 72 (Kan. 2013). What did the U.S. Supreme Court in *Kentucky v. King* (discussed in this chapter) tell lower courts to do when the "police created exigent circumstances" argument is made? Did the Kansas Supreme Court get it right?

3. Police knew the defendant was travelling by train, and when the defendant exited the train the officers arrested him on an outstanding warrant, and handcuffed him. The officers then searched a roller luggage bag, and found illegal drugs. At his trial on the drug charges the defendant moved to suppress the illegal drugs found in his luggage, contending that the U.S. Supreme Court's decision in *Arizona v. Gant* (discussed in this chapter) made the search of his luggage unreasonable, because when the search occurred he was handcuffed and could not therefore gain access to the luggage. Good argument? Why or why not? *People v. Cregan*, 10 N.E.3d 1196 (Ill. 2014).

4. A police officer stopped the defendant after observing a traffic violation. When the officer approached the defendant's car he saw an artificial bladder device the officer knew could be used to cheat on a drug-urine test. He therefore began

investigating to see if the defendant was on probation, and when told he was, continued the traffic stop while the probation officer came to the scene. The probation officer then searched the defendant's car, and found illegal drugs and a handgun. Based on this evidence, the defendant was convicted of federal drug and firearm

offenses. On appeal the defendant argued that the officer unreasonably extended the traffic stop, and that as a result the evidence found in the subsequent search should be suppressed. How should the appeals court address this argument? *United States v. Cash*, 733 F.3d 1264 (10th Cir. 2013), *cert. denied* 134 S. Ct. 1569 (2014).

Notes

1. *Floyd v. City of New York*, 959 F. Supp.2d 540 (S.D. N.Y. 2013).
2. *Ligon v. City of New York*, 736 F.3d 118 (2nd Cir. 2013).
3. *Ligon v. City of New York*, 743 F.3d 362 (2nd Cir. 2014).
4. *Terry v. Ohio*, 88 S. Ct. 1868 (1968).
5. Witnesses to crimes or accidents have a civic obligation as good citizens to provide what information they have to law officers who are investigating the incident. If a material witness will not provide identification, the witness may be detained and could, if necessary, be taken to a police station and charged. See the box, "Obeying Lawful Police Orders," on page 246 in Chapter 9 of *Criminal Law: Principles and Cases*, 12th ed., by Thomas Gardner and Terry Anderson (Cengage Learning, 2015).
6. *Florida v. Royer*, 103 S. Ct. 1319 (1983).
7. Courts will consider the following in determining whether a citizen-police encounter is voluntary or an illegal police seizure:

   - Was there physical contact (touching, holding) by the officer or private security person?
   - How many police officers were present (1 or 10)? Backup officers should stay in the background unless safety is a problem.
   - Were weapons unnecessarily displayed or pointed?
   - Did the officers or their vehicle block a clear path for the suspect to leave the area? Was the person free to leave?
   - Was the suspect told to go to another location or asked to voluntarily move to another place?
   - Were the language and tone of voice intimidating? Was a police badge flashed repeatedly?
   - If the police officer examined identification or plane or bus tickets, were they returned promptly? Because a citizen will need his driver's license or bus ticket, he is not free to leave until the item is returned.
   - See the *FBI Law Enforcement Bulletin* article entitled "Voluntary Encounter or Fourth Amendment Seizure?" (January 1992) for a further discussion and case citations of these factors.

8. *United States v. Mendenhall*, 100 S. Ct. 1870, 1877 (1980).
9. 122 S. Ct. 2105 (2002).
10. *Gomph v. State*, 120 P.3d 980, 986 (Wyo. 2005).
11. *Terry v. Ohio*, 88 S. Ct. 1868 (1968).
12. 534 U.S. 266, 274 (2002).
13. 134 S. Ct. 1683.
14. 448 U.S. 438 (1980).
15. 561 So.2d 1139 (Fla. 1990).
16. *Snow v. State*, 578 A.2d 816 (Md. App. 1990).
17. *United States v. Hernandez-Alvarado*, 891 F.2d 1414 (9th Cir. 1989).
18. *United States v. Tapia*, 912 F.2d 1367 (11th Cir. 1990).
19. *United States v. Millan*, 912 F.2d 1014 (8th Cir. 1990).
20. 124 S. Ct. 2451 (2004).
21. Nevada Statutes § 171.123.
22. Cited in *FBI Law Enforcement Bulletin*, "Police Intervention Short of Arrest" (November 2006, p. 31).
23. 124 S. Ct. at 2458, citing other cases.
24. *Terry v. Ohio*, 88 S. Ct. 1868 (1968).
25. 113 S. Ct. 2130 (1993). A situation similar to *Minnesota v. Dickerson* was before the U.S. Supreme Court in April 2000. In *Bond v. United States*, 120 S. Ct. 1462 (2000), the defendant was a passenger in a public bus. He placed carry-on luggage in a public luggage rack. When the bus properly stopped at a border checkpoint, a border patrol officer entered the bus and verified immigration status. After doing so, the officer "squeezed" soft carry-on luggage in the public bins. He detected a hard, bricklike object in Bond's luggage, which on inspection turned out to be illegal drugs. Bond was convicted over his Fourth Amendment objection to the search of his luggage.

    The Supreme Court reversed, finding that Bond had sought to preserve privacy in his luggage by placing it in the bin above him, and he did not expect the kind of exploratory touching done by the border officer. As a result, Bond's reasonable expectation of privacy was violated without probable cause, and the Fourth Amendment required exclusion of the drugs.

The rule in *Bond* may have little effect on airline security cases. Passengers who have soft carry-on luggage on airline flights must expect careful scrutiny of such bags, and thus they have no reasonable expectation of privacy.

26. Citizen's arrest goes back to England and early America when law officers were scarce or did not exist in some areas. Under such circumstances, private citizens had to assume the burden of maintaining public order. The common-law doctrine of *private person arrest* usually limits the authority to misdemeanor breaches of the peace committed in the presence of the private person and to felonies committed in the presence of the private person. Check the law of your state before assuming this authority exists.

In some states, the general authority of a private citizen to make a citizen's arrest is set forth in a statute. In most states, the authority to make a citizen's arrest is part of the common law of that state (that is, it is found in the court decisions of that state).

State statutes that give private persons the authority to make arrests include some or all of the following:

- Shoplifting statutes give merchants and their adult employees authority to either arrest or detain a person where there is solid probable cause to believe the person has shoplifted.
- Statutes that govern railroad and bus employees give them authority.
- Private citizens who are asked or ordered to aid and assist a law officer could be given the "same power as that of a law enforcement officer" Wisconsin Statute 968.07(2).
- Surety or extradition statutes could give private citizens authority to make an arrest under circumstances set forth in such statutes.

Law officers who are off duty or out of their jurisdiction (city or state) may have the authority to make a citizen's arrest in another city or state.

27. *Henry v. United States*, 361 U.S. 98 (1959).
28. *Chimel v. California*, 89 S. Ct. 2034 (1969).
29. 525 U.S. 113 (1998).
30. *Id.* at 119.
31. *United States v. Weeks*, 232 U.S. 383 (1914).
32. 414 U.S. 218 (1973).
33. 134 S. Ct. 2473, 2489 (2014).
34. *New York v. Belton*, 101 S. Ct. 2860 (1981).
35. *Arizona v. Gant*, 129 S. Ct. 1710 (2009).
36. *Id*, at 1719.
37. 134 S. Ct., at 2494.
38. 494 U.S. 325, 334 (1990).
39. The federal decisions are collected in *United States v. Hassock*, 631 F.3d 79 (2nd Cir. 2011).

40. *Id.* Some state courts have held protective sweeps improper when officers are present only by consent. *See Guzman v. Commonwealth*, 375 S.W.3d 805 (Ky. 2012).
41. *Illinois v. Lafayette*, 462 U.S. 640, 103 S. Ct. 2605 (1983).
42. *Id.*
43. *Id.*
44. *Katz v. United States*, 389 U.S. 347, 357 (1967), quoted in *Arizona v. Gant*, 129 S. Ct. 1710, 1716 (2009). See Appendix A for relevant sections of the U.S. Constitution.
45. *Payton v. New York*, 445 U.S. 573, 585, 100 S. Ct. 1371–79 (1980).
46. In the 1958 case of *Miller v. United States*, 357 U.S. 301, 78 S. Ct. 1190 (1958), the U.S. Supreme Court quoted from the *Oxford Dictionary of Quotations* (2d ed., 1953), attributing the statement to William Pitt in 1763. The Supreme Court traces the history of the Fourth Amendment in the case of *Stanford v. Texas*, 379 U.S. 476, 85 S. Ct. 506 (1965).
47. 6 F.3d 673 (9th Cir. 1993).
48. 762 F.2d 1318 (9th Cir. 1985).
49. In the 1991 case of *State v. Mooney*, 588 A.2d 145 (Conn.), law officers searched under a highway bridge in a place they knew the defendant regarded as his home. They found additional evidence of the crime for which the defendant had been arrested. The majority of the Supreme Court of Connecticut (three judges dissenting) held that the defendant had a reasonable right and expectation of privacy in the duffel bag and cardboard box from which the officers obtained the evidence. The evidence was suppressed and could not be used against the defendant.

Mobile homes are homes to some people. However, the U.S. Supreme Court has held that mobile motor homes are motor vehicles if they can be quickly driven away. In the 1985 case of *California v. Carney,* 471 U.S. 386, 105 S. Ct. 2066, the U.S. Supreme Court held that mobile motor homes have a reduced expectation of privacy and are classified under the law as motor vehicles, where the automobile exception can apply.

50. *Payton v. New York*, 445 U.S. 573, 100 S. Ct. 1371 (1980).
51. *Steagald v. United States*, 451 U.S. 204, 101 S. Ct. 1642 (1981).
52. U.S. Supreme Court in *Ker v. California*, 83 S. Ct. 1623, 1641 (Brennan, Justice, concurring) (1963).
53. U.S. Supreme Court in *Miller v. United States*, 78 S. Ct. 1190 (1958).
54. See *Ker v. California*, 83 S. Ct. 1623 (1963).
55. 531 U.S. 326.
56. 452 U.S. 692 (1981).

57. 403 U.S. 388 (1971).
58. *Georgia v. Randolph*, 547 U.S. 103 (2006).
59. 93 S. Ct. 2523 (1973).
60. *See United States v. Quezada*, 448 F.3d 1005 (8th Cir. 2006).
61. 63 A.3d 175 (N.J. 2013).
62. 440 U.S. 653 (1979).
63. 468 U.S. 420 (1984).
64. 468 U.S. at 436, quoting from *Delaware v. Prouse, supra.*
65. 116 S. Ct. 1769.
66. The facts and ruling of the U.S. Supreme Court in the 1986 case of *New York v. Class*, 475 U.S. 106, 106 S. Ct. 960, follow: After New York police officers stopped the defendant for exceeding the speed limit and driving with a cracked windshield (both are offenses in New York), one of the officers looked for the VIN (vehicle identification number) on the defendant's car. Because some papers were obscuring the area of the dashboard where the VIN should be located, the officer reached in to move the papers. As he did so, he saw the handle of a gun protruding about an inch from under the driver's seat. The officer seized the gun, and the defendant was arrested. In holding that law enforcement officers making a lawful stop of a vehicle have a right and duty to inspect the VIN, the Court affirmed the defendant's conviction of criminal possession of a gun, ruling,

> We hold that this search was sufficiently unintrusive to be constitutionally permissible in light of the lack of a reasonable expectation of privacy in the VIN and the fact that the officers observed respondent commit two traffic violations. Any other conclusion would expose police officers to potentially grave risks without significantly reducing the intrusiveness of the ultimate conduct— viewing the VIN—which, as we have said, the officers were entitled to do as part of an undoubtedly justified traffic stop.

> We note that our holding today does not authorize police officers to enter a vehicle to obtain a dashboard-mounted VIN when the VIN is visible from outside the automobile. If the VIN is in the plain view of someone outside the vehicle, there is no justification for governmental intrusion into the passenger compartment to see it.

67. See *Berkemer v. McCarty*, 468 U.S. 420, 104 S. Ct. 9 (1984).
68. In the 1988 case of *Pennsylvania v. Bruder*, 488 U.S. 9, 109 S. Ct. 205, a police officer stopped Bruder, who was driving erratically and ran a red light. Because the officer smelled alcohol and observed Bruder's stumbling movements, he administered field sobriety tests, which included reciting the alphabet and answering questions regarding alcohol. When Bruder failed the sobriety tests, he was placed under arrest and given *Miranda* warnings. Because of Bruder's intoxicated condition, however, waiver or understanding of the warnings could not be shown, and Bruder's answers were suppressed for lack of *Miranda* warnings. The U.S. Supreme Court held that Bruder's answers to the roadside questions were admissible. The Court compared this case to *Berkemer v. McCarty*, holding that:

> In Berkemer v McCarty, which involved facts strikingly similar to those in this case, the Court concluded that the "noncoercive aspect of ordinary traffic stops prompts us to hold that persons temporarily detained pursuant to such stops are not 'in custody' for the purposes of Miranda." 468 U.S. at 440.

> The Court reasoned that although the stop was unquestionably a seizure within the meaning of the Fourth Amendment, such traffic stops typically are brief, unlike a prolonged station house interrogation. Second, the Court emphasized that traffic stops commonly occur in the "public view," in an atmosphere far "less 'police dominated' than that surrounding the kinds of interrogation at issue in Miranda itself." The detained motorist's "freedom of action [was not] curtailed to 'a degree associated with formal arrest.'"...

> Accordingly, Bruder was not entitled to a recitation of his constitutional rights prior to arrest, and his roadside responses to questioning were admissible.

69. *Schneckloth v. Bustamonte*, 412 U.S. 218, 93 S. Ct. 2041 (1973).
70. In the 1990 case of *Horton v. California,* 496 U.S. 128, 110 S. Ct. 2301, the U.S. Supreme Court gave the following requirements for a plain-view or open-view seizure of evidence by law officers:

- Officers must be in a place where they have a right to be.
- The object or evidence must be in plain or open view and "immediately apparent" to be illegal or evidence of a crime.
- Not only must the officer be lawfully located to see the object, but the officer must also have a lawful right of access to the object. (For example, an officer who is where he or she has a right to be and sees contraband in a home but has no authority to enter the home does not have a lawful right of access to the immediately apparent evidence.)

71. 124 S. Ct. 2127.
72. 124 S. Ct. at 2131.
73. 96 S. Ct. 3092 (1976).

74. 471 U.S. 386 (1985).
75. The U.S. Supreme Court affirmed the criminal convictions of Drayton and his companions and held that the evidence showed the bus passengers were free to leave. The Court held:

> Law enforcement officers do not violate the Fourth Amendment's prohibition of unreasonable seizures merely by approaching individuals on the street or in other public places and putting questions to them if they are willing to listen. Even when law enforcement officers have no basis for suspecting a particular individual, they may pose questions, ask for identification, and request consent to search luggage provided they do not induce cooperation by coercive means. (See *Florida v. Bostick*, 5501 U.S., at 434–435, 111 S. Ct. 2382. (Citations omitted.)) If a reasonable person would feel free to terminate the encounter then he or she has not been seized.
>
> ... (This) Court has rejected in specific terms the suggestion that police officers must always inform citizens of their right to refuse when seeking permission to conduct a warrantless consent search. "While knowledge of the right to refuse consent is one factor to be taken into account, the government need not establish such knowledge as the sine qua non of an effective consent." Nor do this Court's decisions suggest that even though there are no per se rules, a presumption of invalidity attaches if a citizen consented without explicit notification that he or she was free to refuse to cooperate. Instead, the Court has repeated that the totality of the circumstances must control, without giving extra weight to the absence of this type of warning. Although Officer Lang did not inform respondents of their right to refuse the search, he did request permission to search, and the totality of the circumstances indicates that their consent was voluntary, so the searches were reasonable.
>
> In a society based on law, the concept of agreement and consent should be given a weight and dignity of its own. Police officers act in full accord with the law when they ask citizens for consent. It reinforces the rule of law for the citizen to advise the police of his or her wishes and for the police to act in reliance on that understanding. When this exchange takes place, it dispels inferences of coercion.

Obtaining Evidence by Use of Search Warrants, from Computers, Wiretapping, or Dogs Trained to Indicate an Alert

A DISMANTLED HARD DRIVE

© Yomka/Shutterstock.com

LEARNING OBJECTIVES

In this chapter we examine other methods of obtaining evidence, including search warrants, electronic surveillance, and canine alerts. The learning objectives for this chapter are

List the various types of search warrants and their requirements.

Assuming officers are entitled to look at a computer's files, describe the limits on that examination.

List some situations where officers may hear or record statements without the need for a court order.

State the differences in terms of reliability and the need for a search or arrest warrant between a known informant and an anonymous informant.

State the rules on the police use of trained dogs to "sniff" a vehicle or luggage.

Assume an employer gives a laptop computer to an employee for use by the employee in his work. The employer owns the computer, but the employee keeps possession of the computer both at work and at home. The employee is on probation for a forgery conviction, and as a condition of that probation signed a consent form giving probation officers permission to search his person and residence, without any need to show probable cause or reasonable suspicion. During a routine visit to the employee's home probation officers observed a backpack on a table. After asking if it belonged to the employee, they opened the backpack and discovered airline receipts showing the employee had traveled outside the state without permission, a violation of probation. They also discovered the employer-owned computer. Officers seized the backpack and the computer. Assuming the search of the backpack was lawful (it was), can the officers search the computer (without a warrant) for evidence of other probation violations? Does it matter that the employee told officers the computer belonged to his employer? *See State v. Ruck*, 314 P.3d 157 (Idaho 2013) Based on the reasoning of the court in *Ruck*, what could the officers have done differently to avoid the need for a search warrant?

SEARCH WARRANTS

The Fourth Amendment to the U.S. Constitution states that "no Warrant shall issue, but upon probable cause supported by Oath, or affirmation, and particularly describing the place to be searched and the persons or things to be seized" (see Appendix A). One of the most hated practices of the British officers in colonial America was the general warrant. Pursuant to these warrants, Crown officers conducted searches and seizures of colonial homes with no limits on their actions. The framers of the Constitution had those general warrants in mind when they wrote the Fourth Amendment. As a result, U.S. Supreme Court cases have established "the basic principle of Fourth Amendment law that searches and seizures inside a home without a warrant are presumptively unreasonable."[1]

When evidence is obtained without a search warrant, the burden is on the government to show that the evidence was obtained under one of the "established and well-delineated exceptions" to the search warrant requirement. The U.S. Supreme Court pointed out that the exceptions to the search warrant requirement are "jealously and carefully drawn."[2]

A search warrant must be issued by a neutral and detached judge or magistrate who determines that probable cause exists to issue the search or arrest warrant.[3] The oath or affirmation supporting the search warrant is in most instances made by a law enforcement officer, based on information known to that officer. Typically, the facts that support the issuance of a search warrant show that the officer has probable cause to believe that the premises to be searched contain evidence of a crime, such as contraband, or instruments used in a crime, such as weapons, or fruits of a crime, such as stolen property.

The Fourth Amendment states that search warrants must "particularly [describe] the place to be searched and the persons or things to be seized." If a search warrant does not contain such a particular description, it is invalid, even if in fact the officer who obtained the search warrant had probable cause, and even if the search that was made was limited in scope. The following case illustrates the "particular description" requirement.

Groh v. Ramirez

United States Supreme
Court, 540 U.S. 551 (2004)

Federal and county officers were told by a reliable informant that the Ramirezes had illegal automatic weapons at their ranch in Montana. Based on an affidavit that recited these facts, a search warrant was issued by a magistrate. The search warrant was on a form used by the officers and stated in the box where the "person or property to be seized" was to be listed only the address and location of the Ramirez house. The warrant did not mention the stockpile of weapons, nor did it incorporate the affidavit of the officers supporting the warrant.

The U.S. Supreme Court held that the search warrant violated the Fourth Amendment, even though the affidavit supporting the warrant recited probable cause and described particularly the place to be searched. In rejecting the officers' argument that the presence of specific descriptions in the affidavit of the "things to be seized" saved the search warrant, the Court stated,

> The fact that the application adequately described the "things to be seized" does not save the warrant from its facial invalidity. The Fourth Amendment by its terms requires particularity in the warrant, not in the supporting documents. (citations omitted)... "The presence of a search warrant serves a high function," (citation omitted), and that function is not necessarily vindicated when some other document, somewhere, says something about the objects of the search, but the contents of that document are neither known to the person whose home is being searched nor available for her inspection.

The Court noted that although a search warrant can incorporate other documents, such documents must be attached to the search warrant and available for inspection. That was not the case here. The Court also held that the facts that the magistrate actually knew of the specific things to be seized and that the search was limited to a search for those things did not save the search warrant. Moreover, the error in the search warrant was obvious on its face, and not a mere technical mistake or typographical error. As a result, the Court said, the good faith exception (see Chapter 10) was inapplicable.

Luggage or a package may be detained to obtain a search warrant where probable cause exists to believe that the package or luggage contains evidence of a crime. However, as the Supreme Court said in *Illinois v. McArthur*,[4] officers must act diligently to obtain a warrant within a reasonable time. In the case of *United States v. Van Leeuwen*,[5] a package was held up in the U.S. mail for 29 hours, and in the case of *State v. Morrison*,[6] the delay was 3 hours. The U. S. Supreme Court found both delays to be reasonable and necessary under the existing circumstances.

The U.S. Supreme Court has stated that "a seizure lawful at its inception can nevertheless violate the Fourth Amendment because its manner of execution unreasonably infringes possessory interests protected by the Fourth Amendment's prohibition on 'unreasonable searches.'" *United States v. Jacobson*, 466 U.S. 109, 124 (1984). The extent of the infringement on that "possessory interest" can be difficult to evaluate, as two recent cases from the Eleventh Circuit Court of Appeals illustrate.

In the first case, *United States v. Mitchell*, 565 F.3d 1347 (11th Cir. 2009), federal agents who detained a lawfully seized computer for 21 days before obtaining a search warrant to search the computer were held to have unreasonably infringed on the owner's possessory interest in the computer. In the second case, *United States v. Laist*, 702 F.3d 608 (11th Cir. 2012), the court held that detaining a defendant's lawfully seized computer for 25 days was not an unreasonable infringement of his possessory interest in the computer. The court distinguished the case from the facts in *Mitchell* by noting that in *Laist* the defendant was given the opportunity to download any material from the computer for his own purposes, and that the officer seeking the warrant began work on the necessary affidavits and documents needed for the warrant at once.

You be the JUDGE: SEARCH WARRANT

When prosecutions are based on evidence found through use of a search warrant, a defendant might seek to exclude the evidence by attacking the validity of the warrant. The principal requirements for a search warrant under the Fourth Amendment are (1) probable cause, (2) oath or affirmation supporting the application, and (3) particular description of the place to be searched. Assume you are the judge in the following criminal cases, and in each case the defendant has challenged the search warrant under which evidence of crimes was discovered as failing to satisfy the Fourth Amendment requirements:

1. Based on a tip that the defendant had uploaded a video containing child pornography to an image-sharing website, federal agents obtained a search warrant to search his house for the computer to which the video was traced. They obtained the warrant, and found the computer in the defendant's possession. Child pornographic images were found stored in the computer and the defendant was charged under federal child pornography laws. At his trial, the defendant contended the search warrant lacked probable cause because the warrant was based on a tip that the defendant had downloaded the video seven months earlier, and thus the tip was "stale." This showed the warrant lacked probable cause, the defendant argued, because no reasonable magistrate could conclude the computer would still contain evidence of criminal activity seven months later. Should you exclude the evidence found in the computer? See *United States v. Seiver*, 692 F.3d 774 (7th Cir. 2012), *cert. denied* 133 S. Ct. 915 (2013).

2. A confidential informant (CI) told police officers that he witnessed the defendant in possession of an ounce of crack cocaine at the defendant's residence. Based on this tip, officers obtained a search warrant for the defendant's residence, and found illegal drugs. The defendant moved to exclude that evidence, contending the CI's affidavit supporting the warrant application was defective because it stated, "Within the last 10 days..." the CI observed the crack cocaine in the defendant's residence. The defendant argued the affidavit did not show probable cause, because there was no showing it was likely that the illegal drugs would still be at the residence. Should you admit the evidence? See *United States v. Sutton*, 742 F.3d 770 (7th Cir. 2014). These first two cases are both from the Seventh Circuit Court of Appeals. Which "stale" argument do you find more persuasive?

3. If a search warrant is based on a police dog's drug alert, what must the affidavit say to establish probable cause? In *United States v. Grupee*, 682 F.3d 143 (1st Cir. 2012), *cert. denied* 133 S. Ct. 581 (2012), the defendant contended the search warrant obtained to search his car based on the dog alert was defective because it failed to show the dog was trained for drug alerts, and was reliable in his alerts.

Do you agree? Are you helped by the U. S. Supreme Court's opinion in *Florida v. Harris*, 133 S. Ct. 1050 (2013), upholding the dog alert there?

4. Does the judge or magistrate issuing the search warrant have to sign it for it to be valid? Does the Fourth Amendment explicitly impose such a requirement? If not, should you read such a requirement into the Amendment? In *United States v. Lyons*, 740 F.3d 702 (1st Cir. 2014), *cert. denied* 134 S. Ct. 2743 (2014) the defendant contended the absence of the judge's signature on the search warrant rendered it invalid. Do you agree?

5. Do e-warrants satisfy the Fourth Amendment's "oath and affirmation" requirement, which is normally satisfied by the applicant's affirmation under oath before the judge issuing the search warrant? Is it enough that the officer seeking the e-warrant checks the box that says the applicant declares that the application is true and correct? See *State v. Guitierrez-Perez*, 323 P.3d 1017 (Utah 2014). Do the reasons the U. S. Supreme Court gave for its decision in *Missouri v. McNeeley*, 133 S. Ct. 1552 (2013) (discussed in Chapter 14), requiring a search warrant to draw blood in the usual DUI case, guide your analysis?

Types of Search Warrants

Nighttime Search Warrants Most states and the federal government have statutes requiring that search warrants be served and executed during daylight hours. However, such laws permit a magistrate or judge to authorize a nighttime search. Federal Rule of Criminal Procedure 41(e) permits the authorization of a nighttime search when "there be cause for carrying on the unusual nighttime ... search ... upon a showing (that) convinces the magistrate that it is reasonable."

In suspected illegal drug cases, the possibility that the defendant will destroy the illegal drugs before officers can conduct the search is frequently used as the justification for a nighttime search. In *United States v. Kotoa*,[7] police officers obtained a search warrant to search the defendant's home for illegal drugs. The affidavit asked for no-knock and nighttime authorization, and the application was presented to a state district court judge on that basis. However, the warrant issued actually authorized a search "in the daytime with unannounced authority." A police SWAT team executed the search warrant at night and found illegal drugs. During the search, the officers discovered the mistaken omission of "nighttime" from the warrant. They called the district court judge who issued the warrant, and he instructed them to write in "nighttime" in the warrant and said that he would subsequently sign the warrant authorizing the change, which he did. The defendant moved to suppress the evidence found during the search, contending that a nighttime search under a daytime warrant violated the Fourth Amendment. The district court refused to suppress the evidence, and the defendant entered a conditional guilty plea, reserving his right to appeal the suppression ruling.

The court of appeals affirmed the conviction, holding that the mistake in the warrant was cured by the telephone call to the issuing judge. The court distinguished the case from the Supreme Court's decision in *Groh* (discussed previously), noting that because the Fourth Amendment does not explicitly require the warrant to indicate the time of day or night, the holding in *Groh*—that the absence of "the things to be seized" made the warrant invalid—did not apply. The court held that the general reasonableness requirement determined that the search was valid and on that question held that the telephone call to the issuing judge that corrected the defect in the warrant made the search reasonable.

The Fourth Circuit Court of Appeals held in the 2006 case of *United States v. Rizzi*[8] that 21 U.S.C. § 879, which applies to search warrants in illegal drug cases and authorizes daytime or nighttime executions of the search warrant, "trumps" Rule 41(e). Thus, even though the search warrant in *Rizzi* authorizing a search for illegal drugs failed to state that a nighttime search was permitted, section 879 did not require that specific statement, the court concluded.

In states that do not have a statute like 21 U.S.C. § 879, search warrants require a showing of "good cause" if they are to be executed at night. Thus, in *State v. Zeller*, 845 N.W.2d 6 (N.D. 2014) the court suppressed evidence of illegal drug sales found in the defendant's residence based on a 3:00 AM nighttime search warrant. The affidavit supporting the search warrant failed to show any reason to believe evidence likely held in the residence would be lost or destroyed before morning, the court said.

No-Knock or Unannounced Entries   Law enforcement officers must knock, identify themselves, state their purpose, and await a refusal or silence before they enter private premises. An unannounced or no-knock entry can be made if it is specifically authorized by the search warrant or if the officers can show that notice by knocking would be likely to

- Endanger the safety of the officers or another person
- Result in the evidence subject to seizure being easily and quickly destroyed or disposed of
- Enable the party to be arrested or searched to escape
- Be a useless gesture

When officers knock and identify themselves, they are permitted to forcibly enter the premises under certain circumstances. The following U.S. Supreme Court case discusses the rules that determine when an officer may use force in entering premises to conduct a search.

United States v. Banks United States Supreme Court, 540 U.S. 31 (2003)	Police officers obtained a search warrant to search Banks's apartment for evidence of cocaine and drug dealing. At two o'clock in the afternoon, officers went to Banks's apartment, knocked loudly on his door, and after a wait of 15 to 20 seconds with no response from inside, broke down Banks's door with a battering ram. In fact, Banks was in the shower and did not hear the police announcing their presence. The search yielded evidence of drug dealing, which Banks moved to suppress. The district court denied the motion, but on appeal the Ninth Circuit Court of Appeals reversed, holding that waiting only 15 to 20 seconds before breaking down the apartment door was unreasonable, and thus violated the Fourth Amendment. The Supreme Court reversed, finding the decision to make the forced entry reasonable under the circumstances known to the officers. In doing so, the Court reviewed the rules courts use to determine the reasonableness of the manner in which a search warrant is executed. The Court said, The Fourth Amendment says nothing specific about formalities in exercising a warrant's authorization, speaking to the manner of searching as well as the legitimacy of searching at all simply in terms of the right to be "secure ... against unreasonable searches and seizures." Although the notion of reasonable execution must therefore

be fleshed out, we have done that case by case, largely avoiding categories and protocols for searches. We have, however, pointed out factual considerations of unusual, albeit not dispositive, significance.

One such factual consideration, the Court noted, was the presence of exigent circumstances that led the officers to believe that knocking or waiting to enter might result in the destruction of evidence. Where those circumstances are reasonable and expected in the warrant application, a magistrate is justified in authorizing a no-knock warrant: "And even when executing a warrant silent about that, if circumstances support a reasonable suspicion of exigency when the officers arrive at the door, they may go straight in." Under that reasoning, the Court stated, when the exigent circumstances became known to the officers in this case, after knocking and announcing, they could do the same.

The Court concluded that although "this call is a close one," given the nature of the criminal evidence—cocaine—and the ease of its disposal, the officers acted reasonably in waiting only 15 to 20 seconds before making a forced entry. The Court also held that 18 U.S.C. § 3109, which permits forced entry "if, after notice of his authority and purpose, [an officer] is refused admittance," is subject to the "exigent circumstances" exception. (See Chapter 9 for *Hudson v. Michigan,* the Supreme Court case on the "knock-and-announce" rule and its relationship to the exclusionary rule.)

Anticipatory Search Warrants On occasion, law enforcement officers have information that evidence—usually illegal drugs—will be at a particular place at a future time. For example, police might have specific, reliable information that a large shipment of drugs will come into a city to a specific address in the next few days. However, the officers might not have reliable information about where the drugs are presently located, what day and time the drugs will arrive, and how they are being transported.

Because most stocks of illegal drugs are dispersed rapidly due to the danger of a police raid or a snatching by a rival gang, an anticipatory search warrant solves the problem law enforcement officers face in such situations. The police may obtain a search warrant directed at the person and place where it is reliably anticipated the illegal drugs will be located.

In these warrants, the affidavits accompanying the application for the search warrant commonly describe the basis for the officer's belief that some illegal contraband or other evidence of a crime will be located at some specific place in the future. An anticipatory search warrant may be directed toward the search of a person, or it may be used for a "controlled delivery,"[9] as in the following case.

United States v. Grubbs

United States Supreme
Court, 547 U.S. 90 (2006)

The defendant, Grubbs, purchased a child pornography videotape online from a website operated by an undercover postal inspector. The videotape was mailed to Grubbs, and Postal Inspection Service officers obtained an anticipatory search warrant from a federal magistrate in California to search Grubbs's residence after the video arrived. An affidavit accompanying the application for the search warrant stated that execution of the warrant would not occur unless the videotape was received by someone at Grubbs's residence and taken inside the residence. The magistrate issued the warrant, but the "triggering" condition set forth in the affidavit was not incorporated into the warrant.

The video was delivered, and Grubbs's wife took delivery and brought the package into the residence. The police then executed the search warrant and discovered evidence of child pornography in the residence. Grubbs was charged with one count of receiving a visual depiction of a minor engaged in sexually explicit conduct, and he moved to suppress the videotape because the search warrant did not contain the "triggering" condition language. As a result, Grubbs argued, on its face the warrant was a violation of the Fourth Amendment. The district court denied the motion, and Grubbs pleaded guilty, reserving the right to contest the Fourth Amendment claim. The Ninth Circuit Court of Appeals reversed, holding that the absence of the affidavit language in the search warrant rendered the warrant "inoperative." The U.S. Supreme Court granted certiorari and reversed the Ninth Circuit.

The Supreme Court first considered whether "anticipatory search warrants are categorically unconstitutional." The argument against such warrants, the Court said, is that because at the time the search warrant is issued probable cause to suspect that a crime had occurred or contraband was located at a particular place did not exist, anticipatory search warrants violate the Fourth Amendment's requirement that "no Warrants shall issue, but upon probable cause." The Court said, "We reject this view, as has every Court of Appeals to confront the issue."[10]

The Court stated that the probable cause requirement looks to whether probable cause exists to believe evidence will be found when the search is conducted. As a result, the Court said, "all warrants are, in a sense, 'anticipatory.' In the typical case … the Magistrate's determination that there is probable cause for the search amounts to a prediction that the item will still be there when the warrant is executed."[11] An anticipatory warrant is no different from an ordinary warrant, the Court concluded, because based on the "triggering" condition, the magistrate can determine that probable cause exists to believe the contraband will be on the described property when the search warrant is executed. Probable cause in anticipatory search warrants requires only that supporting affidavits provide the issuing magistrate with sufficient information to show that, if the "triggering" condition occurs, contraband or evidence of a crime will be found at the designated place, and it is probable that the "triggering" condition will occur. Here, the Court said, such probable cause existed.

The Court also rejected the Ninth Circuit's conclusion that the search warrant was defective because it failed to explicitly specify the "triggering" condition in the search warrant. The Supreme Court noted that there is no requirement in the Fourth Amendment that the search warrant specify the basis for the warrant's issuance, but only "the place to be searched" and "the persons or things to be seized." "The language of the Fourth Amendment is likewise decisive here; its particularity requirement does not include the conditions precedent to execution of the warrant."[12] As a result, the Supreme Court reversed the Ninth Circuit and upheld the search warrant.

Sneak-and-Peek Entry Warrants Sneak-and-peek warrants permit law officers to enter premises for various reasons. In the case of *United States v. Pangburn*, the entry was made to photograph the contents of a suspected clandestine methamphetamine lab.[13]

Law officers may enter private premises to plant listening devices, as was done in the Waco, Texas, Branch Davidian compound and also the Arlington, Virginia, home of Aldrich Ames, a high-ranking officer of the CIA who was arrested in 1994 for spying against the United States for the Russians.

In the 1979 U.S. Supreme Court case of *Dalia v. United States*,[14] a search warrant was issued to implant a listening device in a business office. Three weeks later, another entry was made to remove the device. The U.S. Supreme Court affirmed the defendant's conviction, holding that

> Nothing in the language of the Constitution or in this Court's decisions ... suggest that ... search warrants ... must include a specification of the precise manner in which they are to be executed. It is generally left to the discretion of the executing officers to determine the details of how best to proceed with the performance of a search authorized by warrant—subject of course to the general Fourth Amendment protection "against unreasonable searches and seizures."

Administrative Search Warrants Under most state laws, fire, health, building, and food inspectors, as well as many other state administrative agencies, may obtain administrative search warrants to determine whether a person or business is violating state laws designed to protect the public. These include health regulation violations, fire hazards, food services, and structural concerns in buildings open to the public.

A lower standard of probable cause than that required in the traditional probable cause search warrant requirement applies to administrative search warrants. In *Camara v. Municipal Court*,[15] the U.S. Supreme Court held that "(if) a valid public interest justifies the intrusion contemplated, then there is probable cause to issue a suitable restricted search warrant."

Health and food inspectors have the authority to close a restaurant or food processing facility that is in serious violation of the health and sanitation codes of a city or state. For lesser violations, health, fire, and building and housing inspectors generally issue summonses or warnings directing the violator to cure the violations.

The New York City Fire Department conducts about 300,000 inspections each year for compliance with fire codes, and each month it issues about 900 summonses for violations. Most offenders answer the summons by appearing in court and providing evidence of efforts to comply with the regulations violated. In 2008, however, the *New York Times*[16] reported that a backlog of about 4,000 persons and businesses had not appeared in court to address fire code violations. More than 200 arrests were made by mid-2008 for the misdemeanor of failing to appear, and more arrest warrants have since been issued.

OBTAINING EVIDENCE FROM COMPUTERS

More than half the homes in the United States, and virtually all the businesses, use computers. Computers store vast amounts of financial and other information and enable us to communicate via e-mail, chat rooms, websites, and the Internet.

Criminals can also put computers to a wide variety of criminal uses. Financial accountings of criminal enterprises, inventories of illegal drugs or contraband, records of money laundering, lists of customers, and records of criminal transactions are just some of the records stored in computers. Communications about pornography are widely seen on computers, and pedophiles (adults who sexually desire children) frequently use computers to communicate with their victims.

Computers thus can be a fertile place for law officers to find evidence of criminal activity. Because people generally have an expectation of privacy in their personal computers, and to a lesser extent in their workplace computers, however, the

Fourth Amendment applies to any search of a computer where such an expectation of privacy exists. The following cases and examples illustrate searches of computers:

- *Search warrants:* A search warrant authorizing officers to enter a home or office does not authorize the officers to search a computer found in the premises, unless the search warrant identifies the computer as part of the authorized search. Moreover, even if the search warrant authorizes the officers to search a computer, it does not follow that the officers can open and look at every piece of information stored in the computer.

  Two cases in the Tenth Circuit Court of Appeals illustrate this distinction. In *United States v. Carey,*[17] officers obtained a search warrant that authorized them to search a defendant's computer for evidence of illegal drug trafficking. While looking at the computer files, an officer inadvertently opened a file that contained child pornography images. The officer then conducted a wholesale search of all computer files. The court held that the subsequent general search of the computer files was a violation of the Fourth Amendment.

  By contrast, in *United States v. Walser,*[18] the officer searching a computer pursuant to a search warrant authorizing the search for evidence of illegal drugs immediately stopped the search when he inadvertently opened a file containing child pornographic images. The officer went to a magistrate and, armed with the information gained during his lawful search of the computer, obtained a search warrant to search the computer files for evidence of child pornography. The court said that search was lawful.

- *Consent:* The person who has the sole control and access to a computer can authorize a computer search, if the consent is given voluntarily. If more than one person has such control or access, the search of the computer files cannot extend to files or information accessed only through use of the non-consenting person's password. The case of *United States v. Block*[19] is often used to illustrate the limits of consent searches. There, the court said that although the "defendant's mother had authority to consent to a search of his room which was located in the home that they shared, ... the mother's authority did not extend to a search of a locked footlocker located within the room."

  Consent to search a computer permits officers to look at computer files, but only consistent with the scope of the consent. For example, in *State v. Bailey,* 989 A.2d 716 (Me. 2010), the court held that a search of computer files exceeded the consent given, and ordered evidence discovered in the search suppressed. Police officers were aware that someone in a neighborhood was using a router at one residence to access child pornography files. They canvassed the neighborhood, asking for consent to look at computers to see if "someone has been wrongfully accessing" the computer. The defendant agreed to let the officers look at his computer for that purpose. When officers searched the computer, they found child pornography files, and the defendant was charged with possession of child pornography. The appeals court reversed his conviction, and ordered the files be suppressed because the officers exceeded the consent given.

- *The workplace:* (See the discussion of the *Ortega* case in Chapter 11.) Employers and supervisors have wide authority to make warrantless searches of the offices, desks, files, and computers of private and public employees. However, this authority does not extend to areas where the employee has a legitimate expectation of privacy, such as a purse or personal briefcase.

  In the case of government employees, courts generally hold that the employee has no legitimate expectation of privacy in a computer used in that employment. For example, in the 2004 case of *United States v. Thorn,*[20] a supervisor in a state agency believed Thorn was sending personal e-mails to other employees, a violation of agency policy. The supervisor checked Thorn's computer to determine whether he had sent e-mails as suspected. While looking at the computer files, the supervisor found evidence that Thorn had visited Internet pornography sites. The supervisor turned this information over to the police, who obtained a search warrant and found evidence of child pornography. Thorn was charged with possession of child pornography, and at his trial he moved to suppress all the evidence taken from his computer. His motion was denied, and he was convicted. On appeal, the court held that Thorn had no legitimate expectation of privacy in his computer. The court noted that the state agency had a policy that employees were not to use their computers for personal purposes and that the agency reserved the right to access the computers to determine whether any unauthorized use had occurred. Because Thorn knew these rules, the court said, he could not expect that his use of the computer was private.

- *Private search.* Generally, searches of computers by private persons are not violations of the Fourth Amendment and thus evidence discovered is not subject to the exclusionary rule. Thus, if a computer is brought to a repair shop, and the technician working on the computer looks in the files and sees child pornography, that search is not governed by the Fourth Amendment.

- *Plain view:* If a law officer is where he or she is entitled to be, then any evidence the officer sees may be seized under the plain view rule (discussed in Chapter 10). In the case of a computer, that might include information an officer viewed on a monitor screen that showed evidence of a crime.

  For example, in *United States v. Tucker,*[21] police were lawfully in the defendant's home conducting a search for evidence of child pornography. An officer noticed that the defendant's computer was connected to the Internet, accessing a website called alt.sex.preteen. The officer then seized the computer, and a subsequent search uncovered evidence of child pornography. The court held that the evidence found after the seizure of the computer was admissible because, under the plain view rule, the officer saw sufficient evidence of a crime to seize the computer and conduct a more thorough search.

Obtaining Evidence from the Internet (Cyberevidence)

Millions of people use the Internet daily. AOL alone has 20 million customers; its permanent staff answers more than a thousand requests each month for information in criminal and civil cases. The most frequently asked questions concern crimes against children, threats, abductions, and pornography, followed by identity theft and computer hacking crimes.

The Internet has become a common avenue for the exchange of child pornography. Attempts to contact and entice children through Internet chat rooms occur almost constantly. An *FBI Law Enforcement Bulletin* article titled "Child Pornography Web Sites" (July 2007) estimates that more than 100,000 national and international websites are devoted to child pornography; these sites generate more than $3 billion annually of illegal money. The subtitle of the article, "Techniques Used to Evade Law Enforcement," explains in detail how "savvy pornographers" are able to sell their illegal products worldwide with almost "no fear of capture by law enforcement."

PROCEDURES & PROCESSES

Computer Searches and the "Plain View" Doctrine

The plain view doctrine states that if a police officer is lawfully in a place where evidence of a crime is in plain view, the evidence may be seized and used in a criminal trial. Police have used the doctrine to justify seizure of computer files with evidence of child pornography, contending that if the police are lawfully searching computer files for evidence of crimes covered by a search warrant, they must open files to see if the evidence is in the files. If they then see evidence of other crimes, such as child pornography, they may seize the computer. Thus, the court in *United States v. Williams*[a] held that "Once it is accepted that a computer search must, by implication, authorize at least a cursory review of each file on the computer, then the criteria for applying the plain view exception are readily satisfied."

Courts have struggled with the plain view doctrine in computer searches, because the prospect of looking at every file on a computer sounds much like the "general warrant" used by the British government prior to 1776, and the basis for the prohibitions in the Fourth Amendment. Most courts have adopted a position like that suggested in *United States v. Mann*[b]: Search warrants authorizing computer searches must be "narrowly tailored" to look only at files that may contain the things described in the warrant.

In *United States v. Comprehensive Drug Testing Inc.*,[c] the Ninth Circuit Court of Appeals set forth guidelines for use in computer searches. There, federal officers investigating BALCO, a suspected supplier of steroids to professional baseball players, obtained a search warrant to search records, including computer files, of a drug testing company. The officers had probable cause to believe the files would disclose a list of 10 players who tested positive to steroid use. However, the officers seized computer files of hundreds of other players tested at the company, and those players moved to quash subpoenas based on information in those files. The government contended the plain view doctrine applied to all the computer files inspected by the officers.

The court of appeals disagreed. It held the subpoenas should be quashed. The court also identified the following guidelines for issuance of computer search warrants:

1. Segregation and redaction of all seized files must be done by a computer specialist, who will turn over only files containing things described in the search warrant.
2. The government's search protocol must be stated in the warrant as being designed to uncover only information for which it had probable cause.
3. Warrants and subpoenas must disclose any risk that information may be destroyed during the search.
4. The government must destroy, or return to the owner if legal, any nonresponsive information discovered in the computer files.

Other federal courts have declined to follow the Ninth Circuit's lead, in particular the suggestion in a concurring opinion in the decision that officers seeking warrants to search computer files agree to waive reliance on the plain view doctrine. In *United States v. Stabile*[d] the Third Circuit said "We decline to follow the Ninth Circuit's suggestion to 'foreswear reliance on the plain view doctrine' in computer search warrants." In *United States v. Galpin*, 720 F.3d 436 (2nd Cir. 2013) a Second Circuit panel also declined to establish special "protocols" for computer searches. Rather, the court said, district judges should look with "heightened sensitivity" at the manner of the forensic search of computer files conducted under a valid search warrant.

[a]593 F.3d 511 (4th Cir. 2010).
[b]592 F.3d 779 (7th Cir. 2010).
[c]621 F.3d 1162 (9th Cir. 2010).
[d]633 F.3d 219 (3rd Cir. 2011).

The article also points out that, although illegal, child pornography is one of the fastest-growing businesses on the Internet, most of the illegal websites are overseas, and thus neither the websites nor the persons who maintain the websites are within U.S. jurisdiction.

Because those websites that are within U.S. jurisdiction are national in scope, it is difficult for individual states to respond to this growing problem. As a result, the U.S. government has created federal task forces to coordinate the enforcement of state and federal criminal laws that pertain to the Internet. This coordination among federal, state, and local law enforcement is detailed in the December 2007 U.S. Department of Justice publication "Federal Prosecution of Child Exploitation Offenders" (NCJ 219412). According to that report,

- All 56 FBI field offices have specialized units that investigate crimes against children.
- The Cyber Tipline, part of the National Center for Missing and Exploited Children, coordinates tips from the public on the sexual exploitation of children on the Internet.
- There are currently 56 Internet Crimes Against Children (ICAC) task forces composed of federal, state, and local law enforcement agencies located in all 50 states.
- Child-sex tours and child pornography networks are targeted by Homeland Security's Operation Predator. This project acts as a clearinghouse of seized images that can be used to assist in identifying and locating child victims.
- Prosecution of child sex exploitation is emphasized and maximized in the Department of Justice's "Project Safe Childhood."

Posts on social media sites, like Facebook, can be admitted as evidence in criminal trials. While it is doubtful looking at a Facebook page open to the public constitutes a search, it is clear one cannot have any reasonable expectation of privacy in such postings. As a result, law enforcement officers should not need a search warrant to access a suspect's social media pages. Courts do require, however, that if a posting is offered as incriminating evidence against a defendant the prosecution must authenticate the defendant's creation of the posting. *See Parker v. State*, 85 A.3d 682 (Del. 2014) for a discussion of the various means open to the prosecution to accomplish such authentication.

Obtaining Evidence from Other Personal Electronic Devices

Many electronic devices have electronic storage capability; laptop computers, cellular telephones, pagers, flash drives, and MP3 players are just some of these devices.

Evidence of criminal activity may be stored in these devices, and law enforcement officers want access to the stored information. Law enforcement can obtain access through search warrants based on probable cause or through consent searches, as is often done with computer files. Prior to the U. S. Supreme Court's decision in *California v. Riley*[22] (discussed in Chapter 14), many courts upheld warrantless searches of cell phones and other electronic devices in the arrested person's possession. That is no longer permitted. Officers finding such devices must hold them until a search warrant is obtained to open them and look at files, messages, and so forth. As the *Riley* opinion succinctly stated, to search a cell phone seized during an arrest, police must "get a warrant."

Not every use police put to a lawfully seized cell phone constitutes a search. For example, in *United States v. Lawing*, 703 F.3d 229 (2nd Cir. 2012), *cert. denied* 133 S. Ct. 1851 (2013), the court held that when officers who had lawfully stopped a defendant called his cell phone to confirm the number given by an informant, the call did not constitute a search of the cell phone.

WIRETAPPING AND ELECTRONIC SURVEILLANCE

wiretapping
According to the U.S. Supreme Court, writing in *Dalia v. United States*, 99 S. Ct. 1682 (1979), this means "interception of communication by telephone and telegraph."

electronic surveillance
Secret interception of communications by wiretapping or bugging, which "typically is accomplished by installation of a small microphone in the room (or vehicle) to be bugged." *Dalia v. United States*, 99 S. Ct. 1682 (1979).

Prior to 1968 the United States did not have any laws governing **wiretapping** and **electronic surveillance**. However, the 1967 case of *Katz v. United States*[23] caused the U.S. Congress to act. In the *Katz* case, FBI agents attached an electronic listening and recording device to the outside of a public telephone booth that Katz was using to lay off Los Angeles gambling bets in Miami, Florida. The U.S. Supreme Court held that the FBI violated Katz's Fourth Amendment privacy rights and that the evidence obtained could not be used to obtain Katz's criminal gambling conviction.

In 1968 Congress enacted the Federal Wiretapping and Electronic Surveillance Act.[24] Most states followed by enacting similar state laws, making the following changes in the laws on electronic surveillance:

- The laws authorize court orders permitting wiretapping and/or electronic surveillance by law enforcement officers in much the same manner as search warrants are issued.[25]
- The act makes wiretapping and electronic surveillance done in violation of the act a felony. The distribution, possession, and advertising of mechanical and electronic devices used for wiretapping and electronic surveillance is also made a felony (section 2513).

The federal wiretapping act includes a specific section providing for the suppression of evidence obtained in violation of the act. 18 U.S.C. § 2518 (10) (a) states that evidence may be suppressed if "(i) the evidence was unlawfully intercepted; (ii) the order of authorization or approval under which it was intercepted is insufficient on its face; or (iii) the interception was not made in conformity with the order of authorization or approval."

The "insufficient on its face" language has proved troublesome in federal court cases considering suppression of wiretapping evidence. The act requires that the application and order granting the wiretap request identify the Department of Justice officer who authorized the wiretap. If that is not done, but the judge signs the wiretap order, courts are split on the result for suppression purposes. While the application and order are in violation of the act's requirements, some courts have held these mere "technical" violations do not require suppression of evidence acquired under the order. *See, e.g., United States v. Gray*, 521 F.3d 514 (6th Cir. 2008) (judge issuing order had knowledge outside application of identity of official who authorized wiretap). Other courts have ordered suppression under these circumstances; *see United States v. Lomeli*, 676 F.3d 734 (8th Cir. 2012) (application said only "approved by authorized official" but did not identify official, and there was no evidence issuing judge otherwise knew identity of official).

Suppression of wiretapping evidence under state wiretap laws has similar limitations. For example, in *People v. Rodriguez,* 970 N.E.2d 816 (N.Y. 2012) the New York Court of Appeals refused to order suppression of evidence obtained pursuant to the New York wiretapping statute. That statute requires police to inform a target of a wiretap within 90 days of the termination of the wiretap warrant. The police failed to do so, but the defendant was informed of the wiretap at his arraignment. The court said without a showing the lack of notice prejudiced the defendant in defense of the charges, suppression was not appropriate.

Finally, not every instance of a law enforcement officer listening to a phone conversation constitutes a wiretap. Most state wiretapping statutes prohibit electronic eavesdropping by use of a "manual or electronic device or apparatus." In *Commonwealth v. Spence*, 91 A.3d 44 (Pa. 2014) the court held that an officer who instructed a confidential informant to use his cell phone to call his drug dealer, and then placed the call on speakerphone, did not violate the Pennsylvania wiretap statute. The CI's cell phone, the court held, was not a "device" under the wiretap statute.

Thermal-Imaging Devices

Advances in technology now make it possible to obtain information about activities that occur in houses, cars, and other places. The question of whether police may use such technological advances in investigations of crimes without traditional search warrants has been before the Supreme Court many times. In some cases technology opens what were once private spaces to public, and hence official, observation. For example, in *California v. Ciraolo,*[26] the Court held that the uncovered portions of a house and its curtilage have become open to general observation by air travel and are thus no longer private for purposes of the Fourth Amendment.

To what extent may police use technological advances that enable an observer to sense what is inside a private place, like a house? A website maintained by the National Law Enforcement and Corrections Technology Center (www.nlectc.org/technproj) describes radar and ultrasound devices that enable an observer to detect individuals through interior walls. The Supreme Court considered one of these technologies, thermal imaging, in the following case.

Kyllo v. United States

United States Supreme Court, 533 U.S. 27 (2001)

Federal agents suspected that Kyllo was growing marijuana in his home. Using a thermal-imaging device, which detects infrared radiation and converts it to a colored image based on the intensity of the radiation, the police believed that Kyllo was using high-intensity lamps to grow marijuana. Based on this and other evidence, the police obtained a search warrant and searched Kyllo's home, discovering more than a hundred marijuana plants. At his trial for the illegal manufacture of marijuana, Kyllo moved to suppress the evidence seized from his home. The trial court and the court of appeals upheld the validity of the search warrant, holding that it did not expose any intimate details of Kyllo's life but only "hot spots" on the roof and exterior walls.

The Supreme Court reversed, holding that use of the thermal-imaging device constituted a search of Kyllo's house and could not be used without a search warrant:

> We think that obtaining by sense-enhancing technology any information regarding the interior of the home that could not otherwise have been obtained without physical "intrusion into a constitutionally protected area" ... constitutes a search—at least where (as here) the technology in question is not in general public use.

Obtaining Evidence from Tracking Devices

Global positioning system (GPS) devices have been in commercial and private use for years. Rental vehicles have them installed both for the convenience of their customers and to enable the rental company to locate and monitor the vehicles. Employers use them to track company equipment and their employees, and parents use them to monitor their children, particularly in family vehicles. Law enforcement officials have found that GPS devices can be very useful tools in investigating both major and minor crimes and also for locating missing persons and investigating employee misconduct.

In December 2006 the Federal Rules of Criminal Procedure, which serve as guidelines for federal law enforcement officers conducting criminal investigations, were revised as to procedures for the installation and use of tracking devices, including GPS devices. The revised rules follow.

- Rule 41(b)(4). Who can issue a warrant for installation? A federal district court magistrate judge.
- Rule 41(e)(2)(B). Contents of the warrant. Must identify the person or property to be tracked, not to exceed 45 days unless extended for good cause.
- Rule 41(f)(2). Return on warrant. Within 10 days after use ended.
- Rule 41(f)(3). Delay in return. Available upon request.

An article in the February 2007 issue of the *FBI Law Enforcement Bulletin* titled "Legal Brief" states,

> The new rule does not address whether law enforcement officers need a warrant to install or monitor a tracking device. Whether a warrant is required to install a tracking device, or track a vehicle or other object, revolves around expectations of privacy. If an intrusion into an area where there is a privacy expectation is necessary to install the device, or the vehicle or object will be tracked in an area where one has a privacy expectation, a warrant is required. If there is no such intrusion or tracking the device will not infringe on privacy, a warrant is not required.

The revised federal rules are in compliance with the U.S. Supreme Court's decisions in *United States v. Knotts*, 460 U.S. 276 (1983), and *United States v. Karo*, 468 U.S. 705 (1984), where the Court held that attaching a device to a vehicle and monitoring it while used on public roads was not a search, and did not require a warrant, but a warrant is required when a vehicle is in a garage or other private place. Thus, in *United States v. McIver*, 186 F.3d 1119 (9th Cir. 1999), the court upheld placing a tracking device in the undercarriage of a vehicle while it was in a public place; the device produced evidence of illegal growing of marijuana. Going into a private garage to place the device, or otherwise intruding into a vehicle, would require a warrant, as was the case in the California murder trial of Scott Peterson.

In *United States v. Maynard*, 615 F.3d 544 (C.A.D.C. 2010), the court held that a GPS tracking unit attached to a defendant's vehicle and used to monitor the defendant's movements 24 hours a day for a month violated the Fourth Amendment. The court found that *Knotts* was not controlling, because that case involved the use of a "beeper" to track the single movement of chemicals used in drug from their point of sale to the defendant's home. Because that one-time trip was over public highways, the driver of the vehicle carrying the chemicals had no reasonable expectation of privacy of his participation in the trip.

In *Maynard* the court said an entirely different kind of surveillance was involved. The defendant's movements were monitored for an entire month, and such constant monitoring did violate a reasonable expectation of privacy, the court held. The court believed the circumstances were the sort contemplated by the Supreme Court in *Knotts* when it said "if such dragnet-type law enforcement practices as respondent envisions should eventually occur, there will be time enough then to determine if different constitutional principles may be applicable. *Maynard*, 615 F.3d, at 556.

In *United States v. Jones*, 132 S. Ct. 945 (2012), the Supreme Court affirmed the *Maynard* court's decision. It held that attachment of the GPS device to Jones's car was a search under the Fourth Amendment: "The Government physically occupied private property for the purpose of obtaining information. We have no doubt that such a physical intrusion would have been considered a 'search' within the meaning of the Fourth Amendment when it was adopted." 132 S. Ct. at 949.

The majority opinion in *Jones* reached its decision based on the "common-law trespassory" test for Fourth Amendment violations, rather than the "expectation of privacy" test of *Katz v. United States* (discussed in this chapter). Under the

 DEVELOPMENT OF FOURTH AMENDMENT PROTECTION

It is clear the Fourth Amendment's search warrant requirements were directed to the British practice of issuing "general" warrants that permitted soldiers to invade a colonist's residence or workplace and conduct a general search for evidence of unlawful activity. As a result, for most of this country's existence cases involving violations of the Fourth Amendment focused on police actions that constituted physical trespasses on a citizen's property, mostly real estate. Where such trespasses did not occur, no Fourth Amendment violation was found. Called the "physical intrusion theory," it was exemplified by the decision in *Olmstead v. United States*, 277 U.S. 438 (1928). There, police officers tapped into a defendant's telephone conversations by cutting into a telephone line not on the defendant's property. The court held this was not a Fourth Amendment violation because it did not involve intrusion on the defendant's property.

The physical intrusion theory was challenged in *Katz v. United States*, discussed earlier in this text. There, police placed a warrantless wiretap on a public phone booth and used the taped conversations in the criminal case against the defendant. Under the physical intrusion theory, the wiretap would not be a violation of the Fourth Amendment, since the public phone booth was not the property of the defendant. The Supreme Court in *Katz* held the wiretap was a Fourth Amendment violation, famously saying, "the Fourth Amendment protects people, not places." The *Katz* ruling created the "reasonable expectation of privacy" theory for Fourth Amendment violations, which was generally seen as discrediting the physical intrusion theory.

The majority opinion in *Jones*, by focusing on the "trespass" that occurred when officers placed the GPS device on the defendant's automobile, shows that the physical intrusion theory was not discarded, but only lay dormant. There are now two ways in which a Fourth Amendment violation may occur: a physical trespass, or an invasion of a reasonable expectation of privacy. It remains to be seen where those theories will take Fourth Amendment jurisprudence.

"trespassory" test, a search that violates a private property right violates the Fourth Amendment, the Court said. Since the government agents were trespassing on the defendant's property—his car—when they attached the GPS device, the attachment violated the Fourth Amendment.

The Supreme Court rejected the Government's argument that the decision in *United States v. Knotts* controlled the case. The Court noted that in *Knotts* it held that the *Katz* expectation of privacy test applied, and that persons have no expectation of privacy for information gained while they are on public roads. However, the Court said, the "common law possessory" test did not apply in *Knotts* because the electronic "beeper" used to trace the defendant's movements in that case was placed in the container *before* the container was in the defendant's possession. As a result, no "trespass" occurred. Here, the Court said, a "trespass" did occur when the agents invaded the defendant's private space to install the GPS device, making the "common law trespassory" test applicable. The Court said: "...The *Katz* reasonable-expectation-of-privacy test has been *added to,* not *substituted for,* the common-law trespassory test." *Id*, at 952. (Emphasis in the original).

In concurring opinions several Justices stated they would have decided the case under the "expectation of privacy" test, mainly because many kinds of electronic monitoring can be done without a physical "trespass" to property, which would make the majority test inapplicable. Those justices would have made the decision stand on the extent of the monitoring—28 days—and expectations of privacy people have against such extensive monitoring.

TECHNIQUES OF LAWFUL ELECTRONIC SURVEILLANCE

Not only are telecommunications corporations required by federal law to cooperate in conducting lawfully authorized electronic surveillances, but they are also required to modify their equipment, facilities, and services to ensure that lawful electronic surveillance actually can be performed. The primary techniques of electronic surveillance available to law enforcement agencies are pen registers, trap and trace devices, and interception of the content of the message.

- Pen registers and trap and trace devices are the most frequently used surveillance techniques. They identify calling numbers or dialed numbers (outgoing or incoming). They can trap or lock lines when threatening or harassing calls are made, if necessary.
- Another form of lawful electronic surveillance is identification of outgoing and incoming calls and also the content of messages. The federal government and 45 states permit this technique but only in investigations to obtain evidence of felony offenses, such as kidnapping, extortion, murder, illegal drug trafficking, organized crime, terrorism, and national security matters. Court authorization is granted only when it is shown that the needed evidence cannot be obtained by other means or it is too dangerous to obtain by other means.

Electronic Surveillance and the USA PATRIOT Act

Following the terrorist attacks of 9/11, Congress passed the USA PATRIOT Act. This act has far-reaching provisions that affect both foreign and domestic criminal investigations. It made many changes in the way electronic surveillance is permitted and conducted in such investigations. Although some sections of the act relating to electronic surveillance had a "sunset" provision of December 31, 2005, at which time the sections would terminate, this "sunset" provision has been extended. It is therefore likely that many of the provisions regulating electronic surveillance will stay in force for some time. What follows is a brief summary of the federal laws that regulated electronic surveillance prior to the USA PATRIOT Act and the changes the act made to those laws.

Wiretapping The 1968 federal wiretap law, discussed earlier in this chapter, originally prohibited only the intentional interception of wire (telephone) and oral communications. That law gave various federal officials the power to obtain judicial authorization to conduct wiretaps as part of the investigation of designated crimes. The authorization required a showing that the wiretap was likely to produce information relating to the criminal investigation, that other methods for obtaining the information had failed or were too dangerous, and that the location where the communications were being intercepted was being used in the commission of the crime.

Cell Phones In 1986 the Electronic Communications Privacy Act amended the Federal Wiretapping and Electronic Surveillance Act to make its prohibitions applicable to cellular phones, although it exempted the broadcast portion of cellular conversations. This was changed in 1994 when the Communications Assistance for Law Enforcement Act made the wiretap law's rules applicable to the broadcast portion of cellular phone conversations. (These amended statutes appear at 18 United States Code, section 2510(1).)

E-Mail The 1986 act also extended the prohibition against interceptions to e-mail, though with slightly different rules. For one thing, the statutory exclusionary rule for unlawfully intercepted telephone conversations does not apply to e-mail. Also, an e-mail may be intercepted as part of the investigation of any federal felony and may be procured by a wider range of federal officials. Parts of the 1986 act, generally referred to as the Stored Communications Act, governed law enforcement access to e-mail stored for the recipient by an Internet service provider (ISP). To access a stored e-mail message less than six months old, the government must obtain a search warrant. For older messages, the ISP may be forced to provide access through a subpoena or court order. Under these provisions, it was generally easier for the government to gain access to stored e-mail than to intercept it during transmission.

Other Surveillance It was not clear whether voicemail was covered by the provisions of the amended wiretap act or the more relaxed provisions of the Stored Communications Act. The 1986 act placed some limitations on the use by law enforcement officers of pen registers and trap and trace devices. The U.S. Supreme Court held in *Smith v. Maryland*[27] that the use of these devices does not constitute violation of either the wiretap law or the Fourth Amendment because the devices disclose only the number dialed or received, and a person has no expectation of privacy in such numbers. The 1986 act's limitations on the use of these devices were thus minimal: All that was needed was a court authorization based on a claim by the state or federal official that the information obtained was relevant to an ongoing criminal investigation.[28]

USA PATRIOT Act Changes The PATRIOT Act made several changes to these laws:[29]

- Section 202 of the Act adds violations of the Computer Fraud and Abuse Act to the list of crimes for which interceptions of telephone calls or e-mail may be authorized.
- Section 209 makes it clear that the lesser requirements of the Stored Communications Act apply to government requests to access voicemail.
- Section 210 amends existing law to permit law enforcement officers to use subpoenas to acquire information about persons' Internet use. Previously, such access had been limited to telephone company records.
- Section 212 permits an Internet service provider to volunteer information about a subscriber's communications if the ISP discovers information about an immediate risk of death or serious physical injury.
- Section 216 makes it clear that law enforcement officers may use pen registers or trap and trace devices to obtain certain information from e-mail, such as Internet addresses. It also authorizes the national use of such devices in large-scale investigations, which means law enforcement officers need not seek multiple court orders to use these devices.
- Section 217 allows an ISP to enlist law enforcement help in dealing with a "computer trespasser." Law enforcement officers are permitted to monitor communications to or from the trespasser, but not those of authorized users.

Tactics Used by Suspects to Avoid Electronic Surveillance

To avoid having conversations regarding criminal activities intercepted and used as evidence against them, suspects who are aware of government electronic surveillance try the following tactics:

- *"Walk and talk" meetings to avoid bugged rooms, vehicles, and other types of electronic surveillance:* The suspect talks in the middle of a busy city street with trucks, buses, and cars coming dangerously close on either side. This tactic makes the use of a parabolic directional mike more difficult, and the surrounding noise level interferes with reception to a wire planted on a person cooperating with the government.
- *Use of a series of public or private telephones:* To counteract this tactic, in 1986 the U.S. Congress enacted a federal statute authorizing "roving wiretaps,"[30] which permit authorized law officers to anticipate and follow a suspect using a series of public or private telephones.

Situations Where Court Orders Are Not Required

Overheard Conversations (Plain Hearing) Law enforcement officers may use artificial means of aiding their vision, such as bifocals, binoculars, or telescopes, but they may not use mechanical or electronic listening devices that intrude upon and violate the privacy of another person without a court order.

People who are talking about criminal activity sometimes become careless and do not exercise a right of privacy. We have all been in restaurants, hotel rooms, taverns, airplanes, or other places where we have overheard conversations. If law enforcement officers are where they have a right to be,[31] they may testify in court about statements that they overheard or heard inadvertently. The following cases illustrate.

Examples
- Law enforcement officers were invited into an apartment where they could hear the defendant talking in a loud voice in the next apartment about illegal drug transactions. The conversations were heard without the use of anything but the human ear. Based on this information, the officers obtained a wiretap warrant and then a search warrant. In affirming the defendant's convictions in the 1988 case of *State v. Benton,*[32] the Court held,

    It has widely been recognized, in cases involving apartments and hotel or motel rooms, that ... overhearing of statements does not constitute a search under the Fourth Amendment. This view has been consistently upheld regardless of whether the eavesdropper was positioned in a common hallway of an apartment building, motel or hotel, or in an adjoining motel or hotel room. These cases do not hinge upon the single fact that the defendant is within the confines of his dwelling, but rather rely for their determination upon the conjunction of various facts, including especially the lack of sensory enhancement, the fact that the eavesdropping government agent was lawfully in position to overhear the statements, and that the presence of a person in that place could reasonably be anticipated.

- Law enforcement officers rented the motel room next to the defendants and listened to their conversations as the defendants were having a party and talking in loud voices.[33]
- A federal narcotics agent stood in the hall of an apartment and listened to the loud voices of the defendants within the apartment. Because the apartment door was hanging imperfectly, the officer could also see the defendants through a small crack in the door. The court held that such evidence was admissible because the "conversations [were] knowingly exposed to the public."[34]
- Testimony of what an officer heard coming from a motel room as the officer stood in the motel parking lot was held to be admissible as evidence.[35]
- The defendant's yelling during a telephone conversation was overheard by a law enforcement officer.[36]

Undercover Officers May Testify About What Was Said in Their Presence

All witnesses, including undercover officers, may testify about what was said in their presence unless a privilege exists (husband-wife and so on). The following two U.S. Supreme Court cases illustrate this type of testimony.

Lewis v. United States

United States Supreme Court, 385 U.S. 206, 87 S. Ct. 424 (1966)

An undercover federal narcotics officer was invited into the defendant's home, where the defendant sold narcotics to the officer. In affirming the defendant's conviction and in holding that testimony about what the defendant said and did was properly used as evidence, the U.S. Supreme Court ruled:

A government agent, in the same manner as a private person, may accept an invitation to do business and may enter upon the premises for the very purposes contemplated by the occupant. Of course, this does not mean that, whenever entry is obtained by invitation and the locus is characterized as a place of business, an agent is authorized to conduct a general search for incriminating materials.

Hoffa v. United States

United States Supreme Court, 385 U.S. 293, 87 S. Ct. 408 (1966)

A former union official, James Hoffa, made incriminating statements in the presence of a paid government informer. Testimony about what Hoffa said was permitted as evidence in Hoffa's trial on criminal charges. The U.S. Supreme Court affirmed Hoffa's conviction, holding that no violation occurred of his Sixth Amendment right to confer privately with his attorneys out of the presence of government agents and informers.

Use of Pocket Tape Recorders and the Crime of Bribery The availability of inexpensive pocket tape recorders makes it easy to secretly record conversations. The *Wall Street Journal* reports that secret recordings of conversations are on the rise in the United States.[37]

Federal law allows such secret taping as long as one of the parties to a conversation knows about it. In more than a dozen states, however, the law requires that *all* the parties to a conversation must know about the recording in order to use it as evidence in a civil or criminal trial if no prior court order has been obtained.

Bribery has always presented a problem for law enforcement investigators, whether the case involves a government official seeking to bribe a private citizen or vice versa. The offender will likely deny the wrongdoing, and unless corroborating evidence is available, the word of the victim standing alone may be insufficient evidence to sustain a conviction. The following U.S. Supreme Court case illustrates the usual solution to the problem.

United States v. Caceres

United States Supreme Court, 440 U.S. 741, 99 S. Ct. 1465 (1979)

The defendant was having federal tax problems and offered to bribe a federal tax agent to fix his tax audits. Unknown to the defendant, three of his face-to-face conversations with the IRS agent were recorded by means of a radio transmitter concealed on the agent's person. However, IRS regulation required that prior authorization be obtained before taping, and the tax agent did not obtain the required permission. The U.S. Supreme Court held that the evidence was admissible despite the IRS requirement. The Court referred to and quoted a similar case (*Lopez v. United States*) and stated,

> Nor does the Constitution protect the privacy of individuals in respondent's position. In *Lopez v. United States*, 373 U.S. 427, 439, 83 S. Ct. 1381, 1388, 10 L.Ed.2d 462, we held that the Fourth Amendment provided no protection to an individual against the recording of his statements by the IRS agent to whom he was speaking. In doing so, we repudiated any suggestion that the defendant had a "constitutional right to rely on possible flaws in the agent's memory, or to challenge the agent's credibility without being beset by corroborating evidence that is not susceptible of impeachment," concluding instead that "the risk that petitioner took in offering a bribe to [the IRS agent] fairly included the risk that the offer would be accurately reproduced in court, whether by faultless memory or mechanical recording."

Do Suspects Have a Right of Privacy in Conversations Held in Police Vehicles, Jails, or Other Police Buildings? Suspects and other people do *not* have a right of privacy in police vehicles, jails, or police or sheriff stations. An article in the September 1993 issue of the *FBI Law Enforcement Bulletin* titled "Surreptitious Recording of Suspects' Conversations" points out that the "effective investigative technique" of surreptitiously recording conversations of suspects in such places will be admissible as evidence if the following points are followed:

(1) Because the technique does not amount to "interrogation" for purposes of *Miranda,* it is not necessary to advise suspects of their constitutional rights and obtain a waiver prior to using this technique. (2) To avoid a Sixth Amendment problem, this technique should not be used following the filing of formal charges or the initial appearance in court, unless the conversation does not involve a government actor, the conversation involves a government actor who has assumed the role of a "listening post," or the conversation pertains to a crime other than the one with which the suspect has been charged. (3) Suspects should not be given any specific assurances that their conversations are private.

In the following cases, either the recordings of conversations were held to be admissible or a witness was permitted to testify about what was said:

- Two robbery suspects were arrested, placed in the back seat of a squad car, and left unattended. Before leaving, one of the officers activated a tape recorder on the front seat of the car. Unaware that their conversation was being recorded, the suspects engaged in an extremely incriminating conversation that was used in their criminal trial.[38]
- Perkins was in jail for aggravated assault. Because he was suspected of a murder unrelated to the assault, an undercover officer was placed in the cell with him. During the planning of a prison break, the undercover officer asked Perkins whether he had ever "done" anyone. Perkins then described in detail the murder-for-hire killing he had committed. The testimony of the officer was held admissible by the U.S. Supreme Court.[39]
- An informer was placed in a jail cell with instructions to just listen and not to question his cellmate. The cellmate, who was formally charged with a crime, made incriminating statements. The U.S. Supreme Court affirmed the defendant's conviction, holding that "the defendant must demonstrate that the police and their informant took some action, beyond merely listening."[40]
- A juvenile who was arrested for murder asked to speak with his mother after being given the *Miranda* warnings. The defendant and his mother talked alone in an interrogation room with the door closed. The juvenile admitted his part in the murder, not knowing the conversation was being recorded. In holding that the recording could be used as evidence, the Court held that "no representations or inquiries were made as to privacy or confidentiality" and that "walls have ears."[41]
- During an investigative stop on reasonable suspicion, the police were given consent to search the suspect's car. The two suspects were asked to sit in the back of a police car while the officers searched the car. Not knowing that a tape recorder was turned on, the two suspects made incriminating statements in their conversation while being left alone in the police car. The court held that the statements could be used as evidence against them.[42]

When One Party to a Telephone Conversation Consents to the Police Listening to and/or Recording the Conversation The Federal Wiretapping Act of 1968 provides that a person who is a party to a wire, oral, or electronic communication may intercept such conversation "unless [the interception] is … for the purpose of committing any crime or tortious act."[43]

Therefore, one of the parties to a telephone call may consent to a law enforcement officer listening to or recording the call without disclosing this fact to the other party. Most states follow this rule, although a few states require a court order for this procedure. The following cases illustrate the use of this investigative technique.

Examples
- In a drug investigation, law enforcement officers recorded telephone conversations with the consent of one of the parties to the conversations. The use of the evidence and the conviction were affirmed.[44]
- A cooperative witness consented to the tape recording of telephone conversations with a murder suspect. The tape recording, along with the testimony of an Illinois assistant state's attorney who had listened to the defendant's confession in the telephone conversations, were held to be properly admitted as evidence.[45]
- In a tax fraud investigation, evidence of the tax fraud was obtained by tape-recording a telephone conversation with the consent of one of the parties to the conversations.[46]
- An interpreter listened from an extension telephone while an informant talked in Spanish with a suspected drug dealer. The Supreme Court of Nevada held that the resulting evidence was admissible.[47]

Obtaining Evidence by Use of the Confrontational Telephone Call If the victim of a crime or a witness is cooperative, law enforcement officers may ask the person to telephone a suspect in a *confrontational call.* Such telephone calls must be made before criminal charging. The following cases illustrate situations in which this technique was used successfully.

Examples
- A minor who was a victim of sexual abuse telephoned her stepfather, who made incriminating admissions while unaware that the conversation was being recorded and a law officer was listening. The stepfather's admission corroborated the victim's accusations and led to criminal charging and conviction.[48]
- In a child molestation case, the child's mother telephoned the defendant, who admitted that he had fondled the child. The defendant was charged with child molestation, and the tape recording of the telephone call was used as evidence to obtain a conviction.[49]
- A woman who participated in the armed robberies of convenience stores agreed to telephone Walton, who made incriminating statements not knowing that the conversation was being recorded and that a police officer was listening.[50]
- Minnesota officers investigating a murder went to Wisconsin to talk to a woman who was being used as an alibi. After the woman admitted she was being paid $1,000 for her story, she agreed to telephone the two defendants, who made incriminating statements in conversations that were recorded. The defendants were then charged with murder and convicted in Minnesota. Because Wisconsin is one of the few states where evidence obtained in this manner is not admissible unless a prior court order is obtained, the question before the Minnesota courts was whether Wisconsin law or Minnesota law should be used. The Minnesota Supreme Court affirmed the murder convictions, holding that Minnesota law would be used in a Minnesota murder trial.[51]

Defendants who have been charged with a crime have the right to an attorney, however, and the use of a confrontational call after a defendant has been charged with a crime violates the *Massiah* limitation in most instances (see Chapter 12). The following case is an exception.

Jenkins v. Leonardo Second Circuit Court of Appeals, 991 F.2d 1033 (1993)	After the defendant was charged with rape and was represented by an attorney, he began calling the victim to harass her. The victim contacted the police, who provided her with recording equipment and encouraged her to have the defendant talk about the facts of the crime. During the next telephone call, the recorder was activated, and the defendant made incriminating statements, unaware that his statements were being recorded. The victim testified about the statements, and the recording was used as evidence in the trial, which resulted in the defendant's conviction. The court of appeals held that the defendant waived his right to an attorney when he made such telephone calls to harass the rape victim.

Using Body Wires or Radio Transmitters Undercover officers, informants, or other people are sometimes fitted with "body wires" or radio transmitters for any or all of the following reasons:

- To alert backup officers if the undercover officer or the police agent is in danger or needs assistance
- To keep nearby officers informed about what is being said and the events that are occurring (with informants, this is a method of controlling the informant and preventing double dealing)
- To enable the listening officers to testify in court about what they heard

Federal law permits the use of radio transmitters, as demonstrated by the following U.S. Supreme Court cases. Most states follow the federal rule, but in some states a prior court order must be obtained to permit the use of such evidence in a criminal trial.

On Lee v. United States United States Supreme Court, 343 U.S. 747, 72 S. Ct. 967 (1952)	Federal narcotics agents wired an undercover agent with a small microphone and radio transmitter. The agent then purchased a pound of opium from the defendant after having conversations with the defendant in his laundry and on the streets in New York City. The undercover agent did not testify at the defendant's trial, but one of the federal narcotics agents who overheard the conversations by means of the radio transmitter was permitted to testify about what he heard and saw. In affirming the defendant's conviction and the use of this evidence, the Supreme Court held: "No good reason of public policy occurs to us why the Government should be deprived of the benefit of On Lee's admissions because he made them to a confidante of shady character."

United States v. White United States Supreme Court, 401 U.S. 745, 91 S. Ct. 1122 (1971)	A government informant made a drug buy while federal drug agents listened to the conversations between the informant and the defendant by means of a concealed radio transmitter worn by the informant. At the time of the defendant's trial, the informer could not be located to testify, and the narcotics agents were permitted to testify about what they heard. The Supreme Court affirmed the defendant's conviction and the use of the officers' testimony as evidence, holding that Concededly a police agent who conceals his police connections may write down for official use his conversations with a defendant and testify concerning them, without a warrant authorizing his encounters with the defendant and without otherwise violating

the latter's Fourth Amendment rights. For constitutional purposes, no different result is required if the agent instead of immediately reporting and transcribing his conversations with defendant, either (1) simultaneously records them with electronic equipment which he is carrying on his person, (2) or carries radio equipment which simultaneously transmits the conversations either to recording equipment located elsewhere or to other agents monitoring the transmitting frequency. *On Lee v. United States.* If the conduct and revelations of an agent operating without electronic equipment do not invade the defendant's constitutionally justifiable expectations of privacy, neither does a simultaneous recording of the same conversations made by the agent or by others from transmissions received from the agent to whom the defendant is talking and whose trustworthiness the defendant necessarily risks.

May One Family Member Wiretap and Record Telephone Calls of Another Family Member? Electronic surveillance and wiretapping are governed by Title III of the 1968 Omnibus Crime Control and Safe Streets Act.[52] The Act makes it unlawful for any person to intercept or attempt to intercept any wire, oral, or electronic communication "except as otherwise specifically permitted" by the Act. Willful disclosure of the contents of communications by a person who knows or has reason to know that the information was obtained through an unlawful interception is also forbidden.[53] No exception in federal law permits electronic surveillance or wiretapping by one family member on another. The following cases illustrate.

Examples
- In the case of *Heggy v. Heggy*,[54] a woman sued her former husband and won a money award against him for recording her telephone conversations.
- After a mother used a microcassette device attached to an extension telephone and recorded conversations between her son and a drug dealer, she turned the recordings over to the police. The recordings were used to obtain a search warrant. In holding that the search warrant was invalid, the North Carolina court cited *Rickenbaker v. Rickenbaker.*[55]
- A California man recorded telephone conversations between his wife and her lover. The husband was then murdered, and his wife and her lover were convicted of the murder; the telephone recordings were used as evidence. The California Supreme Court reversed the convictions following the majority rule, holding that because the recordings were unlawful, they could not be used as evidence.[56]

In discussing listening in on an extension telephone and wiretapping, the Supreme Court of California said,

The differences between casually overhearing part of a conversation on an extension phone and intentionally wiretapping all incoming and outgoing calls are substantial;

In sum, we follow a majority of the courts in declining to read into Title III an exception for interspousal or domestic wiretapping. Neither the text, the history nor the purposes of Title III permit the conclusion that defendants' conversations were lawfully intercepted.

Appraising the Reliability of Informants' Tips

Both search warrants and arrests require the existence of probable cause; that evidence of a crime will be found in the search, or that the person to be arrested has committed a crime. In a great many cases, the required probable cause comes from

PROCEDURES & PROCESSES

Obtaining Evidence by Overhearing, Monitoring, and/or Recording Statements or Conversations

Law enforcement officers sometimes hear or record highly incriminating statements, or private citizens overhear or otherwise monitor conversations. If statements made in such monitored conversations are admitted as evidence in criminal cases, they can have a powerful effect on the judge or jury finding the facts, because the defendant's own words can be used to incriminate him, without the presence of the police. The following examples present the circumstances under which such evidence may be admitted in criminal cases:

Evidence Obtained	Requirements	Evidence Inadmissible
Overheard conversations (plain hearing) in public or private place	The officer must be where he or she has the right to be and cannot use any mechanical or electronic listening device.	Evidence is not admissible if there is violation of right to privacy or trespass—for example, by going on another person's property to listen to conversations.
Statements made to undercover officers or others in their presence	The suspect may not already have been charged with crime and the questions relate to that crime.	Some states have laws prohibiting the use of tape recordings of such conversations.
Tape recordings where the suspect has no expectation of privacy (police vehicles, jail cells, etc.)	See the Massiah rule (Chapter 12) where statements are made in response to questions after a crime has been charged.	Assuring suspects that conversations are private can render statements inadmissible.
Consent by one party to telephone conversation to the police recording or listening to the conversation	Consent by one party is sufficient, but the *Massiah* rule prohibits the police from using the conversation to ask questions about crimes charged.	This is permitted under federal law, but some states require consent by all parties to conversation (e.g., Conn. Gen. Stat. 55-570(d)).
"Confrontational" telephone call or face-to-face meeting with suspect	If the call or meeting is made by the police, the *Massiah* rule applies.	Such call or meeting is not permitted in states that require both parties' consent to record telephone conversations.

tips from an informant. The same is true for satisfying the reasonable suspicion requirement for investigative stops. Before such a tip can satisfy the probable cause or reasonable suspicion requirement, it must be shown to have some reliability.

The December 2003 issue of the *FBI Law Enforcement Bulletin* includes an article titled "When an Informant's Tip Gives Officers Probable Cause to Arrest Drug Traffickers." The article's author provides standards for police officers to use in appraising the reliability of information obtained from informants.

- *The concerned citizen:* "If a concerned citizen is known to the police, he [or she] is presumed credible." "To be considered a concerned citizen informant by the courts, an informant must not be involved in the criminal milieu [environment or setting]." This standard does not apply to the credibility of statements like "The bank was just robbed." Such statements should be investigated immediately to determine the accuracy of the statement.

- *Corroboration of information:* "Once an officer corroborates innocent future conduct of the suspect as predicted by the informant, it would be reasonable for the officer to conclude that the informant is being accurate regarding the suspect's involvement in the alleged crime."

- *Information given to seek a benefit or made against the penal interest of the informant:* "An informant could be considered credible even if he [or she] does not have a track record for reliability, if he [or she] made a statement against his [or her] penal interest, or if it can be established that he has a strong motive to be truthful. It is reasonable to believe that an informant has a motive to be truthful when he [or she] is expecting some leniency for pending [criminal] charges and the circumstances suggest that any benefit expected by him [or her] would only inure to him if the information supplied is accurate." An example of a statement against penal interest is "Joe Smith is a crack dealer. I buy crack from him every day, including last night." Because the statement exposes the speaker to criminal prosecution, which could result in a prison sentence, it is against his penal interest. The fact that he nonetheless made the statement is a sign of its truthfulness.

- *How much corroborating evidence is needed?* "The degree of corroboration necessary to establish probable cause is dependent on the credibility and basis of knowledge of the informant." The "basis of knowledge" looks to how the informant acquired the information the informant provides to an officer. Was the informant a party to the crime? Was he a witness to the crime? Is it first-hand knowledge or hearsay? Is it "hearsay on hearsay," just "street talk," or a rumor? Depending on the basis for an informant's information, an officer may or may not have probable cause to take additional action.

anonymous tip A tip given to police about criminal activity by a person unknown to the police.

If police receive an **anonymous tip** and then through investigation corroborate the tip, a *Terry* stop can be justified. For example, in *United States v. Bullock*, 632 F.3d 1004 (7th Cir. 2011), police received an anonymous tip that a person known as "Quick" was selling drugs out of a residence. Officers used police files to identify the defendant as "Quick," observed him frequently entering and exiting the premises, and observed him exhibiting behavior that was common in drug deals. The court upheld the *Terry* stop, and after other evidence that provided probable cause to arrest the defendant was found in the residence, the court held the police conducted a valid search of the defendant, which uncovered illegal drugs on his person.

Where the "tip" is not anonymous and the identity of the tipster is known to the police, information given by the tipster is often held sufficient to satisfy the reasonable suspicion requirement for a *Terry* stop. In *United States v. Griffin*, 589 F.3d 148 (4th Cir. 2009), *cert. denied*, 131 S. Ct. 1599 (2011), the court upheld a *Terry* stop based on a tip from an identified person. The Court said such tips have greater reliability because the officer can evaluate the demeanor of the tipster, and the tipster can be held accountable if the tip was false. The Court also said the search of the defendant's automobile during the *Terry* stop, which turned up a pistol, was justified based on the officer's reasonable concern for his own safety. The Court said the holding in *Arizona v. Gant* (discussed in Chapter 14) did not apply, because the defendant had not been arrested, and when permitted to leave after a brief detention could easily access any weapons in his automobile. The defendant's conviction for being a felon in possession of a firearm was affirmed.

PROCEDURES & PROCESSES

Admissible Evidence Resulting From Informants' Tips

Informants come from all walks of life. Private citizens may contact the police or call 911 with information regarding a crime. Other informants are persons who could be involved in crime and are providing information for money or to avoid a long prison term.

Some informants are known to law officers and have provided reliable information in the past. Other callers remain anonymous. A caller who is reporting drug or other criminal activity by a neighbor may fear retaliation if his or her identity is disclosed. Some anonymous calls are maliciously made to harm another person or to harass the police. Police must respond to 911 calls, however, because as the court stated in the case of *United States v. Holloway*, 290 F.3d 1331 at 1339, *cert. denied,* 123 S. Ct. 966 (2003), "If law enforcement could not rely on information conveyed by anonymous 911 callers, their ability to respond effectively to emergency situations would be severely curtailed."

Much of the information from informants is of no or little value to a law enforcement agency. Some information, however, could start an investigation that results in curtailing serious criminal activity. Other information could establish reasonable suspicion to make an investigative stop of a person or vehicle. Information from an informant could also establish probable cause to make an arrest or to obtain a search warrant.

Tips from Known Informants

Case and Crime	Type of Tip	Additional Information and Action by Law Officers
Draper v. United States, 79 S. Ct. 329 (1959) drug peddler	Known paid informer who had provided accurate and reliable information in the past	Detailed information corroborated by federal agents, justified arrest
McCray v. Illinois, 87 S. Ct. 1056 (1967) drug trafficking	Specific information from known, reliable informant	"Officers did rely in good faith upon credible information by reliable informant," justified arrest
Adams v. Williams, 92 S. Ct. 1921 (1972) concealed weapon and possession of drugs	"Given in person by known informant who had provided information in the past"	"Carried sufficient indicia of reliability to justify forcible stop." Protective search revealed illegal weapon; search incident to arrest resulted in finding illegal drugs

Anonymous Tips

In *Alabama v. White*, 110 S. Ct. 2412 (1990) the U.S. Supreme Court stated,

> Unlike a tip from a known informant, whose reputation can be assessed and who can be held responsible if her allegations turn out to be fabricated, an anonymous tip alone seldom demonstrates the informant's basis of knowledge or veracity.

In the following cases the Supreme Court evaluated the reliability of an anonymous tip used to satisfy the probable cause or reasonable suspicion requirements:

Case and Crime	Type of Tip	Was Sufficient Indicia of Reliability Shown?
Illinois v. Gates, 103 S. Ct. 2317 (1983) trafficking in drugs	An Illinois police department received handwritten letter telling how Mr. and Mrs. Gates (address given) were buying and selling drugs out of their home. The letter stated detailed facts and information.	Yes, extensive police investigation corroborated major portions of the letter, causing an Illinois judge to issue search warrant for the Gates's home and car, where drugs were found. Convictions affirmed.
Alabama v. White, 110 S. Ct. 2412 (1990) possession of cocaine and marijuana	Police received an anonymous tip asserting that woman was carrying cocaine and predicting that she would leave an apartment building at specific time, get into car matching particular description, and drive to named motel.	Yes, the Court held that the informant's knowledge about the defendant's future movements, when confirmed, showed some familiarity with the person's affairs, and gave the tip sufficient reliability. The Court did say it was a "close" case.
Florida v. J. L., 120 S. Ct. 1375 (2000) illegal possession of firearm (minor)	An anonymous caller reported to the police that a young black male standing at particular bus stop and wearing plaid shirt was carrying gun. Six minutes later, officers arrived at the bus stop and saw J. L. but did not see firearm. J. L. made no threatening or otherwise unusual movements. A frisk revealed a concealed weapon.	No, the Court held that "all the police had to go on in this case was the bare report of an unknown, unaccountable informant who neither explained how he knew about the gun nor supplied any basis for believing he had inside information about J. L."
Navarette v. California, 134 S. Ct. 1683 (2014)	An anonymous caller to a 911 operator reported that a few minutes earlier a car ran her off the road. She described the car, and police stopped defendant's car that matched the description. A search revealed illegal drugs.	Yes. The court said that (1) the person reporting the acts was an eyewitness, since it was her car the other car ran off the road, and (2) the short time between the incident and the call gave little time for fabrication of the report. Conviction affirmed.

OBTAINING EVIDENCE BY THE USE OF DOGS TRAINED TO INDICATE AN ALERT

Dogs have a sense of smell that is reported to be several thousand times stronger than the average human's. For years, dogs have been used to pursue fugitives, locate escaped convicts, find missing persons, detect drugs and explosives, and, in recent years, identify suspects in a lineup.

Drug and bomb detection dogs have become a common and very effective tool used by law enforcement agencies throughout the United States. It is now common practice for trained dogs to be used to "sniff" suspicious luggage or vehicles for evidence of drugs or explosives. When the dog smells the substance it is trained to find, it "alerts," usually by sitting down at the strongest point where it smelled the

Dogs trained to "alert" when they smell illegal drugs are used by U.S. Customs agents to search for such drugs in containers brought across U.S. borders. The use of dog detection evidence in court is dependent on up-to-date records verifying the dog's reliability.

substance. The dog's handler, based on the dog's training, can then interpret the dog's behavior as showing evidence of the substance.

When a dog sniff occurs, one question that arose early on was whether or not the dog's actions constituted a "search" for purposes of the Fourth Amendment. The initial answers given by the U. S. Supreme Court held it was not a search. In *United States v. Place*, the U.S. Supreme Court held that luggage exposed to a trained drug detection dog in a public place "did not constitute a search within the meaning of the Fourth Amendment." [57] The Court reasoned that since the dog was trained to alert only to the presence of illegal drugs, the owner of the luggage had no reasonable expectation of privacy for illegal drugs.

In *Illinois v. Caballes* the U.S. Supreme Court considered the constitutionality of dog sniffs during a routine traffic stop.

Illinois v. Caballes United States Supreme Court, 125 S. Ct. 834 (2005)	An Illinois state trooper stopped Caballes for speeding on an interstate highway. When the trooper called in to report the stop, an officer in the Illinois State Police Drug Interdiction Team overheard the call and went to the scene with his drug detection dog. While Caballes sat in the first trooper's car, the dog sniffed the exterior of his vehicle and alerted at its trunk. The entire stop and sniff lasted about 10 minutes. A subsequent search turned up marijuana in the trunk, and Caballes was arrested and charged with drug violations. At his trial, he moved to suppress the drugs, contending that the dog sniff and resulting search were unconstitutional. The trial court denied the motion, and Caballes was convicted. On appeal, the Illinois Supreme Court reversed, holding that because the dog sniff was based on no "specific and articulable facts" suggesting illegal drug activity, the use of the dog was unjustified. The U.S. Supreme Court granted certiorari on the precise question of "Whether the Fourth Amendment requires reasonable, articulable suspicion to justify using a drug detection dog to sniff a vehicle during a legitimate traffic stop."

The Court answered that question in the negative. After noting that the total duration of the traffic stop and dog sniff was less than 10 minutes, the Court concluded that the detention of Caballes was lawful. In response to the opinion of the Illinois Supreme Court that the dog sniff turned the detention into an unlawful drug investigation without articulable, reasonable suspicion, the Court said,

> In our view, conducting a dog sniff would not change the character of a traffic stop that is lawful at its inception and otherwise executed in a reasonable manner, unless the dog sniff itself infringed respondent's constitutionally protected interest in privacy. Our cases hold that it did not.

The Court noted that in *United States v. Place* (discussed more fully in note 57 of this chapter) it held that because the alert of a well-trained drug detection dog discloses only illegal contraband, no legitimate expectation of privacy is violated. In contrast, devices like the thermal-imaging device whose use was held to be an unlawful search in *Kyllo v. United States* (discussed earlier in this chapter) had the potential to disclose "intimate details in the home," the Court reasoned. Because the traffic stop was lawful and the detention pursuant to that stop reasonable, conducting the dog sniff did not itself infringe on any constitutionally protected privacy interest: "a dog sniff conducted during a concededly lawful traffic stop that reveals no information other than the location of a substance that no individual has any right to possess does not violate the Fourth Amendment."

Justice Souter dissented, contending that the assumption upon which *Place* was based was wrong. He noted that since *Place* was decided, studies have shown that even experienced drug detection dogs give false positives. He cited K. Garner et al., *Duty Cycle of the Detector Dog: A Baseline Study* (April 2001), which stated that the error rate for dog alerts is from 12 to 60 percent, depending on the length of the search. Because of that, Justice Souter was of the opinion that using such dogs incident to a simple traffic stop was an unauthorized search.

Both *Place* and *Caballes* were decided under the *Katz* reasonable expectation of privacy test. One does not have a reasonable expectation of privacy to possess illegal contraband. Those cases thus stand for the proposition that *if the dog is in a place where it is entitled to be* a resulting sniff is not a search for purposes of the Fourth Amendment.

In the 2013 case of *Florida v. Jardines*, 133 S. Ct. 1409, the Supreme Court held that when police, without a search warrant or probable cause, enter a defendant's premises with a police dog and bring the dog to the front door for the purpose of a dog sniff, their actions constitute a search under the Fourth Amendment. Thus, when the dog alerted and the police used the alert as the basis for a search warrant, the search warrant was illegal because the initial search upon which it was issued was illegal, the Court held.

The Court was careful to make it clear the basis of its decision, like the decision in the *Jones* case discussed earlier in this chapter, was the physical intrusion by the officers for the purpose of investigating the defendant's premises. As in *Jones*, it was the physical intrusion, not the violation of a legitimate expectation of privacy, which constituted the Fourth Amendment violation:

> Thus, we need not decide whether the officers' investigation of Jardines's home violated his expectation of privacy under *Katz*. One virtue of the Fourth Amendment's property-rights baseline is that it keeps easy cases easy. That the officers learned what they learned

only by physically intruding on Jardines's property to gather evidence is enough to establish that a search occurred.[58]

It is important to stress that *Jardines* did not change the rule that dog sniffs by themselves do not constitute searches under the Fourth Amendment. It was not the character of the instrumentality used by the police that was the problem in *Jardines*. Rather, it was the fact the police made an unwanted, uninvited physical intrusion on the defendant's premises to use the instrument (the dog) that constituted the violation.

Assuming that a dog sniff did not occur under circumstances that were themselves violations (e.g., unlawful physical intrusion, or traffic stop without reasonable suspicion), police may use the dog sniff as the basis for a search warrant, or as probable cause to search a vehicle in a traffic stop. The dog's alert, like an informant's tip, must have some evidence of reliability in order to satisfy the probable cause requirement.

In the 2013 case of *Florida v. Harris*, 133 S. Ct. 1050, the Supreme Court rejected a rigid, strict method of determining a drug dog's reliability adopted by the Florida Supreme Court. That court had required the state to meet a checklist of reliability factors before a dog's alert could be sufficient probable cause to support a warrant or a search. The Supreme Court said such an inflexible approach was inconsistent with the "totality of circumstances" approach used in assessing probable cause in other contexts. Rather, the Court said, satisfactory participation by the dog and its trainer in a state training and certification program should be sufficient to make it reasonable for an officer to rely on a dog's alert. The Court said,

> The question—similar to every inquiry into probable cause—is whether all the facts surrounding a dog's alert, viewed through the lens of common sense, would make a reasonably prudent person believe a search would reveal contraband or evidence of a crime. A sniff is up to snuff when it meets that test.[59]

When dog detection evidence is used in criminal courts, keeping and maintaining updated records on the dog and its handler are helpful to establishing the dog's reliability. Dog detection handlers should be prepared to establish the reliability of the dog by testimony regarding

- The training that the dog received to detect the odors of particular drugs
- The dog's success rate in detecting these drugs
- The method used to train the dog to indicate an alert
- Whether the dog alerted in the proper manner
- Proof of the dog's certification
- Proof that the dog has continued to meet certification requirements and has continued to receive necessary training on a regular basis

Where drug detection dogs are used in a valid traffic stop, police need not have probable cause to believe drugs may be found on the vehicle. However, if the lawful stop or detention goes beyond a reasonable time, police must have independent cause or suspicion to extend the detention. What constitutes a reasonable time depends on the circumstances. A normal traffic stop should extend only for the time needed to check the driver's license and registration, conduct a computer check for outstanding warrants, and gather other general information about the driver. Certainly a detention for 10 or 15 minutes would usually be reasonable. If a drug dog can be brought to the site of the detention within that period, the resulting sniff should be reasonable. Longer detentions may be justified. For example, in *United States v. McBride*, 676 F.3d 385 (4th Cir. 2012), the court upheld a detention of a vehicle for 55 minutes while a drug detection dog was brought to the site of the detention. The court said that the wait was reasonable because the vehicle detained was in a parking lot of a nightclub, and the driver was not in the vehicle during the detention. Unlike the agents in *Place*, who failed to diligently request the drug dog's presence, the officer here acted as quickly as he could to obtain the dog's presence, the court said.

SUMMARY

1. **List the various types of search warrants and their requirements.**
   - All search warrants must be issued based on probable cause. The general rule is that warrants be executed during daylight hours, and officers must knock and announce their presence. No-knock or nighttime warrants may be issued where officers show good cause that knocking or executing the warrant in daylight may increase risk for the officers, or result in the destruction of evidence. "Sneak-and-peek" warrants must be supported by probable cause and have a limited objective, such as placing a listening device in a residence. Administrative searches pursuant to administrative search warrants conducted by administrative agencies to enforce state regulations are permitted with a more relaxed probable cause requirement. The legitimate public interest that underlies the regulation serves as the basis for probable cause.

2. **Assuming officers are entitled to look at a computer's files, what are the limits on that examination?**
   - If consent to search was given, the search must conform to the terms of the consent. Where a search warrant authorized the search, many courts hold officers may open files, including those whose names do not connect directly to the subject of the search, to determine if they contain material covered by the warrant. In such case, if the officers see evidence of a crime, such as child pornography, the "plain view" doctrine makes that evidence admissible. Some courts have developed procedures designed to limit either the extent to which all computer files may be opened, or the use of the "plain view" doctrine to permit the discovery of criminal evidence in opened files.

3. **List some circumstances where officers may hear or record statements without the need for a court order.**
   - Statements made in a public place, statements made voluntarily to an undercover officer, statements made in police vehicles or station house rooms (except where speaking to an attorney), and statements made over a telephone to a person who consents to permitting an officer to listen to the statements may be listened to without a court order.

4. **State the difference in terms of reliability and the need for a search or arrest warrant between a known informant and an anonymous informant.**
   - Generally, information in an anonymous tip is not sufficient by itself to justify an arrest or search. Because the informant is not known, officers must obtain corroborating evidence showing the information in the tip to be reliable. Where the informant is known, and has been reliable in the past, the tip alone can serve as the basis for an arrest or search.

5. **State the rules on the police use of trained dogs to "sniff" a vehicle, residence or luggage.**
   - Dogs may "sniff" a vehicle lawfully stopped by officers, so long as doing so does not make the stop unreasonably long or difficult. Luggage in a public place, such as an airport, may be sniffed by drug-detection dogs. Dogs may not be brought onto private premises and used to sniff a residence without probable cause to believe illegal drugs may be found in the residence. An "alert" by a drug-detection dog may serve as probable cause to make a further search, so long as the dog has been tested and found to be reliable.

KEY TERMS

anonymous tip, 410   electronic surveillance, 396   wiretapping, 396

KEY CASES

California v. Riley, 134 S. Ct. 2473 (2014): Police must obtain a warrant before searching the contents of a cell phone seized during a lawful arrest.

Florida v. Harris, 133 S. Ct. 1050 (2013): The reliability of using a drug dog sniff to satisfy probable cause depends on the totality of the circumstances. Normally, the fact that the dog performed satisfactorily in a certified training program is enough to satisfy the reliability requirement.

Florida v. Jardines, 133 S. Ct. 1409 (2013): An uninvited physical intrusion by a police officer with a drug detection dog into a person's residence with the purpose of conducting a sniff is an unlawful search.

Groh v. Ramirez, 540 U.S. 551 (2004): A search warrant must state with particularity the place to be searched and the items to be seized.

Illinois v. Caballes, 125 S. Ct. 834 (2005): A drug-detection dog sniff by itself is not a violation of the Fourth Amendment.

Jones v. United States, 132 S. Ct. 945 (2012): Attachment of a GPS device to a suspect's car by police constituted a physical intrusion in violation of the Fourth Amendment.

Kyllo v. United States, 533 U.S. 27 (2001): Use of thermal-imaging device to view activity in residence requires a search warrant.

Payton v. United States, 455 U.S. 573 (1980): A search inside a residence is presumptively unreasonable without a warrant or under an established exception to the warrant requirement.

United States v. Banks, 540 U.S. 31 (2003): Exigent circumstances can make no-knock and forced entry searches pursuant to a search warrant reasonable.

United States v. Comprehensive Drug Testing, Inc., 621 F.3d 1162 (9th Cir. 2010): Leading case on view that the "plain view" doctrine should be limited in computer searches.

United States v. Grubbs, 547 U.S. 90 (2006): Anticipatory search warrants are not per se unreasonable.

United States v. Knotts, 460 U.S. 276 (1985): Attachment of GPS device to vehicle on public roads is not a search, if done without a physical intrusion into the vehicle.

PROBLEMS

1. Most states have wiretapping statutes modeled after the federal wiretap law, 18 U.S.C.A. § 2510. These laws typically have provisions limiting the use of information gained by a prohibited "interception" of a "wire, oral, or electronic" communication. In *Hentz v. State*, 62 So.3d 1184 (Fla. App. 2011), the court considered the application of the Florida act to a cell phone conversation that took place between a suspect in a police interview room and another suspect not held by the police. What was the "interception," and why did it violate the act?

2. As the text notes, the "plain view" doctrine is often used to justify the admission of evidence of crimes discovered when officers "look" inside a computer file pursuant to a search warrant or in another lawful manner. Because cell phones, in particular smartphones, have video storage capability, many of the computer search rules are applicable to searches of cell phones. In a prosecution for possession of child pornography found on a cell phone, what must the defendant prove to avoid the "plain view" doctrine? What mistakes did the defendant make in the case of *Deaver v. State*, 314 S.W. 3d 481 (Tex. App. 2010)?

3. In *Florida v. J. L*, discussed in this chapter, the U.S. Supreme Court appears to say that anonymous tips are not sufficient to justify police searching or arresting a suspect. However, as the discussion of that case showed, the ruling in the case was carefully tailored to the facts. It is

not uncommon for police to receive anonymous tips that an identified vehicle (such as one identified through the license number) is being driven by a drunk driver. These tips often are received by cell phone calls to 911 operators. May police locate the identified vehicle, stop it based on the tip, and give a sobriety test to the driver? Based on what the Supreme Court said in *Florida v. J. L*, what might be some justifications for such a stop? (See *State v. Elliott*, 35 So. 3d 247 (La. 2010).)

4. As noted in the text, some controversy exists among state courts on whether dog sniffs are searches, in particular when the sniff is not of a vehicle (as was the case in *Illinois v. Caballes*, the U.S. Supreme Court decision on this subject discussed in this chapter). How did the Minnesota court deal with this problem in *State v. Carter*, 697 N.W.2d 199 (Minn. 2005), where a drug-detection dog sniffed a storage locker and alerted to illegal drugs? What do you see as the advantages and disadvantages of the decision?

CASE ANALYSIS

Read Appendix B, Finding and Analyzing Cases (p. 499). With these guidelines in mind, please continue with the Case Analysis selections for Chapter 15.

When the police use searches or surveillance techniques that raise Fourth Amendment concerns, an initial question must usually be answered: Did the person claiming the protection of the Fourth Amendment have an expectation of privacy that was invaded by the police actions? The following cases involve determinations of that expectation of privacy in marginal cases.

1. *Jardines* held a warrantless attachment of a GPS device to a suspect's car was a search, and a violation of property rights of the car's owner protected by the Fourth Amendment. What about passengers in a car to which a GPS device had been attached without a warrant? In *United States v. Davis*, 750 F.3d 1186 (10th Cir. 2014), police suspected Baker to be involved in various armed robberies in the Kansas City area. They attached a GPS device to Baker's car, and monitored the car's position. When the device indicated the car was near the place of a recent armed robbery, police stopped the car and searched it, finding evidence that implicated a passenger, Davis, in the robbery. At his trial, Davis moved to suppress the evidence obtained in the stop and search, contending it was derived from the illegal attachment of the GPS device. Should the evidence be suppressed? How is the passenger's status different here from cases where a traffic stop is not supported by reasonable suspicion?

2. Assume police officers obtain a search warrant based on evidence a defendant had what a witness believed were automatic weapons in his home. The witness saw the "guns" in a hall closet in the defendant's home. The witness was reliable. Officers executed the warrant by first searching the hall closet. They discovered the "guns" were not automatic weapons, but BB guns. The police then searched other parts of the house, and found actual weapons and illegal drugs. At his trial on drug and weapons charges the defendant moved to suppress the evidence found during the search of his home. Should the evidence be suppressed? *See State v. Schulz*, 55 A.3d 933 (N.H. 2012).

3. Could police officers obtain an anticipatory search warrant authorizing a search of a house where, after knocking on doors at random, the police officer was able to execute a "controlled" buy of illegal drugs? Why does *United States v. Grubbs*, discussed in this chapter, say no to that question? What would be wrong with the search warrant's "triggering" condition? Assume an informant reliably told police he saw the owner of a house sell drugs from his car in a public parking lot. Can an anticipatory search warrant be lawfully issued under those circumstances? *See Commonwealth v. Wallace*, 42 A.3d 1040 (Pa. 2012).

4. The decision in *United States v. Jones* no doubt came as a surprise to law enforcement officers. Most decisions before *Jones* had held that attachment of GPS devices and "beepers" to cars were not searches under the Fourth Amendment. In Chapter 10 of this text we

discuss the "good faith" exception to the exclusionary rule, including the decision in *Davis v. United States*, where the U.S. Supreme Court applied the good faith exception to a search based on then-applicable case law that was subsequently overruled. Does the good faith exception apply to GPS searches? That is, for the many cases where officers attached GPS

devices without a warrant because of prevailing belief that such attachments were not searches, does the good faith exception make evidence obtained from the GPS trackers admissible? Should it? In *United States v. Katzin*, 732 F.3d 187 (3rd Cir. 2013), a panel of Third Circuit judges said no. In May 2014 the Third Circuit agreed to an *en banc* review of the issue.

Notes

1. *Payton v. New York,* 445 U.S. 573 (1980).
2. The U.S. Supreme Court has repeatedly held that searches "without prior approval by a judge ... are per se unreasonable under the Fourth Amendment—subject only to a few specifically established and well-delineated exceptions." *Coolidge v. New Hampshire,* 91 S. Ct. 2022 (1971). Therefore, evidence obtained as a result of an unreasonable search is suppressed and may not be used.
3. The U.S. Supreme Court held in the case of *United States v. Leon*, 104 S. Ct. 3405 (1984), that "the courts must also insist that the magistrate purport to perform his neutral and detached function and not serve merely as a rubber stamp for the police."
4. 131 S. Ct. 326 (2001).
5. 90 S. Ct. 1029 (1970).
6. 500 N.W.2d 547 (Nebr. 1993).
7. 379 F.3d 1203 (10th Cir. 2004), *cert. denied,* 125 S. Ct. 1390 (2005).
8. 434 F.3d 669 (4th Cir. 2006), *cert. denied,* 127 S. Ct. 2286 (2007).
9. The U.S. Supreme Court defined "controlled delivery" in the 1983 case of *Illinois v. Andreas*, 463 U.S. 765, 103 S. Ct. 3319, and affirmed the manner in which the law enforcement officers acted: Controlled deliveries of contraband apparently serve a useful function in law enforcement. They most ordinarily occur when a carrier, usually an airline, unexpectedly discovers what seems to be contraband while inspecting luggage to learn the identity of its owner, or when the contraband falls out of a broken or damaged piece of luggage, or when the carrier exercises its inspection privilege because some suspicious circumstance has caused concern that it may unwittingly be transporting contraband. Frequently, after such a discovery, law enforcement agents restore the contraband to its container, then close or reseal the container, and authorize the carrier to deliver the container to its owner. When the owner appears to take delivery he is arrested and the container with the contraband is seized and then searched a second time for the contraband known to be there.

10. 547 U.S. at 95; citations omitted.
11. *Id.*
12. 547 U.S. at 97–98.
13. Federal Rule of Criminal Procedure 41 requires that a covert entry under a sneak-and-peek warrant be followed within seven days by notice to the person whose property has been entered. However, cases where this was not done include *United States v. Pangburn*, 983 F.2d 449, 52 CrL 1417 (2d Cir. 1993), and *United States v. Freitas*, 800 F.2d 1451 (9th Cir. 1986).
14. 441 U.S. 238, 99 S. Ct. 1682.
15. 389 U.S. 523 (1967).
16. See "Crackdown on Violations of Fire Code: Arresting New Yorkers Who Ignore Citations" (June 11, 2008).
17. 172 F.3d 1268 (10th Cir. 1999).
18. 275 F.3d 981 (10th Cir. 2001).
19. 590 F.2d 535 (4th Cir. 1978).
20. 375 F.3d 679 (8th Cir. 2004), *vacated on other grounds*, 543 U.S. 1112 (2005).
21. 305 F.3d 1193 (10th Cir. 2002).
22. 134 S. Ct. 2473 (2014).
23. 88 S. Ct. 507.
24. Title 18 of the Omnibus Crime Control and Safe Streets Act of 1968 (18 U.S.C. § 2510).
25. In footnote 1 of the case of *Dalia v. United States*, 441 U.S. 238, 99 S. Ct. 1682 (1979), the U.S. Supreme Court stated the difference between wiretapping and bugging:

    All types of electronic surveillance have the same purpose and effect: the secret interception of communications. As the Court set forth in *Berger v. New York,* 388 U.S. 41 (1967), however, this surveillance is performed in two quite different ways. Some surveillance is performed by "wiretapping," which is confined to the interception of communication by telephone and telegraph and generally may be performed from outside the premises to be monitored. At issue in the present case is the form of surveillance commonly known as "bugging," which includes the interception of all oral communication in a given location. Unlike wiretapping, this interception typically is accomplished by installation of a small microphone in the room to be bugged and transmission to some nearby receiver.

The issue before the U.S. Supreme Court in *Dalia* was whether a separate court order was necessary to authorize the FBI to enter an office building to place a listening device and then, several weeks later, to enter again at night to remove the device. The majority held that court orders were not necessary.

26. 476 U.S. 207 (1986).

27. 442 U.S. 735 (1979).

28. 18 U.S.C. § 3123(a)(2000).

29. A detailed discussion of these changes is found in Robert A. Pikowsky, *An Overview of the Law of Electronic Surveillance Post September 11*, 94 Law Libr. J. 601 (2002).

30. 18 U.S.C.A. § 2518 (11).

31. The word *eavesdropping* is an old English word meaning "to sneak under the eaves of a home and listen to conversations within the home." This conduct was forbidden under old English law and is forbidden under present law. See the case of *State of Texas v. Gonzales*, 388 F.2d 145 (5th Cir. 1968), where law officers sneaked into the defendant's yard at night and listened to conversations in the house. Because the defendant's Fourth Amendment right of privacy was violated, the evidence obtained was suppressed.

32. 10 Conn. App. 7, 521 A.2d 204 (1987), *review denied*, 486 U.S. 1056, 108 S. Ct. 2823.

33. *United States v. Fisch*, 474 F.2d 1071 (9th Cir. 1973), *review denied*, 412 U.S. 921, 93 S. Ct. 2742 (1973); *United States v. Jackson*, 588 F.2d 1046 (5th Cir. 1979).

34. *United States v. Llanes*, 398 F.2d 880 (2d Cir. 1968).

35. *Ponce v. Craven*, 409 F.2d 621 (9th Cir. 1969).

36. *Pappas v. Municipality of Anchorage*, 698 P.2d 1236 (Alaska App. 1985).

37. See the article "Secret Taping of Supervisors Is on the Rise, Lawyers Say" (*Wall Street Journal*, November 3, 1992), p. B1. The article points out that labor lawyers report an increase in secret taping of supervisors by employees seeking to protect their jobs in a tight labor market.

38. *Stanley v. Wainwright*, 604 F.2d 379 (5th Cir. 1979), *review denied*, 100 S. Ct. 3019 (1980).

39. *Illinois v. Perkins*, 496 U.S. 292, 110 S. Ct. 2394 (1990).

40. *Kuhlmann v. Wilson*, 477 U.S. 436, 106 S. Ct. 2616 (1986).

41. *Ahmad A. v. Superior Court*, 263 Cal. Rptr. 747 (1989), *review denied*, 498 U.S. 834, 111 S. Ct. 102 (1990).

42. *State v. Fedorchenko*, 630 So.2d 213 (Fla. App. 1993).

43. 18 U.S.C.A. § 2511(2)(d).

44. *State v. Kedoranian*, 828 P.2d 45 (Wash. App. 1992).

45. *People v. Griffin*, 592 N.E.2d 930 (1ll. App. 1992). Illinois law requires a prior court order for one-party consent to the monitoring of a private conversation through the use of an eavesdropping device.

While investigating an arson, Illinois police officers listened to a telephone conversation between Shinkle (one of the wrongdoers) and a man who admitted to committing the arson and who allowed the police to listen to the conversation. The police officer picked up an extension phone and placed his hand over the mouthpiece. Shinkle made incriminating statements that were used to convict him. The Illinois Supreme Court held that the extension phone did not become an eavesdropping device because the officer cupped his hand over the mouthpiece in the 1989 case of *People v. Shinkle* (539 N.E.2d 1238, 45 CrL 2211).

46. *United States v. Dale*, 991 F.2d 819 (D.C. Cir. 1993).

47. *State v. Reyes*, 808 P.2d 544 (Nev. 1991).

48. *State v. Allgood*, 831 P.2d 1290 (Ariz. App. 1992).

49. *Lawrence v. State*, 393 S.E.2d 475 (Ga. App. 1990).

50. *State v. Walton*, 809 P.2d 81 (Ore. 1991).

51. *State v. Lucas*, 372 N.W.2d 731 (Minn. 1985).

52. 18 U.S.C.A. § 2510–21.

53. 18 U.S.C.A. § 2511(1)(c).

54. 944 F.2d 1537 (10th Cir.), *review denied*, 112 S. Ct. 1574 (1992).

55. *State v. Shaw*, 404 S.E.2d 887, 49 CrL 1340 (N.C. App. 1991); *Rickenbaker v. Rickenbaker*, 226 S.E.2d 347 (N.C. 1976).

56. *People v. Otto*, 831 P.2d 1178 (Calif. 1992), *review denied*, U.S. 113 S. Ct. 414 (1992).

57. 462 U.S. 696 (1983). The U.S. Supreme Court pointed out that a dog's sniff is nonintrusive and reveals only the presence of illegal drugs. Place was not required to open his luggage and expose his personal belongings to public view. The Supreme Court reversed Place's conviction not because of the dog sniff, but because the 90-minute wait for the arrival of the dog at the airport was held to be too long to be reasonable; the officers did not act with due diligence.

A 90-minute detention based on reasonable suspicion has been held to be reasonable in cases where officers acted with due diligence to get a dog to the scene. In the case of *United States v. $ 64,765.00*, 786 F.Supp. 906 (Ore. 1991), the officers' efforts and diligence in getting a dog to the scene caused the court to rule that the delay was reasonable under the circumstances.

58. 133 S. Ct. at 1413.

59. 133 S. Ct. at 1058.

CHAPTER 16

The Crime Scene, the Chain of Custody Requirement, and the Use of Fingerprints and Trace Evidence

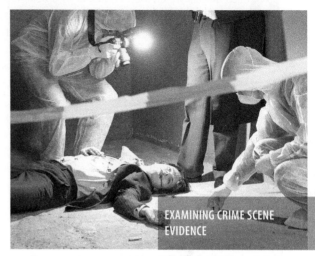

EXAMINING CRIME SCENE EVIDENCE

© Corepics VOF/Shutterstock.com

CHAPTER CONTENTS

Obtaining Evidence from a Crime Scene

The Chain of Custody Requirement

Fingerprints as Evidence

Trace Evidence: The Smallest Things Can Make the Biggest Difference

Other Types of Evidence

LEARNING OBJECTIVES

In this chapter we examine the rules that permit law enforcement officers to obtain evidence from crime scenes and arrests, and how that evidence must be maintained—the "chain of custody" requirement. The learning objectives for this chapter are

Identify the requirements for a warrantless search under the "exigent circumstances" exception.

State the "standing" requirement for objection to search of a crime scene.

List the steps for establishing the chain of custody for evidence found at a crime scene.

State some ways to show that fingerprints taken from a crime scene were left at the scene when the crime occurred.

Compare fingerprint and bite mark evidence to shoe prints and tire tracks.

Police officers were called to a bank by a bank teller reporting a robbery. The police entered the bank and found two female tellers on the floor in the vault room, with their hands and feet bound by plastic zip ties. One officer used a knife to cut the zip ties to free the tellers. The ties remained on the floor until a crime scene technician picked them up several hours later. The ties were bagged, marked, and sent to the police lab for DNA testing. The DNA test results were compared to DNA tests on the defendant, who was a suspect in the case. The tests matched, and the defendant was charged with bank robbery.

At his trial the defendant moved to exclude all the DNA evidence, contending it had been compromised by faulty chain of custody procedures used by the police—mainly that the police erred by leaving the ties on the bank floor for hours without protecting them from contamination. Did the police use a proper chain of custody to preserve the zip ties? If not, should the DNA evidence be excluded? *United States v. Brooks*, 727 F.3d 1291 (10th Cir. 2013), *cert. denied* 134 S. Ct. 835 (2013).

OBTAINING EVIDENCE FROM A CRIME SCENE

Crimes occur in both public and private places. If a crime occurs on a street or sidewalk or in premises open to the public, such as a tavern or store, law officers do not have to show authority such as consent, a search warrant, or an exigency to justify their entry.

When a crime occurs in a private place, such as a home, apartment, office, or factory, law enforcement officers most often enter with the consent of victims, family members, or someone who has control of the premises. Two other situations also confer authority to enter:

- Exigency is where a person's life or safety is endangered: where there is concern for an elderly person or another person; or where a shooting, fire, or explosion has occurred. (See Chapter 14 for cases and the law about exigent entry into private premises.)
- Search warrants are usually necessary to enter premises where there is probable cause to believe that nonemergency crimes have occurred or are occurring (such as drug houses or places where nonviolent crimes are believed to be taking place).

crime scene A location where an illegal act took place and from which law enforcement personnel collect physical evidence.

Law enforcement officers may stay in a **crime scene** for a reasonable period of time to perform whatever tasks they are obligated to do. The question of how long officers may stay on the premises was addressed in the following 1978 case, where the U.S. Supreme Court held that there was no "murder scene exception" to the Fourth Amendment of the U.S. Constitution.

Mincey v. Arizona

United States Supreme Court, 437 U.S.385, 98 S. Ct. 2408 (1978)

In a drug raid of the defendant's apartment in Tucson, Arizona, Officer Headricks was shot and later died. Police officers seized the apartment and held it for four days. The U.S. Supreme Court described the police search as follows:

Their search lasted four days, during which period the entire apartment was searched, photographed, and diagrammed. The officers opened drawers, closets, and cupboards, and inspected their contents; they emptied clothing pockets; they dug bullet fragments out of the walls and floors; they pulled up sections of the carpet and removed them for examination. Every item in the apartment was closely examined and inventoried, and 200 to 300 objects were seized. In short, Mincey's apartment was subjected to an exhaustive and intrusive search. No warrant was ever obtained.

In reversing the defendant's convictions and ordering a new trial, the Court held

In sum, we hold that the "murder scene exception" created by the Arizona Supreme Court is inconsistent with the Fourth and Fourteenth Amendments—that the warrantless search of Mincey's apartment was not constitutionally permissible simply because a homicide had recently occurred there.

What Can Police Search for in Premises Where a Serious Crime Has Recently Occurred?

Police may not, simply because they are present in a home or other building because a serious crime occurred there, conduct an investigatory search of the house or building. However, under some circumstances police may make a limited search of premises in which a serious crime has occurred.

In the *Mincey* case discussed above, the U.S. Supreme Court decided what police may search for in premises where a serious crime has recently occurred. The Court held that law enforcement officers may make "warrantless entries and searches when they reasonably believe that a person within is in need of immediate aid" (**emergency situations**). The Court stated,

emergency situation
A serious and often dangerous situation that requires immediate action, such as "hot pursuit," "now or never," or emergency aid.

- Law officers "may make a prompt warrantless search of the area to see if there are other victims or if a killer is still on the premises...."
- The police "may seize any evidence that is in plain view during the course of their legitimate emergency activities."[1]

In holding that the police search in the *Mincey* case went too far and exceeded the limits of "emergency activities," the Court held:[2]

But a warrantless search must be "strictly circumscribed by the exigencies which justify its initiation," Terry *v. Ohio,* 392 U.S., at 25–26, 88 S. Ct., at 1882, and it simply cannot be contended that this search was justified by any emergency threatening life or limb. All the persons in Mincey's apartment had been located before the investigating homicide officers arrived there and began their search. And a four-day search that included opening dresser drawers and ripping up carpets can hardly be rationalized in terms of the legitimate concerns that justify an emergency search.

The duration of a search made at a crime scene is a factor in determining the reasonableness of the search. Thus, a search lasting 16 hours was held unreasonable in *Flippo v. United States,* 528 U.S. 11 (1999), and a search of 2 hours was held unreasonable in *Thompson v. Louisiana,* 469 U.S. 17 (1984). In both cases the Supreme Court concluded the searches were not limited to looking for "other victims or if a killer is still on the premises," but instead were general searches for evidence of a crime. Where that is the purpose of the search, the officers were required to obtain a search warrant.

When Can Police Search Premises They Have Entered Lawfully?

In *Maryland v. Buie,*[3] the U.S. Supreme Court identified three circumstances where officers may make warrantless searches of premises. First, incident to a lawful arrest, police officers may search the area into which the arrestee might reach in order to grab a weapon or destroy evidence. Second, officers may make a cursory search of the immediate area near the site of the arrest for places a person might be hiding. Third, officers who have lawfully entered a residence may conduct a "protective sweep" of the residence if they reasonably believe that a person posing a threat to the police is on the premises. Any evidence found in plain view during such a sweep is admissible. The sweep must be limited in location and duration, but courts do not require that police have any specific reason to fear that a particular person remains inside the premises. For example, in the 2008 case of *United States v. Mata,*[4] the court upheld a protective search of a repair shop where illegal drugs were known to be stored. Although the police had no reason to expect that a particular person was hiding in the shop, the sweep was justified on the grounds that the police knew that a large amount of illegal drugs had just gone into the shop and that the people there were "keeping an eye out" for law enforcement officers.

A protective sweep is permissible only when police officers have "lawfully entered" a residence. Some courts have limited "lawfully entered" to mean only entering to make an arrest inside a residence. (See *United States v. Torres-Castro*, 470 F.3d 992 (10th Cir. 2006), *cert. denied* 550 U.S. 949 (2007).) Most courts, however, have held that "lawfully entered" includes other reasons for being inside the residence, such as consent or exigent circumstances. In those situations, officers may conduct a protective sweep if, after entry, they have a reasonable belief a person posing a threat is on the premises. (See *United States v. Martin*, 413 F.3d 139 (1st Cir. 2005), *cert. denied* 546 U.S. 1011 (2005).)

A protective sweep is not permitted if police officers do not lawfully enter a residence. In *United States v. Hassock*, 631 F.3d 79 (2d Cir. 2011), federal agents believed the defendant was staying in a bedroom of a private residence. They went to the residence to do a "walk and talk," but the defendant did not answer the door. When a woman answered, officers entered the residence, found the defendant with a firearm in his possession, and arrested him. At a motion to suppress the firearm, the agents stated they conducted a protective sweep and found the firearm. The trial court and court of appeals both held the protective sweep was unreasonable. They held that the voluntary decision by the agents to enter the residence "created the risk" that served as the justification for a protective sweep, not some "lawful" purpose which made the sweep necessary: "But a protective sweep is reasonable only to safeguard officers in the pursuit of an otherwise legitimate purpose. Where no other purpose is being pursued, a sweep is no different from any other search, and, therefore, requires a warrant, exigent circumstances, or authorized consent, none of which were present here." 631 F.3d, at 88.

Obtaining Evidence After a "Hot-Pursuit" Entry into Private Premises

The following U.S. Supreme Court cases state the law about the admissibility of evidence obtained by police in lawful "hot-pursuit" entries into homes.[5]

Warden, Md. Penitentiary v. Hayden

United States Supreme Court, 387 U.S. 294, 87 S. Ct. 1642 (1967)

Immediately after the defendant robbed a Baltimore cab company, his flight was observed by two cab drivers, who reported that he entered a nearby home. Within minutes, police arrived at the home. Having been given a description of the defendant, they requested entrance, and when Mrs. Hayden offered no objections, the police began a search of the home for the defendant. Before the police found Hayden in the home, they found a pistol in a toilet flush tank that was running, and ammunition for the pistol was found under the mattress of Hayden's bed. A shotgun was found, and ammunition for it was found in a bureau drawer. Clothing similar to the type worn by the fleeing felon was found in a washing machine. All the seized items were used as evidence. In affirming the use of the evidence and the conviction of the defendant, the Court held

> They [the police] acted reasonably when they entered the house and began to search for a man of the description they had been given and for weapons which he had used in the robbery or might be used against them. The Fourth Amendment does not require police officers to delay in the course of an investigation if to do so would gravely endanger their lives or the lives of others. Speed here was essential, and only a thorough search of the house for persons and weapons could have insured that Hayden was the only man present and that the police had control of all weapons which could be used against them or to effect an escape.
>
> The permissible scope of search must, therefore, at the least, be as broad as may reasonably be necessary to prevent the dangers that the suspect at large in the house may resist or escape.

United States v. Santana

United States Supreme Court, 427 U.S. 38, 96 S. Ct. 2406 (1976)

In a "buy-and-bust" operation, a police informant bought heroin from Santana and paid for it in marked money. Police officers then had probable cause to arrest Santana. The officers went to Santana's home and identified themselves to the defendant as she stood in her doorway. When the defendant retreated into the house, the officers pursued her and caught her in the vestibule of the home. In a subsequent search, police found additional evidence of illegal drug transactions. Santana successfully moved to suppress the evidence found in the search, contending that the entry into her home was not justified. In holding that the arrest and the evidence obtained in the search incident to the arrest were lawful, the Supreme Court reversed the lower court's ruling suppressing that evidence and held,

> The only remaining question is whether her act of retreating into her house could thwart an otherwise proper arrest. We hold that it could not. In *Warden v. Hayden,* 387 U.S. 294, 87 S. Ct. 1642 (1967), we recognized the right of police, who had probable cause to believe that an armed robber had entered a house a few minutes before, to make a warrantless entry to arrest the robber and to search for weapons. This case, involving a true "hot pursuit," is clearly governed by *Warden*; the need to act quickly here is even greater than in that case while the intrusion is much less. The District Court was correct in concluding that "hot pursuit" means some sort of a chase, but it need not be an extended hue and cry "in and about [the] public streets." The fact that the pursuit here ended almost as soon as it began did not render it any the less a "hot pursuit" sufficient to justify the warrantless entry into Santana's house. Once Santana saw the police, there was likewise a realistic expectation that any delay would result in destruction of evidence. Once she had been arrested the search, incident to that arrest, which produced the drugs and money was clearly justified.
>
> We thus conclude that a suspect may not defeat an arrest which has been set in motion in a public place, and is therefore proper under *Watson v. United States,* 96 S. Ct. 820 (1976), by the expedient of escaping to a private place.

Obtaining Evidence in Now-or-Never Exigency Situations

An exigency exists if law officers have no time to obtain a search warrant and have probable cause to believe that evidence will be destroyed or moved to an unknown place. The burden is on the law officers to show that a now-or-never situation exists; that is, the police must show that they needed to act immediately or else they would lose the opportunity to seize the evidence because it would be destroyed or moved to an unknown place.

In the case of *Schmerber v. California*,[6] the defendant was involved in a car accident where both he and others were injured. Police had probable cause to believe that Schmerber was driving while intoxicated. Because the human body quickly destroys evidence of intoxication and the police did not have time to obtain a search warrant for intoxication evidence within Schmerber's body, police believed a now-or-never situation existed.

The U.S. Supreme Court held in the *Schmerber* case that, because there was no time to obtain a search warrant, immediate action was required by law officers to obtain and preserve evidence of intoxication by obtaining blood or breath for testing and use as evidence. The court noted there had already been a substantial delay caused by the need to get the defendant to a hospital for treatment, and thus the required exigent circumstances existed to have a hospital physician obtain a blood sample. However, as we discussed in Chapter 14, in the 2013 case of *Missouri v. McNeeley*,[7] the Supreme Court was careful to say that while metabolization of alcohol can in some circumstances support a warrantless blood draw, there is no categorical rule that metabolization is always enough by itself to support such a result.

All states have now passed an implied consent law: Drivers who use the highways imply their consent to such tests if probable cause exists to believe that the driver is operating a motor vehicle while intoxicated. Failure to consent to testing under such circumstances is a crime.

In the following case, the U.S. Supreme Court held that a now-or-never entry into an apartment was lawful to seize illegal drugs as evidence.

Ker v. California

United States Supreme Court, 374 U.S. 23, 83 S. Ct. 1623 (1963)

Law enforcement officers observed Ker make a large illegal drug buy from a drug dealer. They followed Ker's car but lost it in traffic when Ker made a sudden turn. Believing that Ker knew that he was being followed, the officers then obtained the address of Ker's apartment from his automobile license number. When Ker's car was found parked at his apartment, the officers obtained a key to his apartment from the apartment manager. Believing that evidence would be destroyed if they made an entry by knocking, the officers used the key to make a no-knock entry into Ker's apartment. In holding that the officers' testimony sustained an exception to the California "knock" requirement, the Supreme Court affirmed the defendant's conviction and the use of the narcotics seized as evidence in Ker's trial, holding,

> Here ... the criteria under California law clearly include an exception to the notice requirement where exigent circumstances are present.
>
> Here justification for the officers' failure to give notice is uniquely present. In addition to the officers' belief that Ker was in possession of narcotics, which could be quickly and easily destroyed, Ker's furtive conduct in eluding them shortly before the arrest was ground for the belief that he might well have been expecting the police. We therefore hold that in the particular circumstances of this case the officers'

> method of entry, sanctioned by the law of California, was not unreasonable under the standards of the Fourth Amendment as applied to the States through the Fourteenth Amendment.

Obtaining Evidence in Emergency Aid Situations

Thousands of emergency aid cases have come before U.S. courts.[8] Evidence found when police are responding to an emergency may be used in criminal trials. The courts sustained police action in the following examples:

Examples

- To aid physicians who are treating a person suffering from a drug overdose, police may search for the substance the person took and seize it to assist in the person's treatment. In the case of *State v. Follett,*[9] police arrested a driver who was under the influence of some substance. Police could search for and seize the substance the person took (cocaine) to aid the treating physician and to use as evidence. This also has been done in attempted suicides.
- The Supreme Court of Delaware held that when police receive a report indicating that emergency aid might be needed, "it was the duty of the police to act forthwith upon the report of the emergency—not to speculate upon the accuracy of the report or upon legal technicalities regarding search warrants."[10]
- An injured driver left the scene of a vehicle accident and was traced by a police officer to his home. When the officer observed the man through a window lying on a bed unconscious and bleeding, an emergency entry into the home was authorized. Evidence of drunk driving was then lawfully obtained.[11]
- Police had reasonable suspicion to stop cars leaving an area where shots were heard. In the 1993 case of *United States v. Reedy,*[12] a citizen told the police of the gunshots; in the 1992 case of *Williamson v. United States*[13] a police officer heard the shots fired. Evidence obtained in the car stops could be used.

Obtaining Scent Evidence from the Crime Scene

Crime scenes differ greatly, depending on the type of crime committed and the setting in which the crime occurred. Some crime scenes, such as the location of a drive-by shooting, may yield little physical evidence, whereas others, like a residential or rural setting of homicide or rape, might yield many types of physical evidence.

DNA evidence is reported to be available in only about 10 percent of the scenes of violent felonies, and where that evidence is available, other kinds of physical evidence, such as fingerprints, blood spatters, and other bodily fluids, are also likely to be found. In a large number of crime scenes, however, these kinds of evidence are not present, which makes the identification of the perpetrator more difficult.

One method of identifying a suspect is through the use of scent evidence. Although scent evidence is not always available, if the crime scene holds clothing a suspect has touched or worn, particularly if worn close to the body, or if blood or other bodily fluids are found, then a trained tracking dog can be used to follow the scent of a suspect and lead law enforcement officers to the suspect.

An example of the use of scent evidence is found in the 2007 case of *State v. St. John.*[14] There, a masked man wearing a knit cap robbed a convenience store at gunpoint. The robber was seen running from the store and taking off his mask and cap.

Police quickly arrived at the store with a tracking dog, which sniffed the scent from the cap and followed the scent to a location about a mile away where the police had detained a suspect. A witness from the store observed the suspect in a showup and stated that she was "pretty sure" he was the robber. At the man's trial, the tracking dog's trainer testified that the dog went directly from the store to the defendant, the dog following the scent the whole way, and when the dog approached the defendant, the dog jumped on the defendant's chest, as the dog was trained to do to indicate the source of the scent. This evidence corroborated the identification evidence, and the defendant was convicted of armed robbery.

A trained dog can use scent evidence to

1. Follow the trail of a suspect from the crime scene, where objects dropped might be found, footprints or tire tracks discovered, or witnesses found who may have seen the fleeing suspect.
2. Identify a suspect in a "scent" lineup. In the 2006 case of *Risher v. State,*[15] a trained bloodhound used a "scent pad" from a brick of cocaine discarded by the driver of a car during a police chase to identify the driver in a scent lineup as the person who had touched the cocaine. Evidence showed that the dog had participated in 74 scent lineups and had identified the person whose scent was on a scent pad in 63 cases. The dog had never made a false identification.
3. Place a suspect at or near the scene of the crime.
4. Establish probable cause to make an arrest or obtain a search warrant. In the 2004 case of *Fitzgerald v. State,*[16] the Maryland Supreme Court held that an alert outside a defendant's apartment by a dog trained to sniff marijuana was sufficient probable cause to obtain a search warrant.
5. Locate a missing person, who might be a hostage or dead. Specially trained "cadaver" dogs can be used to find a body or confirm that a body was once at a particular location. In the 2007 case of *Trejos v. State,*[17] evidence that two trained cadaver dogs alerted to a spot where a body of a murder victim that had never been found but had been buried and later moved was admitted to corroborate other evidence that the defendant had murdered the victim.

Defendants Must Have Standing to Challenge the Use of Evidence Obtained from Crime Scenes

To have *standing* and challenge the manner in which police obtained evidence from a crime scene, a defendant must show that he or she had a legitimate expectation of privacy in the crime scene.

A burglar who illegally entered a home has no legitimate expectation or right of privacy in the home and therefore no standing to challenge evidence against him that police obtained from the home. The following cases illustrate:

Examples

*   Michael Perry was convicted of five murders and sentenced to death. Among the murder victims were his mother and father, who had their own home, which the defendant could not enter without the consent of his parents and in which he had no belongings. In the 1986 case of *State v. Perry,*[18] the Supreme Court of Louisiana held, "There was no living person who had a privacy interest in the house at 810 Seventh Street." (Defendant had killed all of the occupants of the house.) "Therefore the entries of the house were not in violation of anyone's privacy interest."

THE CRIME OF OBSTRUCTING, ALTERING, RIGGING, OR ENGINEERING A CRIME SCENE TO MISLEAD INVESTIGATORS

Law officers are called to investigate serious accidents, deaths, shootings, and fires, and to render aid for serious injuries. In such cases, whether or not the area investigated is a "crime scene" depends on the officers' determination of whether a crime occurred. Where they have suspicion a crime occurred, the area becomes a suspected "crime scene."

It is a crime (often a misdemeanor) in all states for a person to obstruct a law enforcement officer in pursuit of an investigation. (See e.g., R.C.W.A. §9A.76.020 (Wash).) In most states it is a felony to tamper with evidence, including evidence at a crime scene. (See e.g., Ohio R.C. § 2921.12.) Persons who have committed crimes may attempt to alter the crime scene to mislead investigators. Ways of altering or rigging crime scenes include

Staging the Crime Scene to Cause Confusion

An offender might attempt to "stage" the crime scene to lead investigators in the wrong direction. In *People v. Jackson*, 165 Cal. Rptr. 3d 70 (Cal App. 2013), the defendant, the murder victim's husband, killed his wife at their residence. He then dressed the victim in running clothes, put her in the trunk of her car, and drove the car to an area near a beach. He took the victim's credit cards and purse, and left her in the locked trunk, hoping to convince police the murder was a crime of opportunity committed while the victim was running at the beach. At his murder trial a former FBI agent who worked with the FBI's Behavioral Science Unit (the profiling unit) testified as an expert for the prosecution. The former agent showed how the physical facts staged at the beach did not comport with the behavior of an opportunistic killer who has committed either a sexual assault crime or a crime for financial gain. The husband's murder conviction was affirmed.

Altering Crime Scenes by Destroying Evidence

Alteration of physical evidence left at a crime scene, such as blood, fingerprints, or other bodily fluids from which DNA may be extracted, is a crime. In *State v. Hardger*, 2008 WL 4724692, a defendant was convicted under the Ohio tampering statute when he forced a rape victim to scrape her fingernails to remove any skin tissue that could be used to identify the defendant's DNA. Moving a murder victim by propping the victim in a car and driving from the murder scene was ground for conviction under the New York tampering law. (See *People v. Nicholas*, 417 N.Y.S.2d 495 (1979).) Flushing methamphetamine down a toilet constituted a violation of the Montana tampering statute in *State v. Nalder*, 37 P.3d 661 (Mont. 2001).

Rigging a Crime Scene

Arsonists often attempt to make a fire appear to be accidental, such as by a malfunctioning electrical or heating system. Investigators at a fire look at the "fire triangle"–oxygen, fuel source, and heat source—to determine the cause of the fire. Thus, while a rigged electrical box could be the heat source, evidence that windows were opened to supply more oxygen, or that the heat source had been accelerated by other substances, could prove the fire had been rigged. Murders can be rigged to look like suicides. In September 2011 a group of forensic scientists concluded that the junior welterweight champion boxer Arturo Gatti did not hang himself in 2009, as the crime scene was made to look, but was in fact murdered. Injuries to the back of Gatti's head, and the weight-bearing ability of the leather strap found around his neck, did not support the finding that Gatti hanged himself, the experts said.

The Discovery That DNA Evidence Can Be Faked

Investigators now believe it is easier to plant false DNA at a crime scene than it is to plant false fingerprints, based on a 2009 study conducted by Israeli scientists. The results of the study, reported in an August 18, 2009, article in the *New York Times* titled "Scientists Show That It's Possible to Create Fake DNA Evidence," demonstrated that fake DNA can be created two ways. One way is to take DNA from an innocent person and then amplify the sample into a larger sample, using standard technology. Another method is to "clone" DNA from tiny snippets of DNA profiles in a DNA database, representing the common variants at the key 13 spots in the human genome, and then amplifying the clone.

- In a Tennessee case, the defendant's girlfriend was murdered in a house that the defendant had built for her, to which he possessed a key and in which he occasionally stayed overnight. The defendant lived elsewhere, however, and the victim paid for the building supplies used to build the home. The defendant was charged with the murder and challenged the evidence the police had obtained from the victim's home, which was going to be used against him. The Tennessee courts held that the defendant did not have standing to challenge the use of the evidence because he was only a casual visitor who had no right to exclude others from the premises and he had insufficient interest to object to the search that turned up the evidence.[19]

Protecting and Searching a Crime Scene

Testimony of a trained law enforcement officer about the observations and findings from a crime scene is vitally important in many criminal cases. Improper protection of a crime scene could result in the contamination, loss, or unnecessary movement of physical evidence.[20] Therefore, the first officer to arrive at the scene of the crime automatically incurs the serious and critical responsibility of securing the crime scene from unauthorized intrusions. Even though the officer who arrives first will also search it for physical evidence, it is most important that the officer immediately take precautions to protect the scene.

To prove that evidence is genuine and authentic and to show that the object is what it is claimed to be, a witness in court must be able to

- Testify about where and how the object was obtained.
- Identify the object by a serial number if a serial number is on the object. For example, a handgun probably has a serial number, and the gun would be identified in this manner.
- Identify the object based on personal knowledge and observations. This could be done by an officer scratching his or her initials and the date on the object to make it readily identifiable.[21] A *chain of custody* (see below) is not needed if the object is positively identified at trial and the evidence is not susceptible to tampering, contamination, substitution, or mistake.[22]
- Testify about the chain of custody. "If the evidence is not readily identifiable or is susceptible to alteration by tampering, substitution, or contamination, the party must establish a chain of custody; in this event, the chain of custody must be of sufficient completeness to render it improbable that the evidence has been tampered with or substituted."[23]

Crime Scenes Are No Place for a Crowd

A Michigan forensic scientist asked many of his fellow technicians to name the biggest problem on the job. The same answer came from technicians around the country: "crime scenes contaminated by curious officers, detectives, and supervisors."[24] The technician wrote the following description of the problems caused by "pointless tourism":

Lost Evidence, Lost Opportunities

Widespread trampling of crime scenes can prove very damaging to investigations. Often, it results in several of the more sensitive forensic techniques—such as trace analysis, bloodspatter interpretation, and DNA comparison—not being used to their fullest potential. Crime scene technicians know the futility of collecting hair or fiber samples after a roomful of officers have shed all over the scene. Footwear and tire track evidence is rarely recognized as valuable in departments where officers routinely wander unimpeded through crime scenes. On occasion, this can seriously hamper investigations.

Not long ago, a sheriff's department was forced to conduct a mass fingerprinting of its detective unit after a particularly sensational homicide crime scene became overrun with curious personnel. Considerable time and effort went into eliminating officers' fingerprints from the pool of legitimate prints. In another case involving a different agency, a set of crime scene photographs showed supervisory personnel standing on a blood-soaked carpet.

THE CHAIN OF CUSTODY REQUIREMENT

To use physical evidence in a criminal or civil trial, the party offering the evidence has the burden of proving that the evidence is genuine and authentic. This requires testimony establishing an adequate foundation about where and how the object was obtained and that the object offered in evidence is the object that it is claimed to be.

chain of custody The set of procedures that accounts for the integrity of evidence by tracking its handling and storage from the time it was obtained to the time it is offered at trial.

If the evidence (such as fingerprints or illegal drugs) could be subject to alteration by tampering, substitution, or contamination, a **chain of custody** must be shown. All persons who had possession of the evidence must appear as witnesses to testify that the fingerprints or illegal drugs have not been tampered with, substituted, or contaminated while each witness had custody and control of the evidence. For evidence that requires a chain of custody, it is therefore best that as few people as possible come in contact with the evidence.

Besides illegal drugs and fingerprints (regular and DNA), courts have held that chains of custody must be presented for the use of the following as evidence: videotapes,[25] a crack pipe,[26] a suitcase full of marijuana,[27] forensic evidence,[28] a shell casing,[29] blood samples,[30] a note found next to the murder victim,[31] human hair and fibers from carpet,[32] semen and blood,[33] a forged check,[34] specimens from a human body,[35] and the body of the murder victim.[36]

Failing to Show a Sufficient Chain of Custody

To use evidence that could be subject to tampering, substitution, or contamination, the state must, by the use of witnesses, establish a chain of custody to "show a reasonable probability that the [evidence] was not tampered with."[37] In the following examples, the state did *not* prove a sufficient chain of custody for critical evidence in criminal cases.[38]

Examples
- A rape victim identified her panties and blouse in the criminal trial. The semen and bloodstains on the panties and the wool fiber on the blouse seriously incriminated the defendant, but there was no showing about where the clothing was during the time between the commission of the crime and the trial. The Supreme Court of Virginia reversed the defendant's conviction of rape and remanded for a new trial in the case of *Robinson v. Commonwealth.*[39]
- In an illegal drug prosecution the court reversed and remanded for a new trial because the state did not show where the cocaine used as evidence was or how it was kept for a period of 20 days.[40]

- A gap in the chain of custody between the seizure of drugs and the vouching for them at the police station caused reversal for a new trial in the 1993 case of *People v. Rivera.*[41]
- Failure of the drug-testing laboratory to complete the chain of custody form for a urine sample caused reversal for a new trial.[42]

Situations That Do Not Require a Chain of Custody

A chain of custody is *not* required if the object to be used as evidence is not subject to alteration by tampering, substitution, or contamination.

Examples

- A chain of custody is not required in most shoplifting and theft cases. The Supreme Court of Nebraska held that a chain of custody was not required in the shoplifting case of *State v. Sexton.*[43]
- A pistol was held to be admissible without showing a chain of custody (no fingerprint or ballistics testimony) in the 1991 case of *Outland v. State.*[44]
- Twenty-two silver dollars stolen from a pawnshop were admitted for use in evidence, although the victim could not specifically identify them as the silver dollars stolen. In affirming the defendant's conviction, the court in the 1991 case of *State v. Simmons*[45] stated:

> The court does not need a positive and indisputable description of the object in order to admit it into evidence. *Gresham v. State,* 456 P.2d 119 (Okla. 1969). Lack of positive identification goes to weight, not admissibility. (See also *State v. Amaya-Ruiz,* 166 Ariz. 152, 800 P.2d 1260 (1990), *cert. denied,* 111 S. Ct. 2044, 114 L.Ed.2d 129 (1991); *State v. Skelton,* 129 Ariz. 181, 629 P.2d 1017 (App. 1981); *State v. Baker,* 219 Kan. 854, 549 P.2d 911 (1976); *Young v. State,* 701 P.2d 415 (Okla. 1985); *State v. Mitchell,* 56 Wash. App. 610, 784 P.2d 568 (1990).) Further, because of the physical nature of coins and currency, to sufficiently identify the money to make it admissible as relevant evidence, it is not necessary that the witness identify each bill or coin separately, rather, the witness may testify that the money appears to be the same money alleged to have been stolen after considering its amount, denomination, packaging, and general appearance.

Managing the Crime Scene, Chain of Custody, and Scientific Evidence

Physical evidence obtained from a crime scene can be a valuable tool for investigators. But when it comes to introduction of such evidence at a criminal trial, it must be remembered such evidence is circumstantial, and must be carefully connected to a defendant charged with a crime. Careful management of the crime scene to preserve evidence, accurately recording the chain of custody of evidence found at the scene, and proper use of scientific expert testimony are vital to the admissibility of such evidence. In the Casey Anthony murder trial, which received intense national coverage, failures by the prosecution in all three areas were the likely cause of a not guilty verdict.

Caylee Anthony went missing in June of 2008. Six months later her decomposed body was discovered in a wooded area near her home. Her mother, Casey Anthony, was arrested and charged with murder. Investigators believed Casey used chloroform and duct tape to asphyxiate Caylee. While Casey gave several contradictory answers to questions about Caylee's disappearance, ultimately the defense theory was that Caylee accidently drowned and Casey's father buried her to hide her death.

Literally hundreds of exhibits were introduced, but the main evidence for the prosecution was a strand of hair found in the trunk of Casey's car, duct tape found at the crime scene where Caylee's body was discovered, and scientific evidence about DNA and "air sampling tests for decomposition" in the car trunk. Whatever strength this circumstantial evidence might have had was weakened by problems with the evidence. They included the following:

Crime Scene The forensic pathologist could not unequivocally state the cause of death, due to the decomposition of the body. Duct tape was found at the crime scene, which the prosecution contended was attached to the skull over the nose and mouth openings, showing asphyxiation as the cause of death. However, some crime scene photos showed the duct tape on the skull, and others showed the tape alongside the skull. The discrepancy supported witnesses who testified they believed the tape was attached to the skull to hold the jaw together after the body was found.

The Chain of Custody Scrapings from the trunk carpet, wheel well, and spare tire were sent to an expert to test them for evidence of decomposition. The expert's opinion was challenged in part by the defense based on the prosecution's failure to show who collected and transmitted the scrapes, and how and when they were transmitted to the expert for testimony.

Scientific Evidence The scientific evidence introduced by the prosecution was faulty. First, a strand of hair found in the car trunk was submitted for DNA analysis to show it came from Caylee. However, the prosecution did not conduct nuclear DNA testing, which could point virtually exclusively to one person as the source of the hair sample, but instead performed mitochondrial (mtDNA) testing, which could only show that the hair sample came from the maternal line of Caylee's parents, which meant the hair could have come from either Caylee, Casey, or Casey's mother.

Second, the prosecution's expert testified that tests showed evidence of decomposition in the car trunk. However, the tests used had not been subjected to standard reliability criteria, and the expert could not state unequivocally that any decomposition was human decomposition. It was called "junk science" by the defense.

The jury acquitted Casey Anthony of murder, and found her guilty only of giving false information to the police. With time served, she was released from jail shortly after the verdict.

FINGERPRINTS AS EVIDENCE

Historians believe that the Chinese used thumbprints to sign important documents before the birth of Christ. But it was not until the 1870s that a British civil servant in India used fingerprints to record persons on pensions and prisoners in jail. Police in Argentina were reportedly the first law officers to use fingerprinting in 1891.

A criminal who carelessly leaves fingerprints at the scene of a crime leaves what are called **latent fingerprints**. Latent fingerprints taken from a crime scene can be compared with fingerprints on file in local, state, and FBI files. The FBI has millions

latent fingerprints
Fingerprints left by a person on a surface other than one designed for recording fingerprints.

of fingerprints on file and receives more than 20,000 fingerprints a day from law enforcement agencies throughout the country.

> Fingerprints are perhaps the most common form of physical evidence, and certainly one of the most valuable. They relate directly to the ultimate objective of every criminal investigation ... the identification of the offender. Since a print of one finger has never been known to exactly duplicate another fingerprint, even of the same person or identical twin, it is possible to identify an individual with just one impression ... a person's fingerprints have never been known to change. The unchanging pattern thus provides a permanent record of the individual throughout life.[46]

The U.S. Supreme Court stated in the case of *Davis v. Mississippi*[47] that "fingerprinting is an inherently more reliable and effective crime-solving tool than eyewitness identification or confessions and is not subject to such abuses as the improper lineup and the 'third-degree.'"

Because of the serious problems of forged, stolen, or lost driver's licenses, passports, and other forms of identification, law enforcement officers are taking increased security measures to identify persons using their fingerprints. Not only are police cars equipped to take the fingerprints of persons detained on the street, but those same fingerprints can be transmitted electronically to police headquarters for a prompt positive identification of the person detained.

Obtaining Fingerprints

In 2008 Interpol (International Criminal Police Organization) reported that more than six million passports have been lost or stolen in recent years. U.S. officers are now testing new biometric systems of identification that can, in less than a minute, record all ten fingerprints of a person entering this country at one of its 311 air and sea entry points.[48]

Another innovation in fingerprint analysis introduced in 2008 is equipment that can analyze fingerprints and not only identify the person leaving the fingerprints but also determine whether that person has touched drugs, explosives, poisons, or other substances. This equipment, which costs about $60,000 per machine, was developed during efforts to build a new surgical tool that could test body tissues for the presence of cancer cells.[49]

Persons in lawful police custody are routinely fingerprinted and photographed. Persons who have served in the military have their fingerprints on file, as do many government employees and people who receive licenses for such occupations as bartending, taxicab driving, private security, or jobs that require government security clearance.

People can also consent to having their fingerprints taken, as occurred in the Gainesville, Florida, area in 1990 when five college students were slain in a two-month period. Law officers focused on persons on foot, mopeds, bicycles, and motorcycles. If any question arose concerning why the person was in the area, a voluntary stop was made, and the individual was asked to consent to fingerprinting. In 1994 the killer was apprehended and confessed to the killings.

Several states have statutes that authorize juvenile judges to order a juvenile who is not arrested or in custody to submit to fingerprinting when probable cause does not exist. The Supreme Court of Colorado[50] and the Supreme Court of Ohio[51] found such statutes constitutional.

A crime scene examiner dusts for fingerprints on shields that had been used to reflect light on marijuana plants. Fingerprints are a highly reliable form of physical evidence because each person's fingerprints are unique and unchanging.

AP Images/The Plain Dealer/Lisa DeJong

The U.S. Supreme Court held in the cases of *Hayes v. Florida*[52] and *Davis v. Mississippi*[53] that courts may order fingerprinting "under narrowly defined circumstances ... found to comply with the Fourth Amendment even though there is no probable cause in the traditional sense." Rapes had occurred in both the *Davis* and *Hayes* cases, where the police had fingerprints of the offenders but could not match them up with and identify the defendants, who were not in custody. The Supreme Court held in both cases that the Fourth Amendment was violated by the police when they took the defendants into custody, brought them to the station house, and obtained their fingerprints to see if they matched those found near the victims. The Supreme Court "suggested" that a temporary stop "in the field" to obtain fingerprints may be permitted, where there is reasonable suspicion but less than probable cause.

Proving That Fingerprints Were Impressed at the Time of the Crime

Fingerprints are circumstantial evidence from which inferences must be drawn. It is "impossible ... to determine the age of [a] latent print" because the print could have been on an object for a long time before the crime was committed.

As a general rule, the prosecution must first introduce fingerprint evidence by use of an expert witness and then show a chain of custody to prove that the evidence is authentic and genuine and has not been tampered with. The government must then show that the fingerprints "could only have been impressed at the time when the crime was committed." The U.S. Department of Justice work entitled *Crime Scene Search and Physical Evidence Handbook* states that: "It is impossible ... to determine the age of a latent print to determine the age or sex of the person leaving the print ... (or) to identify the race of the suspect, nor the (suspect's) occupation (unless they are a bricklayer)."[54]

To prove that fingerprints were impressed at the time of the crime, the following evidence may be used:

- In rape, assault, theft, or robbery cases where the victim or witness was present at the time of the crime and is available as a witness, testimony of the victim or a witness that the defendant touched or handled the object on which the fingerprints were found.
- Testimony that the surface had been washed or cleaned just prior to the crime.
- Fingerprints found in a home or an area to which the defendant did not have access (burglary, theft, and sometimes homicide cases). In *Com. v. Netto*, 783 N.E.2d 439 (Mass. 2003), the court held that evidence of fingerprints made by the defendant and found at a crime scene was "fairly fresh," based on the speed with which it reacted to chemicals. The defendant had been prohibited by the victim from entering his apartment and, as a result, the court concluded sufficient evidence existed to prove the defendant made the fingerprint at the time of the victim's murder.
- Fingerprints found in a victim's blood smear that could not have been made prior to the blood smear. In *State v. Williams*, 2010 WL 3971765 (N.M. App. 2010), *cert denied* 228 P.3d 488 (N.M. 2010), the court held that expert blood splatter and fingerprint testimony established that defendant's fingerprint found on the victim's car could only have been made at the same time a blood smear on the car occurred.

However, a murder conviction was reversed in the 1991 California case of *Mikes v. Borg*.[55] The court held that the mere fact that the defendant's fingerprints were found on the murder weapon was not sufficient to prove that the defendant was the murderer. The court stated: "[T]he prosecution introduced no evidence placing the defendant at the scene of the crime—either on the day of the murder or on any other occasion."[56]

Automated Fingerprint Identification Systems

For years, fingerprints found at a crime scene had to be compared manually with cards on file—one card at a time. The search was a slow, time-consuming process, limiting fingerprint searches in most cities to only the most serious crimes. Victims of burglaries were often shocked to find that burglary was not considered serious enough to qualify in most instances.

In 1985 the Automated Fingerprint Identification System (AFIS) for the Los Angeles Police Department was activated. The AFIS uses a computer with a large database to compare latent fingerprints electronically.

The first assignment given to the Los Angeles AFIS was fingerprints found at the scene of one of the killings by the "Night Stalker," who had terrorized Los Angeles for months. Within three minutes, AFIS identified a suspect.

In Los Angeles, like other large American cities, thousands of people are arrested each month. Comparing fingerprints from these people to fingerprints found at the scenes of crimes and fingerprints of suspects on wanted lists would be an impossible task without AFIS. The largest database in the United States is at the FBI, with 41 million fingerprint files and 24 million crime history records.

Today, all states and all large cities have their own databases (or have access to a database) that can electronically identify fingerprints lifted at a crime scene—often within hours. AFIS also processes fingerprints found in old cases. With fingerprint and other circumstantial evidence, states have been taking cases into criminal courts that have been unsolved for months and years.

Fingerprints and the *Daubert* Test

Prior to 1993, defense lawyers rarely attacked fingerprint evidence, unless there was a break or weakness in the chain of custody foundation necessary to qualify the fingerprints as admissible evidence. This is because the two basic assumptions underlying fingerprint identifications—that every person's fingerprint is unique and that an expert can distinguish between two persons' fingerprints—were accepted as true.

In the 1993 case of *Daubert v. Merrill Dow Pharmaceuticals Co.*[57] (discussed in Chapter 18), the U.S. Supreme Court said there are no certainties in science, only probabilistic results. Scientific theories must be demonstrated as being reliable, not simply assumed to be true, the Court said. After *Daubert*, the theory of forensic fingerprint identification evidence came under attack, and courts began requiring fingerprint experts to demonstrate that the procedures used were reliable and that test results had a high probability of accuracy.

Since 1993, higher standards for fingerprint technicians and experts have been established. New proficiency testing and new qualitative and quantitative analyses have been established. Fingerprint science has had to "reconstruct itself." Where these standards have been followed, most courts have concluded that fingerprint evidence is reliable and admissible.[58] Where the testimony of the fingerprint expert is based on a comparison of rolled fingerprints rather than a comparison of a latent print to a rolled print, the evidence has been found to be especially reliable. An FBI study discussed in *United States v. Sanchez-Birruetta*[59] found that in a comparison of 50,000 rolled fingerprints, not one false-positive identification was made.

TRACE EVIDENCE: THE SMALLEST THINGS CAN MAKE THE BIGGEST DIFFERENCE

When two objects come in contact, small amounts of material are often transferred from one to the other. This is nearly always the case when fabrics come in contact with a rough surface. Therefore, when a suspect comes in contact with the victim and objects at the crime scene, he frequently leaves behind traces of himself and takes with him traces of the things he has touched. Materials transferred in this way are normally referred to as **trace evidence**.

trace evidence Small amounts of material that a suspect leaves or acquires when he or she comes in contact with another object.

The term *trace evidence* is usually very loosely defined; however, it most often is applied to minute or microscopic bits of materials that are not immediately apparent to even a trained investigator. Thus, trace evidence is usually in the hard-to-find category. Because trace materials resulting from exchanges are less likely to excite the attention of the criminal, or even to be apparent to him, there is far less probability that the criminal will deliberately eliminate these materials than is the case with larger items of evidence or latent fingerprints.

The following hypothetical situation illustrates the potential for the exchange of physical evidence during fairly typical criminal actions.

The criminal crosses the back porch of a residence and steps on a brown paper bag lying on the floor. To gain entry, he breaks a small glass pane in the back door and reaches in to unlock the door. After gaining entry, he is surprised by the home-owner and a struggle follows. During the struggle, the victim's nose begins to bleed. The suspect flees the scene.

In this situation, the following exchanges of materials are entirely possible:

- The suspect's shoe print to the brown paper bag on the back porch
- Fibers from the suspect's clothing to the edge of the broken pane of glass in the back door (or blood on the glass from a cut on the suspect's arm)
- Fingerprints to the glass on the back door and possibly to other surfaces along the suspect's route of entry
- Fibers from the suspect's clothing to the victim's clothing during the struggle, and vice versa

The following (transferred) evidence may be found on or in possession of the suspect:

- Glass fragments or small paint chips on the outer garments of the suspect from the back door windowpane and frame
- Blood or hair from the victim on the suspect's clothing
- Bruises or lacerations on the suspect from the struggle with the victim
- Fibers from the rug or furniture at the crime scene on the shoes or garments of the suspect

It is apparent from this example that the possibilities for exchanges of trace materials are great. Even if the shoe prints and fingerprints are excluded from the potential array of physical evidence, there are still abundant opportunities to link the suspect with the crime scene, if proper collections are made at the scene and from the person of the suspect.

OTHER TYPES OF EVIDENCE

Palm Prints and Lip Prints as Evidence

Palm prints are considered part of fingerprinting and in some cases are found at crime scenes or on victims of crimes. Cases where palm prints were important evidence in obtaining criminal convictions are the armed robbery of a post office in the case of *United States v. Moore*[60] (palm print found on stolen postal money order) and the rape and robbery case of *Yelder v. State*[61] (palm print from known offender found in victim's home where rape occurred). In the 2010 case of *White v. State*[62] expert testimony showed that a palm print left on a window of a victim's resident was made by the defendant, and that based on the testimony of the expert that the print was facing into the residence, proved the defendant left the palm print as he entered the residence through the window.

In the 2005 case of *Barber v. State,*[63] the Alabama Court of Criminal Appeals upheld the admissibility of testimony of a fingerprint expert who testified that a bloody palm print found on the wall in a murder victim's house was made by the defendant.

In an article entitled "Focus on Forensics: Lip Prints," published in the November 1992 issue of the *FBI Law Enforcement Bulletin,* the author reported that studies of lip prints indicate that "every individual has unique lip prints—no two were identical in any case." Although lip print cases are rare, at least one state appellate court has determined that lip print identification evidence is reliable and admissible. In the case of *People v. Davis*,[64] the defendant was charged with robbery and murder. Duct tape used to bind the victim contained lip prints of the person who used the duct tape. Experts for the prosecution were permitted to testify that the lip prints on the duct tape were made by the defendant, and the defendant was convicted of murder. On appeal, the court held that lip print identification was sufficiently reliable to be admitted. The court accepted the prosecution expert's statement that "[t]he basis for identification of impression evidence is that everything is unique if looked at in sufficient detail, and if two things are sufficiently similar, they must have come from the same source."

Footprints and Shoe Prints as Evidence

Very few footprint cases exist because the majority of criminals wear shoes! One of the more notable cases is the 1984 murder case of *State v. Bullard*,[65] where the Supreme Court of North Carolina discussed the art of footprint identification in affirming the defendant's conviction.

In many cases, however, shoe prints provide important identification evidence. Shoe prints are obtained from surfaces covered with snow, mud, dust, dirt, paint, or other substances in which an imprint can be made. Identification testimony must include enough characteristics—such as size, length, width, type, wear patterns, and individual characteristics such as nicks, cuts, and scratches—to establish a match between the print or prints left at the crime scene and the defendant's shoes. Testimony of experts trained in other kinds of forensic print analysis was admitted to connect a shoe print at a crime scene to shoes worn by a defendant in the 2011 case of *Rodriguez v. State*.[66] A California court of appeals held in *People v. Maglaya*[67] that a police officer would be permitted to testify about similarities between a shoe print and shoes worn by the defendant.

In the 1992 home burglary case of *People v. Campbell*[68] the Supreme Court of Illinois held that "shoe-print evidence, standing alone, is sufficient to convict." The court pointed out that shoe-print evidence, like fingerprint evidence, is circumstantial evidence. Supporting the evidence of the shoe prints was further evidence that the defendant had the opportunity to commit the burglary as well as evidence of flight.

In the 1990 murder case of *State v. Jells*,[69] the Supreme Court of Ohio affirmed the defendant's conviction and permitted a lay witness (a police officer) to testify as to the similarities between the prints and the defendant's shoes. The Supreme Court of Nebraska affirmed the attempted sexual assault conviction in the 1989 case of *State v. Rhodes*,[70] where shoe-print evidence was used. Burglary convictions that were affirmed on shoe-print evidence include *State v. Tincher*,[71] *State v. Ingold*,[72] and *State v. Johnson*.[73]

Bite Marks as Evidence

To use bite-mark evidence, a chain of custody must be shown and an expert witness must be used, such as a dentist with training and experience as a forensic odontologist.

Bite marks could result from fighting; they could be sexual, attacking, or sadistic. In the 1990 case of *Commonwealth v. Henry,*[74] the Supreme Court of Pennsylvania stated:

> The essence of the distinction is that fighting bite marks are less well defined because they are done carelessly and quickly, whereas attacking or sadistic bite marks are made slowly and produce a clearer pattern. According to Dr. Asen, the sadistic bite mark is one of the most well-defined. Sexual bite marks are also well defined, but usually have a red center, produced by sucking tissue into the mouth. The dentist testified that the bite marks produced in this case were extremely well-defined, and were attacking or sadistic in nature. The legal significance of this testimony is that it might have been considered by the jury as part of their determination that the homicide was committed by means of torture.

In the 2000 case of *Seivewright v. State,*[75] the court stated that every court considering the issue has permitted the introduction of expert testimony on bite mark evidence. It noted that the usual method of evaluating a bite mark was (1) to register both the bite mark and the suspect's dentition (i.e., the suspect's dental mark pattern); (2) compare the bite mark to the suspect's dentition; and (3) evaluate similarities or dissimilarities between the two.

Bite-mark evidence is used primarily in criminal homicide cases in which police need to establish the identity of the defendant. Examples of such murder cases are *State v. Richards*[76] and *People v. Marsh.*[77]

Tire Tracks as Evidence

In the 1974 U.S. Supreme Court case of *Cardwell v. Lewis,*[78] the defendant parked his car in a commercial parking lot and then went into a police building for questioning regarding a murder. After the police arrested the defendant for the murder, they took his car keys and, without a court order or warrant, had his car towed to a police lot, where tire prints and paint scrapings were taken. This evidence was used to obtain the murder conviction of the defendant.

The U.S. Supreme Court affirmed the conviction and held that no right of privacy was violated, saying,

> In the present case, nothing from the interior of the car and no personal effects, which the Fourth Amendment traditionally has been deemed to protect, were searched or seized and introduced in evidence. With the "search" limited to the examination of the tire on the wheel and the taking of paint scrapings from the exterior of the vehicle left in the public lot, we fail to comprehend what expectation of privacy was infringed.
>
> Under circumstances such as these, where probable cause exists, a warrantless examination of the exterior of a car is not unreasonable under the Fourth and Fourteenth Amendments.[79]

In the 1991 case of *State v. Tillman,*[80] the manager of a Goodyear tire store was held to have sufficient training and experience in tire tread patterns to testify as an expert witness on tire tracks. The witness testified as to the similarities between tire tracks found at the scene of a murder and tires on the defendant's car. The defendant's conviction for murder was affirmed. In the 2007 case of *Brown v. State*[81] the court upheld the admission of testimony by a state police officer that tire tracks found at a crime scene matched the tires on the defendant's vehicle. The defendant contended the tire track evidence did not show a "unique" characteristic that proved only his tires could have made the track. The court said the testimony was admissible circumstantial evidence to show similarities because other evidence was introduced that linked the defendant to the crime scene. Some "unique" characteristic of the tire would be required only if the tire tracks had been the only evidence connecting the defendant to the crime scene, the court said.

SUMMARY

1. **Identify the requirements for a warrantless search of a crime scene under the "exigent circumstances" exception.**
   - Police may enter a residence where a crime occurred and search for victims, injured persons, or perpetrators of the crime. They may seize any evidence in "plain view" during such a search. Police may not make a general search of the residence simply to discover if any evidence of other crimes may be found.

2. **State the "standing" requirement for objecting to searches of a crime scene.**
   - Only persons who have a reasonable expectation of privacy in the area where a crime scene is located may object to a search of that area.

3. **List the steps in establishing the chain of custody for evidence found at a crime scene.**
   - Persons having control of evidence that is susceptible to tampering, substitution, or contamination must testify on how and when they gained control of the evidence, what they did with the evidence, and if they transferred the evidence how and when the transfer occurred. Each person having such control

from the crime scene to the trial must show how the "chain" was maintained.

4. **State some ways it can be shown fingerprints taken from a crime scene were left at the scene when the crime occurred.**
   - Testimony that the person who matched the fingerprints was present at the scene when the crime occurred; testimony that the crime scene had been cleaned just prior to the time the crime occurred; testimony showing the person who matched the fingerprints could not have been at the crime scene at any time other than when the crime occurred; or testimony that the crime scene location was not accessible at any other time.

5. **Compare fingerprints and bite mark evidence to shoe prints and tire tracks.**
   - Fingerprints and bite marks can, through expert testimony, be used to positively identify an individual as the person who left the fingerprints or bite marks. Shoe-prints and tire tracks, unless they exhibit unique characteristics, are only circumstantial evidence connecting a person to a crime scene.

KEY TERMS

chain of custody, 431
crime scene, 422

emergency situations,
   423

latent fingerprints, 433
trace evidence, 437

KEY CASES

Mincey v. Arizona, 437 U.S. 385 (1978) A general, warrantless search of a residence is not permitted simply because a crime was committed in the residence.

Missouri v. McNeeley, 133 S. Ct. 1552 (2013): Police may not take warrantless blood sample from suspected intoxicated driver simply because the alcohol

dissipates over time. Other circumstances must make the circumstances "exigent".

Thompson v. Louisiana, 105 S. Ct. 409 (1984)
The duration of a search of a crime scene residence may cause the search to be unreasonable, and make it a general search for evidence of any crime.

United States v. Hassock, 631 F.3d 79 (2d Cir. 2011): A "protective sweep" is permissible only if police lawfully enter a residence. The police may not "create the risk" a sweep is designed to uncover.

United States v. Santana, 427 U.S. 38 (1976): Police may enter premises during a "hot pursuit" and make a warrantless search for weapons, dangerous persons, or persons needing emergency aid.

PROBLEMS

1. The application of the Fourth Amendment, under *Davis v. Mississippi* and *Hayes v. Florida* (discussed in this chapter), to fingerprints taken from a suspect after an illegal arrest or detention is not uniform in lower federal courts. Compare the holdings of the courts in *United States v. Plaza-Leon*, 2011 WL 3510944 (D. Ariz. 2011), and *United States v. Guevara-Martinez*, 262 F.3d 751 (8th Cir. 2001). How do they differ? Which seems more consistent with the Supreme Court's "suggestion" in *Hayes* and *Davis*?

2. Fingerprints found at a crime scene must match those of a defendant before they can be admitted as evidence. However, the prosecution must also prove the fingerprints were left at the time the crime occurred. That can be a problem where a defendant had access to the place where the fingerprints were found prior to the time the crime occurred. In those cases, circumstantial evidence must be used to convince the jury the fingerprints were made at the time of the crime. What circumstantial evidence was introduced in the cases of *Crawford v. State*, 664 S.E.2d 820 (Ga. App. 2008), and *State v. Moore*, 626 S.E.2d 876 (N.C. App. 2006)? Which is more persuasive?

3. Fortin was convicted of sexual assault on a woman, which included bite marks on the victim's chin and left breast. After this conviction, Fortin was charged with the murder of another woman. At his trial on the murder charge, the prosecution wanted to introduce the evidence of the prior assault, contending it was a "signature crime" because the murder victim also had bite marks on her chin and left breast. What should the prosecution be required to prove before introducing the evidence of the prior crime? How exactly are the "bite marks" being used by the prosecution? What proof will be needed for the bite marks to be admitted into evidence? *State v. Fortin*, 917 A.2d 746 (N.J 2007).

4. In *People v. Davis*, 879 N.E.2d 996 (Ill. App. 2007), *review denied*, 888 N.E.2d 1186 (Ill. 2008), the defendant was convicted of murder. The only physical evidence connecting him to the murder was a lip print on a roll of duct tape found near the victim, which the state's expert testified were identical to defendant's lip prints. On direct appeal the state appeals court upheld the conviction, including admission of the lip print evidence. In a subsequent petition for post-conviction relief (similar to a habeas corpus petition in federal court) the appeals court reversed the conviction and ordered a new trial. What role did the lip print evidence play in the decision to reverse the conviction? Why didn't the appeals court reverse the conviction in the direct appeal?

CASE ANALYSIS

Read Appendix B, Finding and Analyzing Cases (p. 499). With these guidelines in mind, please continue with the Case Analysis selections for Chapter 16.

1. In 1994 a rape victim was brought to a hospital after the assault, and a rape kit was used to hold sperm and blood samples taken from the victim. Later, the sperm samples were subjected to DNA tests, and a male DNA "profile" was created and filed in databases, including the CODIS federal DNA database. In 2008 CODIS reported a "hit" on the sperm sample profile logged as recovered from the 1994 rape. The defendant was then arrested and charged with rape. At his trial, he objected to admission on the profile documents, because documents showing chain of custody of the rape kit had been destroyed by Hurricane Katrina.

How could the prosecution deal with this problem? *See State v. Taylor,* 118 So.3d 65 (La. App. 2013).

2. Many, perhaps even most, murders are solved by circumstantial evidence. Physical evidence like fingerprints or DNA found at a crime scene requires a two-step process for using such evidence at a criminal trial. First, the defendant must be linked to the evidence by appropriate fingerprint or DNA tests. Second, it must be shown the evidence was left at the crime scene when the crime was committed. If it could have been left earlier the evidence loses much of its probative value to the prosecution. In *State v. Carter,* 725 S.E.2nd 902 (N.C. App 2012), virtually the only evidence that linked the defendant to a murder victim was fingerprints on the victim's car, and DNA tests of substances left by the fingerprints. How did the prosecution satisfy the second requirement, showing when the evidence was left on the car? Did the defendant make that easier for the prosecution?

3. Defendant was admitted to a hospital after a traffic accident where three occupants of another vehicle died after colliding with the vehicle driven by defendant. Paramedics drew samples of the defendant's blood and placed them in tubes held in a collection bag. Police investigators interviewed the defendant, and detected the smell of alcohol on her breath. They thus asked for a blood sample to be sent to be tested for alcohol. The test results showed alcohol beyond the permissible limit, and the defendant was charged with motor vehicle manslaughter. At her trial she objected to the introduction of the blood tests' results, because the technician doing the tests stated in the test chart that the blood came from a tube different from the kind of tubes normally placed in collection bags. How did the prosecution get around this problem? *State v. Coccomo,* 31 A.3d 1012 (Conn. 2012).

4. When police chase a suspect in "hot pursuit" and in the process enter a residence, they obviously do so without a warrant. However, in a sense the residence is now the crime scene, and at least to some degree police should be entitled to enter the crime scene to apprehend the criminal. What if police, while in hot pursuit of a person who has committed a misdemeanor, enter a person's property, and in the process damage either the property or its owner? Are they entitled to do so? If not, they have committed a Fourth Amendment violation, and can be held civilly liable for the damage caused. The U.S. Supreme Court had occasion to visit this issue in the 2013 case of *Stanton v. State,* 134 S. Ct. 3. (1) Did the court decide if the officer was entitled to enter the premises in a hot pursuit? (2) If not, and the officer was mistaken in his belief that he was entitled to enter, what was the standard used to judge the police officers' mistake in order to escape civil liability.

Notes

1. To seize evidence in plain view, it must be "immediately apparent" to the law officer that the object is evidence of a crime. In the U.S. Supreme Court case of *Arizona v. Hicks* [107 S. Ct. 1149 (1987)], police officers were in an apartment building because a man was wounded when a bullet came through the ceiling of his apartment. The police immediately went into Hicks's apartment, where the bullet came from, to search "for the shooter, for other victims, and weapons."

   While they were lawfully in Hicks's apartment, police saw expensive stereo equipment that they suspected was stolen property. To determine whether the stereo equipment was stolen, an officer picked up stereo parts to read and record the serial numbers, which he called in to the stolen property division.

The U.S. Supreme Court held that as it was not "immediately apparent" that the equipment was stolen; thus, the seizure was unlawful and the evidence could not be used against Hicks on the criminal charge of possession of stolen property.

2. An example of a state case in which the police exceeded the limits of an emergency search is *People v. Williams* [557 P.2d 399 (Colo. 1976)]. After Claudine Longet (Mrs. Andy Williams) shot her lover, professional skier "Spider" Sabich, police were in the couple's home after the body was removed. The gun used in the shooting had been seized, and photographs of the crime scene had been taken. The police then went into dresser drawers, where they found Longet's diary, which they seized. The Colorado Supreme Court held that the diary could not be used

as evidence in the homicide case because it was seized without consent or a search warrant.

Can the police cordon off and maintain control of major crime scenes so they may reenter without consent or a search warrant? This issue was before a number of California courts. In the 1991 case of *People v. Boragno* [49 CrL 1394], police officers continued to enter a murder scene for 13 hours after the apartment was cordoned off and the police retained exclusive control of the apartment. The police continued to take photographs and search for blood and hair samples. The California Court of Appeals held that searches after the first sweep of the apartment were invalid. But the valid and good evidence against the defendant was so overwhelming that "it is not reasonably probable a result more favorable to [the defendant] would have occurred."

In the case of *People v. Neulist*, 43 A.D.2d 150, 350 N.Y.S.2d 178 (1973), medical examiners first said that the death of a woman in her home was from natural causes. The police still posted a guard at the room where the body was found. However, a physician then discovered that a murder had occurred. The police returned to the crime scene within an hour, and the highest court in New York held that the evidence obtained could be used against the defendant.

3. 494 U.S. 325 (1990).
4. 517 F.3d 279 (5th Cir. 2008).
5. Most (if not all) states authorize "hot-pursuit" entries into private premises for misdemeanor crimes, such as drunk driving, that threaten public safety. However, "hot pursuit" of a person who had committed a civil offense is not justified. The U.S. Supreme Court reversed the conviction in *Welsh v. Wisconsin* [104 S. Ct. 2091 (1984)], holding that, at the time of Welsh's arrest for first-offense drunk driving, the offense was a civil offense punishable in civil court. No imprisonment was possible for the noncriminal, civil forfeiture offense. At the time, Wisconsin was the only state that made first-offense drunk driving a civil offense.
6. 86 S. Ct. 1826.
7. 133 S. Ct. 1552 (2013).
8. The U.S. Supreme Court held in two cases that when law enforcement officers make a lawful entry into private premises because of an emergency, they may not make a second entry after the emergency no longer exists without a search warrant or consent. In the case of *Michigan v. Tyler* [98 S. Ct. 1942 (1978)], the Supreme Court held that an entry 27 days after a fire to obtain evidence of arson was not a lawful entry. The Court held: "... we hold that an entry to fight a fire requires no warrant, and that once in the building, officials may remain there for a reasonable time to investigate the cause of the blaze. Thereafter, additional entries to investigate the cause of the fire must be made pursuant to the warrant procedures governing administrative searches."

9. 840 P.2d 1298 (Ore. App.).
10. *Patrick v. State*, 227 A.2d 486 (Del. 1967).
11. *City of Troy v. Oblinger*, 475 N.W.2d 54, 50 CrL 1006 (Mich. 1991).
12. 990 F.2d 167 (4th Cir.).
13. 607 A.2d 471 (D.C. App.).
14. 919 A.2d 452 (Conn. 2007).
15. 227 S.W.3d 133 (Tex. App. 2006).
16. 864 A.2d 1006 (Md. 2004).
17. 243 S.W.3d 30 (Tex. App. 2007).
18. 502 So.2d 453 (La.), *cert. denied,* 108 S. Ct. 205 (1987).
19. *State v. Vann,* 1990 WL 51763, 49 CrL 3042 (Tenn. Crim. App. 1990), *cert. denied,* 111 S. Ct. 2015 (1991).
20. Much of the following material in this section is taken from U.S. Department of Justice Law Enforcement Assistance Administration book entitled *Crime Scene Search and Physical Evidence Handbook* (Government Printing Office, 1973).
21. Police training manuals and directives recommend that objects likely to be used as evidence be identified by having the collecting officer scratch his initials or name and date on the object if practical. The officer can then readily identify the object as the evidence recovered at the crime scene or other place. Firearms, spent cartridges, bullets, clothing, currency, and many other objects have been identified and authenticated as genuine in this manner. Weapons used in the commission of a felony are ordinarily identified not only by the serial number but also by initials and date scratched on the object by a law enforcement officer.

If the weapon is also to be used as the basis for evidence, such as fingerprints or ballistics reports, a chain of custody must then be established and used to show that the evidence has not been altered or tampered with.
22. See *State v. Gustin,* 826 S.W.2d 409 (Mo. App.); *People v. Winters,* 422 N.E.2d 972 (Ill. App. 1981); and *United States v. Clonts,* 966 F.2d 1366 (10th Cir. 1992).
23. *People v. Kabalia,* 587 N.E.2d 1210 (Ill. App. 1992).
24. D. H. Garrison, Jr., "Sound Off: Protecting the Crime Scene," *FBI Law Enforcement Bulletin* (September 1994). Although this problem was noted in 1994, there is reason to believe that it continues today (hopefully, to a lesser degree).
25. *Schultz v. State,* 811 P.2d 1322 (Okla. Crim. App. 1991).
26. *Hunter v. State,* 805 S.W.2d 918 (Tex. App. 1991).

27. *United States v. Clonts,* 966 F.2d 1366 (10th Cir. 1992).

28. *United States v. Gilliam,* 975 F.2d 1050 (4th Cir. 1992).

29. *Van Pelt v. State,* 816 S.W.2d 607 (Ark. 1991); *State v. Clay,* 817 S.W.2d 565 (Mo. App. 1991).

30. *Moorman v. State,* 574 So.2d 953 (Ala. Crim. App. 1990).

31. *English v. State,* 575 N.E.2d 14 (Ind. 1991).

32. *Kennedy v. State,* 578 N.E.2d 633 (Ind. 1991); *Davasher v. State,* 823 S.W.2d 863 (Ark. 1992).

33. *State v. Jackson,* 821 P.2d 1374 (Ariz. App. 1991).

34. *Turner v. State,* 610 S.2d 1198 (Ala. Crim. App. 1992).

35. *Snowden v. State,* 574 So.2d 960 (Ala. Crim. App. 1990).

36. *Holder v. State,* 584 So.2d 872 (Ala. Crim. App. 1991).

37. *Bell v. State,* 339 So.2d 96 (Ala. Crim. App. 1976).

38. One of the authors sat on a jury in 1999 where the defendant was charged criminally for dealing rock cocaine. Because two adjournments had already been granted in the case, the trial judge announced in open court that both parties and the court had agreed that no further adjournments would be granted.

    After the rock cocaine was legally seized by the police under the authority of a search warrant, it was delivered to a young lab technician at the state crime lab. The lab technician testified that she received the evidence, she performed two different tests on the substance, and both tests showed that the substance was rock cocaine. After testifying that the rock cocaine was stored in a secured locker, the lab technician was asked whether the storage area was locked at all times and who had a key to the locker. The lab technician answered that the storage area was locked at all times and that she and her two supervisors all had keys to the storage locker. Because the two supervisors who had access to the storage locker were not in court to testify and show a sufficient chain of custody, the charges against the defendant were dismissed, and the state could not file new criminal charges because of the doctrine of double jeopardy.

    When a defendant appeals a criminal conviction and wins a reversal of the conviction, as in the cases cited and used in this section, the state may retry the case. The prosecutors in those cases had another chance to prove the chain of custody for the critical evidence. Today, prosecutors in busy criminal courts had better do a good job at the first trial, or they are going to lose cases because they fail to prove a chain of custody for evidence that can be falsified or tampered with.

39. S.E.2d 179 (Va. 1971).

40. *Laws v. State,* 562 So.2d 305 (Ala. Crim. App. 1990).

41. 184 A.D.2d 153 (N.Y.A.D.).

42. *Byerly v. Ashley,* 825 S.W.2d 286 (Ky. App. 1991).

43. 482 N.W.2d 567 (Nebr. 1992).

44. 810 S.W.2d 474 (Tex. App.).

45. 818 P.2d 787 (Idaho App.).

46. R. H. Fox & C. L. Cunningham, *Crime Scene Search and Physical Evidence Handbook* 48, National Institute of Law Enforcement and Criminal Justice (1985).

47. 394 U.S. 721 (1969).

48. See "At Airport, 2 Fingerprints Are Not Enough," *New York Times* (March 26, 2008).

49. See "Fingerprint Test Shows Not Only Who, But What," *New York Times* (August 8, 2008).

50. *People v. Madson,* 638 P.2d 18 (Colo. 1981).

51. *In re Order Requiring Fingerprinting of a Juvenile,* 537 N.E.2d 1286, 45 CrL 2164 (1989).

52. 105 S. Ct. 1643 (1985).

53. 89 S. Ct. 1394, 1398 (1969).

54. *Crime Scene Search and Physical Evidence Handbook, supra,* at 48, n. 20. See the 1992 case of *State v. Hamilton,* 827 P.2d 232, where the Supreme Court of Utah reviewed many cases from throughout the United States concerning the general approaches to the weight that may be afforded fingerprint evidence.

55. 947 F.2d 353 (9th Cir.), *review denied,* 112 S. Ct. 3055 (1992).

56. Cases where the state was able to obtain convictions by proving that fingerprints of the defendant were made at the time of the crime (or created a strong inference to that effect) include: murder and theft case of *Commonwealth v. Servich,* 602 A.2d 1338 (Pa. Super. 1992), where a glass touched by the defendant was washed on the morning of the murder; *Commonwealth v. Hall,* 590 N.E.2d 1177 (Mass. App. 1992), where the robber touched a lavatory doorknob while forcing a witness into a room; *State v. Jackson,* 582 So.2d 915 (La. App. 1991), a case of theft from a supermarket where the general public did not have access to the area and the defendant was not an employee of the store and had never been seen in the store before; the home burglary case of *Tyler v. State,* 402 S.E.2d 780 (Ga. App. 1991), where the defendant testified that he had never been in the home and did not know where it was located, but his fingerprints were found in the home; the burglary of an auto sales and repair business in *Commonwealth v. Baptista,* 585 N.E.2d 335 (Mass. App. 1992), where fingerprints found inside a closed, locked Pepsi vending machine justified the inference that the defendant had cut the lock and entered the machine; a home burglary case of *Jones v. State,* 825 S.W.2d 529 (Tex. App. 1992),

where fingerprints on a kitchen window screen and mud marks showed that the screen was laid in the mud; the home burglary case of *State v. Evans*, 392 S.E.2d 441 (N.C. App. 1990), where the defendant's fingerprints were found on a piece of glass from the window broken to gain entry; a car theft case, *In the Interest of N. R.*, 402 S.E.2d 120 (Ga. App. 1991), where juvenile fingerprints were found on the inside of the driver's window of a recently stolen car; the burglary case of *Brown v. State* 837 S.W.2d 457 (Ark. 1992), where fingerprints were found inside the broken glass door of a home; the murder case of *Hanson v. Commonwealth* [416 S.E.2d 14 (Va. App. 1992)], where police went into the murder victim's trash and found the defendant's fingerprints on envelopes, which were used to show his presence at the crime scene; the murder case of *Cavazos v. State*, 779 P.2d 987 (Okla. Crim. App. 1989), where the defendant's fingerprints were found on the victim's unclothed back; and the rape and robbery case of *People v. Himmelein*, 442 N.W.2d 667 (Mich. App. 1989), where the defendant's fingerprints were found on a yardstick used to strike a rape victim.

57. 509 U.S. 579 (1993). (See *United States v. Plaza,* 188 F.Supp.2d 549 (2002), for a discussion of fingerprinting.)

58. See, for example, *United States v. Crisp*, 3242 F.3d 261 (4th Cir. 2003), *cert. denied,* 124 S. Ct. 220 (2003).

59. 128 Fed. Appx. 571 (9th Cir. 2005).

60. 936 F.2d 1508 (7th Cir. 1991).

61. 575 So.2d 131 (Ala. Crim. App. 1990).

62. 40 So.3d 879 (Fla. App. 2010).

63. 2005 WL 125745 (Ala. Crim. App.).

64. 710 N.E.2d 1251 (Ill. App. 1999), *review denied,* 720 N.E.2d 1251 (1999).

65. 322 S.E.2d 370 (N.C.).

66. 2011 WL 5992325 (Del. Sup. 2011).

67. 6 Cal. Rptr. 3d 155 (Cal. App. 2003).

68. 586 N.E.2d 1261 (Ill.).

69. 559 N.E.2d 464 (Ohio).

70. 445 N.W.2d 622 (Nebr.).

71. 797 S.W.2d 794 (Mo. App. 1990).

72. 450 N.W.2d 344 (Minn. App. 1990).

73. 464 N.W.2d 167 (Nebr. 1991).

74. 569 A.2d 929.

75. 7 P.3d 24, 30 (Wyo. 2000).

76. 804 P.2d 109 (Ariz. App. 1990).

77. 441 N.W.2d 33 (Mich. App. 1989).

78. 417 U.S. 583, 94 S. Ct. 2464.

79. 417 U.S. at 592, 94 S. Ct. at 2470.

80. 405 S.E.2d 607 (S.C. App.).

81. 650 S.E.2d 780 (Ga. App. 2007).

CHAPTER 17

Videotapes, Photographs, Documents, and Writings as Evidence

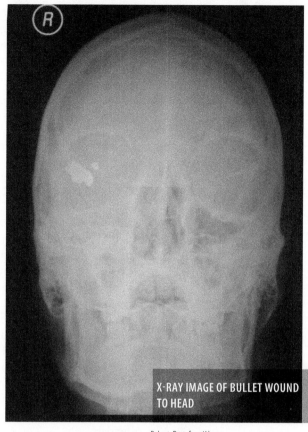

X-RAY IMAGE OF BULLET WOUND TO HEAD

Robert Destefano/Alamy

LEARNING OBJECTIVES

In this chapter we discuss when and how recordings, photographs, and copies of things or events may be introduced as evidence. The learning objectives for this chapter are

State when search warrants are required or not for electronic surveillance.

State the requirements for the introduction into evidence of videotapes, photographs, and other electronic records.

Explain the "best evidence" rule.

Explain how the Fifth Amendment applies to documents.

N ot everyone carries a video recorder into a public event, but most carry a cell phone. Smart phones have video capability, and people use it to record events, including crimes. That was the case at a basketball tournament where a homicide occurred. In *State v. Torres*, 813 N.W.2d 148 (S.D. 2012), a spectator entering a basketball arena spotted a fight brewing, and turned on his cell phone camera. He then captured images of a shooter firing a gun that killed the victim. Other evidence pointed to the defendant as the shooter, and he was charged with murder. At the defendant's trial the cell phone video was introduced into evidence. How did the prosecution use the video? How was the video relevant, given it was "pixilated" and did not show individual faces? Do you agree with the court's decision?

PHOTOS AND VIDEOTAPES AS EVIDENCE

Public surveillance cameras, video cameras, and cell phone cameras are everywhere in the United States. Thousands of people carry cell phones equipped with cameras, and thousands more possess video cameras. Banks, stores, private businesses, schools, and apartment buildings have installed cameras as part of security systems. Some squad cars and buses have them. They are commonly used in drunk-driving cases as well as traffic and investigative stops by the police. Video cameras have filmed murders, armed robberies, shoplifting, and other crimes (see Federal Rule of Evidence 1001 in Appendix C).

Since the Zapruder film of the assassination of President John F. Kennedy in 1963, and later the video footage of the Los Angeles beatings of Rodney King and Reginald Denny, videotapes have brought street events to the American public and evidence into criminal trials. Fixed surveillance cameras and handheld video cameras regularly provide information to law officers for the identification and arrest of offenders.

If the filming is done in a public place where a defendant does not have a right of privacy and if a witness verifies that the tape is a reliable reproduction of the events that occurred, the tape is ordinarily admissible as evidence. The following examples illustrate the thousands of cases where photos and videotapes are used as evidence each year.

Examples

- In the case of *Pennsylvania v. Muniz,*[1] the U.S. Supreme Court held that a videotape of the defendant's answers to routine booking questions at a police station were admissible as evidence. The tape showing the defendant's slurred speech, his poor performance on sobriety tests, and his unsolicited incriminating statements was used in evidence, which resulted in his conviction. The tape was held not to violate his *Miranda* rights, except for the incriminating statement the defendant made when he was asked the year of his sixth birthday.

- In the case of *CBS, Inc. v. Jackson*,[2] the Florida Supreme Court pointed out that either the person taping a street arrest can be ordered to appear as a witness or the tape can be ordered to be produced. Television news reporters do not enjoy a First Amendment privilege when they are eyewitness observers to an event that is relevant in a criminal trial.

- A murder victim's videotaped dying declaration was held admissible in the murder case of *Grayson v. State.*[3] The victim's physician withheld all pain medication prior to the videotaping, and the victim responded to most questions by nodding his head and sometimes motioning with his hands.

- An undercover officer's videotape of a drug buy and the videotape of a controlled drug buy were used as evidence in the cases of *Hall v. State*[4] and *Edwards v. State.*[5]
- A videotape of the defendant cultivating marijuana in a field was used as evidence in the case of *Pfaff v. State.*[6]
- A defendant, while being booked on an assault charge, became disruptive and was also charged with disorderly conduct. The videotape of the scene was admitted as evidence in the case of *State v. Warmsbecker.*[7]
- Surveillance evidence is important in civil personal injury trials as well as in criminal cases. For example, if an insurance company suspects that a personal injury claim is fraudulent, it might use a video camera to conduct surveillance of the claimant in public places to determine whether injuries are faked or exaggerated. For interesting insights into this practice, see the article titled "Disclosing Surveillance Evidence: 'I've Got a Secret'" in *Wisconsin Lawyer* (September 2006).
- Videotapes of the defendant refusing to submit to blood alcohol testing and refusing to perform field sobriety tests while in police custody were admissible as evidence to obtain a criminal conviction in the case of *Commonwealth v. McConnell.*[8]
- A videotape of the defendant's arrest and a search of the immediate premises were admissible in the case of *People v. Schaaefer.*[9]
- A videotape simulation of a highway accident by the Minnesota Highway Patrol was held admissible in the case of *State v. Rasinski.*[10] In reconstructing the accident, the state stayed within the objective evidence (measurements, placement of the skid marks, and the final resting place of the vehicles at the accident). But video reenactment of a fight at a jail was held inadmissible because the version was biased in favor of what the state believed had occurred (*State v. Hopperstad*).[11]
- When the defendant approached a man with regard to committing an armed robbery, the man went to the police. A video recorder then captured the defendant soliciting a police informant for armed robbery. The authenticated videotape was used in evidence, resulting in the defendant's conviction (*Powell v. State*).[12]
- Store security videotapes and apartment lobby videotapes were held admissible for use as evidence in the cases of *MacFarland v. State*[13] and *Smith v. United States.*[14]
- Videotapes of drug dealers, prostitutes, and car thieves taken by people living in the neighborhood are sometimes turned over to local police.

WHEN IS A WARRANT NEEDED TO INSTALL AND CONDUCT VIDEOTAPE SURVEILLANCE?

videotape surveillance Close observation by use of video cameras.

Search warrants must be obtained to conduct **videotape surveillance** when a suspect has a right of privacy in the place where the videotape surveillance is to be conducted (for instance, the suspect's home, apartment, or office).

Examples
- Law enforcement officers obtained a warrant to install a hidden microphone and video camera in a hotel room that the officers had rented. The defendant came to the room and offered to buy 185 pounds of marijuana for $121,000. The defendant was arrested when he returned with the money and bought the marijuana. Because the defendant did not have a right of privacy in the hotel room rented by the law officers, the Supreme Court of Massachusetts held that the defendant did not have standing in court to challenge the use of the surveillance tapes as evidence against him (*Commonwealth v. Price*).[15]
- As a general rule, a search warrant is not necessary to search a public employee's workplace (desk, files, and so on) to investigate work-related misconduct under the U.S. Supreme Court case of *O'Connor v. Ortega.*[16]

- In the case of *United States v. Taketa,*[17] federal agents suspected Taketa (a law officer) of improper wiretapping. The federal agents entered Taketa's office at night to investigate possible work-related misconduct. This was lawful without a warrant under *O'Connor v. Ortega,* but the federal agents also placed a hidden video camera in the office without a warrant. Their failure to obtain a warrant for the video surveillance spoiled the evidence obtained by the camera.
- A hidden video surveillance camera was installed in the employee break room of a Hawaii post office, where it operated for a year. The camera picked up evidence of illegal gambling against the defendant. The Supreme Court of Hawaii held that the postal employees had a reasonable expectation of privacy in the break room, which was neither a public place nor open to public view or hearing. Because the offense was not related to postal work, it was held not to fall under *O'Connor v. Ortega (State v. Bonnell).*[18]
- Secret Service agents permitted a CBS camera crew to go with them in the search of a New York home under the authority of a search warrant. The agents had the authority to search for illegal credit cards; however, they had no authority under a search warrant to permit private citizens to accompany them. Only a woman and her 4-year-old son were present in the home, and no evidence of any crime was found. A civil lawsuit against CBS and the federal government was settled by damage payments to the family. The trial judge, in the case of *Ayeni v. CBS et al.,*[19] stated that "CBS had no greater right than that of a thief to be in the home. [T]he television crew took from the home, for the purpose of broadcasting them to the world at large, pictures of intimate secrets of the household, including sequences of a cowering mother and child resisting the videotaping."

Where Can Videotaping Be Done Without a Warrant?

Videotaping may be conducted in places where the people being filmed do not have a reasonable expectation of privacy. The following cases further illustrate.

McCray v. State

Maryland Court of Special Appeals, 84 Md. App. 513, 581 A.2d 45 (1990)

The defendant was suspected of being involved in a scheme to provide false driver's licenses for money. Investigating officers videotaped him walking from his home across the public street to the motor vehicle office. This tape was used as evidence in a trial that resulted in the defendant's conviction. In holding that a court order or search warrant was not needed, the court held:

[o]ne walking along a public sidewalk or standing in a public park cannot reasonably expect that his activity will be immune from the public eye or from observation by the police. Consequently, any justified expectation of privacy is not violated by the video-taping of activity occurring in full public view.

Thus, the videotape surveillance of McCray, in public view, walking across the street to the MVA poses no Fourth Amendment problem. Clearly, the videotape of McCray was captured in a public place and in public view. Consequently, McCray had no reasonable expectation of privacy when he walked on public sidewalks, streets, and parking lots, because he voluntarily exposed to anyone interested the fact that he was traveling to a particular destination and meeting a particular individual in a public place. (See *Sponick v. City of Detroit Police Dept.,* 49 Mich. App. 162, 211 N.W.2d 674 (1973) (where police officer videotaped in a bar talking with known criminals did not have a "reasonable expectation of privacy" because the observations occurred in a public place).)

Here, the police officers were engaged in a legitimate investigation, and upon first utilizing various investigative activities to ferret out this licensing scheme, the police officers then chose to record their own visual observations with a video camera rather than with a note pad. The officers were observing a public place and positioned the video camera to observe the activities in this public place. As such, any visual observations were not an intrusion into an area where appellant possessed a "reasonable expectation of privacy." The videotape surveillance did not, therefore, constitute a search in violation of the Fourth Amendment. The videotaping of that which is lawfully observed is not more invasive or unreasonable than personal observation and is just as lawful. Consequently, neither a court order nor a search warrant was required. The trial court, therefore, did not err in admitting into evidence the videotapes.

People v. Lynch

Michigan Court of Appeals, 445 N.W.2d 803 (1989)

Because of unlawful homosexual activity taking place in a men's public restroom on a public highway, police obtained a search warrant to install video cameras in the ceiling above the toilet stalls because a person in a toilet stall with the door closed has a right of privacy. The defendant was convicted of two counts of gross indecency between males in the common area (the open area a person walks into from outside) of the public restroom, and he appealed, arguing that a right of privacy also exists in the common area. In holding that a warrant was not needed for the common area, the court held:

This was a public bathroom in a public rest area off a public highway. Any member of the public could feel free to enter that restroom. While the structure itself preserves a certain amount of privacy to those using the facilities, it can be presumed that any member of the public would expect that in the common area of the facility their privacy is not absolute and that any activity in that area is open to public examination.

The common area was readily accessible to anyone needing to use the facility. The public's expectation that they were entering a public facility certainly was not extinguished because they had to open two doors rather than one. To the extent that the videotapes were made of activities in the common area of the rest-room, we cannot find that they invaded a constitutionally protected expectation of privacy.

As applied to this case, our holding means that the police did not need a warrant to monitor or videotape the common area.

An employee's office can be a place where a reasonable expectation of privacy exists, although the *Ortega* rule discussed in Chapter 11 makes it clear that a public employee's office may generally be searched without the need for a search warrant. Where the intrusion is video surveillance of an employee and the employee's office, courts continue to determine whether a reasonable expectation of privacy exists in relation to the video surveillance. In *Cowells v. State,*[20] the court concluded that a University of Alaska employee had no reasonable expectation of such privacy in her office in the university's ticket office. The court noted that people passing her office could see her desk and other parts of the office and that other employees made frequent and regular entrances to her office. As a result, the court concluded, she could not reasonably expect any privacy for her actions in the public view of her office, including by a hidden video camera.

A video surveillance camera caught this woman in the act of stealing. Such cameras can provide information that leads to the identification and arrest of suspects. Videotapes are admissible as evidence in court if the incident occurred where the defendant had no right to privacy and if a witness can verify that the tape is a reliable reproduction of the events. Without a witness, the videotape must meet defined standards in order to be admitted as evidence in court.

 ## THE CRIME OF VIDEO VOYEURISM

Devices capable of video recording are everywhere. In some circumstances making the video infringes on reasonable expectations of privacy held by the persons captured on the video. One such situation involves taking videos of unsuspecting subjects as they do intimate things, like remove their clothes. To combat this "video voyeurism," in 2003 New York passed "Stephanie's Law," which makes "unlawful surveillance" a crime. The act was named after a woman whose landlord installed a video recorder in a smoke detector in her bedroom to film her intimate acts. It makes it a crime to use an imaging device to "surreptitiously" view another person dressing or undressing, or to view a person's sexual or intimate parts.

In the 2014 case of *People v. Schreier*, 5 N.E.3d 985, the New York Court of Appeals considered whether this law applied to one who stood outside a woman's house and made a video recording of her exiting her bathroom, which was visible through a window in her front door. The issue for the court was the meaning of "surreptitiously"; the defendant argued that because he was standing in public view with his video camera, his actions were not surreptitious. The court disagreed, noting that the window in the door required the defendant to hold his camera over his head to see into the bathroom. That was enough to make the statute applicable, the court held.

USING PHOTOGRAPHS AS EVIDENCE

Photographs and videotapes are **demonstrative evidence** because they portray (demonstrate) objects, persons, or events not in the courtroom. Videotapes present many pictures of an event or object, whereas a photo presents only one picture. Diagrams,

demonstrative evidence Evidence that portrays objects, persons, or events not in the courtroom—for example, photographs and videotapes.

maps, drawings, models, and sketches are also demonstrative evidence in that they present information needed to understand events, places, or objects relevant to a case. A Texas court of appeals made the following statement regarding the use of photographs as evidence:

> Photographs are admissible in evidence on the theory that they are pictorial communications of a witness who uses them instead of, or in addition to, some other method of communication. Thus, they are admissible on the same grounds and for the same purposes as are diagrams, maps, and drawings of objects or places, and the same rules of admissibility applicable to objects connected with the crime apply to photographs of such objects. This is true whether they are originals or copies, black and white or colored. So, a photograph, proved to be a true representation of the person, place, or thing that it purports to represent, is competent evidence of those things of which it is material and relevant for a witness to give a verbal description.[21]

Introducing Photographs and Videotapes into Evidence

Photographs and videotapes are admissible into evidence to explain or illustrate anything that a witness could testify to or describe in words. It is not necessary to have the person who took the photo or video introduce the picture or pictures into evidence. Any witness who can testify from firsthand knowledge that the photograph or video accurately portrays and represents the object, place, person, or event may introduce the photo or video. In many instances, the person who took the photo or video introduces it into evidence, but this is not necessary.

When a video recording is offered into evidence, the party offering it must show a proper foundation for the video. In *State v. Sibley*,[22] the court stated that showing a proper foundation for a video recording requires (1) testimony from someone with firsthand knowledge that the video accurately and fairly illustrates the event that appears in the video; (2) testimony that the video recorder was checked and operating properly; and (3) testimony that the video introduced was the same video previously seen by the witness, or that the video had not been edited after it was first recorded. In *Sibley* the court reversed a conviction for possession of illegal weapons, stating that a video recording showing the defendant holding an illegal weapon was inadmissible because no witness testified about either the accuracy of the video, or the operation of the video recorder.

The extent to which the verifying witness must testify about the accuracy of a photograph varies, depending on the importance of each photograph to the issues before the court. Some photographs might be admitted by stipulation (agreement between the parties) or with no challenge, whereas other photographs might be sharply contested and challenged. A photograph that incriminates a defendant is more likely to be contested and therefore requires more testimony about verification. Conversely, minimal proof of accuracy may be sufficient for a photograph that illustrates something not seriously contested.

All evidence sought to be admitted for use in criminal or civil trials must be relevant to at least one of the issues before that court. In determining the admissibility of a photograph or videotape, the trial judge must determine whether the photo or video has probative, or evidentiary, value and tends to prove or disprove some issue in dispute. The Supreme Court of Minnesota stated: "Photographs are admissible if they accurately portray what a witness would be permitted to describe or if they aid a description, provided they are relevant.[23]

In many cases photographs taken by a police officer are offered as evidence. The officer must establish the foundation for the photograph. After verifying the accuracy of a photograph, the officer may be asked to state how he or she knows that the photograph is the one the officer took. The witness may identify the photograph by testimony showing any one or more of the following:

- Sole continuous possession of the photograph between the time the photo was taken and its presentation in court.
- The chain of possession for the time between the taking of the photograph and the presentation in court.
- The presence of an identifiable object in the picture that the officer placed at the scene before taking the photograph. The identifiable object could be an information data board or a measuring device with the initials of the officer and the date and place that the photograph was taken.

Gruesome Photographs and Videotapes

gruesome photographs
Photographs that are shocking and repulsive.

Photographs of some crime scenes and victims are shocking and horrible. Such videotapes or **gruesome photographs** may be used as evidence if they are relevant to some issue before the court. The trial judge has a great deal of discretion in determining whether such photos are needed and how many photos may be shown. In the case of *Young v. State,*[24] a Florida Court of Appeals held as follows:

> The fact that the photographs are offensive to our senses and might tend to inflame the jury is insufficient by itself to constitute reversible error, but the admission of such photographs, particularly in large numbers must have some relevancy, either independently or as corroborative of other evidence.
>
> The very number of photographs of the victim in evidence here, especially those taken away from the scene of the crime, cannot but have had an inflammatory influence on the normal fact-finding process of the jury. The number of inflammatory photographs and resulting effect thereof was totally unnecessary to a full and complete presentation of the state's case. The same information could have been presented to the jury by use of the less offensive photographs whenever possible and by careful selection and use of a limited number of the more gruesome ones relevant to the issues before the jury.

The Supreme Court of North Carolina gave reasons why photographs of a victim's body could be admitted as evidence in the case of *State v. Robinson:*[25]

> Photographs are usually competent to explain or illustrate anything that is competent for a witness to describe in words ... and properly authenticated photographs of a homicide victim may be introduced into evidence under the trial court's instructions that their use is to be limited to illustrating the witness's testimony.
>
> Thus, photographs of the victim's body may be used to illustrate testimony as to the cause of death. Photographs may also be introduced in a murder trial to illustrate testimony regarding the manner of killing so as to prove circumstantially the elements of murder in the first degree and for this reason such evidence is not precluded by a defendant's stipulation as to the cause of death. Photographs of a homicide victim may be introduced even if they are gory, gruesome, horrible or revolting, so long as they are used for illustrative purposes and so long as their excessive or repetitious use is not aimed solely at arousing the passions of the jury.
>
> This Court has recognized, however, that when the use of the photographs that have inflammatory potential is excessive or repetitious, the probative value of such evidence is eclipsed by its tendency to prejudice the jury.

PROCEDURES & PROCESSES

The "Silent Witness" Method for Introducing Videotapes

When the prosecution plans to introduce a videotape as evidence in a criminal trial, it must lay the proper foundation for its admission. Federal Rule of Evidence 901(A), applicable in federal courts and adopted by many states, requires that all evidence must be "authenticated" before it can be admitted and then presents a nonexclusive list of how such authentication can occur.

In the case of videotape evidence, two methods of authentication have developed in the federal and state courts. The first is generally called the "pictorial communication" method. Under this method, a live witness must testify that the videotape accurately depicts an event that the witness actually saw. If such a witness can be found, no other authentication of the videotape is required, although the chain of custody requirements discussed in this section may be applicable.

In many situations a live witness may not be available for this kind of authentication. For example, video cameras may be placed in a location and programmed to film events that occur at that location, without a person operating the video recorder. Where videotapes of this type are offered as evidence, they are authenticated through the "silent witness" method. The following case illustrates this second method of authentication.

Straughn v. State Court of Criminal Appeals of Alabama, 876 So.2d 492 (2003)	Police officers discovered a marijuana field, and in an effort to identify the persons cultivating the marijuana, they set up video recorders near the field to record persons using the road leading to the field and inside the field. The cameras were programmed to begin recording when motion was detected. The cameras subsequently recorded the defendant stopping on the road leading to the field, entering the field, and working on the marijuana plants. At his trial for unlawful possession of marijuana, the defendant moved to suppress the videotapes, contending that they were not properly authenticated. The trial court admitted the videotapes, and the defendant was convicted. On appeal, the court held that the admission of the videotapes was proper under the "silent witness" method.

Under the "silent witness" theory, a witness must explain how the process or mechanism that created the item works and how the process or mechanism ensures reliability.

The court stated that the standards for admission of a videotape under the "silent witness" method were

1. A showing that the device that produced the videotape was capable of recording what a witness would have seen had a witness been present
2. A showing that the operator of the video camera was competent
3. A showing that the resulting videotape was correct and authentic
4. A showing that no changes or deletions had been made
5. A showing of the manner in which the videotapes were preserved

6. An identification of the persons depicted in the videotapes
7. If statements are made in the recording, a showing that such statements were made voluntarily

The court held that because a police officer was able to provide the appropriate testimony meeting the standards set forth above, the videotape was properly admitted into evidence.

X-ray Films as Evidence

Rule 1001(2) of the Federal Rules of Evidence (see Appendix C) defines photographs as including still photographs, X-ray films, videotapes, and motion pictures. Therefore, X-ray films, videotapes, and motion pictures are introduced into evidence on the same basis and principles as still photographs. X-ray films—radiographs, roentgenograms, and skiagrams—are different from ordinary photographs in the following respects:

- An untrained person may take a photograph, but a trained technician or a physician must take an X-ray. Therefore, the photographer of the X-ray must testify in court unless the defense stipulates or agrees to the admission of the X-ray film.
- Unlike most photographs, X-ray films require an expert to explain and interpret them. Therefore, in most situations a licensed physician who has had experience with X-rays must be qualified as an expert witness to testify about the content of the X-ray film.
- Because no witness is capable of testifying to actually seeing the injury depicted by the X-ray, the picture must be admitted as original evidence in order to provide the basis for the opinion of the expert trained in the interpretation of X-rays.

In the case of *State v. Wilson*, 200 P.3d 417 (Hawaii App. 2009), the court upheld a trial court's decision admitting into evidence an X-ray of a victim taken in a hospital in Japan. The court said that the prosecution showed a proper chain of custody of the X-ray from the date it was taken until its admission at the trial. It held that the testimony of an expert who examined the X-ray established that it had not been altered, and that it accurately pictured the internal injuries of the victim. The expert compared the Japan X-ray to an X-ray of the same part of the victim taken in a Hawaii hospital, and confirmed they were of the same person.

USING DOCUMENTS AND WRITINGS AS EVIDENCE

document A piece of written or printed matter that provides information or evidence or that serves as an official record.

Documents and writings are involved in almost all civil cases and in many criminal cases. Generally, anything that conveys a message is a **document**. In criminal cases, documents could include such things as written confessions, bad checks, drug records and accounts, written evidence of fraud, business and hospital records, betting slips, altered prescriptions, incriminating statements found in notes and letters, demand notes used in kidnapping and robbery cases, and computer printouts relating to a criminal case.

The party seeking to use documents (or writings) as evidence must show that the document or writing is not only relevant and material but also genuine and authentic. Some documents and writings can prove their own authenticity. A prosecutor or defense attorney seeking to use a public record, whether sealed or not, or a newspaper or periodical as evidence may use a state rule of evidence similar to Federal Rule of Evidence 902 (self-authentication; see Appendix C). Authenticity may also be agreed upon by a stipulation between the parties that the document is genuine and authentic, leaving only the question whether the document is relevant and material.

Although a document or writing may be shown to be authentic and genuine, this is not proof about statements and assertions made in the document or writing. For example, a newspaper may be shown to be genuine and authentic and accepted for use in evidence as such. However, a jury or judge could find that statements made in the newspaper are not true.

Some documents are admissible as evidence as "self-authenticated." Rule 902 of the Federal Rules of Evidence states that "extrinsic evidence of authenticity" is not required for certain kinds of documents. The list includes certain public documents either certified or under seal, and similar foreign documents. The authenticity of a birth certificate issued by a foreign government, such as Mexico, is sometimes an issue in criminal prosecutions for violation of immigration laws, including illegal reentry after deportation. In *United States v. Pintado-Isiordia*, 448 F.3d 1155 (9th Cir. 2006), the court held that a Mexican birth certificate that had been certified by the proper Mexican official was admissible under Rule 902. In *United States v. Torrez-Reyes*, 46 Fed. Appx. 925 (10th Cir. 2002), the court held that even if a birth certificate had not been finally certified by a proper official, it would be "presumptively" authenticated under Rule 902 if the certificate had been available for inspection of the authenticity and accuracy of the certificate.

Using Direct Evidence to Prove That Documents Are Authentic and Genuine

Documents and writings may be proven genuine and authentic by any of the following forms of direct evidence:

- Testimony of a witness who observed the signing or the writing of the document—for example, an officer who observed the defendant writing or signing a consent form or a confession.
- Testimony of the person who wrote or signed the document acknowledging that the writing is genuine and authentic.
- Regularly kept business records that are authenticated by witnesses who are custodians or supervisors of such records and who can testify that the writing offered for use in evidence is actually part of the records of the business. In such cases, the custodian or supervisor may not have actually seen the writing or document written or signed. However, the trustworthiness of the writing may be established with testimony that the writing was a regularly kept business record. The *regularly kept business record exception* is also sometimes referred to as the *shop book rule* or the *business record exception.* (See Chapter 8 on "regularly kept records" as a major exception to the hearsay rule.)
- Testimony establishing proof of handwriting by an expert witness who is qualified to testify as to the identity of the writer of the document or writing.
- For example, an expert could testify about the identity of the writer of a check, a demand note in a robbery case, or a threat found in a writing sent to a victim.

- Testimony of a person who is not a handwriting expert but is well acquainted with the handwriting of the signer or writer of the document or writing. This could be a member of the family, a friend, or another person who has seen the handwriting of the writer frequently.[26]
- The contents of the document or writing—for example, a demand note or a check may be easily recognized by the contents and form of the writing.[27]

Using Circumstantial Evidence to Prove That Documents Are Authentic and Genuine

The majority of documents and writings introduced for use as evidence in criminal trials are proven authentic and genuine by direct evidence or by the contents of the document or writing itself. If the document or writing cannot be proven authentic and genuine by direct evidence or by its contents, then *circumstantial evidence* may be used. The following types of circumstantial evidence may be used:

- Circumstantial evidence such as the fact that the writing was in the custody of the defendant, the victim,[28] or the deceased; or that the defendant, victim, or deceased acted in response to the writing; or that the defendant, victim, or deceased referred to the document or writing in oral or written communications with other persons; or that the document or writing did not appear to be forged or have any other suspicious appearance.

ancient document rule The rule that a piece of written or printed matter may be deemed authentic and genuine without a witness to attest to the circumstances of its creation because its age suggests that it is unlikely to have been falsified.

- The **ancient document rule**, which permits the use of circumstantial evidence where the document has been in existence for a number of years (20 years or more under Federal Rule of Evidence 901(8); see Appendix C). Circumstantial evidence may be derived from the fact that the document or writing was in the custody of a public official. Statements made in a will, an income tax return, a bill of sale, or a deed may be used in evidence. If there is any question about the authenticity or genuineness of such documents, circumstantial evidence may be used.
- The reply doctrine, which permits the use of circumstantial evidence to show that a writing was in response to other communication. Writings in response to other communications often indicate this in their contents. The following case illustrates a situation in which the writing was shown to be a reply communication.

Winel v. United States

Eighth Circuit Court of Appeals, 365 F.2d 646, 648 (1966)

In holding that a postcard was properly admitted for use in evidence in a mail fraud case, the court held:

It has long been recognized that one of the principal situations where the authenticity of a letter is provable by circumstantial evidence arising out of the letter's context, other than proof of handwriting or the business records exception, is where it can be shown that the letter was sent in reply to a previous communication.

… In the instant case the inherent nature of the communication makes it absolutely certain that it is a reply communication. The only question that can then arise with respect to its admissibility would be whether there was proof of its mailing and receipt. This is clearly answered by the record…. It is not necessary that there be direct testimony of placing in the mails or removing from the mails if there is a full showing of the customs and usage relating to this type of communication."

Regularly Kept Records

All large businesses, hospitals, law enforcement agencies, and other organizations have regularly kept records. More than 300 years ago, English courts recognized the shop book rule, which is now a well-recognized exception to the hearsay rule. A writing is in most instances recognized as authentic and genuine if it is shown to be a regularly kept record.

Police reports and police records meet the requirements of regularly kept records. Records of illegal sales and shipments of drugs have been held to fall within the hearsay exception.[29] In recognizing computer printouts as a regularly kept business record, the Superior Court of New Jersey held:

> We hold that as long as a proper foundation is laid, a computer printout is admissible on the same basis as any other business record.
>
> Computerized bookkeeping has become commonplace. Because the business records exception is intended to bring the realities of the business world into the courtroom, a record kept on computer in the ordinary course of business qualifies as competent evidence. This result is in accordance with that reached in other jurisdictions. Of course, if the computer printout at issue here is admitted at trial, it will constitute only prima facie evidence of an account stated. Defendant will have the opportunity to refute plaintiff's evidence.[30]

The Best Evidence, or Original Document, Rule

The famous English lawyer and writer, Sir William Blackstone, wrote in the 1760s that "the best evidence the nature of the case will admit of shall always be required, if possible to be had; but if not possible then the best evidence that can be had shall be allowed."[31]

best evidence rule (original document rule) The rule of evidence that requires the original of a writing, photograph, or other document to prove the content, unless the original is unavailable.

Federal Rules of Evidence 1002–1006 state the **best evidence rule (original document rule)** used today in federal courts and most state courts (see Appendix C). Rule 1002 provides that the best evidence rule applies to "writing(s), recording(s), or photograph(s)" and requires the original unless "(1) Originals lost or destroyed. (2) Original not obtainable. (3) Original in possession of opponent. (4) The writing, recording, or photograph is not closely related to a controlling issue" (Rule 1004).

Carbon or photographic copies of an original document or writing are secondary evidence of the original. The requirement that the original be offered as evidence is an ancient requirement that originated in English law prior to the American Revolution. Some writers state that the reason for the rule was to prevent fraud. Most modern writers, however, state that the primary purpose of the rule was to ensure the most accurate written version, which is the original document or writing.

The rule requires that the best evidence available be used. This preference for the original of any document or writing is a commonsense attempt to minimize the possibilities of errors or fraud in seeking the truth. Possibilities of errors certainly existed years ago when all copies of original documents were made by hand. With modern copy machines, the margin of error has been minimized but still exists. The rule, which originated centuries ago, continues to require that the best available evidence be used.

The best evidence rule applies only to writings, recordings, or photographs (Rule 1002). In the 2010 case of *United States v. Buchanan*,[32] the court held that the best evidence rule applies only to writings and not to other evidence. In that

PROCEDURES & PROCESSES

The Use of Writings or Documents as Evidence

Documents and writings may be admissible for use as evidence if

- The document or writing is shown to be genuine and authentic.
- The evidence contained in the document or writing is relevant, material, and competent.
- The document or writing does not contain inadmissible hearsay. (Part of a writing may be held to be inadmissible for this reason.)
- The requirements of the best evidence or original document rule are met.

After the writing or document has been admitted for use as evidence, the jury or judge as fact finder then determines:

- The author and person who wrote the writing, if this question and issue are unresolved
- The truth and credibility of the statements and assertions made in the document or writing
- The weight to be given to the statements and assertions made in the document or writing
- The issue of guilt or innocence of each charge made against the defendant

case, police officers testified that a key in the defendant's possession marked "2010" matched a safe bearing an inscription "2010" inside the safe. Illegal drugs were found in the safe, but the safe was not entered into evidence. The defendant contended that the written inscription "2010" in the safe was a "writing," and thus had to be produced under the best evidence rule. The court rejected that contention, stating the safe was not a "writing," but a chattel (personal property), and not subject to the best evidence rule. It also stated that the policy reasons behind the rule do not apply to written "marks" on chattels, because there is little likelihood a mistake would be made about the mark, and little chance of fraud because an instructional manual inside the safe, that was admitted, also carried the "2010" mark.

Failure to comply with the best evidence rule could create problems unless one of the reasons listed in Rule 1004 is shown. The following case illustrates.

Commonwealth v. Lewis

Pennsylvania Superior Court, 623 A.2d 355 (1993)

A shoplifting was recorded by a video camera in a Sears retail store. At the trial, a police officer who had not viewed the theft testified about what he observed on the store videotape, but the videotape was not introduced for use as evidence.

A store security guard testified that he was unable "to locate the videotape of [defendant's] action." The court held that this explanation was unsatisfactory and reversed the conviction and remanded the case for a new trial, holding that "whatever knowledge [the police officer] possessed was gained from his viewing of the videotape. Thus, the original tape should have been produced."

The Fourth Amendment Protection of Writings, Records, and Documents

The Fourth Amendment provides that "The right of the people to be secure in their persons, houses, papers and effects, against unreasonable searches and seizures, shall not be violated." Therefore, law enforcement officers and other governmental officials cannot intrude into a "zone of privacy" of a person to seize documents, writings, or records without a showing of proper authority.

The plain view and public view doctrines apply to documents and writings as follows:

- *Plain view:* If officers are where they have a right to be and they see a document or writing in plain view that is immediately apparent to be evidence of a crime, they may seize the document or writing.
- *Public view:* Handwriting, like the tone of a person's voice, is constantly exposed to public view, and therefore samples may be compelled by court or grand jury order.

In addition, the business records of banks, stock brokerage houses, and other financial institutions are available to governmental authorities because such records are not private papers of individual investors and account holders. The following U.S. Supreme Court cases state the law concerning this.

United States v. Dionisio

United States Supreme Court, 410 U.S.1, 93 S. Ct. 764 (1973)

The Supreme Court held that handwriting, like speech, is a characteristic that is continually on display to the public, and people can have no greater expectation of privacy to their writings than to the tone quality of their voices. A grand jury can therefore order people to submit samples of their handwriting, just as a person can be requested to talk for identification purposes.[33]

United States v. Miller

United States Supreme Court, 425 U.S. 435, 96 S. Ct. 1619 (1976)

The defendant was charged with various federal offenses. The government obtained microfilms of checks, deposit slips, and other records by means of subpoenas duces tecum served upon officials of two banks where the defendant had accounts. The Supreme Court held that these documents and records were properly used as evidence in the defendant's trial because

- The evidence was business records of the banks and was not private papers of the defendant.
- The defendant had no legitimate expectation of privacy in the original checks and deposit slips because these writings were not confidential communications but instead were negotiable instruments used in commercial transactions.

The Court ruled:

> The depositor takes the risk, in revealing his affairs to another, that the information will be conveyed by that person to the government.... This Court has held repeatedly that the Fourth Amendment does not prohibit the obtaining of information revealed to a third party and conveyed by him to government authorities, even if the information is revealed on the assumption that it will be used only for a limited purpose and the confidence placed in the third party will not be betrayed.

The Fifth Amendment Protection of Writings, Records, and Documents

The Fifth Amendment provides that "No person shall … be compelled in any criminal case to be a witness against himself." The Fifth Amendment therefore forbids demanding that a suspect write out a confession or otherwise incriminate himself by producing a writing. The U.S. Supreme Court stated the Fifth Amendment privilege against self-incrimination as follows:

> [T]he constitutional privilege against self-incrimination is designed to prevent the use of legal process to force from the lips of the accused individual the evidence necessary to convict him or to force him to produce and authenticate any personal documents or effects that might incriminate him.[34]

Although the government cannot force a suspect to produce a document that incriminates the suspect, this does not mean that the government cannot lawfully seize a document that incriminates the defendant. U.S. Supreme Court Justice Holmes stated this principle of law in 1913: "A party is privileged from producing the evidence but not from its production."[35] The following U.S. Supreme Court case illustrates.

Andresen v. Maryland

United States Supreme Court, 427 U.S. 463, 96 S. Ct. 2737 (1976)

The defendant, an attorney who practiced alone, was convicted of real estate fraud. Business records were obtained from the defendant's office under the authority of a search warrant. The trial court permitted these records to be used as evidence, holding that the defendant had not been compelled to do anything that incriminated himself. At the trial the records were authenticated by prosecution witnesses, not by the defendant. In affirming the defendant's conviction, the Supreme Court held:

> There is no question that the records seized from petitioner's offices and introduced against him were incriminating. Moreover, it is undisputed that some of these business records contain statements made by petitioner.
>
> This case thus falls within the principle stated by Mr. Justice Holmes: "A party is privileged from producing the evidence but not from its production." *Johnson v. United States,* 228 U.S. 457, 458, 33 S. Ct. 572, 57 L. Ed. 919 (1913). This principle recognizes that the protection afforded by the self-incrimination clause of the Fifth Amendment "adheres basically to the person, not to information that may incriminate him." *Couch v. United States,* 409 U.S. at 328, 93 S. Ct. at 611. Thus, although the Fifth Amendment may protect an individual from complying with a subpoena for the production of his personal records in his possession because the very act of production may constitute a compulsory authentication of incriminating information, a seizure of the same materials by law enforcement officers differs in a crucial respect—the individual against whom the search is directed is not required to aid in the discovery, production, or authentication of incriminating evidence.
>
> Accordingly, we hold that the search of an individual's office for business records, their seizure, and subsequent introduction into evidence does not offend the Fifth Amendment's prescription that "[n]o person shall be compelled in any criminal case to be a witness against himself."

◼ TERMS USED IN THE EXAMINATION OF DOCUMENTS AND WRITINGS

- *Questioned document:* A document or writing is questioned when questions are raised about who wrote, typed, or made the writing; whether the document is genuine and authentic; or whether the writing is totally or partially forged or altered.
- *Questioned document examiner:* A person who has the special training and experience necessary to examine questioned documents to determine the author or the genuineness of the document. To make this determination, the questioned document is often compared with one or more other documents.
- *Graphologist:* A person who studies one or more documents written by a known person and, from the writing or penmanship, infers personality traits of the writer of the document. Because courts do not recognize graphology as a reliable science, such evidence is not admissible.
- *Indented writings:* Writing on a sheet of a note pad or telephone pad that is under the paper on which a person originally wrote. Indented writing may provide valuable information in the investigation of a crime.
- *Charred document:* A writing or document that has been partially or completely burned. If the document is left undisturbed or can be preserved, a document examiner can usually determine the written contents.
- *Linguistics analysis:* The study of language usage. Linguistics analysis may be used to determine the genuineness of a document or to determine who wrote a document. The defense in the Patty Hearst case used linguistic evidence of writings and tape recordings in an attempt to prove that Patty did not participate voluntarily in the bank robbery. (See *United States v. Hearst,* 412 F.Supp. 893 (N.D. Calif. 1976).)

SUMMARY

1. **State when search warrants are required or not for electronic surveillance.**
   - Any person, including law enforcement officers, may make videos of public places. Videos or electronic surveillance of persons in places where they do not have a reasonable expectation of privacy are also permitted without a search warrant. However, electronic surveillance that crosses into private places, such as listening devices that can hear what is said in a residence, require court approval.

2. **State the requirements for the introduction into evidence of videotapes, photographs, and other electronic records.**
   - The two main requirements are establishing that the videotape or photograph accurately depicts the events that are the subject of the video or photograph, and that the videotape or photograph had not been altered, usually established by showing the chain of possession.

3. **Explain the "best evidence" rule.**
   - The original of a writing or document introduced as evidence must be presented, unless one of the exceptions to the rule, such as a lost or destroyed document, is established.

4. **Explain how the Fifth Amendment applies to documents.**
   - Compelling a witness to produce documents that serve to incriminate the witness violates the Fifth Amendment just as much as compelling a witness to make incriminating statements. As a result, the U.S. Supreme Court has held the Fifth Amendment applies to prohibit such compulsion. However, if the prosecution can obtain incriminating writings or documents in some fashion other than compulsion of the witness, the Fifth Amendment does not bar their use in a criminal prosecution.

KEY TERMS

ancient document
  rule, 458

best evidence rule
  (original document
  rule), 459

demonstrative
  evidence, 453

document, 456

gruesome
  photographs, 454

videotape
  surveillance, 449

PROBLEMS

1. To be admissible in a criminal trial, a video purporting to depict a defendant must have sufficient clarity to be understood by the jury. If a video lacks that clarity, can the prosecution produce a witness to testify that he is able to recognize the defendant in the video, even though others may not? If so, what must the prosecution establish about the witness? How did it fail in *Grimes v. State*, 662 S.E.2d 346 (Ga. App. 2008)?

2. Courts often say the fact that photographs of the victim are gruesome and upsetting does not alone require their exclusion from a trial. In *United States v. Salim*, 189 F. Supp. 2d 93 (S.D.N.Y. 2002), the trial court did refuse to admit photographs of a victim's head, showing damage inflicted by a criminal assault by the defendant, taken after surgery to save his life. Before reading the case, why do you think the judge thought this was a proper case to exclude the photographs?

3. Border patrol officers routinely inspect a database called "CLAIMS," which contains names of persons who have filed applications to reenter the United States after having been deported. If the search comes up empty, the suspect is charged with illegal reentry. May the officer who searched the database testify that his search came up empty? What might be the problem with that testimony? (See *United States v. Diaz-Lopez*, 625 F.3d 1198 (9th Cir. 2010).)

4. Federal officers suspected the defendant was acting as an agent for Iraq in the United States. An American counterintelligence officer working in Iraq obtained a file (the "Baghdad file") that contained documents that incriminated the defendant. Are the documents admissible? (See *United States v. Dumeisi*, 424 F.3d 566 (7th Cir. 2007).)

CASE ANALYSIS

Read Appendix B, Finding and Analyzing Cases (p. 499). With these guidelines in mind, please continue with the Case Analysis selections for Chapter 17.

1. Photographs and videotapes can serve the same function as live witnesses; that is, they can show by pictures what a witness might otherwise describe in words. But more dramatically than words, photographs and videotapes have the potential to unfairly influence or prejudice the jury. This is nowhere more apparent than in the admission of gruesome photographs. In a child abuse case, where the child died as a result of the abuse, should the prosecution be permitted to introduce autopsy photographs that show the injuries to the child? Should the answer be different if the defendant admits to the cause of death and that she did it? *See Burnette v. Commonwealth*, 729 S.E.2d 740 (Va. App. 2012).

2. Three men are murdered in their hotel room. Based on hotel surveillance video tapes, one of the men is seen entering an elevator with the defendant, and the defendant is later seen leaving the hotel carrying a cooler identified as belonging to one of the victims. The hotel security staff did not monitor the surveillance cameras, and could not authenticate the images captured on the videotapes based on date and time. The time/date stamp on the videos was not accurate compared to real time. Can the prosecution get the videotapes into evidence? How?

See Dawson v. State, 658 S.E.2d 755 (Ga. 2008), *cert. denied* 555 U.S. 871 (2008).

3. In child sexual abuse prosecutions, evidence of the abuse is frequently captured on videotape. However, the videotape is also commonly made by the defendant. Fed. R. Evid. 901 (a), and most state evidence rules, require the proponent of a videotape to produce evidence showing the video accurately depicts what the proponent claims it depicts. The person making the video can normally do that, but in child sexual abuse cases the defendant is unlikely to do so. How does the prosecution satisfy the Rule 901 authentication requirement? *See State v. Berke,*

992 A.2d 1290 (Me. 2010) for an example of how that can be accomplished.

4. Shoplifters are not always discovered by personal observation of store employees. As a result, a store "loss prevention officer" often reviews store videotapes to determine if any illegal activity in the store occurred. When the video shows suspicious activity, how does the officer determine the identity of the person depicted, and how does she authenticate the various videos she used to reach her conclusion a person stole store property? Look at the case of *State v. Stangle,* 97 A.3d 634 (N.H. 2014) to see how the officer did it in that case.

Notes

1. 496 U.S. 582 (1990).
2. 578 So.2d 698, 49 CrL 1169 (Fla. 1991).
3. 611 So.2d 422 (Ala. Crim. App. 1992).
4. 829 S.W.2d 407 (Tex. App. 1992).
5. 583 So.2d 740 (Fla. App. 1991).
6. 830 P.2d 193 (Okla. Crim. App. 1992).
7. 466 N.W.2d 105 (N.D. 1991).
8. 591 A.2d 288 (Pa. Super. 1991).
9. 577 N.E.2d 855 (Ill. App. 1990).
10. 464 N.W.2d 517 (Minn. App. 1990).
11. 367 N.W.2d 546 (Minn. App. 1985).
12. 808 S.W.2d 102 (Tex. App. 1990).
13. 581 So.2d 1249 (Ala. Crim. App. 1991).
14. 561 A.2d 468 (D.C. App. 1989).
15. 562 N.E.2d 1355 (Mass. 1990).
16. 480 U.S. 709, 107 S. Ct. 1492 (1987).
17. 923 F.2d 665 (9th Cir. 1991).
18. 856 P.2d 1265 (Hawaii 1993).
19. 848 F.Supp. 362 (E.D.N.Y. 1994).
20. 23 P.3d 1168 (Alaska 2001).
21. *Terry v. State,* 491 S.W.2d 161 (Tex. Crim. App. 1973).
22. 537 S.E.2d 835 (N.C. App. 2000).
23. *State v. DeZeler,* 41 N.W.2d 313, 319 (1950).
24. 234 So.2d 341 (Fla. 1970).
25. 395 S.E.2d 402 (N.C. 1990).
26. See the 1990 case of *State v. Glidden,* 459 N.W.2d 136 (Minn. App.), where the Minnesota Court of Appeals quoted *McCormick on Evidence*: "generally anyone familiar with the handwriting of a given person may supply authenticating testimony in the form of his opinion that a writing or a signature is the handwriting of that person." In the *Glidden* case, an office manager who was familiar with the defendant's

handwriting identified the handwriting on questioned documents as being the defendant's.

27. Records and writings concerning drug transactions are often found in raids on drug houses and apartments. In the 1991 case of *United States v. Jaramillo-Suarez,* 942 F.2d 1412 (9th Cir.), a "pay/owe" sheet was held admissible; in *United States v. Lai,* 934 F.2d 1414 (9th Cir. 1991), "what appeared to be hand-written and computer summaries of drug transactions" were allowed in evidence; and in *State v. Lewis,* 567 So.2d 726 (Fla. App. 1990), writings of the drug transactions between the defendant and the undercover officers were admitted into evidence.

28. In the 1990 case of *State v. Boppre,* 453 N.W.2d 406, a murder victim wrote the defendant's name on the floor and on a door casement as he was dying. The Supreme Court of Nebraska held that the writing was admissible in evidence as both a dying declaration and an excited utterance. In this case, in which the floor and the door could not be brought into court, a photograph of the writings was introduced as evidence.

For cases where the contents of a writing were used as evidence to identify the writer, see *United States v. Sutton,* 426 F.2d 1202 (D.C. Cir. 1969), where four handwritten, unsigned notes found on the body of a murdered woman revealed knowledge identifying and incriminating the defendant of the murder of the woman, and *People v. Faircloth,* 599 N.E.2d 1356 (Ill. App. 1992), where letters signed using a nickname showed that the defendant sold the illegal drugs that caused the death of the victim. The letters were admitted for use as evidence in the case where the defendant was convicted of the drug-induced death of a woman.

29. See *United States v. Grossman,* 614 F.2d 295 (1st Cir. 1980).

30. *Sears, Roebuck & Co. v. Merla,* 361 A.2d 68 (1976).

31. Blackstone, *Commentaries,* 368.

32. 604 F.3d 517 (8th Cir. 2010). Rule 1002 of the Federal Rules of Evidence, which is followed by most states, now requires "the original writing, recording, or photograph."

33. See also *United States v. Mara,* 410 U.S. 19, 93 S. Ct. 774 (1973).

34. *Bellis v. United States,* 417 U.S. at 88, 94 S. Ct. at 2183.

35. *Johnson v. United States,* 228 U.S. 457, 458, 33 S.Ct. 572 (1913).

Scientific Evidence

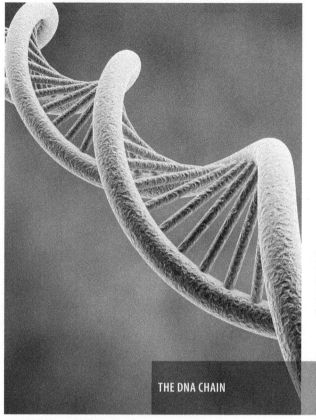

THE DNA CHAIN

© Sashkin/Shutterstock.com

LEARNING OBJECTIVES

In this chapter we examine a particular kind of evidence that is produced by scientific methods and tests. The learning objectives for this chapter are

State the requirements for admissibility of scientific evidence under Rule 702 of the Federal Rules of Evidence.

Explain the difference between the *Frye* test and the *Daubert* test.

Explain how DNA evidence is used to identify a suspect in a crime.

State both the logistical and the theoretical problems with ballistic fingerprinting.

s we saw earlier in this book, courts virtually never allow results from traditional lie detector tests to be admitted as evidence in criminal trials. What about new, non-traditional tests which claim to use "functional magnetic resonance imaging" (called here fMRI) to identify deception in a subject's answers to questions? In *United States v. Semrau*, 693 F.3d 510 (6th Cir. 2012), a federal court was called on to answer this question, a question it said was presented there for the first time in any jurisdiction. The court said no, and in doing so gave us a detailed and thoughtful review of (1) how the proponent of the fMRI theory tested his theory, and (2) why the theory did not pass the *Daubert* test for the admissibility of scientific evidence.

THE IMPORTANCE OF SCIENTIFIC EVIDENCE

scientific evidence

Evidence, usually in the form of expert testimony, that relates to scientific theory, experiments, or tests.

The American criminal justice system relies on the knowledge and equipment of many sciences and skills—chemistry, physics, mathematics, medicine, and dentistry, to name just a few. Crime laboratories with sophisticated equipment are used every day; highly skilled techniques and specialized training are often required to analyze and support evidence.

In this chapter we examine a variety of kinds of **scientific evidence** and the rules courts use to determine the admissibility of scientific evidence. DNA evidence is discussed in some detail, owing to the frequency and importance of that evidence in criminal prosecutions.

The Use of Scientific Evidence

Experienced law enforcement officers state that most crimes are solved through the use of common sense and hard work. An officer who is investigating a crime may obtain enough information to identify the perpetrator of the offense but may have insufficient evidence to charge and obtain a conviction. In such situations, scientific techniques may provide the additional evidence necessary to carry the burden of proving guilt beyond a reasonable doubt.

Sometimes an investigating officer may have only the evidence obtained from crime laboratories. When no additional evidence is available, scientific evidence may be the starting point or the link that leads to the solution of the crime.

For these reasons, scientific evidence has become one of the strongest weapons available for the successful prosecution of criminal offenders. Judges and juries may overestimate the reliability of scientific evidence, however. This problem caused the Supreme Judicial Court of Massachusetts to state: "We are aware that scientific proof may in some instances assume 'a posture of mystic infallibility in the eyes of a jury of laymen.'"[1]

Even though scientific evidence is not infallible, it may contribute to an investigation by

- Providing a lead or leads that point a criminal investigation in the right direction.
- Providing information that eliminates a suspect as the person who committed the crime being investigated. For example, DNA evidence, standard fingerprinting, or a surveillance videotape could show that the suspect did not commit the crime.

Scientists and technicians in crime laboratories use sophisticated equipment to analyze and provide evidence that can be crucial in solving cases and convicting offenders. Here a toxicologist awaits the results of a lab procedure that extracts drug and poison from biosamples.

AP Images/Mary Ann Chastain

- Providing corpus delicti, or proof that a crime was committed, such as scientific evidence that a fire was intentionally started, (in arson cases), or that death was caused by poisoning.
- Providing the independent corroborative evidence necessary to support a confession, or to corroborate and support other evidence presented by the prosecutor or the defense attorney.
- Establishing a link between the crime scene and the suspect or between the suspect and the victim of the crime.
- Providing one of the essential elements of the crime being investigated.
- Affirming or disproving an alibi.
- Establishing the innocence of people not involved in the crime.
- Encouraging or inducing a person to make a confession or an incriminating admission when the person is confronted with scientific evidence that incriminates him or her. (If such a person were being held in custody, *Miranda* warnings would have to be given before the confrontation.)
- Providing reasonable suspicion (for an investigative stop), probable cause (to make an arrest, obtain a search warrant, and so on), or sufficient proof beyond a reasonable doubt (necessary for a criminal conviction).
- Building such strong cases against defendants that the number of guilty pleas increases, thus clearing court calendars and permitting faster trials of contested cases.

THE ADMISSIBILITY OF SCIENTIFIC EVIDENCE

Traditional evidence usually comes from a witness giving testimony in a criminal trial based on "personal knowledge," usually acquired by firsthand observation of facts or events. The reliability of the witness's testimony can then be tested in a courtroom by close scrutiny of the circumstances surrounding the witness's acquisition of that firsthand knowledge. Scientific evidence differs from traditional evidence because it does not involve testimony based on personal knowledge, and because it

"COLD CASE" FILES AND SCIENTIFIC EVIDENCE

There are more than three-quarters of a million law enforcement officers in the United States, working on more than 24 million violent and felony-property crimes that occur each year. Although many crimes are solved soon after they are committed, a significant number of crimes go unsolved. For law enforcement officers, these "cold cases" remain open and are a source of concern. In recent years, the use of scientific techniques and technology has made it possible for investigators to solve many cold cases. The following two cases illustrate how DNA databases and high-tech equipment have led to closure on cold cases:

- *DNA:* In 1988 three people were killed in two separate incidents in northern Virginia. Two of the victims were women who were raped by their murderer. Police were able to collect crime-scene samples that produced a DNA profile of the rapist in each incident, but they were unable to match the DNA to any other DNA sample stored in a DNA database. In 2000 these DNA samples were entered into the new Virginia DNA database, which quickly showed that the DNA samples from both crime scenes came from the same man. However, the identity of the man was not established. In 2005 California collected DNA samples from all 70,000 inmates in the California Penal System and entered DNA profiles from these samples into the federal DNA database, CODIS (see the discussion of CODIS). In September 2005 the CODIS database indicated that the DNA sample taken from Alfredo Prieto, a convicted killer on California's death row, matched the DNA taken from the Virginia rapes and murders. In 2006 Prieto was returned to Virginia, and in 2010 (a 2007 conviction was overturned by the trial judge, and a 2008 death sentence remanded by the Virginia Supreme Court) he was sentenced to death. Prieto has been convicted of three murders, and is a suspect in four others.
- *High-tech equipment:* A young girl was reported missing in Spokane, Washington, in 1999. Extensive searches for the girl or her body came up empty. Although some evidence pointed to the girl's father as a possible suspect in the girl's disappearance, searches of his home and truck produced nothing. When the father picked up his truck after it was searched, police officers said they believed the girl was buried in a shallow grave and that the police would find the body after animals dug it up. Unknown to the father, the police had, pursuant to a court order, placed a GPS device in his truck. The father then went to the spot where he had buried the girl, dug her body up, and moved it to a new burial site. The police retrieved the GPS device, which showed the movements of the truck. By tracing the truck's movement through the GPS device, officers were able to locate the girl's body. This and other evidence collected from the body resulted in the father's first-degree murder conviction. *State v. Jackson,* 76 P.3d 217 (Wash. 2003).

often includes expert opinion testimony about the meaning of the scientific evidence. As a result, courts and legislatures have developed specific rules for determining the reliability of scientific evidence.

What Is Scientific Evidence?

Scientific evidence is most often presented in court by an expert witness testifying about expert opinions. When, for example, a person trained in science or technology gives his or her opinion about the chemical or biological composition of a substance, the testimony is scientific evidence. If the scientist has the necessary education, training, and experience to test the substance and if the scientist has conducted suitable tests of the substance, the testimony is usually admissible as expert testimony. Most states have rules identical or similar to Federal Rule of Evidence 702 (see Appendix C), which permits such expert testimony.

Scientific evidence also includes expert testimony that goes beyond science. The scientific expert is frequently called upon to interpret results and draw conclusions about what results mean in the case being tried. This is very common in criminal trials, where experts in a wide variety of scientific disciplines offer comparison testimony linking a defendant to a crime, crime scene, or victim. For example, the fingerprint expert may testify that the defendant's fingerprints match those found on a murder weapon; the ballistics expert may testify that bullets found in the victim were fired from the defendant's pistol; the forensic odontologist may testify that bite marks on the victim's body were made by the defendant's teeth; and a voice identification expert may testify that a recorded voice matches the defendant's voice.

The central issue for this kind of scientific evidence is the reliability of the theory and testing on which the conclusions are based. If the scientific theory is flawed or the tests unpredictable, then the conclusions are unreliable and should not be admitted as evidence.

Some scientific theories and tests are so widely accepted and verified that they are virtually beyond criticism. The theory that each person's fingerprints are unique, for example, has universal acceptance. Similarly, tests used to link bullets to the gun that fired them are rarely questioned (but see the discussion of ballistic fingerprinting later in this chapter).

Other scientific theories have been rejected as unreliable. Voiceprint comparisons, for example, have been found inadmissible on both theoretical and testing grounds.[2] Many courts have rejected the theory that voiceprints are unique, as well as rejecting the tests by which experts match voice spectrograms.

Thus, an important question in the admissibility of scientific evidence is the theoretical and experimental basis of the scientific expert's testimony. Courts traditionally use one of the following three rules for the admissibility of scientific evidence.

The *Frye* Test   In *Frye v. United States*,[3] the U.S. Court of Appeals refused to admit the results of a lie detector test given to a defendant in a murder trial. In rejecting the scientific basis for lie detector results, the court formulated what has become known as the *general acceptance test*:

> Just when a scientific principle or discovery crosses the line between the experimental and demonstrable stages is difficult to define. Somewhere in this twilight zone the evidential force of the principle must be recognized, and while courts will go a long way in admitting expert testimony deduced from a well-recognized scientific principle or discovery, the thing from which the deduction is made must be sufficiently established to have gained general acceptance in the particular field in which it belongs.[4]

Frye test The general acceptance test: scientific evidence presented to the court must result from tests and theories that are generally accepted by a meaningful segment of the associated scientific community.

Prior to 1993, when the U.S. Supreme Court decided *Daubert v. Merrill Dow Pharmaceuticals*,[5] the federal courts and most state courts applied the **Frye test** to determine the admissibility of scientific evidence. The *Frye* general acceptance test was subject to significant criticisms. Some thought the test was too broad because it permitted expert scientific testimony in areas where no real scientific methods had been followed. For example, in *Commonwealth v. Lykus*,[6] the Massachusetts Supreme Judicial Court admitted voice spectrographic identification evidence, stating "the requirement of the *Frye* rule of general acceptance is satisfied, in our opinion, if the principle is generally accepted by those who would be expected to be familiar with its use."[7] As critics observed, the only people "familiar with the use" of voiceprint analysis are the voiceprint experts themselves.

The *Frye* test was also criticized as too narrow because otherwise reliable scientific evidence might be inadmissible even though it had sound theoretical and experimental foundations. Indeed, some courts rejected *Frye* for this reason. In *State v. Hall*,[8] the Iowa Supreme Court permitted an expert witness to testify about blood-spatter analysis. In this analysis the expert reached conclusions about the direction, force, and other physical characteristics of the crime based on the pattern of the victim's blood spatter. Although such evidence is not generally accepted, the Iowa court permitted the evidence because it was otherwise shown to be reliable.

The *Frye* Plus Test   In the 1980s when prosecutors began using DNA test results to link defendants to crime scenes, some courts modified the *Frye* test by adding other requirements to it. In the leading case of *People v. Castro*,[9] the New York Supreme Court held that DNA evidence[10] is admissible if (1) the theory is generally accepted, (2) procedures for testing the theory are generally accepted, and (3) the testing is shown to have followed those procedures.

In the case of DNA evidence, the theory is generally accepted. Most courts and scientists agree that the DNA chain of an individual can be analyzed and compared with the DNA chain found in crime-scene evidence.[11] Moreover, there is general acceptance for some, but not all, procedures for testing DNA. The RFLP test (see the discussion below) has general acceptance.[12] The PCR test has not been generally accepted by some courts.[13]

In courts that use the *Frye* Plus test, the admissibility question frequently turns on how accurately and faithfully the testing laboratory followed accepted procedures.

The *Daubert* Test   The U.S. Supreme Court decision in *Daubert v. Merrill Dow Pharmaceuticals Co.*[14] rejected the *Frye* test and held that Federal Rule of Evidence 702 created its own standard for the introduction of scientific evidence. Under Rule 702, the Court said, scientific evidence is admissible if:

> the expert is proposing to testify to (1) scientific knowledge that (2) will assist the trier of fact to understand or determine a fact in issue. This entails a preliminary assessment of whether the reasoning or methodology underlying the testimony is scientifically valid and of whether that reasoning or methodology properly can be applied to the facts in issue.[15]

The *Daubert* Court suggested that the trial court consider various factors in assessing scientific validity: (1) Has the theory been tested? (2) Has the theory been subjected to peer review by other scientists? (3) What is the theory's or technique's known or potential rate of error? (4) Do standards controlling the application of the theory or technique exist? (5) Is the theory or technique generally accepted?

Daubert test   The principle that scientific evidence presented to the court must result from tests and theories that are testable, have been reviewed by peers, have high reliability rates, and are generally accepted by the associated scientific community.

In 1999 the U.S. Supreme Court held that the **Daubert test** was applicable to technical as well as scientific evidence. In *Kumho Tire Co. v. Carmichael*,[16] the Court held that an engineer's testimony concerning a tire failure was inadmissible under the *Daubert* test.

Kumho and *Daubert* are decisions that interpret Federal Rule of Evidence 702 and are binding only in federal prosecutions. Because most states have adopted a rule similar to Rule 702, *Daubert* and *Kumho* are influential in state cases. In a 2010 study,[17] it was reported that 30 states had specifically adopted *Daubert* and an evidence rule similar to Rule 702. The other states continue to use the *Frye* test or a specific state-created test, or have announced no final decision.[18] However, a 2006 study published by the American Bar Association Committee on Continuing Legal Education notes that many states use parts of the *Daubert* test but have not adopted the complete test.[19]

As pointed out in Chapter 16, fingerprint science has reconstructed itself in recent years. New proficiency testing and new qualitative and quantitative analyses have been established. These changes can be attributed to *Daubert,* which emphasizes rigorous testing and organized skepticism and points out that there are no certainties in science, only probabilistic results. Although it is still widely accepted that no two people have the same fingerprints, it is now known that the same finger does not produce the same print twice in a row and that the impression of a small area of a fingerprint may match any number of different fingers.

In 2000, Federal Rule of Evidence 702 was amended to incorporate the reliability tests mandated by *Daubert.* Effective December 1, 2011, the Federal Rules of Evidence were amended to achieve primarily stylistic changes. Appendix C includes the most recent changes to the Federal Rules, including Rule 702.

Many of the states that have adopted the *Daubert* decision will likely make similar amendments to their evidence rules. Rule 702 has already resulted in changes in how scientific evidence is received. For example, the horizontal gaze nystagmus (HGN) sobriety test (discussed below) was once such well-regarded scientific evidence that courts took judicial notice of its reliability.[20] Since the incorporation of the *Daubert* requirements into Rule 702, however, courts have taken a more cautious approach to that test. In *United States v. Horn,*[21] the court refused to take judicial notice of the reliability of the HGN test and permitted the introduction of test results only as evidence of probable cause for arrest, not as proof of intoxication.

The Use of Judicial Notice for Accepted Scientific Techniques

After a scientific technique has been found by the highest court to be reliable under Rule 702 or the standard required in a specific state, judicial notice can be made of that court's ruling. As a result, the reliability of the technique itself need not be established, although its application in the case at issue could be attacked.

In the 1993 case of *United States v. Jakobetz,*[22] a woman was abducted from a rest area along Interstate 91 in Vermont. After she was repeatedly raped, the woman was released in New York. The federal trial court used Rule 702 in admitting DNA evidence in the trial of the defendant. In holding that the scientific technique was reliable and did not unfairly prejudice the defendant's case, the Second Circuit Court of Appeals stated,

> [I]t appears that in future cases with a similar evidentiary issue, a court could properly *take judicial notice of the general acceptability of the general theory and the use of these specific techniques.* Beyond such judicial notice, the threshold for admissibility should require only a preliminary showing of reliability of the particular data to be offered, i.e., some indication of how the laboratory work was done and what analysis and assumptions underlie the probability calculations. *Affidavits should normally suffice to provide a sufficient basis for admissibility.* (emphasis added)

The extent to which judicial notice of a scientific theory is taken can change. For example, the science of handwriting analysis has been the subject of judicial notice.[23] However, as a result of the *Daubert* case and independent handwriting analysis studies,[24] handwriting expert testimony has come under attack. One court concluded that handwriting analysis is not scientific knowledge at all but only technical knowledge.[25] After the *Kumho* decision, which made *Daubert*'s rules applicable to technical evidence, expert handwriting testimony has to meet the *Daubert* reliability tests. The following case illustrates how expert handwriting evidence can satisfy the *Daubert* reliability test.

United States v. Crisp

Fourth Circuit Court of Appeals, 324 F.3d 261 (2003), cert. denied, 124 S. Ct. 220 (2003)

Crisp was charged with bank robbery with a dangerous weapon. Part of the evidence against him included the note used by the robber during the bank robbery. The prosecution produced a handwriting expert, who had examined both the note and a sample of Crisp's handwriting given for purposes of the examination. Over Crisp's objection under *Daubert,* the expert was permitted to testify. Crisp was convicted and on appeal contended that the trial court was wrong in admitting the handwriting expert's testimony:

> Crisp contends that, like fingerprinting identifications, the basic premise behind handwriting analysis is that no two persons write alike, and thus that forensic document examiners can reliably determine authorship of a particular document by comparing it with known samples. He maintains that these basic premises have not been tested, nor has any error rate been established. In addition, he asserts that handwriting experts have no numerical standards to govern their analyses and that they have not subjected themselves and their science to critical self-examination and study.

The court rejected these contentions. It noted that the expert, Officer Currin, had 24 years of experience with the North Carolina State Bureau of Investigation. Currin testified that every questioned document was first examined by a "questioned document examiner" and then reviewed by another examiner. He testified that he had passed numerous proficiency tests in handwriting analysis and that document examiners followed a "consistent methodology of handwriting examination." He also testified that studies existed showing that experienced document examiners consistently scored higher on identification of handwriting than laypersons.

Based on this testimony, the court concluded that handwriting analysis was reliable scientific knowledge and admissible. It also noted that every circuit court of appeals that addressed the question after the *Daubert* decision had reached the same conclusion.

The court gave the following description of Currin's tests of the handwriting samples, and the reasons given by him for his expert opinion:

> At trial, Currin drew the jury's attention to similarities between Crisp's known handwriting exemplars and the writing on the note. Among the similarities that he pointed out were the overall size and spacing of the letters and words in the documents; the unique shaping of the capital letter "L" in the name "Lamont"; the spacing between the capital letter "L" and the rest of the word; a peculiar shaping to the letters "o" and "n" when used in conjunction with one another; the v-like formation of the letter "u" in the word "you"; and the shape of the letter "t," including the horizontal stroke. Currin also noted that the word "tomorrow" was misspelled in the same manner on both the known exemplar and the note.

The court affirmed the defendant's conviction.

A FEW OF THE SCIENCES AND SCIENTIFIC TECHNIQUES USED IN THE CRIMINAL JUSTICE SYSTEM

Scientific evidence covers a range of evidence that varies widely in probative value, weight, and persuasiveness. Some sciences permit the formulation of an opinion with almost mathematical certainty, whereas others are less precise and become more of an art than a science. For example, polygraph testing is widely used in the United States, yet very few state courts permit the results of lie detector tests to be used as evidence because of the reasons stated in Chapter 12.

A scientific theory that was novel only a few years ago but is now widely accepted by the scientific, legal, and law enforcement community is the DNA test and technique. DNA easily passes the *Daubert* test. It is reported that DNA was first used as evidence in a criminal court in 1987, and the FBI first began analyzing DNA in casework in 1996.

DNA Genetic Profiling

forensic Belonging to or connected with a court; for example, forensic fingerprints are fingerprints used as evidence in a civil or criminal trial.

DNA genetic profiling A method for identifying individuals by the unique structure of their DNA; used for both identifying the person who committed a crime and clearing innocent suspects.

locus points Points in the sequence of base pairs in human DNA where individual DNA chains vary.

Deoxyribonucleic acid (DNA) testing has become an important **forensic** tool for linking suspects to a crime. Equally important, DNA testing has made it possible to eliminate a suspect in a crime, sometimes even after the suspect has been convicted of that crime.[26] **DNA genetic profiling** has received such wide acceptance among criminal justice professionals that it is frequently called *genetic fingerprinting*.

DNA testing is in many ways similar to fingerprint testing. In both, samples found at the crime scene or on the victim are collected and stored. In the crime of rape, where DNA testing is widely used, most police departments or hospitals have a "rape kit," in which blood or semen samples from the victim are collected and stored. This procedure begins a proper chain of custody, a vital ingredient in any DNA evidence.

Two major tests are used on DNA: polymerase chain reaction (PCR) (see Figure 18.1) and restriction fragment length polymorphism (RFLP) analysis. Although these tests are conducted differently, they have a common goal: to identify the genetic code in the crime-scene sample and compare it with the genetic code in the suspect's (and victim's) samples.

The human body consists of billions of cells, most of which carry chromosomal DNA. Human genetic information is encoded in the DNA found in chromosomes. The DNA in chromosomes is arranged in a sequence of paired organic bases, called base pairs, which form the well-known twisted double-helix DNA chain. A set of chromosomes (one from the mother, one from the father) might contain 3 billion base pairs arranged in sequences on the DNA chain. Knowledge about these sequences in chromosomes makes DNA matching possible.

If we compare DNA chains from two people who are not identical twins, we discover two things. First, the chains, or sequences of base pairs, are identical for more than 99 percent of the base pairs. Humans are, after all, more alike than different. Second, at certain identifiable sites, called **locus points**, base pairs vary from one individual to another. At such a locus, for example, where eye color is determined, base pairs join in a sequence that is repeated; measuring the size of a repetitive sequence of base pairs at many such locations gives a fingerprint-like picture of the DNA chain, since at these locations the sequence of base pairs varies among different

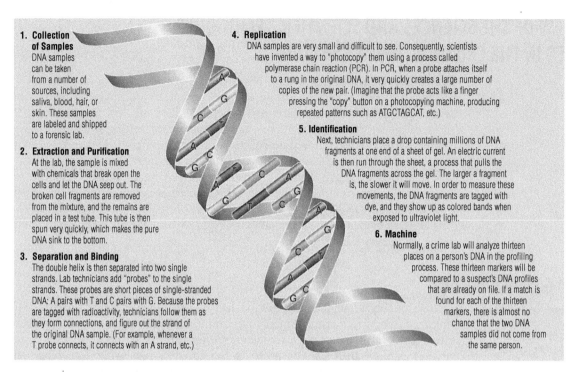

Figure 18.1 | The Polymerase Chain Reaction

Source: L. Gaines and R. Miller, *Criminal Justice in Action*, 4th ed. (Belmont, CA, Wadsworth, 2002).

individuals. Thus, like fingerprints, if we have a picture of enough of these locations where human DNA varies, then we have an individual's genetic fingerprint.

When a suspect's DNA profile matches the crime-scene sample's DNA profile, it means that the two profiles appear the same at several key points in the DNA chain where individual differences occur. Because databases do not have millions of individual DNA profiles on file, in most cases one cannot simply search a database and see whether another person's DNA profile matches the suspect's. Instead, DNA profiles taken from a selected sample of the population are compared with the suspect's profile. Based on the number of times at each of the locus points tested a match in the selected sample is found, a probability estimate can be made.

Experts who perform DNA tests and later testify to test results and meaning usually give probability estimates, taking into account different population samples, as the following example demonstrates:

> Deoxyribonucleic acid (DNA) profiles for [the specific sites tested] were developed from specimens obtained from the crime scene, from the victim, and from the suspect. Based on these results, the DNA profiles from the crime scene match those of the suspect. The probability of selecting at random from the population an unrelated individual having a DNA profile matching the suspect's is approximately 1 in 200,000 in Blacks, 1 in 200,000 in Whites, and 1 in 100,000 in Hispanics.[27]

Figure 18.2 shows the types and sources of DNA.

The previous example shows an expert giving the "random match" probability that a person selected at random would possess a DNA fingerprint that matched the crime scene sample. Thus, an expert might reliably testify that the likelihood a

DNA is the hereditary material that contains instructions to build a human being. DNA can be collected from very small amounts of blood, mouth (cheek) scrapings, hair roots, or other samples. There are two kinds of DNA in the body: nuclear DNA and mitochondrial DNA. Both kinds of DNA can be used for DNA identification.

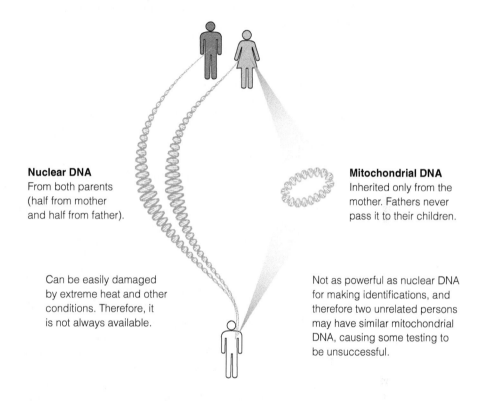

Nuclear DNA
From both parents (half from mother and half from father).

Can be easily damaged by extreme heat and other conditions. Therefore, it is not always available.

Mitochondrial DNA
Inherited only from the mother. Fathers never pass it to their children.

Not as powerful as nuclear DNA for making identifications, and therefore two unrelated persons may have similar mitochondrial DNA, causing some testing to be unsuccessful.

Sources of other DNA samples include bone marrow, biopsy samples, and toothbrush and hairbrush samples. (Urine samples will not work.)

Figure 18.2 | Types and Sources of DNA

Source: NCJ 209493, *Identifying Victims Using DNA* (2005).

person selected at random would have a DNA profile that matched a crime scene DNA profile is 1 in 1,000,000. If the DNA profile of a suspect matches the crime scene DNA profile, is it logical to conclude the likelihood is 1,000,000 to 1 that the suspect is the source of the DNA?

The equation of "random match probability" with "source probability" was called the "prosecutor's fallacy" by the U.S. Supreme Court in the 2010 case of *McDaniel v. Brown*, 130 S. Ct. 665, 670. Prosecutors commit error when they tell the jury that the probability of finding a DNA match in a random sample is also the probability the suspect is the source of the DNA, the Court said. A simple example illustrates the fallacy. Assume a defendant can prove he could not possibly have been at the crime scene where DNA evidence was found. However, the DNA profile matches the defendant's profile. The "random match probability" of 1 in 1,000,000 means only that *if an innocent person* was tested, the odds are 1,000,000 to 1 the person would have a matching DNA profile. However, in this example, the "source probability," that the defendant was the source of the DNA, is 0, because other evidence makes it impossible the DNA was left by the defendant. It would thus be illogical to say the probability the defendant is the "source" of the DNA is 1,000,000 to 1. Prosecutors must therefore offer other evidence showing the likelihood the defendant left the DNA at the crime scene.

At present, DNA profiles have a wide variety of uses:

- To identify air crash victims and other dead people from bits of bones or charred flesh. For example, casualties from Operation Desert Storm and the Vietnam War have been identified by obtaining DNA samples from family members. Bones thought to be from former Russian Czar Nicholas II and his family, who were executed in 1917, were proven to be the remains of the Russian royal family through blood donated by British Prince Philip, who is a distant relative of the former Russian royalty.[28]
- To identify offenders from blood, semen, and hair left at the scene of a crime. The FBI reports that more than 80 percent of the DNA samples they receive from state and local police are from rape cases.
- To clear suspects who are innocent. The FBI reports that in 20 to 25 percent of the cases sent to them, the suspect is cleared. An FBI official stated that in one case the standard blood tests did not eliminate the suspect and two victims of a serial rapist had identified the suspect, with "one of them fairly positive. He certainly would have gone to trial and probably would have been convicted, but the DNA evidence eliminated him as a suspect."[29]
- To establish proof of corpus delicti, which is proof that a crime was committed. Missing persons are a problem in every American city. To charge murder, the state must prove that the missing person is dead and was killed by the defendant. In the 1991 case of *State v. Davis*,[30] a woman was missing. She was last seen going to work, but her body was never found. However, DNA from dried blood, skull bone fragments, and blood-encrusted tissue was compared with DNA from her children and husband and showed that the woman had been murdered. The conviction of her husband was affirmed.
- To identify missing persons. More than 88,000 U.S. people who served in the Vietnam War, the Korean War, and World War II are still missing. The military services are asking family members of people listed as missing to submit DNA samples to aid in identifying the remains found. Each service has its own casualty office. The telephone number for the U.S. Army office is 800-892-2490.

The U.S. armed forces are building a DNA database by collecting blood and saliva from all service personnel. The reason for this database is that military dog tags can be lost, switched, or counterfeited, and fingerprinting and dental records are not always reliable.

The creation of DNA databases also affects statutes of limitation. Many states are abolishing, extending, or amending their statutes of limitation for rape; in other states, prosecutors are issuing John Doe criminal complaints or obtaining John Doe indictments when it is determined that they have probable cause based on DNA evidence. New York prosecutors obtained rape indictments against an unknown serial rapist known as the "East Side Rapist" in March 2000. In October 1999 Wisconsin prosecutors filed three rape charges against a man known only by his DNA code, to avoid the expiration of the Wisconsin statute of limitations, and in 1991 Kansas prosecutors filed one rape charge based only on DNA evidence.

LEGAL CASES

Cases Where DNA Evidence Did Not Carry the Burden of Proof

DNA evidence has had a remarkable record of success since it was first used in 1987. It must be remembered, however, that DNA is available in only about 10 percent of crimes committed because sweat, saliva, skin, blood, or some other bodily substance must be found on the victim or at the crime scene in order to create a DNA "fingerprint." Moreover, even where DNA evidence is available, it still is subject to burden of proof requirements, as the following two situations demonstrate:

- In the O.J. Simpson murder trial, investigators stated they had never seen as much blood at a crime scene as was found near the bodies of Nicole Simpson and Ronald Goldman. Both victims resisted the knife attack, and their blood covered the crime scene. A third person's blood was also found at the scene, and DNA tests showed that the blood came from Simpson. Simpson's attorneys did not attack the DNA evidence itself, but rather the way in which investigators collected the evidence. Simpson was found not guilty by a jury in the criminal trial, but subsequently the Goldman family obtained a multimillion-dollar civil judgment against Simpson. The Goldmans have collected little of that judgment. Simpson was convicted in 2008 on charges of robbery and kidnapping; in December 2008 he was sentenced to 16 years in prison. In 2002 a private company hired by the California Department of Justice donated its DNA papers on the 100 items of bloodstained evidence taken in the murder case to the Smithsonian Institution's anthropological archives, where they will join the museum's extensive collection of forensic material. (See "Simpson's Papers Go to Smithsonian," *New York Times* (May 18, 2002).)

- In 1975 former Teamsters Union president James (Jimmy) Hoffa disappeared from the parking lot of an exclusive restaurant during the lunch hour. Because of Hoffa's reputed connection to organized crime, many persons believed he was the subject of a mafia "hit." In 2002 FBI scientists, using new technology, were able to match the DNA from Hoffa's hair to a strand of hair found in a vehicle owned by a reputed mafia family. On the day of Hoffa's disappearance, the car had been loaned to a friend of Hoffa to make a delivery, which placed the friend and the car in the vicinity of the restaurant where Hoffa disappeared. The prosecutors concluded that after 27 years, there was not enough evidence to bring criminal charges. (See "Hoffa DNA Evidence Not Enough for State Charges," *Milwaukee Journal-Sentinel* (August 20, 2002).)

Familial (Kinship-Based) DNA Searching

Until 2011 most computers in the United States, including the FBI's CODIS database (discussed below), could be searched only for exact matches of stored DNA profiles to DNA samples found at crime scenes. With slight modifications, these computers can also expand DNA searches to produce "partial matches," where DNA profiles in the database are a close, but not exact match. Close family members of the partial matches can then be investigated as a possible source of DNA evidence at a crime scene, because the DNA of close family members is genetically very similar. (See Suter, *All in the Family: Privacy and Familial Searching*, 23 Harv. J. L. & Tech. 309 (2010).) This would be particularly helpful in old, "cold" cases, where the victims are women or children and traditional investigative tactics have failed to identify a single suspect.

The two limitations on DNA evidence as of 2012 are that (1) DNA evidence becomes available in only about 10 percent of crimes because bodily fluids such as blood, sweat, semen, hair, or skin fragments needed for crime lab testing are not always present in a crime scene; and (2) a significant number of criminals who leave DNA evidence at a crime scene are not in a DNA database, and therefore cannot be immediately identified by a "match."

Familial DNA searching was developed by British investigators in 2006 during an investigation of the "Dearne Valley Shoe Rapist" crimes. DNA left at the crimes scenes did not yield an exact match, and for 20 years police had no firm suspects. By searching for partial matches, police found 43 persons in DNA databases who were partial matches to the crime scene DNA. Police investigated these people, and ultimately determined a brother of one of them was the rapist. The following case is one of the growing number of cases that have been solved by the use of the familial DNA search technique.

For more than 20 years a serial killer stalked a poor area of South Los Angeles, murdering at least 10 people. The killer, known as the "Grim Sleeper" because of a gap in killings between 1988 and 2002, was finally caught in 2010, using the familial DNA search technology. Semen found at many of the crimes scenes had not yielded an exact match to any DNA profile in either the FBI or California DNA databases, so police began searching the databases for partial matches. Under California law, as one of the few states with such restrictions, familial search technology could not be used unless all other investigative leads had been exhausted, and only then in the crimes of rape or murder when the perpetrator was still committing crimes and was a threat to public safety.

Using DNA samples the "Grim Sleeper" had left at several crime scenes, a familial DNA search in 2010 produced a close, partial match to Christopher Franklin, incarcerated in a California prison on a weapons conviction, whose DNA profile was in the California DNA database. Believing the "Grim Sleeper" was a close relative of Christopher Franklin, police focused their investigation on his father, Lonnie Franklin, Jr.

Police surveillance of Lonnie Franklin (see "surreptitious sampling" in the following box) observed him as he discarded the remains of a slice of pizza. Police seized the discarded pizza, and saliva from the pizza yielded DNA that was an exact match to the DNA left by the "Grim Sleeper," and was a critical link in ending some of the fear that existed in Los Angeles during the killings.

The July 9, 2010, *New York Times* article, "Arrest in 'Grim Sleeper' Killings Fans Debate on DNA Procedure," reports that debates are ongoing in many states on what restrictions should be placed on the use of familial DNA searches to avoid unnecessary harassment of innocent people. At present, most "partial matches" are not the result of deliberate familial searches, but of inadvertent or accidental discoveries. Only three states—California, Nebraska, and New York—permit deliberate familial searches. Other states permit investigators to use partial matches to identify family members as potential suspects where the match is "very close." (Suter, *All in the Family*, *supra*, at 327.) For those interested in the debate, David Kaye, the author of "The Genealogy Detectives: A Constitutional Analysis of 'Familial Searching'", 50 Am. Crim. L. Rev. 109 (2013) believes that a properly implemented "near-miss" or "kinship matching" (his preferred terms) program could be a valuable investigative tool without unnecessarily treading on constitutional principles.

DNA Forensic Laboratories and the Work They Do There are now hundreds of state, federal, and private DNA laboratories in the United States, many of which do only forensic work for law enforcement agencies. The work of these forensic DNA labs is generally of two types: (1) casework on pending criminal cases and (2) classi-fication of DNA samples taken from persons convicted of certain serious offenses.

In addition to fingerprinting, it is now standard practice for state and federal officers to take blood samples from felons who have been convicted of serious offenses, such as rape, homicide, or sexual assault, and those who are serving prison terms for such offenses. These samples are then stored in state and federal databases. Pursuant to federal statute,[31] the FBI maintains a national DNA database, the Com-bined DNA Index System (CODIS). Many states maintain similar systems. Blood samples taken from convicted felons are analyzed and classified according to the samples' DNA. The samples' DNA can then be compared with any DNA evidence found in prior or subsequent crimes and help law enforcement officers identify sus-pects. The National DNA Index System (NDIS) holds DNA profiles created by fed-eral and state law enforcement agencies. The FBI reported that as of July 2014, 11,074,565 offender DNA profiles were stored in NDIS, and that there have been 253,757 "hits," matching a forensic sample (from a crime scene) to an offender sample. These "hits" have aided 242,241 investigations. (See CODIS-NDIS statis-tics, at www.fbi.gov/about-us/codis/ndis/statistics.)

The federal DNA act was amended in 2006 to require persons arrested for felo-nies to submit DNA samples, and 24 states have passed similar laws. As stated in Chapter 11, the federal act has been upheld (*United States v. Mitchell*, 652 F.3d 387 (3d Cir. 2011), *cert. denied,* 132 S. Ct. 1741 (2012).) Also in Chapter 11, we noted that the U. S. Supreme Court, writing in *Maryland v. King,* upheld a state law that requires those arrested for serious offenses to submit to a buccal swab DNA test as part of the booking process.

In *People v. Buza*, 129 Cal. Rptr. 3d 753 (Cal. App. 2011), a California Court of Appeals held that the California DNA act, which requires all persons arrested on a felony charge to give a DNA sample, was invalid under the Fourth Amendment. In 2013 the California Supreme Court remanded the case to the Court of Appeals for review in light of the U.S. Supreme Court's decision in *Maryland v. King*, 302 P.3d 1051 (Cal. 2013).

DNA evidence has been an important development in criminal investigations. In the 2005 case of *United States v. Sczubelek*,[32] the court made the following com-ments about the role and importance of DNA testing:

> DNA testing has changed the criminal justice system. All 50 states and the federal gov-ernment have enacted DNA collection and database statutes. To date, 143 people have been exonerated by DNA evidence, 13 of whom were sentenced to death. 38 states have enacted some form of a DNA statute, allowing for post-conviction DNA testing, com-pensation for wrongful conviction, or preservation of evidence. In 2003 the House of Representatives passed the Advancing Justice Through DNA Technology Act (HR3214), a federal statute which would give prisoners the right to petition for DNA testing in support of a claim of innocence.

An example of how a DNA database was used to aid law enforcement officers in solving a crime is a 2002 bank robbery that occurred in Milwaukee, Wisconsin. The bank robbery was well planned and well executed, leaving little evidence for the police. However, one of the bank robbers left gloves that he wore during the robbery in a car stolen for that robbery. Sweat residue from the robber's hands remained in the gloves, enabling investigators to conduct DNA tests. The test results were compared with DNA samples stored in a DNA database, and a match was found. The police arrested the man identified in the database, and after the police

PROCEDURES & PROCESSES

Other Means of Obtaining and Other Uses of DNA Evidence

DNA Source or Technique	Use of DNA Evidence
Using surreptitious samples (surveillance of a person of interest)	When the DNA of a suspect or a person of interest is not in a national or state database, police sometimes attempt "surreptitious sampling" to obtain the biological material necessary for a DNA profile. A minute amount of saliva, sweat, or other bodily fluid is sufficient for a laboratory to project a full DNA profile, which may clear or incriminate the person. Objects that are thrown away, abandoned, or left behind may possibly provide sufficient genetic material. The "abandoned" material could be a discarded tissue, cigarette butt, soda can, coffee cup, straw, fork, or napkin with a minute amount of biological material. Lower courts have generally held that persons who discard such genetic material have no subjective expectation of privacy in the material object. In a 2007 Washington State case, Seattle police sent a murder suspect a fictitious letter inviting him to join a class-action lawsuit with a return envelope. The DNA on the return envelope (sealed by the suspect) matched the DNA in the semen found at the scene of the 1982 rape and murder of a 13-year-old Seattle girl. In Buffalo, New York, police waited until a person of interest left a restaurant and then obtained the suspect's glass. The DNA profile was used as evidence to convict the suspect of the murder of three women.
Linking a suspect to a crime scene or victim of a crime by DNA from the victim's pet	Animals also have distinct DNA fingerprints. Because animals constantly shed hair, animal hair is found at crime scenes where animals have been kept. The hair is on furniture, rugs, carpets, and the clothing of persons in the home. A criminal coming onto the property could pick up not only hair on his clothing and shoes but also saliva, feces, or animal blood, which could be critical evidence in linking him to the crime scene and victim.
Do prisoners have a right to access DNA to challenge their convictions?	Almost all states have laws making DNA evidence available to prisoners who want to challenge their convictions. Most states also have laws allowing prisoners access to biological material found at crime scenes. In 2006 the U.S. Supreme Court ruled unanimously that defendants have a right to introduce this type of evidence to assert "third-party guilt." (See the box in Chapter 6 titled "The Defense that Someone Else Committed the Crime.")
Is DNA evidence always foolproof?	DNA evidence is powerful evidence that has been used to convict thousands of defendants, and to free hundreds of prisoners wrongfully convicted. It has been called a "truth machine." But mistakes made by people collecting samples, transporting them to crime labs, testing DNA evidence, or preparing reports of such tests can limit the value of DNA evidence. The human factor can be a spoiler.
If DNA evidence suggests that a prisoner is innocent, should there be any doubt?	The November 16, 2011 New York Times article "When DNA Evidence Suggests 'Innocent'; Some Prosecutors Cling to Maybe" raised this question. The article cited studies of situations where prosecutors have questioned or disputed the significance of DNA evidence found at a crime scene that did not "match" the defendant. This tends to happen where other evidence against a defendant is strong, or the defendant has confessed to the crime. There might be good reasons why the DNA evidence did not match the defendant. In such cases a new trial might be the answer, if the original witnesses are available.

showed him the DNA results and offered him a plea bargain, he pled guilty and identified the other robber, who also pled guilty.[33]

In addition to DNA forensic evidence work, crime labs do work in many other scientific fields to produce evidence for law enforcement agencies. The U.S. Department of Justice (NCJ 191191) lists the following kinds of work done by crime labs, in the order of most to least evidence handled:

1. Controlled substance evidence
2. Firearm/tool mark/footwear/tire print evidence
3. Fire debris for arson analysis
4. Crime-scene material
5. Latent fingerprints
6. Blood alcohol evidence
7. Serology (analysis of blood spattering, rape kits, etc.)
8. Explosive residue
9. Toxicology (fluid analysis, such as blood, saliva, semen, etc.)
10. Questioned documents (see Chapter 17)
11. Computer crime investigations
12. Others

Determining the Time of Death in Criminal Cases

When law enforcement officers arrive at a crime scene where a dead person has been found, it is important to the investigation that the officers determine the time the death occurred. Witnesses might be available to provide information about the victim's movements, or an estimate might be made at the crime scene based on the lividity of the body or the advance of rigor mortis.

Lividity and Rigor Mortis *Lividity* is the process of blood settlement within a body after death. Within 30 minutes of death, gravity causes the blood in the body to settle in the lowest part. A body found on its back will have blood gathered in the body's back surfaces. By looking at the state of lividity, investigators can sometimes determine how long the victim has been dead and in what position he or she died.

FORENSIC CRIME LABS AND ACCREDITATION PROBLEMS

Perhaps what comes to mind first when we see reference to a "forensic crime lab" is the FBI crime lab, or an important state crime lab. Results from these places of high science are given the force of realized truth, or so it may seem in criminal jury trials. The reality may not be the same as the perception, however, as a recent Massachusetts crime lab scandal demonstrates.

In November 2013 Anne Dookhan, a chemist at a forensic drug testing lab run by the Massachusetts Department of Public Health began serving a 3–5 year prison sentence for issuing false drug-test reports used in criminal prosecutions. During the period in question she performed over 58,000 tests on drug evidence; she admitted that in many cases she either did not perform the tests she reported performing, or falsified test results. As a result, the Massachusetts Public Defender office believes as many as 190,000 criminal convictions may be compromised.

There is no widely used national accreditation program for monitoring forensic crime labs. Many of the over 400 publicly funded crime labs are unaccredited. As a result, the testing practices are controlled by the crime lab, which is often run by or closely associated with law enforcement.

Rigor mortis is the stiffening of the body's muscles that occurs after death. Human bodies produce a substance called *adenosine triphosphate*, which enables energy to flow to the muscles. At death, this substance is no longer produced, and as a result the muscles begin to stiffen. This process affects the small muscles, such as those in the face or neck, first, and becomes noticeable within about two hours of death. By looking at the extent to which rigor mortis has set in, investigators can sometimes determine how long the victim has been dead.

Investigators at the crime scene must determine whether the death was accidental, by natural causes, or a homicide, and knowing the time of death is critical to that determination. Where neither lividity nor rigor mortis can accurately determine the time of death, investigators may look to forensic entomology to estimate the time of death.

forensic entomology

The study of insects to provide scientific evidence to aid legal investigations.

Forensic Entomology Entomology is the study of insects. **Forensic entomology** is used to determine the amount of time that has passed since a person's death and also other facts surrounding the death, such as location, placement, movement of the body, and the manner of death.

Because insects can be present on a cadaver for as long as two and a half years, entomological analysis can provide useful information (evidence) concerning the cause and manner of death as well as the approximate time of death when bodies are found or missing persons are found dead.

Extensive studies and experiments have identified five stages in the decomposition process of human corpses and animal remains:

1. *Fresh stage*: In warm temperatures, blowflies can arrive within 10 minutes of death.
2. *Bloated stage*: The body inflates as the result of the release of gas from bacterial composition in the body.
3. *Decay stage*: The odors of decomposition are overwhelming.
4. *Post-decay stage*: Insects such as cloth moths and hide beetles are present.
5. *Skeletal stage*: Insects are usually gone except for wasps and spiders; animals such as mice, foxes, and dogs gnaw on and scatter bones.

The presence of insects in a body can provide information to investigators about many circumstances surrounding the body and the crime scene in which the body was found. Here are some ways in which investigators can learn about the time of death and the movement of the body:

- *Time of death (postmortem interval, or PMI)*: From controlled laboratory studies, it can be determined exactly, at various temperatures, how long it takes a fly's eggs to hatch, a maggot to grow through its three larval stages, or a fly pupa to mature into an adult. By observing the presence of these insects and the body's stage of decomposition, investigators can establish the length of the decomposition process. They can then reach a close approximation of the time of death.
- *Movement of the body*: It is important in a homicide investigation to determine whether a body has been moved after death has occurred. Entomologists can assist in this determination by identifying the habitat of insects present in the body. Forest, meadow, swamp, farm field, and water-based insects are normally not found in urban areas. The presence of these insects in a body found on a city street, for example, might indicate that the body was moved from

another place. Also, the presence of some insects in the body could indicate the time of year the crime took place. Because some insects that have fed on a corpse, such as maggots, retain traces of chemicals taken from the corpse, testing for chemicals in the insects can assist investigators in determining whether those chemicals were present in the corpse.

Entomological evidence is widely accepted as scientific evidence in courts. A May 2002 U.S. Department of Justice publication (NCJ 191717) used the following example to illustrate. An Oklahoma woman's claim about when she last saw her husband was disproved by the third-stage maggot accumulation on his body. The analysis included critical climatological data, the time delay from death until colonization, the effect of the maggot mass temperature on development, and the nocturnal absence of blowflies. The woman was eventually convicted of murdering her husband.

Forensic examination and forensic entomology can provide information that aids investigators in identifying unidentified bodies that are found. Assistance in identifying bodies can also be obtained from the Forensic Anthropology Computer Enhancement Service (FACES) laboratory, which can construct a clay model of what the victim's face may have looked like. Photographs of the clay model and any clothing, jewelry, or available personal belongings are then shown on the FBI website at www.fbi.gov. Identity can be confirmed by DNA testing.

Autopsies as a Source of Evidence

All states have laws regarding autopsies and when public officials may order them. Forensic autopsies can provide valuable evidence in accident, assault, or suicide cases. What may appear to be an accidental death or a suicide might be shown to be a criminal homicide based on results from an autopsy. Autopsy results may also be used to determine the time of death, which could connect a defendant to the death. In *United States v. Williams*, 740 F. Supp. 2d 4 (D.D.C. 2010), the autopsy report was used to show the injury to the victim was one to three days before death, which included the time the defendant assaulted the victim. (Most courts treat autopsy reports as "testimonial" under the Confrontation Clause, see Chapter 8, and require the person performing the autopsy to be present in court if an autopsy is offered as evidence.)

The National Center for Health Statistics issued a report in 2011 (NCHS Data Brief, No. 67, August 2011) based on studies of autopsies conducted from 1972 to 2007. It concluded that the total number of autopsies declined by about 50 percent in that period, mainly because of limited use of autopsies in deaths caused by disease. In cases of death due to external causes, autopsies were performed in 97.1 percent of cases of assault, 80.8 percent where the cause of death was undetermined, 79 percent of suspected poisonings, and 59.9 percent of suicides. The report also found that autopsies were ordered in 60 percent of the deaths of persons in the 15-to-24 age group, but the percentage of autopsies declined with age. In the 65-to-74 age group only 4.2 percent of deaths were followed by an autopsy. Autopsies may be performed at the request of law enforcement officers, or under rules of the hospital where the death occurred. The next of kin may also order and pay for an autopsy.

Most autopsies provide forensic answers to the cause of death, though it is estimated that in 1 to 2 percent of the autopsies done the cause of death remains unknown or ill defined.

▮ FRACTURE MATCHING

Fingerprints or DNA evidence that confirms a "match" between evidence found at a crime scene and fingerprints or DNA of a suspect are compelling evidence of guilt. Experts are routinely permitted to testify about such "matches," because the theory on which the "match" is based has been shown to be scientifically valid.

Other kinds of physical evidence found at crime scenes may also be used to provide a "match" to physical evidence linked to a suspect. Ropes, tape, clothing, knife blades, and other objects found at a crime scene are sometimes used to prove a suspect's connection to the crime by a method called "fracture matching." If the object found at the crimes scene has been cut, torn, or ripped, experts can compare the object to similar objects found in the suspect's possession. By comparing the fractures on each object, experts can determine if the objects were once joined together.

The theory underlying "fracture matching" is that molecular structure of physical objects is essentially random, and that when it is torn or cut the molecules break apart in ways that are unique to each fracture. Inspection of the fractures, using molecular microscopes, can thus "match" two pieces of a material that has been cut or torn.

Some courts admit expert testimony on fracture matching, when given by a criminalist with a degree in forensic chemistry and practical experience. In the 2011 case of *Com. v. Gomes*,[a] the Massachusetts Supreme Judicial Court upheld the admission of expert testimony that a torn piece of electrical tape found on a murder weapon "fracture matched" a roll of electrical tape in the possession of the defendant. The court said that the expert's testimony that "fracture match" theory was "generally accepted" in the scientific community was not disputed by the defendant. Other courts have reached similar results: *Davis v. State*[b] (Pa. 2008—broken knife blade); *State v. Smith*[c] (La. 2008—wood board); *State v. Zubiga*[d] (N.C. 1987—torn newspaper).

In 2011 the Georgia Court of Appeals, using factors similar to the *Daubert* tests, held that it was an error to admit the testimony of an expert that based on "fracture matching," a ripped piece of duct tape found at a crime scene matched a roll of duct tape in the possession of the defendant. The court said that the state failed to produce any evidence establishing the reliability of the theory that fractures are unique, even though the expert testified that examination of fractures could produce "definitive results akin to DNA testing." The court said that unless a scientific theory had achieved the status of "verifiable certainty," such as DNA theory, the party seeking admission of expert testimony based on the theory must prove its reliability.

[a] 944 N.E.2d 1007 (Mass. 2011);
[b] 2 So.3d 952 (Fla. 2008), *cert. denied,* 129 S. Ct. 2872 (2009);
[c] 988 So. 2d 861 (La. Ct. App. 2008); 357 S.E.2d 8898 (N.C. 1987);
[d] *Jefferson v. State,* 720 S.E.2d 184 (Ga. App. 2011).

Ballistic Fingerprinting or Firearm Fingerprinting

Because 40 percent of criminal homicides go unsolved, identification of the weapons used by the criminal is critical. With 200 million guns in public hands and an estimated 30,000 gangs with 800,000 members, drive-by shootings and other violent crimes have become all too common. It is often vital to an investigation to link the weapon used in a crime to the person who used it. Moreover, rapid identification of a weapon may also permit law enforcement officers to prevent further killings.

In the 2002 sniper shootings near Washington, D.C., law enforcement officers, National Guard troops, and medical personnel worked together to try to identify the sniper. The victims were hit by .223-caliber bullets moving at about 2,000 miles per hour, which on impact caused the bullets to shatter into fragments inside the victims. Emergency medical workers as well as doctors and nurses at hospitals where the gunshot victims were taken treated the victims as a "crime scene" and attempted to find bullet fragments for transfer to the U.S. Bureau of Alcohol, Firearms, Tobacco and Explosives (ATF) ballistics laboratory in Rockville, Maryland.[34] It was hoped that tests on the bullet fragments could result in a match with data on weapons maintained by state and federal law enforcement agencies.

These tests, called **ballistic fingerprinting**, can sometimes lead to a match between the bullet fragments and the weapon used to fire the bullet. When rifles and gun barrels are manufactured, the machines producing the barrels leave identifiable "tool" or "rifling" marks in the barrels. In these tests, the subject weapon is fired, yielding a bullet that shows the tool marks of the weapon. This bullet can then be compared microscopically to a bullet recovered from a crime scene, and an expert witness can make a match.

The usefulness of such tests have limitations. First, in the case of bullet fragments, unless the bullet recovered is substantial, marks on the bullet may match rifling marks in multiple weapons. One observer compared this to finding a shoe print of a size 10 Nike shoe at a crime scene: Too many shoes would match the print to make it worthwhile. Moreover, the *Journal of the Association of Firearms and Toolmark Examiners* (AFTA) has concluded that there is no "perfect match" test such as is available in fingerprint tests, and that a ballistic expert should declare a "match" only when there is a "substantial duplication of random tool-marks" in the bullets compared. Thus, although courts continue to admit expert testimony on ballistic matching, some courts limit the conclusions the expert may state. The federal trial court in *United States v. Taylor*, 663 F. Supp. 2d 1170, 1180 (D. N.M. 2009), following what the trial court stated other federal courts were doing, held that the ballistics expert "will not be allowed to testify that he can conclude that there is a match to the exclusion, either practical or absolute, of all other guns. He may only testify that, in his opinion, the bullet came from the subject rifle to within a reasonable degree of certainty in the firearms examination filed."

Second, even if a substantial bullet is found at a crime scene, it is helpful only if it can be compared to weapons data maintained by law enforcement agencies. Although a national database that includes rifling data on every new weapon manufactured has been proposed, groups such as the National Rifle Association have fought efforts to create such a database. A few states have compiled a database of guns used in crimes in those states, but no national database exists.[35] In 2003, after conducting about 2,500 bullet-lead tests of bullets recovered from crime scenes, the FBI notified some 300 law enforcement agencies that it was abandoning tests that attempted to identify the chemical composition of a bullet and match it with the gun that fired it.[36]

It is possible to match a shell casing found at a crime scene to the gun that fired it based on tool marks impressed on the shell casing. When a gun is fired, expanding gases in the barrel cause the cartridge shell to forcefully strike parts of the rifle. This collision results in tool marks from the rifle being impressed on the shell casing, and then the casing and the rifle can be matched by scientific testing.[37]

Like bullet fragment matching, however, a shell casing is helpful only if a database of rifle markings exists. There has been encouragement for a law that creates a national database that would require every gun manufactured to have a microstamp inside the gun that would enable the gun to be matched to a shell casing,[38] but again, organizations like the NRA have resisted microstamping.

In 2007 California passed a law requiring that, beginning in 2010, all new semi-automatic pistols sold in California must be microstamped. In this process, a laser

---

ballistic fingerprinting

Identification of the gun that fired a bullet from an analysis of the marks that every gun makes on the bullet it fires and on the shell ejected from it.

engraves a microscopic mark in the firing pin of each weapon when it is manufactured. When the weapon is fired, the firing pin and the breech face transfer the mark to the cartridge. This permits police to match shell casings to the weapons that fired them. The new law is prospective only and does not require retrofitting for existing guns. Because of problems with the patents held on the microstamping process, the California Attorney General did not declare the law in force until May 2013. Following the law's implementation, several gun manufacturers declared they would no longer sell guns in California. (San Francisco Chronicle, January 26, 2014).

GUNSHOT RESIDUE EVIDENCE (GSR)

A person who fires a gun will have gunshot residue on their hands and clothing, as will persons standing within three feet of the shooter. Gunshot residue cannot identify a shooter, but it can be good circumstantial evidence that a suspect either fired a gun, or was very close to a person who did fire a gun.

An article in the May 2011 issue of the *FBI Law Enforcement Bulletin* entitled "The Current Status of GSR (Gunshot Residue) Examinations" points out that persons standing 10 or more feet from a gunshot will not have residue (unburned particles) fall on them. The article also identified some of the many variables that must be considered when examining GSR, such as the number of shots fired; the type of gun and ammunition used (handguns leave more residue than rifles and shotguns); where the weapon was fired (out-of-doors or in a small room); and if out-of-doors, environmental factors such as wind (how strong and in what direction).

Unburned gunshot residue particles can be removed easily from the surface on which they land; they can also be lost very easily. If the shooter puts his or her hands in a pocket, or if the shooter's hands are rubbed together, the particles could be wiped away. Gunshot residue particles can remain on a shooter's hands for up to four or five hours after a shooting, if the hands are not washed or rubbed. Immediate measures to preserve the GSR are thus very important. The FBI article pointed out that GSR evidence can be transferred from one surface to another, or from one person to another, with some loss of GSR with each transfer.

Sources of Other Scientific Evidence

Almost every known science, and sometimes what is called "junk science",[39] have been presented to courts for use as evidence. The U.S. Supreme Court has stressed the obligation of trial judges as gatekeepers to screen expert witnesses so that unreliable evidence is not presented to juries and judges. Since *Daubert,* the U.S. Supreme Court has issued two additional opinions dealing with the admissibility of scientific evidence.[40]

Other scientific evidence used regularly in courts throughout the United States includes the following:

- *Tests for alcohol intoxication:* Used in drunk-driving and other cases. It is necessary in most cases to present evidence showing that the officer had probable cause to arrest the defendant for operating under the influence. This is done by having the officer, and in some cases witnesses, testify about what they saw and smelled. Field tests include performance tests, the horizontal gaze nystagmus (HGN) test,[41] and alcohol screening devices that sample the air around the suspect, including air from the person. Video pictures of the driver or other person may also be used as evidence. If probable cause exists, the driver

PROCEDURES & PROCESSES

Obtaining Evidence from Drug Testing

A 2002 study by the National Highway Traffic Safety Administration and the Robert Wood Johnson Foundation estimated that 9 million Americans a year drive while under the influence of illegal drugs. It has been recognized for some time that drunk drivers are detected far more often than drugged drivers, even though both are very serious dangers on American highways. In 2003 only eight states had laws that made it illegal for a person to drive with any measurable amount of illegal drugs in his or her system. In the other states, prosecutors must prove that the illegal drugs caused the reckless conduct for which a driver was stopped.

This is very difficult to prove in many cases. The following chart describes samples that may be used for drug testing:

Sample Used for Testing	Advantages	Detection Times	Disadvantages
Urine—privacy intrusion	Is accurate and economical; contains high concentrations of drugs used by person	Hours to days	Cannot indicate blood levels; is easy to falsify
Blood—highly invasive	Indicates the extent of the person's impairment at the time the sample is taken	Variable	Not recommended for use as evidence in court because of the potential for infection
Breath—noninvasive	Indicates ethanol concentrations and the extent of the person's impairment from alcohol (not other drugs)	Hours	Very short time frame for detection; detects only volatile compounds
Hair	Indicates long-term drug use; is difficult to adulterate	Weeks to months	Can be contaminated by external products; has potential racial bias because dark pigmented hair absorbs drugs more readily than blonde or bleached hair
Sweat—obtained from patches placed on person for days	Is difficult to adulterate	Days to weeks	May be biased because persons differ in manner of sweat production
Saliva—easily obtained	Provides estimates of blood levels and indicates degree of impairment	Hours to days	Can be contaminated by smoking and other substances as well as pH changes

Sources: "Drug Testing in a Drug Court Environment," NCJ 1811103 (May 2000); "Many, Undetected, Use Drugs and Then Drive, Report Says," *New York Times* (November 15, 2002).

is then arrested and informed that under the "implied consent" statute of that state or jurisdiction, the person is obligated to submit to a Breathalyzer test, a blood-alcohol test, or a urine test.

- *Fire and explosive science evidence*: Used in arson and civil lawsuit cases.
- *Forensic pathology*: Used in determining the cause of death, time of death, and identity of the deceased.

- *Chemistry, toxicology, serology, and hematology tests*: Used for identifying bloodstains, human blood types, blood spatters, and age of bloodstains; for identifying seminal fluid, sperm cells, saliva, fecal matter, and perspiration; for identifying opiates, hallucinogens, barbiturates, and amphetamines; and for determining narcotic addiction.
- *Microanalysis*: Used to identify and compare small objects and particles, including hair, fibers, paint, glass, soil and dust, cosmetics, wood, and trace evidence.
- *Neutron activation analysis (NAA)*: Used for testing gunshot residue.
- *Tests used in questioned documents*: Used for handwriting and typing comparisons, analysis of inks, examination of papers and watermarks, and forensic linguistics.
- *Scientific detection of speeding*: By use of radar, VASCAR (Visual Average Speed Computer and Recorder), and other speed detection devices.
- *Forensic odontology*: Used for identification by dental characteristics, bite-mark analysis, and dental comparisons.
- *Accident reconstruction techniques*: By use of skid marks, tire imprints, and scuff marks.
- *Physical anthropology*: Used to determine time of death and age, sex, race, and identification of victim.

COMPUTER SYSTEMS USED BY LAW ENFORCEMENT

Large American cities have increased their use of computers to perform the functions listed here:[a]

- All large departments use computer-aided dispatch systems.
- Enhanced 911 emergency systems are capable of pinpointing a caller's location automatically.
- Almost all large departments use in-field computers or terminals.
- Almost all have exclusive or shared ownership of an Automated Fingerprint Identification System (AFIS), which matches fingerprints from a crime scene with a known person (if the person's fingerprints are on file) within minutes.
- The National Crime Information Center (NCIC) provides information to police agencies on wanted suspects, stolen firearms, stolen property and securities, unidentified bodies, and computerized criminal histories. Members enter information into the system for use by other law enforcement agencies.

During the 21 days in which snipers terrorized the Washington, D.C., area, investigators from a dozen law agencies worked together, sharing ballistics testing information, geographic and criminal profiling, thousands of tips from citizens, and police files and computer information. To coordinate all of this information, an Internet-based system called Coplink was used that allows police agencies to establish links quickly to their own files and to those of other departments. With resources from the military, federal, state, and local departments, Coplink interconnected files through new computer systems.

Will evidence be excluded if computer error is attributed to court officials rather than to a police record-keeping system?

The purpose of the exclusionary rule is to deter police misconduct. The U.S. Supreme Court held in the 1995 case of *Arizona v. Evans*, 115 S. Ct. 1185, that the rule does not apply when the mistake is made by employees of a court. Evidence, therefore, can be used under the good faith exception when the police rely on computerized information.

[a]See the U.S. Department of Justice report at NCJ 175703 (May 2002).

PROCEDURES & PROCESSES

Correlating, Coordinating, and Collecting Evidence

The following agencies, technology, and databases assist law enforcement officials in gathering and analyzing evidence:

- National Law Enforcement Data Exchange System (N-Dex): N-Dex correlates data from all major FBI databases. It provides "one-stop shopping," where an initial search provides combined data in about 30 seconds. Information on crimes from different states and cities can identify trends and allow immediate response. FBI Director Robert Mueller said of the new system: It "provides unprecedented access to information allowing us to link cases, solve crimes, and form broader investigative partnerships." N-Dex began operation in 2005.

- Terrorist Screening Center: Begun in December 2004 and operating 24 hours a day, 7 days a week, the Center maintains the most up-to-date terrorist watch list in the United States and enables federal, state, and local officials to respond quickly where a known or suspected terrorist is encountered during a routine law enforcement stop or in an airport, bus, or train station. The Center provides a strong link between the FBI, military, and civil intelligence agencies and state and local law enforcement.

- Combined DNA Index System (CODIS): CODIS has been in operation since 1998, and as of August, 2014 has helped solve or aided in more than 246,334 investigations nationwide (www.fbi.gov/CODIS). DNA technology has helped solve serial rape cases that were more than 25 years old. Because of CODIS, rapists or killers who travel from state to state can be apprehended more easily.

- National Gang Threat Assessment and Database: The database provides information and helps coordinate and target efforts of federal, state, and local law enforcement agencies against the active gangs operating in the United States. The Department of Justice's 2009 National Youth Gang Survey reported that there were 28,100 active gangs in the United States, with 731,000 members. In the largest U.S. cities, between 1,000 and 1,300 gang-related homicides occurred each year. Chicago and Los Angeles accounted for about one-third of all gang homicides. The number of gang-related homicides increased by 7 percent between 2005 and 2009. See www.nationalgangcenter.gov/Survey-Analysis.

- Hazardous Devices School: Located in Redstone Arsenal, Alabama, the school provides training, information, and instruction on the latest tools and techniques for confronting suicide bombers, large vehicle bombs, weapons of mass destruction, and other threats. The FBI trains more than 1,100 students every year at the school and has provided millions of dollars of equipment for more than 400 bomb squads in the United States.

- Federal Bureau of Investigation (FBI): The Laboratory Division provides technical and scientific response and forensic support to investigations that involve hazardous materials, including weapons of mass destruction. It offers the capability to disrupt explosive devices and perform forensic examination of explosives in post-blast situations. The division also provides expertise in processing crime scenes. The Engineering Research Facility (ERF) supplies technical support for secure and nonsecure communications, computer hardware and software, and feasibility assessments for proposed command post sites. The Critical Incident Response Group (CIRG) provides subject-matter expertise in counterterrorism tactics, crisis management, hostage negotiations, logistics, and behavioral analysis. FBI Headquarters offers language specialists, intelligence analysis, and activation of the Strategic Information and Operations Center (SIOC) in support of special events. The Cyber Division evaluates emerging cyberthreats and performs forensic examinations of digital evidence. The Counterterrorism Division provides financial and administrative support.

SUMMARY

1. **State the requirements for admissibility of scientific evidence under Rule 702 of the Federal Rules of Evidence.**
   - A qualified expert may testify about scientific evidence if the testimony is (1) based on sufficient facts or data, (2) is the product of reliable principles and methods, and (3) the expert witness reliably applied the principles and methods to the facts of the case.

2. **Explain the difference between the *Frye* test and the *Daubert* test.**
   - Under the *Frye* test, scientific theories that have received general acceptance by experts in the field of science at issue may be used as the basis for expert opinions. Under *Daubert*, a scientific theory may be used for an expert opinion only if the theory has been shown to be reliable, using factors such as peer review, test results, standard of error, and acceptance of the theory.

3. **Explain how DNA evidence is used to identify a suspect in a crime.**
   - If a DNA profile exists in a database like CODIS, the DNA "fingerprint" taken from the crime scene can be matched to the DNA "fingerprint" in the database. This is done by comparing the base pairs at various points in the DNA chains of the sample and the profile in the database where individual differences in the DNA chain occur. If the DNA fingerprint in the sample from the crime scene does not match an existing DNA profile in a database, a DNA sample from a suspect may be compared to the crimes scene sample. If they match, experts are then able to calculate the probability a person selected at random would match the DNA profile. That probability is usually several million to one. If other evidence can connect the defendant to the crime scene, (the "prosecutor's fallacy problem"), the jury can use the probability estimates as a factor in determining the defendant was the source of the DNA.

4. **State both the logistical and the theoretical problems with ballistic fingerprinting.**
   - One logistical problem is that a bullet fragment may be too small to have enough identifiable tool marks to match a bullet fired from a suspect's weapon. A theoretical problem is that unlike with fingerprints, experts agree there is no perfect match connection between bullets and barrels of weapons. As a result, even if a bullet can be shown to have all the tool marks of a particular weapon, an expert cannot say with absolute certainty that no other weapon could also match the bullet.

KEY TERMS

ballistic fingerprinting, 487

Daubert test, 472

Frye test, 471

DNA genetic profiling, 475

forensic, 475

forensic entomology, 484

locus points, 475

scientific evidence, 468

KEY CASES

Com. v. Gomes, 944 N.E.2d 1007 (Mass. 2011): Accepted theory of "fracture matching" to permit expert testimony linking crime scene material to material possessed by a defendant. *Compare*

Jefferson v. State, 720 S.E.2d 184 (Ga. App. 2011): "Fracture matching" must be shown to be reliable under *Daubert*-type tests before expert may testify to a "match."

Daubert v. Merrill Dow Pharmaceuticals, 509 U.S. 579 (1993): Established the tests for admissibility of scientific evidence in federal courts, and is followed by most state courts.

Frye v. United States, 293 Fed. 1013 (D.C. Cir. 1923): The origin of the "general acceptance" test for admissibility of scientific evidence.

McDaniel v. Brown, 130 S. Ct. 665 (2010): Discussed the nature of the "prosecutor's fallacy" in DNA probability testimony.

United States v. Taylor, 663 F. Supp.2d 1170 (D.N.M. 2009): An example of a trial court that limited expert testimony on "ballistic fingerprinting."

PROBLEMS

1. Not every state has a rule of evidence patterned after Rule 702 of the Federal Rules, and thus not every state court uses the tests identified in the *Daubert* case for admissibility of scientific evidence. In *State v. Jones*, 681 S.E. 2d 580 (S.C. 2009) the prosecution attempted to prove the defendant was the person who left a bloody boot print at a murder scene by offering expert testimony on "barefoot insole impressions." The expert proposed to testify that a particular steel-toed boot left the bloody impression, and based on "barefoot insole impressions" in the boot, the boot was worn by the defendant. What did the South Carolina Supreme Court conclude about the admissibility of this testimony? What standards did it sue? Did it adopt *Daubert*?

2. In Chapter 16 we discussed palm print evidence as a method of identifying a suspect in a crime. Experts who give testimony on palm prints must show their testimony is based on reliable scientific theories and methods. Human palms have creases and ridgelines, which are used to make comparisons between a suspect and a palm print. How much of a palm must be left in the print to make a comparison? What did the expert use as the basis for his palm print identification in *State v. Bickart*, 963 A.2d 183 (Me. 2009)? What test did the court say must be used to determine the reliability of palm print evidence?

3. Bank robbery trials often include video evidence of the robbery. (The admissibility of such videos was discussed in Chapter 17.) Where the facial image on the video does not clearly match the defendant's face, what may the prosecution do to otherwise use the video to connect the defendant to the robbery? In *United States v. Williams*, 235 Fed. Appx. 925 (3d Cir. 2007), witnesses to a bank robbery described the robber as being between 5'2" and 5'7". The defendant was 6 feet tall. May the prosecution introduce expert testimony that using the "reverse projection photogrammetry" technique, the figure in the bank video was closer to 6 feet tall than to 5 feet 2 inches? Because it was a federal trial, *Daubert* applied to the expert testimony. How did the court apply the *Daubert* tests? Do you agree?

4. A defendant was charged with murder in a shotgun slaying at a residence. Although fingerprints and shoeprints were found at the crime scene, they were not shown to match defendant's fingerprints or shoes. The prosecution offered testimony by a state police officer who was a qualified firearm and toolmark examiner. The officer testified that two spent shotgun shell casings found at the murder scene "were discharged from [defendant's] shotgun." Should the trial court have permitted the officer to give that expert testimony? What test did the appeals court use to answer that question? If you were the trial judge, what limit, if any, would you have put on the expert's testimony? (See *Com. v. Whitacre*, 878 A.2d 96 (Pa. Super. 2005), *appeal denied*, 892 A.2d 823 (Pa. 2005).)

CASE ANALYSIS

Read Appendix B, Finding and Analyzing Cases (p. 499). With these guidelines in mind, please continue with the Case Analysis selections for Chapter 18.

1. The *Daubert* rules for the prevention of the admission of "junk science" go beyond classic chemical, biological, or physical science theories. They also apply to the reliability of the premises an expert relies on for an expert opinion. An example is the case of *State v. Perea*, 322 P.3d 624 (Utah 2013). There, a trial judge in a murder trial refused to let a defense expert testify on his "false confession" theory, holding it was not scientifically reliable. On appeal, the Utah Supreme Court held that the expert should have been allowed to testify. Why did it think the expert's theory passed the *Daubert* tests?

2. Compare the opinion in the Utah case discussed above to the opinion of the Michigan Supreme Court in *People v. Kowalski*, 821 N.W.2d 14 (Mich. 2012), where the court refused to allow expert testimony on false confession theories. Which court has the better argument?

3. In child sexual abuse cases, where the victim (now an adult) first reports the abuse years after the event is alleged to have happened, the reliability of the victim's memory of the event is central to the case against the alleged assailant. To bolster the victim's testimony, the prosecution often seeks to introduce expert testimony on "repressed memory syndrome," the theory that traumatic events in a child's life can be repressed and only surface much later when triggered by another event, such as psychiatric therapy. How did the court in *State v. King*, 733 S.E.2d 535 (N.C. 2012), decide the defendant's claim that the state's proposed expert testimony was insufficiently reliable? Did the court use the *Daubert* test, or some other test?

4. Most states use some form of breathalyzer device like the BAC Datamaster machine to test for blood/alcohol concentration (BAC). However, these machines give only estimates of the BAC, and are subject to error. States also rely on the HGN test in DUI prosecutions. At least one state, South Dakota, has rejected breath tests, and requires blood samples be used to determine if a driver was over the legal limit. In *State v. Yuel*, 840 N.W.2d 680 (S.D. 2013), the court considered the reliability of the HGN test and the accuracy of the blood sample BAC test. What did it decide?

Notes

1. *Commonwealth v. Lykus*, 327 N.E.2d 671 (Mass. 1975), quoting *United States v. Addison*, 498 F.2d 741 (D.C. Cir. 1974).
2. See, e.g., *State v. Cortarez*, 686 P.2d 1224 (Ariz. 1984), and *Cornet v. State*, 450 N.E.2d 498 (Ind. 1983).
3. 293 Fed. 1013 (D.C. Cir. 1923).
4. 293 Fed. 1013, 1014 (D.C. Cir. 1923).
5. 509 U.S. 579 (1993).
6. 327 N.E.2d 671 (Mass. 1975).
7. *Id.* at 677.
8. 297 N.W.2d 80 (Iowa 1980).
9. 545 N.Y.S.2d 985 (Sup. Ct. 1989).
10. DNA, DNA tests, and probability estimates are discussed on pages 475–480.
11. In *Hayes v. State*, 660 So. 2d 257 (Fla. 1995), the Florida Supreme Court stated that it could take judicial notice of the general theory of DNA. It also held that one testing procedure sometimes used to explain minor variances in DNA results, the band-width connection procedure, was not generally accepted.
12. See, e.g., *State v. Cauthron*, 846 P.2d 502 (Wash. 1993).
13. See, e.g., *State v. Carter*, 524 N.W.2d 763 (Neb. 1994) Other courts have found the PCR test generally accepted. See *State v. Russell*, 882 P.2d 742 (Wash. 1994).
14. 509 U.S. 579 (1993).
15. 509 U.S. 592–93.
16. 119 S. Ct. 1167 (1999).
17. Nash, *Are We There Yet? Gatekeepers,* Daubert, *and an analysis of* State v. White, 61 S.C.L.R. 897 (2010).
18. Hamilton, *The Movement from Frye to Daubert: Where Do the States Stand?* Jurimetrics J. 38 (1998): 201, 209.
19. See Daubert *in the States,* SLO84 ALI–ABA 273 (2006).

20. See, e.g., *Emerson v. State,* 880 S.W.2d 759 (Tex. Crim. App. 1994).

21. 185 F. Supp. 2d 530 (D. Md. 2002).

22. 955 F.2d 786 (2d Cir.).

23. See, e.g., *Greenberg Gallery Inc. v. Bauman,* 817 F. Supp. 167, 172 (D.D.C. 1993).

24. See, for example, M. Kam, G. Fielding, and R. Conn, *Written Identification by Professional Document Examiners,* J. Forensic Sci. 42 (1997): 778. The Kam study found that some, but not all, handwriting professionals were superior to laypersons on matching handwriting samples. Those professionals made mistaken matches on 6.5 percent of 144 samples. Laypersons made mistaken matches on 38.3 percent of those same samples.

25. *United States v. Starzecpyzel,* 880 F. Supp. 1027 (S.D.N.Y. 1995).

26. Between 1988 and 1998, fifty-six wrongfully convicted people were exonerated based on DNA tests that showed they could not have committed the crime for which they were charged. Ten of those exonerated were awaiting the death penalty. (See L. Gaines, M. Kaune, and R. Miller, *Criminal Justice in Action* (Belmont, CA: Wadsworth, 2000).) That number had increased to 143 as of March 2005.

27. J. McKenna, J. Cecil, and P. Coukos, *Reference Manual on Scientific Evidence,* Federal Judicial Center (St. Paul, MN: West, 1994), p. 278.

28. See "Scientists Identify Bones as Those of the Czar," *New York Times* (July 10, 1993), p. 1.

29. See National District Attorneys' Association Bulletin (November 1990), 7.

30. 814 S.W.2d 593 (Mo.).

31. 42 U.S.C. § 14135.

32. 402 F.3d 175, 185 (3d Cir. 2005).

33. "DNA Helps Solve Bank Robbery," *Milwaukee Journal-Sentinel* (July 16, 2002).

34. See the articles "Sniper Case Renews Debate over Firearm Fingerprinting," *New York Times* (October 18, 2002), and "Doctors Help Gather Evidence," *Washington Post* (October 23, 2002).

35. See "Technology: Now, 4 States Look to Start Tracing Shells and Bullets," *New York Times* (October 24, 2002).

36. See "FBI Bullet Tests Found to Be Flawed," *New York Times* (November 22, 2003).

37. See, e.g., *United States v. Monteiro,* 407 F.Supp.2d 351 (D. Mass. 2006).

38. See "A Crime-Fighting Opportunity," *New York Times* (February 15, 2008).

39. Some or all of the following could be called junk science, depending on who makes the judgment call: narcoanalysis ("truth serum"), hypnosis, voice-stress analysis, polygraph (lie detector), spectrographic voice recognition, and handwriting analysis.

40. The two additional cases are *General Electric v. Joiner,* 522 U.S. 136 (1997), and *Kumho Tire Co. v. Carmichael,* 526 U.S. 137 (1999).

41. When police officers stop a driver who has been drinking beer or most other alcoholic beverages, smell will cause the officer to suspect a driving violation. Most illegal drugs do not have a smell, however, and the person's behavior may be tranquil and calm. It is therefore necessary to use the horizontal gaze nystagmus test. The horizontal gaze nystagmus (HGN) test is a field sobriety test in which a person is requested to follow an object with his eyes. When a person's central nervous system is depressed by alcohol, barbiturates, phencyclidine (PCP), or certain inhalants, rapid involuntary jerking of the eyeballs occurs as the eyes seek to follow a pencil or finger moved before them. In the 1960s California police observed this involuntary jerking in the eyes of barbiturate users. Later, East Coast law enforcement officers began applying the concept to intoxicated drivers. The HGN test is administered in conjunction with other field sobriety tests such as the one-leg-stand test and the walk-and-turn test. Many state courts have held that HGN test results can be used with other information to establish probable cause.

APPENDIX **A**

SECTIONS OF THE U.S. CONSTITUTION

APPLICABLE SECTIONS OF THE U.S. CONSTITUTION, RATIFIED IN 1788

Preamble

We the People of the United States, in Order to form a more perfect Union, establish Justice, insure domestic Tranquility, provide for the common defence, promote the general Welfare, and secure the Blessings of Liberty to ourselves and our Posterity, do ordain and establish this CONSTITUTION for the United States of America.

Article I

Section 1. All legislative Powers herein granted shall be vested in a Congress of the United States, which shall consist of a Senate and House of Representatives...

Article II

Section 1. The executive Power shall be vested in a President of the United States of America....

Article III

Section 1. The judicial Power of the United States, shall be vested in one supreme Court, and in such inferior Courts as the Congress may from time to time ordain and establish....

Article IV

Section 4. The United States shall guarantee to every State in this Union a Republican Form of Government, and shall protect each of them against Invasion; and on Application of the Legislature, or of the Executive (when the Legislature cannot be convened) against domestic Violence....

Article VI

This Constitution, and the Laws of the United States which shall be made in Pursuance thereof; and all Treaties made, or which shall be made, under the Authority of the United States, shall be the supreme Law of the Land; and the Judges in every State shall be bound thereby, any Thing in the Constitution or Laws of any State to the Contrary notwithstanding....

AMERICAN BILL OF RIGHTS, RATIFIED 1791

Amendment I

Congress shall make no law respecting an establishment of religion, or prohibiting the free exercise thereof; or abridging the freedom of speech or of the press; or the right of the people peaceably to assemble and to petition the Government for a redress of grievances.

Amendment II

A well-regulated Militia, being necessary to the security of a free State, the right of the people to keep and bear Arms, shall not be infringed.

Amendment III

No Soldier shall, in time of peace be quartered in any house, without the consent of the Owner, nor in time of war, but in a manner to be prescribed by law.

Amendment IV

The right of the people to be secure in their persons, houses, papers, and effects, against unreasonable searches and seizures, shall not be violated, and no Warrants shall issue, but upon probable cause, supported by Oath, or affirmation, and particularly describing the place to be searched and the persons or things to be seized.

Amendment V

No person shall be held to answer for a capital, or otherwise infamous crime, unless on a presentment or indictment of a Grand Jury, except in cases arising in the land or naval forces, or in the Militia, when in actual service in time of War or public danger; nor shall any person be subject for the same offence to be twice put in jeopardy of life or limb; nor shall be compelled in any criminal case to be a witness against himself, nor be deprived of life, liberty, or property, without due process of law; nor shall private property be taken for public use, without just compensation.

Amendment VI

In all criminal prosecutions, the accused shall enjoy the right to a speedy and public trial, by an impartial jury of the State and district wherein the crime shall have been committed, which district shall have been previously ascertained by law, and to be informed of the nature and cause of the accusation; to be confronted with the witnesses against him; to have compulsory process for obtaining witnesses in his favor, and to have the Assistance of Counsel for his defence.

Amendment VII

In suits at common law, where the value in controversy shall exceed twenty dollars, the right of trial by jury shall be preserved, and no fact tried by jury, shall be otherwise reexamined in any Court of the United States, than according to the rules of the common law.

Amendment VIII

Excessive bail shall not be required, nor excessive fines imposed, nor cruel and unusual punishments inflicted.

Amendment IX

The enumeration in the Constitution, of certain rights, shall not be construed to deny or disparage others retained by the people.

Amendment X

The powers not delegated to the United States by the Constitution, nor prohibited by it to the States, are reserved to the States respectively, or to the people....

Amendment XIV, Ratified 1868

Section 1. All persons born or naturalized in the United States, and subject to the jurisdiction thereof, are citizens of the United States and of the State wherein they reside. No State shall make or enforce any law which shall abridge the privileges or immunities of citizens of the United States; nor shall any State deprive any person of life, liberty, or property, without due process of law; nor deny to any person within its jurisdiction the equal protection of the laws....

FINDING AND ANALYZING CASES

CASE ANALYSIS

In the end materials of each chapter in this text we have included citations to (mostly) recent cases in which issues presented in the chapters are discussed in appellate court opinions. Although criminal evidence, like criminal law, includes many statutory rules, court opinions interpreting and applying those rules continue to play a vital role in the development of the law. We therefore believe the time spent reading and analyzing appellate court opinions will be rewarded with a better understanding of the law of criminal evidence. In each of the eighteen chapters, we recommend that the student find the cases cited in the Case Analysis section, read them carefully, and give some thought to the questions posed.

Understanding Citations

Appellate court cases have both a name and a citation. The name of a case includes the two main parties in the case, usually called the *appellant* and the *appellee,* but sometimes the *petitioner* and the *respondent.* The citation of the case is a reference to a place where the full text of the opinion in the case can be found. For example, the first case in Chapter 1's Case Analysis section is titled *Pierce v. Commonwealth.* Pierce is the person appealing the decision of a trial court. The citation is 652 S.E.2d 785 (Va. App. 2007). That means this opinion can be found in volume 652 of the Southeastern Reporter system, second series, page 785. The parenthetical information identifies the appellate court that issued the opinion, here the Virginia Court of Appeals. 2007 is the date of the opinion. The Southeastern Reporter includes opinions from several states in the southeastern United States. Other regional reporter systems exist for other parts of the United States. In addition, many states maintain their own reporter system for opinions of appellate courts in that state. For example, *Pierce v. Commonwealth* may also be found in the Virginia State Reporter system at 50 Va. App. 609.

Kinds of Appellate Courts: States

The highest appellate court in most states is called the state supreme court. Some states, such as New York, call the highest appellate court the court of appeals. Many states have more than one level of appellate courts. When a citation is to an opinion of the highest state court, it usually ends with the date of the case and the state's abbreviation. For example, a citation might read "—N.W.2d— (Iowa 2008)." If the citation is to a lower appellate court, "App." is added to the state abbreviation: "—N.W.2d— (Iowa App. 2008). This tells us the case was decided by the Iowa Court of Appeals. The losing party in a court of appeals may petition the state supreme court for review of the court of appeals decision. These petitions are not routinely granted, and when they are denied the case citation reflects that denial. Thus, if a petition for review in *Pierce v. Commonwealth* had been filed but denied, the final citation would look like this: *Pierce v. Commonwealth,* 652 S.E.2d 785 (Va. App. 2007), *review denied,* ___S.E.2d___, (Va. 2007).

Federal Trial and Appellate Courts

Each state in the United States has at least one Federal District Court that serves as a trial court in that state. Many states have several district courts. Many, but not all, decisions of Federal District Courts are reported in the Federal Supplement Reporter, first or second series. In a state that has multiple districts, a case citation might look like this: *United States v. Smith,* 450 F. Supp. 2d 234 (N.D. Cal. 2009). That means the case can be found in volume 450 of the Federal Supplement reporter, second series, page 234. The parenthetical language tells us it was a 2009 decision of the Federal District Court sitting in the Northern District of California.

Decisions of Federal District Courts can be appealed to Federal Circuit Courts of Appeals. There are eleven federal circuits in the United States, plus the District of Columbia Circuit and the Federal Circuit.

Each circuit has a Circuit Court of Appeals. A decision of a Circuit Court of Appeals might look like this: *United States v. Jones*, 345 F.3d 221 (8th Cir. 2010). This means the case can be found in volume 345 of the Federal Reporter, third series, at page 221. It was decided by a panel of Eighth Circuit judges in 2010.

The losing party may petition the full Circuit Court to rehear the case heard by a three-judge panel. These petitions are not routinely granted. When denied, the final citation of the case records the denial: *United States v. Jones*, 345 F.3d 221 (8th Cir. 2010), *rev. denied*, 365 F.3d 446 (8th Cir. 2011).

Decisions of the Courts of Appeals (and in some cases of state supreme courts) can be appealed through the certiorari process to the United States Supreme Court. These petitions are rarely granted. Thus, when a petition for certiorari has been filed and denied, the full case citation might look like this: *United States v. Doe,* 546 F.3d 124 (3rd Cir. 2009), *cert. denied* 125 S. Ct. 1456 (2009). Decisions of the Supreme Court can be found either in the Supreme Court Reporter, or the United States Reports. Thus, an opinion of the Supreme Court might look like this: *United States v. White*, 457 U.S. 213, 115 S. Ct. 1134 (2010).

Reading an Appellate Opinion

We recommend the student consider the following aspects of each appellate opinion:

1. What are the relevant facts of the case? In this text, the exclusion or introduction of some evidence in a criminal trial is important, so try to determine the exact evidence that was under consideration.

2. What did the trial court do (or fail to do) that is challenged on appeal? Did it admit evidence over a party's objection? Did it refuse to permit evidence to be admitted?

3. What is the basis for the appellant's (usually the defendant's) claim that the trial court committed reversible error? Is it a constitutional claim? Is it a procedural error?

4. What did the appellate court decide? Did it affirm the trial court, or reverse it? Did it send the case back (called "remand") to the trial court for more hearings? If so, what precise question must be determined on remand?

5. What were the appellate court's reasons for its decision? The appellate court rarely simply affirms or reverses a trial court's decision on guilt or innocence. The reasons given by the appellate court are really the most important part of the decision, at least for our purposes. Once we pin down the reasons for a decision, we can use those reasons to figure what might happen in related cases. This is how court opinions contribute to the development of the law. Sometimes the members of an appellate court cannot agree on a decision. When that happens, the majority of the judges write their opinion, and that becomes the rule of the case. The minority judges may also write a dissenting opinion, which sometimes influences other courts to disagree with the result ordered by the majority. A concurring opinion is an opinion written by a judge who agrees with the result ordered by the majority, but who wants to state different or more detailed reasons for the result.

FEDERAL RULES OF EVIDENCE

ARTICLE I. GENERAL PROVISIONS

Rule 101. Scope; Definitions

(a) **Scope.** These rules apply to proceedings in United States courts. The specific courts and proceedings to which the rules apply, along with exceptions, are set out in Rule 1101.

(b) **Definitions.** In these rules
  (1) "civil case" means a civil action or proceeding;
  (2) "criminal case" includes a criminal proceeding;
  (3) "public office" includes a public agency;
  (4) "record" includes a memorandum, report, or data compilation;
  (5) a "rule prescribed by the Supreme Court" means a rule adopted by the Supreme Court under statutory authority; and
  (6) a reference to any kind of written material or any other medium includes electronically stored information.

Rule 102. Purpose

These rules should be construed so as to administer every proceeding fairly, eliminate unjustifiable expense and delay, and promote the development of evidence law, to the end of ascertaining the truth and securing a just determination.

Rule 103. Rulings on Evidence

(a) **Preserving a Claim of Error.** A party may claim error in a ruling to admit or exclude evidence only if the error affects a substantial right of the party and:
  (1) if the ruling admits evidence, a party, on the record:
    (A) timely objects or moves to strike; and
    (B) states the specific ground, unless it was apparent from the context; or
  (2) if the ruling excludes evidence, a party informs the court of its substance by an offer of proof, unless the substance was apparent from the context.

(b) **Not Needing to Renew an Objection or Offer of Proof.** Once the court rules definitively on the record—either before or at trial—a party need not renew an objection or offer of proof to preserve a claim of error for appeal.

(c) **Court's Statement About the Ruling; Directing an Offer of Proof.** The court may make any statement about the character or form of the evidence, the objection made, and the ruling. The court may direct that an offer of proof be made in question-and-answer form.

(d) **Preventing the Jury from Hearing Inadmissible Evidence.** To the extent practicable, the court must conduct a jury trial so that inadmissible evidence is not suggested to the jury by any means.

(e) **Taking Notice of Plain Error.** A court may take notice of a plain error affecting a substantial right, even if the claim of error was not properly preserved.

Rule 104. Preliminary Questions

(a) **In General.** The court must decide any preliminary question about whether a witness is qualified, a privilege exists, or evidence is admissible. In so deciding, the court is not bound by evidence rules, except those on privilege.

(b) **Relevance That Depends on a Fact.** When the relevance of evidence depends on whether a fact exists, proof must be introduced sufficient to support a finding that the fact does exist. The court may admit the proposed evidence on the condition that the proof be introduced later.

(c) **Conducting a Hearing So That the Jury Cannot Hear It.** The court must conduct any hearing on a preliminary question so that the jury cannot hear it if:
  (1) the hearing involves the admissibility of a confession;

(2) a defendant in a criminal case is a witness and so requests; or

(3) justice so requires.

(d) **Cross-Examining a Defendant in a Criminal Case.** By testifying on a preliminary question, a defendant in a criminal case does not become subject to cross-examination on other issues in the case.

(e) **Evidence Relevant to Weight and Credibility.** This rule does not limit a party's right to introduce before the jury evidence that is relevant to the weight or credibility of other evidence.

ARTICLE II. JUDICIAL NOTICE

Rule 201. Judicial Notice of Adjudicative Facts

(a) **Scope.** This rule governs judicial notice of an adjudicative fact only, not a legislative fact.

(b) **Kinds of Facts That May Be Judicially Noticed.** The court may judicially notice a fact that is not subject to reasonable dispute because it:

(1) is generally known within the trial court's territorial jurisdiction; or

(2) can be accurately and readily determined from sources whose accuracy cannot reasonably be questioned.

(c) **Taking Notice.** The court:

(1) may take judicial notice on its own; or

(2) must take judicial notice if a party requests it and the court is supplied with the necessary information.

(d) **Timing.** The court may take judicial notice at any stage of the proceeding.

(e) **Opportunity to Be Heard.** On timely request, a party is entitled to be heard on the propriety of taking judicial notice and the nature of the fact to be noticed. If the court takes judicial notice before notifying a party, the party, on request, is still entitled to be heard.

(f) **Instructing the Jury.** In a civil case, the court must instruct the jury to accept the noticed fact as conclusive. In a criminal case, the court must instruct the jury that it may or may not accept the noticed fact as conclusive.

ARTICLE III. PRESUMPTIONS IN CIVIL CASES

Rule 301. Presumptions in Civil Actions Generally

In a civil case, unless a federal statute or these rules provide otherwise, the party against whom a presumption is directed has the burden of producing evidence to rebut the presumption. But this rule does not shift the burden of persuasion, which remains on the party who had it originally.

ARTICLE IV. RELEVANCE AND ITS LIMITS

Rule 401. Test for Relevant Evidence

Evidence is relevant if:

(a) it has any tendency to make a fact more or less probable than it would be without the evidence; and

(b) the fact is of consequence in determining the action.

Rule 402. General Admissibility of Relevant Evidence

Relevant evidence is admissible unless any of the following provides otherwise:

* the United States Constitution;
* a federal statute;
* these rules; or
* other rules prescribed by the Supreme Court.

Irrelevant evidence is not admissible.

Rule 403. Excluding Relevant Evidence for Prejudice, Confusion, Waste of Time, or Other Reasons

The court may exclude relevant evidence if its probative value is substantially outweighed by a danger of one or more of the following: unfair prejudice, confusing the issues, misleading the jury, undue delay, wasting time, or needlessly presenting cumulative evidence.

Rule 404. Character Evidence; Crimes or Other Acts

(a) **Character Evidence.**

(1) *Prohibited Uses.* Evidence of a person's character or character trait is not admissible to prove that on a particular occasion the person acted in accordance with the character or trait.

(2) *Exceptions for a Defendant or Victim in a Criminal Case.* The following exceptions apply in a criminal case:

(A) a defendant may offer evidence of the defendant's pertinent trait, and if the evidence is admitted, the prosecutor may offer evidence to rebut it;

(B) subject to the limitations in Rule 412, a defendant may offer evidence of an alleged victim's pertinent trait, and if the evidence is admitted, the prosecutor may:

(i) offer evidence to rebut it; and

(ii) offer evidence of the defendant's same trait; and

(C) in a homicide case, the prosecutor may offer evidence of the alleged victim's trait of peacefulness to rebut evidence that the victim was the first aggressor.

(3) *Exceptions for a Witness.* Evidence of a witness's character may be admitted under Rules 607, 608, and 609.

(b) **Crimes, Wrongs, or Other Acts.**

(1) *Prohibited Uses.* Evidence of a crime, wrong, or other act is not admissible to prove a person's character in order to show that on a particular occasion the person acted in accordance with the character.

(2) *Permitted Uses; Notice in a Criminal Case.* This evidence may be admissible for another purpose, such as proving motive, opportunity, intent, preparation, plan, knowledge, identity, absence of mistake, or lack of accident. On request by a defendant in a criminal case, the prosecutor must:

(A) provide reasonable notice of the general nature of any such evidence that the prosecutor intends to offer at trial; and

(B) do so before trial—or during trial if the court, for good cause, excuses lack of pretrial notice.

Rule 405. Methods of Proving Character

(a) **By Reputation or Opinion.** When evidence of a person's character or character trait is admissible, it may be proved by testimony about the person's reputation or by testimony in the form of an opinion. On cross-examination of the character witness, the court may allow an inquiry into relevant specific instances of the person's conduct.

(b) **By Specific Instances of Conduct.** When a person's character or character trait is an essential element of a charge, claim, or defense, the character or trait may also be proved by relevant specific instances of the person's conduct.

Rule 406. Habit; Routine Practice

Evidence of a person's habit or an organization's routine practice may be admitted to prove that on a particular occasion the person or organization acted in accordance with the habit or routine practice. The court may admit this evidence regardless of whether it is corroborated or whether.

Rule 410. Pleas, Plea Discussions, and Related Statements

(a) **Prohibited Uses.** In a civil or criminal case, evidence of the following is not admissible against the defendant who made the plea or participated in the plea discussions:

(1) a guilty plea that was later withdrawn;

(2) a nolo contendere plea;

(3) a statement made during a proceeding on either of those pleas under Federal Rule of Criminal Procedure 11 or a comparable state procedure; or

(4) a statement made during plea discussions with an attorney for the prosecuting authority if the discussions did not result in a guilty plea or they resulted in a later-withdrawn guilty plea.

(b) **Exceptions.** The court may admit a statement described in Rule 410(a)(3) or (4):

(1) in any proceeding in which another statement made during the same plea or

plea discussions has been introduced, if in fairness the statements ought to be considered together; or

(2) in a criminal proceeding for perjury or false statement, if the defendant made the statement under oath, on the record, and with counsel present.

Rule 412. Sex-Offense Cases: The Victim's Sexual Behavior or Predisposition

(a) **Prohibited Uses.** The following evidence is not admissible in a civil or criminal proceeding involving alleged sexual misconduct:

(1) evidence offered to prove that a victim engaged in other sexual behavior; or

(2) evidence offered to prove a victim's sexual predisposition.

(b) **Exceptions.**

(1) *Criminal Cases.* The court may admit the following evidence in a criminal case:

(A) evidence of specific instances of a victim's sexual behavior, if offered to prove that someone other than the defendant was the source of semen, injury, or other physical evidence;

(B) evidence of specific instances of a victim's sexual behavior with respect to the person accused of the sexual misconduct, if offered by the defendant to prove consent or if offered by the prosecutor; and

(C) evidence whose exclusion would violate the defendant's constitutional rights.

(2) *Civil Cases.* In a civil case, the court may admit evidence offered to prove a victim's sexual behavior or sexual predisposition if its probative value substantially outweighs the danger of harm to any victim and of unfair prejudice to any party. The court may admit evidence of a victim's reputation only if the victim has placed it in controversy.

(c) **Procedure to Determine Admissibility.**

(1) *Motion.* If a party intends to offer evidence under Rule 412(b), the party must:

(A) file a motion that specifically describes the evidence and states the purpose for which it is to be offered;

(B) do so at least 14 days before trial unless the court, for good cause, sets a different time;

(C) serve the motion on all parties; and

(D) notify the victim or, when appropriate, the victim's guardian or representative.

(2) *Hearing.* Before admitting evidence under this rule, the court must conduct an in camera hearing and give the victim and parties a right to attend and be heard. Unless the court orders otherwise, the motion, related materials, and the record of the hearing must be and remain sealed.

(d) **Definition of "Victim."** In this rule, "victim" includes an alleged victim.

Rule 413. Similar Crimes in Sexual-Assault Cases

(a) **Permitted Uses.** In a criminal case in which a defendant is accused of a sexual assault, the court may admit evidence that the defendant committed any other sexual assault. The evidence may be considered on any matter to which it is relevant.

(b) **Disclosure to the Defendant.** If the prosecutor intends to offer this evidence, the prosecutor must disclose it to the defendant, including witnesses' statements or a summary of the expected testimony. The prosecutor must do so at least 15 days before trial or at a later time that the court allows for good cause.

(c) **Effect on Other Rules.** This rule does not limit the admission or consideration of evidence under any other rule.

(d) **Definition of "Sexual Assault."** In this rule and Rule 415, "sexual assault" means a crime under federal law or under state law (as "state" is defined in 18 U.S.C. § 513) involving:

(1) any conduct prohibited by 18 U.S.C. chapter 109A;

(2) contact, without consent, between any part of the defendant's body—or an object—and another person's genitals or anus;

(3) contact, without consent, between the defendant's genitals or anus and any part of another person's body;

(4) deriving sexual pleasure or gratification from inflicting death, bodily injury, or physical pain on another person; or

(5) an attempt or conspiracy to engage in conduct described in subparagraphs (1)-(4).

Rule 414. Similar Crimes in Child-Molestation Cases

(a) **Permitted Uses.** In a criminal case in which a defendant is accused of child molestation, the court may admit evidence that the defendant committed any other child molestation. The evidence may be considered on any matter to which it is relevant.

(b) **Disclosure to the Defendant.** If the prosecutor intends to offer this evidence, the prosecutor must disclose it to the defendant, including witnesses' statements or a summary of the expected testimony. The prosecutor must do so at least 15 days before trial or at a later time that the court allows for good cause.

(c) **Effect on Other Rules.** This rule does not limit the admission or consideration of evidence under any other rule.

(d) **Definition of "Child" and "Child Molestation."** In this rule and Rule 415:

(1) "child" means a person below the age of 14; and

(2) "child molestation" means a crime under federal law or under state law (as "state" is defined in 18 U.S.C. § 513) involving:

(A) any conduct prohibited by 18 U.S.C. chapter 109A and committed with a child;

(B) any conduct prohibited by 18 U.S.C. chapter 110;

(C) contact between any part of the defendant's body—or an object—and a child's genitals or anus;

(D) contact between the defendant's genitals or anus and any part of a child's body;

(E) deriving sexual pleasure or gratification from inflicting death, bodily injury, or physical pain on a child; or

(F) an attempt or conspiracy to engage in conduct described in subparagraphs (A)–(E).

Rule 415. Similar Acts in Civil Cases Involving Sexual Assault or Child Molestation

(a) **Permitted Uses.** In a civil case involving a claim for relief based on a party's alleged sexual assault or child molestation, the court may admit evidence that the party committed any other sexual assault or child molestation. The evidence may be considered as provided in Rules 413 and 414.

(b) **Disclosure to the Opponent.** If a party intends to offer this evidence, the party must disclose it to the party against whom it will be offered, including witnesses' statements or a summary of the expected testimony. The party must do so at least 15 days before trial or at a later time that the court allows for good cause.

(c) **Effect on Other Rules.** This rule does not limit the admission or consideration of evidence under any other rule.

ARTICLE V. PRIVILEGES

Rule 501. Privileges in General

The common law—as interpreted by United States courts in the light of reason and experience—governs a claim of privilege unless any of the following provides otherwise:

- the United States Constitution;
- a federal statute; or
- rules prescribed by the Supreme Court.

But in a civil case, state law governs privilege regarding a claim or defense for which state law supplies the rule of decision.

Rule 502. Attorney-Client Privilege and Work Product; Limitations on Waiver

The following provisions apply, in the circumstances set out, to disclosure of a communication or information covered by the attorney-client privilege or work-product protection.

(a) **Disclosure Made in a Federal Proceeding or to a Federal Office or Agency; Scope of a Waiver.** When the disclosure is made in a federal proceeding or to a federal office or agency and waives the attorney-client privilege or work-product protection, the waiver extends to an undisclosed communication or information in a federal or state proceeding only if:

(1) the waiver is intentional;

(2) the disclosed and undisclosed communications or information concern the same subject matter; and

(3) they ought in fairness to be considered together.

(b) **Inadvertent Disclosure.** When made in a federal proceeding or to a federal office or agency, the disclosure does not operate as a waiver in a federal or state proceeding if:

(1) the disclosure is inadvertent;

(2) the holder of the privilege or protection took reasonable steps to prevent disclosure; and

(3) the holder promptly took reasonable steps to rectify the error, including (if applicable) following Federal Rule of Civil Procedure 26(b)(5)(B).

(c) **Disclosure Made in a State Proceeding.** When the disclosure is made in a state proceeding and is not the subject of a state-court order concerning waiver, the disclosure does not operate as a waiver in a federal proceeding if the disclosure:

(1) would not be a waiver under this rule if it had been made in a federal proceeding; or

(2) is not a waiver under the law of the State where the disclosure occurred.

(d) **Controlling Effect of a Court Order.** A federal court may order that the privilege or protection is not waived by disclosure connected with the litigation pending before the court—in which event the disclosure is also not a waiver in any other federal or state proceeding.

(e) **Controlling Effect of a Party Agreement.** An agreement on the effect of disclosure in a federal proceeding is binding only on the parties to the agreement, unless it is incorporated into a court order.

(f) **Controlling Effect of This Rule.** Notwithstanding Rules 101 and 1101, this rule applies to state proceedings and to federal court-annexed and federal court-mandated arbitration proceedings, in the circumstances set out in the rule. And notwithstanding Rule 501, this rule applies even if State law provides the rule of decision.

(g) **Definitions.** In this rule:

(1) "attorney-client privilege" means the protection that applicable law provides for confidential attorney-client communications; and

(2) "work-product protection" means the protection that applicable law provides for tangible material (or its intangible equivalent) prepared in anticipation of litigation or for trial.

ARTICLE VI. WITNESSES

Rule 601. Competency to Testify in General

Every person is competent to be a witness unless these rules provide otherwise. But in a civil case, state law governs the witness's competency regarding a claim or defense for which state law supplies the rule of decision.

Rule 602. Need for Personal Knowledge

A witness may not testify to a matter unless evidence is introduced sufficient to support a finding that the witness has personal knowledge of the matter. Evidence to prove personal knowledge may, but need not, consist of the witness' own testimony. This rule is subject to the provisions of Rule 703, relating to opinion testimony by expert witnesses.

Rule 603. Oath or Affirmation to Testify Truthfully

Before testifying, a witness must give an oath or affirmation to testify truthfully. It must be in a form designed to impress that duty on the witness's conscience.

Rule 604. Interpreter

An interpreter must be qualified and must give an oath or affirmation to make a true translation.

Rule 605. Judge's Competency as a Witness

The presiding judge may not testify as a witness at the trial. A party need not object to preserve the issue.

Rule 606. Who May Impeach a Witness

(a) **At the Trial.** A juror may not testify as a witness before the other jurors at the trial. If a juror is called to testify, the court must give a party an opportunity to object outside the jury's presence.

(b) **During an Inquiry into the Validity of a Verdict or Indictment.**

    (1) *Prohibited Testimony or Other Evidence.* During an inquiry into the validity of a verdict or indictment, a juror may not testify about any statement made or incident that occurred during the jury's deliberations; the effect of anything on that juror's or another juror's vote; or any juror's mental processes concerning the verdict or indictment. The court may not receive a juror's affidavit or evidence of a juror's statement on these matters.

    (2) *Exceptions.* A juror may testify about whether:

        (A) extraneous prejudicial information was improperly brought to the jury's attention;

        (B) an outside influence was improperly brought to bear on any juror; or

        (C) a mistake was made in entering the verdict on the verdict form.

Rule 607. Who May Impeach a Witness

Any party, including the party that called the witness, may attack the witness's credibility.

Rule 608. A Witness's Character for Truthfulness or Untruthfulness

(a) **Reputation or Opinion Evidence.** A witness's credibility may be attacked or supported by testimony about the witness's reputation for having a character for truthfulness or untruthfulness, or by testimony in the form of an opinion about that character. But evidence of truthful character is admissible only after the witness's character for truthfulness has been attacked.

(b) **Specific Instances of Conduct.** Except for a criminal conviction under Rule 609, extrinsic evidence is not admissible to prove specific instances of a witness's conduct in order to attack or support the witness's character for truthfulness. But the court may, on cross-examination, allow them to be inquired into if they are probative of the character for truthfulness or untruthfulness of:

    (1) the witness; or

    (2) another witness whose character the witness being cross-examined has testified about.

By testifying on another matter, a witness does not waive any privilege against self-incrimination for testimony that relates only to the witness's character for truthfulness.

Rule 609. Impeachment by Evidence of a Criminal Conviction

(a) **In General.** The following rules apply to attacking a witness's character for truthfulness by evidence of a criminal conviction:

    (1) for a crime that, in the convicting jurisdiction, was punishable by death or by imprisonment for more than one year, the evidence:

        (A) must be admitted, subject to Rule 403, in a civil case or in a criminal case in which the witness is not a defendant; and

        (B) must be admitted in a criminal case in which the witness is a defendant, if the probative value of the evidence outweighs its prejudicial effect to that defendant; and

    (2) for any crime regardless of the punishment, the evidence must be admitted if the court can readily determine that establishing the elements of the crime required proving—or the witness's admitting—a dishonest act or false statement.

(b) **Limit on Using the Evidence After 10 Years.** This subdivision (b) applies if more than 10 years have passed since the witness's conviction or release from confinement for it, whichever is later. Evidence of the conviction is admissible only if:

    (1) its probative value, supported by specific facts and circumstances, substantially outweighs its prejudicial effect; and

(2) the proponent gives an adverse party reasonable written notice of the intent to use it so that the party has a fair opportunity to contest its use.

(c) **Effect of a Pardon, Annulment, or Certificate of Rehabilitation**. Evidence of a conviction is not admissible if:

(1) the conviction has been the subject of a pardon, annulment, certificate of rehabilitation, or other equivalent procedure based on a finding that the person has been rehabilitated, and the person has not been convicted of a later crime punishable by death or by imprisonment for more than one year; or

(2) the conviction has been the subject of a pardon, annulment, or other equivalent procedure based on a finding of innocence.

(d) **Juvenile Adjudications.**
Evidence of a juvenile adjudication is admissible under this rule only if:

(1) it is offered in a criminal case;

(2) the adjudication was of a witness other than the defendant;

(3) an adult's conviction for that offense would be admissible to attack the adult's credibility; and

(4) admitting the evidence is necessary to fairly determine guilt or innocence.

(e) **Pendency of an Appeal.** A conviction that satisfies this rule is admissible even if an appeal is pending. Evidence of the pendency is also admissible.

Rule 610. Rule 610. Religious Beliefs or Opinions

Evidence of a witness's religious beliefs or opinions is not admissible to attack or support the witness's credibility.

Rule 611. Mode and Order of Examining Witnesses and Presenting Evidence

(a) **Control by the Court; Purposes.** The court should exercise reasonable control over the mode and order of examining witnesses and presenting evidence so as to:

(1) make those procedures effective for determining the truth;

(2) avoid wasting time; and

(3) protect witnesses from harassment or undue embarrassment.

(b) **Scope of Cross-Examination.** Cross-examination should not go beyond the subject matter of the direct examination and matters affecting the witness's credibility. The court may allow inquiry into additional matters as if on direct examination.

(c) **Leading Questions.** Leading questions should not be used on direct examination except as necessary to develop the witness's testimony. Ordinarily, the court should allow leading questions:

(1) on cross-examination; and

(2) when a party calls a hostile witness, an adverse party, or a witness identified with an adverse party.

Rule 612. Writing Used to Refresh a Witness's Memory

(a) **Scope.** This rule gives an adverse party certain options when a witness uses a writing to refresh memory:

(1) while testifying; or

(2) before testifying, if the court decides that justice requires the party to have those options.

(b) **Adverse Party's Options; Deleting Unrelated Matter.** Unless 18 U.S.C. § 3500 provides otherwise in a criminal case, an adverse party is entitled to have the writing produced at the hearing, to inspect it, to cross-examine the witness about it, and to introduce in evidence any portion that relates to the witness's testimony. If the producing party claims that the writing includes unrelated matter, the court must examine the writing in camera, delete any unrelated portion, and order that the rest be delivered to the adverse party. Any portion deleted over objection must be preserved for the record.

(c) **Failure to Produce or Deliver the Writing.** If a writing is not produced or is not delivered as ordered, the court may issue any appropriate order. But if the prosecution does not comply in a criminal case, the court must strike the witness's testimony or—if justice so requires—declare a mistrial.

Rule 613. Witness's Prior Statement

(a) **Showing or Disclosing the Statement During Examination.** When examining a witness about the witness's prior statement, a party need not show it or disclose its contents to the witness. But the party must, on request, show it or disclose its contents to an adverse party's attorney.

(b) **Extrinsic Evidence of a Prior Inconsistent Statement.** Extrinsic evidence of a witness's prior inconsistent statement is admissible only if the witness is given an opportunity to explain or deny the statement and an adverse party is given an opportunity to examine the witness about it, or if justice so requires. This subdivision (b) does not apply to an opposing party's statement under Rule 801(d)(2).

Rule 614. Court's Calling or Examining a Witness

(a) **Calling.** The court may call a witness on its own or at a party's request. Each party is entitled to cross-examine the witness.

(b) **Examining.** The court may examine a witness regardless of who calls the witness.

(c) **Objections.** A party may object to the court's calling or examining a witness either at that time or at the next opportunity when the jury is not present.

Rule 615. Excluding Witnesses

At a party's request, the court must order witnesses excluded so that they cannot hear other witnesses' testimony. Or the court may do so on its own. But this rule does not authorize excluding:

(a) a party who is a natural person;

(b) an officer or employee of a party that is not a natural person, after being designated as the party's representative by its attorney;

(c) a person whose presence a party shows to be essential to presenting the party's claim or defense; or

(d) a person authorized by statute to be present.

ARTICLE VII. OPINIONS AND EXPERT TESTIMONY

Rule 701. Opinion Testimony by Lay Witnesses

If a witness is not testifying as an expert, testimony in the form of an opinion is limited to one that is:

(a) rationally based on the witness's perception;

(b) helpful to clearly understanding the witness's testimony or to determining a fact in issue; and

(c) not based on scientific, technical, or other specialized knowledge within the scope of Rule 702.

Rule 702. Testimony by Expert Witnesses

A witness who is qualified as an expert by knowledge, skill, experience, training, or education may testify in the form of an opinion or otherwise if:

(a) the expert's scientific, technical, or other specialized knowledge will help the trier of fact to understand the evidence or to determine a fact in issue;

(b) the testimony is based on sufficient facts or data;

(c) the testimony is the product of reliable principles and methods; and

(d) the expert has reliably applied the principles and methods to the facts of the case.

Rule 703. Bases of an Expert's Opinion Testimony

An expert may base an opinion on facts or data in the case that the expert has been made aware of or personally observed. If experts in the particular field would reasonably rely on those kinds of facts or data in forming an opinion on the subject, they need not be admissible for the opinion to be admitted. But if the facts or data would otherwise be inadmissible, the proponent of the opinion may disclose them to the jury only if their probative value in helping the jury evaluate the opinion substantially outweighs their prejudicial effect.

Rule 704. Opinion on an Ultimate Issue

(a) **In General—Not Automatically Objectionable.** An opinion is not objectionable just because it embraces an ultimate issue.

(b) **Exception.** In a criminal case, an expert witness must not state an opinion about whether the defendant did or did not have a mental state or condition that constitutes an element of the crime charged or of a defense. Those matters are for the trier of fact alone.

Rule 705. Disclosing the Facts or Data Underlying an Expert's Opinion

Unless the court orders otherwise, an expert may state an opinion—and give the reasons for it—without first testifying to the underlying facts or data. But the expert may be required to disclose those facts or data on cross-examination.

Rule 706. Court-Appointed Expert Witnesses

(a) **Appointment Process.** On a party's motion or on its own, the court may order the parties to show cause why expert witnesses should not be appointed and may ask the parties to submit nominations. The court may appoint any expert that the parties agree on and any of its own choosing. But the court may only appoint someone who consents to act.

(b) **Expert's Role.** The court must inform the expert of the expert's duties. The court may do so in writing and have a copy filed with the clerk or may do so orally at a conference in which the parties have an opportunity to participate. The expert:

    (1) must advise the parties of any findings the expert makes;

    (2) may be deposed by any party;

    (3) may be called to testify by the court or any party; and

    (4) may be cross-examined by any party, including the party that called the expert.

(c) **Compensation.** The expert is entitled to a reasonable compensation, as set by the court. The compensation is payable as follows:

    (1) in a criminal case or in a civil case involving just compensation under the Fifth Amendment, from any funds that are provided by law; and

    (2) in any other civil case, by the parties in the proportion and at the time that the court direct—and the compensation is then charged like other costs.

(d) **Disclosing the Appointment to the Jury.** The court may authorize disclosure to the jury that the court appointed the expert.

(e) **Parties' Choice of Their Own Experts.** This rule does not limit a party in calling its own experts.

ARTICLE VIII. HEARSAY

Rule 801. Definitions That Apply to This Article; Exclusions from Hearsay

(a) **Statement.** "Statement" means a person's oral assertion, written assertion, or nonverbal conduct, if the person intended it as an assertion.

(b) **Declarant.** "Declarant" means the person who made the statement.

(c) **Hearsay.** "Hearsay" means a statement that:

    (1) the declarant does not make while testifying at the current trial or hearing; and

    (2) a party offers in evidence to prove the truth of the matter asserted in the statement.

(d) **Statements That Are Not Hearsay.** A statement that meets the following conditions is not hearsay:

    (1) *A Declarant-Witness's Prior Statement.* The declarant testifies and is subject to cross-examination about a prior statement, and the statement:

        (A) is inconsistent with the declarant's testimony and was given under penalty of perjury at a trial, hearing, or other proceeding or in a deposition;

        (B) is consistent with the declarant's testimony and is offered to rebut an express or implied charge that the declarant recently fabricated it or acted from a recent improper influence or motive in so testifying; or

        (C) identifies a person as someone the declarant perceived earlier.

(2) ***An Opposing Party's Statement.*** The statement is offered against an opposing party and:
 (A) was made by the party in an individual or representative capacity;
 (B) is one the party manifested that it adopted or believed to be true;
 (C) was made by a person whom the party authorized to make a statement on the subject;
 (D) was made by the party's agent or employee on a matter within the scope of that relationship and while it existed; or
 (E) was made by the party's coconspirator during and in furtherance of the conspiracy.

The statement must be considered but does not by itself establish the declarant's authority under (C); the existence or scope of the relationship under (D); or the existence of the conspiracy or participation in it under (E).

Rule 802. The Rule Against Hearsay

Hearsay is not admissible unless any of the following provides otherwise:

- a federal statute;
- these rules; or
- other rules prescribed by the Supreme Court.

Rule 803. Exceptions to the Rule Against Hearsay—Regardless of Whether the Declarant Is Available as a Witness

The following are not excluded by the rule against hearsay, regardless of whether the declarant is available as a witness:

(1) ***Present Sense Impression.*** A statement describing or explaining an event or condition, made while or immediately after the declarant perceived it.

(2) ***Excited Utterance.*** A statement relating to a startling event or condition, made while the declarant was under the stress of excitement that it caused.

(3) ***Then-Existing Mental, Emotional, or Physical Condition.*** A statement of the declarant's then-existing state of mind (such as motive, intent, or plan) or emotional, sensory, or physical condition (such as mental feeling, pain, or bodily health), but not including a statement of memory or belief to prove the fact remembered or believed unless it relates to the validity or terms of the declarant's will.

(4) ***Statement Made for Medical Diagnosis or Treatment.*** A statement that:
 (A) is made for—and is reasonably pertinent to—medical diagnosis or treatment; and
 (B) describes medical history; past or present symptoms or sensations; their inception; or their general cause.

(5) ***Recorded Recollection*** A record that:
 (A) is on a matter the witness once knew about but now cannot recall well enough to testify fully and accurately;
 (B) was made or adopted by the witness when the matter was fresh in the witness's memory; and
 (C) accurately reflects the witness's knowledge. If admitted, the record may be read into evidence but may be received as an exhibit only if offered by an adverse party.

(6) ***Records of a Regularly Conducted Activity.*** A record of an act, event, condition, opinion, or diagnosis if:
 (A) the record was made at or near the time by—or from information transmitted by—someone with knowledge;
 (B) the record was kept in the course of a regularly conducted activity of a business, organization, occupation, or calling, whether or not for profit;
 (C) making the record was a regular practice of that activity;
 (D) all these conditions are shown by the testimony of the custodian or another qualified witness, or by a certification that complies with Rule 902(11) or (12) or with a statute permitting certification; and
 (E) neither the source of information nor the method or circumstances of preparation indicate a lack of trustworthiness.

(7) ***Absence of a Record of a Regularly Conducted Activity.*** Evidence that a matter is not included in a record described in paragraph (6) if:
 (A) the evidence is admitted to prove that the matter did not occur or exist;

(B) a record was regularly kept for a matter of that kind; and

(C) neither the possible source of the information nor other circumstances indicate a lack of trustworthiness.

(8) ***Public Records.*** A record or statement of a public office if:

   (A) it sets out:

     (i) the office's activities;

     (ii) a matter observed while under a legal duty to report, but not including, in a criminal case, a matter observed by law-enforcement personnel; or

     (iii) in a civil case or against the government in a criminal case, factual findings from a legally authorized investigation; and

   (B) neither the source of information nor other circumstances indicate a lack of trustworthiness.

(9) ***Public Records of Vital Statistics.*** A record of a birth, death, or marriage, if reported to a public office in accordance with a legal duty.

(10) ***Absence of a Public Record.*** Testimony—or a certification under Rule 902—that a diligent search failed to disclose a public record or statement if the testimony or certification is admitted to prove that:

   (A) the record or statement does not exist; or

   (B) a matter did not occur or exist, if a public office regularly kept a record or statement for a matter of that kind.

(11) ***Records of Religious Organizations Concerning Personal or Family History.*** A statement of birth, legitimacy, ancestry, marriage, divorce, death, relationship by blood or marriage, or similar facts of personal or family history, contained in a regularly kept record of a religious organization.

(12) ***Certificates of Marriage, Baptism, and Similar Ceremonies.*** A statement of fact contained in a certificate:

   (A) made by a person who is authorized by a religious organization or by law to perform the act certified;

   (B) attesting that the person performed a marriage or similar ceremony or administered a sacrament; and

   (C) purporting to have been issued at the time of the act or within a reasonable time after it.

(13) ***Family Records.*** A statement of fact about personal or family history contained in a family record, such as a Bible, genealogy, chart, engraving on a ring, inscription on a portrait, or engraving on an urn or burial marker.

(14) ***Records of Documents That Affect an Interest in Property.*** The record of a document that purports to establish or affect an interest in property if:

   (A) the record is admitted to prove the content of the original recorded document, along with its signing and its delivery by each person who purports to have signed it;

   (B) the record is kept in a public office; and

   (C) a statute authorizes recording documents of that kind in that office.

(15) ***Statements in Documents That Affect an Interest in Property.*** A statement contained in a document that purports to establish or affect an interest in property if the matter stated was relevant to the document's purpose—unless later dealings with the property are inconsistent with the truth of the statement or the purport of the document.

(16) ***Statements in Ancient Documents.*** A statement in a document that is at least 20 years old and whose authenticity is established.

(17) ***Market Reports and Similar Commercial Publications.*** Market quotations, lists, directories, or other compilations that are generally relied on by the public or by persons in particular occupations.

(18) ***Statements in Learned Treatises, Periodicals, or Pamphlets.*** A statement contained in a treatise, periodical, or pamphlet if:

   (A) the statement is called to the attention of an expert witness on cross-examination or relied on by the expert on direct examination; and

   (B) the publication is established as a reliable authority by the expert's admission or testimony, by another expert's testimony, or by judicial notice.

   If admitted, the statement may be read into evidence but not received as an exhibit.

(19) ***Reputation Concerning Personal or Family History.*** A reputation among a person's family by blood, adoption, or marriage—or among a

person's associates or in the community—concerning the person's birth, adoption, legitimacy, ancestry, marriage, divorce, death, relationship by blood, adoption, or marriage, or similar facts of personal or family history.

(20) ***Reputation Concerning Boundaries or General History.*** A reputation in a community—arising before the controversy—concerning boundaries of land in the community or customs that affect the land, or concerning general historical events important to that community, state, or nation.

(21) ***Reputation Concerning Character.*** A reputation among a person's associates or in the community concerning the person's character.

(22) ***Judgment of a Previous Conviction.*** Evidence of a final judgment of conviction if:
   (A) the judgment was entered after a trial or guilty plea, but not a nolo contendere plea;
   (B) the conviction was for a crime punishable by death or by imprisonment for more than a year;
   (C) the evidence is admitted to prove any fact essential to the judgment; and
   (D) when offered by the prosecutor in a criminal case for a purpose other than impeachment, the judgment was against the defendant.
   The pendency of an appeal may be shown but does not affect admissibility.

(23) ***Judgments Involving Personal, Family, or General History, or a Boundary.*** A judgment that is admitted to prove a matter of personal, family, or general history, or boundaries, if the matter:
   (A) was essential to the judgment; and
   (B) could be proved by evidence of reputation.

(24) *[Other Exceptions.]* [Transferred to Rule 807.]

Rule 804. Exceptions to the Rule Against Hearsay—When the Declarant Is Unavailable as a Witness

(a) **Criteria for Being Unavailable.** A declarant is considered to be unavailable as a witness if the declarant:
   (1) is exempted from testifying about the subject matter of the declarant's statement because the court rules that a privilege applies;

   (2) refuses to testify about the subject matter despite a court order to do so;
   (3) testifies to not remembering the subject matter;
   (4) cannot be present or testify at the trial or hearing because of death or a then-existing infirmity, physical illness, or mental illness; or
   (5) is absent from the trial or hearing and the statement's proponent has not been able, by process or other reasonable means, to procure:
      (A) the declarant's attendance, in the case of a hearsay exception under Rule 804(b)(1) or (6); or
      (B) the declarant's attendance or testimony, in the case of a hearsay exception under Rule 804(b)(2), (3), or (4). But this subdivision (a) does not apply if the statement's proponent procured or wrongfully caused the declarant's unavailability as a witness in order to prevent the declarant from attending or testifying.

(b) **The Exceptions.** The following are not excluded by the rule against hearsay if the declarant is unavailable as a witness:
   (1) ***Former Testimony.*** Testimony that:
      (A) was given as a witness at a trial, hearing, or lawful deposition, whether given during the current proceeding or a different one; and
      (B) is now offered against a party who had—or, in a civil case, whose predecessor in interest had—an opportunity and similar motive to develop it by direct, cross-, or redirect examination.
   (2) ***Statement Under the Belief of Imminent Death.*** In a prosecution for homicide or in a civil case, a statement that the declarant, while believing the declarant's death to be imminent, made about its cause or circumstances.
   (3) ***Statement Against Interest.*** A statement that:
      (A) a reasonable person in the declarant's position would have made only if the person believed it to be true because, when made, it was so contrary to the declarant's proprietary

or pecuniary interest or had so great a tendency to invalidate the declarant's claim against someone else or to expose the declarant to civil or criminal liability; and

(B) is supported by corroborating circumstances that clearly indicate its trustworthiness, if it is offered in a criminal case as one that tends to expose the declarant to criminal liability.

(4) ***Statement of Personal or Family History.*** A statement about:

(A) the declarant's own birth, adoption, legitimacy, ancestry, marriage, divorce, relationship by blood, adoption, or marriage, or similar facts of personal or family history, even though the declarant had no way of acquiring personal knowledge about that fact; or

(B) another person concerning any of these facts, as well as death, if the declarant was related to the person by blood, adoption, or marriage or was so intimately associated with the person's family that the declarant's information is likely to be accurate.

(5) ***[Other Exceptions.]*** [Transferred to Rule 807.]

(6) ***Statement Offered Against a Party That Wrongfully Caused the Declarant's Unavailability.*** A statement offered against a party that wrongfully caused— or acquiesced in wrongfully causing—the declarant's unavailability as a witness, and did so intending that result.

Rule 805. Hearsay Within Hearsay

Hearsay within hearsay is not excluded by the rule against hearsay if each part of the combined statements conforms with an exception to the rule.

Rule 806. Attacking and Supporting the Declarant's Credibility

When a hearsay statement—or a statement described in Rule 801(d)(2)(C), (D), or (E)—has been admitted in evidence, the declarant's credibility may be attacked, and then supported, by any evidence that would be admissible for those purposes if the declarant had testified as a witness. The court may admit evidence of the declarant's inconsistent statement or conduct, regardless of when it occurred or whether the declarant had an opportunity to explain or deny it. If the party against whom the statement was admitted calls the declarant as a witness, the party may examine the declarant on the statement as if on cross-examination.

Rule 807. Residual Exception

(a) **In General.** Under the following circumstances, a hearsay statement is not excluded by the rule against hearsay even if the statement is not specifically covered by a hearsay exception in Rule 803 or 804:

(1) the statement has equivalent circumstantial guarantees of trustworthiness;

(2) it is offered as evidence of a material fact;

(3) it is more probative on the point for which it is offered than any other evidence that the proponent can obtain through reasonable efforts; and

(4) admitting it will best serve the purposes of these rules and the interests of justice.

(b) **Notice.** The statement is admissible only if, before the trial or hearing, the proponent gives an adverse party reasonable notice of the intent to offer the statement and its particulars, including the declarant's name and address, so that the party has a fair opportunity to meet it.

ARTICLE IX. AUTHENTICATION AND IDENTIFICATION

Rule 901. Authenticating or Identifying Evidence

(a) **In General.** To satisfy the requirement of authenticating or identifying an item of evidence, the proponent must produce evidence sufficient to support a finding that the item is what the proponent claims it is.

(b) **Examples.** The following are examples only— not a complete list—of evidence that satisfies the requirement:

(1) ***Testimony of a Witness with Knowledge.*** Testimony that an item is what it is claimed to be.

(2) ***Nonexpert Opinion About Handwriting.*** A nonexpert's opinion that handwriting is genuine, based on a familiarity with it that was not acquired for the current litigation.

(3) ***Comparison by an Expert Witness or the Trier of Fact.*** A comparison with an authenticated specimen by an expert witness or the trier of fact.

(4) ***Distinctive Characteristics and the Like.*** The appearance, contents, substance, internal patterns, or other distinctive characteristics of the item, taken together with all the circumstances.

(5) ***Opinion About a Voice.*** An opinion identifying a person's voice—whether heard firsthand or through mechanical or electronic transmission or recording—based on hearing the voice at any time under circumstances that connect it with the alleged speaker.

(6) ***Evidence About a Telephone Conversation.*** For a telephone conversation, evidence that a call was made to the number assigned at the time to:

   (A) a particular person, if circumstances, including self-identification, show that the person answering was the one called; or

   (B) a particular business, if the call was made to a business and the call related to business reasonably transacted over the telephone.

(7) ***Evidence About Public Records.*** Evidence that:

   (A) a document was recorded or filed in a public office as authorized by law; or

   (B) a purported public record or statement is from the office where items of this kind are kept.

(8) ***Evidence About Ancient Documents or Data Compilations.*** For a document or data compilation, evidence that it:

   (A) is in a condition that creates no suspicion about its authenticity;

   (B) was in a place where, if authentic, it would likely be; and

   (C) is at least 20 years old when offered.

(9) ***Evidence About a Process or System.*** Evidence describing a process or system and showing that it produces an accurate result.

(10) ***Methods Provided by a Statute or Rule.*** Any method of authentication or identification allowed by a federal statute or a rule prescribed by the Supreme Court.

Rule 902. Evidence That Is Self-Authenticating

The following items of evidence are self-authenticating; they require no extrinsic evidence of authenticity in order to be admitted:

(1) ***Domestic Public Documents That Are Sealed and Signed.*** A document that bears:

   (A) a seal purporting to be that of the United States; any state, district, commonwealth, territory, or insular possession of the United States; the former Panama Canal Zone; the Trust Territory of the Pacific Islands; a political subdivision of any of these entities; or a department, agency, or officer of any entity named above; and

   (B) a signature purporting to be an execution or attestation.

(2) ***Domestic Public Documents That Are Not Sealed but Are Signed and Certified.*** A document that bears no seal if:

   (A) it bears the signature of an officer or employee of an entity named in Rule 902 (1)(A); and

   (B) another public officer who has a seal and official duties within that same entity certifies under seal—or its equivalent—that the signer has the official capacity and that the signature is genuine.

(3) ***Foreign Public Documents.*** A document that purports to be signed or attested by a person who is authorized by a foreign country's law to do so. The document must be accompanied by a final certification that certifies the genuineness of the signature and official position of the signer or attester—or of any foreign official whose certificate of genuineness relates to the signature or attestation or is in a chain of certificates of genuineness relating to the signature

or attestation. The certification may be made by a secretary of a United States embassy or legation; by a consul general, vice consul, or consular agent of the United States; or by a diplomatic or consular official of the foreign country assigned or accredited to the United States. If all parties have been given a reasonable opportunity to investigate the document's authenticity and accuracy, the court may, for good cause, either:

(A) order that it be treated as presumptively authentic without final certification; or

(B) allow it to be evidenced by an attested summary with or without final certification.

(4) *Certified Copies of Public Records.* A copy of an official record—or a copy of a document that was recorded or filed in a public office as authorized by law—if the copy is certified as correct by:

(A) the custodian or another person authorized to make the certification; or

(B) a certificate that complies with Rule 902 (1), (2), or (3), a federal statute, or a rule prescribed by the Supreme Court.

(5) *Official Publications.* A book, pamphlet, or other publication purporting to be issued by a public authority.

(6) *Newspapers and Periodicals.* Printed material purporting to be a newspaper or periodical.

(7) *Trade Inscriptions and the Like.* An inscription, sign, tag, or label purporting to have been affixed in the course of business and indicating origin, ownership, or control.

(8) *Acknowledged Documents.* A document accompanied by a certificate of acknowledgment that is lawfully executed by a notary public or another officer who is authorized to take acknowledgments.

(9) *Commercial Paper and Related Documents.* Commercial paper, a signature on it, and related documents, to the extent allowed by general commercial law.

(10) *Presumptions Under a Federal Statute.* A signature, document, or anything else that a federal statute declares to be presumptively or prima facie genuine or authentic.

(11) *Certified Domestic Records of a Regularly Conducted Activity.* The original or a copy of a domestic record that meets the requirements of Rule 803(6)(A)-(C), as shown by a certification of the custodian or another qualified person that complies with a federal statute or a rule prescribed by the Supreme Court. Before the trial or hearing, the proponent must give an adverse party reasonable written notice of the intent to offer the record—and must make the record and certification available for inspection—so that the party has a fair opportunity to challenge them.

(12) *Certified Foreign Records of a Regularly Conducted Activity.* In a civil case, the original or a copy of a foreign record that meets the requirements of Rule 902(11), modified as follows: the certification, rather than complying with a federal statute or Supreme Court rule, must be signed in a manner that, if falsely made, would subject the maker to a criminal penalty in the country where the certification is signed. The proponent must also meet the notice requirements of Rule 902(11).

Rule 903. Subscribing Witness's Testimony

A subscribing witness's testimony is necessary to authenticate a writing only if required by the law of the jurisdiction that governs its validity.

ARTICLE X. CONTENTS OF WRITINGS, RECORDINGS, AND PHOTOGRAPHS

Rule 1001. Definitions That Apply to This Article

In this article:

(a) A "writing" consists of letters, words, numbers, or their equivalent set down in any form.

(b) A "recording" consists of letters, words, numbers, or their equivalent recorded in any manner.

(c) A "photograph" means a photographic image or its equivalent stored in any form.

(d) An "original" of a writing or recording means the writing or recording itself or any counterpart intended to have the same effect by the person who executed or issued it. For electronically stored information, "original" means any printout—or other output readable by sight—if it accurately reflects the information.

An "original" of a photograph includes the negative or a print from it.

(e) A "duplicate" means a counterpart produced by a mechanical, photographic, chemical, electronic, or other equivalent process or technique that accurately reproduces the original.

Rule 1002. Requirement of the Original

An original writing, recording, or photograph is required in order to prove its content unless these rules or a federal statute provides otherwise.

Rule 1003. Admissibility of Duplicates

A duplicate is admissible to the same extent as the original unless a genuine question is raised about the original's authenticity or the circumstances make it unfair to admit the duplicate.

Rule 1004. Admissibility of Other Evidence of Content

An original is not required and other evidence of the content of a writing, recording, or photograph is admissible if:

(a) all the originals are lost or destroyed, and not by the proponent acting in bad faith;

(b) an original cannot be obtained by any available judicial process;

(c) the party against whom the original would be offered had control of the original; was at that time put on notice, by pleadings or otherwise, that the original would be a subject of proof at the trial or hearing; and fails to produce it at the trial or hearing; or

(d) the writing, recording, or photograph is not closely related to a controlling issue.

Rule 1005. Copies of Public Records to Prove Content

The proponent may use a copy to prove the content of an official record—or of a document that was recorded or filed in a public office as authorized by law—if these conditions are met: the record or document is otherwise admissible; and the copy is certified as correct in accordance with Rule 902(4) or is testified to be correct by a witness who has compared it with the original. If no such copy can be obtained by

reasonable diligence, then the proponent may use other evidence to prove the content.

Rule 1006. Summaries to Prove Content

The proponent may use a summary, chart, or calculation to prove the content of voluminous writings, recordings, or photographs that cannot be conveniently examined in court. The proponent must make the originals or duplicates available for examination or copying, or both, by other parties at a reasonable time and place. And the court may order the proponent to produce them in court.

Rule 1007. Testimony or Statement of a Party to Prove Content

The proponent may prove the content of a writing, recording, or photograph by the testimony, deposition, or written statement of the party against whom the evidence is offered. The proponent need not account for the original.

Rule 1008. Functions of the Court and Jury

Ordinarily, the court determines whether the proponent has fulfilled the factual conditions for admitting other evidence of the content of a writing, recording, or photograph under Rule 1004 or 1005. But in a jury trial, the jury determines—in accordance with Rule 104(b)—any issue about whether:

(a) an asserted writing, recording, or photograph ever existed;

(b) another one produced at the trial or hearing is the original; or

(c) other evidence of content accurately reflects the content.

ARTICLE XI. MISCELLANEOUS RULES

Rule 1101. Applicability of the Rules

(a) To Courts and Judges. These rules apply to proceedings before:

- United States district courts;
- United States bankruptcy and magistrate judges;
- United States courts of appeals;
- the United States Court of Federal Claims; and

- the district courts of Guam, the Virgin Islands, and the Northern Mariana Islands.

(b) To Cases and Proceedings. These rules apply in:

- civil cases and proceedings, including bankruptcy, admiralty, and maritime cases;
- criminal cases and proceedings; and
- contempt proceedings, except those in which the court may act summarily.

(c) Rules on Privilege. The rules on privilege apply to all stages of a case or proceeding.

(d) Exceptions. These rules—except for those on privilege—do not apply to the following:

(1) the court's determination, under Rule 104 (a), on a preliminary question of fact governing admissibility;

(2) grand-jury proceedings; and

(3) miscellaneous proceedings such as:

- extradition or rendition;
- issuing an arrest warrant, criminal summons, or search warrant;
- a preliminary examination in a criminal case;
- sentencing;
- granting or revoking probation or supervised release; and
- considering whether to release on bail or otherwise.

(e) Other Statutes and Rules. A federal statute or a rule prescribed by the Supreme Court may provide for admitting or excluding evidence independently from these rules.

Rule 1102. Amendments

These rules may be amended as provided in 28 U.S.C. § 2072.

Rule 1103. Title

These rules may be cited as the Federal Rules of Evidence.

GLOSSARY

abandoned property Property that a person has deserted or thrown away and thereby disclaims interest in; may be used as evidence against the former owner.

administrative functions Functions such as screening at airports and courthouses and many fire, health, housing, and school services.

adversary system The judicial system in which opposing parties present evidence, and an impartial judge or jury weighs the evidence; contrasts with the inquisitorial system, where the judge actively questions the accused and witnesses.

affirmative defense A defense that admits the defendant committed the crime charged but asserts that the defendant should not be convicted.

Alford guilty plea A guilty plea that permits the accused to maintain innocence.

ancient document rule The rule that a piece of written or printed matter may be deemed authentic and genuine without a witness to attest to the circumstances of its creation because its age suggests that it is unlikely to have been falsified.

anonymous tip Information from an unknown person; could be received in a 911 call or another telephone call.

arraignment The formal proceeding following the indictment or information, where a plea is entered and the defendant is bound over for trial.

arrest Defined in 1760 by Sir William Blackstone as "the apprehending or restraining of one's person, in order to be forthcoming to answer an alleged or suspected crime."

arrest warrant An order signed by a judge or magistrate authorizing the arrest of a named person or persons.

assertive statement A statement by which a person intends to communicate a thought or belief.

attorney-client privilege The oldest of the evidentiary privileges.

ballistic fingerprinting Identification of the gun that fired a bullet from an analysis of the marks that every gun makes on the bullet it fires and on the shell ejected from it.

best evidence rule (original document rule) The rule of evidence that requires the original of a writing, photograph, or other document to prove the content, unless the original is unavailable.

beyond a reasonable doubt The burden that the prosecution must meet in proving guilt in criminal cases; applies to every element of the crime charged.

Bill of Rights The first 10 amendments to the U.S. Constitution.

Brady **rule** The rule that requires the prosecution to disclose upon request evidence favorable to the accused.

Bruton **rule** The rule that a criminal tribunal may not hear a confession or incriminating statement against a defendant that was made by another party to the crime unless the proponent produces the speaker.

burden of persuasion That part of the burden of proof that requires a party to persuade the jury that a fact exists.

burden of production That part of the burden of proof that requires a party to produce sufficient evidence to establish the fact at issue.

chain of custody The set of procedures that accounts for the integrity of evidence by tracking its handling and storage from the time it was obtained to the time it is offered at trial.

circumstantial evidence Evidence from which proof of the fact in question may be inferred.

closely regulated businesses Businesses that are subject to careful oversight by laws and codes, such as liquor stores, firearms dealers, coal mines, and pharmacies.

common law Legal rules that evolved over many years in English and American court opinions.

competency The fitness or ability of an individual to participate in legal proceedings.

competent evidence Any evidence that is relevant and reliable and not otherwise excludable; see Chapter 5.

confession A direct acknowledgment of guilt; generally viewed the same as a guilty plea in open court.

Confrontation Clause The clause in the U.S. Constitution that entitles a defendant in a criminal case to demand witnesses to testify against him in his presence.

conspiracy An agreement by two or more people to commit an illegal act.

corpus delicti The body of the crime; the requirement that the government must prove that the crime charged has been committed.

courtroom identification A prescribed series of steps used during a trial to identify the defendant as the person who committed the crime or was a party to the crime charged.

credibility Believability.

crime–fraud exception The exception made to attorney–client privilege when a client consults with an attorney for the purpose of committing a future crime such as perjury; communication and documents relating to this fraud are not protected.

crime scene A location where an illegal act took place and from which law enforcement personnel collect physical evidence.

criminal complaint The formal charge made by the prosecution against a defendant, which begins criminal proceedings.

criminal indictment The formal charge issued by a grand jury, listing crimes believed to have been committed by the named defendant.

cross-examination Re-examination of a witness by the opposing attorney following the direct examination of the witness.

curtilage The area close to a home where persons have a right of privacy.

custody Under police control, whether or not physically constrained.

Daubert test The principle that scientific evidence presented to the court must result from tests and theories that are testable, have been reviewed by peers, have high reliability rates, and are generally accepted by the associated scientific community.

declarant A person who makes a statement, either in or out of court.

demonstrative evidence Evidence that portrays objects, persons, or events not in the courtroom—for example, photographs and videotapes.

derivative evidence rule Another term for the fruit of the poisonous tree doctrine.

direct evidence Evidence that proves or disproves a fact in question with no need for inferences.

direct examination Questioning of a witness by the lawyer who subpoenaed the witness.

discovery Formal procedures used by prosecution and defense attorneys to gather documents, witnesses, and other evidence.

DNA genetic profiling A method for identifying individuals by the unique structure of their DNA; used for both identifying the person who committed a crime and clearing innocent suspects.

document A piece of written or printed matter that provides information or evidence or that serves as an official record.

due process The minimum procedural protections courts must afford those charged with crimes; guaranteed by the Fifth and Fourteenth Amendments to the U.S. Constitution.

dying declaration exception The exception defined by Rule 804(b)(2), making admissible statements made by a victim or other person under the belief of impending death.

electronic surveillance Secret interception of communications by wiretapping or bugging, which "typically is accomplished by installation of a small microphone in the room (or vehicle) to be bugged." *Dalia v. United States*, 99 S. Ct. 1682 (1979).

emergency situation A serious and often dangerous situation that requires immediate action, such as "hot pursuit," now or never, or emergency aid.

evidence The means of establishing the truth or untruth of any fact that is alleged.

exclusionary rule A judicial rule that makes evidence obtained in violation of the U.S. Constitution, state or federal laws, or court rules inadmissible.

exigent circumstances A court-recognized exception to the warrant

requirement of the Fourth Amendment; authorizes entry not only by law enforcement officers but also by firefighters and emergency medical personnel.

expert witness A witness who has special knowledge or training in a specialized area.

federalism Division of power between state governments and the federal government, in which the federal government has specified powers delegated to it, with the remaining powers vested in the states.

Federal Rules of Evidence Codification in 1975 of common-law rules of evidence; applicable only in federal courts but the model for most state evidence codes.

forensic Belonging to or connected with a court; for example, forensic fingerprints are fingerprints used as evidence in a civil or criminal trial.

forensic entomology The study of insects to provide scientific evidence to aid legal investigations.

forfeiture by wrongdoing A rule permitting the admission of hearsay evidence as a penalty against a defendant who wrongfully made the declarant unavailable; often used in murder cases.

free-to-leave test The test used to determine whether a conversation between a person and a law officer is voluntary; a reasonable person must believe he is free to leave.

fruit of the poisonous tree Evidence obtained legally through the use of evidence obtained illegally.

Frye test The general acceptance test; scientific evidence presented to the court must result from tests and theories that are generally accepted by a meaningful segment of the associated scientific community.

good faith exception The exception that makes admissible evidence that was obtained under a search warrant that has a technical error if that error was unknown to the law officers executing the warrant.

grand jury A jury that hears evidence presented by the prosecution and determines whether to charge persons with crimes; used in federal and many state criminal proceedings.

grand jury secrecy requirement The mandate that persons serving on grand juries will not disclose "matters occurring before" the grand jury on which they serve.

gruesome photographs Photographs that are shocking and repulsive.

habeas corpus Latin name of the writ used to compel a government official, such as a prison warden, to show cause why the official is holding a person in custody.

hearsay Secondhand testimony; reports by one person about what another person said.

honest mistake rule The U.S. Supreme Court's ruling that courts must "allow some latitude for honest mistakes that are made by officers in the dangerous and difficult process of making arrests and executing search warrants."

impeachment Calling into question the truth or accuracy of direct testimony by cross-examination or introduction of contradictory evidence.

impermissible inference An inference a fact finder may not draw; an example is inferring guilt because the defendant does not testify.

incriminating statement "Any statement or conduct from which guilt of the crime can be inferred." *People v. Stanton*, 158 N.E.2d 47 (Ill. 1959).

independent source doctrine An exception to the exclusionary rule where evidence obtained lawfully by one source is admissible even though another source (law officers) obtained the same evidence improperly.

indicia of reliability Characteristics of a statement, otherwise inadmissible as hearsay, which courts believe sufficiently establish the statement's reliability so that cross-examination is not required.

inevitable discovery rule An exception to the exclusionary rule where illegally discovered evidence would certainly have been discovered legally.

inferences Conclusions that may be drawn from facts.

informants Persons who provide information to law officers.

initial appearance The first appearance by an accused before a judge or magistrate; a plea is entered and bail is set at this hearing.

insanity plea A plea to a criminal charge of not guilty because of mental disease or defect.

inventory searches The procedure that law officers use to account for the property of people who are in their custody.

judgment NOV A post-trial judgment made by a judge changing or reversing the jury decision; literally, *non obstante veredicto* ("notwithstanding the verdict").

judicial notice The doctrine that evidence of well-accepted facts may be introduced in court without proof; a judicial shortcut.

latent fingerprints Fingerprints left by a person on a surface other than one designed for recording fingerprints.

lineup An identification procedure in which six or more persons are shown to witnesses to or the victim of a crime.

locus point A point in the sequence of base pairs in human DNA where individual DNA chains vary.

Magna Carta The Great Charter signed by King John of England and his barons in 1215; created the first

standards for arresting and imprisoning those accused of crimes.

***Massiah* limitation** The holding that after a person has been charged with a crime, law officers cannot question the person or otherwise obtain incriminating statements regarding that crime without the person's attorney present.

material evidence Evidence that will affect the result of a trial.

***Miranda* requirements** The procedural safeguards established by the U.S. Supreme Court in 1966.

motion to suppress evidence A written or oral request to a judge to keep out evidence at a trial or hearing; often made when a party believes the evidence was unlawfully obtained.

news reporter's privilege A privilege that does not exist in common law; created by statute in many states.

no contest or nolo contendere plea A plea in which the accused neither contests nor admits the charges against him; treated as a guilty plea.

nonverbal communication Acts that do not involve words or speech but that may be assertive and therefore hearsay.

objections Formal statements made by attorneys during trials, objecting to the form or substance of a question or to the answer given by a witness to a question.

open field An unoccupied or undeveloped area outside of the curtilage; objects found there may be used as evidence.

ordeal A medieval method of proof that was an appeal to God to determine guilt or innocence.

ordinary (lay) witness Witness who has firsthand information about a fact gained by personal observation.

partner-in-crime exception The exception to the marital privilege that arises if a husband and wife commit a crime together.

passage-of-time rule (attenuation) An exception to the exclusionary rule where the "taint" from the improper conduct is dissipated over a significant period of time after the improper conduct.

permissible inferences Inferences made from proof of facts that a fact finder may, but need not, draw.

photographic array A group of photographs shown to witnesses or the victim of a crime for identification purposes.

physical evidence (real evidence) Physical objects, such as weapons, drugs, and clothing.

physician–patient privilege The privilege created, not by common law, but by state law for state courts; belongs to the patient and may be waived by the patient.

plain view or open view doctrine The principle that if a law officer is where he or she has a right to be and sees evidence or contraband in plain view, then the evidence may be seized and used in a criminal trial.

plea bargaining Agreement to enter a guilty plea in return for a reduction in the charge or sentence. For example, first-offense shoplifters are often given the opportunity to plead to disorderly conduct in a municipal court instead of going to trial for a theft charge. First-offense drunk drivers are often permitted to enter a guilty plea in return for the dropping of one of the three or four criminal charges that they face.

preliminary hearing Full adversarial hearing with a lawyer present.

presentment juries English forerunners to grand juries; gave information that crimes had been committed.

presumption of innocence The legal presumption required in all criminal courts that the defendant is innocent until sufficient credible evidence is produced to carry the burden of proving guilt beyond a reasonable doubt.

prima facie case A civil or criminal case that is so strong that the opponent must respond with rebutting evidence to avoid losing the case.

private search A search by a private person that is not subject to the exclusionary rule.

privilege A benefit or right enjoyed by a person; for example, the privilege of a witness not to answer a question might be based on the privilege against self-incrimination or the marital privilege.

probable cause The quantum (amount) of evidence required by the Fourth Amendment to make an arrest or to issue a search warrant; must be greater than reasonable suspicion but can be less than proof or reasonable doubt.

proof The result of evidence; evidence is the means of attaining proof.

protective search A search limited in purpose to discovering threatening weapons.

protective sweep or safety check An investigation of a building or vehicle to determine whether other persons or weapons are present that could jeopardize safety.

psychotherapist–patient privilege A privilege created by statute in many states.

reasonable doubt The standard for evidence that fact finders (juries or judges) must use in criminal cases to find a defendant guilty of the crime charged.

reasonable suspicion The amount of evidence a law enforcement officer needs to make an investigative stop (a *Terry* stop); less than probable cause but more than a hunch or mere suspicion.

regularly kept records exception The exception defined by Rule 803, which allows the use of regularly kept business records and public, religious, and family records.

relevant evidence Evidence that has a tendency to make a material issue before the court more or less probable; see Chapter 5.

reliable evidence Evidence that possesses a sufficient degree of likelihood that it is true and accurate.

reversible errors Errors that occur at a trial that might have had a bearing on the outcome. If the outcome clearly would have been the same without the error, it is not reversible error.

relevant, material, and competent Evidence that will affect the result of a trial.

scientific evidence Evidence, usually in the form of expert testimony, that relates to scientific theory, experiments, or tests.

search warrant An order signed by a judge or magistrate identifying the place to be searched and the persons or things to be seized.

sexual assault counselor's privilege The privilege for counselors of victims of sexual assault and crimes of violence; also applies to records and testimony by counselors, and can be invoked without the consent of the victim or patient.

showup An identification procedure in which only one subject is shown to witnesses or the victim of a crime.

sketches Drawings made by an artist or with an Identi-Kit for use in identification.

"special needs" of government The basic government requirements of safety, health, education, and concern for the well-being of the society as a whole.

spectrograms or voiceprints Voice graphs made on a spectrograph, which analyzes voice recordings based on intensity, frequency, and time gaps.

standing Possession of the necessary relationship to an issue to be permitted to raise that issue in a court of law.

statement-against-penal-interest exception The exception defined by Rule 804(b)(3) making admissible a statement that exposes the speaker to criminal liability.

statements for purposes of medical diagnosis or treatment exception The exception defined by Rule 803(4); for example, statements by doctors and nurses are admissible in child abuse cases.

subpoena An order compelling a person to appear as a witness; defense lawyers and prosecutors may have subpoenas issued for witnesses needed in either criminal or civil cases.

subpoena duces tecum A subpoena that not only requires the appearance of a witness but also requires the witness to bring relevant and competent documents or writings that may be in his or her possession.

sufficiency-of-evidence requirement The demand for a reasonably substantial foundation of evidence to support a verdict or finding.

***Terry* stop** An investigative street detention named after the 1968 U.S. Supreme Court case of *Terry v. Ohio*.

then existing mental, emotional, or physical condition The exception defined by Rule 803(3); for example, testimony that the victim stated that she was going to visit her boyfriend is admissible under this exception to show intent.

totality of the circumstances test The test that looks at the whole picture—all factors—in determining whether a confession, incriminating statement, or consent was freely and voluntarily given.

trace evidence Small amounts of material that a suspect leaves or acquires when he or she comes in contact with another object.

truth of the matter asserted The subject to be proved in an assertive statement.

videotape surveillance Close observation by use of video cameras.

voir dire The preliminary examination of a prospective juror or a child who is going to be a witness to determine qualifications.

voluntariness test The requirement that confessions, incriminating statements, and consent be voluntary and freely given and not obtained by means that overwhelmed the will of the accused or another person.

wiretapping According to the U.S. Supreme Court in *Dalia v. United States*, 99 S. Ct. 1682 (1979), "interception of communication by telephone and telegraph."

witnesses Persons who appear and testify under oath or affirmation before civil and criminal courts and other hearings.

work-related searches A search of a worker's desk and workstation for necessary records or equipment so that another employee can fill in for the absent worker or the employer can check for theft or fraud.

writ of certiorari Formal notice from the U.S. Supreme Court to a lower federal court or state court that a decision of that court has been accepted for review by the Supreme Court.

CASE INDEX

SUBJECT INDEX

Pages in notes are followed by n and the note number.